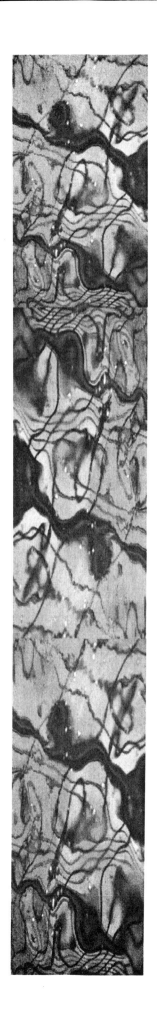

KEYS TO SUCCESSFUL SOFTWARE DEVELOPMENT

Edited by
Dr. Phillip Laplante

IEEE

Networking
the World™

The Institute of Electrical and Electronics Engineers, Inc.

CHAPTER 5   RELIABILITY, RISK MITIGATION AND AVOIDANCE

CHAPTER 6   USING METRICS

CHAPTER 7   PROCESS MEASUREMENT AND COST ESTIMATION

Introduction

KEYS TO SUCCESSFUL SOFTWARE DEVELOPMENT

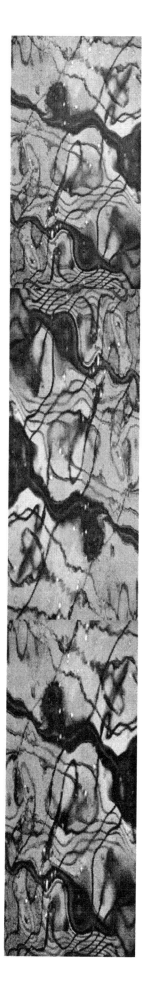

Why this Collection?

Virtually no one will argue that the vast majority of software projects are delivered late and over budget. Consequently, late software projects cost corporations hundreds of millions of dollars per year—and cost many project managers their jobs. Obviously, these companies wish they could control their software development costs through better management practices. Why, then, haven't more of them done something about it?

Well, many firms have tried to improve their software project management practices through the adoption of one or more fashionable techniques. But this often lead to failure and abandonment of those techniques. The truth is that there is no magic elixir; no silver bullet for improving software project management practices. Bad management habits take a long time to develop and even longer to break.

This collection is intended to provide an introduction to software project management by reviewing best practices and the theoretical foundations. It is intended for new software project managers and experienced ones. Project team members, even though they are not managers, can benefit from this collection too.

What Makes Software Project Management So Special?

Although there are many similarities between software project management and other types of project management, software project management has several unique aspects. These are directly related to the uniqueness of software.

First, software includes the translation of information from one representation to another. This includes translation of:

- requirements into design
- design into code
- code into assembly or machine language
- machine language into ones and zeros

At each translation step there is room for error and mistranslation.

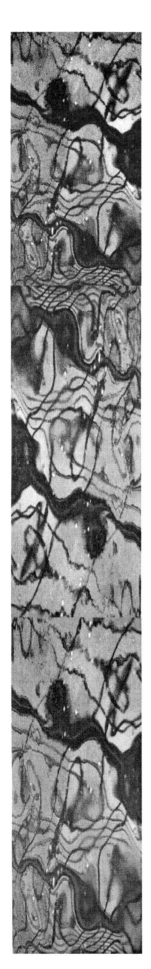

Additionally software designers build software knowing that it will have to change. Hence the project manager has to think about both the design and redesign. That adds a level of complication.

Finally, software development involves novelty, which, of course, introduces uncertainty. It can be argued that there is a higher degree of novelty in software than in other forms of engineering. Why else are there so few reusable and off-the-shelf software components?

How Were the Papers Selected?

This collection is intended to serve as a focused primer on software project management. Only high quality journal articles and magazine pieces are included. In order to keep this collection timely, the papers selected were less than ten years old and most are less than five years old. In addition, the increasing prevalence of object-oriented software development suggested the inclusion of a significant number of papers that addressed that approach.

What Makes a Good Software Project Manager?

The skills that make a good software engineer are not necessarily the skills needed to be a good project manager. Nevertheless, many companies promote good software engineers to project management positions without the necessary training. Unfortunately, it is usually too late when senior management discovers that a software project is headed for disaster because of poor management. Sadly, last minute heroics are a poor substitute for careful planning and execution throughout the early phases of software development.

This reader is organized into the following sections:

- Managing people and projects
- Software life cycle processes
- Requirements engineering
- Reuse and reengineering
- Reliability
- Using metrics
- Process measurement and cost estimation

These sections reflect my understanding of important aspects of software project management. Each section can be used as a focused introduction to its respective area.

Other Resources

This reader was developed to accompany a multimedia self-study course in software project management. See the IEEE Web site www.ieee.org/organizations/eab for more information.

About the Author

Phil Laplante has been a software engineer, project manager, teacher, researcher, and author for over 15 years. He currently consults to numerous industrial and military organizations on a wide range of software design and engineering topics.

His experience includes designing software for embedded avionics like the Space Shuttle; building computer aided design software for commercial use; developing software and best practices for software testing; and managing database systems.

He has also written 10 books and numerous refereed journal and magazine articles on computing, software engineering and electrical engineering.

He holds a bachelor's degree in systems planning and management; a master's degree in electrical engineering; and a doctorate in computer science all from Stevens Institute of technology. He also holds a master's degree in business administration from the University of Colorado at Colorado Springs.

Acknowledgements

Thanks to Barbara Stoler of IEEE for conceiving of this project and commissioning me to do it.

Many thanks to Jill Bagley for assisting me in tracking down most of the papers and for guiding me through the development of this collection.

Finally, thanks to my family—my wife, Nancy, and kids, Christopher and Charlotte for their long-suffering patience.

Phillip A. Laplante
March 1999

x

Chapter 1

MANAGING PEOPLE AND PROJECTS

One of the most important elements of software project management is the human element. The first paper by Boehm and Ross illustrates a wonderful understanding of the role that people play with respect to the software project. The three remaining papers in this section provide useful frameworks for managing software projects in the ubiquitous presence of unreliable data, for object-oriented projects and through the use of engineering data. Read them as a unit and try to take the best elements of each and see how they might be applied to your current project.

Theory-W Software Project Management: Principles and Examples

BARRY W. BOEHM, SENIOR MEMBER, IEEE, AND RONY ROSS

Abstract—A good software project management theory should be simultaneously simple, general, and specific. To date, those objectives have been difficult to satisfy. This paper presents a candidate software management theory and shows that it satisfies those objectives reasonably well. Reflecting various alphabetical management theories (X, Y, Z), it is called the Theory W approach to software project management.

Theory W: Make Everyone a Winner

The paper explains the key steps and guidelines underlying the Theory W statement and its two subsidiary principles: *plan the flight and fly the plan*; and, *identify and manage your risks*.

Several examples illustrate the application of Theory W, and an extensive case study is presented and analyzed: the attempt to introduce new information systems to a large industrial corporation in an emerging nation. The case may seem unique, yet it is typical. The analysis shows that Theory W and its subsidiary principles do an effective job both in explaining why the project encountered problems, and in prescribing ways in which the problems could have been avoided.

Index Terms—Project management, software case studies, software development, software maintenance, software management, software personnel management, software planning and control.

I. Introduction

SOFTWARE project management today is an art. The skillful integration of software technology, economics and human relations in the specific context of a software project is not an easy task. The software project is a highly people-intensive effort that spans a very lengthy period, with fundamental implications on the work and performance of many different classes of people.

A. The Software Project Manager's Problem

The software project manager's primary problem is that a software project needs to simultaneously satisfy a variety of constituencies: the users, the customers, the development team, the maintainance team, the management. As seen in Fig. 1, each of these constituencies has its own desires with respect to the software project. The *users*—sometimes too enthusiastic, sometimes too skeptical—desire a robust, user-friendly system with many functions supporting their mission. The *customers* desire a product delivered reliably to a short schedule and low budget. The *bosses* of the project manager desire a project with am-

Manuscript received October 30, 1987; revised February 29, 1988.
B. W. Boehm is with TRW Defense Systems Group, One Space Park, Redondo Beach, CA 90278, and the Department of Computer Science, University of California, Los Angeles, CA 90024.
R. Ross is with the Department of Computer Science, University of California, Los Angeles, CA 90024.
IEEE Log Number 8928293.

bitious goals, no overruns, and no surprises. The *maintainers* of the product desire a well-documented, easy-to-modify system with no bugs. The *development team* members—often brilliant, sometimes unmanageable—desire interesting technical challenges and fast career paths, generally with a preference for design and an inclination to defer documentation.

These desires create fundamental conflicts when taken together (e.g., many functions versus a low budget and no overruns). These conflicts are at the root of most software project management difficulties—both at the strategic level (setting goals, establishing major milestones and responsibilities) and at the tactical level (resolving day-to-day conflicts, prioritizing assignments, adapting to changes).

B. The Software Management Theory Problem

A good software management theory should help the project manager navigate through these difficulties. As seen in Fig. 2, a software management theory has a similar challenging set of simultaneous objectives to satisfy. It should be simple to understand and apply; general enough to cover all classes of projects and classes of concerns (procedural, technical, economic, people-oriented); yet specific enough to provide useful, situation-specific advice.

Several attempts have been made to provide a relatively small set of software project management principles which can be easily recalled and applied, and which cover all of the important aspects. Thayer *et al.* [21] and Reifer [18] provide sets of principles largely organized around the five overall management principles in Koontz-O'Donnell [12] of planning, staffing, organizing, controlling, and directing. Boehm [3] provides a set of seven fundamental principles of software development. Although these have been very useful in many situations, none of these to date have produced a sufficient combination of simplicity, generality and specificity to have stimulated widespread use.

This paper presents a candidate fundamental principle for software project management developed by one of the authors (Boehm), and shows how it would apply in avoiding the software project management problems encountered in a case study analyzed by the other author (Ross).

The fundamental principle is called the Theory W approach to software project management.

Theory W: Make Everyone a Winner.

Reprinted from *IEEE Transactions on Software Engineering*, Vol. SE-15, July 1989, pp. 902-916.

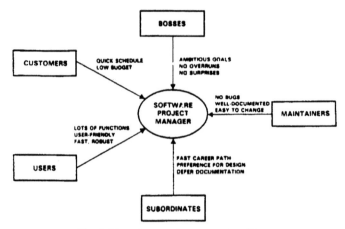

Fig. 1. The software project manager's problem.

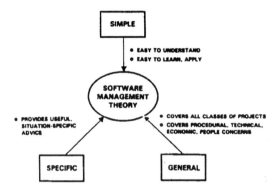

Fig. 2. The software management theory problem.

It holds that the primary job of the software project manager is to make winners of each of the parties involved in the software process: the project manager's subordinates and managers; the customers; the users and maintainers of the resulting product; and any other significantly affected people, such as the developers or users of interfacing products.

Making everyone a winner has a number of implications which will be discussed below, including the use of two subsidiary principles:
- Plan the flight and fly the plan.
- Identify and manage your risks.

Section II of this paper elaborates on the overall Theory W approach and the software project implications of making everyone a winner. Section III elaborates on the two subsidiary principles. Section IV provides the history of the system involved in the case study. Section V analyzes the case study with respect to Theory W and the subsidiary principles, and Section VI presents the resulting conclusions.

II. THEORY W: MAKE EVERYONE A WINNER

This section elaborates on Theory W's major principle. We begin in Section II-A by placing Theory W in the context of other management theories, particularly Theories X, Y, and Z. Section II-B presents the key concept involved in Theory W: the distinction between win–win, win–lose, and lose–lose situations. Section II-C summarizes the three primary steps suggested to achieve the desired goal of making everyone a winner, and the nine substeps involved in implementing Theory W. Section II-C also elaborates on the first three substeps: those that deal with creating win–win situations, the strongest distinguishing feature of Theory W as a management approach. Section II-D elaborates on all of the substeps, and shows how a set of strategic principles for software project management can be generated by applying each of the substeps to each of the project manager's constituencies identified in Fig. 1 above. Section II-E shows via an example how the Theory W steps can be used to solve day-to-day tactical project management problems as well as strategic problems.

A. Comparison to Theories X, Y and Z

The Theory X approach to management built largely on the "scientific management" ideas of Frederick Taylor [20]. It held that the most efficient way to get a job done was to do more and more precise time and motion studies, and to organize jobs into well-orchestrated sequences of tasks in which people were as efficient and predictable as machines. Management consisted of keeping the system running smoothly, largely through coercion.

Theory Y, introduced in [8], held that Theory X was a poor long-term strategy because it stunted people's creativity, adaptiveness, and self esteem, making the people and their organizations unable to cope with change. Theory Y held that management should stimulate creativity and individual initiative. This led to organizations which were much more adaptive and personally satisfying, but created difficulties in dealing with conflict. This was not a problem in Theory X, but became a major concern in Theory Y organizations, with many individual initiatives competing for resources and creating problems of coordination.

Theory Z, described in [10], holds that much of the conflict resolution problem can be eliminated by up-front investment in developing shared values and arriving at major decisions by consensus. It focuses largely on doing this within an organization, and does not say much about how to deal with other organizations with different objectives and cultures—a particularly common situation with software managers and their diverse constituencies (developers, customers, users, etc.). Overall, Theory Z's primary emphasis is at the corporate-culture level rather than at the intercompany level or the individual project level.

Theory W's fundamental principle is well-matched to the problems of software project management. It holds that software project managers will be fully successful if and only if they make winners of all the other participants in the software process: superiors, subordinates, customers, users, maintainers, etc. This principle is particularly relevant in the software field, which is a highly people-intensive area whose products are largely services or decision aids, and whose performers are often unfamiliar with user and management concerns. However, Theory W can be applied to other fields as well.

Rather than characterizing a manager as an autocrat (Theory X), a coach (Theory Y), or a facilitator (Theory Z), Theory W characterizes a manager's primary role as a negotiator between his various constituencies, and a packager of project solutions with win conditions for all parties. Beyond this, the manager is also a goal-setter, a monitor of progress towards goals, and an activist in seeking out day-to-day win–lose or lose–lose project conflicts, confronting them, and changing them into win–win situations.

B. Win–Win, Win–Lose, and Lose–Lose Situations

Making everyone a winner may seem like an unachievable objective. Most situations tend to be zero-sum, win–lose situations. Building a quick and sloppy product may be a low-cost, near-term "win" for the software developer and customer, but it will be a "lose" for the user and the maintainer. Adding lots of marginally useful software "bells and whistles" to a product on a cost-plus contract may be a win for the developer and some users, but a lose for the customer.

At worst, software projects can be lose–lose situations. Setting unrealistic schedule expectations; staffing with incompatible people; poor planning; or trying to catch up on a schedule by adding more people will generally make losers of all the participants.

Nonetheless, win–win situations exist, and often they can be created by careful attention to people's interests and expectations. Creating a profit-sharing arrangement for a software subcontractor provides the subcontractor with a motivation to develop a high-quality, widely-sold product, thus increasing the size of the profit pie for both the subcontractor and the top-level product developer. Using better software technology such as structured pro-

gramming, early error detection techniques, or information hiding will also create wins for all parties.

C. Creating Win–Win Situations

The best work on creating win–win situations has been done in the field of negotiation. The book *Getting to Yes* [9] is a classic in the area. Its primary thesis is that successful negotiations are not achieved by haggling from preset negotiating positions, but by following a four-step approach whose goal is basically to create a win–win situation for the negotiating parties:

1) Separate the people from the problem.
2) Focus on interests, not positions.
3) Invent options for mutual gain.
4) Insist on using objective criteria.

The Theory W approach to software project management expands on these four steps to establish a set of win–win preconditions, and some further conditions for structuring the software process and the resulting software product, as shown in Table I.

The remainder of this section elaborates on the first three substeps in Table I which deal primarily with the process of creating win–win situations.

1) Understand How People Want to Win: One important subprinciple here is to *make sure you identify the key people.* Often, software projects have failed because a key constituency (users' bosses, hardware procurement personnel, subcontractors) has not been included in the win–win scheme.

Another important subprinciple is to *project yourself into others' win situations.* This is often difficult for people to do because it runs counter to strongly implanted notions of goodness such as the Golden Rule: "Do unto others as you would have others do unto you." But, others may not want what you want as win conditions. Some frequent examples:

• Managers frequently assume that software professionals win by getting "promoted" to management. However, the motivating-factors studies done by Couger and Zawacki [6] indicate that the typical data processing professional has a much stronger need for professional growth than for social interaction, while the average manager has the opposite profile. Thus, promotions to management can be quite harmful to software people's careers, and dual-track (technical and managerial) career-path ladders can be much more successful in software organizations.

• Computer-science majors brought up on canonical applications such as compilers and operating systems, where users are programmers, implicitly build up a set of assumptions about software users: that software users like to program, and prefer powerful and terse (but perhaps obscure) command languages and users' manuals. Well-meaning attempts to apply those assumptions to such software users as nurses, doctors, pilots and bank tellers have led to numerous software disasters.

Thus, Theory W suggests a modified form of the Golden Rule: "Do unto others as you would have others do unto you—if you were like them."

TABLE I
THEORY W WIN-WIN STEPS

1. Establish a set of win-win preconditions
a. Understand how people want to win;
b. Establish reasonable expectations;
c. Match people's tasks to their win conditions;
d. Provide a supportive environment.
2. Structure a win-win software process.
a. Establish a realistic process plan;
b. Use the plan to control the project;
c. Identify and manage your win-lose or lose-lose risks;
d. Keep people involved;
3. Structure a win-win software product.
a. Match product to users', maintainers' win conditions.

Another key subprinciple is the Peters-Waterman [17] maxim to *get close to the customer*. This involves getting software people to operate more like marketing personnel than like people who wait around to code up whatever specification is provided. It involves much more proactive use of interviews, surveys, tours of duty, prototypes, scenarios, operations analysis, user-culture analyses, and understanding of users' previous experiences with automation (scars, bruises, traumas, triumphs).

Overall, the field of motivational analysis provides the most comprehensive set of insights on understanding how people want to win. Gellerman [10] provides a good early survey of the field; more recently, Couger and Zawacki [6] have provided a good set of insights related specifically to data processing people.

2) Establish Reasonable Expectations: Many software problems stem from the fact that software customers and users frequently have little feel for what is easy and what is hard to achieve with computers and software. This leads to a set of unrealistic expectations: either thinking things are too hard to implement (complex scheduling or file management) or too easy (pattern recognition or building 150 man-months worth of software in 6 months). Similarly, software people often have unrealistic expectations of what is easy and what is hard for users to do.

Some important subprinciples here are:
• Bring your constituencies together to identify and resolve expectation mismatches.
• Have people look at issues from the other constituents' viewpoints.
• Have people look for objective, mutually relevant solution criteria.
• Relate people's expectations to experience: benchmarks, reference checks, expert judgment.
• Relate people's expectations to well-calibrated models: computer-performance models, software project cost and schedule estimation models.

A related management insight is that "hard-soft works better than soft-hard." A manager who overpromises to his various constituencies and then has to deflate their expectations has an easier time initially, but a much rougher time in the long run, than a manager who deflates initial expectations and provides some management reserve to soften his position later where necessary.

A good recent example of establishing reasonable soft-

ware project expectations involved the need for improvements in the on-board software of the F-16 aircraft. The aircraft users expected a long list of additional software capabilities to be delivered in 12 months. The developers' expectations were in terms of previous software productivity rates, and indicated a much longer development period. Rather than conduct a positional bargaining exercise resulting in unsatisfied expectations on both sides, the users and developers decided to explore their options using COCOMO, a software cost and schedule estimation model calibrated to experience in similar projects [2].

As a result, both groups developed a much better understanding of the relationships between software functionality, cost, and schedule. The developers found options to increase their software productivity capabilities and expectations. The users were able to establish a series of prioritized annual software increments whose achievability was keyed to their developer-shared productivity expectations. After two years of software deliveries, both groups have experienced satisfactory results relative to their revised expectations.

Overall, the process of reconciling people's expectations is dealt with in the fields of conflict resolution and teambuilding. Walton [22], Kirchof and Adams [11], and Dyer [7] are good sources of additional insight.

3) Match People's Tasks to Their Win Conditions: The key principles here involve *searching out win-win situations* and *expanding the option space to create win-win situations*.

Some effective techniques available to the software project manager for searching out win-win situations include:
• Breaking options into parts (functions, activities, increments, phases), and configuring combinations of suboptions into win packages for each participant. For example, under some conditions, establishing a separate leader for successive software increments has worked well, particularly if the increments are large, with different technical and/or organizational centers of gravity.
• Realigning options along win-win axes. For example, some projects have successfully shifted the authority and responsibility for software quality assurance from the developer (who may consider it a bore) to the maintainer, who has considered it a major win-leverage opportunity.

Some effective techniques available to the software project manager for expanding the option space to create win-win situations are:
• Linking tasks to future options and career paths ("Quality assurance may be a bore, but it's a ticket to a fast-track career path").
• Expanding the scope of a task ("Quality Assurance should not be a bore. I think you could lead the way in helping us make quality assurance a more proactive function in getting us quality products. That would be a real achievement").
• Linking tasks to extra rewards ("Rescuing this integration and test mess will be a killer, but I'll make sure you get a good bonus and lots of kudos if you succeed").
• Providing extra support ("This schedule is very am-

4

bitious, but I'll provide your team with the first-class workstations and facilities you'll need to meet it'').

• Surfacing new options (''We can't develop all the functions in 12 months, but if we do an incremental development, we can satisfy your top-priority needs in 12 months'').

Overall, the field of negotiation provides the best additional sources of insight in matching tasks to win conditions. Some good books are Fisher and Ury [9] and Nierenberg [15].

D. Deriving Strategic Project Guidelines from Theory W Win–Win Steps

Most current software management directives, and many of the textbooks, present strategic software management guidelines as a series of relatively unconnected what-to-do lists of activities to perform (e.g., prototype the user interface, configuration-manage the baselined items, set up and follow a set of programming standards).

The power of Theory W becomes evident in Tables II and III, which show that one can derive most of the apparently unconnected what-to-do activities by applying the Theory W win–win steps in Table I to the various constituencies involved in the software process. Prototyping is a way of understanding the users' win conditions (Table II). Configuration management is partly establishing a supportive environment for the developers and maintainers, and partly participation in change control by all parties impacted by a proposed change (Table II). Programming standards contribute to structuring a software product so that its maintainers will be winners (Table III).

Further, Tables II and III provide stronger guidance than usual for allocating life-cycle responsibilities to the various software parties. An example is the allocation of the quality assurance responsibility to the maintainers, as their win conditions are most strongly affected by product quality.

Tables II and III also show that Theory W provides not just a ''what'' for the process activities, but also the underlying ''why.'' This is very important in the frequent situations of tailoring the process activities to special circumstances, and determining how much of a given process activity is enough. For example, if the inclusion of machine-generated flowcharts in the maintainance documentation does not help the maintainers become winners, it is not necessary to require their delivery.

E. Theory W: A Tactical Management Example

Theory W provides specific useful guidance in tactical as well as strategic project management situations. The resulting solutions are often preferable to those derived from previous management theories. Consider the following example:

XYZ Corp. has been developing a large financial system for a Boston bank. A new position on the project is being created to lead a system analysis ef-

TABLE II
STRATEGIC GUIDELINES DERIVED FROM WIN–WIN PRECONDITIONS

Win-Win Precondition	Users	Maintainers	Customers	Developer Team
Understand win conditions	Mission anal. Ops. concept Prototyping Rqts. spec Early users' manual	Ops. concept Ops. procedures	Cost-benefit analysis	Career path develop.
Reasonable expectations	*Teambuilding, Negotiating, Conflict resolution*			
	Rqts. scrub		Resource allocation	
Match tasks to win conditions	*Change control participation*			
	User-spec reviews Prototype exercise	Quality assurance	Status tracking	Staffing, organizing
			Early Error Detection	
Supportive environment preparation	User training Cutover preparation	Maint. training Conversion Deliverable support envir. Config. mgmt.	Customer training	Developer training Support envir. Config. mgmt.
	Modern programming practices			

TABLE III
STRATEGIC GUIDELINES DERIVED FROM PRODUCT, PROCESS GUIDELINES

Guideline	Users	Maintainers	Customers	Developers
Process planning	Operational plan Installation & training plans	Life-cycle support plan	Development plans	
Process control	*Teambuilding, Negotiating, Communicating*			
	Reviews	Reviews	Status tracking,	Controlling Perform. feedback
	Sensitivity analysis			
	Risk management plans			
Risk management	User rqts. validation, stability	Quality assurance	Budget, schedule Validation	staffing
Process involvement	Sys. engr. plan participation Review participation Prototype exercise	Sys. engr. plan participation Review participation Quality assurance	Cost-benefit reviews, approvals	Delegation Planning particip.
Product structuring	Service oriented Efficient Easy to learn Easy to use Tailorable	Easy to modify Prog. standards	Efficient Correct Feasible	Easy to Modify Balanced Correct

fort. George and Ann are the two primary candidates for the job. They are equally well qualified: George has somewhat more overall experience, while Ann has more experience specific to this type of application. The project manager must decide whom to chose.

Using Theory X, the manager would make a choice, based on some arbitrary criterion such as seniority. Using Theory Y, the manager would likely ask George and Ann for proposals on how they would do the job, and pick the most ambitious one. Using Theory Z, the manager would likely concentrate on prebuilding a consensus on team objectives, and make a choice based on team priorities.

Theory W would try to avoid the above situations, each of which creates a win–lose situation between George and Ann. By following the Theory W steps in Table I, the manager would try to create a win–win situation as follows:

1) Understand how people want to win. In talking with George and Ann, the manager finds that George greatly wants the job because of the extensive travel to Boston, where he has a daughter in college. Ann greatly wants the job because it would provide a career path toward marketing.

2) Match people's tasks to their win conditions. The manager expands the option space by considering comparable jobs with Boston travel for George and comparable marketing-oriented jobs for Ann.

Frequently, the Theory W approach will help the manager to find and establish such win–win solutions, creating more satisfaction and personal commitment among the participants, fewer disaffected and uncooperative participants, and more satisfactory all-around outcomes.

F. Connections between Theory W and Game Theory

Theory W also has fruitful connections to game theory. For example, the case of George and Ann can be formulated as a nonzero-sum game involving three players: George, Ann, and the customer. By using the concept of Rational Offer Groups formulated by Rosenschein and Genesereth [19], one can analyze the conditions under which the expansion of George's and Ann's option spaces will produce a win–win–win situation for George, Ann, and the customer. An example result is that if the project manager is too successful in finding alternate jobs for George and Ann, neither will take the systems analysis job, and the customer will become a loser.

III. Theory W Subsidiary Principles

Because of their particular importance to the management of the software process, the first three Theory W win–win process substeps in Table I are highlighted and combined into two key Theory W subsidiary principles. These are:
- Plan the flight and fly the plan (steps 2a, 2b).
- Identify and manage your risks (step 2c).

A. Planning the Flight

Establishing a realistic process plan is crucial to the success of the project. As indicated in Table III, there are several types of plans involved in making everyone a winner: operational plans, installation and training plans, life-cycle support plans, and development plans. Each of these may have a number of subsidiary plans: configuration management plans, quality assurance plans, test plans, conversion plans, etc.

Plans are important in Theory W because:
- They record the mutual commitment of the project participants to a set of win–win conditions and their implications.

- They provide a framework for detecting deviations from the win–win conditions which require corrective action.

Frequently, each software subplan is organized around a totally different outline, making the various plans more difficult to develop, assimilate, and query. Each Theory W plan is organized around a common outline, reflecting a small number of universal interrogatives (why, what, when, who, where, how, and how much):

1) Objectives (*Why* is the activity being pursued?)
2) Products and Milestones (*What* is being produced by when?)
3) Responsibilities (*Who* is responsible for each result? *Where* are they located organizationally?)
4) Approach (*How* is each result being achieved?)
5) Resources (*How much* of each scarce resource is required to achieve the results?)

Fig. 3 presents the outline for one of the key software management plans: the software development plan. It shows that the subsections of the plan are particular to software development issues (requirements, product design, programming, configuration management, quality assurance, etc.), but that the major sections of the plan follow the common Theory W outline.

Space limitations preclude further discussion of software project planning here; some good references are [8] and [14]. Also, some similar concepts are being developed in the draft IEEE Standard for Software Project Management Plans.

B. Flying the Plan

Developing a plan which satisfies everyone's win conditions is not enough to make everyone a winner. You also need to use the plan to manage the project.

This involves making a particular effort to monitor the project's progress with respect to the plan. The nature of this effort should be specified in the plan; see section 5.3 of the plan outline in Fig. 3. If the project's progress continues to match its plans, the project is in good shape. But usually, there will be some mismatches between the progress and the plans. If so, the manager needs to assess the reasons for the mismatches. It may be that the plans are flawed or out of date, in which case the plans need to be modified. Or the project's progress may be deficient, in which case the project manager needs to apply corrective action.

Applying corrective action is one of the most critical situations for using the "make everyone a winner" principle. It is all too easy to apply snap-judgment corrective actions with win–lose or lose–lose outcomes, or to heap public blame on people so that they feel like losers rather than winners. But it is generally possible to follow the Theory W win–win steps in Table I to find a corrective action strategy which either preserves everyone as winners, or convinces them that their losses are minimal with respect to other strategies. (An example is provided in the case study analysis in Section V-A.) And it is generally possible to reprimand people's behavior without making

1. Objectives (the "why")
    1.1. Software Product Objectives
    1.2. Development Plan Objectives
2. Milestones and Products (the "what" and "when")
    2.1. Overall Development Strategy
    2.2. Detailed Schedule of Deliverables
    2.3. Detailed Development Milestones and Schedules
3. Responsibilities (the "who" and "where")
    3.1. Organizational Responsibilities
        3.1.1. Global Organization Charts
        3.1.2. Organizational Commitment Responsibilities
    3.2. Development Responsibilities
        3.2.1. Development Organization Charts
        3.2.2. Staffing
        3.2.3. Training
4. Approach (the "how")
    4.1. Risk Management
    4.2. Development Phases
        4.2.1. Plans and Requirements Phase
        4.2.2. Product Design Phase
        4.2.3. Programming Phase
        4.2.4. Integration and test Phase
        4.2.5. Implementation Phase
    4.3. Reviews
    4.4. Documentation
    4.5. Configuration Management
    4.6. Quality Assurance
    4.7. Facilities and Related Concerns
5. Resources (the "how much")
    5.1. Work Breakdown Structure
    5.2. Budgets
    5.3. Status Monitoring and Control

Fig. 3. Theory W outline for the software development plan.

them feel like losers. A good example is the "one-minute reprimand" in the book *The One-Minute Manager* [1].

C. Risk Management

Planning the flight and flying the plan will make everyone a winner if the plans reflect the participants' win conditions and if the plans are realistic. Ensuring that the plans are realistic is the province of risk management.

Risk management focuses the project manager's attention on those portions of the project most likely to cause trouble and to compromise the participants' win conditions. Risk management considerations can also help the project manager to determine the appropriate sequence of performing project activities. The spiral model of software development [4] discusses risk-driven sequencing of project activities in more detail.

Webster defines "risk" as "the possibility of loss or injury." The magnitude of a risk item is generally defined as a quantity called Risk Exposure *RE*:

$$RE = (LP) * (LM).$$

The Loss Probability factor *LP* represents the probability of an unsatisfactory outcome. The Loss Magnitude factor *LM* represents the magnitude of the loss if the outcome is unsatisfactory. The magnitude of the loss is best expressed in terms of the participants' utility functions, which measure the degree to which the participants become losers rather than winners.

There are two primary classes of project risk:

1) *Generic risks*, which are common to all projects, and which are covered by standard development plan techniques.

2) *Project-specific risks*, which reflect a particular aspect of a given project, and which are addressed by project-specific risk management plans. The most common project-specific risks are personnel shortfalls, unrealistic schedules and budgets, inappropriate requirements, shortfalls in external components and tasks, and technology shortfalls or unknowns.

D. Risk Management Steps

The practice of risk management involves two primary steps, Risk Assessment and Risk Handling, each with three subsidiary steps. Risk Assessment involves risk identification, risk analysis, and risk prioritization. Risk Handling involves risk management planning, risk management execution, and risk monitoring and control.

Risk Identification produces lists of the project-specific items likely to compromise a project's win–win conditions. Typical risk identification techniques include checklists, decomposition, comparison with experience, and examination of decision drivers.

Risk Analysis produces assessments of the loss-probability and loss-magnitude associated with each of the identified risk items, and assessments of compound risks involved in risk-item interactions. Typical techniques include network analysis, decision trees, cost models, and performance models.

Risk Prioritization produces a prioritized ordering of the risk items identified and analyzed. Typical techniques include risk leverage analysis and Delphi or group-consensus techniques.

Risk Management Planning produces plans for addressing each risk item, including the coordination of the individual risk-item plans with each other and with the overall project plan (e.g., to ensure that enough up-front schedule is provided to properly develop, exercise, and learn from a prototype). Typical techniques include risk-resolution checklists such as the one in Table IV, showing the top 10 primary sources of software project risk and the most effective approaches for resolving them. Other techniques include cost-benefit analysis and statistical decision analysis of the relative cost and effectiveness of alternative risk-resolution approaches. The best form for a risk management plan is the general "why, what, when, who, where, how, how much" plan template discussed above.

Risk Management Execution produces a resolution of the risk items. Typical techniques are the ones shown in Table IV.

Risk Monitoring and Control completes the "flying the plan" counterpart of risk management planning. It involves tracking the progress toward resolving high-risk items and taking corrective action where appropriate. A most effective technique is a Top Ten Risk Item list which

TABLE IV
A Top Ten List of Software Risk Items

A Top Ten List of Software Risk Items	
RISK ITEM	RISK MANAGEMENT TECHNIQUES
1. Personnel shortfalls	-Staffing with top talent; job matching; teambuilding; key-personnel agreements; cross-training; prescheduling key people
2. Unrealistic schedules and budgets	-Detailed multisource cost & schedule estimation; design to cost; incremental development; software reuse; requirements scrubbing
3. Developing the wrong software functions	-Organization analysis; mission analysis; ops-concept formulation; user surveys; prototyping; early users' manuals
4. Developing the wrong user interface	-Prototyping; scenarios; task analysis; user characterization (functionality, style, workload)
5. Gold plating	-Requirements scrubbing; prototyping; cost-benefit analysis; design to cost
6. Continuing stream of requirements changes	-High change threshold; information hiding; incremental development (defer changes to later increments)
7. Shortfalls in externally furnished components	-Benchmarking; inspections; reference checking; compatibility analysis
8. Shortfalls in externally performed tasks	-Reference checking; pre-award audits; award-fee contracts; competitive design or prototyping; teambuilding
9. Real-time performance shortfalls	-Simulation; benchmarking; modeling; prototyping; instrumentation; tuning
10. Straining computer science capabilities	-Technical analysis; cost-benefit analysis; prototyping; reference checking

is highlighted at each weekly, monthly, or milestone project review.

These steps are supported by a variety of techniques. Space limitations preclude further discussion of the issues here. Further details on each of the software risk management steps are given in [5].

IV. THE CASE STUDY

A. Corporate Background

BBB Industries is one of the largest manufacturers in the small, yet advanced emerging nation named Optimia. The company started out in the 1950's as a privately owned workshop, and has gone through periods of prosperity and periods of recession. During one of the recession periods in the early seventies, the owners sold their shares to MMM corporation, one of Optimia's largest investment corporations.

In 1983, BBB Industries' sales volume reached $100 million a year, with over 3000 employees. The manufacturing was carried out in several factories while the Marketing, Production Planning, and Financial Services functions were all concentrated at the company's headquarters. BBB Industries manufactured various consumer products that were marketed through diverse distribution channels, including the company's own store. Over half of the sales were directed to export markets in the USA and Europe.

The profitability of the company was very unstable: the world demand for BBB's product line is subject to frequent ups and downs, and BBB Industries was unable to adjust in time to these dynamic changes. This inability was attributed mainly to BBB's old-fashioned production and organizational methods.

BBB's Information Systems in 1983 were of the most archaic type. In the early 1970's a major effort was made to computerize the production and control systems by using a card-operated computer. This effort failed, and a decision was made to transfer the information processing to a service bureau. For technical and political reasons, the various departments adopted different service bureaus, so that in 1983 each of the General-Ledger, Accounts-Receivables, Payroll and Inventory systems used the services of a different service bureau.

B. The New Management's Attitude

In 1984, a new General Manager was appointed to BBB Industries. The business results of 1984 were good, and the General Manager decided that the time had come to do something about BBB's Information Systems. To achieve that result, he hired a new manager for the Data Processing department, Mr. Smith.

"It's not going to be an easy job," he told Mr. Smith, "But this is a big challenge. I know this company cannot go on without proper information systems. However, my middle management does not understand information systems concepts. It is up to you to show us the way, and to help me convince the other managers in this company to give a hand to this effort. However—you should not forget that BBB's budget is limited, and that 1985 is not going to be as profitable as 1984. So, we shall have to do our best with a minimal budget. And, of course, since I am trying to cut down on all personnel, you cannot hire any more people to the data processing department right now. First, I want to see some results, and then—the sky is the limit."

C. The Initial Survey

The initial survey was done by Mr. Smith himself. The survey consisted of two parts:
a) A study of BBB's existing systems.
b) An outline of BBB's requirements for new Information Systems.

The survey's findings can be summed up as follows:
- Except for the Payroll system, all the existing data-processing systems of BBB did not serve their purposes. These systems were not used in the day-to-day operations, their accuracy was very low, and they therefore required a lot of manual processing.
- The vital Production Design and Control operation could not benefit at all from any of the computer systems, and therefore was slow, inflexible, and inefficient.
- There was practically no integration between the different systems, and each served the specific, limited needs of the department that was in charge of it.
- BBB's productivity, manageability, and profitability depended on the replacement of these systems by new, better ones.
- The potential users of the systems were quite ignorant of what modern information systems concepts are, and how they could be of use for them in their daily ac-

tivities. Furthermore, the factory workers had little faith in BBB's ability to adopt new, modern methods.

The survey's recommendations were:

• There is immediate need to replace the existing systems by on-line, interactive systems, based on in-house computers, that will supply the information by both operational and management levels in a timely, accurate, and comprehensive fashion. This effort can be done in stages, and the first system to be implemented should be a relatively simple, low-risk system. The success of this implementation will improve the ability to continue with other, more complex systems.

• The development of the first system should be done by an outside contractor, preferably a software house that already has a package for that purpose.

• BBB's middle management personnel should receive special training that will enable them to better understand the potential of on-line computer systems and their applicability to their own problems.

• The problems of the factories are complex, and require more detailed research to analyze and define the information systems requirements of the factories and to evaluate the various modes of operations that are amenable for this problem (distributed processing versus centralized processing, interactive versus autonomous, data collection techniques, etc.).

• Even though the task of computerizing BBB is complex, such projects are common nowadays, and the overall timetable should not exceed three years.

The survey was presented to BBB's management, and its conclusions were approved enthusiastically. The Finished-Goods Sales and Marketing system (FGSM) was chosen for first implementation, primarily because it was the easiest to implement, and because the FGSM managers were the strongest in expressing their need for and support of a new system. Mr. Smith was charged with preparing a Request for Proposal that would be presented to potential suppliers of software and hardware. There was no discussion of the required budget, nor additional personnel.

D. The Request for Proposal (RFP)

The RFP was based on the initial survey and on the findings of a subsequent two-week survey of the Finished-Goods Sales and Marketing organization. It consisted of the following parts:

a) A general description of BBB, its organization, operations, and goals.

b) A thorough, although not detailed, description of the Finished-Goods Marketing and Sales Organization.

c) A list of the requirements for the new system for FGSM:

• The system should be an on-line, interactive system.

• The system shall handle all the different types of items and incorporate all the different types of Catalog Codes that are in current use.

• The system shall handle the Finished Goods inventory in various levels of detail.

• The system shall handle the various types of clients (retailers, wholesalers, department stores, company-owned stores).

• The system shall produce automatic billings to the various clients (some of the department stores required predefined forms).

• The system shall be able to produce different sales and inventory reports.

• The system shall be able to integrate in the future into the General Ledger and Accounts Receivable Systems

d) A four-page outline of the requirements for the new Financial Systems for BBB.

The RFP was presented to the three leading hardware suppliers in Optimia, and to five software companies that had previous experience in similar systems.

E. The Proposals

After the first elimination process, three proposals were left in the game. Since the RFP was rather open-ended, the proposals varied in their scopes and in the extent to which they covered the requirements mentioned. The price quotations ranged from $70,000 to $450,000. The final competitors were as follows.

1) Colossal Computers: The leading hardware distributor in Optimia. Colossal Computers proposed their popular System C computer, and recommended the software packages of SW1 Software as the basis for the implementation. (Colossal refused to take full commitment for both hardware and software.)

2) Big Computing Computers: The second largest hardware distributor in Optimia, distributors of Big computers, with their own Financial and Marketing packages.

3) Fast Computing Computers: The distributors of world renowned Fast computers. There were only few installations of Fast computers in Optimia, even though the equipment was excellent. As a result, there were no software packages available on Fast Computers. The owners of Fast Computing Computers was MMM Corp., the owners of BBB Industries. MMM Corp. was deliberating at the time how to increase the sales of Fast Computers.

Table V summarizes the results of the evaluation process among the three competitors, as presented to BBB's management.

Mr. Smith's recommendation was to buy Colossal's equipment and to engage SW1 Software as subcontractor for the Marketing and Financial Systems, relying on SW1's existing Financial package. Mr. Smith had met with two of SW1's executives and was very impressed with their familiarity with Sales and Marketing Systems. It turned out that SW1 had considerable previous experience in developing Marketing systems similar to that required by BBB.

BBB's management informed the three competitors of BBB's choice, and started final negotiations with Colossal Computers.

TABLE V
PROPOSALS EVALUATION—THE FGSM SYSTEM FOR BBB INDUSTRIES

	Colossal	Big Computing	Fast Computing
HARDWARE EVALUATION			
Speed Factor	Average	Average	V. Good
Memory Factor	Average	Low	V. Good
# of installations (Optima)	200	50	5
Growth Factor	Average	Low	High
PROPOSED SW SOLUTION			
Financial Package	SW1's package	Own Package	To be developed
Marketing System	SW1	Own devlp.	BBB devlp.
SOFTWARE EVALUATION			
Financial Package	Good	Good	?
Marketing Solution	Good	Average	None
Addt'l Packages	Many	A few	None
GENERAL FACTORS			
Familiarity with Equip.	High	Low	Low
Compatibility with			
BBB's Inventory Sys.	None	None	High
# of SW houses	15	5	2
COMPANY FACTORS			
Company Stability	High	Average	Average
Maintenance Organization	High	Low	Average
Company Commitment	Average	Average	High
ESTIMATED COSTS			
Hardware	$170K	$130K	$140K
Marketing System	$50K	$40K	?
Financial Package	$30K	$30K	$40K
Estimated Modifications to			
Financial Package	$20K-$40K	$30K-$50K	?
TOTAL COSTS	$270K-$290K	$240K-$260K	$180K+?

The next day, BBB's General Manager got a call from Fast Computing Computers' General Manager, and a meeting was set where BBB was asked to clarify why Colossal was chosen. Fast Computing's General Manager explained that the BBB account had a crucial significance to Fast Computing's future. "If in-house companies (that is—MMM owned) won't buy our equipment, who will? Colossal will use this fact as a weapon to beat us even in places where they don't have such an advantage," he said.

"The solution offered by Colossal answers most of our needs," replied BBB's General Manager, "Your equipment may be good, but you simply do not have enough software packages to attract new clients in our line of business."

The following day, BBB's General Manager got a call from MMM's Chairman: "I would hate to interfere with BBB's internal management, but will you please give Fast Computers another chance? There must be a way for them to get this account."

BBB's General Manager's reply to that was simple: "Only if we can get the same solution as is available on Colossal equipment, within no more than two months delay, and provided that the software is developed by SW1 and that we get all the required modifications to the financial package for free."

When informed by BBB's General Manager of this conversation, Mr. Smith protested: "This is an infeasible solution! It is too expensive for Fast Computing, and I don't believe we will get our system within this time frame."

"Are you sure it cannot be done?" asked BBB's manager.

"Well—It's not impossible, but it sure requires an extraordinary effort," replied Mr. Smith.

"So, we must make sure that Fast Computing does this extraordinary effort."

"If that's what you want, we can put a clause in the agreement that we will not pay unless we get satisfactory results within a predescribed timeframe. However—I still recommend that we take Colossal's proposal," said Mr. Smith.

A couple of days later BBB signed an agreement with Fast Computing Computers. One of the preconditions for payments for both Hardware and Software was that BBB must receive a software solution that satisfied its needs, within the outlined timetable. The total cost of the project to BBB (Hardware, Marketing System, Financial Package and all the required modifications to the Financial Package) was to be $230,000.

F. The Detailed Requirements Specifications for the FGSM System

Fast Computing Computers engaged SW1 Software to develop both the Marketing and the Financial Systems. The Marketing system was to be developed according to BBB's requirements, and the Financial System was to be converted from the Colossal Computer version.

Since the project was to be carried out on Fast computers, SW1 decided not to allocate the same project manager that was proposed to manage the development on Colossal computers (Mr. Brown). A new project manager was recruited to SW1—Mr. Holmes. Mr. Smith was disappointed, since his decision to choose SW1 as software developer was based partly on Mr. Brown's capabilities and familiarity with marketing systems. But, SW1 insisted (they did not want to waste Mr. Brown's familiarity with Colossal equipment).

A Technical Committee was formed: Mr. Smith, Mr. Holmes and Mr. Watson, the representative of Fast Computing Computers. The Committee agreed upon the timetable outlined in Table VI for the development of the FGSM system. It was further agreed that, if feasible, the design and development would be divided into modules (increments), thus enabling starting 1986 with the new inventory system for FGSM (the beginning of the 10th month from the start of the project).

The analysis of FGSM's requirements specifications started off on the right foot. The Specifications Document was ready in time for the Design Review scheduled for month 4. The Design Review lasted two whole days: on top of the technical and supervisory committee members, additional representatives from FGSM's organization participated and contributed their comments and clarifications. However, Mr. Holmes expressed his concern regarding the difficulty in handling the complex form required for the Catalog Number. He complained about the lack of appropriate software tools on Fast Computers: his people were having difficulties in adjusting to the new development environment. They were very hopeful that the new version of operating system, due to be released the next month, would solve these problems. When the discussion narrowed down on the format of the sales reports, it turned out that there was no easy way to develop a report-writer similar to report-writers found in Colossal applications, and SW1 refused to commit to develop a report-writer within the existing budget for the FGSM system. They were willing to commit only to 4 predefined

10

TABLE VI
ORIGINAL TIMETABLE FOR THE FGSM PROJECT

Months	Subject
1 - 3	Detailed System Requirements Document for FGSM
4	Requirements Review
5 - 6	Detailed Design of FGSM
7 - 9	Programming
10	Acceptance Tests
11-12	New and Old Systems running concurrently

TABLE VII
UPDATED TIMETABLE FOR THE INCREMENTAL DEVELOPMENT OF THE FGSM SYSTEM

Months (From beginning of Project)	Subject
5 - 6	Module # 1 - Detailed Design
7 - 9	Module # 1 - Programming and Test
10	Module # 1 - Acceptance Tests
7 - 9	Module # 2 - Detailed Design
10 - 11	Module # 2 - Programming and Test
12	Module # 2 - Acceptance Tests
10	Module # 3 - Detailed Design
11 - 12	Module # 3 - Programming and Test
13	Module # 3 - Acceptance Test

sales reports. Mr. Smith would not agree, and the issue remained unsolved. A similar problem arose regarding the development of special reports to Department-Stores, and this issue remained unsolved as well.

The disagreements were outlined in the document that summarized the Design Review.

G. The Design and Development of the FGSM System

The real problems started at the detailed design phase. SW1's people discovered that the differences between the Fast computer and other computers were more than they had planned for. SW1 did not have people with previous experience in Fast computers, and so the original estimates, that were prepared for the Colossal computer, were not accurate. So as to enable BBB to start 1986 with a new Inventory system, the development was partitioned into 3 increments. The Inventory Module, the Operations Module, the Sales Reports Module. Mr. Holmes presented to Mr. Smith the updated timetable outlined in Table VII.

Mr. Smith pointed out that even though he understood the difficulties SW1 had run into, these problems should be addressed to Fast Computing, and they should be able to help SW1 to keep the original timetables. BBB was willing to accept only one month of delay in the delivery of the total system, and had agreed to break the system into increments so as to receive the first module sooner, not later, than the original timetable. After a couple of meetings between Mr. Smith, Mr. Holmes and Mr. Watson, the parties agreed that it was possible to improve the timetables by 6 weeks, delivering the first module to BBB before the end of the 8th month.

Meanwhile, the people of FGSM were full of enthusiasm towards the prospect of the forthcoming installation. Being aware that once the system was installed, it would be hard to request changes and improvements, they began asking for all sorts of small improvements and minor changes. Both Mr. Holmes and Mr. Smith were very satisfied with the users' attitude, and made every possible effort to please the people of FGSM, by incorporating most of these changes into the design.

H. The Installation of Module #1

Module #1 was installed in the middle of the 9th month—two weeks before the beginning of the New Year. Mr. Holmes, Mr. Smith, and the people of FGSM exerted enormous efforts to have the system up and running in time for the New Year. It turned out, however, that the

acceptance tests were not comprehensive enough, and after the system was already installed and running, many problems and bugs would still pop up during operations. The many minor design changes that had accumulated in the last 3 months did not help the SW1 programmers to correct these bugs and problems in time, and it was hard to tell which was the latest version of every program. Though the FGSM people were pleased with having an on-line system, they began to feel pretty uneasy about the system when it went through a whole series of corrections, errors, and crashes.

By early 1986, the development of Module #2 was almost complete, but the amount of man-months invested by SW1 had already exceeded the original estimates that were presented to Fast Computing. When SW1's General Manager discussed this problem with Mr. Watson, Mr. Watson explained that there was not much they could do for the time being: Fast Computing still had not received any money from BBB, and its own investments in support and management attention to this project were very high. Mr. Watson's recommendation was to wait for the successful installation of the 2nd and 3rd module before approaching BBB's higher management.

Mr. Holmes discussed these problems with Mr. Smith. Mr. Smith expressed his opinion, that Fast Computing had misled his management into believing that an impossible effort was possible, and that now Fast Computers were not doing their very best to keep their promise. Mr. Holmes remarked that his company did not like to be in such a situation either: lagging behind timetables and exceeding cost estimates. Both felt pretty bitter about the situation they found themselves in. Mr. Holmes, who was not party to the original cost estimates, began to feel that he was going to be blamed for something that was not of his doing, and secretly began looking for another job. One month later Mr. Holmes announced his decision to resign from SW1. One of SW1's senior Systems Analysts who participated in the project was made Project Manager.

I. The Installation of Modules #2 and #3

The installation of Module #2, though two months later than scheduled, was smoother than the installation of Module #1: the acceptance tests were ready, and were carried out properly. However the integration with Module #1 was not an easy task: it was hard to locate the latest versions of the software that were currently in use. Thus, the installation required a lot of time from SW1 programmers. It became evident that Module #3 would not be ready on time; in fact, the delay was estimated at 6 months.

All the partners to the effort were in bad shape. On one hand, the expenses of SW1 and Fast Computing exceeded even the worst projections, and it was obvious that both companies were going to lose money on this project. On the other hand, BBB was not getting the systems according to the promised timetables, and people started to compare the project to former unsuccessful attempts to introduce new systems to BBB.

The disagreements regarding the contents and form of the Sales Reports now surfaced. FGSM was not willing to settle for the 4 reports suggested by SW1. "The system is completely useless unless we get the reports we want," said Mr. Jones. "Not only that, but the Department Stores are threatening to close their account with us unless we automate the special reports they required, like all their other customers."

SW1 claimed that these reports were not part of their original agreement with Fast Computing. In fact, they blamed the Initial Survey for being vague on these points. "Heaven knows how much money we are going to lose in this project," said their General Manager to Mr. Smith, "Either BBB or Fast Computing must make it up to us."

J. The Financial Systems Design

The problems of the FGSM system were minor relative to the problems that arose during the analysis of BBB's requirements for the Financial Systems. Fast Computing's commitment was to deliver a complete system, tailored to BBB's requirements, and at the price of an "off-the-shelf" product. An initial survey of BBB's requirements, carried out by SW1's professionals, estimated the cost of this project at $150K.

The three General Managers of the three companies were summoned by Mr. Watson to a special meeting. BBB was asked to lower its level of requirements from the Financial System, so as to minimize the projected expenses. BBB's General Manager was furious: "We could have had a working system by now, had we purchased Colossal equipment," he exclaimed. "My people want nothing but the best. It took me a great effort to raise their expectations, and I am not going to let them down. Fast Computers knew exactly what they were up against when they signed the agreement with us. They cannot disregard their commitments now!"

"Our original estimates regarding the scope of the project were based upon the prices quoted by SW1 Software," replied Fast Computing's General Manager "We never intended to make money on this project, but we also never intended to lose that much."

"We based our estimates on BBB's initial survey," retorted SW1's General Manager. "As it turned out, there were too many TBD's, and the problem was that BBB's people wanted the maximum in every case, and would not settle for anything less. They kept coming with more requirements and endless modifications. One of my people has already resigned. We will not take the responsibilities that you two should have taken."

The meeting lasted for four hours, but the parties could not reach an agreement on how to proceed.

V. CASE STUDY ANALYSIS

Clearly, in this case, none of the parties came out a winner. BBB Industries ended up with unsatisfied users, mistrust in information systems, delays, partial systems, low morale, and major unresolved problems. Fast Computing ended up with significant unreimbursed expenditures, a poor reputation in the Sales Information Systems marketplace, and some useless partial products. SW1 also ended up with unreimbursed expenditures, and also a tarnished reputation in Sales Information Systems and poor prospects for future business in the Fast computer user community.

Below is an analysis of how these problems can be traced to lack of responsiveness to the Theory W fundamental principle (*make everyone a winner*) and to the two subsidiary principles (*identify and manage your risks*, and *plan the flight and fly the plan*). The analysis also indicates ways in which the principles could have been used to avoid the problems and to make the participants winners.

A. Make Everyone a Winner

The major source of difficulty was the win-lose contract established between BBB and Fast Computing: no payment unless BBB got everything it asked for, on schedule (Section IV-E). Fast Computing should have made a more thorough analysis of their overrun potential (risk assessment), and a thorough assessment of the benefits of entering the Sales Information System market. If the benefits were high enough, they should have approached MMM's Chairman to authorize their spending additional profit dollars to cover the added costs of software development. Otherwise, they should have dropped out. BBB's General Manager should have heeded Mr. Smith's cautions, and either required a more detailed and realistic plan and cost estimate from Fast Computers, or gone ahead with Colossal. BBB could have made a better win-win situation by not coupling system delivery and cutover to the New Year at a time when the likely development schedules were not well known.

Another major difficulty was SW1's use of Mr. Holmes. If SW1 seriously wanted to penetrate the Fast Computers market, they should have used Mr. Brown (Section IV-F). Holmes should not have accepted responsibility for making people winners until he understood the situation better (Section IV-F). SW1 management should have done more to make Holmes a winner: apprised him of the risks, done a better job of recognizing his good work in getting Module 1 running (Section IV-H), and of monitoring his frustration level and likelihood of leaving SW1 (Section IV-H).

As indicated in Section II, making people winners involves seeking out day-to-day conflicts and changing them into win-win situations. An excellent opportunity to do this occurred at the Design Review (Section IV-F), when SW1 balked at producing more than four sales reports, and at producing any Department Store reports at all. However, the conflict was not addressed, and the project continued to inflate users' expectations without any attempt to get SW1 to provide the promised capabilities.

A Theory W solution to this problem would consider the conditions necessary to make winners of each of the interested parties:

- *BBB and Its Customers:* Furnish the most important reports in the initial delivery, with the other reports as soon as possible thereafter.
- *SW1:* Provide a realistic schedule and budget for producing the desired reports (and other capabilities).
- *Fast Computing:* Develop a strong system with further sales potential, within a realistic and affordable budget and schedule.

Subsequently, a much more thorough analysis would be done to determine realistic budget and schedule estimates as functions of the amount of functionality to be delivered at each increment. These levels of functionality, their associated schedules, and Fast Computing's definition of "affordability" provide some degrees of freedom within which may be possible to define a win-win solution. If so, the project can go forward on such a basis. If not, the project should be disbanded: everyone would not be a winner, but they would minimize their losses.

A similar day-to-day problem which was deferred rather than addressed was the Fast Computing payments problem (Section IV-H). A related problem was the addition of changes and improvements to the system without changing the budget or schedule (Section IV-G). This usually leads to a lose-lose situation when the budget and schedule give out and all the original and new capabilities are not completed. A Theory W solution would involve prioritizing the proposed changes with respect to the original desired capabilities, reallocating the top priority capabilities to remain consistent with the three scheduled increments; then defining an Increment 4 and assuring the users that their remaining features would definitely be incorporated in Increment 4 if BBB's management agreed to provide the budget for them.

Some other problems were created by establishing unrealistic expectations. Issuing vague Requests for Proposal (Section IV-D) is a classical example: users tend to interpret the requirements expansively, while developers interpret them austerely, creating an inevitable lose-lose situation. The cost underestimate and specification interpretation for the Financial System is another example (Section IV-J).

On the other hand, some Theory W principles were followed well. The BBB General Manager's initial conversation with Mr. Smith (Section IV-B) established a realistic climate of expectations. The choice of FGSM as the initial system to implement (Section IV-C) was good, given that FGSM's managers were enthusiastic product

champions. Had the other situations been handled in similar ways, with the participants trying harder to accommodate the others' interests, the project could have had a good chance of making the participants winners.

B. Plan the Flight and Fly the Plan

The project's planning was seriously deficient with respect to the elements of a Software Development Plan shown in Fig. 3. Some top-level milestones were established, but no attempt was made to identify dependencies and critical-path items. As discussed in the previous section, the imprecise allocation of responsibilities (e.g., SW1's responsibilities for sales reports) led to serious problems downstream. Several approach and resources problems (configuration management, verification, and validation planning, reviews, resource control) will be discussed further below.

But the major problem here was in putting the plans on a realistic basis. Budgets and schedules were determined more from optimistic target figures than from any rationale based on cost estimation techniques or task dependency analyses. Thus, although more elaborate approach plans would have avoided some problems, they would not have cured the budget-schedule-functionality mismatch problems.

For example, SW1's projected productivity for the Fast Computer development was considered to be equal to their productivity on Colossal Computer projects. Even a rough analysis using the COCOMO cost model [2] indicated a factor of 3 likely reduction in productivity due to personnel capability and experience, support system volatility, reduced tool support, and schedule compression.

1) Configuration Management: In this area, we can easily count the following shortcomings from the part of the project management:

- No change control system.
- No configuration management and control.
- No baselined master version of the specs or programs.
- No quality assurance (project standards, technical audits).

All those led to confusion, multiple bugs, problems in integration, installation, unmaintainability of the system, additional costs, and errors. There was no controlled mechanism for product changes, no track of product status, and no product integrity.

2) Verification and Validation Planning:

Most of the basic principles of V&V planning were not implemented in this case:

- No verification of the initial survey or the detailed design.
- Insufficient, late test plans (due to untimely, careless preparation).
- No acceptance criteria.
- No integration and test plans.
- Test phase and system acceptance combined.

As a result, the users got their system before it was completely verified, and were confronted with bugs and problems. The system's reliability was undermined, and the operations forced into a haphazard process.

3) Review Plans: No product review was held, only a requirements review. However, the problems that arose in the review were not assigned, nor tracked. It is no wonder that most problems were left unattended. The results were that on one hand there were missing capabilities, and on the other that some of the requirements were not really needed. The users were not committed to the final product. Attempts to correct the problems of missing capabilities at later stages were very expensive. A proper treatment of the problem at an earlier stage would have been less costly.

4) Resources, Status Monitoring, and Control: The main problems in the area were:

- Only high-level milestone charts were available.
- No work breakdown structure was prepared.
- No budget allocations were established.

Therefore, no cost versus progress monitoring and control was possible, and only when the overall budget was exceeded were the problems surfaced. Problems of insufficient personnel and inappropriate budget were discovered only when it was too late. In short, the visibility was poor, both at the overall progress level and the individual trouble-spot level.

C. Identify and Manage Your Risks

In some cases, the participants did a good job of identifying and managing risks. In particular, Mr. Smith's recommendation in Section IV-C to start and pursue an incremental development was very good. But there were many situations in which the lack of risk management caused serious problems.

Allowing two weeks to prepare the RFP (Section IV-D) reflects a serious neglect of risk management. BBB's General Manager should have done a risk analysis on hearing Mr. Smith assess Fast Computing's need for "extraordinary effort" to succeed (Section IV-E); in particular, to carry out an independent estimate of the development cost and schedule.

BBB also did not risk assessment by looking behind the interface between Fast Computing and SW1. They did not investigate whether SW1 would use Mr. Brown on their job, and were taken by surprise when SW1 assigned the unknown Mr. Holmes. Holmes himself did very little analysis of the risks he was getting into.

BBB did not assess the risk of the highly optimistic, highly overlapped incremental development schedule proposed by SW1 (Table V, Section IV-G). They were too preoccupied with establishing an ambitious schedule for Increment 1 to meet their New Year deadline. Such overlapping increments are major sources of risk, as changes in the earlier increments usually have serious ripple effects on the later increments under development.

In one case, risk avoidance caused an "everyone a winner" problem. Mr. Smith identified several risks due to lack of user management commitment, and addressed these by a strong effort to sell the users on the advantages of information technology. This backfired when the users compared their unrealistic expectations to the project's results. A preferred Theory W solution would be to couch user benefit projections more realistically in terms of expected near-term and long-term benefits, and to involve the users more closely in analyzing and preparing for the benefits.

VI. CONCLUSIONS

When applied to a project case study, a good management theory should be able to do two things:

1)To explain why the project encountered problems.

2) To prescribe improved approaches which would have avoided the problems.

Analysis of the BBB case study indicates that the Theory W fundamental principle (*Make everyone a winner*) and its two subsidiary principles (*Plan the flight and fly the plan; identify and manage your risks*) did a good job on both counts. The case study and the other examples provided earlier also indicate that Theory W does a reasonably good job in satisfying the management theory objectives of being simultaneously simple, general, and specific.

REFERENCES

[1] K. Blanchard and S. Johnson. *The One Minute Manager.* Berkeley, CA: Berkeley Books, 1982.

[2] B. W. Boehm, *Software Engineering Economics.* Englewood Cliffs, NJ: Prentice-Hall, 1981.

[3] ——, "Seven basic principles of software engineering," *J. Syst. Software*, vol. 3, pp. 3-24, 1983.

[4] ——, "A spiral model of software development and enhancement." *Computer*, pp. 61-72, May 1988.

[5] ——, "Tutorial volume: Software risk management," IEEE Computer Society, 1989 (in publication).

[6] J. D. Couger and R. A. Zawacki, *Motivating and Managing Computer Personnel.* New York: Wiley, 1980.

[7] W. G. Dyer, *Team Building.* Reading, MA: Addison-Wesley, 1987.

[8] M. W. Evans, P. Piazza, and B. Dolkas, *Principles of Productive Software Management.* New York: Wiley, 1983.

[9] R. Fisher and W. Ury, *Getting to Yes.* Boston, MA: Houghton-Mifflin, 1981; also, Baltimore, MD: Penguin Books, 1983.

[10] S. W. Gellerman, *Motivation and Productivity.* New York: American Books, 1978.

[11] N. J. Kirchof and J. R. Adams, *Conflict Management for Project Managers,* Project Management Inst., Feb. 1986.

[12] H. Koontz and C. O'Donnell, *Principles of Management: An Analysis of Managerial Functions,* 5th ed. New York: McGraw-Hill, 1972.

[13] D. McGregor, *The Human Side of Enterprise.* New York: McGraw-Hill, 1960.

[14] P. W. Metzger, *Managing a Programming Project,* 2nd ed. Englewood Cliffs, NJ: Prentice-Hall, 1981.

[15] G. I. Nierenberg, *The Art of Negotiating.* Pocket Books, 1984.

[16] W. G. Ouchi, *Theory Z.* Reading, MA: Addison-Wesley, 1981; also Avon, 1982.

[17] T. J. Peters and R. H. Waterman, *In Search of Excellence.* New York: Harper & Row, 1982.

[18] D. J. Reifer, *Tutorial: Software Management,* 3rd ed., IEEE Catalog No. EHO 189-1, 1986.

[19] J. S. Rosenschein and M. R. Genesereth, "Deals among rational agents," in *Proc. IJCAI-85,* pp. 91-99.

[20] F. W. Taylor, *The Principles of Scientific Management.* New York: Harper and Brothers, 1911.

[21] R. H. Thayer, A. Pyster, and R. C. Wood, "The challenge of software engineering project management," *Computer,* pp. 51-59, Aug. 1980.

[22] R. E. Walton, *Managing Conflict.* Reading, MA: Addison-Wesley, 1987.

Barry W. Boehm (SM'84) received the B.A. degree in mathematics from Harvard University, Cambridge, MA, in 1957, and the M.A. and Ph.D. degrees in mathematics from the University of California, Los Angeles, in 1961 and 1964, respectively.

He is an Adjunct Professor of Computer Science at UCLA, and also Chief Scientist of TRW's Defense Systems Group. He has served as the manager of several TRW software development projects, and also directed the development of TRW's software management policies and standards.

Within the IEEE Computer Society, Dr. Boehm has served as Chairman of the Technical Committee on Software Engineering, a member of the Governing Board, and an editorial board member of *Computer*, *IEEE Software*, and IEEE TRANSACTIONS ON SOFTWARE ENGINEERING.

Rony Ross was born in Tel Aviv. She received the B.Sc. degree in mathematics from Tel Aviv University in 1972, the M.Sc. degree in computer science from the Weizmann Institute of Science, Rehovot, Israel, in 1976, and the M.B.A. degree in business administration from the Graduate School of Management, Tel Aviv University, in 1980.

From 1971 to 1980, she was a Teaching Assistant at Tel Aviv University Department of Computer Science. From 1975 to 1980, she was employed by Mini-Systems Computers Ltd. as a Systems Analyst and Real-Time Programmer, working for Sci-Tex Corp. From 1980 to 1983, she was Manager of Data Processing and Information Systems Department of Kitan Ltd. From 1983 to 1986, she was in charge of new business development for Contahal Ltd. Currently, she is studying toward the Ph.D. degree in the Department of Computer Science at the University of California, Los Angeles.

15

The Impact of Unreliable Information on the Management of Software Projects: A Dynamic Decision Perspective

Kishore Sengupta and Tarek K. Abdel-Hamid, *Member, IEEE*

Abstract—The task of managing software projects is universally plagued by cost and schedule overruns. A fundamental problem in software projects is the presence of unreliable information, in initial information as well as in subsequent status reports. We report an experiment that investigates decision making in software projects as exemplars of complex, dynamic environments reactive to the actions of the decision maker. The experiment shows that in coping with unreliable information in such environments, decision makers are susceptible to *self-fulfilling prophesies* created by the environment, and are prone to demonstrate *conservatism*. A process tracing extension of the experiment shows that subjects demonstrate a low capacity for handling complexity. The implications of the results for managing software projects and for research in dynamic decision making are discussed.

I. INTRODUCTION

SEVERAL articles in the trade and research literature have documented a serious and persistent problem in managing software projects: such projects routinely incur significant over-runs in cost and schedule [16], [21], [43, p. 18]. In attempting to address this problem, researchers in software engineering have sought to improve the effectiveness of estimation and control tools that are used for managing software projects [6], [29]. Another emerging area of research has taken a different approach to the problem. Its objective is to explore the micro-structure of decisions made by managers in software projects, identify the associated dysfunctionalities, and prescribe methods for minimizing them [4], [5], [47]. The research reported in this paper is in the latter category. Specifically, we seek to identify the dysfunctionalities that result when decision makers must manage software projects with unreliable information. The research question is addressed from the conceptual standpoint of dynamic decision making.

The management of software projects can be viewed as a case of decision making in reactive, dynamic environments. Such environments are distinguished by three salient features [11], [22]. First, the task requires making a series of decisions over time. For example, a project manager is required to decide on the size of the software development team for a project at several points over the life of the project. Second,

the decisions are not independent, i.e., decisions made at time t are constrained by decisions already made at time $t - n$. Thus, in deciding on the staffing level at any point in the project, the manager must consider existing staff levels and past hiring decisions, because repeated hiring and attrition can have an adverse impact on a project. Finally, the decision environment changes over time, autonomously as well as in reaction to a manager's decisions. For example, a project's environment may change autonomously because of changes in the requirements' specifications. At the same time, staffing decisions made in a particular period may affect the progress of the project, thereby impacting such decisions in subsequent periods.

This research is the second in a series of studies examining how decision makers react to unreliable feedback in complex, dynamic tasks. The first study (reported in [5]) examined how subjects performed the task of productivity estimation over the life of a project. Subjects in different experimental groups were given different initial estimates of the development staff's productivity. At periodic intervals, the system provided feedback on reported productivity, based on which subjects made new estimates of future productivity. The results show that subjects resorted to a strategy wherein their estimates over time were strongly influenced by the initial estimates of productivity provided to them. The experiment contained a major simplification in that it employed a *nonreactive* decision environment. That is, while subjects were told that their estimates would be used in determining future staffing levels, in practice the system disregarded the subjects' estimates and calculated its own staffing levels—a fact that was not known to the subjects. This ensured that all subjects received the same feedback on reported productivity. Thus, any differences in decisions across groups could be attributed to the initial estimates.

However, in reality, software project environments, like many dynamic environments, are *reactive* in the sense that the actions of the decision maker can change the environment, often in unanticipated ways (cf. [11]). In such environments, the actions of decision makers in a particular period can have the effect of changing outcomes in subsequent periods [25]. When different decision makers start by making different decisions in reactive environments, the underlying environment changes; thereby altering in different ways, the feedback they receive. As a result, their downstream decisions can be quite

Manuscript received November 5, 1994; revised March 31, 1995.
The authors are with the Naval Postgraduate School, Department of Systems Management, Monetery, CA 93943 USA (e-mails: kishore@nps.navy.mil; 3991p@navpgs.bitnet).
Publisher Item Identifier S 1083-4427(96)01391-4.

Reprinted from IEEE Transactions on Systems, Man and Cybernetics, Part A, Vol. 26, No. 2, Mar. 1996, pp. 177-189.

17

different. In such environments, decision makers can be seen to adopt different trajectories through a large decision space, depending substantially on how the environment reacts to their earlier decisions.

What are the implications of this distinction between reactive and nonreactive environments? While decision making in nonreactive environments is similar to chasing a moving target [30], the task of decision making in reactive environments can be likened to a target that not only moves *but also reacts* to the actions of the pursuer. Thus, the fundamental mechanisms that drive decisions in the two environments are different. Consequently, decision strategies (and dysfunctionalities) associated with the two environments are distinct, and strategies that are effective in one type of environment may not necessarily succeed in the other. Second, in reactive environments, we *expect* different subjects to adopt different trajectories. In a sense, therefore, decision makers create their own environments, depending on the trajectories of their respective decisions. In such environments, decisions should be considered from a cybernetic perspective [11]. Thus, decisions cannot be viewed in isolation, but should rather be studied in systematic terms as an interaction of the decision maker and the environment.

In this paper, we report an experiment that employs a reactive dynamic environment. It explores the consequences of unreliability of information in managing software projects—unreliability with respect to initial information as well as subsequent outcome feedback. The experiment focuses on the task of estimating the productivity of a software development team. To assess progress on a software project, a manager needs to track work accomplished as well as resources utilized. Combining both "measures" (by dividing the former with the latter) yields an estimate of the team's productivity. The amount of effort still needed to complete the project may then be estimated as a function of the tasks that remain to be accomplished (total project size minus work already completed) and the estimated productivity. As Howes [31] observes, productivity assessment plays a central role in the planning and control of software projects. The reactive nature of the underlying environment affects the manner in which productivity is assessed over the lifecycle of a project. For example, the decisions that managers make at the beginning of a project are significantly influenced by the pressures and perceptions created by initial estimates of project schedules [2]. Initial perceptions of staff productivity may form the basis for hiring new staff, thereby affecting productivity in the immediate future. This, in turn, can change feedback on reported productivity. Therefore, different starting points represented by different initial estimates can, in a very real sense, create different projects [2].

The paper proceeds as follows. In the next section, we employ dynamic decision making as a conceptual basis to lay out *a priori* assertions on decision behavior specific to reactive environments. Section III describes the method. Sections IV and V report the results of the experiment. Section VI outlines the implications of the results, for research as well as for managing software projects.

II. MANAGING SOFTWARE PROJECTS: A DYNAMIC DECISION PERSPECTIVE

A. Operating Effectively in Dynamic Environments: The Case of Software Projects

From a control theory perspective, dynamic decision making is analogous to controlling a dynamic system [11]. The key requirement for effective control of a dynamic system is the operator's ability to incorporate an adequate model of the system [17]. The availability of an adequate model enables a decision maker to assess the action possibilities in the environment, and thus devise appropriate decision strategies for coping with it. In control theoretic terms, this means finding the right match between the characteristics of the processes to be controlled and those of the controlling process [10].

When decision makers begin to operate in a dynamic environment, they initially apply sketchy and rudimentary models of the environment to the task at hand [34]. These initial models, which are necessarily incomplete, are progressively refined over time through a feedback control strategy, i.e., through initial information on the environment, and continuous outcome feedback on the state of the environment. An individual's ability to acquire a refined model through feedback control is affected by the *complexity* of the environment, the degree to which it is *observable*, and the extent to which the environment *changes* over time [11]. Past research has shown that subjects have great difficulty in acquiring adequate models of environments that are complex, relatively opaque, and subject to continuous change [11], [20]. This finding has been established across a variety of tasks and settings, with experienced and inexperienced decision makers alike (cf. [20]).

What does the nature of software environments generally imply for the ability of project managers to acquire adequate models? Software project environments are typically complex, because they are endowed with time lags, nonlinearities and interactions [3]. Second, software is an intangible product for which it is difficult to establish and verify milestones. As a consequence, software projects are hampered by poor observability [13]. Finally, software project environments are highly dynamic because they are continually accompanied by changes in requirements' specifications, schedules and personnel [19], [29]. On the basis of past research on analogous environments, we conclude that subjects relying on outcome feedback are liable to develop incomplete and inadequate models of the environment.

B. Estimating Software Productivity: The Impact of Unreliable Information

In addition to being complex, opaque and dynamic, software environments are also characterized by information that is *unreliable*, with respect to initial estimates as well as outcome feedback available over the life of the project. The unreliability in initial estimates is due to the inability of extant forecasting techniques to provide accurate projections [33]. The unreliability in outcome feedback results from the difficulty in assessing how much of the work has been completed during a particular time period, especially for intermediate products such as design specifications and undebugged programs [39]. This is particularly true in the early stages of the project, where much of the work is in unverified stages and the cumulative extent of its contribution to the final product is not clear. This inherent lack of accuracy in measurement is compounded by the tendency of project staff to report favorable information (which is relatively unimportant for control purposes) and to withhold unfavorable information (which, on the other hand, is critical for taking corrective action).

The effect of unreliable information on productivity estimation can be posited in terms of two factors: unreliable initial information, and unreliable outcome feedback. First, consider the impact of *unreliable initial information*. An example of this would be a situation where at the inception of a project, the manager is provided with an unduly low initial estimate of the development staff's productivity.[1] Faced with a low initial estimate, the manager would plan to recruit a large staff in order to get the project completed on time. Doing so would increase the communication and training overheads, which in turn would depress productivity—at least in the short run. Therefore, outcome feedback received by the manager over time would serve to create and reinforce a *self-fulfilling prophesy* (cf. [45, p. 84]). Self-fulfilling prophesies refer to situations where an initial false belief or perception of a situation creates new behavior which reinforces the original (false) perception [38]. In this case, the initial false perception (of low staff productivity) would create behavior (i.e., hiring large staff), which in turn would produce outcome feedback (of low productivity) that would reinforce the initial perception.

In reactive environments, therefore, initial information is critical in that it represents a *starting point* which shapes the environment for subsequent decisions. The effect of unreliable initial information (such as an understated estimate of productivity) is to *shift* the starting point. This, in turn, creates a self-fulfilling prophesy that changes the environment accordingly and affects the subsequent decisions of the decision maker.

Hypothesis 1: Initial estimates in software projects create self-fulfilling prophesies.

Consider next, the effect of *unreliable outcome feedback*, i.e., where the estimates of reported productivity over time are unreliable. The impact of unreliable outcome feedback in dynamic decision making can be specified as follows. Multiple cue probability learning studies in static environments show that subjects have great difficulty in learning cue-cue and cue-criterion relations in environments where outcome feedback is characterized by even modest amounts of error [9], [24]. In complex, dynamic environments, we can expect unreliability in outcome feedback to pose a similar impediment to subjects in inferring these relationships.

How do subjects cope with unreliable feedback when they lack an adequate model of the environment? When confronted with unreliable information, decision makers resort to incremental behavior, in the belief that when the information is

unreliable, dramatic changes can have large, unanticipated and dysfunctional consequences [30], [35]. Furthermore, in complex dynamic environments, subjects are often found to move toward a "ballistic" strategy in which prior beliefs (in this case, induced by the self-fulfilling prophesy) become increasingly influential while outcome feedback is increasingly ignored [40]. Thus, when faced with unreliable outcome feedback, subjects' decisions at any point of time will be *conservative* (cf. [23]), and made by small, incremental adjustments from previous decisions, even when the outcome feedback may suggest larger revisions.

Hypothesis 2: In software projects, the presence of unreliable outcome feedback will induce conservative behavior on the part of subjects.

III. METHOD

A. Task Environment

We employed an experimental microworld for conducting the experiment. Experimental microworlds enable replication of complex, dynamic environments, and provide researchers with a degree of control not easily obtained in field settings [11], [50]. As a result, such microworlds have gained increasing acceptance as a tool for research in dynamic decision making. The task environment is embodied in a systems dynamics model of the software development process, developed from a battery of 27 field interviews of software project managers in five software producing organizations, and supplemented by an extensive database of empirical findings from the literature. The model is described in detail elsewhere [1], [3], and a summary of the model's structure is provided in the Appendix. The task environment changes autonomously as well as in consequence of the subject's actions. The environment as represented by the model is complex (with more than 100 causal links), relatively opaque (in the sense that very little of the model is actually observable by the decision maker), and dynamic (the nature of the project can change over time). As in most software real-life projects, the project status reports are not completely reliable, especially in the early phases of a project.

In the experiment, subjects were told to play the role of project management staff with the objective of helping the manager make decisions on staffing levels for the projects. Their role was to track the progress of the project using a set of reports delivered in intervals of every two months (40 work days). Specifically, subjects were required to provide an estimate of the productivity of the project staff for the next period, in tasks per person-day. They were told that the project manager would then use the estimate to decide on the staffing level for the next period.[2] Subjects were provided with an initial estimate of the team's productivity for the type of project they were to manage. Subjects were told that these estimates were derived from a database of historical project

---

[1] Productivity in software projects can vary widely across projects and development teams [7]. Thus, an estimate that is unduly low for a particular situation would not in itself raise questions about the credibility of that estimate.

[2] Note that the staffing decisions were made by the system. In making the decisions, the subjects' productivity estimates were used as inputs by the system in the following manner: (a) Effort remaining = no. of tasks remaining/productivity, (b) Staffing level required = Effort remaining/time remaining.

TABLE I
PROFILES OF PROJECTS

	UnderSize	FixedSize
Initial estimate of project size (number of tasks)	397	1,866
Actual project size (number of tasks)	610	1,866
Initial estimate of project duration (work days)	362	380
Initial estimate of the effort required (person-days)	1,460	2,792

Note: A task is a unit of work, the equivalent of a software module 50 lines of code long. Using a task as the unit of work for reporting and estimating future resources is a common practice in software projects [18].

TABLE II
EXPERIMENTAL DESIGN

	Project 1		Project 2	
	Initial Estimate of Productivity	Project	Initial Estimate of Productivity	Project
Combination 1	High	FixedSize	Low	UnderSize
Combination 2	Low	FixedSize	High	UnderSize
Combination 3	High	UnderSize	Low	FixedSize
Combination 4	Low	UnderSize	High	FixedSize

statistics that the organization had developed over the past five years.

The projects used in the experiment—hereinafter referred to as *UnderSize* and *FixedSize*—are simulations of real software development efforts at NASA in the early 1980's. They have been employed in prior studies on decision making (e.g., [47]), and were selected in an attempt to cover the spectrum of situations that typically confront software project managers. The initial size of the *UnderSize* project was underestimated. The size of this project grew over time because of additional requirements imposed during its lifecycle. The size of the *FixedSize* project remained constant over its lifecycle. Giving subjects multiple projects enabled us to test the robustness of the findings across varying levels of task difficulty. Table I contains the profiles of the projects.

B. Experimental Design

The experiment had two independent variables: the *initial estimate* of productivity, and the *type of project*. The initial estimate provided to the subjects was unreliable, and its treatment was operationalized at two levels: *high* (i.e., the initial estimate of productivity was overstated) and *low* (the initial estimate was understated). As stated above, each subject worked on two projects: *UnderSize*, and *FixedSize*. Table II shows the experimental design, which was obtained by crossing the values of initial estimate and type of project. Thus, each subject worked on two projects, one with a high initial estimate and one with a low initial estimate. Participants were randomly assigned to one of four initial estimate-project combinations.

The high and low initial estimates for each project were calculated by scaling the actual average staff productivity for that project by a factor of 0.5. The factor was chosen on the basis of Boehm's finding [7], replicated in other studies, that deviations between the estimates for a project in the design

stage and the actual values, lie within a bandwidth of 50 per cent error in either direction. The actual productivity attained by the staff implementing the (real) *UnderSize* project was 0.27 tasks per person-day. Thus, the high and low initial estimates were 0.41 (0.27*1.5) and 0.18 (0.27/1.5), respectively. In the *FixedSize* project, the actual staff productivity in the (real) project was 0.37 tasks per person-day. Thus, the high and low initial estimates were 0.55 and 0.25 tasks per person-day, respectively.

C. Experimental Setting and Participants

The experiment was conducted with graduate students at a U.S. university. The subjects were masters' students in a computer systems management curriculum, and had an average of 10 years' full time work experience. The experiment was part of a course in software engineering. Students received credit for participating in the assignment.

Before conducting the experiment, we ran a pilot study with 6 subjects. The purpose of the pilot was to ensure that the software worked as intended and that the instructions were understood by the subjects.

The actual experiment was conducted with 72 subjects. The experiment was conducted in two parts—the main experiment and a process tracing extension. The objective of the main experiment was to test the hypotheses. The objectives of the process tracing extension were to: (a) glean insights into the cognitive processes that subjects use in dynamic tasks such as managing software projects, and (b) ascertain how subjects cope with unreliable information. Accordingly, subjects were divided into two pools—64 for the main experiment, and 8 for the process tracing extension. Of the subjects in the main experiment, 16 were assigned to each initial estimate-project combination. Of the subjects in the process tracing extension, 2 were assigned to each initial estimate-project combination. All assignments were made randomly. Two days before the experiment, all students were given a one-hour briefing, in which they were introduced to the simulation and shown how to play the game. Prior to the start of the actual experiment, subjects conducted a trial run on a project different from the ones used for experimental purposes.

The experiment was conducted on desktop computers with interactive simulation software written in Dynamo. For each 40-day interval in a project, subjects estimated the average staff productivity (in tasks per person-day) for the next interval, recorded the number in the instruction set provided and then entered the number in the computer. The software ran the simulation for that interval, and provided outcome feedback on the project through a set of on-line reports, which are described below. Subjects then made another productivity estimate for the next interval. The process continued until the project was completed. The software recorded keystroke, timing, and other process information on the use of feedback. In addition to the instructions given to all subjects, those assigned to the process-tracing extension were told to provide concurrent "think aloud" protocols in the course of performing the task. The instructions given to these subjects were standard protocol analysis instructions, as specified in [26]. In order to

TABLE III
INITIAL ESTIMATES REPORT (FIXED SIZE PROJECT, HIGH INITIAL ESTIMATE)

Project Size	1,866	Tasks
Project Duration	380	Days
Staff Productivity	0.55	Tasks/Person-Day

TABLE IV
CURRENT STATUS REPORT

Elapsed Time	80	Days
No. of Tasks Reported Complete to Date	416.01	Tasks
Percent Development Reported Complete	67.68	Percent
Percent Testing Reported Complete	16.27	Percent
Person-Days Expended to Date	1376.09	Person-Days
Current Staff Size	4	Full-time Staff
Reported Productivity to date	0.31	Tasks/Person-Days

TABLE V
ACTUAL PRODUCTIVITY — MEANS (AND STANDARD DEVIATIONS)

	UnderSize Project	*FixedSize* Project
Initial Estimate: High	0.3581 (0.0621)	0.4536 (0.0798)
Initial Estimate: Low	0.2096 (0.0452)	0.2545 (0.0498)

become familiar with the software, all subjects played for one interval on a trial project before starting on the actual projects.

Two on-line reports containing information on the project were available to subjects after every interval. The *Initial Estimates Report* (Table III) simply contained information provided to subjects at the inception of the project.

The *Current Status Report* (Table IV) provided information available to-date on the status of the project. This report incorporated a critical piece of information: the reported productivity of the team as of the previous interval. *Reported productivity to date* was calculated by dividing the *number of tasks reported accomplished to date* by the *number of person-days expended to date*.

After completing each project, each subject filled out a one-page questionnaire describing his/her decision process in arriving at the productivity estimate. Subjects also answered a debriefing questionnaire upon completion of the experiment.

Subjects in the main experiment took between 50 and 80 min in completing the task. Subjects in the process tracing extension took between 90 and 145 min.

D. Dependent Measures

Evidence of self-fulfilling prophesies was obtained through two measures. The first measure for self-fulfilling prophesies examined the actual project productivity attained. Actual productivity for a project was obtained by dividing the number of tasks in the project by the effort expended to complete the project. In the presence of a self-fulfilling prophesy, the productivity levels attained in low initial estimate conditions would be lower than those starting with higher initial estimates. Thus a significant difference in overall actual productivity between the high and low initial estimate conditions would provide evidence of self-fulfilling prophesies. The second measure compared the productivity estimates of subjects in the high and low initial estimate conditions, respectively. In the presence of a self-fulfilling prophesy, the productivity estimates in the low initial estimate condition would continue to be low, whereas those in the high initial estimate condition would remain high. Thus, a significant difference in the productivity estimates between the high initial estimate and

the low initial estimate conditions would constitute further evidence of self-fulfilling prophesies.

Evidence of conservative behavior was obtained from two measures. The first measure ascertained for each period, the *normalized value* of the absolute difference between the reported productivity and the subsequent productivity estimate made by the subject.[3] A value significantly greater than zero of this absolute difference measure, would indicate that subjects' estimates did not adhere to the feedback they received. This would suggest insufficient revision of opinion in response to outcome feedback (cf. [23], [41], [42]), and thus, would constitute evidence of conservative behavior. The second measure for conservative behavior compared the fluctuation in the reported productivity from one period to another with the corresponding fluctuation in the subject's productivity estimates. If the fluctuation in the subject's estimates between two consecutive periods is less than the fluctuation in outcome feedback (reported productivity) in the corresponding interval, then the subject can be said to have acted conservatively. Thus, a frequency count of the number of times the fluctuation in a subject's estimate was *less* than that of the report would indicate the extent of conservative behavior present.

IV. RESULTS

Some subjects completed the task by day 240 (as opposed to an overall average of 387 days). In order to avoid problems in interpretation due to missing values, all data analyses with a *repeated-measures component* were conducted with data up to day 240.

A. Productivity: Actual and Subjects' Estimates

Actual Productivity: Table V shows the actual project productivity attained by subjects. As Table VI shows, actual productivity attained in the low initial estimate conditions was significantly lower than that in the with high initial estimate conditions. There were significant main effects for initial estimate and project. All other effects were nonsignificant. Thus evidence indicates support for Hypothesis 1.

Estimates of Productivity: Fig. 1 shows the mean productivity estimates made by subjects for the *UnderSize* project. An inspection of Fig. 1 indicates that subjects whose initial estimates were high continued making high estimates of productivity. Conversely, subjects given a low initial estimate provided estimates that were usually lower than those made

---

[3] Since the range of possible deviations in the reported productivity is greater around a high initial estimate than around a low initial estimate, we calculated a normalized value of the actual absolute difference. Thus, Normalized Value of Absolute Difference

$$= \frac{\text{Absolute Value (Productivity estimate} - \text{Reported Productivity)}}{\text{Value of Initial Estimate}}.$$

TABLE VI
ANALYSIS OF VARIANCE ON SUBJECTS' ACTUAL PRODUCTIVITY

Explanatory Variable	df	F	p
Initial Estimate	1	15.97	0.0002
Project	1	5.61	0.021
Combination	1	0.12	0.7355
Initial Estimate*Project	1	0.35	0.5567
Initial Estimate*Combination	1	1.81	0.1256
Project*Combination	1	0.45	0.5039
Subjects within cells	57		
$R^2 = 0.5962; p < 0.001$			

TABLE VII
REPEATED MEASURES ANALYSIS OF VARIANCE FOR PRODUCTIVITY ESTIMATES

Explanatory Variable	df	F	p
Between Projects			
Initial Estimate	1	199.66	0.0001
Project	1	13.93	0.0003
Combination	1	0.40	0.5275
Initial Estimate*Project	1	0.02	0.8870
Initial Estimate*Combination	1	0.03	0.8728
Project*Combination	1	0.39	0.5360
Subjects within cells	121		
Within Projects			
Time	5, 117	4.4974	0.0009
Time*Initial Estimate	5, 117	0.3704	0.8680
Time*Project	5, 117	1.8832	0.1027
Time*Combination	5, 117	1.3012	0.2106

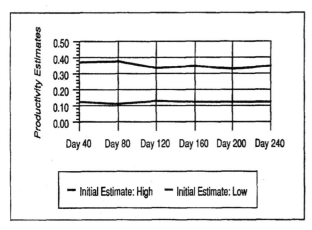

Fig. 1. *UnderSize* project—subjects' productivity estimates over time.

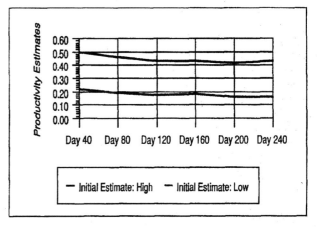

Fig. 2. *FixedSize* project—subjects' productivity estimates over time.

by high initial estimate subjects. Visual evidence suggests a self-fulfilling prophesy. Note that the mean estimates in neither condition approached the nominal productivity of 0.27 tasks/person-day attained in the real-life project, lending further credence to the notion that different estimates create different projects.

Fig. 2 depicts the mean productivity estimates made by subjects in the *FixedSize* project. As in the *UnderSize* project, estimates in the high initial estimate condition remained high, and the estimates in the low initial estimate condition remained low. Thus, inspection indicates the presence of self-fulfilling prophesies. Again, neither group's mean estimates approached the nominal productivity estimate (of 0.37 tasks/person-day).

Table VII, which reports the statistical analysis, indicates a significant main effect for the initial estimate. Thus, the productivity estimates in the high initial estimate condition were significantly different from those in the low initial estimate condition. There was also a significant main effect for project. None of the interactions was significant. Given this further evidence of a self-fulfilling prophesy, we conclude that Hypothesis 1 is supported.

The *within-projects* analysis showed a significant main effect for time, thereby indicating that subjects' decisions changed over time. This is probably because of a general downward drift in subjects' estimates. A nonsignificant time*initial estimate effect indicates that the manner in which the decisions changed did not depend on whether the initial estimate was high or low. A nonsignificant time*project effect shows that the manner in which subjects' decisions

changed over time did not vary from one project to another. Finally, a nonsignificant time*combination effect indicates that the subjects' decisions over time did not depend on the experimental combination to which they were assigned.

B. Productivity Estimates Versus Outcome Feedback

Figs. 3 and 4 show normalized values of the absolute difference between the productivity estimates made by the subjects and the outcome feedback, i.e., reported productivity estimates as of the previous interval. In both projects, the absolute difference was greater than zero, indicating that the decisions made by the subjects did not converge to the outcome feedback. A visual inspection of the two projects, therefore, suggests that the subjects' estimates were different from the reports they received.

T-tests show that the null hypothesis of the difference being equal to zero is rejected for every mean (i.e., each time interval), at a 0.05 level. A *between-subjects* analysis indicated nonsignificant main effects of initial estimate, project and combination, as well as for the initial estimate*project, initial estimate*combination and project*combination interactions. A significant time effect in the *within-subjects* analysis indicated that the differences indeed oscillated over

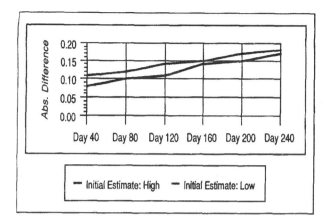

Fig. 3. *UnderSize* project—(normalized) absolute difference between reported productivity and subjects' productivity estimates.

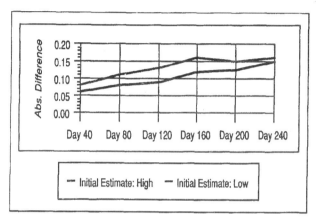

Fig. 4. *FixedSize* project—(normalized) absolute difference between reported productivity and subjects' productivity estimates.

time $(F = 5.5562; \mathrm{df} = 5, 117; p < 0.0001)$. There was a weak interaction effect between time and initial estimate $(F = 2.1601; \mathrm{df} = 5, 117; p < 0.0737)$ and non significant interactions for time*project and time*combination. Thus, (a) subjects' estimates were significantly different from that of the reports, (b) the extent of the difference did not depend on the project, and (c) that the difference persisted over time. Subjects increasingly ignore the growing weight of evidence in the productivity reports in favor of their prior beliefs. This is consistent with prior evidence [40].

We then compared fluctuations in subject's estimates with fluctuations in the reported productivity in the corresponding period.[4] The fluctuations in the estimates were lower than that of the report 467 times (73%). The fluctuations in the reports were lower than that of the estimates in 130 instances (20%), and the respective fluctuations were equal on 43 occasions. Thus, in an overwhelming majority of the cases, the behavior of the subjects was conservative. Hypothesis 2 is supported.

Relative Weighting of Cues by Subjects: As shown in Figs. 3 and 4, subjects appear to ignore the evidence of

---

[4] We examined 768 instances of productivity estimates (i.e., the first six estimates of 64 subjects in each of two projects). That is, there were 640 opportunities for fluctuation (five for each subject in each project).

productivity reports in favor of their prior beliefs. To what extent did the subjects perceive the outcome feedback to be unreliable (and therefore choose to undervalue it)? In order to get some insights on how subjects used the information they received, we conducted a regression analysis. Subjects' written descriptions of their decision processes indicate that they relied primarily on two information cues in arriving at their estimates: the *reported productivity*, and their *prior estimate of productivity*. Therefore, for any period, a subject's productivity estimate can be viewed as a trade-off between the reported productivity estimate of the previous period, and the subject's estimate of the previous period. The trade-off can be represented through the following formulation

$$\begin{aligned} \text{Productivity Estimate}_t \\ = \beta_0 + \beta_1 * \text{ Productivity Estimate}_{t-1} \\ + \beta_2 * \text{Reported Productivity}_{t-1} + \varepsilon \end{aligned} \quad (1)$$

where β_i denote the weights attached to each factor, and ε is an error term representing a subject's inconsistency in executing his/her decision rule.

From (1), we can test for the following relationships:

a) $\beta_1 = 0$, $\beta_2 = 1$: This is equivalent to support for the null form of Hypothesis 2. Support for this relationship implies that a subjects relied completely on the outcome feedback (reported productivity estimate), and placed no reliance on their previous estimates.

b) $\beta_1 = 1$, $\beta_2 = 0$: This is equivalent to support for the alternative form of Hypothesis 2. Support for this relationship indicates that a subject relied entirely on his/her previous estimate and ignored the reported estimate.

c) $0 < \beta_1 < 1$, $0 < \beta_2 < 1$: Support for this relationship implies support for the alternative form of Hypothesis 2. This relationship implies that for values between 0 and 1, a higher value represents heavier reliance on that cue. In general, situations where β_1 is greater than β_2 indicate greater reliance on the productivity estimate.

These predictions were tested through a series of regressions. The data from both projects were pooled into a cross-sectional time series design, with each productivity estimate made by each subject (along with the corresponding reported productivity estimate) constituting an observation (estimates for $t = 0$ do not constitute a data point except for providing values of Productivity Estimate$_{t-1}$ for $t = 40$). The pooling of cross-sectional and time series data can cause estimation problems such as heteroscedasticity and autocorrelated disturbances. Johnston [32] suggests using the Cochrane-Orcutt method in such cases.

Table VIII summarizes the results of the regression. An application of the decision rules suggested by Gujarati [28] on the Durbin-Watson statistics indicates that a two-sided null hypothesis of (positive or negative) serial correlation cannot be rejected at a 0.05 level. Thus, auto-correlation does not appear to be a problem. However, tests of the first and second moment specification show that a null hypothesis of no heteroscedasticity is rejected at a 0.05 level. Therefore, to the extent that heteroscedasticity is present in the data, the OLS estimator may be biased in a positive direction.

TABLE VIII
RELATIVE WEIGHTING OF CUES BY SUBJECTS

Explanatory Variable	Estimated Coefficient	Standard Error	Hypothesis Test
β_0: Constant	0.0003	0.0064	H_0: $\beta_0 = 0$. $T = 0.046$; $p < 0.9635$
β_1: Subject's Productivity Estimate$_{(t-1)}$	0.7985	0.0271	H_0: $\beta_1 = 0$. $F = 870.26$; $p < 0.0001$ H_0: $\beta_1 = 1$. $F = 55.38$; $p < 0.0001$
β_2: Reported Productivity$_{(t-1)}$	0.1943	0.0385	H_0: $\beta_2 = 0$. $F = 25.43$; $p < 0.0001$ H_0: $\beta_2 = 1$. $F = 437.45$; $p < 0.0001$
Adjusted $R^2 = 0.8308$; $p < 0.0001$. $DW = 1.819$.			

Table VIII indicates no support for predictions (a) and (b) in (1). Prediction (c) is supported, thus demonstrating that subjects relied on both cues in making their decisions, and providing further support for Hypothesis 2. An inspection of the values shows that the coefficient for the prior estimate was substantially more than the coefficient for the reported productivity. We therefore conclude that while subjects relied on both cues in making their decisions, the reliance on their own prior productivity estimates was greater than on reported productivity estimates. This is consistent with the findings reported by Paich and Sterman [40].

C. Transition Effect in Switching Initial Estimates Between Projects

In switching from a high estimate in the first project to a low estimate in the second, did subjects continue to provide estimates of high productivity—or vice versa? Here, we test for a *transition effect*. Evidence of a transition effect can be ascertained by examining the last few estimates of subjects in their first project and the first few estimates in the second project. The absence of a transition effect would establish the strength of the phenomenon, i.e., indicate that the presence of unreliable information could cause the same subject to fall victim to self-fulfilling prophesies in both directions.

Fig. 5 shows the last three decisions of subjects in their first project and the first three decisions in their second project.[5] An inspection of the figure suggests that the productivity decisions with high initial estimates in the first project (i.e., combinations 1 and 3—Table II) were no different from those with high initial estimates in the *second* project (combinations 2 and 4). Similarly, productivity decisions with low initial estimates were similar whether the estimates were provided in the first or the second project. Statistical tests confirm the observations. The productivity decisions for high initial estimate conditions in either sequence were similar ($F(1, 26) = 0.16$, $p > 0.69$), as were the productivity decisions in the low initial estimate conditions ($F(1, 26) = 0.33$, $p > 0.57$). We conclude that there was no transition effect.

V. PROCESS TRACING EXTENSION

A. Protocol Analysis

The protocol analysis primarily entailed disaggregating the transcripts into "semantic elements" (cf. [8]). The elements

[5] Some subjects completed their first project *after* day 240. In order to be consistent with the other analyses, we represent decisions in days 160, 200 and 240 as their last three decisions.

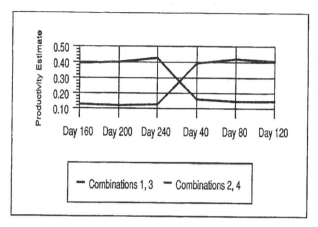

Fig. 5. Transition effect in switching initial estimates from the first project to the second project.

were classified as an *item* of information, an *operator* on item/s, or the *result* of an operator on item/s. These elements were then aggregated into functional groups by linking an operator element to the item/s it operated on in order to produce the result. Functional groups were found by examining the transcripts for repetitive operations that were employed by subjects to acquire information and make judgments. The analysis also extracted the reasoning process underlying the use of each functional group.

The transcripts were analyzed independently by the first author and an assistant who was blind to the purpose of the study. The analyses were aggregated into an agreement matrix. The raw proportion of agreement was 0.86. The Kappa coefficient, which measures the proportion of agreement obtained after separating the agreement attributable to chance (cf. [14]), was 0.79, with a less than 0.01 probability that the true Kappa coefficient was outside the range 0.765 and 0.843.

We compared the performance of the eight protocol subjects with the other 64 experimental subjects in the following manner. First, the eight protocol analysis subjects were added to the pool of 64 subjects and the statistical analysis recomputed with 72 subjects. Next, we dropped two experimental subjects from each initial estimate-project combination, replacing them with the appropriate protocol analysis subjects, and repeated the analyses. The inferences in both cases were similar to results reported in Section IV. The evidence, therefore, indicates that the exercise of thinking aloud did not affect the decision behavior of subjects. However, given the discrepancy in the respective sizes of the experimental and protocol pools, it is difficult to make a definitive assertion in this respect.

B. Decision Behavior of Subject S

In this section, we convey a qualitative view of how a subject, selected at random (and hereinafter referred to as S), made his productivity estimates in the *UnderSize* project, starting from a *high initial estimate*.

In making his productivity estimates, S consistently used two cues throughout the project: his *previous productivity estimate*, and the *reported productivity*. Fig. 6 shows a flowchart of how S traded off various cues available in each time period.

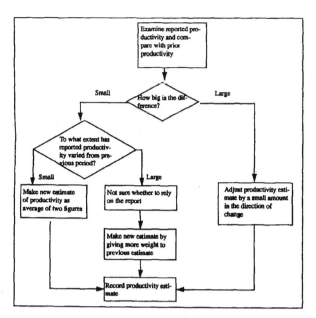

Fig. 6. Decision process of subject S, high initial estimate, *UnderSize* Project.

TABLE IX
ADJUSTMENT OF PRODUCTIVITY ESTIMATES VERSUS FEEDBACK

Adjustment of new estimate from prior estimate	Difference between prior estimate and reported productivity		
	Small	Large	Total
Small	35	44	79
Large	5	19	24

Notes: 1. The table represents the productivity estimates of seven protocol analysis subjects.
2. Subjects' estimates of "small" differences were up to 0.04 for the low initial estimate condition, and up to 0.075 for the high initial estimate condition.
3. $\chi^2 = 4.269; p < 0.039$.

At each interval, S compared the reported productivity with his previous estimate, and ascertained if the difference was "small" or "large".[6] (This particular subject took eight periods to complete the project. In three instances, the differences were considered to be small. In the other five instances, the differences were considered to be large.)

If the difference was small, S checked for the fluctuation of the reported productivity estimate from the prior period to this period. A "small" fluctuation indicated to S that the report was relatively reliable, in which case, S made the next productivity estimate fairly quickly, usually by settling on a number that was midway between the two estimates. If, on the other hand, the fluctuation of the reported productivity was thought to be "large," then S perceived the reported productivity figure to be much less reliable. In that case, the next productivity estimate was made by considering both figures, but giving greater weight to S's own prior estimate. (Note here that S did not explicitly state the weights he was using, but used phrases to the effect that he was weighing one cue less than the other).

However, S had greater difficulty in arriving at an estimate when the difference (between his prior estimate and the reported productivity) was large. Typically, a large difference was also accompanied by a high fluctuation in the reported productivity (from the previous report), often as a result of S's own actions a few periods earlier. For example, S changed his estimate at Day 40 from 0.43 to 0.37. This resulted in more staff being hired, thereby resulting in a drop in productivity a few periods later. However, S had difficulty inferring the reasons for the variability in productivity. Typically, his first reaction was to question the reliability of the reported estimate,

after which he expressed exasperation at not being able to ascertain the environment. Eventually, rather than relying on a report that he thought to be unreliable, S decided to take his prior estimate and adjust it upward or downward by a "small" amount.

Thus, the dynamic decision behavior displayed by S was conservative. In operational terms, the strategy followed by S was to make small adjustments from his previous estimate, even when the difference between that previous estimate and the reported productivity was large.

S displayed little grasp of the action-outcome aspects of the dynamic environment. As is reflected in the example above, S appeared to have difficulty in understanding the time lag between his actions at time t and the corresponding effect at time $t + n$. This lack of understanding and a continuing inability to grapple with the dynamic elements of a complex environment, left S frustrated and bewildered. This is consistent with research findings showing that individuals typically display low *heuristic competence*, i.e., lack a grasp of the dynamic aspects of the system [20].

The inability to infer the crucial relationships in the task environment led S to perceive the outcome feedback as being unreliable, and consequently to diminish his reliance on it. This is manifested in the change in his decision behavior over time with respect to how he integrated the cues. For example, by day 120, dissatisfaction with the reported productivity figure had started to set in, and S increasingly attached greater weight to his own prior estimates. Thus, S altered his decision strategy to take progressively less account of the feedback. Ironically, even as the reported productivity figure became more reliable with the progress of the project, S's perception of its unreliability increased.

C. Decision Behavior of Other Protocol Subjects

To what extent was this pattern of decision making replicated in the decision behavior of other subjects?

Conservative Behavior: Other subjects adopted an approach similar to S in comparing their prior estimates with the reported productivity, determining if the difference was "small" or "large," and then behaving accordingly. Table IX provides a summary of how the other seven subjects compared their prior estimates with the reported productivity, i.e., how they handled differences that they considered to be "small" or "large." Once again, in the vast majority of instances (79 times out of 103), the adjustment made by subjects was small. This was so, even if the difference between the prior estimate and the feedback was considered by the subject to be large.

[6] An examination of the corresponding values indicates S generally considered differences up to 0.02 to be small for the low initial estimate condition, and 0.05 in the high initial estimate condition.

TABLE X
INFERRED WEIGHTS ACCORDED BY SUBJECTS TO INFORMATION AVAILABLE

Explanatory Variable	Periods 40-120	Periods 160-240
β_0: Constant	0.0023	0.0002
β_1: Subject's Productivity Estimate$_{(t-1)}$	0.63	0.72
β_2: Reported Productivity$_{(t-1)}$	0.43	0.25

 The weights were obtained from a regression following procedures detailed in section 4.6.

Thus, in a broad sense, the decision strategies of the other individuals were similar to that depicted in Fig. 6.

The same trend was visible with respect to how subjects handled fluctuations in reported productivity. As long as the reported productivity was stable from one period to another or changed gradually in the same direction, subjects felt comfortable using the figure in their subsequent judgments. However when the change was drastic and/or was in a different direction from the change, the subjects' typical reaction was to express frustration at the figure. Thus, the perception of the unreliability of feedback increased over time, even though the actual feedback grew more reliable.

Decision Behavior Over Time: How did the subjects' reliance on the information cues change over time? Table X shows weights accorded to cues in the first three and last three periods, respectively. The differences in the weights were tested according to the following equation suggested by Cohen and Cohen [15]: $z = (\beta_{i1} - \beta_{i2})/\sqrt{SE^2\beta_{i1} + SE^2\beta_{i2}}$. The differences were significant at $p < 0.05$. Thus, the change in decision behavior over time appears to have been widespread.

VI. DISCUSSION

A. Limitations of Results

An overall discussion of the results should be prefaced by stating the limitations of the study. The study was conducted in an experimental setting (as opposed to a field setting), with students as subjects, and with a well-defined task. While the use of experimental settings raises questions of external validity, past research has demonstrated the utility of studying dynamic decision making in such settings through simulations of rich, complex decision making environments (e.g., [10], [27], [36], [49], [50]). Indeed, as noted earlier, such settings enable researchers to represent the structure and complexity of dynamic systems with great fidelity and permit controlled manipulations of the decision context and information presented to the subject.

Second, the use of students as subjects raises the question of the generalizability of the results to actual managers. We note that all subjects had substantial prior managerial experience (4–16 yrs.), often in managing large projects. As a group, therefore, the subject pool had a degree of *heuristic competence* (cf. [11]) normally associated more with managers than with typical student populations. (the manner in which they differed from actual software project managers was in their *epistemic competence*.) Also, a study by Remus [44] found no significant differences between students and managers in making production scheduling decisions. Although

software project management decisions are somewhat different from production scheduling decisions, they are similar enough to apply his findings and assume that software engineering graduate students used here are acceptable surrogates in this experimental investigation.

Finally, there is the issue of task design. The task was an abstraction of real life projects, the subjects' role was constrained to making a single decision, and the information provided was limited. Admittedly, project managers rely on more than status reports in making their decisions. However, the premise of the study—that unreliable information affects decision making in dynamic environments—is equally applicable to real life projects, where software project visibility continues to be rather poor. This suggests that even with additional cues, status information remains unreliable, especially in the earlier stages of the project. Thus, it is reasonable to assume that the availability of additional information that managers may have access to in actual projects would not change the fundamental nature of the task.

B. Summary of Findings

The results of the experiment support our basic argument that in reactive environments, the presence of unreliable information engenders specific types of decision behavior. In the task of estimating software productivity, the presence of unreliable initial estimates led to the creation of self-fulfilling prophesies. Because of the dynamics of reactive environments, initial decisions affected subsequent feedback that subjects received, which in turn impacted subsequent decisions, and in time propagated a self-fulfilling prophesy. Thus, subjects who started out with low initial estimates made decisions that led to low productivity in the short term. This was reflected in the outcome feedback, which reinforced the perception, thereby leading subjects to continue providing low assessments of productivity. In the final analysis, self-fulfilling prophesies affected the overall productivity attained. Thus, subjects who started out with low initial estimates attained lower overall productivity than those who were provided with high initial estimates.

In addition, unreliability in outcome feedback caused subjects to resort to conservative behavior, and to undervalue their reliance on the outcome feedback. This is evidenced by systematic differences between the feedback that subjects received and their subsequent decisions, in the fluctuations in their decisions, as well as in regression models of subjects' use of information.

The results of the process tracing exercise show that none of the process tracing subjects exhibited much understanding of the complexity of the environment. This is consistent with past research on dynamic decision suggesting that subjects do not acquire adequate mental models in environments that are complex, opaque and dynamic [11], [12], [49], [50]. This inadequacy impinged on the performance of subjects, who had great difficulty in detecting the effects of the time lags and delays. The results of the process-tracing exercise also confirm the basic premise that unreliable information can lead to self-fulfilling prophesies and foster conservative behavior. Subjects perceived the information they received to be unreliable, as a result of which they did not place much emphasis on them. Instead, they adopted a conservative approach in which their decisions were made through incremental adjustments from their past decisions.

How robust are the phenomena identified? Evidence indicates persistence across different projects, regardless of the order in which they were executed. Also, there is no evidence of a transition effect. Thus, when subjects switched from a high to a low initial estimate condition, they did not continue making high estimates of productivity. Rather, their behavior in the new project created self-fulfilling prophesies in the *other* direction, i.e., they persistently made low estimates of productivity. We conclude that the phenomena are indeed robust.

C. Implications for Research in Dynamic Decision Making

This study has uncovered a general dysfunctionality in dynamic decision making occurring in reactive environments characterized by the presence of unreliable information. A fruitful extension of this research would be to conduct a fine-grained examination of the decision strategies that individuals use in a variety of software management tasks. For example, how do individuals handle tasks that require the accomplishment of multiple goals? Previous research in other task domains suggests that they resort to "thematic vagabonding," or tend to shift from one goal to another in the course of the task [20]. Besides raising the cognitive issue of *focus* of *attention* in dynamic tasks (cf. [37]), evidence of such behavior in the context of software project management implies disquieting consequences for effective management.

One prominent line of research in dynamic decision behavior has been a search for factors that enable some individuals to handle such environments better than others can. As Brehmer [11] notes, superior performance, at least in the experimental settings, does not appear to have an association with standard psychological variables such as tests of intelligence or personality. Dorner and associates show that subjects with putatively superior heuristic competence (executives in business organizations) performed better than students [20]. In contrast, higher epistemic competence did not necessarily translate into superior performance. Interestingly, the role of experience has not been examined in any detail. The issue of individual differences is an important one, and the identification of relevant factors has significant implications for training.

The task of productivity estimation is a judgment task, as opposed to a choice task. Researchers in behavioral decision theory have long debated about the distinctions between the two types of tasks and the cognitive mechanisms underlying each task. However, as Hogarth [30] observes, the distinction is difficult to make in static contexts, because in such contexts judgment also implies commitment, and therefore, choice. In dynamic situations, however, "judgment can be thought of as providing a temporal background of mental activity that is punctuated by particular choices" [30, p. 201]. The relationship between judgment and choice constitutes an important problem for further research, and can be examined profitably in dynamic contexts.

D. Implications for Software Project Management

As has been noted earlier, a typical software project is highly likely to cost more than budgeted, and take more time to complete than scheduled. Given that software project estimates are notoriously unreliable, managers often opt for what is generally considered to be prudent behavior. Thus, in making their decisions, they settle for conservative estimates. However, this study demonstrates that such behavior can alter the essential dynamic of the project, thereby leading to consequences not anticipated by the prudent manager. Indeed, "safe" (i.e., understated) estimates can become self-fulfilling, thereby leading to suboptimal performance. Thus, while decision heuristics that tend toward the conservative are "safe" and indeed serve the individual manager well, the potential risk to the organization is that a depressed productivity benchmark can be deleterious to performance.

Such dysfunctional managerial behavior, however, is often difficult to discern in real life [46]. The causal links in organizational settings are sufficiently dispersed in time and space as to make it very difficult to detect them in actual project settings. This study suggests that controlled experiments under laboratory settings offer a better prospect for managers to tease out such links (which can then be used for the purposes of planning and implementing actual projects).

APPENDIX
OVERVIEW OF MODEL

Fig. 7 shows a high-level view of the model's four subsystems: human-resource management, software production, control, and planning, and some of the relations between them. The actual model is very detailed and contains more than 100 causal links. A full description of the model's structure, its mathematical formulation, and its validation can be found elsewhere [3].

A. Human Resource Subsystem

This subsystem captures the hiring, assimilation, and transfer of people. We segregate the project's work force into employee types, such as newly hired and experienced. This distinction is necessary because new team members are usually less productive than veterans. This segregation also lets us capture the training process for assimilating new members. The veterans usually train the newcomers, both technically and socially. This is important, because this training can significantly affect a project's progress by reducing the veteran's productivity.

In deciding how big a work force they need, project managers typically consider several factors. One, of course, is the project's scheduled completion date. Another is the work force's stability, so managers try to predict project employment time for new members before they are hired. In general, the relative weight managers give to stability versus completion date changes as the project progresses.

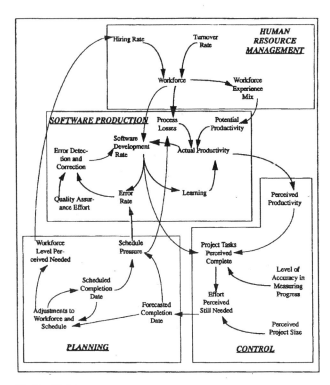

Fig. 7. Model structure.

B. Software Production

This subsystem models development; it does not include the operation and maintenance phases. The development phases included are designing, coding, and testing.

As software is developed, it is reviewed by using quality assurance activities such as structured walkthroughs. Errors detected through such activities are reworked. Not all software errors are detected during development, however; some escape detection until the testing phase.

The software production subsystem models productivity and its determinants in great detail. Productivity is defined as potential productivity minus the loss from faulty processes. Potential productivity is the maximum level of productivity that can occur when an individual or group makes the best possible use of its resources, and is a function of the nature of the task and the group's resources [48]. Losses from faulty processes are losses in productivity from factors such as communication and coordination overhead and low motivation.

C. Control Subsystem

As progress is made, it is reported. A comparison of the degree of project progress to the planned schedule is captured within the control subsystem.

In all organizations, decisions are based on the information available to the decision maker. Often, this information is inaccurate. Apparent conditions may be far removed from those actually encountered, depending on information flow, time lag and distortion.

The rate of progress is a good example of a variable that is difficult to assess during the project. Because software is essentially an intangible product during most of the development, it is difficult to measure things like programming performance and intermediate work. In the earlier phases of development, progress is typically measured by the rate of resource expenditure rather than accomplishments. But as the project advances toward its final stages, though, work accomplishments become relatively more visible and project members better perceive how productive the work force has actually been.

D. Planning Subsystem

In the Planning Subsystem, managers can make project estimates, revising them as the project progresses. For example, when a project is behind schedule, a manager can revise the plan to hire more people, extend the schedule, or both.

By dividing the value of person-days remaining at any point in the project by the time remaining, a manager can determine the indicated work force level, which is the work force needed to complete the project on time. However, hiring decisions are not made solely on the basis of scheduling requirements. Managers must also consider the training requirements and the work force's stability. Thus, before adding new project members, the management assesses the project employment time for new members. In general, the relative weighting between the desire for work force stability and the desire to complete the project on time is not static; it changes throughout the project's life.

Although management determines the work-force level needed to complete the project, this level does not necessarily translate into the actual hiring goal. The hiring goal is constrained by the ceiling on new hires. This ceiling represents the highest work force-level management believes can be adequately handled by its experienced project members.

Thus, three factors—scheduled completion time, work-force stability, and training requirements—affect the work-force level.

REFERENCES

[1] T. Abdel-Hamid, "The dynamics of software project staffing: a system dynamics based simulation approach," *IEEE Trans. Software Eng.*, vol. 15, pp. 109–119, 1989.
[2] T. Abdel-Hamid and S. Madnick, "Impact of schedule estimation on software project behavior," *IEEE Software*, pp. 70–75, July 1986.
[3] ——, *Software Project Dynamics: An Integrated Approach*. Englewood Cliffs, NJ: Prentice-Hall, 1991.
[4] T. Abdel-Hamid, K. Sengupta, and M. Hardebeck, "The impact of reward structures on staff allocations in a multi-project software development environment," *IEEE Trans. Eng. Manag.*, vol. 41, pp. 115–125, 1994.
[5] T. Abdel-Hamid, K. Sengupta, and D. Ronan, "Software project control: An experimental investigation of judgment with fallible information," *IEEE Trans. Software Eng.*, vol. 19, pp. 603–612, 1993.
[6] B. Boehm, *Software Engineering Economics*. Englewood Cliffs, NJ: Prentice-Hall, 1981.
[7] ——, "Software engineering economics," *IEEE Trans. Software Eng.*, vol. SE-10, pp. 4–21, 1984.
[8] M. Bouwman, "Human diagnostic reasoning by computer: An illustration from financial analysis," *Manag. Sci.*, vol. 29, pp. 653–672, 1983.
[9] B. Brehmer, "In one word: Not from experience," *Acta Psychologica*, vol. 45, pp. 223–241, 1980.
[10] ——, "Strategies in real-time, dynamic decision making," in *Insights in Decision Making: A Tribute to Hillel J. Einhorn*, R. Hogarth, Ed. Chicago: University of Chicago Press, 1990.

[11] _____ , "Dynamic decision making: The control of complex systems," *Acta Psychologica*, vol. 81, pp. 211–241, 1992.

[12] D. E. Broadbent, P. Fitzgerald, and M. H. P. Broadbent, "Implicit and explicit knowledge in the control of complex systems," *British J. Psychol.*, vol. 77, pp. 33–50, 1986.

[13] F. P. Brooks, "No silver bullet: Essence and accidents of software engineering," *IEEE Computer*, vol. 20, pp. 10–19, 1987.

[14] J. Cohen, "A coefficient of agreement for nominal scales," *Educational Psycholog. Meas.*, vol. 20, pp. 37–46, 1960.

[15] J. Cohen and P. Cohen, *Applied Multiple Regression/Correlation Analysis for the Behavioral Sciences*. Hillsdale, NJ: Lawrence Erlbaum, 2nd ed., 1983.

[16] Committee on Government Operations, "DoD automated information systems experience runaway costs and years of schedule delays while providing little capability," U.S. H. Rep. Rept., pp. 101–382, Nov. 20, 1989.

[17] R. Conant and W. Ashby, "Every good regulator of a system must be a model of the system," *Int. J. Syst. Sci.*, vol. 1, pp. 89–97, 1970.

[18] J. Cooper, "Software development management planning," *IEEE Trans. Software Eng.*, vol. SE-10, pp. 22–26, 1984.

[19] B. Curtis, "Three problems overcome with behavioral models of the software development process," in *Proc. Eleventh Int. Conf. Software Engineering*, 1989.

[20] D. Dörner and J. Schölkopf, "Controlling complex systems," *Toward a General Theory of Expertise*, K. Ericsson and J. Smith, Eds. Cambridge: Cambridge University Press, 1991.

[21] *The Economist*, "All fall down," p. 89, Mar. 20, 1993.

[22] W. Edwards, "Dynamic decision theory and probabilistic information processing," *Human Factors*, vol. 4, pp. 59–73, 1962.

[23] W. Edwards, "Conservatism in human information processing," *Formal Representation of Human Judgment*, B. Kleinmuntz, Ed. New York: Wiley, 1968.

[24] H. Einhorn and R. Hogarth, "Confidence in judgment: Persistence of the illusion of validity," *Psycholog. Rev.*, vol. 85, pp. 395–416, 1978.

[25] _____ , "Prediction, diagnosis and causal thinking in forecasting," *J. Forecasting*, vol. 1, pp. 23–36, 1982.

[26] K. Ericsson and H. Simon, *Protocol Analysis: Verbal Reports as Data*. Cambridge, MA: MIT Press, 1984.

[27] J. Funke, "Solving complex problems: Exploration and control of complex systems," *Complex Problem Solving: Principles and Mechanisms*, R. J. Sternberg and P. A. Frensch, Eds. Hillsdale, NJ: Lawrence Erlbaum, 1991.

[28] D. Gujarati, *Basic Econometrics*. New York: McGraw-Hill, 1978.

[29] W. Humphrey, *Managing the Software Process*. Reading, MA: Addison-Wesley, 1989.

[30] R. Hogarth, "Beyond discrete biases: Functional and dysfunctional aspects of judgmental heuristics," *Psycholog. Bulletin*, vol. 90, pp. 197–217, 1981.

[31] N. R. Howes, "Managing software development projects for maximum productivity," *IEEE Trans. Software Eng.*, vol. SE-10, pp. 27–35, 1984.

[32] J. Johnston, *Econometric Methods*. New York: McGraw-Hill, 3rd ed., 1984.

[33] C. Kemerer, "An empirical validation of software cost estimation models," *Comm. ACM*, vol. 30, pp. 416–429, 1987.

[34] L. Ketscher, "Knowledge structure in a computer-simulated environment," *Systems Analysis Department Annual Progress Report*, H. Larsen and K. E. Petersen, Eds., Risø National Laboratory, Roskilde, Denmark, pp. 27–28, 1992.

[35] C. Lindblom, "The science of 'muddling through,'" *Public Admin. Rev.*, vol. 19, pp. 79–88, 1959.

[36] L. Løvborg and B. Brehmer, "NEWFIRE: A flexible system for running simulated fire-fighting experiments," Rept. M-2953, Risø National Laboratory, Roskilde, Denmark, 1992.

[37] J. G. March and Z. Shapira, "Variable risk preferences and the focus of attention," *Psycholog. Rev.*, 1992.

[38] R. Merton, "Self-fulfilling prophesies," in *Social Theory and Social Structure*. New York: Free Press, 1948.

[39] H. Mills, *Software Productivity*. Toronto: Little, Brown, 1983.

[40] M. Paich and J. Sterman, "Boom, bust, and failures to learn in experimental markets," *Manag. Sci.*, vol. 39, pp. 1439–1458, 1993.

[41] L. Phillips and W. Edwards, "Conservatism in a simple probability inference task," *J. Experimental Psychol.*, vol. 72, pp. 346–57, 1966.

[42] L. Phillips, W. Edwards, and W. Hays, "Conservatism in complex probabilistic inference," *IEEE Trans. Human Factors Electron.*, vol. 7, pp. 7–18, 1966.

[43] R. Pressman, *Software Engineering: A Practitioner's Guide*. New York: McGraw-Hill, 3rd ed., 1992.

[44] W. E. Remus, "Graduate students as surrogates for managers in experiments on business decision making," *J. Business Res.*, vol. 14, pp. 19–25, 1986.

[45] G. Richardson, *Feedback Thought in Social Science and Systems Theory*. Philadelphia: University of Pennsylvania Press, 1991.

[46] G. Richardson and A. Pugh, *Introduction to System Dynamics Modeling With Dynamo*. Cambridge, MA: MIT Press, 1981.

[47] K. Sengupta and T. Abdel-Hamid, "Alternative conceptions of feedback in dynamic environments: An experimental investigation," *Manag. Sci.*, vol. 39, pp. 411–428, 1993.

[48] J. Steiner, *Group Process and Productivity*. New York: Academic, 1972.

[49] J. D. Sterman, "Modeling managerial behavior: Misperceptions of feedback in a dynamic decision making experiment," *Manag. Sci.*, vol. 35, pp. 321–339, 1989a.

[50] _____ , "Misperceptions of feedback in dynamic decision making," *Organizational Behavior and Human Decision Processes*, vol. 43, pp. 301–335, 1989b.

Kishore Sengupta received the Ph.D. in management information and decision systems from Case Western Reserve University, Cleveland, OH.

He is currently an Associate Professor of Information Systems, Naval Postgraduate School, Monterey, CA. His research interests are in decision support for dynamic tasks, multimedia and intelligent tutoring, and computer supported cooperative work. Dr. Sengupta's research has appeared in *Decision Support Systems*, IEEE TRANSACTIONS ON SOFTWARE ENGINEERING, IEEE TRANSACTIONS ON ENGINEERING MANAGEMENT, *Management Science, MIS Quarterly*, and other journals, conference proceedings and book chapters.

Tarek K. Abdel-Hamid (M'83) received the B.S. degree in aeronautical engineering from Cairo University, Cairo, Egypt, in 1972, and the Ph.D. in management information systems from the Massachusetts Institute of Technology, Cambridge, in 1984.

He is a Professor of Information Systems, Department of Systems Management, Naval Postgraduate School, Monterey, CA. Prior to joining NPS, he spent two and a half years at the Stanford Research Institute. He is an advisor to NASA's Jet Propulsion Lab (since 1986) on the development of computer-based tools for software project management. His research interests focus on software project management, software reuse, and system dynamics. He is the coauthor of *Software Project Dynamics: An Integrated Approach*, published by Prentice-Hall, 1991. In addition to his book, he has authored or coauthored more than 30 papers, published in journals such as the *Communications of the ACM*, IEEE COMPUTER, *Management Science*, and IEEE TRANSACTIONS ON SOFTWARE ENGINEERING.

Dr. Abdel-Hamid was awarded the 1994 Jay Wright Forrester Award, which recognizes "The best contribution to the field of System Dynamics in the preceding five years." He is a member of the ACM, SIM, the IEEE Computer Society, and the System Dynamics Society.

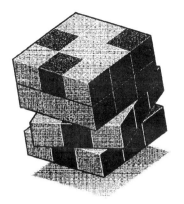

An OO Project Management Strategy

Babak Sadr
PARTA Corporation

Patricia J. Dousette
Litton Data Systems

O bject technology is seen by many as the Yellow Brick Road to improved productivity, reliability, maintainability, and software reusability. Because of this, the software development community rushed to adopt OT.

As with all technological breakthroughs, OT has yielded successes and failures. The failures have been due largely to inexperience and a lack of planning by project managers for the transition to OT.

OT is tremendously helpful in achieving strategic goals and fulfilling business needs. However, because it is relatively new, it requires a transition plan, and its implementation must be closely supervised.

NEEDS ASSESSMENT

We developed our strategy to manage OO projects while working on a project that involved more than 100 engineers and development centers throughout the world. However, the strategy can be tailored for use in projects of any size.

Our strategy grew out of the challenges we faced, including the need to overcome coordination, logistical, and communication problems caused by having development personnel in various locations. In addition, to minimize development risks, we used Barry Boehm's spiral development model,[1] which calls for OO projects to be developed iteratively.

We also designed our strategy to solve the type of problems we, and many others, have encountered during OO projects[2]:

- A lack of coherency in methodology and process across the enterprise causes backward incompatibility and product-line integration problems. For customers, it reduces plug-and-play capabilities and makes it harder to upgrade to newer product lines.
- Architectural instability and incompleteness cause schedule delays and results in software components that must be redesigned for each development iteration. This also results in throwaway code and, therefore, low developer morale.
- A lack of staff familiarity with OT requires a substantial investment in training. A software developer typically needs six months of training to understand OO methodology, C++, and development tools. This must be included in the development schedule to avoid project delays.
- Staff inexperience with OT leads to an overly complex system architecture and implementation, which can degrade maintainability, performance, and reliability.
- Because it is new, distributed OT software development is hard to learn and use. Support tools are generally slow and unreliable, so their use will hurt system performance.

This strategy solves many problems typically encountered during large OO projects by creating specialized work teams and by dividing projects into strategic and tactical areas.

Reprinted from IEEE Computer, Vol. 29, No. 8, Sept. 1996, pp. 33-38.

- Lack of a code reuse strategy leads to redundant implementations.
- Developers who inadequately evaluate off-the-shelf products' applicability to their projects may spend time developing capabilities when existing products already provide them (thus reinventing the wheel). They may also use inappropriate product features in system design, which may cause performance and reliability problems.
- Not having an OO test environment and strategy affects software implementation stability and reliability.

PROJECT ORGANIZATION

We recommend that a project be divided into *strategic* and *tactical* processes. This division will determine the way you organize and manage the project.

Strategic process

This process addresses global concerns that have systemwide ramifications.[3] Strategic concerns include reuse strategy, the definition of project deliverables, and the system architecture, which guides system development. A technical manager coordinates strategic activities.

Tactical process

This process defines the development team's day-to-day operations.[3] Tactical concerns include software analysis, design, implementation, and testing, which are carried out iteratively until each object's dynamic and static behavior has been fully defined and implemented. A project manager coordinates tactical activities.

Staff organization

The traditional organizational hierarchy for a software development project does not work well for a large OO project, particularly one that has team members spread out in a variety of locations.

It is better to use a group of cohesive, specialized, and focused teams, each working on its own set of strategic and tactical activities. This divides and thereby reduces problems caused by the project's complexity and requirements, and also minimizes dependencies, which makes the teams more self-sufficient. In addition, this maximizes the degree to which tasks can be performed in parallel, thereby reducing dead time and increasing productivity.

PROJECT PLANNING

In keeping with our strategy, you should divide project planning into strategic and tactical focus areas.

Strategic planning

You use strategic planning to develop a stable system architecture, which provides the road map for developing an OO system.

Strategic project planning partitions project development into three phases. The setup phase and architecture definition phase generate the system architecture and requirements, while the development phase implements the software. Dividing your project into three phases partitions its logistical and technical needs, which also reduces risk factors.

Figure 1 provides an overview of strategic planning activities, showing the order in which teams perform various activities.

SETUP PHASE. In this phase, system engineers specify system requirements, which will be used in the next phase to design the system architecture. The rest of the development organization works on the project's infrastructural needs by, for example, undergoing training, preparing standards, establishing a documentation control system, and installing a configuration management system.

We assume here that project management, systems engineers, and support personnel (such as test, software quality assurance, and software configuration management) have already received OT training.

Since team dependencies are not critical in the setup phase, teams can move on to the next phase's activities as soon as they accomplish their objectives for this phase.

- *Systems engineering team:* The systems engineers define system requirements based on customer and marketing needs. For consistency, the format of the system requirements and specifications should be based on a development standard, such as the IEEE Software Standards[4] or the US Department of Defense's Mil-Std-498.[5] Although these standards do not explicitly support the OO paradigm, they add structure and definition to any development process.

Generally, there is no object model during requirements definition, so it is difficult and usually unnecessary to prepare object specifications at this time.

- *Development teams:* Team members are trained in the areas of analysis, design, language, and tools. Developers who do not have OO backgrounds generally need three months of training and three months to refine and sharpen their new skills.

They should attend a class to learn about OO analysis and design, and such methodologies and notations as the Unified Modeling Language, the Object Modeling Technique, Booch, and Real-time Object Oriented Modeling (ROOM).[2-3, 6-7]

An OO programming class should relate OO concepts to the features of the chosen language. Developers can use OO languages such as C++, Java, and Ada 95 to implement an object model. By taking a class that emphasizes OO programming instead of language syntax, developers will be better able to move from analysis to implementation.

In addition, developers will need software training from vendors on the use of software configuration management and CASE tools, which are essential parts of an organization's infrastructure.

For companies that will be using distributed objects and applications based on CORBA (Common Object Request Broker Architecture), formal training in these areas is also essential.[8]

Meanwhile, developers should be trained in software standards and processes, which define the rules for development activities.

We have found that about 80 hours of classroom train-

> **A project should be divided into strategic and tactical processes. This division will determine the way you organize and manage the project.**

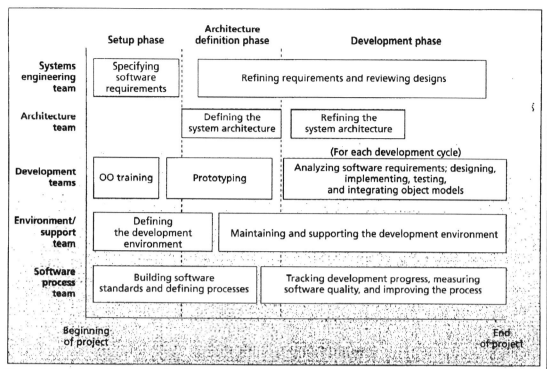

Figure 1. Overview of strategic development program. You divide strategic planning into three phases—setup, architecture definition, and development. You also divide the people working on your project into teams. The chart shows what each team works on during each phase, with the earliest activities on the left.

ing per person is necessary for a smooth transition to OT. Training costs can be significant and must be planned for.

• *Environment/support team:* This team installs and tests new computing systems, software products, and tools. These include the compiler and its supporting development environment, development frameworks and tools (such as GUI builders), an OO CASE tool, document generation software tools, and software for tracking and reporting problems. The environment/support team must integrate commercial software tools into the development environment and solve compatibility problems before formal development begins.

If the organization does not have an adequate communications system, the environment/support team must establish it now. E-mail, electronic file transfer, telephone conferencing and videoconferencing capabilities, and fax machines are critical, particularly when project members are in different locations.

The environment/support team also must establish an electronic documentation control system. A configuration management tool works well as the foundation for the documentation control system. Such tools help the organization control the data and documents that will be produced and disseminated later in the development cycle.

• *Software process team:* The SPT plans, tracks, and oversees software development. The team builds an OO project's development standards and processes around the OO paradigm. Development organizations must have formal software standards and processes to promote communication and avoid confusion in the execution of development tasks.[9,10] This improves the quality of prod-

ucts and organizational processes.

The SPT, which should consist of OO and software process experts, also specifies the criteria for measuring the effectiveness of managerial and technical activities.

Specifically, the team works on software-design document formats, which capture an object model's dynamic and static behavior. Their content should be object-focused rather than procedural, in contrast to traditional design documents.

The SPT also works on the organization's software coding standard, which creates a homogeneous style and presentation format for all program source files and which can support a formal test environment by creating test interfaces that are not intrusive.[11]

By standardizing source file content, layout, and documentation style, team members can use software tools to generate high-level documents, such as a software reference manual, from source files. These tools streamline the documentation process by incorporating function comment blocks in source files and by extracting and exporting applicable information to a word processor file.[11]

In addition, the SPT builds software test standards, which identify the testing strategy and environment for deliverable software. The team also specifies development processes by identifying the organization's teams, membership, roles, responsibilities, and intergroup relations.

ARCHITECTURE DEFINITION PHASE. In this phase, the system architecture is developed from the system requirements. A specialized team of systems engineers and developers focus on defining a stable system architecture.

Initiation of system development without this stable framework greatly increases development risk and leads to quality-related problems and nonreusable components.

While the architecture team is designing the system architecture, other teams are preparing for the development phase. In addition, software processes, standards, and development methods are prototyped and instantiated. This refines key processes, reveals obstacles and problems, resolves organizational and staffing needs, and gives development teams more experience with OT and support tools.

• *Architecture team:* This team consists of systems engineers and designers who analyze system requirements and define the system architecture. By defining the major software components (such as subsystems, modules, and their interfaces), the system architecture defines the framework from which development teams will work. For projects based on Boehm's spiral model,[1] project management uses this framework to specify each development cycle's software deliverables.

• *Development teams:* These teams develop software prototypes. For instance, one team may create a preliminary GUI specification.

By creating prototypes, developers gain experience with OO analysis, design, and programming, as well as support tools. Although these work products are not reusable, the process lets developers validate basic concepts in key areas of the system and generate early feedback on technical issues and development processes.

• *Environment/support team:* This team continues to establish a mature development environment, and defines and develops the environment for unit and integration testing.

• *Software process team:* This team refines software standards and processes by validating them. Selected development teams test the standards on a limited basis. For example, the GUI team will develop the software for the GUI prototype based on the specified coding standards. This approach provides early feedback on the effectiveness of the standards and processes.

DEVELOPMENT PHASE. Using the system architecture, the technical management team begins a series of development cycles, using Boehm's spiral model.[1] For each development cycle, management identifies subsystems and modules that must be developed, tested, and integrated. Meanwhile, processes and standards are further refined.

At the end of each development cycle, project teams should meet to discuss the obstacles they encountered and the lessons they learned. This creates a system for tracking problems and resolutions.

• *Systems engineering team:* Systems engineers turn their attention to refining and updating software requirements. They also determine whether object models created by the development teams comply with system requirements.

• *Development teams:* During each development cycle, these teams analyze the software requirements and

design object models for the architectural components on which they are working. Peer reviews are conducted to ensure that each component design provides the features and interfaces required to meet the client component's needs.

The development teams also implement object models and subject them to unit and integration testing.

• *Environment/support team:* This team provides the traditional system "housekeeping" and administrative support, and also maintains configuration management of object models, documentation, and source code.

• *Software process team:* This team performs risk assessment for future development cycles, tracks the progress of development, and collects data for measuring software quality.

Tactical planning

Because each phase builds on the previous phase, the project must have a technical management team to prioritize and focus on each phase's key areas. Companies will decide many of the details of tactical planning based on their standard operating procedures. However, some general principles apply.

SETUP PHASE. Without proper logistical support by the environment/support team, a project may encounter severe configuration and integration problems in the development phase. Meanwhile, the software processes that the SPT is putting in place must streamline development by specifying only processes and tasks that are necessary to enhance work on the project. These processes must be tested on a limited basis and then must be refined before they are fully adopted.

ARCHITECTURE DEFINITION PHASE. Project management must make sure the architecture team addresses nine key issues. This will refine the system architecture and establish the details of the software architecture.

• *Performance:* For real-time applications, an object model must encompass the system's timing aspect, which includes the real-time computational and operational requirements for the applicable subsystems and modules.[6] The development teams accommodate performance requirements in the component design, thus minimizing the need for subsequent redesigns and modifications.

The software-development platforms, tools, and methodologies used must support the system performance requirements. For example, you must determine the effect of a CORBA platform on a distributed application's performance prior to selecting the platform.

• *Error handling:* When an error occurs, the objects within a module may need to notify objects in other modules. Sharing and propagating errors is part of the modules' design interface, which means error detection and recovery are critical. Development teams can accomplish this by using a systemwide interface provided by a standardized error detection and reporting mechanism.

• *Fault tolerance:* Using the system requirements, the architecture team specifies fault modes and identifies the affected modules' behavior.

• *Concurrency:* In the case of distributed systems, the object model must address concurrency issues and incor-

Because each phase builds on the previous phase, the project must have a technical management team to prioritize and focus on each phase's key areas.

porate strategies for avoiding deadlocks caused when multiple processes try to access an object.

• *Connectivity:* A network interface may affect the system architecture. By considering data bandwidth and related connectivity issues during high-level analysis and design, the architecture team can avoid architectural design flaws and shortcomings.

• *User interface:* An easy-to-use interface is a key marketing requirement, so the user interface's design should start in the early stages of system development. This lets customers work with the interface early enough in the process to provide useful feedback. This also gives the interface time to evolve and mature before reaching the market.

• *Off-the-shelf products:* The use of these products can significantly reduce development time. In addition, the use of generic interfaces can minimize dependencies on vendor products.

A project team should learn about off-the-shelf operating systems, hardware platforms, development tools, software development environments, databases, and other tools that can be used on the project.[2]

For the software components that will use off-the-shelf products, the team must specify design requirements and guidelines that will minimize dependencies between the products and the components under development. This will minimize the number of changes that product upgrades will cause.

• *System requirements traceability:* Analyzing requirements and verifying a design is tedious in large-scale system development. Manual verification is neither feasible nor desirable. Instead, you should use a database to map system and software requirements to the appropriate modules. Using an off-the-shelf database, the requirements are documented in requirements traceability matrix tables (see the sidebar "Requirements traceability"). These tables typically list, for each testable requirement, its source, its title and description, the design component to which it is allocated, the class and object that implements it, and the test reference that verifies it.

The quality assurance team also uses the matrix to verify object models' adherence to system requirements. Most importantly, by specifying relevant requirements for a module, the matrix lets development teams focus their OO analysis and design on the applicable requirements.

• *Interoperability:* To achieve interoperability, the common features and capabilities of a company's product lines are specified in a set of core components. Using core software components in various products enhances software reusability and enterprise coherency.

DEVELOPMENT PHASE. In the development phase, the development teams develop an object model for their assigned modules and subsystems. Because this phase can be divided into several development cycles, you must insti-

---

Requirements traceability

Requirements traceability is an important part of any OO development strategy. You use the process, which begins in the requirements analysis phase, to verify the correct and complete implementation of the system software.

Requirements analysis allocates system requirements to software components. The correct allocation of these requirements can be documented using a commercial database that produces a requirements traceability matrix (RTM). The database provides automation and flexibility.

The RTM provides the project's design and implementation history and must be maintained for the entire project. In the matrix, you list information for each testable requirement, such as the requirement's source, its title and description, the design component (such as the subsystem or module) to which the requirement is allocated, the class and object that implements the requirement, and the test reference that verifies the requirement.

The matrix specifies relevant requirements for a module and thus lets developers focus on the applicable requirements. The RTM also lets the quality assurance and test teams verify whether object models adhere to system requirements.

If an RTM is not used, the requirements traceability and system verification processes will be disorganized and probably ineffective.

---

tute appropriate reviews to ensure coherency between the object modules developed in each cycle.

• *Design coherency and reuse strategy:* You should adopt a reuse strategy early in the design process. For example, you should review the object models created by different development teams for common design patterns.[10] The creation of common libraries could eliminate redundancies and enhance coherency across module boundaries.

Because developers use an iterative approach to design and implement OO projects, you should review the design of new modules in terms of previously developed class libraries, to identify similarities and differences.

Changes to an existing class library may require substantial interface and design changes. You should evaluate the extent of the redevelopment, retesting, and revalidation that would be necessary to determine whether it would be better to modify and reuse a class library or to develop a new library.

• *Standard class libraries:* Some classes in the model can be implemented by using standard class libraries. In terms of maintainability, testability, reusability, and portability, this is better than using custom implementations.

• *Legacy software:* Using existing non-OO software libraries eases a development organization's transition to OO methodology. An OO software wrapper can use an adapter class to hide the use of a non-OO legacy component in the system implementation. This adapter class does not provide any additional functionality except for minor and hidden data transformations that its member functions may perform to accommodate the use of existing products.[12] If the legacy software implementation is later replaced by an internal implementation or another vendor's tool, the adapter class keeps this from affecting the rest of the software design.

OUR STRATEGY IS BASED on our experiences and is not meant to be used like a recipe in a cookbook. You must build on this blueprint and customize it to meet the needs of your projects and your work environment.

In addition, if you are considering an OT project, you should hire an industry expert on OO adaptation and training. This expert can help design a transition program for your company.[2] ❙

References

1. B. Boehm, "A Spiral Model of Software Development and Enhancement," *Computer*, May 1988, pp. 61-72.
2. M.F. Fayad, W. Tsai, and M.L. Fulghum, "Transition to Object-Oriented Software Development," *Comm. ACM*, Feb. 1996, pp. 108-121.
3. G. Booch, *Object-Oriented Analysis and Design with Applications*, Addison-Wesley, Reading, Mass., 1994.
4. *IEEE Software Standards*, IEEE, Piscataway, N.J., 1994.
5. *Mil-Std-498, Military Standard: Defense System Software Development*, US Dept. of Defense, Washington, D.C., 1995.
6. B. Selic, G. Gullekson, and P. Ward, *Real-Time Object-Oriented Modeling*, John Wiley and Sons, New York, 1994.
7. G. Booch and J. Rumbaugh, *Unified Method for Object-Oriented Development Documentation Set, Version 0.8*, Rational Software, Santa Clara, Calif., 1995.
8. *Common Object Request Broker Architecture (CORBA): Architecture and Specification, Version 2.0*, Object Management Group, Framingham, Mass., 1995.
9. *ISO-9000, International Standard: Quality-Management and Quality-Assurance Standards*, ISO, Geneva, 1987.
10. M. Paulk and C. Weber, *Key Practices of the Capability Maturity Model*, Software Eng. Inst., Pittsburgh, 1993.
11. B. Sadr, *Fundamentals and Applications of Object-Oriented Programming Using C++*, UCLA Academic Publishing Services, Los Angeles, 1995.
12. E. Gamma et al., *Design Patterns: Elements of Object-Oriented Software*, Addison-Wesley, Reading, Mass., 1994.

Babak Sadr *is an electrical engineer at PARTA Corp., a software development consulting and research company. He also teaches OO-related classes at UCLA. His expertise is in software development, parallel processing, and OO design. He received a BS and an MS in electrical engineering from the University of Southern California.*

Patricia J. Dousette *is a senior technical staff member at Litton Data Systems, where she is a member of the Advanced Products Group. She also teaches programming language courses at UCLA. Her expertise is in software process definition and instantiation. She received a BS and an MS in mathematics from California State Polytechnic University, San Luis Obispo, and California State University, Los Angeles, respectively.*

Contact Sadr at (818) 889-5333 or Dousette at (818) 597-5388.

The use of software engineering data in support of project management

by Ole Andersen

Based on software metrics data from a large (19 working-years) software development project, a number of analyses have been carried out. The results reveal the causes for cost overruns, show how effort planning can be refined during development, and identify a relationship between the quality of the design documents and the effort consumed for their production. This gives an insight into the development process and establishes norms for interpreting metrics values obtained in future projects. In this way, it is a first step for a company towards increasing its software development process maturity level.

1 Introduction

The main activities of software project managers include planning, estimating, tracking and decision making. It is a characteristic of a mature engineering discipline that the end-product quality level is planned, reliable project plans are made, progress is tracked on a detailed level, and estimates and decisions can be made, based on well documented experience with previous successful projects.

This situation is not usually found in the relatively new discipline of software engineering. One reason is that, over the years, software engineering has adapted to a rapid technological development. This, together with the fact that the end product is intangible, has led to a situation where many software development projects are carried out in an *ad hoc* fashion and very often fail to meet their success criteria.

For software development, the important management parameters are project cost and duration, and product quality. Measurements of cost and calendar time are fairly easy. Control of these parameters is often attempted and is possible within limits, although most managers have difficulties predicting project cost and duration. Discussion of the quality of the end product starts with defining the relevant quality factors and their measurement units. However, the next steps of predicting, at the start of the project, the expected end-product quality factor levels, and controlling progress towards specified quality factor levels during the project, are not usually attempted.

To improve the present state of affairs, it is necessary, during a software development project, to collect data that describe the various production processes, as well as the resulting partial and intermediate products. Thereby, the technical achievements, as well as the overall project status and progress, can be assessed. By analysing the data, a quantitative basis for decisions can be established, with results improving as norms for interpreting measurement values become available from finished projects.

When selecting data and analyses for use in a project, or across projects in an organisation, the emphasis should be on data that are simple and easy to collect and analyses giving results that can easily be understood. The benefits of introducing a software metrics programme will then include

- improved tracking and control of a development project;
- early identification of atypical measurement values, which may indicate a previously undiscovered problem;
- an accumulated set of data describing completed projects, for use in planning and estimation of future projects;
- the possibility of optimising the software development process, since the problem areas can be identified and the results of changes to the existing process can be documented.

The last three points require that norms for measurement values are available and, in many cases, such norms must be derived from data collected during previous projects.

This paper will describe a number of data analyses, together with the conclusions that may be drawn from their results. The analyses are performed on a very comprehensive data set collected during a 19-working-year software development project. The analyses demonstrate how the experience can help the company to improve project planning and monitoring, through the establishment of company norms and by introducing specific changes to the development process.

2 Monitoring of software development

The work reported here is one result of a concerted effort to improve the prediction, monitoring and assessment of soft-

Reprinted from IEEE *Software Engineering Journal*, Vol. 5, No. 6, Nov. 1990, pp. 350-356.

ware product quality. This was undertaken as part of the ESPRIT project REQUEST (REliability and QUality of European Software Technology). In the area of software quality, work has concentrated on developing COQUAMO (COnstructive QUAlity MOdel) [1].

The original idea of COQUAMO was to transfer the approach that had been successfully applied in COCOMO (COst MOdel) [2] to the field of software quality. COQUAMO has now been developed into three models, the first of which is a predictive model for software quality (using an approach similar to that of COCOMO) to be applied in the early phases of development. The second part consists of a monitoring model for use during the project, and the third part is a quality assessment model for the later stages in the development.

Introduction of the monitoring model [3] as part of COQUAMO enables it to support the natural activities of a project manager during a software development project. In this way, software metrics are utilised in software project control activities, based on the general project control procedure of setting quantitative targets, measuring against these targets and responding to deviations. The approach aims to work at a more detailed level and include more metrics than other software metrics programmes [4] and [5].

In support of the development of COQUAMO, large-scale data collection and storage have been carried out for software metrics data as part of REQUEST [6]. For the monitoring model, this allows significant metrics and relationships to be identified. In-depth analyses have been carried out for a number of project data sets, with the aims of developing the model and investigating the assumptions behind it, as well as investigating the possibilities for automating the analyses of project data.

One set of analyses has been based on the ideas of using anomalies [7], i.e. atypical metric values, to detect the deviations that, at an early stage, may indicate potential quality problems [8]. This paper shows how detailed analyses of data from a large software development project may be used to support general project management, by establishing quantitative norms, and how they may also be used to improve the software development process in a company.

Collection and analysis of software engineering data from just one project allow initial norms to be established. These can be used to support planning, as well as interpretation of data, in subsequent projects. The data collected from these projects may then be used to check, refine and expand the set of norms.

To begin with, the empirical foundation for the norms is naturally weak, since they are based on the information extracted from one project. It is, however, an advantage to utilise this quantified experience as support in the next project, rather than continuing a purely qualitative approach. As data become available from more projects, the initial assumptions concerning relationships between parameters can be verified and the uncertainties of numerical values can be reduced. In addition, the coverage of the norms can be expanded, and gradually this will lead to a set of company norms, in which the project manager can have confidence, and which will help managers of future projects to learn from the experience gained in previous projects.

This process does not follow a strict scientific approach, of first establishing a number of hypotheses, then collecting a statistically sufficient number of datasets and finally verifying or rejecting the hypotheses based on data analyses. In a commercial environment, the attitude will be to analyse the first available data set, draw conclusions from (or base decisions on) the results of the analyses and then introduce changes to optimise the development process.

The description below is concerned with the first step a company must take in order to introduce a quantitative basis for the management of software development projects. This includes the collection of a first data set, which describes one of the company's own projects, together with a number of analyses of the data, leading to the establishment of a first set of norms for software engineering data.

3 The product and the development process

The software development project from which data were obtained can be characterised in the following way.

● *The product:* the software product is a real-time information system for use in a highly integrated, but geographically widespread, environment. Requirements for total system reliability are very high, since the consequences of severe faults are critical. It was developed for one customer, consists of four subsystems and has a total (all inclusive) size of 73 000 lines of code.

● *The process:* the development process followed an in-house software development handbook prescribing a life-cycle, documentation level and V & V activities, corresponding to a standard third-generation development

Table 1 Summary of task categories

Category	Plan man-hours	Number of tasks	Overrun man-hours	Number [2,6[tasks	Overrun [2,6[%	Number [0.8,1.2] tasks
Unplanned	0	21	5455	—	—	—
S	855	23	565	7	98	1
A	1909	23	203	3	270	6
L	2626	17	1341	5	104	3
VL	5965	19	374	1	114	5

For the unplanned tasks, as well as for the tasks in the four categories, the Table shows the total planned effort in man-hours, the number of tasks of each kind and the total overrun of effort in man-hours. For each category, the number of tasks where the ratio actual man-hours/planned man-hours is > =2, as well as the overrun caused by these tasks in percentage of the total overrun for the category, are shown. The last column gives the number of tasks in each category where the actual effort is within ±20% of the planned value.

38

approach. In practice, this was followed fairly strictly. This was the case, despite the fact that it was the first time the project group had followed the already existing development handbook, which was well tested in use by other development groups. The development was based on detailed plans, with effort allocated to tasks in the range of 20–600 man-hours and follow-up supported by an extensive data collection. The code was written in a high-level dedicated application language and supported by dedicated tools, as well as host and target environments.

- *The personnel:* all developers were involved in most of the project, and the majority had several job functions. The average experience among the developers in the application area and in the software development was fairly high.
- *The project:* the project was carried out by 20–25 developers from one department at one site, delivering a total of 19 working years within a calendar time of two years. The period covered the activities from analysis until the product was released to the customer. The delivery took place on time, and the total cost (−overrun) was kept within acceptable limits.
- *The organisation:* the company has an experience of many (>20) years in the development of systems in the application area.

4 The data and data collection

A large amount of data was collected as an integrated part of the development process and the project management. This was supported by existing administrative procedures and viewed by all involved as a necessity for successful project management. The following data items were among those made available to REQUEST, subject to the condition that the identity of the provider remains undisclosed for commercial reasons:

☐ planned and actual effort for each development and inspection task broken down, so that the planned task effort is in the range of 20–600 man-hours;
☐ size of documents (pages);
☐ number of errors detected by inspection of documents.

Information was made available so that it was possible to link the effort consumed to produce a specific document or module to its size, the effort consumed by V & V activities (inspections), as well as the number of errors detected.

5 Data analyses and results

Results are presented below from a number of analyses which have been chosen so as to focus on the establishment of company norms. The norms can be used to interpret measurements made in future projects, and further data from these can then be used to check and improve the norms. Furthermore, some of the analyses give an insight into the development process and show how the process may be optimised. The analyses include

- *detailed comparisons between planned and actual effort for tasks occurring up to the end of coding* (see Section 5.1). The results are used to highlight the sources of significant overruns in expenditure, when compared to the planned cost, and to determine how this can be avoided in future projects.

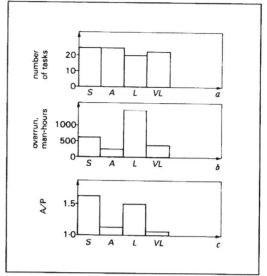

Fig. 1 Effort overrun for planned tasks

a The number of tasks in each of the four categories of effort planned for the tasks
b The total overrun in man-hours over the planned effort, observed for all tasks in each category
c The ratio between the total actual and planned efforts (A/P) in each category

- *comparisons of different activities within one phase and across phases* (see Section 5.2). This allows sets of activities for which the effort consumptions are mutually related to be identified. This, in turn, allows plans to be refined during future projects.
- *comparisons of the complexity of document-producing tasks and the quality of the resulting documents* (see Section 5.3). In future projects, the identified relationship can be used to evaluate the documents produced, the inspection procedure, or to plan or evaluate results of individual inspections.

All of the analyses are concerned with issues that may vary from company to company. For example, the activities which have mutually related efforts may not be the same in different companies. This depends on the lifecycle used, the availability of internal standards and the strictness with which such standards are adhered to. It is therefore necessary for each company to go through the process of establishing their own norms, based on data describing their own projects, rather than relying on industry averages extracted from the literature. Only in this way is it possible to arrive at detailed norms that, in the given environment, give relevant management support.

5.1 Planned and actual effort

Analysis of the relationships between the effort planned and actually occurring for development tasks will enable the company to improve the evaluation of similar plans prepared in future projects. They may learn how to limit the number of unplanned tasks, as well as the total overrun occurring in the planned tasks.

For each task, from the start of high-level design until the end of coding, the effort planned, as well as that actually

352

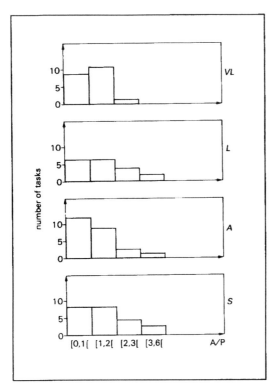

Fig. 2 Distribution of tasks in each of the four categories S, A, L and VL, according to the ratio between actual and planned effort (A/P)

consumed, is available in man-hours for all four subsystems. Planning was done in an empirical fashion, with effort allocation to each task based on consultations between the project manager and the task leader. The plan, which was made before finishing the high-level design, included 82 tasks out of the 103 tasks which were planned or actually did occur in these phases. Of the tasks originally in the plan, five were later found to be superfluous and two (inspection) tasks were not carried out.

The tasks included, for each subsystem, the production of

☐ high-level design
   subsystem design
   interface design
   user manual
   test specification
   test design
☐ detailed design
   module design
   test design
☐ coding
   module code

as well as the inspection of each document (except the test design documents) and the module code.

In Fig. 1 the tasks are shown categorised according to their planned size.

• S = small (1–50 man-hours)
• A = average (51–100 man-hours)

• L = large (101–200 man-hours)
• VL = very large (201–600 man-hours)

excluding the tasks not originally included in the plan. The categories have been chosen so that the number of tasks (Fig. 1a) in each is roughly the same. Figs. 1b and c show the overrun in man-hours observed for all the tasks in each category, as well as the relative overrun in units of the total planned effort for the category.

Fig. 2 shows the distribution of tasks in each of the four categories used in Fig. 1, according to the ratio between the actual and planned effort (A/P = actual man-hours/planned man-hours):

☐ [0,1[: 0 < = A/P < 1
☐ [1,2[: 1 < = A/P < 2
☐ [2,3[: 2 < = A/P < 3
☐ [3,6[: 3 < = A/P < 6

The unplanned tasks are shown in Table 1, together with the tasks in the four categories. For each task category, the planned man-hours, the number of tasks and the overrun in man-hours observed in each category are shown. Furthermore, the Table contains, for each of the task categories, the number of tasks where A/P > = 2 (i.e. those which cost twice the planned effort or more), together with the overrun caused by these tasks as a percentage of the total overrun recorded in the category, and the number of tasks where 0.8 < = A/P < = 1.2. Of these well planned tasks, there are a total of 15 where 8 have A/P < = 1 and 7 have A/P > 1, with the symmetry around 1 supporting the statement that the efforts were indeed well estimated.

The data illustrate the relative importance of the two causes for deviations between actual and planned effort for the project as a whole.

• Approximately 20% of the tasks carried out were not included in the original plan. This caused an overrun of 5455 man-hours or close to 30% of the total costs.
• For the tasks that did appear in the plan, with a total planned effort of 11355 man-hours, an overrun of 2483 man-hours or 22% was recorded.

The majority of the unplanned tasks were concerned with either the test design documents (none of which were included in the original plan [approx. 2000 man-hours]) or the production of graphical documentation of the design (approx. 3300 man-hours). Omission of the test design documents from the plan was caused by the fact that the development group was following the development handbook for the first time. They were therefore not familiar with the requirements for early test planning. This shortcoming of the project plan can be easily avoided in future projects.

The reason why a number of design tasks were omitted from the plan is that the planning was based on the assumption that a specific design method could be applied. When it later became clear that this was not possible, a fallback was necessary to the use of a more traditional and complicated method.

There is no general way in which to avoid a situation where assumptions concerning the basic design approach do not hold. Decisions regarding the way to perform the design are based on an analysis of the system and software requirements, and the effort invested in such an analysis should be weighed against the cost incurred if incorrect decisions are made.

With regard to the planned tasks, the largest total overrun in man-hours is seen in the L (101–200 man-hours) category of tasks, and the next largest in the S (1–50 man-hours) category. In both cases, the relative overrun is more than 50% of the planned effort. Only small overruns were recorded in the other two categories, both in absolute and relative terms.

In addition, the S and L categories show the largest number of tasks with an actual effort of more than twice the planned level and the smallest number of well planned tasks with the actual effort within ±20% of the planned level. The overrun in the S and L categories corresponds to the amount that is recorded for the tasks where the actual effort is larger than twice the planned level. This is also the case in the VL category, but it is hardly significant with only one task showing such an overrun in the category.

The *a priori* credibility of planned effort values therefore depends on the category in which it falls. In the S and L categories there is a larger risk that a given task has been underestimated by a significant fraction. The underestimation is seen to give rise to the largest overruns, not only in relative terms but also on an absolute scale, in the S and L categories, when compared to the A and VL tasks. If these underestimated tasks can be identified early in the process and re-estimated, the planned effort in the two categories will be very close to reflecting the actual effort needed.

Two different strategies must therefore be applied in the short-term to reduce the uncertainty of the effort estimates for the tasks in the plan.

☐ When the planned effort for a task falls in the S or L

categories, it must be carefully reviewed to ensure that no gross underestimation has been made.

☐ For tasks in the A and VL categories the easiest approach is to increase the estimates by 5–10% to cover for the slight underestimations that occur for such tasks.

It should also be considered if the estimation process is carried out so as to induce the developers to estimate the 'minimum time to complete', rather than the actual size of the task. If this is the case, a long-term response to the planning difficulties must include a change in attitude to the planning process and possibly also training in the estimation process.

An attempt to identify a pattern of which tasks display the large overruns does not give a clear picture. The 11 module coding tasks were the ones most consistently showing large overruns (80% total — in agreement with the old adage of making an estimate of coding time and then doubling it), and the company could therefore consider emphasising the reviewing of the coding task effort allocations, taking experience values into account.

5.2 *Relationships between activities*

By establishing a set of experience values for expansion ratios (e.g. the ratios between the efforts used in producing the high-level design, the detailed design and the code) it is possible to create a basis for revision of effort allocations during future projects in those cases where overruns occur in the early phases.

The actual effort used in the phases of high-level design, detailed design and coding for the production of the design descriptions, test specifications, test designs and module code have been used in Table 2. The Table contains the

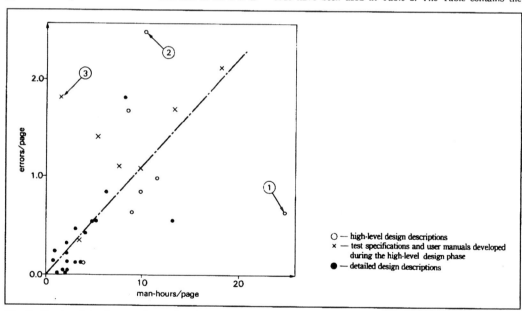

Fig. 3 Scatterplot of errors/page found in inspections against production effort man-hours/page for the majority of documents from the two design phases

The line is based on a least-square fit to all the points, except the three pronounced outliers marked 1, 2 and 3, with no constraints that it should pass the origin

354

Software Engineering Journal   November 1990

41

Table 2 ·Summary of expansion ratios

Ratio	Sub1	Sub2	Sub3	Sub4	Total
DD/HLD	0.68	0.89	1.44	0.27	0.73
CODE/DD	1.23	0.85	0.92	0.95	1.00
CODE/(HLD + DD)	0.50	0.40	0.54	0.20	0.42
TP/(HLD + DD)	0.31	0.24	0.15	0.21	0.24

The ratios between the total effort used for production of the high-level design documents (HLD), the detailed design documents (DD), the module code (CODE) and the test plans (TP), including test specifications and test design documents from both design phases. The ratios are calculated for each of the four subsystems (Sub1, Sub2, Sub3, Sub4), as well as for the system as a whole.

'expansion ratio' between actual effort in detailed design (DD) and high-level design (HLD), between code (CODE) and detailed design, and between code and the total design effort (HLD + DD), for each of the four subsystems, as well as for the total system. Furthermore, the Table contains the total actual effort used for test planning (TP, i.e. specification and design) in the two design phases, in relation to the total design effort (HLD + DD) for the subsystems and the total system.

A relatively large variation is seen for the ratio DD/HLD, whereas this is less pronounced for the CODE/DD ratio. One cause of the variation is that a serious deficiency was detected at the inspection of the high-level design of subsystem 4 (Sub4), causing a substantial effort to be used for a total redesign of this subsystem. Another cause seems to be that the level of design details to be included in the high-level design documents, as described in the software development handbook. has not been interpreted in the same way for all four subsystems.

When comparing the coding effort to the total design effort for each subsystem (CODE/(HLD + DD)), the variation is less, except for subsystem 4 where this ratio is also affected by the redesign. This ratio, however, is insensitive to the point of transition between high-level and detailed design.

In the comparison of the ratios between test planning and total design effort (TP/(HLD + DD)), subsystem 4 does not show a large deviation. This reflects the fact that, when the high-level design had to be changed, so did the test specification and test design documents.

If the company, in future projects, strengthens the definitions of the content of high-level and detailed design documents, the expansion ratios can be used to support the initial planning activity, as well as revisions of the plan during development. Assuming that an overrun (caused by the task being larger than anticipated, rather than by design faults) is recorded for the high-level design, the expansion ratios can be used to re-estimate the effort for the test planning, detailed design and coding.

Until this change of design standards has been implemented, the ratio between coding and total design effort can be used in the same way. This is of less value, however, than using the DD/HLD and CODE/DD ratios, since the total design effort becomes available at a later time than the high-level design effort, causing responses to overruns to be less effective.

5.3 Document complexity and quality

A detailed analysis of the production process has been performed for documents from the design phases, and a relationship established between production process parameters and the quality of the produced documents, measured as the number of errors found by inspections. For the majority of documents produced in the high-level and detailed design phases, the following three measures are available:

● effort (man-hours) consumed in the production of the document;
● document size in pages;
● total number of errors found during inspections.

Fig. 3 shows a scatter plot which, for each document,· displays errors per page against the effort consumed to produce one page, thereby normalising out effects caused by the mere size of the documents. The Figure also shows the least-square line fitted to all data points, excluding the three most pronounced outliers (1, 2, 3) detected by visual inspection. The line was not constrained to pass through the origin.

The trend of the data leads to the interpretation that a large effort per page for a document from the design phases implies that the task of producing the document was a complex one, and the document therefore contains a relatively large number of errors. This interpretation is supported by the background information relating to the documents causing the outliers (the numbers refer to Fig. 3)

☐ 1: this document contains the high-level design of the subsystem which is the corner-stone of the entire system. The designer has taken extra time to arrive at a good design, and consequently fewer errors were found.

☐ 2: this was the first interface design to be produced and inspected. The large number of errors are indicative of the ensuing discussion about the right level of detail to aim for in such documents.

☐ 3: this was the first test specification to be produced and inspected. As a result, it was realised that the task of test planning was far greater than anticipated and that it required the production of test design documents, which, so far, had not been included in the project plan.

The general trend is observed for all the documents from the design phases, although they are of different type and their size is measured in primitive units. A first assumption would be that the number of pages is too simple a measure to be involved in the capture of the complexity of tasks as different as the production of design descriptions, user manuals and test specifications. However, no pattern related to document type has been identified for the documents, as can be seen from the different markings used for three kinds of documents in Fig. 3. The only exception is that documents from the high-level design phase tend to have a larger value of the man-hours/page than those from the detailed design phase. This is in agreement with the expectation that tasks in the high-level design phase, in general, are more complex than those involved in the detailed design.

It should be noted that the trend seen in Fig. 3 need not be valid for all companies. The trend depends on the way the task breakdown is performed and on the management follow-up on plans, assuming the same inspection procedure for all documents. A large number of tasks showing large values of man-hours/page and a correspondingly small number of errors/page could result from costly gold-plating of the documents. On the other hand, a large number of documents with low man-hours/page values and high number of errors/page indicate that the necessary care was not applied in the corresponding task.

The knowledge that the relationship between man-hours/page and errors/page is as shown in Fig. 3 can, in future projects, be used for

- planning of inspections when a document has been produced and the man-hours/page is known. Maximum effort may be allocated to the inspection of complex documents, i.e. those with a large value of man-hours/page, and the participants in such reviews selected with care.
- assessment of inspection efficiency, by comparing the number of errors found to the norm.
- assessment of documents, by comparing the effort consumed for the document production to the norm.

Concerning the two last points, it should be noted that, with regard to outliers in two-dimensional plots, there is generally no indication of whether the outlier is caused by one or other parameter having an atypical value. The identification of an outlier merely focuses the project management's attention on, for example, a given document. It is then up to the manager to decide, among a number of possible causes, the reason for the anomaly.

6 Conclusion

Collection and analysis of software metrics data, even from just one software development project, will provide a company with an improved insight into their development process. This insight will develop further as more data sets become available and they are used to check and improve the initial norms. The analyses of the data may indicate that the underlying part of the process is performed in an acceptable way. In such cases, the data may be used as norms within the company for planning of future projects, or so that data values from future projects can be compared to the norms.

An example is the trend seen in Fig. 3. When the average effort required to produce one page in a document is influenced by the complexity of writing the document, the higher error rates recorded for high values of man-hours/page are acceptable, and the trend may be used as a norm as described above.

On the other hand, the analyses may reveal problems with an aspect of the development process and possibly may also point to the cause of the problems. In such cases, the increased insight may be used to plan and implement changes to the development process, and to document the impact of the changes by repeating the analyses on data from projects carried out under the changed conditions.

As an example, the tasks in categories S and L on Fig. 1 may be considered. The severe overruns seen for these tasks indicate that the effort allocation should be improved to avoid gross underestimations for some tasks (i.e. the planning process must be changed), rather than to continue

using the same planning process and then increase the planned values by 50–60%.

The data, analyses and results presented here will, in a future project, provide important guidance on how to

- [ ] plan the required effort with confidence;
- [ ] refine the effort allocation during the development;
- [ ] assess the produced documents and inspection results.

By collecting and analysing a detailed data set, the company has taken a first step towards increasing their software development process maturity level [9], and ultimately, their productivity and end-product quality. The description of the data collection and analysis can therefore serve as an example of the activities that many companies must undertake in the near future, in order to build up quantitative support for project management, in the form of norms for interpreting data from future projects.

7 Acknowledgments

This paper is based on results obtained in REQUEST Subproject 1. The author wishes to thank the many contributors to the general approach and ideas outlined above: Poul Grav Petersen, Susanne Klim, Johanne Schmidt, Jens Heile Heilesen, ElektronikCentralen, Denmark; Stephen Linkman, Lesley Pickard, Niall Ross, STC Technology, UK; Peter Mellor, The City University, UK; and Barbara Kitchenham, National Computing Centre, UK. The work has been supported by the EEC ESPRIT programme (Grant ESP/300) and the Danish Council of Technology (Grant 840563.0).

8 References

[1] PETERSEN, P.G.: 'Software quality: The COnstructive QUAlity MOdelling System' in Directorate General XIII (Eds.): 'ESPRIT '86: Results and Achievements' (Elsevier Science Publishers B.V., North-Holland, 1987)
[2] BOEHM, B.W.: 'Software engineering economics' (Prentice-Hall Inc., 1981)
[3] KITCHENHAM, B.A., and WALKER, J.G.: 'A quantitative approach to monitoring software development', Soft. Eng. J., 1989, 4, (1), pp. 2–13
[4] GRADY, R.B., and CASWELL, D.L.: 'Software metrics: establishing a company-wide program' (Prentice-Hall Inc., 1987)
[5] DUNCAN, A.S.: 'Software development productivity tools and metrics'. Proc. 10th Int. Conf. on Software Engineering, Singapore, April 1988, pp. 41–48
[6] DALE, C.: 'The REQUEST database for software reliability and software development data' in Directorate General XIII (Eds.): 'ESPRIT '87: achievements and impact (Elsevier Science Publishers B.V., North-Holland, 1987)
[7] DOERFLINGER, C.W., and BASILI, V.R.: 'Monitoring software development through dynamic variables'. IEEE Trans., 1985, SE-11, (9), pp. 978–985
[8] KITCHENHAM, B.A., ANDERSEN, O., and KLIM, S.: 'Interpreting software metrics data: a case study'. REQUEST document R1.10.3, 1989
[9] HUMPHREY, W.S., and SWEET, W.L.: 'A method for assessing the software engineering capability of contractors'. Software Engineering Institute Technical Report CMU/SEI-87-TR-23, 1987

The author is with ElektronikCentralen, Venlighedsvej 4, DK-2970 Horsholm, Denmark.

The paper was first received on 2nd January and in revised form on 19th March 1990.

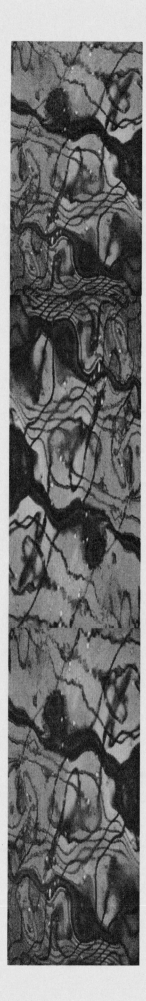

Chapter 2

SOFTWARE LIFE CYCLE PROCESSES

No project manager can operate efficiently without a plan. This plan must include an understanding of the formal life cycle of the software project to be managed. This section includes two important papers on software life cycle models.

The first paper is one of my favorite all-time papers. In "A Rational Design Process—How and Why to Fake it," Parnas and Clements show us how even "faking" a formal life cycle model is better than adhering to no formal model. The second paper by Boehm is one of the most famous papers on software engineering. In it, Boehm introduces the well-known Spiral model, a significant advancement over the standard waterfall model.

A Rational Design Process: How and Why to Fake It

DAVID LORGE PARNAS AND PAUL C. CLEMENTS

Abstract—Many have sought a software design process that allows a program to be derived systematically from a precise statement of requirements. This paper proposes that, although we will not succeed in designing a real product in that way, we can produce documentation that makes it appear that the software was designed by such a process. We first describe the ideal process, and the documentation that it requires. We then explain why one should attempt to design according to the ideal process and why one should produce the documentation that would have been produced by that process. We describe the contents of each of the required documents.

Index Terms—Programming methods, software design, software documentation, software engineering.

I. THE SEARCH FOR THE PHILOSOPHER'S STONE: WHY DO WE WANT A RATIONAL DESIGN PROCESS?

A PERFECTLY rational person is one who always has a good reason for what he does. Each step taken can be shown to be the best way to get to a well defined goal. Most of us like to think of ourselves as rational professional. However, to many observers, the usual process of designing software appears quite irrational. Programmers start without a clear statement of desired behavior and implementation constraints. They make a long sequence of design decisions with no clear statement of why they do things the way they do. Their rationale is rarely explained.

Many of us are not satisfied with such a design process. That is why there is research in software design, programming methods, structured programming, and related topics. Ideally, we would like to derive our programs from a statement of requirements in the same sense that theorems are derived from axioms in a published proof. All of the methodologies that can be considered "top down" are the result of our desire to have a rational, systematic way of designing software.

This paper brings a message with both bad news and good news. The bad news is that, in our opinion, we will never find the philosopher's stone. We will never find a process that allows us to design software in a perfectly rational way. The good news is that we can fake it. We can present our system to others as if we had been rational designers and it pays to pretend to so during development and maintenance.

Manuscript received March 18, 1985. This work was supported by the U.S. Navy and by the National Science and Engineering Research Council (NSERC) of Canada.

D.L. Parnas is with the Department of Computer Science, University of Victoria, Victoria, B.C. V8W 2Y2, Canada, and the Computer Science Naval Systems Branch, Naval Research Laboratory, Washington DC 20375.

P.C. Clements is with the Computer Science and Systems Branch, Naval Research Laboratory, Washington, DC 20375.

IEEE Log Number 8405736.

II. WHY WILL A SOFTWARE DESIGN "PROCESS" ALWAYS BE AN IDEALIZATION?

We will never see a software project that proceeds in the, "rational" way. Some of the reasons are listed below:

1) In most cases the people who commission the building of a software system do not know exactly what they want and are unable to tell us all that they know.

2) Even if we know the requirements, there are many other facts that we need to know to design the software. Many of the details only become known to us as we progress in the implementation. Some of the things that we learn invalidate our design and we must backtrack. Because we try to minimize lost work, the resulting design may be one that would not result from a rational design process.

3) Even if we knew all of the relevant facts before we started, experience shows that human beings are unable to comprehend fully the plethora of details that must be taken into account in order to design and build a correct system. The process of designing the software is one in which we attempt to separate concerns so that we are working with a manageable amount of information. However, until we have separated the concerns, we are bound to make errors.

4) Even if we could master all of the detail needed, all but the most trivial projects are subject to change for external reasons. Some of those changes may invalidate previous design decisions. The resulting design is not one that would have been produced by a rational design process.

5) Human errors can only be avoided if one can avoid the use of humans. Even after the concerns are separated, errors will be made.

6) We are often burdened by preconceived design ideas, ideas that we invented, acquired on related projects, or heard about in a class. Sometimes we undertake a project in order to try out or use a favorite idea. Such ideas may not be derived from our requirements by a rational process.

7) Often we are encouraged, for economic reasons, to use software that was developed for some other project. In other situations, we may be encouraged to share our software with another ongoing project. The resulting software may not be the ideal software for either project, i.e., not the software that we would develop based on its requirements alone, but it is good enough and will save effort.

For all of these reasons, the picture of the software designer deriving his design in a rational, error-free way from a statement of requirements is quite unrealistic. No

Reprinted from *IEEE Transactions on Software Engineering*, Vol. 12, No. 2, Feb. 1986, pp. 351-357.

47

system has ever been developed in that way, and probably none ever will. Even the small program developments shown in textbooks and papers are unreal. They have been revised and polished until the author has shown us what he wishes he had done, not what actually did happen.

III. WHY IS A DESCRIPTION OF A RATIONAL IDEALIZED PROCESS USEFUL NONETHELESS?

What is said above is quite obvious, known to every careful thinker, and admitted by the honest ones. In spite of that we see conferences whose theme is the software design process, working groups on software design methods, and a lucrative market for courses purporting to describe logical ways to design software. What are these people trying to achieve?

If we have identified an ideal process, but cannot follow it completely, we can still follow it as closely as possible and we can write the documentation that we would have produced if we had followed the ideal process. This is what we mean by "faking a rational design process."

Below are some of the reasons for such a pretense:

1) Designers need guidance, When we undertake a large project we can easily be overwhelmed by the enormity of the task. We will be unsure about what to do first. A good understanding of the ideal process will help us to know how to proceed.

2) We will come closer to a rational design if we try to follow the process rather than proceed on an ad hoc basis, For example, even if we cannot know all of the facts necessary to design an ideal system, the effort to find those facts before we start to code will help us to design better and backtrack less.

3) When an organization undertakes many software projects, there are advantages to having a standard procedure. It makes it easier to have good design reviews, to transfer people, ideas, and software from one project to another. If we are going to specify a standard process, it seems reasonable that it should be a rational one.

4) If we have agreed on an ideal process, it becomes much easier to measure the progress that a project is making. We can compare the project's achievements to those that the ideal process calls for. We can identify areas in which we are behind (or ahead) .

5) Regular review of the project's progress by outsiders is essential to good management. If the project is attempting to follow a standard process, it will be easier to review.

IV. WHAT SHOULD THE DESCRIPTION OF THE DEVELOPMENT PROCESS TELL US?

The most useful form of a process description will be in terms of work products. For each stage of the process, this paper describes:

1) What product we should work on next.
2) What criteria that work product must satisfy.
3) What kind of persons should do the work.
4) What information they should use in their work.

Management of any process that is not described in terms of work products can only be done by mind-readers.

Only if we know which work products are due and what criteria they must satisfy, can we review the project and measure progress.

V. WHAT IS THE RATIONAL DESIGN PROCESS?

This section describes the rational, ideal software design process that we should try to follow. Each step is accompanied by a detailed description of the work production associated with that step.

The description of the process that follows includes neither testing nor review. This is not to suggest that one should ignore either of those. When the authors apply the process described in this paper, we include extensive and systematic reviews of each work product as well as testing of the executable code that is produced. The review process is discussed in [1] and [17].

A. Establish and Document Requirements

If we are to be rational designers, we must begin knowing what we must do to succeed. That information should be recorded in a work product known as a requirements document. Completion of this document before we start would allow us to design with all the requirements in front of us.

1) Why do we need a requirements document?

1) We need a place to record the desired behavior of the system as described to us by the user; we need a document that the user, or his representative, can review.

2) We want to avoid making requirements decisions accidentally while designing the program. Programmers working on a system are very often not familiar with the application. Having a complete reference on externally visible behavior relieves them of any need to decide what is best for the user.

3) We want to avoid duplication and inconsistency. Without a requirements document, many of the questions it answered would be asked repeatedly throughout the development by designers, programmers and reviewers. This would be expensive and would often result in inconsistent answers.

4) A complete requirements document is necessary (but not sufficient) for making good estimates of the amount of work and other resources that it will take to build the system.

5) A requirements document is valuable insurance against the costs of personnel turnover. The knowledge that we gain about the requirements will not be lost when someone leaves the project.

6) A requirements document provides a good basis for test plan development. Without it, we do not know what to test for.

7) A requirements document can be used, long after the system is in use, to define the constraints for future changes,

8) A requirements document can be used to settle: arguments among the programmers; once we have a complete and accurate requirements document, we no longer need to be, or consult, requirements experts.

Determining the detailed requirements may well be the most difficult part of the software design process because there are usually no well-organized sources of information.

2) What goes into the requirements document?

The definition of the ideal requirements document is simple: it should contain everything you need to know to write software that is acceptable to the customer, and no more. Of course, we may use references to existing information, if that information is accurate and well organized. Acceptance criteria for an ideal requirements document include the following:

1) Every statement should be valid for all acceptable products; none should depend on implementation decisions.

2) The document should be complete in the sense that if a product satisfies every statement, it should be acceptable.

3) Where information is not available before development must begin, the areas of incompleteness should be explicitly indicated.

4) The product should be organized as a reference document rather than an introductory narrative about the system. Although it takes considerable effort to produce such a document, and a reference work is more difficult to browse than an introduction, it saves labor in the long run. The information that is obtained in this stage is recorded in a form that allows easy reference throughout the project.

3) Who writes the requirements document?

Ideally, the requirements document would be written by the users or their representatives. In fact, users are rarely equipped to write such a document. Instead, the software developers must produce a draft document and get it reviewed and, eventually, approved by the user representative.

4) What is the mathematical model behind the requirements specification?

To assure a consistent and complete document, there must be a simple mathematical model behind the organization. The model described here is motivated by work on real-time systems but, because of that, it is completely general. All systems can be described as real-time systems—even if the real-time requirements are weak.

The model assumes that the ideal product is not a pure digital computer, but a hybrid computer consisting of a digital computer that controls an analog computer. The analog computer transforms continuous values measured by the inputs into continuous outputs. The digital computer brings about discrete changes in the function computed by the analog computer. A purely digital or purely hybrid computer is a special case of this general module. The system that will be built is a digital approximation to this hybrid system. As in other areas of engineering, we can write our specification by first describing this "ideal" system and then specifying the allowable tolerances. The measurements document treats outputs as more important than inputs. If the value of the outputs is correct, nobody will mind if the inputs are not even read, Thus, the key step is identifying all of the outputs. The heart of the requirements document is a set of mathematical functions described in tabular form. Each table specifies the value of a single output as a function of external state variables.

5) How is the requirements document organized?

Completeness in the requirements document is obtained by using separation of concerns to obtain the following sections:

a) Computer Specification: A specification of the machines on which the software must run. The machine need not be hardware-for some software this section might simply be a pointer to a language reference manual.

b) Input/Output Interfaces: A specification of the interfaces that the software must use in order to communicate with the outside world.

c) Specification of Output Values: For each output, a specification of its value in terms of the state and history of the system's environment.

d) Timing Constraints: For each output, how often, or how quickly, the software is required to recompute it.

e) Accuracy Constraints: For each output, how accurate it is required to be.

f) Likely Changes: If the system is required to be easy to change, the requirements should contain a definition of the areas that are considered likely to change. You cannot design a system so that everything is equally easy to change. Programmers should not have to decide which changes are most likely.

g) Undesired Event Handling: The requirements should also contain a discussion of what the system should do when, because of undesired events, it cannot fulfill its full requirements, Most requirements documents ignore those situations; they leave the decision about what to do in the event of partial failures to the programmer.

It is clear that good software cannot be written unless the above information is available, An example of a complete document produced in this way is given in [9] and discussed in [8].

B. Design and Document the Module Structure

Unless the product is small enough to be produced by a single programmer, one must give thought to how the work will be divided into work assignments, which we call modules. The document that should be produced at this stage is called a module guide. It defines the responsibilities of each of the modules by stating the design decisions that will be encapsulated by that module. A module may consist of submodules, or it may be considered to be a single work assignment. If a module contains submodules, a guide to its substructure is provided.

A module guide is needed to avoid duplication, to avoid gaps, to achieve separation of concerns, and most of all, to help an ignorant maintainer to find out which modules are affected by a problem report or change request. If it is kept up-to-date, this document, which records out initial design decisions, will be useful as long as the software is used.

If one diligently applies "information hiding" or "separation of concerns" to a large system, one is certain to end up with a great many modules, A guide that was simply a list of those modules, with no other structure, would help only those who are already familiar with the system. The module guide should have a tree structure, dividing the system into a small number of modules and treating each such module in the same way until all of the modules are quite small. For a complete example of such a document. see [3]. For a discussion of this approach and its benefits, see [6], [15].

C. Design and Document the Module Interfaces

Efficient and rapid production of software requires that the programmers be able to work independently. The module guide defines responsibilities, but it does not, provide enough information to permit independent implementation. A module interface specification must be written for each module. It must be formal and provide a black box picture of each module, Written by a senior designer, it is reviewed by both the future implementers and the programmers who will use the module. An interface specification for a module contains just enough information for the programmer of another module to use its facilities, and no more. The same information is needed by the implementers.

While there will be one person or small team responsible for each specification, the specifications are actually produced by a process of negotiation between implementers, those who will be required to use it, and others interested in the design, e.g., reviewers, The specifications include:

1) a list of programs to be made invokable by the programs of other modules (called "access programs");

2) the parameters for the access programs;

3) the externally visible effects of the access programs;

4) timing constraints and accuracy constraints, where necessary;

5) definition of undesired events.

In many ways this module specification is analogous to the requirements document. However, the notation and organization used is mom appropriate for the software-to-software interface than is the format that we use for the requirements.

Published examples and explanations include [1], [2], [51-[11].

D. Design and Document the Uses Hierarchy

The "uses" hierarchy [13] can be designed once we know all of the modules and their access programs, It is conveniently documented as a binary matrix where the entry in position (A, B) is true if and only if the correctness of program A depends on the presence in the system of a correct program B. The "uses" hierarchy defines the set of subsets that can be obtained by deleting whole programs without rewriting any programs, It is important for staged deliveries, fail soft systems, and the development of program families [12], The "uses" hierarchy is determined by the software designers, but must allow the subsets specified in the requirements document.

E. Design and Document the Module Internal Structures

Once a module interface has been specified, its implementation can be carried out as an independent task except for reviews, However, before coding the major design decisions are recorded in a document called the module design document [16]. This document is designed to allow an efficient review of the design before the coding begins and to explain the intent behind the code to a future maintenance programmer.

In some cases, the module is divided into submodules and the design document is another module guide in which case the design process for that module resumes at step B above. Otherwise, the internal data structures are described; in some cases, these data structures are implemented (and hidden) by submodules. For each of the access programs, a function [10] or LD-relation [14] describes its effect on the data structure. For each value returned by the module to its caller, another mathematical function, the abstraction function, is provided. This function maps the values of the data structure into the values that are returned. For each of the undesired events, we describe how we check for it. Finally, there is a "verification," an argument that programs with these properties would satisfy the module specification.

The decomposition into and design of submodules is continued until each work assignment is small enough that we could afford to discard it and begin again if the programmer assigned to do it left the project.

Each module may consist of one or more processes. The process structure of the system is distributed among the individual modules.

When one is unable to code in a readable high-level language, e.g., if no compiler is available, pseudocode must be part of the documentation. It is useful to have the pseudocode written by someone other than the final coder, and to make both programmers responsible for keeping the two versions of the program consistent [7].

F. *Write Programs*

After all of the design and documentation has been carried out, one is finally ready to write actual executable code. Because of the preparatory work, this goes quickly and smoothly. The code should not include comments that are redundant with the documentation that has already been written. It is unnecessary and makes maintenance of the system more expensive. Redundant comments increase the likelihood that the code will not be consistent with the documentation.

G. *Maintain*

Maintenance is just redesign and redevelopment. The policies recommended here for design must be continued after delivery or the "fake" rationality will disappear. If a change is made, all documentation that is invalidated must be changed. If a change invalidates a design document, it and all subsequent design. documents must be faked to look as if the change had been the original design. If two or more versions are being maintained, the system should be redesigned so that the differences are confined to small modules. The short term costs of this may appear high, but the long term savings can be much higher.

VI. WHAT IS THE ROLE OF DOCUMENTATION IN THIS PROCESS?

A. *What is wrong with most documentation today? Why is it hard to use? Why is it not read?*

It should be clear that documentation plays a major role in the design process that we are describing. Most programmers regard documentation as a necessary evil, written as an afterthought only because some bureaucrat requires it. They do not expect it to be useful.

This is a self-fulfilling prophecy; documentation that has not been used before it is published, documentation that is not important to its author, will always be poor documentation.

Most of that documentation is incomplete and inaccurate, but those are not the main problems. If those

were the main problems, the documents could be easily corrected by adding or correcting information. In fact, there ire underlying organizational problems that lead to incompleteness and incorrectness and those problems, which are listed below, are not easily repaired.

1) Poor Organization: Most documentation today can be characterized as "stream of consciousness," and "stream of execution." "Stream of consciousness" writing puts information at the point in the text that the author was writing when the thought occurred to him, "Stream of execution" writing describes the system in the order that things will happen when it runs. The problem with both of these documentation styles is that subsequent readers cannot find the information that they seek. It will therefore not be easy to determine that facts are missing, or to correct them when they are wrong. It will not be easy to find all the parts of the document that should be changed when the software is changed. The documentation will be expensive to maintain and, in most cases, will not be maintained.

2) Boring Prose: Lots of words are used to say what could be said by a single programming language statement, a formula, or a diagram. Certain facts are repeated it many different sections. This increases the cost of the, documentation and its maintenance. More importantly, it leads to inattentive reading and undiscovered errors,

3) Confusing and Inconsistent Terminology: Any complex system requires the invention and definition of new terminology. Without it the documentation would be far too long. However, the writers of software documentation often fail to provide precise definitions for the terms that they use. As a result, there are many terms used for the same concept and many similar but distinct concepts described by the same term.

4) Myopia: Documentation that is written when the project is nearing completion is written by people who have lived with the system for so long that they take the major decisions for granted. They document the small details that they think they will forget. Unfortunately, the result is a document useful to people who know the system well, but impenetrable for newcomers.

B. *How can one avoid these problems?*

Documentation in the ideal design process meets the needs of the initial developers as well as the needs of the programmers who come later. Each of the documents mentioned above records requirements or design decisions and is used as a reference document for the rest of the design. However, they also provide the information that the maintainers will need. Because the documents are used as reference manuals throughout the building of the software, they will be mature and ready for use in the later work. The documentation in this design process is not an afterthought; it is viewed as one of the primary products of the project. Some systematic checks can be applied to increase completeness and consistency.

One of the major advantages of this approach to documentation is the amelioration of the Mythical Man Month effect (4). When new programmers join the project they do not have to depend completely on the old staff for their information. They will have an up-to-date and rational sot of documents available.

"Stream of consciousness" and "stream of execution" documentation is avoided by designing the structure of each document. Each document is designed by stating the questions that it must answer and refining the questions until each defines the content of an individual section. There must be one, and only one, place for every fact that will be in the document. The questions are answered, i.e., the document is written, only after the structure of a document has been defined. When there are several documents of a certain kind, a standard organization is written for those documents [5]. Every document is designed in accordance with the same principle that guides our software design: separation of concerns. Each aspect of the system is described in exactly one section and nothing else is described in that section. When documents are reviewed, they are reviewed for adherence to the documentation rules as well as for accuracy.

The resulting documentation is not easy or relaxing reading, but it is not boring. It makes use of tables, formulas, and other formal notation to increase the density of information. The organizational rules prevent the duplication of information. The result is documentation that must be read very attentively, but rewards its reader with detailed and precise information.

To avoid the confusing and inconsistent terminology that pervades conventional documentation, a system of special brackets and typed dictionaries is used. Each of the many terms that we must define is enclosed in a pair of bracketing symbols that reveals its type. There is a separate dictionary for each such type. Although beginning readers find the presence of !+terms+!, %terms%, #terms#, etc., disturbing, regular users of the documentation find that the typo information implicit in the brackets makes the documents easier to read. The use of dictionaries that are structured by types makes it less likely that we will define two terms for the same concept or give two meanings to the same term. The special bracketing symbols make it easy to institute mechanical checks for terms that have been introduced but not defined or defined but never used.

VII. FAKING THE IDEAL PROCESS

The preceding describes the ideal process that we, would like to follow and the documentation that would be produced during that process. The process is "faked" by producing the documents that we would have produced if " had done things the ideal way. One attempts to produce the documents in the order that we have described. If a

piece of information is unavailable, that fact is noted in the part of the document where the information should go and the design proceeds as if that information were expected to change. If errors are found, they must be corrected and the consequent changes in subsequent documents must be made. The documentation is our medium of design and no design decisions are considered to be made until their incorporation into the documents. No matter how often we stumble on our way, the final documentation will be rational and accurate.

Even mathematics, the discipline that many of us regard as the most rational of all, allows this procedure. Mathematicians diligently polish their proofs, usually presenting a proof very different from the first one that they discovered. A first proof is often the result of a tortured discovery process. As mathematicians work on proofs, understanding grows and simplifications are found. Eventually, some mathematician finds a simpler proof that makes the truth of the theorem more apparent, The simpler proofs arc published because the readers are interested in the truth of the theorem, not the process of discovering it.

Analogous reasoning applies to software, Those who read the software documentation want to understand the programs, not to relive their discovery. By presenting rationalized documentation we provide what they need.

Our documentation differs from the ideal documentation in one important way. We make a policy of recording all of the design alternatives that we considered and rejected. For each, we explain why it was considered and why it was finally rejected. Months, weeks, or even hours later, when we wonder why we did what we did, we can find out. Years from now, the maintainer will have many of the same questions and will find his answers in our documents.

An illustration that this process pays off is provided by a software requirements document written some years ago as part of a demonstration of the ideal process [9]. Usually, a requirements document is. produced before coding starts and is never used again. However, that has not been the case for [9]. The currently operational version of the software, which satisfies the requirements document, is still undergoing revision. The organization that has to test the software uses our document extensively to choose the tests that they do. When new changes are needed, the requirements document is used in describing what must be changed and what cannot be changed. Here we see that a document produced at the start of the ideal process is still in use many years after the software went into service. The clear message is that if documentation is produced with care, it will be useful for a long time. Conversely, if it is going to be extensively used, it is worth doing right.

VIII.   CONCLUSION

It is very hard to be rational designer; even faking that process is quite difficult. However, the result is a product that can be understood, maintained, and reused. If the project is worth doing, the methods described here are worth using.

ACKNOWLEDGMENT

R. Faulk, J. Shore, D, Weiss. and S. Wilson of the Naval Research Laboratory provided thoughtful reviews of this paper. P. Zave and anonymous referees provided some helpful comments.

REFERENCES

[1] D. L. Parnas, D. M. Wells, P. C, Clements, and K. H. Britton, "Interface specifications for the SCR (A-7E) extended computer module," NRL Memor. Rep. 5502, Dec. 31,1984 (major revisions to NRL Rep. 4843).

[2] K. H. Britton, R. A, Parker, and D. L. Parnas, "A procedure for designing abstract interfaces for device-interface modules." in *Proc. 5th Int. Conf. Software Eng.*, 1981,

[3] K. H. Britton and D. L, Parnas, "A-7E software module guide," NRL Memo. Rep. 4702, Dec, 1981.

[4] F. P. Brooks, Jr., *The Mythical Man-Month: Essays on Software Engineering.* Reading, MA: Addison-Wesley, 1975.

[5] P. Clements, A. Parker, D, L. Parnas, J. Shore and K. Britton. "A standard organization for specifying abstract interfaces," NRL Rrp. 8815, June 14, 1984.

[6] P. Clements. D, Parnas, and D. Weiss, "Enhancing reusability with Information hiding," in *Proc. Workshop Reusability in Program.* Sept. 1983, pp. 240-247.

[7] H, S. Blovitz, "An experiment in software engineering: The architecture research facility as a case study," in *Proc. 4th Int. Conf. Software Eng.*, Sept. 1979.

[8] K. L, Heninger, "Specifying software requirements for complex systems: New techniques and their application," IEEE Trans. Software Eng., Vol. SE-6, pp. 2-13, Jan. 1980.

[9] K. Heninger, J, Kallander, D. L Parnas. and J. Shore, "Software requirements for the A-7E aircraft, "NRL Memo. Rep. 3876, Nov. 27, 1979.

[10] R.C. Linger, H. D. Mills, B.I. Witt, *Structure Programming: Theory and Practice.* Reading, MA! Addison-Wesley, 1979.

[11] A. Parker, K. Heninger, D. Parnas. and J. Shore, "Abstract interface specifications for the A-7E device interface module," NRL Memor. Rep, 4385, Nov, 20. 1980.

[12] D.L. Parnas, "On the design and development of program families," *IEEE Trans. Software Eng.*, vol. SE-2, Mar. 1976.

[13] ___ "Designing software for case of extension and contraction." In *Proc. 3rd Int. Conf Software Eng.*, May 10-12, 1973, pp. 264-277.

[14] ___ "A generalized control structure and its formal definition," *Commun. ACM*, vol. 26, no. 8, pp. 572-581. Aug. 1983.

[15] D. L. Farms, P. Clements and D. Weiss. "The modular structure of complex systems," in *Proc. 7th Int. Conf. Software Eng.*, Mar. 1984, pp. 408-417.

[16] S. Faulk. B. Labaw, and D. Parnas. "SCR module implementation document guidelines," NRL Tech. Memor. 7590-072: SR_GL_DP, April 1, 1983.

[17] D, L, Parnas and D.M. Weiss, "Active design reviews: Principles and practices," in *Proc. 8th Int. Conf. Software Eng.*, London, Aug. 1985.

David Lorge Parnas was born in Plattsburgh, NY, on February 10, 1941.

He is currently Lansdown Professor of Computer Science at the University of Victoria, Victoria, BC, Canada, as well as Principle Consultant of the Software Cost Reduction Project at the Naval Research Laboratory, Washington, DC. He has also taught at Carnegie-Mellon University, the University of Maryland, the Technische Hochschule Darmstadt, and the University of North Carolina at Chapel Hill. He is interested in all aspects f software engineering. His special interests include program semantics, language design, program organization, process structure, process synchronization, and precise abstract specification. He is currently leading an experimental redesign of a hard-real-time system in order to evaluate a number of software engineering principles. He is also involved in the design of a language involving new control structures and abstract data types.

Paul C. Clements received the B.S. degree in mathematical sciences and the M.S. degree in computer science from the University of North Carolina at Chapel Hill in 1977 and 1980, respectively.

Since 1980 he has worked in software engineering research at the Naval Research Laboratory, Washington, DC. In 1982 he became the Technical Director of the Software Cost Reduction Project, whose purpose is to provide a well-engineered model of a complex real-time system. He is interested in most areas of software engineering, but most of his time is spent working on problems in modularization and specification of software designs.

A Spiral Model of Software Development and Enhancement

Barry W. Boehm, TRW Defense Systems Group

This evolving risk-driven approach provides a new framework for guiding the software process.

"Stop the life cycle—I want to get off!"
"Life-cycle Concept Considered Harmful."
"The waterfall model is dead."
"No, it isn't, but it should be."

These statements exemplify the current debate about software life-cycle process models. The topic has recently received a great deal of attention.

The Defense Science Board Task Force Report on Military Software[1] issued in 1987 highlighted the concern that traditional software process models were discouraging more effective approaches to software development such as prototyping and software reuse. The Computer Society has sponsored tutorials and workshops on software process models that have helped clarify many of the issues and stimulated advances in the field (see "Further reading").

The spiral model presented in this article is one candidate for improving the software process model situation. The major distinguishing feature of the spiral model is that it creates a *risk-driven* approach to the software process rather than a primarily *document-driven* or *code-driven* process. It incorporates many of the strengths of other models and resolves many of their difficulties.

This article opens with a short description of software process models and the issues they address. Subsequent sections outline the process steps involved in the spiral model; illustrate the application of the spiral model to a software project, using the TRW Software Productivity Project as an example; summarize the primary advantages and implications involved in using the spiral model and the primary difficulties in using it at its current incomplete level of elaboration; and present resulting conclusions.

Background on software process models

The primary functions of a software process model are to determine the *order of the stages* involved in software development and evolution and to establish the *transition criteria* for progressing from one stage to the next. These include completion criteria for the current stage plus choice criteria and entrance criteria for the next stage. Thus, a process model addresses the following software project questions:

(1) What shall we do next?
(2) How long shall we continue to do it?

Consequently, a process model differs from a software method (often called a methodology) in that a method's primary focus is on how to navigate through each phase (determining data, control, or "uses" hierarchies; partitioning functions; allocating requirements) and how to represent phase products (structure charts; stimulus-response threads; state transition diagrams).

Why are software process models important? Primarily because they provide guidance on the order (phases, increments, prototypes, validation tasks, etc.) in which a project should carry out its major tasks. Many software projects, as the next section shows, have come to grief because they pursued their various development and evolution phases in the wrong order.

Evolution of process models. Before concentrating in depth on the spiral model, we should take a look at a number of others: the code-and-fix model, the stagewise model and the waterfall model, the evolutionary development model, and the transform model.

The code-and-fix model. The basic model used in the earliest days of software

Reprinted from *IEEE Computer*, Vol. 21, no. 5, May 1988, pp. 61-72.

55

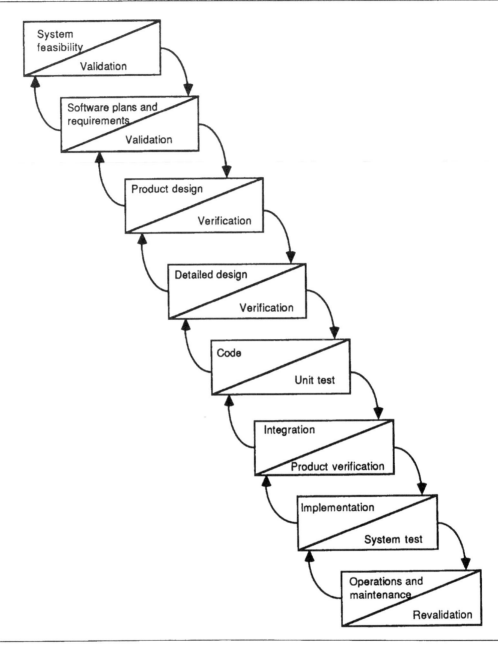

Figure 1. The waterfall model of the software life cycle.

development contained two steps:

(1) Write some code.

(2) Fix the problems in the code.

Thus, the order of the steps was to do some coding first and to think about the requirements, design, test, and maintenance later. This model has three primary difficulties:

(a) After a number of fixes, the code became so poorly structured that subsequent fixes were very expensive. This underscored the need for a design phase prior to coding.

(b) Frequently, even well-designed software was such a poor match to users' needs that it was either rejected outright or expensively redeveloped. This made the need for a requirements phase prior to design evident.

(c) Code was expensive to fix because of poor preparation for testing and modification. This made it clear that explicit recognition of these phases, as well as test-and-evolution planning and preparation tasks in the early phases, were needed.

The stagewise and waterfall models. As early as 1956, experience on large software systems such as the Semi-Automated Ground Environment (SAGE) had led to the recognition of these problems and to the development of a stagewise model[2] to address them. This model stipulated that software be developed in successive stages (operational plan, operational specifications, coding specifications, coding, parameter testing, assembly testing, shakedown, system evaluation).

The waterfall model,[3] illustrated in Figure 1, was a highly influential 1970 refinement of the stagewise model. It provided two primary enhancements to the stagewise model:

(1) Recognition of the feedback loops between stages, and a guideline to confine the feedback loops to successive stages to minimize the expensive rework involved in feedback across many stages.
(2) An initial incorporation of prototyping in the software life cycle, via a "build it twice" step running in parallel with requirements analysis and design.

The waterfall model's approach helped eliminate many difficulties previously encountered on software projects. The waterfall model has become the basis for most software acquisition standards in government and industry. Some of its initial difficulties have been addressed by adding extensions to cover incremental development, parallel developments, program families, accommodation of evolutionary changes, formal software development and verification, and stagewise validation and risk analysis.

However, even with extensive revisions and refinements, the waterfall model's basic scheme has encountered some more fundamental difficulties, and these have led to the formulation of alternative process models.

A primary source of difficulty with the waterfall model has been its emphasis on fully elaborated documents as completion criteria for early requirements and design phases. For some classes of software, such as compilers or secure operating systems, this is the most effective way to proceed. However, it does not work well for many classes of software, particularly interactive

---

The waterfall model has become the basis for most software acquisition standards.

---

end-user applications. Document-driven standards have pushed many projects to write elaborate specifications of poorly understood user interfaces and decision-support functions, followed by the design and development of large quantities of unusable code.

These projects are examples of how waterfall-model projects have come to grief by pursuing stages in the wrong order. Furthermore, in areas supported by fourth-generation languages (spreadsheet or small business applications), it is clearly unnecessary to write elaborate specifications for one's application before implementing it.

The evolutionary development model. The above concerns led to the formulation of the *evolutionary development* model,[4] whose stages consist of expanding increments of an operational software product, with the directions of evolution being determined by operational experience.

The evolutionary development model is ideally matched to a fourth-generation language application and well matched to situations in which users say, "I can't tell you what I want, but I'll know it when I see it." It gives users a rapid initial operational capability and provides a realistic operational basis for determining subsequent product improvements.

Nonetheless, evolutionary development also has its difficulties. It is generally difficult to distinguish it from the old code-and-fix model, whose spaghetti code and lack of planning were the initial motivation for the waterfall model. It is also based on the often-unrealistic assumption that the user's operational system will be flexible enough to accommodate unplanned evolution paths. This assumption is unjustified in three primary circumstances:

(1) Circumstances in which several independently evolved applications must subsequently be closely integrated.
(2) "Information-sclerosis" cases, in which temporary work-arounds for software deficiencies increasingly solidify into

unchangeable constraints on evolution. The following comment is a typical example: "It's nice that you could change those equipment codes to make them more intelligible for us, but the Codes Committee just met and established the current codes as company standards."

(3) Bridging situations, in which the new software is incrementally replacing a large existing system. If the existing system is poorly modularized, it is difficult to provide a good sequence of "bridges" between the old software and the expanding increments of new software.

Under such conditions, evolutionary development projects have come to grief by pursuing stages in the wrong order: evolving a lot of hard-to-change code before addressing long-range architectural and usage considerations.

The transform model. The "spaghetti code" difficulties of the evolutionary development and code-and-fix models can also become a difficulty in various classes of waterfall-model applications, in which code is optimized for performance and becomes increasingly hard to modify. The transform model[5] has been proposed as a solution to this dilemma.

The transform model assumes the existence of a capability to automatically convert a formal specification of a software product into a program satisfying the specification. The steps then prescribed by the transform model are

- a formal specification of the best initial understanding of the desired product;
- automatic transformation of the specification into code;
- an iterative loop, if necessary, to improve the performance of the resulting code by giving optimization guidance to the transformation system;
- exercise of the resulting product; and
- an outer iterative loop to adjust the specification based on the resulting operational experience, and to rederive, reoptimize, and exercise the adjusted software product.

The transform model thus bypasses the difficulty of having to modify code that has become poorly structured through repeated reoptimizations, since the modifications are made to the specification. It also avoids the extra time and expense involved in the intermediate design, code, and test activities.

Still, the transform model has various

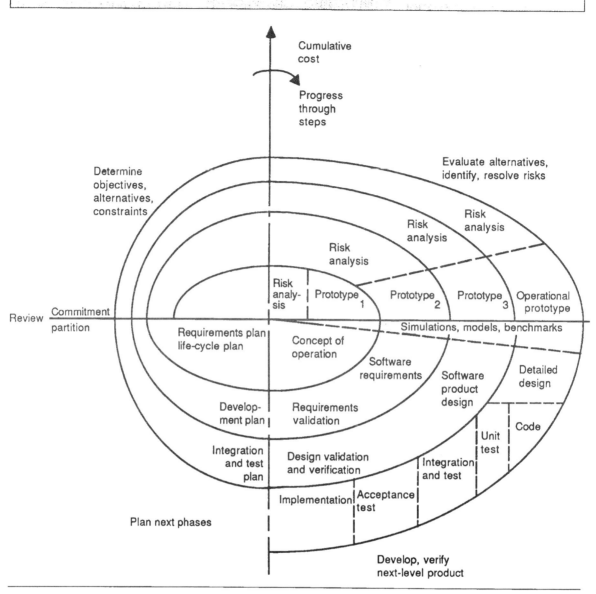

Figure 2. Spiral model of the software process.

difficulties. Automatic transformation capabilities are only available for small products in a few limited areas: spreadsheets, small fourth-generation language applications, and limited computer-science domains. The transform model also shares some of the difficulties of the evolutionary development model, such as the assumption that users' operational systems will always be flexible enough to support unplanned evolution paths.

Additionally, it would face a formidable knowledge-base-maintenance problem in dealing with the rapidly increasing and evolving supply of reusable software components and commercial software products. (Simply consider the problem of tracking the costs, performance, and features of all commercial database management systems, and automatically choosing the best one to implement each new or changed specification.)

The spiral model

The spiral model of the software process (see Figure 2) has been evolving for several years, based on experience with various refinements of the waterfall model as applied to large government software projects. As will be discussed, the spiral model can accommodate most previous models as special cases and further pro-

64

COMPUTER

vides guidance as to which combination of previous models best fits a given software situation. Development of the TRW Software Productivity System (TRW-SPS), described in the next section, is its most complete application to date.

The radial dimension in Figure 2 represents the cumulative cost incurred in accomplishing the steps to date; the angular dimension represents the progress made in completing each cycle of the spiral. (The model reflects the underlying concept that each cycle involves a progression that addresses the same sequence of steps, for each portion of the product and for each of its levels of elaboration, from an overall concept of operation document down to the coding of each individual program.) Note that some artistic license has been taken with the increasing cumulative cost dimension to enhance legibility of the steps in Figure 2.

A typical cycle of the spiral. Each cycle of the spiral begins with the identification of

- the objectives of the portion of the product being elaborated (performance, functionality, ability to accommodate change, etc.);
- the alternative means of implementing this portion of the product (design A, design B, reuse, buy, etc.); and
- the constraints imposed on the application of the alternatives (cost, schedule, interface, etc.).

The next step is to evaluate the alternatives relative to the objectives and constraints. Frequently, this process will identify areas of uncertainty that are significant sources of project risk. If so, the next step should involve the formulation of a cost-effective strategy for resolving the sources of risk. This may involve prototyping, simulation, benchmarking, reference checking, administering user questionnaires, analytic modeling, or combinations of these and other risk-resolution techniques.

Once the risks are evaluated, the next step is determined by the relative remaining risks. If performance or user-interface risks strongly dominate program development or internal interface-control risks, the next step may be an evolutionary development one: a minimal effort to specify the overall nature of the product, a plan for the next level of prototyping, and the development of a more detailed prototype to continue to resolve the major risk issues.

If this prototype is operationally useful and robust enough to serve as a low-risk base for future product evolution, the subsequent risk-driven steps would be the evolving series of evolutionary prototypes going toward the right in Figure 2. In this case, the option of writing specifications would be addressed but not exercised. Thus, risk considerations can lead to a project implementing only a subset of all the potential steps in the model.

On the other hand, if previous prototyping efforts have already resolved all of the performance or user-interface risks, and program development or interface-control risks dominate, the next step follows the basic waterfall approach (concept of operation, software requirements, preliminary design, etc. in Figure 2), modified as appropriate to incorporate incremental development. Each level of software specification in the figure is then followed by a validation step and the preparation of plans for the succeeding cycle. In this case, the options to prototype, simulate, model, etc. are addressed but not exercised, leading to the use of a different subset of steps.

This risk-driven subsetting of the spiral model steps allows the model to accommodate any appropriate mixture of a specification-oriented, prototype-oriented, simulation-oriented, automatic transformation-oriented, or other approach to software development. In such cases, the appropriate mixed strategy is chosen by considering the relative magnitude of the program risks and the relative effectiveness of the various techniques in resolving the risks. In a similar way, risk-management considerations can determine the amount of time and effort that should be devoted to such other project activities as planning, configuration management, quality assurance, formal verification, and testing. In particular, risk-driven specifications (as discussed in the next section) can have varying degrees of completeness, formality, and granularity, depending on the relative risks of doing too little or too much specification.

An important feature of the spiral model, as with most other models, is that each cycle is completed by a review involving the primary people or organizations concerned with the product. This review covers all products developed during the previous cycle, including the plans for the next cycle and the resources required to carry them out. The review's major objective is to ensure that all concerned parties are mutually committed to the approach for the next phase.

The plans for succeeding phases may also include a partition of the product into increments for successive development or components to be developed by individual organizations or persons. For the latter case, visualize a series of parallel spiral cycles, one for each component, adding a third dimension to the concept presented in Figure 2. For example, separate spirals can be evolving for separate software components or increments. Thus, the review-and-commitment step may range from an individual walk-through of the design of a single programmer's component to a major requirements review involving developer, customer, user, and maintenance organizations.

Initiating and terminating the spiral. Four fundamental questions arise in considering this presentation of the spiral model:

(1) How does the spiral ever get started?
(2) How do you get off the spiral when it is appropriate to terminate a project early?
(3) Why does the spiral end so abruptly?
(4) What happens to software enhancement (or maintenance)?

The answer to these questions involves an observation that the spiral model applies equally well to development or enhancement efforts. In either case, the spiral gets started by a hypothesis that a particular operational mission (or set of missions) could be improved by a software effort. The spiral process then involves a test of this hypothesis: at any time, if the hypothesis fails the test (for example, if delays cause a software product to miss its market window, or if a superior commercial product becomes available), the spiral is terminated. Otherwise, it terminates with the installation of new or modified software, and the hypothesis is tested by observing the effect on the operational mission. Usually, experience with the operational mission leads to further hypotheses about software improvements, and a new maintenance spiral is initiated to test the hypothesis. Initiation, termination, and iteration of the tasks and products of previous cycles are thus implicitly defined in the spiral model (although they're not included in Figure 2 to simplify its presentation).

Using the spiral model

The various rounds and activities involved in the spiral model are best understood through use of an example. The spiral model was used in the definition and development of the TRW Software Productivity System (TRW-SPS), an integrated software engineering environment.[6] The initial mission opportunity coincided with a corporate initiative to improve productivity in all appropriate corporate operations and an initial hypothesis that software engineering was an attractive area to investigate. This led to a small, extra "Round 0" circuit of the spiral to determine the feasibility of increasing software productivity at a reasonable corporate cost. (Very large or complex software projects will frequently precede the "concept of operation" round of the spiral with one or more smaller rounds to establish feasibility and to reduce the range of alternative solutions quickly and inexpensively.)

Tables 1, 2, and 3 summarize the application of the spiral model to the first three rounds of defining the SPS. The major features of each round are subsequently discussed and are followed by some examples from later rounds, such as preliminary and detailed design.

Round 0: Feasibility study. This study involved five part-time participants over a two- to three-month period. As indicated in Table 1, the objectives and constraints were expressed at a very high level and in qualitative terms like "significantly increase," "at reasonable cost," etc.

Some of the alternatives considered, primarily those in the "technology" area, could lead to development of a software product, but the possible attractiveness of a number of non-software alternatives in the management, personnel, and facilities areas could have led to a conclusion not to embark on a software development activity.

The primary risk areas involved possible situations in which the company would invest a good deal only to find that

- resulting productivity gains were not significant, or

- potentially high-leverage improvements were not compatible with some aspects of the "TRW culture."

The risk-resolution activities undertaken in Round 0 were primarily surveys and analyses, including structured interviews of software developers and managers, an initial analysis of productivity leverage factors identified by the constructive cost model (Cocomo)[7]; and an analysis of previous projects at TRW exhibiting high levels of productivity.

The risk analysis results indicated that significant productivity gains could be achieved at a reasonable cost by pursuing an integrated set of initiatives in the four major areas. However, some candidate solutions, such as a software support environment based on a single, corporate, maxicomputer-based time-sharing system, were found to be in conflict with TRW constraints requiring support of different levels of security-classified projects. Thus, even at a very high level of generality of objectives and constraints, Round 0 was able to answer basic feasibility questions and eliminate significant classes of candidate solutions.

The plan for Round 1 involved commitment of 12 man-months compared to the two man-months invested in Round 0 (during these rounds, all participants were part-time). Round 1 here corresponded fairly well to the initial round of the spiral model shown in Figure 2, in that its intent was to produce a concept of operation and a basic life-cycle plan for implementing whatever preferred alternative emerged.

Round 1: Concept of operations. Table 2 summarizes Round 1 of the spiral along the lines given in Table 1 for Round 0. The features of Round 1 compare to those of Round 0 as follows:

- The level of investment was greater (12 versus 2 man-months).

- The objectives and constraints were more specific ("double software productivity in five years at a cost of $10,000 a person" versus "significantly increase productivity at a reasonable cost").

- Additional constraints surfaced, such as the preference for TRW products (particularly, a TRW-developed local area network (LAN) system).

- The alternatives were more detailed ("SREM, PSL/PSA or SADT, as requirements tools etc." versus "tools"; "private/shared" terminals, "smart/dumb" terminals versus "workstations").

- The risk areas identified were more specific ("TRW LAN price-performance

Table 1. Spiral model usage: TRW Software Productivity System, Round 0.

Objectives	Significantly increase software productivity
Constraints	At reasonable cost
	Within context of TRW culture
	• Government contracts, high tech., people oriented, security
Alternatives	Management: Project organization, policies, planning, control
	Personnel: Staffing, incentives, training
	Technology: Tools, workstations, methods, reuse
	Facilities: Offices, communications
Risks	May be no high-leverage improvements
	Improvements may violate constraints
Risk resolution	Internal surveys
	Analyze cost model
	Analyze exceptional projects
	Literature search
Risk resolution results	Some alternatives infeasible
	• Single time-sharing system: Security
	Mix of alternatives can produce significant gains
	• Factor of two in five years
	Need further study to determine best mix
Plan for next phase	Six-person task force for six months
	More extensive surveys and analysis
	• Internal, external, economic
	Develop concept of operation, economic rationale
Commitment	Fund next phase

within a $10,000-per-person investment constraint'' versus "improvements may violate reasonable-cost constraint'').

• The risk-resolution activities were more extensive (including the benchmarking and analysis of a prototype TRW LAN being developed for another project).

• The result was a fairly specific operational concept document, involving private offices tailored to software work patterns and personal terminals connected to VAX superminis via the TRW LAN. Some choices were specifically deferred to the next round, such as the choice of operating system and specific tools.

• The life-cycle plan and the plan for the next phase involved a partitioning into separate activities to address management improvements, facilities development, and development of the first increment of a software development environment.

• The commitment step involved more than just an agreement with the plan. It committed to apply the environment to an upcoming 100-person testbed software project and to develop an environment focusing on the testbed project's needs. It also specified forming a representative steering group to ensure that the separate activities were well-coordinated and that the environment would not be overly optimized around the testbed project.

Although the plan recommended developing a prototype environment, it also recommended that the project employ requirements specifications and design specifications in a risk-driven way. Thus, the development of the environment followed the succeeding rounds of the spiral model.

Round 2: Top-level requirements specification. Table 3 shows the corresponding steps involved during Round 2 defining the software productivity system. Round 2 decisions and their rationale were covered in earlier work[6]; here, we will summarize the considerations dealing with risk management and the use of the spiral model:

• The initial risk-identification activities during Round 2 showed that several system requirements hinged on the decision between a host-target system or a fully portable tool set and the decision between VMS and Unix as the host operating system. These requirements included the functions needed to provide a user-friendly front-end, the operating system to be used by the workstations, and the functions necessary to support a host-target

operation. To keep these requirements in synchronization with the others, a special minispiral was initiated to address and resolve these issues. The resulting review led to a commitment to a host-target operation using Unix on the host system, at a point early enough to work the OS-dependent requirements in a timely fashion.

• Addressing the risks of mismatches to the user-project's needs and priorities resulted in substantial participation of the user-project personnel in the requirements definition activity. This led to several significant redirections of the requirements, particularly toward supporting the early phases of the software life-cycle into which the user project was embarking, such as an adaptation of the software requirements engineering methodology (SREM) tools

for requirements specification and analysis.

It is also interesting to note that the form of Tables 1, 2, and 3 was originally developed for presentation purposes, but subsequently became a standard "spiral model template" used on later projects. These templates are useful not only for organizing project activities, but also as a residual design-rationale record. Design rationale information is of paramount importance in assessing the potential reusability of software components on future projects. Another important point to note is that the use of the template was indeed uniform across the three cycles, showing that the spiral steps can be and were uniformly followed at successively detailed levels of product definition.

Table 2. Spiral model usage: TRW Software Productivity System, Round 1.

Objectives	Double software productivity in five years
Constraints	$10,000 per person investment Within context of TRW culture • Government contracts, high tech., people oriented, security Preference for TRW products
Alternatives	Office: Private/modular/. . . Communication: LAN/star/concentrators/. . . Terminals: Private/shared; smart/dumb Tools: SREM/PSL-PSA/. . .; PDL/SADT/. . . CPU: IBM/DEC/CDC/. . .
Risks	May miss high-leverage options TRW LAN price/performance Workstation cost
Risk resolution	Extensive external surveys, visits TRW LAN benchmarking Workstation price projections
Risk resolution results	Operations concept: Private offices, TRW LAN, personal terminals, VAX Begin with primarily dumb terminals; experiment with smart workstations Defer operating system, tools selection
Plan for next phase	Partition effort into software development environment (SDE), facilities, management Develop first-cut, prototype SDE • Design-to-cost: 15-person team for one year Plan for external usage
Commitment	Develop prototype SDE Commit an upcoming project to use SDE Commit the SDE to support the project Form representative steering group

Succeeding rounds. It will be useful to illustrate some examples of how the spiral model is used to handle situations arising in the preliminary design and detailed design of components of the SPS: the preliminary design specification for the requirements traceability tool (RTT), and a detailed design rework or go-back on the unit development folder (UDF) tool.

The RTT preliminary design specification. The RTT establishes the traceability between itemized software requirements specifications, design elements, code elements, and test cases. It also supports various associated query, analysis, and report generation capabilities. The preliminary design specification for the RTT (and most of the other SPS tools) looks different from the usual preliminary design specification, which tends to show a uniform level of elaboration of all components of the design. Instead, the level of detail of the RTT specification is risk-driven.

In areas involving a high risk if the design turned out to be wrong, the design was carried down to the detailed design level, usually with the aid of rapid prototyping. These areas included working out the implications of "undo" options and dealing with the effects of control keys used to escape from various program levels.

In areas involving a moderate risk if the design was wrong, the design was carried down to a preliminary-design level. These areas included the basic command options for the tool and the schemata for the requirements traceability database. Here again, the ease of rapid prototyping with Unix shell scripts supported a good deal of user-interface prototyping.

In areas involving a low risk if the design was wrong, very little design elaboration was done. These areas included details of all the help message options and all the report-generation options, once the nature of these options was established in some example instances.

A detailed design go-back. The UDF tool collects into an electronic "folder" all artifacts involved in the development of a single-programmer software unit (typically 500 to 1,000 instructions): unit requirements, design, code, test cases, test results, and documentation. It also includes a management template for tracking the programmer's scheduled and actual completion of each artifact.

An alternative considered during detailed design of the UDF tool was reuse of portions of the RTT to provide pointers to the requirements and preliminary design specifications of the unit being developed. This turned out to be an extremely attractive alternative, not only for avoiding duplicate software development but also for bringing to the surface several issues involving many-to-many mappings between requirements, design, and code that had not been considered in designing the UDF tool. These led to a rethinking of the UDF tool requirements and preliminary design, which avoided a great deal of code rework that would have been necessary if the detailed design of the UDF tool had proceeded in a purely deductive, top-down fashion from the original UDF requirements specification. The resulting go-back led to a significantly different, less costly, and more capable UDF tool, incorporating the RTT in its "uses-hierarchy."

Spiral model features. These two examples illustrate several features of the spiral approach.

• It fosters the development of specifications that are not necessarily uniform, exhaustive, or formal, in that they defer detailed elaboration of low-risk software elements and avoid unnecessary breakage in their design until the high-risk elements of the design are stabilized.

• It incorporates prototyping as a risk-reduction option at any stage of development. In fact, prototyping and reuse risk analyses were often used in the process of going from detailed design into code.

• It accommodates reworks or go-backs to earlier stages as more attractive alternatives are identified or as new risk issues need resolution.

Overall, risk-driven documents, particularly specifications and plans, are important features of the spiral model. Great amounts of detail are not necessary unless the absence of such detail jeopardizes the

Table 3. Spiral model usage: TRW Software Productivity System, Round 2.

Objectives	User-friendly system
	Integrated software, office-automation tools
	Support all project personnel
	Support all life-cycle phases
Constraints	Customer-deliverable SDE ⇒ Portability
	Stable, reliable service
Alternatives	OS: VMS/AT&T Unix/Berkeley Unix/ISC
	Host-target/fully portable tool set
	Workstations: Zenith/LSI-11/. . .
Risks	Mismatch to user-project needs, priorities
	User-unfriendly system
	• 12-language syndrome; experts-only
	Unix performance, support
	Workstation/mainframe compatibility
Risk resolution	User-project surveys, requirements participation
	Survey of Unix-using organizations
	Workstation study
Risk resolution results	Top-level requirements specification
	Host-target with Unix host
	Unix-based workstations
	Build user-friendly front end for Unix
	Initial focus on tools to support early phases
Plan for next phase	Overall development plan
	• for tools: SREM, RTT, PDL, office automation tools
	• for front end: Support tools
	• for LAN: Equipment, facilities
Commitment	Proceed with plans

project. In some cases, such as with a product whose functionality may be determined by a choice among commercial products, a set of weighted evaluation criteria for the products may be preferable to a detailed pre-statement of functional requirements.

Results. The Software Productivity System developed and supported using the spiral model avoided the identified risks and achieved most of the system's objectives. The SPS has grown to include over 300 tools and over 1,300,000 instructions; 93 percent of the instructions were reused from previous project-developed, TRW-developed, or external-software packages. Over 25 projects have used all or portions of the system. All of the projects fully using the system have increased their productivity at least 50 percent; indeed, most have doubled their productivity (when compared with cost-estimation model predictions of their productivity using traditional methods).

However, one risk area—that projects with non-Unix target systems would not accept a Unix-based host system—was underestimated. Some projects accepted the host-target approach, but for various reasons (such as customer constraints and zero-cost target machines) a good many did not. As a result, the system was less widely used on TRW projects than expected. This and other lessons learned have been incorporated into the spiral model approach to developing TRW's next-generation software development environment.

Evaluation

Advantages. The primary advantage of the spiral model is that its range of options accommodates the good features of existing software process models, while its risk-driven approach avoids many of their difficulties. In appropriate situations, the spiral model becomes equivalent to one of the existing process models. In other situations, it provides guidance on the best mix of existing approaches to a given project; for example, its application to the TRW-SPS provided a risk-driven mix of specifying, prototyping, and evolutionary development.

The primary conditions under which the spiral model becomes equivalent to other main process models are summarized as follows:

• If a project has a low risk in such areas

All of the projects fully using the system have increased their productivity at least 50 percent.

---

as getting the wrong user interface or not meeting stringent performance requirements, and if it has a high risk in budget and schedule predictability and control, then these risk considerations drive the spiral model into an equivalence to the waterfall model.

• If a software product's requirements are very stable (implying a low risk of expensive design and code breakage due to requirements changes during development), and if the presence of errors in the software product constitutes a high risk to the mission it serves, then these risk considerations drive the spiral model to resemble the two-leg model of precise specification and formal deductive program development.

• If a project has a low risk in such areas as losing budget and schedule predictability and control, encountering large-system integration problems, or coping with information sclerosis, and if it has a high risk in such areas as getting the wrong user interface or user decision support requirements, then these risk considerations drive the spiral model into an equivalence to the evolutionary development model.

• If automated software generation capabilities are available, then the spiral model accommodates them either as options for rapid prototyping or for application of the transform model, depending on the risk considerations involved.

• If the high-risk elements of a project involve a mix of the risk items listed above, then the spiral approach will reflect an appropriate mix of the process models above (as exemplified in the TRW-SPS application). In doing so, its risk-avoidance features will generally avoid the difficulties of the other models.

The spiral model has a number of additional advantages, summarized as follows:

It focuses early attention on options involving the reuse of existing software. The steps involving the identification and evaluation of alternatives encourage these options.

It accommodates preparation for life-cycle evolution, growth, and changes of the software product. The major sources of product change are included in the product's objectives, and information-hiding approaches are attractive architectural design alternatives in that they reduce the risk of not being able to accommodate the product-change objectives.

It provides a mechanism for incorporating software quality objectives into software product development. This mechanism derives from the emphasis on identifying all types of objectives and constraints during each round of the spiral. For example, Table 3 shows user-friendliness, portability, and reliability as specific objectives and constraints to be addressed by the SPS. In Table 1, security constraints were identified as a key risk item for the SPS.

It focuses on eliminating errors and unattractive alternatives early. The risk-analysis, validation, and commitment steps cover these considerations.

For each of the sources of project activity and resource expenditure, it answers the key question, "How much is enough?" Stated another way, "How much of requirements analysis, planning, configuration management, quality assurance, testing, formal verification, etc. should a project do?" Using the risk-driven approach, one can see that the answer is not the same for all projects and that the appropriate level of effort is determined by the level of risk incurred by not doing enough.

It does not involve separate approaches for software development and software enhancement (or maintenance). This aspect helps avoid the "second-class citizen" status frequently associated with software maintenance. It also helps avoid many of the problems that currently ensue when high-risk enhancement efforts are approached in the same way as routine maintenance efforts.

It provides a viable framework for integrated hardware-software system development. The focus on risk-management and on eliminating unattractive alternatives early and inexpensively is equally applicable to hardware and software.

Difficulties. The full spiral model can be successfully applied in many situations, but some difficulties must be addressed before it can be called a mature, universally applicable model. The three primary challenges involve matching to contract software, relying on risk-assessment expertise, and the need for further elaboration of spiral model steps.

Matching to contract software. The spiral model currently works well on internal software developments like the TRW-SPS, but it needs further work to match it to the world of contract software acquisition.

Internal software developments have a great deal of flexibility and freedom to accommodate stage-by-stage commitments, to defer commitments to specific options, to establish minispirals to resolve critical-path items, to adjust levels of effort, or to accommodate such practices as prototyping, evolutionary development, or design-to-cost. The world of contract software acquisition has a harder time achieving these degrees of flexibility and freedom without losing accountability and control, and a harder time defining contracts whose deliverables are not well specified in advance.

Recently, a good deal of progress has been made in establishing more flexible contract mechanisms, such as the use of competitive front-end contracts for concept definition or prototype fly-offs, the use of level-of-effort and award-fee contracts for evolutionary development, and the use of design-to-cost contracts. Although these have been generally successful, the procedures for using them still need to be worked out to the point that acquisition managers feel fully comfortable using them.

Relying on risk-assessment expertise. The spiral model places a great deal of reliance on the ability of software developers to identify and manage sources of project risk.

A good example of this is the spiral model's risk-driven specification, which carries high-risk elements down to a great deal of detail and leaves low-risk elements to be elaborated in later stages; by this time, there is less risk of breakage.

However, a team of inexperienced or low-balling developers may also produce a specification with a different pattern of variation in levels of detail: a great elaboration of detail for the well-understood, low-risk elements, and little elaboration of the poorly understood, high-risk elements. Unless there is an insightful review of such a specification by experienced development or acquisition personnel, this type of project will give an illusion of progress during a period in which it is actually heading for disaster.

Another concern is that a risk-driven specification will also be people-dependent. For example, a design produced by an expert may be implemented by non-experts. In this case, the expert, who does not need a great deal of detailed documentation, must produce enough additional documentation to keep the non-experts from going astray. Reviewers of the specification must also be

Table 4. A prioritized top-ten list of software risk items.

Risk item	Risk management techniques
1. Personnel shortfalls	Staffing with top talent, job matching; teambuilding; morale building; cross-training; pre-scheduling key people
2. Unrealistic schedules and budgets	Detailed, multisource cost and schedule estimation; design to cost; incremental development; software reuse; requirements scrubbing
3. Developing the wrong software functions	Organization analysis; mission analysis; ops-concept formulation; user surveys; prototyping; early users' manuals
4. Developing the wrong user interface	Task analysis; prototyping; scenarios; user characterization (functionality, style, workload)
5. Gold plating	Requirements scrubbing; prototyping; cost-benefit analysis; design to cost
6. Continuing stream of requirement changes	High change threshold; information hiding; incremental development (defer changes to later increments)
7. Shortfalls in externally furnished components	Benchmarking; inspections; reference checking; compatibility analysis
8. Shortfalls in externally performed tasks	Reference checking; pre-award audits; award-fee contracts; competitive design or prototyping; teambuilding
9. Real-time performance shortfalls	Simulation; benchmarking; modeling; prototyping; instrumentation; tuning
10. Straining computer-science capabilities	Technical analysis; cost-benefit analysis; prototyping; reference checking

Table 5. Software Risk Management Plan.

1.	Identify the project's top 10 risk items.
2.	Present a plan for resolving each risk item.
3.	Update list of top risk items, plan, and results monthly.
4.	Highlight risk-item status in monthly project reviews.
	• Compare with previous month's rankings, status.
5.	Initiate appropriate corrective actions.

sensitive to these concerns.

With a conventional, document-driven approach, the requirement to carry all aspects of the specification to a uniform level of detail eliminates some potential problems and permits adequate review of some aspects by inexperienced reviewers. But it also creates a large drain on the time of the scarce experts, who must dig for the critical issues within a large mass of non-critical detail. Furthermore, if the high-risk elements have been glossed over by impressive-sounding references to poorly understood capabilities (such as a new synchronization concept or a commercial DBMS), there is an even greater risk that the conventional approach will give the illusion of progress in situations that are actually heading for disaster.

Need for further elaboration of spiral model steps. In general, the spiral model process steps need further elaboration to ensure that all software development participants are operating in a consistent context.

Some examples of this are the need for more detailed definitions of the nature of spiral model specifications and milestones, the nature and objectives of spiral model reviews, techniques for estimating and synchronizing schedules, and the nature of spiral model status indicators and cost-versus-progress tracking procedures. Another need is for guidelines and checklists to identify the most likely sources of project risk and the most effective risk-resolution techniques for each source of risk.

Highly experienced people can successfully use the spiral approach without these elaborations. However, for large-scale use in situations where people bring widely differing experience bases to the project, added levels of elaboration—such as have been accumulated over the years for document-driven approaches—are important in ensuring consistent interpretation and use of the spiral approach across the project.

Efforts to apply and refine the spiral model have focused on creating a discipline of software risk management, including techniques for risk identification, risk analysis, risk prioritization, risk-management planning, and risk-element tracking. The prioritized top-ten list of software risk items given in Table 4 is one result of this activity. Another example is the risk management plan discussed in the next section.

Implications: The Risk Management Plan. Even if an organization is not ready to adopt the entire spiral approach, one characteristic technique that can easily be adapted to any life-cycle model provides many of the benefits of the spiral approach. This is the Risk Management Plan summarized in Table 5. This plan basically ensures that each project makes an early identification of its top risk items (the number 10 is not an absolute requirement), develops a strategy for resolving the risk items, identifies and sets down an agenda to resolve new risk items as they surface, and highlights progress versus plans in monthly reviews.

The Risk Management Plan has been used successfully at TRW and other organizations. Its use has ensured appropriate focus on early prototyping, simulation, benchmarking, key-person staffing measures, and other early risk-resolution techniques that have helped avoid many potential project "show-stoppers." The recent US Department of Defense standard on software management, DoD-Std-2167, requires that developers produce and use risk management plans, as does its counterpart US Air Force regulation, AFR 800-14.

Overall, the Risk Management Plan and the maturing set of techniques for software risk management provide a foundation for tailoring spiral model concepts into the more established software acquisition and development procedures.

We can draw four conclusions from the data presented:

(1) The risk-driven nature of the spiral model is more adaptable to the full range of software project situations than are the primarily document-driven approaches such as the waterfall model or the primarily code-driven approaches such as evolutionary development. It is particularly applicable to very large, complex, ambitious software systems.

(2) The spiral model has been quite successful in its largest application to date: the development and enhancement of the TRW-SPS. Overall, it achieved a high level of software support environment capability in a very short time and provided the flexibility necessary to accommodate a high dynamic range of technical alternatives and user objectives.

(3) The spiral model is not yet as fully elaborated as the more established models. Therefore, the spiral model can be applied by experienced personnel, but it needs further elaboration in such areas as contract-

ing, specifications, milestones, reviews, scheduling, status monitoring, and risk-area identification to be fully usable in all situations.

(4) Partial implementations of the spiral model, such as the Risk Management Plan, are compatible with most current process models and are very helpful in overcoming major sources of project risk.☐

Acknowledgments

I would like to thank Frank Belz, Lolo Penedo, George Spadaro, Bob Williams, Bob Balzer, Gillian Frewin, Peter Hamer, Manny Lehman, Lee Osterweil, Dave Parnas, Bill Riddle, Steve Squires, and Dick Thayer, along with the *Computer* reviewers of this article, for their stimulating and insightful comments and discussions of earlier versions of the article, and Nancy Donato for producing its several versions.

References

1. F.P. Brooks et al., *Defense Science Board Task Force Report on Military Software*, Office of the Under Secretary of Defense for Acquisition, Washington, DC 20301, Sept. 1987.
2. H.D. Benington, "Production of Large Computer Programs," *Proc. ONR Symp. Advanced Programming Methods for Digital Computers*, June 1956, pp. 15-27. Also available in *Annals of the History of Computing*, Oct. 1983, pp. 350-361, and *Proc. Ninth Int'l Conf. Software Engineering*, Computer Society Press, 1987.
3. W.W. Royce, "Managing the Development of Large Software Systems: Concepts and Techniques," *Proc. Wescon*, Aug. 1970. Also available in *Proc. ICSE 9*, Computer Society Press, 1987.
4. D.D. McCracken and M.A. Jackson, "Life-Cycle Concept Considered Harmful," *ACM Software Engineering Notes*, Apr. 1982, pp. 29-32.
5. R. Balzer, T.E. Cheatham, and C. Green, "Software Technology in the 1990s: Using a New Paradigm," *Computer*, Nov. 1983, pp. 39-45.
6. B.W. Boehm et al., "A Software Development Environment for Improving Productivity," *Computer*, June 1984, pp. 30-44.
7. B.W. Boehm, *Software Engineering Economics*, Prentice-Hall, 1981, Chap. 33.

Further reading

The software process model field has an interesting history, and a great deal of stimulating work has been produced recently in this specialized area. Besides the references that appear at the end of the accompanying article, here are some additional good sources of insight:

Overall process model issues and results

Agresti's tutorial volume provides a good overview and set of key articles. The three recent *Software Process Workshop Proceedings* provide access to much of the recent work in the area.

Agresti, W.W., *New Paradigms for Software Development*, IEEE Catalog No. EH0245-1, 1986.

Dowson, M., ed., *Proc. Third Int'l Software Process Workshop*, IEEE Catalog No. TH0184-2, Nov. 1986.

Potts, C., ed., *Proc. Software Process Workshop*, IEEE Catalog No. 84CH2044-6, Feb. 1984.

Wileden, J.C., and M. Dowson, eds., Proc. Int'l Workshop Software Process and Software Environments, *ACM Software Engineering Notes*, Aug. 1986.

Alternative process models

More detailed information on waterfall-type approaches is given in:

Evans, M.W., P. Piazza, and J.P. Dolkas, *Principles of Productive Software Management*, John Wiley & Sons, 1983.

Hice, G.F., W.J. Turner, and L.F. Cashwell, *System Development Methodology*, North Holland, 1974 (2nd ed., 1981).

More detailed information on evolutionary development is provided in:

Gilb, T., *Principles of Software Engineering Management*, Addison Wesley, 1988 (currently in publication).

Some additional process model approaches with useful features and insights may be found in:

Lehman, M.M., and L.A. Belady, *Program Evolution: Processes of Software Change*, Academic Press, 1985.

Osterweil, L., "Software Processes are Software, Too," *Proc. ICSE 9*, IEEE Catalog No. 87CH2432-3, Mar. 1987, pp. 2-13.

Radice, R.A., et al., "A Programming Process Architecture," *IBM Systems J.*, Vol. 24, No.2, 1985, pp. 79-90.

Spiral and spiral-type models

Some further treatments of spiral model issues and practices are:

Belz, F.C., "Applying the Spiral Model: Observations on Developing System Software in Ada," *Proc. 1986 Annual Conf. on Ada Technology*, Atlanta, 1986, pp. 57-66.

Boehm, B.W., and F.C. Belz, "Applying Process Programming to the Spiral Model," *Proc. Fourth Software Process Workshop*, IEEE, May 1988.

Iivari, J., "A Hierarchical Spiral Model for the Software Process," *ACM Software Engineering Notes*, Jan. 1987, pp. 35-37.

Some similar cyclic spiral-type process models from other fields are described in:

Carlsson, B., P. Keane, and J.B. Martin, "R&D Organizations as Learning Systems," *Sloan Management Review*, Spring 1976, pp. 1-15.

Fisher, R., and W. Ury, *Getting to Yes*, Houghton Mifflin, 1981; Penguin Books, 1983, pp. 68-71.

Kolb, D.A., "On Management and the Learning Process," MIT Sloan School Working Article 652-73, Cambridge, Mass., 1973.

Software risk management

The discipline of software risk management provides a bridge between spiral model concepts and currently established software acquisition and development procedures.

Boehm, B.W., "Software Risk Management Tutorial," Computer Society, Apr. 1988.

Risk Assessment Techniques, Defense Systems Management College, Ft. Belvoir, Va. 22060, July 1983.

Barry W. Boehm is the chief scientist of the TRW Defense Systems Group. Since 1973, he has been responsible for developing TRW's software technology base. His current primary responsibilities are in the areas of software environments, process models, management methods, Ada, and cost estimation. He is also an adjunct professor at UCLA.

Boehm received his BA degree in mathematics from Harvard in 1957 and his MA and PhD from UCLA in 1961 and 1964, respectively.

Readers may write to Boehm at TRW Defense Systems Group, One Space Park, R2/2086, Redondo Beach, CA 90278.

72

Chapter 3

REQUIREMENTS ENGINEERING

Software requirements represent the blueprints that the project manager must follow in the construction of the system. The first paper by Parnas shows how requirements can and should be written to allow for the inevitable—change. The second paper appeared in a special issue of the journal, Real-Time Systems, which I guest-edited several years ago. Although the title seems slightly out of place here, it is the single best paper describing the rich variety of software specification tools that I have ever seen. The remaining two papers in this section talk about the challenges of dealing with those change requests that never seem to end.

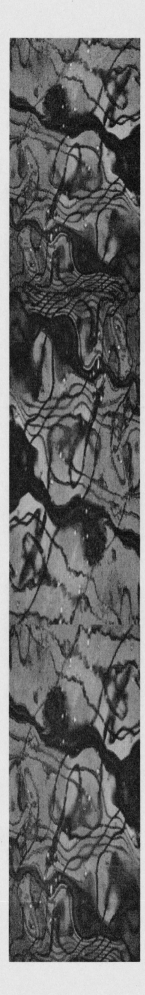

Designing Software for Ease of Extension and Contraction

DAVID L. PARNAS

Abstract—Designing software to be extensible and easily contracted is discussed as a special case of design for change. A number of ways that extension and contraction problems manifest themselves in current software are explained. Four steps in the design of software that is more flexible are then discussed. The most critical step is the design of a software structure called the "uses" relation. Some criteria for design decisions are given and illustrated using a small example. It is shown that the identification of *minimal* subsets and *minimal* extensions can lead to software that can be tailored to the needs of a broad variety of users.

Index Terms—Contractibility, extensibility, modularity, software engineering, subsets, supersets.

Manuscript received June 7, 1978; revised October 26, 1978. The earliest work in this paper was supported by NV Phillips Computer Industrie, Apeldoorn, The Netherlands. This work was also supported by the National Science Foundation and the German Federal Ministry for Research and Technology (BMFT). This paper was presented at the Third International Conference on Software Engineering, Atlanta, GA, May 1978.

The author is with the Department of Computer Science, University of North Carolina, Chapel Hill, NC 27514. He is also with the Information Systems Staff, Communications Sciences Division, Naval Research Laboratory, Washington, DC.

I. INTRODUCTION

THIS paper is being written because the following complaints about software systems are so common.

1) "We were behind schedule and wanted to deliver an early release with only a <proper subset of intended capabilities>, but found that that subset would not work until everything worked."

2) "We wanted to add <simple capability>, but to do so would have meant rewriting all or most of the current code."

3) "We wanted to simplify and speed up the system by removing the <unneeded capability>, but to take advantage of this simplification we would have had to rewrite major sections of the code."

4) "Our SYSGEN was intended to allow us to tailor a system to our customers' needs but it was not flexible enough to suit us."

After studying a number of such systems, I have identified some simple concepts that can help programmers to design software so that subsets and extensions are more easily obtained. These concepts are simple if you think about software in the way suggested by this paper. Programmers do not commonly do so.

Reprinted from *IEEE Transactions on Software Engineering*, Vol. SE-5, Mar. 1979, pp. 128-38.

69

II. SOFTWARE AS A FAMILY OF PROGRAMS

When we were first taught how to program, we were given a specific problem and told to write one program to do that job. Later we compared our program to others, considering such issues as space and time utilization, but still assuming that we were producing a single product. Even the most recent literature on programming methodology is written on that basis. Dijkstra's *A Discipline of Programming* [1] uses predicate transformers to specify *the* task to be performed by *the* program to be written. The use of the definite article implies that there is a unique problem to be solved and but one program to write.

Today, the software designer should be aware that he is not designing a single program but a family of programs. As discussed in an earlier paper [2], we consider a set of programs to be a program family if they have so much in common that it pays to study their common aspects before looking at the aspects that differentiate them. This rather pragmatic definition does not tell us what pays, but it does explain the motivation for designing program families. We want to exploit the commonalities, share code, and reduce maintenance costs.

Some of the ways that the members of a program family may differ are listed below.

1) They may run on different hardware configurations.

2) They may perform the same functions but differ in the format of the input and output data.

3) They may differ in certain data structures or algorithms because of differences in the available resources.

4) They may differ in some data structures or algorithms because of differences in the size of the input data sets or the relative frequency of certain events.

5) Some users may require only a subset of the services or features that other users need. These "less demanding" users may demand that they not be forced to pay for the resources consumed by the unneeded features.

Engineers are taught that they must try to anticipate the changes that may be made, and are shown how to achieve designs that can easily be altered when these anticipated changes occur. For example, an electrical engineer will be advised that the world has not standardized the 60-cycle 110-V current. Television designers are fully aware of the differing transmission conventions that exist in the world. It is standard practice to design products that are easily changed in those aspects. Unfortunately, there is no magic technique for handling unanticipated changes. The makers of conventional watches have no difficulty altering a watch that shows the day so that it displays "MER" instead of "WED," but I would except a long delay for redesign were the world to switch to a ten day week.

Software engineers have not been trained to design for change. The usual programming courses neither mention the need to anticipate changes nor do they offer techniques for designing programs in which changes are easy. Because programs are abstract mathematical objects, the software engineers' techniques for responding to anticipated changes are more subtle and more difficult to grasp than the techniques used by designers of physical objects. Further, we have been led astray by the other designers of abstract objects—mathematicians who state

and prove theorems. When a mathematician becomes aware of the need for a set of closely related theorems, he responds by proving a more general theorem. For mathematicians, a more general result is always superior to a more specialized product. The engineering analogy to the mathematician's approach would be to design television sets containing variable transformers and tuners that are capable of detecting several types of signals. Except for the U.S. armed forces stationed overseas, there is little market for such a product. Few of us consider relocations so likely that we are willing to pay to have the generality present in the product. My guess is that the market for calendar watches for a variable length week is even smaller than the market for the television sets just described.

In [2] I have treated the subject of the design of program families rather generally and in terms of text in a programming language. In this paper I focus on the fifth situation described above; families of programs in which some members are subsets of other family members or several family members share a common subset. I discuss an earlier stage of design, the stage when one identifies the major components of the system and defines relations between those components. We focus on this early stage because the problems described in the introduction result from failure to consider early design decisions carefully.

III. HOW DOES THE LACK OF SUBSETS AND EXTENSIONS MANIFEST ITSELF?

Although we often speak of programs that are "not subsetable" or "not extensible," we must recognize that phrase as inaccurate. It is always possible to remove code from a program and have a runable result. Any software system can be extended (TSO proves that). The problem is that the subsets and extensions are not the programs that we would have designed if we had set out to design just that product. Further, the amount of work needed to obtain the product seems all out of proportion to the nature of the change. The obstacles commonly encountered in trying to extend or shrink systems fall into four classes.

A. Excessive Information Distribution

A system may be hard to extend or contract if too many programs were written assuming that a given feature is present or not present. This was illustrated by an operating system in which an early design decision was that the system would support three conversational languages. There were many sections of the system where knowledge of this decision was used. For example, error message tables had room for exactly three entries. An extension to allow four languages would have required that a great deal of code be rewritten. More surprisingly, it would have been difficult to reduce the system to one that efficiently supported only two of the languages. One could remove the third language, but to regain the table space, one would have had to rewrite the same sections of code that would be rewritten to add a language.

B. A Chain of Data Transforming Components

Many programs are structured as a chain of components, each receiving data from the previous component, processing it (and changing the format), before sending the data to the next program in the chain. If one component in this chain is not needed, that code is often hard to remove because the output of its predecessor is not compatible with the input requirements of its successor. A program that does nothing but change the format must be substituted. One illustration would be a payroll program that assumed unsorted input. One of the components of the system accepts the unsorted input and produces output that is sorted by some key. If the firm adopts an office procedure that results in sorted input, this phase of the processing is unnecessary. To eliminate that program, one may have to add a program that transfers data from a file in the input format to a file in the format appropriate for the next phase. It may be almost as efficient to allow the original SORT component to sort the sorted input.

C. Components That Perform More Than One Function

Another common error is to combine two simple functions into one component because the functions seem too simple to separate. For example, one might be tempted to combine synchronization with message sending and acknowledgment in building an operating system. The two functions seem closely related; one might expect that for the sake of reliability one should insist on a "handshake" with each exchange of synchronization signals. If one later encounters an application in which synchronization is needed very frequently, one may find that there is no simple way to strip the message sending out of the synchronization routines. Another example is the inclusion of run-time type-checking in the basic subroutine call mechanism. In applications where compile-time checking or verification eliminates the need for the run-time type-check, another subroutine call mechanism will be needed. The irony of these situations is that the "more powerful" mechanism could have been built separately from, but *using*, simpler mechanisms. Separation would result in a system in which the simpler mechanism was available for use where it sufficed.

D. Loops in the "Uses" Relation

In many software design projects, the decisions about what other component programs to use are left to individual systems programmers. If a programmer knows of a program in another module, and feels that it would be useful in his program, he includes a call on that program in his text. Programmers are encouraged to use the work of other programmers as much as possible because, when each programmer writes his own routines to perform common functions, we end up with a system that is much larger than it need be.

Unfortunately, there are two sides to the question of program usage. Unless some restraint is exercised, one may end up with a system in which nothing works until everything works. For example, while it may seem wise to have an operating system scheduler use the file system to store its data (rather than use its own disk routines), the result will be that the file system must be present and working before any task scheduling is possible. There are users for whom an operating system subset without a file system would be useful. Even if one has no such users, the subset would be useful during development and testing.

IV. STEPS TOWARDS A BETTER STRUCTURE

This section discusses four parts of a methodology that I believe will help the software engineer to build systems that do not evidence the problems discussed above.

A. Requirements Definition: Identifying the Subsets First

One of the clearest morals in the earlier discussion about "design for change" as it is taught in other areas of engineering is that one must anticipate changes before one begins the design. At a past conference [3] many of the papers exhorted the audience to spend more time identifying the actual requirements before starting on a design. I do not want to repeat such exhortations, but I do want to point out that the identification of the possible subsets is part of identifying the requirements. Treating the easy availability of certain subsets as an operational requirement is especially important to government officials who purchase software. Many officials despair of placing strict controls on the production methods used by their contractors because they are forbidden by law to tell the contractor how to perform his job. They may tell him what they require, but not how to build it. Fortunately, the availability of subsets may be construed as an operational property of the software.

On the other hand, the identification of the required subsets is not a simple matter of asking potential users what they could do without. First, users tend to overstate their requirements. Second, the answer will not characterize the set of subsets that might be wanted in the future. In my experience, identification of the potentially desirable subsets is a demanding intellectual exercise in which one first searches for the *minimal* subset that might conceivably perform a useful service and then searches for a set of *minimal* increments to the system. Each increment is small—sometimes so small that it seems trivial. The emphasis on minimality stems from our desire to avoid components that perform more than one function (as discussed in Section III-C). Identifying the minimal subset is difficult because the minimal system is not usually a program that anyone would ask for. If we are going to build the software family, the minimal subset is useful; it is not usually worth building by itself. Similarly, the maximum flexibility is obtained by looking for the smallest possible increments in capability: often these are smaller increments than a user would think of. Whether or not he would think of them before system development, he is likely to want that flexibility later.

The search for a minimal subset and minimal extensions can best be shown by an example. One example of a minimal subset is given in [4]. Another example will be given later in this paper.

B. Information Hiding: Interface and Module Definition

In an earlier section we touched upon the difference between the mathematician's concept of generality and an engineer's approach to design flexibility. Where the mathematician wants his product, a theorem or method of proof, to be as general as possible, i.e., applicable, without change, in as many situations as possible, an engineer often must tailor his product to the situation actually at hand. Lack of generality is necessary to make the program as efficient or inexpensive as possible. If he must develop a family of products, he tries to isolate the changeable parts in modules and to develop an interface between the module and the rest of the product that remains valid for all versions. The crucial steps are as follows.

1) Identification of the items that are likely to change. These items are termed "secrets."

2) Location of the specialized components in separate modules.

3) Designing intermodule interfaces that are insensitive to the anticipated changes. The changeable aspects or "secrets" of the modules are not revealed by the interface.

It is exactly this that the concept of information hiding [5], encapsulation, or abstraction [6] is intended to do for software. Because software is an abstract or mathematical product, the modules may not have any easily recognized physical identity. They are not necessarily separately compilable or coincident with memory overlay units. The interface must be general but the contents should not be. Specialization is necessary for economy and efficiency.

The concept of information hiding is very general and is applicable in many software change situations—not just the issue of subsets and extensions that we address in this paper. The ideas have also been extensively discussed in the literature [5]-[9]. The special implications for our problem are simply that, as far as possible, even the presence or absence of a component should be hidden from other components. If one program uses another directly, the presence of the second program cannot be fully hidden from its user. However, there is never any reason for a component to "know" how many other programs use it. All data structures that reveal the presence or number of certain components should be included in separate information hiding modules with abstract interfaces [10]. Space and other considerations make it impossible to discuss this concept further in this paper; it will be illustrated in the example. Readers for whom this concept is new are advised to read some of the articles mentioned above.

C. The Virtual Machine (VM) Concept

To avoid the problems that we have described as "a chain of data transforming components," it is necessary to stop thinking of systems in terms of components that correspond to steps in the processing. This way of thinking dies hard. It is almost certain that your first introduction to programming was in terms of a series of statements intended to be executed in the order that they were explained to you. We are goal oriented; we know what we start with and what we want to produce. It is natural to think in terms of steps progressing towards that goal. It is the fact that we are designing a family of systems that makes this "natural" approach the wrong one.

The viewpoint that seems most appropriate to designing software families is often termed the virtual machine approach. Rather than write programs that perform the transformation from input data to output data, we design software machine extensions that will be useful in writing many such programs. Where our hardware machine provides us with a set of instructions that operate on a small set of data types, the extended or virtual machine will have additional data types as well as "software instructions" that operate on those data types. These added features will be tailored to the class of programs that we are building. While the VM instructions are designed to be generally useful, they can be left out of a final product if the user's programs do not use them. The programmer writing programs for the virtual machine should not need to distinguish between instructions that are implemented in software and those that are hardware implemented. To achieve a true virtual machine, the hardware resources that are used in implementing the extended instruction set must be unavailable to the user of the virtual machine. The designer has traded these resources for the new data elements and instructions. Any attempt to use those resources again will invalidate the concept of virtual machine and lead to complications. Failure to provide for isolation of resources is one of the reasons for the failure of some attempts to use macros to provide a virtual machine. The macro user must be careful not to use the resources used in the code generated by the macros.

There is no reason to accomplish the transformation from the hardware machine to a virtual machine with all of the desired features in a single leap. Instead we will use the machine at hand to implement a few new instructions. At each step we take advantage of the newly introduced features. Such a step-by-step approach turns a large problem into a set of small ones and, as we will see later, eases the problem of finding the appropriate subsets. Each element in this series of virtual machines is a useful subset of the system.

D. Designing the "Uses" Structure

The concept of an abstract machine is an intuitive way of thinking about design. A precise description of the concept comes through a discussion of the relation "uses" [11], [12].

1) The relation "uses": We consider a system to be divided into a set of programs that can be invoked either by the normal flow of control mechanisms, by an interrupt, or by an exception handling mechanism. Each of these programs is assumed to have a specification that defines exactly the effect that an invocation of the program should have.

We say of two programs A and B that A uses B if correct execution of B may be necessary for A to complete the task described in its specification. That is, A uses B if there exist situations in which the correct functioning of A depends upon the availability of a correct implementation of B. Note that to decide whether A uses B or not, one must examine both the implementation *and* the specification of A.

The "uses" relation and "invokes" very often coincide, but uses differs from invokes in two ways:

a) Certain invocations may not be instances of "uses." If A's specification requires only that A *invoke* B when certain conditions occur, then A has fulfilled its specification when it has generated a correct call to B. A is correct even if B is incorrect or absent. A proof of correctness of A need only make assumptions about the way to invoke B.

b) A program A may use B even though it never invokes it. The best illustration of this is interrupt handling. Most programs in a computer system are only correct on the assumption that the interrupt handling routine will correctly handle the interrupts (leave the processor in an acceptable state). Such programs use the interrupt handling routines even though they never call them. *"Uses"* can also be formulated as *"requires the presence of a correct version of."*

Systems that have achieved a certain "elegance" (e.g., T.H.E. [5], Venus [6]) have done so by having parts of the system *"use"* other parts in such a way that the "user" programs were simplified. For example, the transput stream mechanism in T.H.E. *uses* the segmenting mechanism to great advantage. In contrast, many large and complex operating systems achieve their size and complexity by having "independent" parts. For example, there are many systems in which "spooling," virtual memory management, and the file system all perform their own backup store operations. Code to perform these functions is present in each of the components. Whenever such components must share a single device, complex interfaces exist.

The disadvantage of unrestrained "usage" of each others facilities is that the system parts become highly interdependent. Often there are no subsets of the system that can be used before the whole system is complete. In practice, some duplication of effort seems preferable to a system in which nothing runs unless everything runs.

2) *The uses hierarchy:* By restricting the relation *"uses"* so that its graph is loop free we can retain the primary advantages of having system parts *"use"* each other while eliminating the problems. In that case it is possible to assign the programs to the levels of a hierarchy by the following rules:

a) level 0 is the set of all programs that *use* no other program;

b) level i (i ⩾ 1) is the set of all programs that *use* at least one program on level i − 1 and no program at a level higher than i − 1.

If such a hierarchical ordering exists, then each level offers a testable and usable subset of the system. In fact, one can get additional subsets by including only parts of a level. The easy availability of these subsets is very valuable for the construction of any software systems and is vital for developing a *broad* family of systems.

The design of the "uses" hierarchy should be one of the major milestones in a design effort. The division of the system into independently callable subprograms has to go on in parallel with the decisions about *uses*, because they influence each other.

3) *The criteria to be used in allowing one program to use another:* We propose to allow A *"uses"* B when all of the following conditions hold:

a) A is essentially simpler because it uses B;

b) B is not substantially more complex because it is not allowed to use A;

c) there is a useful subset containing B and not A;

d) there is no conceivably useful subset containing A but not B.

During the process of designing the "uses" relation, we often find ourselves in a situation where two programs could obviously benefit from using each other and the conditions above cannot be satisfied. In such situations, we resolve the apparent conflicts by a technique that we call "sandwiching." One of the programs is "sliced" into two parts in a way that allows the programs to "use" each other and still satisfy the above conditions. If we find ourselves in a position where A would benefit from using B, but B can also benefit from using A, we may split B into two programs: B1 and B2. We then allow A to use B2 and B1 to use A. The result would appear to be a sandwich with B as the bread and A as the filling. Often, we then go on to split A. We start with a few levels and end up with many.

An earlier report [11] introduced many of the ideas that are in this paper and illustrated them by proposing a "uses" relation for a family of operating systems. It contains several examples of situations where "sandwiching" led us from a "T.H.E.-like structure" [14] to a structure with more than twice as many levels. For example, the virtual memory mechanism was split into address translation and dynamic allocation of memory areas to segments.

The most frequent instances of splitting and sandwiching came because initially we were assuming that a "level" would be a "module" in the sense of Section IV-B. We will discuss this in the final part of this paper.

4) *Use of the word "convenience":* It will trouble some readers that it is usual to use the word "convenience" to describe a reason for introducing a certain facility at a given level of the hierarchy. A more substantial basis would seem more scientific.

As discussed in [11] and [13], we must assume that the hardware itself is capable of performing all necessary functions. As one goes higher in the levels, one can lose capabilities (as resources are consumed)—not gain them. On the other hand, at the higher levels the new functions can be implemented with simpler programs because of the additional programs that can be used. We speak of "convenience" to make it clear that one could implement any functions on a lower level, but the availability of the additional programs at the higher level is useful. For each function we give the lowest level at which the features that are useful for implementing that function (with the stated restrictions) are available. In each case, we see no functions available at the next higher level that would be useful for implementing the functions as described. If we implemented the program one level lower we would have to duplicate programs that become available at that level.

V. EXAMPLE: AN ADDRESS PROCESSING SUBSYSTEM

As an example of designing for extensibility and subsets, we consider a set of programs to read in, store, and write out lists of addresses. This example has also been used, to illustrate a different point, in [10] and has been used in several classroom experiments to demonstrate module interchangeability. This

```
The following items of information will
be found in the addresses to be processed
and constitute the only items of relevance
to the application programs:

  • Last name
  • Given names (first name and possible
      middle names)
  • Organization (Command or Activity)
  • Internal identifier (Branch or Code)
  • Street address or P.O. box
  • City or mail unit identifier
  • State
  • Zip code
  • Title
  • Branch of service if military
  • GS grade if civil service

Each of the above will be strings of
characters in the standard ANSI alphabet,
and each of the above may be empty or blank.
```

Fig. 1.

example is intended as an integral part of this paper; several statements in the final summation are supported only in this section.

A. Our Basic Assumptions

1) The information items discussed in Fig. 1 will be the items to be processed by all application programs.

2) The input formats of the addresses are subject to change.

3) The output formats of the addresses are subject to change.

4) Some systems will use a single fixed format for input and output. Other systems will need the ability to choose from several input or output formats at run-time. Some systems will be required in which the user can specify the format using a format definition language.

5) The representation of addresses in main storage will vary from system to system.

6) In most systems, only a subset of the total set of addresses stored in the system need be in main storage at any one time. The number of addresses needed may vary from system to system, and in some systems the number of addresses to be kept in main memory may vary at run-time.

B. We Propose the Following Design Decisions

1) The input and output programs will be table driven: the table will specify the format to be used for input and output. The contents and organization of these format tables will be the "secrets" of the input and output modules.

2) The representation of addresses in core will be the "secret" of an address storage module (ASM). The implementation chosen for this module will be such that the operations of changing a portion of an address will be relatively inexpensive, compared to making the address table larger or smaller.

3) When the number of addresses to be stored exceeds the capacity of an ASM, programs will use an address file module (AFM). An AFM can be made upward compatible with an ASM; programs that were written to use ASM's could operate using an AFM in the same way. The AFM provides additional

commands to allow more efficient usage by programs that do not assume the random access properties of an ASM. These programs are described below.

4) Our implementation of an AFM would use an ASM as a submodule as well as another submodule that we will call block file module (BFM). The BFM stores blocks of data that are sufficiently large to represent an address, but the BFM is not specialized to the handling of addresses. An ASM that is used within an AFM may be said to have two interfaces. In the "normal interface" that an ASM presents to an outside user, an address is a set of fields and the access functions hide or abstract from the representation. Fig. 2 is a list of the access programs that comprise this interface. In the second interface, the ASM deals with blocks of contiguous storage and abstract from the contents. There are commands for the ASM to input and output "addresses" but the operands are storage blocks whose interpretation as addresses is known only within the ASM. The AFM makes assumptions about the association between blocks and addresses but not about the way that an address's components are represented as blocks. The BFM is completely independent of the fact that the blocks contain address information. The BFM might, in fact, be a manufacturer supplied access method.

C. Component Programs

1) Module: Address Input

INAD: Reads in an address that is assumed to be in a format specified by a format table and calls ASM or AFM functions to store it.

INFSL: Selects a format from an existing set of format tables. The selected format is the one that will be used by INAD. There is always a format selected.

INFCR: Adds a new format to the tables used by INFSL. The format is specified in a "format language." Selection is *not* changed (i.e., INAD still uses the same format table).

INTABEXT: Adds a blank table to the set of input format tables.

INTABCHG: Rewrites a table in the input format tables using a description in a format language. Selection is not changed.

INFDEL: Deletes a table from the set of format tables. The selected format cannot be deleted.

INADSEL: Reads in an address using one of a set of formats. Choice is specified by an integer parameter.

INADFO: Reads in an address in a format specified as one of its parameters (a string in the format definition language). The format is selected and added to the tables and subsequent addresses could be read in using INAD.

2) Module: Address Output

OUTAD: Prints an address in a format specified by a format table. The information to be printed

Access Functions for "Normal Interface"

MODULE: ASM

NAME OF ACCESS PROGRAM*	INPUT PARAMETERS					OUTPUT	
*ADDTIT:	asm	X	integer	X	string	→	asm •
ADDGN:	asm	X	integer	X	string	→	asm •
ADDLN:	asm	X	integer	X	string	→	asm •
ADDSERV:	asm	X	integer	X	string	→	asm •
ADDBORC:	asm	X	integer	X	string	→	asm •
ADDCORA:	asm	X	integer	X	string	→	asm •
ADDSORP:	asm	X	integer	X	string	→	asm •
ADDCITY:	asm	X	integer	X	string	→	asm •
ADDSTATE:	asm	X	integer	X	string	→	asm •
ADDZIP:	asm	X	integer	X	string	→	asm •
ADDGSL:	asm	X	integer	X	string	→	asm •
SETNUM:	asm	X	integer	→	asm •		
FETTIT:	asm	X	integer	→	string		
FETGN:	asm	X	integer	→	string		
FETGN:	asm	X	integer	→	string		
FETLN:	asm	X	integer	→	string		
FETSERV:	asm	X	integer	→	string		
FETBORC:	asm	X	integer	→	string		
FETCORA:	asm	X	integer	→	string		
FETSORP:	asm	X	integer	→	string		
FETCITY:	asm	X	integer	→	string		
FETSTATE:	asm	X	integer	→	string		
FETZIP:	asm	X	integer	→	string		
FETGSL:	asm	X	integer	→	string		
FETNUM:	asm	→	integer				

*These are abbreviations: ADDTIT = ADD TITLE; ADDGN = ADD GIVEN NAME, etc.

Fig. 2. Syntax of ASM functions.

is assumed to be in an ASM and identified by its position in an ASM.

OUTFSL: Selects a format table from an existing set of output format tables. The selected format is the one that will be used by OUTAD.

OUTTABEXT: Adds a "blank" table to the set of output format tables.

OUTTABCHG: Rewrites the contents of a format table using information in a format language.

OUTFCR: Adds a new format to the set of formats that can be selected by OUTFSL in a format description language.

OUTFDEL: Deletes a table from the set of format tables that can be selected by OUTFSL.

OUTADSEL: Prints out an address using one of a set of formats.

OUTADFO: Prints out an address in a format specified in a format definition language string, which is one of the actual parameters. The format is added to the tables and selected.

3) Module: Address Storage (ASM)

FET: (Component Name): This is a set of functions used to read information from an address store. Returns a string as a value. See Fig. 2.

ADD: (Component Name): This is a set of functions used to write information in an address store. Each takes a string and an integer as parameters. The integer specifies an address within the ASM. See Fig. 2.

OBLOCK: Takes an integer parameter, returns a storage block as a value.

IBLOCK: Accepts a storage block and integer as parameters. Its effect is to change the contents of an address store—which is reflected by a change in the values of the FET programs.

ASMEXT: Extends an address store by appending a new address with empty components at the end of the address store.

ASMSHR: "Shrinks" the address store.

ASMCR: Creates a new address store. The parameter specifies the number of components. All components are initially empty.

ASMDEL: Deletes an existing address store.

4) Module: Block File Module

BLFET: Accepts an integer as a parameter and returns a "block."

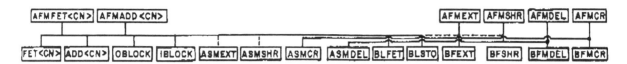

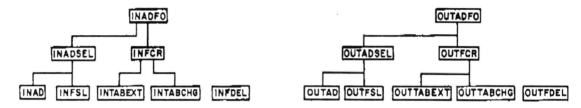

Fig. 3.

BLSTO: Accepts a block and an integer and stores the block.

BFEXT: Extends BFM by adding additional blocks to its capacity.

BFSHR: Reduces the size of the BFM by removing some blocks.

BFMCR: Creates a file of blocks.

BFMDEL: Deletes an existing file of blocks.

5) Module: Address File Module

This module includes implementations of all of the ASM functions except OBLOCK and IBLOCK. To avoid confusion in the diagram showing the uses hierarchy we have changed the names to:

AFMADD (Component Name) defined as in Fig. 2

AFMFET (Component Name) defined as in Fig. 1

AFMEXT defined as in BFM above

AMFSHR defined as in BFM above

AFMCR defined as in BFM above

AFMDEL defined as in BFM above.

D. Uses Relation

Fig. 3 shows the *uses* relation between the component programs. It is important to note that we are now discussing the implementation of those programs, not just their specifications. The *uses* relation is characterized by the fact that there are a large number of relatively simple, *single-purpose* programs on the lowest level. The upper level programs are implemented by means of these lower level programs so that they too are quite simple. This *uses* relation diagram characterizes the set of possible subsets.

E. Discussion

To pick a subset, one identifies the set of upper level programs that the user needs and includes only those programs that those programs use (directly or indirectly). For example, a user who uses addresses in a single format does not need the component programs that interpret format description lan-

guages. Systems that work with a small set of addresses can be built without any BFM components. A program that works as a query system and never prints out a complete address would not need any Address Output components.

The system is also easily extended. For example, one could add a capability to read in addresses with self-defining files. If the first record on a file was a description of the format in something equivalent to the format description language, one could write a program that would be able to read in that record, use INTABCHG to build a new format table, and then read in the addresses. Programs that do things with addresses (such as print out "personalized" form letters) can also be added using these programs and selecting only those capabilities that they actually need.

One other observation that can be made is that the upper level programs can be used to "generate" lower level versions. For example, the format description languages can be used to generate the tables used for the fixed format versions. There is no need for a separate SYSGEN program.

We will elaborate on this observation in the conclusion.

VI. SOME REMARKS ON OPERATING SYSTEMS: WHY GENERALS ARE SUPERIOR TO COLONELS

An earlier report [11] discusses the design of a "uses" hierarchy for operating systems. Although there have been some refinements to the proposals of that report, its basic contents are consistent with the present proposals. This section compares the approach outlined in this paper and the "kernel" approach or "nucleus" approach to OS design [18]-[20]. It is tempting to say that the suggestions in this paper do not conflict with the "kernel" approach. These proposals can be viewed as a refinement of the nucleus approach. The first few levels of our system could be labeled "kernel," and one could conclude that we are just discussing a fine structure within the kernel.

To yield to that temptation would be to ignore an essential difference between the approaches suggested in this paper and the kernel approach. The system kernels known to me are such that some desirable subsets cannot be obtained without major surgery. It was assumed that the nucleus must be in every system family member. In the RC4000 system the inability to separate synchronization from message passing has led some users to bypass the kernel to perform teletype handling functions. In Hydra as originally proposed [19], "type checking" was so intrinsic to the call mechanism that it appeared impossible to disable it when it was not needed or affordable.[1]

Drawing a line between "kernel" and the rest of the system, and putting "essential" services of "critical programs" in the nucleus yields a system in which kernel features cannot be removed and certain extensions are impractical. Looking for a *minimal* subset and a set of *minimal* independent incremental function leads to a system in which one can trim away unneeded features. I know of no feature that is always needed. When we say that two functions are *almost* always used together, we should remember that "almost" is a euphemism for "not."

VII. SUMMATION

This paper describes an approach to software intended to result in systems that can be tailored to fit the needs of a broad variety of users. The points most worthy of emphasis are as follows.

1) The Requirements Include Subsets and Extensions: It is essential to recognize the identification of useable subsets as part of the preliminaries to software design. Flexibility cannot be an afterthought. Subsetability is needed, not just to meet a variety of customers' needs, but to provide a fail-safe way of handling schedule slippage.

2) Advantages of the Virtual Machine Approach: Designing software as a set of virtual machines has definite advantages over the conventional (flowchart) approach to system design. The virtual machine "instructions" provide facilities that are useful for purposes beyond those originally conceived. These instructions can easily be omitted from a system if they are not needed. Remove a jamor box from a flowchart and there is often a need to "fill the hole" with conversion programs.

3) On the Difference Between Software Generality and Software Flexibility: Software can be considered "general" if it can be used, *without change*, in a variety of situations. Software can be considered flexible, if it is *easily changed* to be used in a variety of situations. It appears unavoidable that there is a run-time cost to be paid for generality. Clever designers can achieve flexibility without significant run-time cost, but there is a design-time cost. One should incur the design-time cost only if one expects to recover it when changes are made.

Some organizations may choose to pay the run-time cost for generality. They build general software rather than flexible software because of the maintenance problems associated with maintaining several different versions. Factors influencing this decision include a) the availability of extra computer resources,

b) the facilities for program change and maintenance available at each installation, and c) the extent to which design techniques ease the task of applying the same change to many versions of a program.

No one can tell a designer how much flexibility and generality should be built into a product, but the decision should be a conscious one. Often, it just happens.

4) On the Distinction Between Modules, Subprograms, and Levels: Several systems and at least one dissertation [14]-[17] have, in my opinion, blurred the distinction between modules, subprograms, and levels. Conventional programming techniques consider a subroutine or other callable program to be a module. If one wants the modules to include all programs that must be designed together and changed together, then, as our example illustrates, one will usually include many small subprograms in a single module. If does not matter what word we use; the point is that the unit of change is not a single callable subprogram.

In several systems, modules and levels have coincided [14], [15]. This had led to the phrase "level of abstraction." Each of the modules in the example abstract from some detail that is assumed likely to change. In our approach there is no correspondence between modules and levels. Further, I have not found a relation, "more abstract than," that would allow me to define an abstraction hierarchy [12]. Although I am myself guilty of using it, in most cases the phrase "levels of abstraction" is an abuse of language.

Janson has suggested that a design such as this one (or the one discussed in [11]) contain "soft modules" that can represent a breach of security principles. Obviously an error in any program in one of our modules can violate the integrity of that module. All module programs that will be included in a given subset must be considered in proving the correctness of that module. However, I see no way that allowing the component programs to be on different levels of a "uses" hierarchy makes this process more difficult or makes the system less secure. The boundaries of our modules are quite firm and clearly identified.

The essential difference between this paper and other discussions of hierarchically structured designs is the emphasis on subsets and extensions. My search for a criterion to be used in designing the *uses* hierarchy has convinced me that if one does not care about the existence of subsets, it does not really matter what hierarchy one uses. Any design can be bent until it works. It is only in the ease of change that they differ.

5) On Avoiding Duplication: Some earlier work [21] has suggested that one needs to have duplicate or near duplicate modules in a hierarchically structured system. For example, they suggest that one needs one implementation of processes to give a fixed number of processes at a low level and another to provide for a varying number of processes at a user's level. Similar ideas have appeared elsewhere. Were such duplication to be necessary, it would be a sound argument against the use of "structured" approaches. One can avoid such duplication if one allows the programs that vary the size of a data structure to be on a higher level than the other programs that operate on that data structure. For example, in an operating system, the programs to create and delete processes need not be on the

---

[1] Accurate reports on the current status and performance of that system are not available to me.

same level as the more frequently used scheduling operations. In designing software, I regard the need to code similar functions in two separate programs as an indication of a fundamental error in my thinking.

6) Designing for Subsets and Extensions Can Reduce the Need for Support Software: We have already mentioned that this design approach can eliminate the need for separate SYSGEN programs. We can also eliminate the need for *special*-purpose compilers. The price of the convenience features offered by such languages is often a compiler and run-time package distinctly larger than the system being built. In our approach, each level provides a "language extention" available to the programmer of the next level. We never build a compiler; we just build our system, but we get convenience features anyway.

7) Extension at Run-Time Versus Extension During SYSGEN: At a later stage in the design we will have to choose data structures and take the difference between run-time extension and SYSGEN extension into consideration. Certain data structures are more easily accessed but harder to extend while the program is running; others are easily extended but at the expense of a higher access cost. These differences do not affect our early design decisions because they are hidden in modules.

8) On the Value of a Model: My work on this example and similar ones has gone much faster because I have learned to exploit a pattern that I first noticed in the design discussed in [11]. Low level operations assume the existence of a fixed data structure of some type. The operations on the next level allow the swapping of a data element with others from a fixed set of similar elements. The high level programs allow the creation and deletion of such data elements. This pattern appears several times in both designs. Although I have not designed your system for you, I believe that you can take advantage of a similar pattern. If so, this paper has served its purpose.

ACKNOWLEDGMENT

The ideas presented in this paper have been developed over a lengthy period and with the cooperation and help of many collaborators. I am grateful to numerous Philips employees for thought provoking comments and questions. Price's collaboration was invaluable at Carnegie-Mellon University. The help of W. Bartussek, G. Handzel, and H. Wuerges at the Technische Hochschule Darmstadt led to substantial improvements. Heninger, Weiss, and J. Shore at the Naval Research Laboratory helped me to understand the application of the concepts in areas other than operating systems. B. Trombka and J. Guttag both helped in the design of pilots of the address process system. Discussions with P. J. Courtois have helped me to better understand the relation between software structure and run-time characteristics of computer systems. Dr. E. Britton, H. Rettenmaier, L. Belady, Dr. D. Stanat, G. Fran, and Dr. W. Wright made many helpful suggestions about an earlier draft of this paper. If you find portions of this paper helpful, these people deserve your thanks.

REFERENCES

[1] E. W. Dijkstra, *A Discipline of Programming.* Englewood Cliffs, NJ: Prentice-Hall, 1976.

[2] D. L. Parnas, "On the design and development of program families," *IEEE Trans. Software Eng.*, vol. SE-2, pp. 1-9, Mar. 1976.

[3] 2nd Int. Conf. Software Engineering, Oct. 13-15, 1976; also, *IEEE Trans. Software Eng.*, (Special Issue), vol. SE-2, Dec. 1976.

[4] D. L. Parnas, G. Handzel, and H. Würges, "Design and specification of the minimal subset of an operating system family," presented at the 2nd Int. Conf. Software Engineering, Oct. 13-15, 1976; also, *IEEE Trans. Software Eng.*, (Special Issue), vol. SE-2, pp. 301-307, Dec. 1976.

[5] D. L. Parnas, "On the criteria to be used in decomposing systems into modules," *Commun. Ass. Comput. Mach.*, Dec. 1972.

[6] T. A. Linden, "The use of abstract data types to simplify program modifications," in *Proc. Conf. Data: Abstraction, Definition and Structure,* Mar. 22-24, 1976; also, *ACM SIGPLAN Notices* (Special Issue), vol. II, 1976.

[7] D. L. Parnas, "A technique for software module specification with examples," *Commun. Ass. Comput. Mach.*, May 1972.

[8] ——, "Information distribution aspects of design methodology," in *1971 Proc. IFIP Congr.* Amsterdam, The Netherlands: North-Holland, 1971.

[9] ——, "The use of precise specifications in the development of software," in *1977 Proc. IFIP Congr.* Amsterdam, The Netherlands: North-Holland, 1977.

[10] ——, "Use of abstract interfaces in the development of software for embedded computer systems," Naval Res. Lab., Washington, DC, NRL Rep. 8047, June 1977.

[11] ——, "Some hypotheses about the 'uses' hierarchy for operating systems," Technische Hochschule Darmstadt, Darmstadt, West Germany, Tech. Rep., Mar. 1976.

[12] ——, "On a 'buzzword': Hierarchical structure," in *1974 Proc. IFIP Congr.* Amsterdam, The Netherlands: North-Holland, 1974.

[13] D. L. Parnas and D. L. Siewiorek, "Use of the concept of transparency in the design of hierarchically structured systems," *Commun. Ass. Comput. Mach.*, vol. 18, July 1975.

[14] E. W. Dijkstra, "The structure of the "THE"-multiprogramming system," *Commun. Ass. Comput. Mach.*, vol. 11, pp. 341-346, May 1968.

[15] B. Liskov, "The design of the Venus operating system," *Commun. Ass. Comput. Mach.*, vol. 15, pp. 144-149, Mar. 1972.

[16] P. A. Janson, "Using type extension to organize virtual memory mechanisms," Lab. for Comput. Sci., M.I.T., Cambridge, MA, MIT-LCS-TR167, Sept. 1976.

[17] ——, "Using type-extension to organize virtual memory mechanisms," IBM Zurich Res. Lab., Switzerland, Res. Rep. RZ 858 (#28909), August 31, 1977.

[18] P. Brinch Hansen, "The nucleus of the multiprogramming system," *Commun. Ass. Comput. Mach.*, vol. 13, pp. 238-241, 250, Apr. 1970.

[19] W. Wulf, E. Cohen, A. Jones, R. Lewin, C. Pierson, and F. Pollack, "HYDRA: The kernel of a multiprocessor operating system," *Commun. Ass. Comput. Mach.*, vol. 17, pp. 337-345, June 1974.

[20] G. J. Popek and C. S. Kline, "The design of a verified protection system," in *Proc. Int. Workshop Prot. In Oper. Syst.*, IRIA, pp. 183-196.

[21] A. R. Saxena and T. H. Bredt, "A structured specification of a hierarchical operating system," in *Proc. 1975 Int. Conf. Reliable Software.*

David L. Parnas received the B.S., M.S., and Ph.D. degrees in electrical engineering–systems and communications sciences from the Carnegie Institute of Technology, Pittsburgh, PA.

He held the position of Assistant Professor of Computer Science at the University of Maryland and at Carnegie-Mellon University. During the period 1969-1970 he was employed by Philips-Electrologica, Apeldoorn, The Netherlands, and at the MBLE Research Laboratory, Brussels, Belgium. He then returned to Carnegie-Mellon

University where he held the rank of Associate Professor until 1973. In June of 1973 he was appointed Professor and Head of the Research Group on Operating Systems I at the Technical University of Darmstadt, Germany, where he remained through August 1976. He is presently Professor in the Department of Computer Science, University of North Carolina, Chapel Hill. He is also with the Information Systems Staff, Communications Sciences Division, at the Naval Research Laboratory, Washington, DC. He has published papers in the areas of computer design languages and simulation techniques. His current interests are in the field of software engineering methods, computer system design, abstract specification for programs, verification that a program meets its specifications, and cooperating sequential processes.

Real-Time Systems, 8, 117–172 (1995)

Reprinted by permission from Real-Time Systems: The International Journal of Time Critical Systems, Kluwer Academic Press Publisher, Vol. 8, No. 2/3, pp. 117-172, March/April 1995.

Tools for Specifying Real-Time Systems*

GIACOMO BUCCI

Department of Systems and Informatics, Faculty of Engineering, University of Florence, Florence, Italy.

MAURIZIO CAMPANAI

CESVIT/CQ_ware, Centro per la Qualità del Software, Florence, Italy

PAOLO NESI   nesi@ingfi1.ing.unifi.it
Department of Systems and Informatics, Faculty of Engineering, University of Florence, Florence, Italy.

Abstract. Tools for formally specifying software for real-time systems have strongly improved their capabilities in recent years. At present, tools have the potential for improving software quality as well as engineers' productivity. Many tools have grown out of languages and methodologies proposed in the early 1970s. In this paper, the evolution and the state of the art of tools for real-time software specification is reported, by analyzing their development over the last 20 years. Specification techniques are classified as operational, descriptive or dual if they have both operational and descriptive capabilities. For each technique reviewed three different aspects are analyzed, that is, power of formalism, tool completeness, and low-level characteristics. The analysis is carried out in a comparative manner; a synthetic comparison is presented in the final discussion where the trend of technology improvement is also analyzed.

1. Introduction

In recent years, several techniques for formal specification of real-time systems have been proposed; a large number of tools — ranging from research prototypes to marketed software packages — supporting these specification techniques have also been introduced. The growing interest for specification tools can be explained by considering that they have the potential for improving software quality as well as engineers' productivity. Furthermore, their use may be the only practical way to guarantee that certain quality factors (such as safeness, consistency, timeliness, etc.), which are mandatory for real-time systems, are achieved.

This paper contains a historical review above the tools for the specification of real-time systems, taking into account their evolution in the last 20 years. To this end, a number of well-known proposals are examined and criticized in the light of the classification criteria described in the sequel. The choice of classification criteria has been one of the major concerns of this paper. In fact, space limitations do not allow going into details for each tool under examination. Furthermore, the subject matter is far away from being stable and settled and so we may have overlooked some relevant issues. As a result, we do not claim that the proposed taxonomy is an exhaustive method for classifying real-time specification techniques. However, we believe that this paper provides a reasonable

---

* This work was partially supported by the Italian Research Council, CNR (Consiglio Nazionale delle Ricerche), n. 93.01865.CT12.

picture of their evolution as well as an indication on future developments and research issues.

A popular method for classifying software specification techniques is based on the degree of formality used. *Formal* techniques are based on mathematics, and (pure) *informal* techniques on natural languages. The former are generally preferred, because the latter tend to be incomplete and inconsistent (Meyer, 1985), (Stankovic, 1988), (Levi and Agrawala, 1990), (Stankovic and Ramamritham, 1992). The formalism can cover both syntax and semantics of a technique or only a part of them.

Another method for classifying software specification techniques is based on the extent to which they are *descriptive, operational* or *dual* (that is a mixture of descriptive and operational). *Operational* techniques are those which are defined in terms of states and transitions; therefore, they are intrinsically executable. *Descriptive* techniques are based on mathematical notations (axioms, clauses, etc.) and produce precise, rigorous specifications, giving an abstract view of the state space by means of algebraic or logic equations. These can be automatically processed for verifying the completeness and the consistency of the specification, by proving properties by means of automatic tools. *Dual* techniques tend to integrate both descriptive and operational capabilities, allowing the formal specification by means of clauses or other mathematical formalisms as well as the execution of specifications based on state diagrams or Petri nets. For dual techniques, the main problem is the formal relationship between operational and descriptive notations, which should be interchangeable.

In the literature, there are many other classifications according to which tools are divided in process-, data-, control-, and object-oriented (Dorfman, 1990) or in model-, and property-oriented approaches (Wing, 1990a), (Hall, 1990). In (Zave, 1990), Zave has made a classification by considering the degree of formalism with respect the degree of descriptiveness/operationality. This has resulted in a plot having in the abscissa the formal-informal range, and in the ordinate the descriptive-operational range.

In this paper, a somewhat different approach is taken. The classification is based on the distinction between operational, descriptive and dual techniques; however, for each technique reviewed three different aspects are analyzed, that is, *power of formalism, tool completeness*, and *low-level characteristics*.

In the light of this approach, languages and tools for reactive system specification are historically surveyed. It should be noted that a classification based on the distinction between operational, descriptive and dual aspects quite mirror the historical evolution of the subject matter. The remaining part of this section gives a brief account of the factors which must be considered in assessing tool capabilities. The review is made by presenting several examples in order to better explain the main characteristics of each technique with respect to these factors.

In evaluating the *power of formalism* three different aspects must be considered: the structural, the functional and the behavioral aspect (Harel, 1988), (Wing, 1990a). The *structural* aspect refers to the system decomposition into sub-systems. The *functional* aspect has to do with the transformational activities (on data) performed by individual software components. The *behavioral* aspect (i.e., the system dynamics) refers to the system reaction to external stimuli and internally generated events, either synchronously or asynchronously. The systems in which the behavioral aspect is relevant are usually denoted as reactive; real-time systems belong to this category. Descriptive methods usually fail in modeling structural and functional aspects, but they are suitable for describing system behavior. Operational methods are intrinsically suitable for modeling system behavior in detail, even if they lack in mathematical foundation for describing system behavior at the needed level of abstraction in order to allow validation (i.e., the proving of a required property) without simulation.

Since this paper is focused on tools for real-time systems specification, a particular attention is devoted to identifying the expressivity of tools in modeling the *temporal constraints* (timeout, deadline, etc.) (Stankovic, 1988). At a high level, a formalism can deal with time either in an *explicit* or *implicit* manner. In the first case, the language allows the representation of time through variables which provide an exact time measure. Explicit timing constraints can be expressed in relative or absolute form. When time is expressed in a relative manner, time durations and deadlines are given in time units. In this case, the relationship between these time units and the absolute measure of time expressed in seconds (or milliseconds) is not clear. However, the validation of specifications becomes almost hardware independent. When time is expressed in absolute form, time durations and deadlines are directly given in seconds or milliseconds (i.e., the absolute time of the clock) and therefore the meeting of timing constraints depends on the context (machine type, number of processes, workload, etc.). When time management is implicit, the formalism is able to represent the temporal ordering of events without reporting any quantification on time intervals (i.e., in state machines, and in languages enriched with operators like *next* and *previous*). When time is treated implicitly, the possibility of its exact measure is usually lost.

A tool for specifying real-time system should guarantee both correctness and completeness of the formal specification, as well as the satisfaction of system behavior with respect to both the timing constraints defined and the high-level behavioral descriptions. The *verification* of correctness and completeness is usually performed statically by controlling the syntax and semantics of the model without executing the specification. The system *validation* consists in controlling the conditions of liveness (i.e., absence of deadlock), safety, and the meeting of timing constraints (e.g., deadline, timeout, etc.). It is usually performed statically in descriptive approaches (i.e., by proving properties) and dynamically in operational approaches (i.e., by simulation). The capability of the method for verifying and validating the system specification (by means of mathematical techniques or simulations) must be analyzed in order to establish if the tools are capable of guaranteeing that the specification produced exactly matches the behavior of the system under development, with safety, without deadlocks and by meeting all timing constraints.

Please note that the two terms verification and validation do not always receive the above meaning (Thayer and Dorfman, 1992). For instance, in (Thayer and Dorfman, 1992) the most frequently used definitions for *verification* are reported, while the term validation is mentioned as "final verification".

A specification model may be *executable* or not. Executability is, by definition, a prerogative of operational approaches. On the other hand, some descriptive specifications are also executable. Executable means that the model is focused on defining the possible evolutions of the system state domain, rater than describing what the system should perform.

A model can provide support for defining strategies for *recovering from failures*, such as timeout, overflow, divide by zero, unmet deadline, etc. as well as for managing *external exceptions*. These features are usually available in operational approaches. Since there are some difficulties to guarantee that timing constraints are met, simulation is the way for detecting where the recovering paths must be defined.

Referring to *tool completeness*, an *integrated specification environment* is mandatory. To this end, a formal language must be endowed with a set of features, helping the user in its work. A very relevant feature is the availability of a well-defined *methodology*. In fact, a tool supported by a methodology is easier to be learned and used, while the quality of specification improves, and becomes more stable, irrespective of user's experience. Moreover, a tool should support the analyst in all phases of *software life-cycle*. Operational approaches are mainly based on the design aspect of the problem, while descriptive are better ranked for supporting the analysis phase.

The user interface is also very important. In recent years, graphics user's interfaces and *visual* languages have highly improved user's productivity with respect to *textual* interfaces. From this point of view, the operational approaches are favoured since they are intrinsically endowed with a visual notation, while the definition of visual language supporting the syntax of descriptive approaches is a more difficult task.

Another important factor is the presence of an automatic *generator of documentation* and of a *code generator* for classical high-level languages, like C, C++, ADA, etc. Note that several tools provide the support for generating a skeleton of the final code; in these cases, the verification and validation phases are usually performed without considering the final version of the code. Therefore, its final behavior may be unpredictable.

A further ingredient for improving users' productivity is the support for *simulation*. The simulator may either execute the generated code or interpret the specification itself. The first case is typical of the operational approach, whereas the second corresponds to the descriptive approach. Of course, the first method produces more trustable results, since the specification execution is based on the same code as that which will be executed at run-time. Simulation is usually performed by controlling system behavior with respect to manually or automatically generated test patterns. Of course, the latter are to be preferred; however, automatically generated test patterns should be used judiciously, since they may be affected by vices. The analyst should also check if test patterns provide a sufficient coverage.

In order to guarantee the possibility of *prototype generation*, a tool must provide support for *validating partially defined specifications*, otherwise the prototype might produce an unpredictable behavior.

Reuse of old specifications has become an important issue in software engineering. Many formal methods lead to specifications in which single components are too much coupled to be easily separated for reuse. Recently produced tools incorporate object-oriented concepts, since the object-oriented paradigm provides a number of mechanisms for reuse (e.g., inheritance, instantiation, etc.) (Nierstrasz, 1989), (Booch, 1986), (Meyer, 1988).

With the term *low-level characteristics*, we refer to the underlying assumptions and to the basic environment on which the specified software is to be run.

In many approaches, the system under specification is modeled as a set of communicating sub-systems. The communications among these sub-systems can be synchronous or asynchronous. *Synchronous* mechanisms are more predictable, but also more sensitive to deadlocks; on the contrary, *asynchronous communications* are less predictable and less sensitive to deadlocks. In general, synchronous mechanisms are more suitable for specifying real-time systems — i.e., systems in which predictability is the first goal. Situations leading to deadlocks can be detected during the validation phase.

In order to guarantee the system predictability several *restrictions* are usually imposed. Most of them are devoted to constrain the possibility of changing the operating machine conditions. For example, no dynamic creation of processes or data, no dynamic process priority changes, and no recursion or unbounded loop definition are allowed. In the object-oriented specification tools, the absence of dynamic inheritance is usually supposed, and thus the possibility of defining polymorphic class hierarchies (Nierstrasz, 1989), (Booch, 1986).

Most of the tools proposed in the literature are supported by a specific real-time kernel, which includes a scheduler — e.g., (Sha and Goodenough, 1990), (Forin, 1992), (Liu and Layland, 1973), (Tokuda, Nakajima and Rao, 1990). Others approaches generate a code for platforms in which a real-time operating system is available. A choice among the several solutions is quite difficult. On the other hand, the specification tools take usually into account the features of low-level support in their semantics.

As already mentioned, the survey is focused on the historical evolution of tools and is organized as follows. Section 2 contains a short summary of early supports for modeling communicating concurrent processes. This is useful since in many cases they are the foundation for approaches surveyed in this paper. In Section 3 operational methods are examined, while descriptive methods are discussed in Section 4. Dual methods are treated in Section 5. The impact of CASE (Computer Aid Software Engineering) technology on tools is discussed in this paper with the comments related to the different techniques. In Section 6, the findings of our analysis are synthesized and some conclusions are drawn.

We are aware that many interesting languages, techniques and tools have not been considered. This is not to be viewed as a negative aspect, but rather as a necessity due to space limitations. Moreover, since this paper is mainly focused on tools rather than on languages, the latter are reported when their quotation is needed to explain the historical evolution of tools. A complementary survey focused on real-time languages can be found in (Stoyenko, 1992).

2. Mathematical Supports

In this section, the most frequently used mathematical supports for reasoning on communicating concurrent processes are briefly discussed. In the late 1970s, Hoare, with his work on CSP (Communicating Sequential Processes) (Hoare, 1978), (Hoare, 1985), and Milner, with his work on CCS (Calculus of Communicating Systems) (Milner, 1980), have posed the bases for the verification and validation of concurrent systems. The relationships among these two models have been discussed in (Brookes, 1983). Until (Hoare, 1978) several methods for specifying communicating sequential processes were widely used, including semaphores (Dijkstra, 1968), conditional critical regions (Hoare, 1972), monitors and queues (concurrent Pascal) (Brinch-Hansen, 1975), etc. As observed in (Hoare, 1978), 'most of these are demonstrably adequate for their purpose, but there is no widely recognized criterion for choosing between them'. This consideration led Hoare to attempt to find a single simple solution to all those problems. In the light of the subsequent evolution, CSP is considered as a first rigorous approach to the specification of concurrent systems.

The mathematical bases of CSP have been widely used for defining and analyzing concurrent systems regarded as processes communicating via *channels* (Hoare, 1985). For this reason, the CSP model is denoted as process-oriented, and each process is modeled as a sequential machine. The communication mechanism is completely synchronous — i.e., the transmitter/receiver is blocked until the receiver/transmitter is ready to perform the communication. In the CSP notation, sending a message e on a channel c is denoted by $c!e$, while receiving a message e from a channel c is denoted by $c?e$. This syntax and communication model have been frequently used for defining programming languages (e.g., Occam) and specification tools. In CSP model constructs for modeling parallel ($\parallel$), sequential ($\gg$), and interleaved ($\parallel\parallel$) executions of processes are also defined (Hoare, 1985).

Given its popularity, the original CSP model (Hoare, 1978) has been expanded in many ways, resulting in a set of models of increasing complexity: the Counter Model, the Trace Model, the Divergence Model, the Readiness Model, and the Failure Model (Moore, 1990), (Olderog and Hoare, 1986), (Hoare, 1981), (Hoare, 1985), (Misra and Chandy, 1981). The Failure Model can be profitably used for reasoning about the safety and liveness conditions of the system under specification, even in the presence of divergent models (i.e., having an infinite number of states) and non-deterministic processes (Barringer, 1985), (Hoare, 1985). The Trace Model can be used to analyze the history of events on the system channels, and for verifying if the system satisfies abstract descriptions of system behavior. For these reasons, CSP is an appropriate basis for both operational and descriptive approaches.

The CSP model does not comprise the concept of time and, thus, the system validation does not take into account timing constraints. For these reasons during the 1980s many extensions have been proposed for adding time support — e.g., CSP-R (Koymans, et. al, 1985) (where time managing is added by means of *WAIT t* instruction), Timed CSP (Reed and Roscoe, 1986) (where time managing is added by means of the special function *delay()*), CSR (Communicating Shared Resources) (Gerber and Lee, 1989)and in the CRSM (Communicating Real-time State Machines) (Shaw, 1992) (where time is added by means of time bounds on executions and inputs/outputs), etc.

The syntax and semantics of CCS are based on the concept of *observation equivalence* between programs: a program is specified by describing its observation equivalent class which corresponds to the description of its behavior. This is given by means of a mathematical formalism in which variables, behavior-identifiers and expressions are defined. Behavior-identifiers are used in behavior expressions where the actions performed by the system are described. This makes the CCS model quite operational as pointed out in (Milner, 1980) and (Olderog and Hoare, 1983). This model is based on an asynchronous communication mechanism. The CCS model provided the ground for several models proposed in the late 1980s — e.g., (Bolognesi and Brinksma, 1987).

It should be noted that, the fact that the CSP model is strictly synchronous is not a limitation. In fact, by means of synchronous communicating state machines, asynchronous communications can also be defined. This is done through buffers of infinite capacity which are modeled as state machines as in (Shaw, 1992). In a similar manner, synchronous communications 1:1 (one sender and one receiver) can be expanded to 1:N communications (one sender and N receivers).

3. Operational Approaches

Operational approaches describe the system by means of an executable model. The model can be mathematically verified (for consistency and completeness) by using static analysis, and validated by executing the model (i.e., simulation). Though operational techniques were already introduced in the 1970s (Alford, 1977), it was not after the paper by Zave (Zave, 1982) that they have attracted large research attention. The most innovative aspect of Zave's paper was the embodiment of the operational approach into a programming language named PAISLey.

Operational approaches can be divided in two categories.

The first category comprises languages and methods which are usually based on transition-oriented models, such as state machines (Bavel, 1983) or Petri nets (Reisig, 1985), that is, models naturally oriented towards the description of system behavior.

The second category includes methods which are based on abstract notations especially suitable for supporting the system analysis and design (system decomposition/composition). In these cases, the notations are mainly oriented towards the description of system structure and/or functionality. For this reason, these notations are usually associated with guidelines for system analysis/design and are regarded as methodologies. However, most of them do not model system behavior and, thus, cannot be directly used for system simulation and specification execution. Moreover, since these methods have been developed by starting from visual notations, they lack in formalism and are usually considered as semiformal.

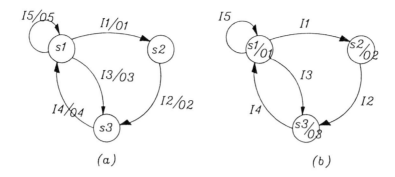

Figure 1. Example of FSM: (a) Mealy model, (b) Moore model, where Ii are input names, Oi outputs and Si names of states. In this example, the two models do not represent the same behavior. On the contrary, the Mealy and Moore models are interchangeable by means of simple rules.

3.1. *Operational Approaches Based on State Machines*

The basic theory of Finite State Machines (FSM) and automata dates back to the 1950s (Moore, 1956), (Mealy, 1955), (Booth, 1967), (Bavel, 1983). Since state machines are intrinsically operational, they have been used as a basis for several operational models.

The classical FSM models (by Mealy and Moore) are suitable for the specification of system behavior. Referring to Fig.1, outputs are produced as a function of the state of the FSM (i.e., Moore model) or of the state and machine inputs (i.e., Mealy model). FSMs can be represented by using two different notations: state transition diagrams (see Fig.1) and state transition matrices (Bavel, 1983).

The definition of FSM can be verified in order to identify its correctness — i.e., the reachability of the states, etc. In addition, the consistency and the congruence of a system description given in term of FSM can be verified by using several mechanisms as in (Jaffe, et. al, 1991). In a system defined as set of communicating state machines the number of states depends on the Cartesian product of the state domain of each machine; therefore, the number of states grows very quickly, and so the complexity of system verification. Moreover, in the presence of a communicating FSM there exists the possibility of deadlock and starvation (Hoare, 1985), (Sifakis, 1989). For this reason, mathematical supports, such as CSP and CCS are useful for reasoning about system and process (i.e., in this case FSM) liveness.

The classical model for FSM is unsuitable to represent the structural and functional aspects of the system under specification. To be profitably adopted as a tool for specifying real-time systems, the FSM model must provide support for describing temporal dependencies and constraints (e.g., timeout, deadline, etc.) among control flows. For these reasons, several extensions have been proposed in the literature.

Moreover, the classical FSM model is unsuitable when the number of states is very high. This problem can be partially avoided by decomposing the system into smaller communicating FSMs. The result is that the complexity of the system corresponds to the Cartesian product the of single machines state domains. Another possibility is to represent the state diagram in a more concise way with respect to the classical notation.

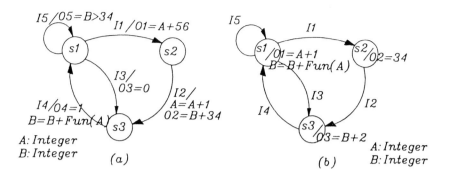

Figure 2. Example of extended FSMs: (a) Mealy model, (b) Moore model. Presence of expressions and of auxiliary variables — i.e., *A, B* of type *Integer*.

Classical FSMs are obviously unsuitable (being called Finite State Machines) to represent systems with a number of infinite states. Some extensions have been defined to give major expressivity to the graphical notation and to allow the definition of auxiliary variables (see Fig.2).

In FSM models the timing relationships among different events are implicitly defined by means of state diagrams. On the other hand, in several cases is not always possible to predict the state trajectory and, thus, the ordering of events. For this reason, an explicit model of time has been added to the FSM models in order to cope with the problems of real-time system specification.

One of the first integrated operational tools for software specification was the SREM (Software Requirement Engineering Methodology) (Alford, 1977). This was sponsored by the Ballistic Missile Defence Advanced Technology Center (BMDATC) in 1973. SREM is based on RSL (Requirement Statement Language) which supports both model-oriented and property-oriented styles of programming, and on REVS (Requirements Engineering Validation System) which is able to control the consistency and completeness of the specification. A system in SREM is decomposed in sub-functions. In SREM, the elementary function is modeled as an extended finite state machine. The state diagram is given in terms of the so-called R-nets. An R-net represents the system evolution starting from a state, by means of reading inputs, producing outputs, iterations, and showing in this way the set of possible next states. Since a finite state machine can have only a single active state, there is only an active R-net. Timing constraints are also defined into the R-nets. It should be noted that, the decomposition of the system in R-nets allows the specification of a distinct behavior for each system state without giving a global view of the system.

SREM, as an operational approach, has been widely used for more than a decade (Alford, 1985), (Scheffer, Stone and Rzepka, 1985). In parallel, several other operational methods sustained by mathematical formalisms were introduced and publicized. In the following subsections, four of them will be discussed — i.e., PAISLey (Zave, 1982), SDL (Rockstrom and Saracco, 1982), Esterel (Berry and Cosserat, 1985), and Statecharts (Harel, 1987).

3.1.1.   PAISLey

PAISLey (Process-oriented Applicative and Interpretable Specification Language) was
introduced in 1982. It is an operational specification model for defining embedded real-
time systems (Zave, 1982), (Zave, 1984), (Zave and Schell 1986). The system under
specification is decomposed in processes which communicate asynchronously. Although
the communications are asynchronous, the model presents several methods for process
synchronization. Each process is equivalent to an extended state machine. State machines
are defined by means of a functional language. On the state domain of the system under
specification, union, Cartesian product, and other operations are possible. In PAISLey,
the external environment is also modeled to avoid misunderstandings in validating the
specification. The number of processes, data structures and state domains are finite; these
assumptions augment the predictability of system behavior. For example (Zave, 1982),
a system decomposed in four processes is declared by means of their initial state:

(terminal_1_cycle[blank_display],
terminal_2_cycle[blank_display],
terminal_3_cycle[blank_display],
database_cycle[initial_database]
);

where *terminal_3_cycle*, etc.. are transition functions, while *blank_display*, *initial_database*
are values of variables. For each process the domain range is defined, such as:

terminal_1_cycle: DISPLAY → DISPLAY;

.   .   .

.   .   .

database_cycle: → DISPLAY;

The single process (i.e., transition function) is defined on the basis of other functions,
e.g.:

terminal_1_cycle[d] = display[display_and_transact[(d,think_of_request[d])]];

represents the internal structure of *terminal_1_cycle* functions.

Communications among processes are obtained from selected combinations between
three modalities: x_-, xm_-, and xr_-, obtaining four type of mechanisms: (i) (x_-, xm_-)
blocked synchronous with mutual exclusion, (ii) (x_-, x_-) blocked synchronous, (iii)
(xm_-, xr_-) mutual exclusion asynchronous, (iv) (x_-, xr_-) simply asynchronous.

The method adopted for modeling temporal characteristics of the system is based on the
theory of random variables. Therefore, PAISLey is primarily operational, but its timing
constraints are mathematical (Zave, 1990). Timing constraints can be associated with
the execution of state transitions, and are given by means of (i) lower and upper bounds,
or (ii) distributions. For this reason, the static verification of time requirements could be
only verified by means of a statistical reasoning. As a consequence, timing constraints

are checked in the phase of simulation, during which time failures are recorded. The final system validation is obtained by simulation, being the simulator an interpreter of the language.

3.1.2. SDL

SDL (Specification and Description Language) is an operational language belonging to the standard FDT (Formal Description Techniques) defined in 1982 within ISO (International Organization of Standardization) (ISO TC97/SC16/WG1) and CCITT (Comité Consultatif International Télégraphique et Téléphonique) for the specification of open distributed systems (Rockstrom and Saracco, 1982). In particular, the subgroups B and C have analyzed the descriptive models which combine the concepts of finite state machines with high-level languages, e.g., Pascal. SDL (Rockstrom and Saracco, 1982), (Sarraco and Tilanus, 1987), Estelle (Budkowski and Dembinski, 1987), and LOTOS (Bolognesi and Brinksma, 1987) (see Section 4.1.2) belong to this category of specification languages. SDL provides both visual and textual representations of its syntax. The textual representation extends Pascal according to the ISO draft.

In SDL, the system under specification is regarded as a block which can be decomposed in sub-blocks, thus modeling the structural aspects of the system (see Fig.3a). Blocks communicate asynchronously by means of strongly typed channels. The language provides support for defining new types of messages modeled as ADTs (Abstract Data Types) (Guttag, 1977), (Guttag and Horning, 1978). A block can be decomposed in sub-blocks or in a set of communicating processes (see Fig.3b). A process is implemented as an extended state machine, where the communication semantics is defined by means of a single buffer of infinite length for each state machine. SDL state machines are a mixture of state diagrams and flow charts (see Fig.3c); in fact, they present states, transitions and selections (equivalent to the "if" statements of high-level languages). In SDL state diagrams, reading of inputs and writing of outputs, as well as the execution of assignments and procedures can be associated with each transition. Reading should always precede writing, since inputs usually represent the condition for transition. If no input reading is defined, the change of state is always performed. For example, the exiting from the initial state is usually performed without reading any input (see Fig.3c).

In SDL, timing constraints are modeled through *timers*. A timer can be considered as a separate process which is able to send messages. A process can have a set of timers, which can be set, read or reset. For example, an SDL state machine that must satisfy a timeout must set a timer and then wait for the message signalling its occurrence. To this end, the state machine must be able to receive input messages from the timer in all its states, and a transition from a state to the next cannot be interrupted. As a result, definition of deadlines may result in somewhat complicated expressions. SDL permits the dynamic generation of processes; this is denoted with a dashed line as in Fig.3b. For the above reasons, the behavior of an SDL specification can be non completely deterministic. On the other hand, the validation is performed by simulation and, thus, the analysts achieve the final version by refinement.

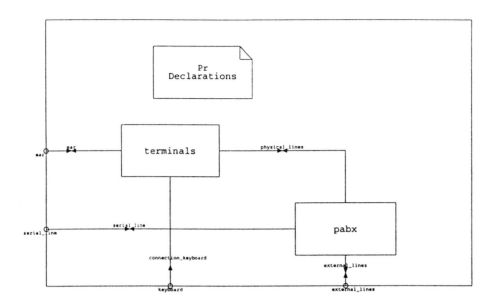

Figure 3a. Example of system specification in SDL 1988: system decomposed in two blocks *terminal* and *pabx*.

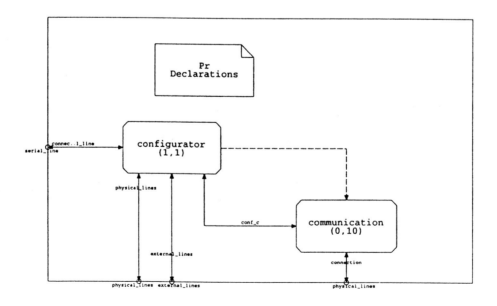

Figure 3b. Specification in SDL 1988: the block *pabx* is decomposed in the processes *configurator* and *communication.*

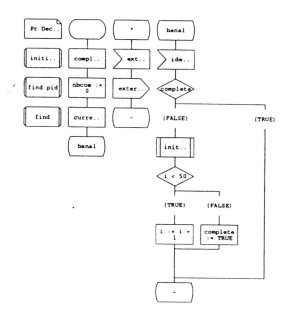

Figure 3c. Specification in SDL 1988: a part of the implementation of process *configurator* as an SDL state machine where: *banal* is a state, the empty rounded box is the initial state of the machine, *ext..* and *ide..* are inputs, *ester..* is an output, simple squared boxes contain assignments, etc..

More recently, an object-oriented extension of SDL (i.e., SDL 1992) has been presented (Braek and Haugen, 1993). This integrates the classical notation of SDL with the power of the object-oriented paradigm (e.g., Object-oriented SDL, OSDL). The major advantage is the presence of the mechanisms of inheritance, polymorphism and instantiation which have been defined for both the block and state machine levels. For example, new blocks and processes can be defined and used in more than one place (i.e., instantiation).

There are many SDL tools — e.g., GEODE (GEODE, 1992) — which cover all features defined in the so-called SDL 88 (version of 1988). Moreover, for supporting the configuration management, versioning, and report generator, other instruments are needed. In order to manage the problems of real-time in telecommunications supporting functional, behavioral and structural aspects, several extensions of SDL, such as (Encontre, et. al, 1990), have been presented.

3.1.3. Esterel

Esterel is an operational programming language introduced in 1985, which supports a set of elementary instructions such as: *loop* (indefinite), *if-then-else*, etc. Among these, there are special instructions for defining expressions of timing requirements (Berry and Cosserat, 1985). A program specifies the deadline for procedure execution and let's suppose that the requirements are met at run-time. Consider for instance the following piece of code:

```
var A, B: int in;
    loop
        do
            A := Fun(B)*5.6;
            .......;
            .......;
        uptonext 10 seconds end;
    end;
end;
```

where: A, B are variables, and *seconds* is a signal. For this program, the instructions inside the **do-uptonext** body are executed for the next 10 *seconds*. By using the elementary instructions, more complex instructions can be defined.

Rather than requiring that all timing behavior be known at compile time, Esterel allows the programmer to specify not only the timing requirements, but also allows the definition of the exception handlers which will be executed if the timing requirements are not met (recovering from time-failure). This approach to validation is very similar to that adopted by SDL. The execution is obtained by translating the Esterel specifications in communicating finite state machines. The number of processes is finite and their communications are through broadcasting. The execution model is synchronous and communications are considered instantaneous. These assumptions imply that the communications can be simply described by a discrete history of events where several events

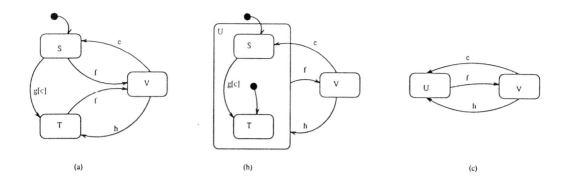

Figure 4. Statecharts notation and the operation of state clustering (i.e., the XOR) (a) Traditional state diagram, (b) Statecharts notations at detailed level, (c) Statecharts notations at abstract level.

can formally occur at the same time instant. As a result, if a message is not received at the same instant in which it is made available, it is lost. Esterel makes no provision for exhaustive static analysis before compilation; therefore, it does not ensure predictability, in the strong meaning of completing without exception. This is essentially due to the adoption of a strongly synchronous model with instantaneous communications.

3.1.4. Statecharts

Statecharts have been firstly introduced in 1987 as a visual notation for representing complex state machines, in a more synthetic manner with respect to the usually adopted notations based on state diagrams (Harel, 1987), (Harel, 1988). With this notation, complex state machines are represented as combinations of simpler machines, through the XOR and AND mechanisms as shown in Fig.4 and Fig.5, respectively. In this way, the explosion of the number of states of conventional state diagrams is strongly reduced. On the other hand, this notation may be less intuitable than conventional state diagrams.

Associated with the notation, an operational semantics has been presented, which describes how single machines are executed in order to model the equivalent complete state machine (Harel, 1987). Following this semantics, the single state machines are considered as concurrent and communicating through broadcasting (similar to Esterel). A state machine can observe both the current status of other state machines and the history of their behavior by using special functions provided by this language. The operational semantics is based on a set of micro-steps in which the execution of a single state machine is decomposed. In some cases, Statecharts can lead to define non-deterministic paths of execution.

In Statecharts, the notion of time is managed through the special function *timeout(E,N)* which becomes true when *N* time units are passed, after the last occurrence of event *E* (STATEMATE, 1987). Statecharts have been defined for modeling only system behavior, they can be profitably used as a specification language only if they are integrated in a CASE tool where the structural and functional aspects are addressed by

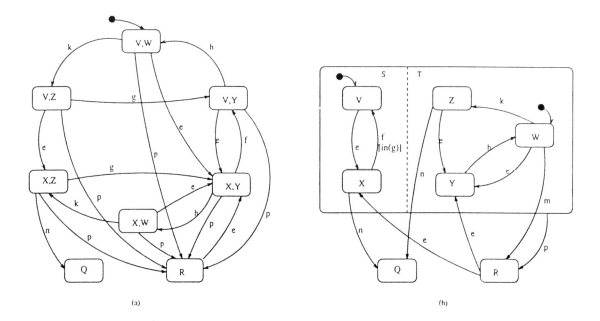

Figure 5. The operation of state machine composition (i.e., the AND operation) of Statecharts (a) Traditional state diagram, (b) Statecharts notations where S and T are orthogonal components of the complete state machine.

means of other notations. This has been done with STATEMATE (STATEMATE, 1987), (Harel, et. al, 1990). This tool makes an explicit distinction among structural, functional and behavioral aspects. These three aspects are described via three different representations, that is, activity-chart, statechart, and module-chart — modeling functional, behavioral and structural aspects, respectively. The activity-chart is a sort of RT-DFT (see Section 3.3.1), while the module-chart is a visual notation for structural decomposition. STATEMATE controls that consistency and completeness are maintained through the three different notations. STATEMATE has the capability of verifying the correctness of a Statecharts by means of exhaustive and sub-exhaustive execution tests. The verification of reachability, the presence of non-deterministic conditions and deadlocks, and the use of transitions, are identified through these tests. Simulation gives the system a great confidence in producing specifications.

More recently, several extensions of the Statecharts model have been proposed for improving its capabilities in modeling timing constraints and functional aspects — e.g., Modecharts (Jahanian and Stuart, 1988), Objectcharts (Coleman, Hayes and Bear, 1992), and ROOMcharts (Selic, 1993). In Objectcharts the model of Statecharts has been ported in an object-oriented environment. The concepts of temporal constraints on state transitions and those of auxiliary variables for state machines have also been added (see Fig.6). Object orientation has solved the problems related to the different views by integrating them in the concepts of classes (objects). Moreover, other classical object-oriented concepts such as inheritance, and instantiation have also been added. ROOMcharts is also supported by an object-oriented methodology (Selic, et. al, 1992) and a CASE tool named ObjecTime (NorthernTelecom, 1993). The Modecharts model is also discussed in Section 4.2.1.

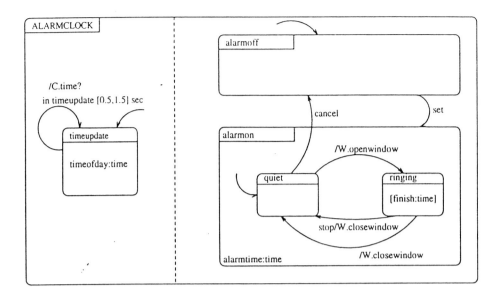

Figure 6. Example of an alarm clock in the Objectcharts notation, where *alarmtime* of type *time* in the state machine *alarmon* is an auxiliary variable.

3.1.5. *Other Operational Approaches Based on State Machines*

In this section, further interesting approaches based on state machines will be discussed for completeness. The classical model of extended state machine has been modified to offer the capability for defining timing constraints — e.g., RTRL (Real-Time Requirements Language) (Taylor, 1980), ESM (Extended State Machine, which will be discussed in Section 5.1) (Ostroff and Wonham, 1987), and CRSM (Communicating Real-time State Machines) (Shaw, 1992).

RTRL was firstly developed by the GTE laboratories, for their internal use (Taylor, 1980). The notion of time is modeled through the concept of timer as SDL (on the other hand, minimum and maximum time constraints on the occurrence of events can be defined in terms of timers (Dasarathy, 1985)). To avoid the problems of several other languages which assume the execution time to be instantaneous, in RTRL, time durations (such as the execution of sending/receiving a signal) are modeled by means of dedicated constructs which consider the execution time.

CRSM is an extension of the classical CSP model, which adds timing constraints on the conditions for the execution of transitions (Shaw, 1992). In particular, the minimum and the maximum time in which the transitions can be enabled is defined. Time is considered as continuous; therefore, it is represented as a real value (in floating point). The value of the current real time is available as the common variable *rt*. In CRSM, the system is described by means of a set of communicating state machines in which communications are strictly synchronous, even if asynchronous communications can be defined by resorting to infinite buffers on the inputs. The system validation is performed via simulation, and by analyzing the history traces.

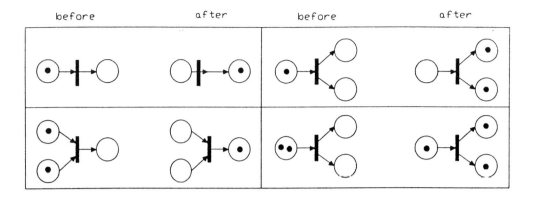

Figure 7. Example of the execution of simple Petri Nets.

3.2. *Operational Approaches Based on Petri Nets*

Petri Nets (PNs) were introduced by Petri as early as 1962 (Petri, 1962). They are more expressive than state machines, which can be proved to be a Petri nets subclass (Murata, 1989). However, given their lower intuitability, PNs have hardly found their way into programming languages.

PNs are an operational formalism, especially suitable for modeling synchronizations among asynchronous processes (Merlin and Faber, 1976), (Reisig, 1985), (Peterson, 1981). A Petri net is a graph comprising a finite number of *places* (circles) and *transitions* (segments) (see Fig.7), connected by oriented arcs. A set of *tokens* can be associated with each place. The state of a PN corresponds to the distribution of tokens on the places (i.e., the *marking* of the net). The operational semantics is that the presence of places with at least a token connected with arcs to a transition makes it "firable" — i.e., executable. The execution of a transition leads to the generation of a token in each place connected by an arc going out of the transition itself. In Fig.7, several examples of executions are reported. When a transition has more outgoing than ingoing arcs, it is a producer of tokens, and when the number of outgoing arcs is lower than that of ingoing arcs, the transition is a consumer of tokens. A review of fundamentals about Petri nets can be found in (Murata, 1989).

A PN is *safe* if the number of tokens is limited in time; in this case, it can be easily transformed in a finite state machine which is called *Token Machine*. On the contrary, if the PN is *unsafe* it corresponds to a state machine having an infinite number of states, defining in this way a divergent behavior. In this case, the verifiability of a PN is impossible. If the number of tokens of a PN is constant for each state, the PN is called *conservative*. On the contrary, PNs are called *inconsistent* when the behavior (i) terminates for token consuming, or (ii) diverges for an uncontrolled production of tokens.

The verification of a PN is based on the analysis of the Token Machine. All the classical verifications, which can be executed on finite state machines to verify reachability, deadlock free, etc. are performed on the Token Machine. If in a PN there is more than one transition enabled by the same *marking*, the execution is non-deterministic (i.e., the PN has more than one possible next state). PNs in which this condition never occurs

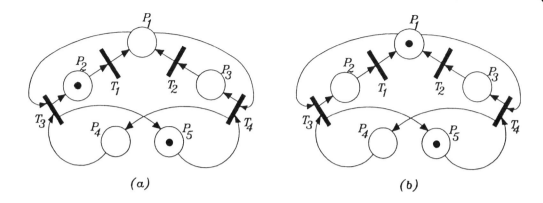

Figure 8. Example of Petri Nets, where T_i are transitions, P_i places, (a) and (b) are two consequent states of the net.

behave in a determinism manner and are called *decision free* nets. The verification of a PN is computationally possible only for *consistent deterministic* nets, while for the non-deterministic nets the problem is NP complete (Willson and Krogh, 1990). For conservative nets, the absence of deadlocks can be demonstrated by using algorithms with exponential complexity. On the other hand, these algorithms cannot be extended to all the extensions of the classical Petri net model.

It should be noted that, a state diagram can be regarded as a particular Petri net where the transitions have only one entering and one outgoing arc. On the other hand, the state diagrams are more intuitive with respect to the visual representation of Petri nets. The classical notation for Petri nets is unsuitable for representing the functional and structural aspects of the system under specification; there is no explicit support for specifying timing constraints, and the tokens are only untyped control messages. For these reasons, many extensions have been proposed for transforming PNs into suitable models for the specification of real-time systems. The following subsections are dedicated to the discussion of several of them.

3.2.1. TPN

The TPN (Time Petri Nets) model has been introduced in 1976. It is an extension of classical Petri nets for treating the timing constraints. These are expressed explicitly for each transition, by means of a minimum and a maximum time ($Tmin$ and $Tmax$, respectively) (Merlin and Faber, 1976). $Tmin$ is the minimum time for which the transition must stay enabled in order to be firable. $Tmax$ is the maximum time for which the transition can stay enabled without firing. If $Tmin = 0$ and $Tmax = \infty$ the TPN corresponds to the classical PN model. The adoption of this time modeling allows the definition of timeouts, deadlines, etc. A TPN, defined on a structurally safe PN, can be verified for controlling the absence of deadlocks and other properties (Berthomieu and Diaz, 1991), (Leveson and Stolzy, 1987). The Token Machine resulting from a TPN is different from that of the corresponding PN (i.e., the same TPN without timing constraints) and may

ble states, thus requiring a more accurate analysis. Moreover, in certain eneration of the Token Machine and the reachability analysis can be

ʝΡΝ

SPNs (Stochastic Petri Nets) are an extension of the classical PN for describing the timing constraints, introduced in 1983 (Marsan, Balbo and Conte, 1983), (Molloy, 1985). In this model, a random variable is assigned to each transition T_i representing the firing delay. In this way, in the presence of several firing conditions in the nets, these are ordered by means of their respective firing delays. SPNs with geometrical or exponential distributed delays are isomorphic to homogeneous Markov chains; therefore, they are appropriate for modeling non-deterministic processes.

PROT nets are an extension of SPN and allow the discovering of critical conditions (Bruno and Marchetto, 1986). These can be easily translated in ADA language, where the interactions between a process and a transition take place through two rendez-vous of ADA. PROT nets are an efficient system for producing the ADA structure of a system by specifying system behavior. For these nets, a simulator is also available to validate the specification. This model is also supported by a CASE tool, named ARTIFEX (ARTIFEX, 1993), which includes the aspects of object-oriented paradigm and methodology called PROTOB (Baldassari and Bruno, 1991).

3.2.3. Other Operational Approaches Based on Petri Nets

For completeness, other approaches based on Petri nets are briefly discussed in this sub-section, in the order of their appearance — i.e., Timed-PN (Timed Petri Nets) (Ramachandani, 1974), CPN (Colored Petri Nets) (Jensen, 1981), (Jensen, 1987), HMS (Hierarchical Multi-State machines) (Gabrielian and Franklin, 1991), ER, TER and TB nets (Ghezzi, et. al, 1991), and CmPN (Communicating Petri Nets) (Bucci, Mattoline, and Vicario, 1993), etc.

In Timed-PNs, a duration time is associated with each transition for modeling the execution time of the transition itself (Ramachandani, 1974), (Ramamoorthy and Ho, 1980). The semantics of classical PNs is modified by assuming that a transition must fire as soon as it is enabled. These nets are mainly suited for performance evaluation.

The HMS model is based on state machines, but presents many characteristics which make this formalism more similar to Petri nets than to state machines (Gabrielian and Franklin, 1991). In fact, as in Petri nets, in a HMS specification several active states (i.e., states with a sort of "token") can exist at the same time. In HMS the system under specification is modeled as a hierarchy of specifications starting from the more abstract to the more detailed one. This layering allows the reduction of diagram complexity, similar to the clustering mechanism of Statecharts formalism (see Section 3.1.4). Moreover, the specification refinement is supported by a process of verification which validates if the conditions (expressed by means of axioms) for any given abstract level are satisfied by

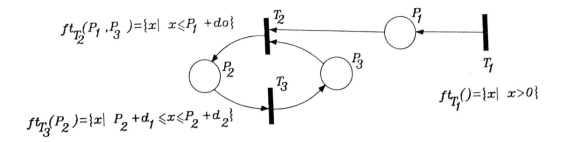

$ft_{T_2}(P_1, P_3) = \{x \mid x \leqslant P_1 + d_0\}$

$ft_{T_3}(P_2) = \{x \mid P_2 + d_1 \leqslant x \leqslant P_2 + d_2\}$

$ft_{T_1}() = \{x \mid x > 0\}$

Figure 9. Example of a TB net.

the specification for the lover level (i.e., more detailed). Timing constraints are defined in Temporal Interval Logic (TIL). Timing constraints can be used for defining conditions on state transitions. The complete model is non-deterministic, but executable, and thus it is suitable for simulation.

In (Ghezzi, et. al, 1991), a collection of extended Petri nets has been presented in order of complexity: ER, TER and TB nets. In the TB model, the time in which a token has been produced (i.e., *timestamp*), is associated with the token itself. In TB nets, tokens are "functions" which associate values with variables. In addition, a Boolean condition based on the presence of tokens with their *timestamps* on the connected places is associated with each transition. The TB model is to be a generalization of the TPN model proposed in (Merlin and Faber, 1976). The transformational aspects (i.e., *functional aspect*) of the system under specification can also be described by the TB model. Fig.9 reports an example presented in (Ghezzi, et. al, 1991). It represents a net that models a data acquisition system which periodically samples data from the environment. Sampled data are modeled by the tokens fired by transition T_1. A controller (represented by a token in place P_3) takes those data (i.e., transition T_2 fires) and then elaborates them, i.e., transition T_3 fires. The sampled data are valid only at most for d_o time units and the elaboration takes a minimum of d_1 and a maximum of d_2 time units.

CmPNs are an object-oriented extension of PN. These are suitable for modeling structural, behavioral aspects of the system under specification (Bucci Mattoline and Vicario, 1993). By means of this model the system is regarded as a set of asynchronously communicating subsystems (which can be placed in a single-processor or distributed environment). In the CmPN model, a *priority* and an *action* are associated with each transition. The scheduler takes into account the priority during its work, and the action corresponds to the execution of a procedure when the transition is fired. For a specification given in terms of CmPNs, the absence of deadlocks can be verified. Moreover, a CmPN specification can be directly translated into C++ code for a heterogeneous environment based on MS-DOS and UNIX machines.

3.3. Operational Approaches Based on Other Notations

Most of the operational models have their own visual notations and this increases specification understandability. Starting with the late 1970s, a number of different notations were introduced as a substantial component of various methodologies for system analysis and design. Most of them, including Structured Analysis (Ross and Schoman, 1977), (Yourdon and Constantine, 1979), Data Flow Analysis (DeMarco, 1979), JSP (Jackson Structured Programming) (Jackson, linebrak 1975), and JSD (Jackson System Development) (Jackson, 1983), have found large acceptance by industry. In addition, because of their expressiveness, these notations have been incorporated in many CASE environments. As a result, the boundaries between the use of these notations and of operational visual specification languages are crumbling. In fact, tools supporting methodologies of the above mentioned category become increasingly similar to visual programming environments, thus allowing the direct manipulation of graphical elements in order to visually describe program aspects like structure, flow of data and the like. Following this trend, conventional approaches like Structured Analysis, have be considered operational, in spite of their informal nature.

The use of visual techniques reduces the effort of user-machine communication. In this way, the ability of the user to describe the system is greatly enhanced, further reducing the intermediation with the system. This aspect has been taken into consideration by the designer of tools like those described in (Jacob, 1985) and (Harel, 1988).

In recent years, the Object-Oriented Paradigm (OOP) has gained large acceptance in software analysis and design (Coad and Yourdon, 1991), (Booch, 1991), (Northern-Telecom, 1993), (Coleman, Hayes and Bear, 1992). This is largely due to the fact that working with classes and objects is an easy and natural way for partitioning large problems. The mechanisms for decomposing a system into objects, makes OOP the natural methods for separating the different activities that can be carried out in parallel. By supporting strong modularity, code reusability, and extendibility, OOP is having quite an impact on design, implementation and maintenance of complex systems, and many formal languages have been extended with object-oriented capabilities, leading to languages like Z++, VDM++, TRIO+, etc. Several object-oriented methodologies for real-time systems have also been introduced — e.g., HOOD (HOOD, 1988), Wirsf-Brock et al. (Wirsf-Brock, Wilkerson and Winer, 1990), Booch (Booch, 1991), OMT (Rumbaugh, et. al, 1991), Coad and Yourdon (Coad and Yourdon, 1991), and these have been adopted as a basis for a number of CASE tools.

3.3.1. Structured Analysis

Structured Analysis is a generic term which denotes a number of analysis and design methodologies, approaching system specification in a *structured* manner.

Historically, SADT (Structured Analysis and Design Technique, introduced in 1977) (Ross and Schoman, 1977) has been the first methodology based on a structured approach and, more specifically, on the concept of functional decomposition. SADT has its own diagrammatic notation, with well-defined syntax, semantics. The notation handles the data and control flows. SADT builds on the concept of *models*. A model corresponds to a hierarchy of diagrams describing the system from a particular point of view (for instance, from the operator's point of view). Models can share common details. A sub-model which is shared by other models or whose implementation can be changed is

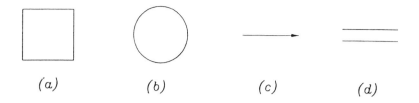

Figure 10. Symbols of DFD: (a) external agent, (b) function or process for data transform, (c) data flow, (d) permanent data repositor.

called a *mechanism*. A mechanism can remain undeveloped until the later stages, thus delaying detailed decisions. SADT is a registered trademark of SofTech and is available commercially.

Structured analysis as publicized by Yourdon and Constantine (Yourdon and Constantine, 1979) and De Marco (DeMarco, 1979) in 1979, is perhaps one of the best known methodologies (Svoboda, 1990). This is essentially a functional decomposition technique, used to identify a number of transforms and the data flowing among them (DeMarco, 1979). This is done by the successive application of the engineering definition of a black box that transforms an input data stream in an output data stream. Data-Flow Diagrams (DFD) and data dictionaries are the most important tools used in carrying out the analysis. Transforms are called processes and represented as bubbles in data flow diagrams, while flows of data are represented as oriented arcs among bubbles. The data dictionary keeps track of any data flowing through the network of processes. The graphic symbols used in Structured Analysis/Data-Flow Analysis are shown in Fig.10.

Data-flow analysis tends to produce a network of (sub)programs corresponding to each transform, but allows the identification of the central transform, that is, the one that accepts the most abstract input stream and produces the most abstract output stream. The central transform corresponds to the most abstract view of the program functionality. By picking up the data-flow diagram from the central transform, a tree representing the hierarchical structure of the program is obtained. Starting from the so-called context diagram, which contains only a single bubble representing the system in its entirety, successive refinements are applied (DeMarco, 1979). This leads to a hierarchical decomposition, where each process is decomposed in a number of lower-level, more detailed data transforms. Of course, consistency must be kept among levels. In particular, input/output data, flowing in/from a given process, must be preserved when the process is decomposed in a number of lower-level processes.

Structured Analysis can be applied in a purely manual fashion or it can be automated to varying degrees (Birrel and Ould, 1985). Almost any CASE tool produced in the last decade includes Structured Analysis — e.g., (Teamwork, 1992), (StP, 1991). In addition, DFDs admit also an operational interpretation.

Structured analysis is still one of the most used techniques for dealing with transformational applications, as found in data-processing environments, where procedural (i.e., static) aspects are relevant. Its strength is also its weakness: it is informal and very intuitive, and thus can be used also by people not keen in mathematics; however, this denies rigorous specification validation.

3.3.2. Real-Time Extensions of Structured Analysis

Several extensions to structured analysis have been proposed in the 1980s, in order to take into account also system dynamics and use it for the specification of real-time systems.

DARTS (Design Approach for Real-time Systems) (Gomaa, 1984), (Gomaa, 1986), and its recent object-oriented extension (Gomaa, 1992), is an example of design techniques which closely follow the Structured Analysis/Data-Flow analysis approach to identify the processes to be implemented in a real-time system, as well as their synchronizations.

Ward and Mellor (Ward and Mellor, 1985), (Ward, 1986), extended data flow diagrams by adding edges representing control. They also used state machines for representing behavior. Many commercial CASE tools, including Teamwork (Teamwork, 1992), StP (Software through Pictures) (StP, 1991) and Excelerator (Excelerator, 1986) have followed this lead.

Hatley and Pirbhai (Hatley and Pirbhai, 1987) performed a data-flow analysis and then proceeded with a control-flow analysis. This leads to augmenting the data flow-diagram with the so-called control bars, which are introduced to represent event occurrences. Additional specification tools (i.e., CSPECS (Hatley and Pirbhai, 1987)) are used in order to express how and when a transformation occurs. As a result, the designer must employ different tools and languages, depending upon the stage of the analysis. In Fig.11a, the top level of a cruise control system according to the Hatley and Pirbay notation, is reported. In the diagram, both data and control flows are shown, where square boxes represent terminal objects. In Fig.11b, the DFD diagram at level 0 shows the decomposition of the system in "processes" (according to Hatley and Pirbay, but called data transformations in the more general meaning), data and control flows (i.e., continuous and dashed lines), data stores (e.g., *mile count*) and a control bar (i.e., *CNT_1*). The control bar encapsulates the system behaviour and process activation in terms of a Mealy state machine (see Fig.11c).

Structured analysis for real-time systems is still based on the notion of the flow of data between successive transforms, and provides little support to identify the concurrent processes (in this paper, the word "process" was used to denote a separate sequential activity, implemented as an independent thread of execution, and not simply a data transform). that must be implemented in a given application. Depending upon the detail of the analysis, there is something arbitrary in identifying the system processes. This may result in the implementation of unnecessary processes and the possibility that a given process needs concurrency internally.

3.3.3. JSD and Entity Life

Jackson System Development (JSD) (Jackson, 1983), (Cameron, 1986) was introduced in 1983, and has become since then a well-known method for software development. It encompasses most of the software life-cycle and, being based on the concept of communicating sequential processes, it can be used for the design of real-time and concurrent software.

JSD is an entity-life modeling approach (Sanden, 1989c) to software analysis and design. In fact, the first phase of the method, the model phase, is devoted to the examination

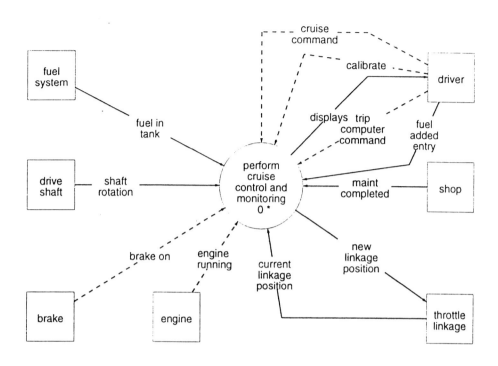

Figure 11a. Example of extended DFD in the Hatley and Pirbay notation: Context Diagram.

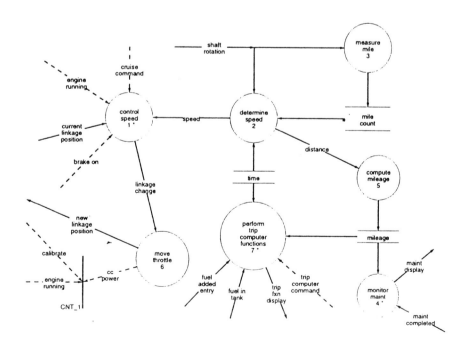

Figure 11b. Example of extended DFD in the Hatley and Pirbay notation: level 0.

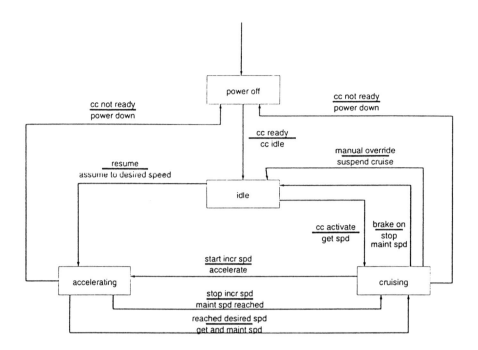

Figure 11c. Example of extended DFD in the Hatley and Pirbay notation: behavior of *control speed.*

of the real-world environment, in order to identify and model the entities belonging to it. Entities that have a strong time dimension, that is, when they make transitions between different states over time, are modeled as software processes. Modeling is done trough an explicit diagrammatic notation in which three basic structuring concepts are used, namely: sequence, iteration and selection. The resulting entity structure describes all the possible life histories of the entity itself. Since JSD makes reference to languages that do not support concurrent programming, processes are implemented as coroutines, managed by a tailor-made scheduler.

Elaborating upon JSD, Sanden has proposed the so-called generic entity-life approach to concurrent software design (Sanden, 1989c), (Sanden, 1989b), (Sanden, 1989a). In this approach, the first step is the identification of each independent and asynchronous thread of events in the problem domain; for any thread of events, a software process is implemented in the system. The generic entity-life approach avoids certain intricacies of JSD, as well as the implementation of unnecessary processes. Furthermore, Sanden uses the ADA language to work out his examples. The task construct of that language avoids another problem of JSD, that is, the implementation of processes as coroutines and the consequent need of a tailor-made scheduler.

Entity-life approaches are a step towards clear specifications of concurrent systems. They take into account functional, structural and behavioral aspects. In the examples presented in (Sanden, 1989c) and (Sanden, 1989b), system behavior is dealt at the level of interactions among tasks. The specification of internal details is left to other techniques, such as state machines.

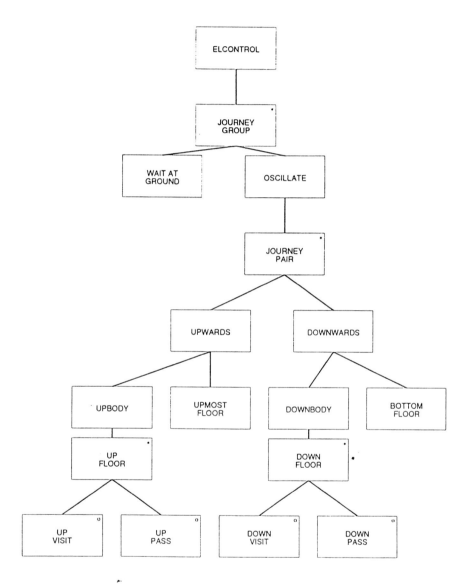

Figure 12. Structure of control software of an elevator in JSD. Operations, represented by square boxes are described by decomposition; at the same level they are executed from left to right; iterative executions are marked by "*"; and selections with an "o".

3.3.4.   Object-Oriented Notations

In recent years, the Object-Oriented Paradigm (OOP) has gained a large acceptance in the software community. Object orientation has also been used for the development of real-time systems, due to the fact that the object-oriented model can be considered intrinsically concurrent. In fact, software objects can be regarded as independent threads of execution which communicate by means of message passing (Cox, 1984), (Diederich and Milton, 1989), (Bihari and Gopinath, 1992). More refined models divide system objects into active and passive, and/or server and client objects (Agha, 1986), (Ellis and Gibbs, 1989), (Booch, 1991). For these reasons, both object-oriented methodologies and languages (e.g., (Ishikawa, Tokuda and Mercer, 1992)), have been defined for modeling real-time systems. Since, this section is devoted to the operational approaches, only methodologies are discussed. Pure languages are not mentioned, even those that are focused on programming distributed and/or real-time systems.

In the early 1990s, many efforts have been made to reuse the good things of the old conventional methodologies, such as DFD, Entity-Relationships diagrams (ER) (Chen, 1976), etc., by reinterpreting them in the context of an object-oriented methodology — e.g., Coad and Yourdon (Coad and Yourdon, 1991), Rumbaugh at al. (OMT) (Rumbaugh, et. al, 1991), and Martin and Odell (Martin and Odell, 1991). Of course, the resulting techniques are influenced by the functional view. More recently, some "pure" object-oriented methodologies have been proposed — e.g., Booch (Booch, 1991), and Wirsf-Brock et al. (Wirsf-Brock, Wilkerson and Winer, 1990). Pure object-oriented methodologies focus only on the definition of objects and relationships among them (Monarchi and Puhr, 1992).

In many of the above-mentioned approaches, the system is decomposed into objects for representing the structural aspects of the system under specification. Object relationships are defined through extended Entity Relationship diagrams (Coad and Yourdon, 1991), (Rumbaugh, et. al, 1991) or by using the so-called Object Diagrams (see Fig.13) (Booch, 1991), (Rumbaugh, et. al, 1991), (HOOD, 1988), (Wirsf-Brock, Wilkerson and Winer, 1990). To support all the features of the OOP, such as inheritance, polymorphism, aggregation, association, etc., special symbols for Entity Relationship diagrams or special diagrams, such as Class Hierarchy, have been defined (see Fig.14). In most of the proposed methodologies, system behavior is encapsulated in the implementation of objects (more specifically in the implementation of class methods). The object behavior is usually described by means of extended state diagrams or state transition matrices. Shlaer and Mellor (Shlaer and Mellor, 1988), (Shlaer and Mellor, 1991) and Booch (Booch, 1991), use a Mealy model; Rumbaugh (OMT) (Rumbaugh, et. al, 1991) uses a notation strongly similar to Statecharts — i.e., the ROOMcharts (see Section 3.1.4); Coad and Yourdon (Coad and Yourdon, 1991) use a state event table.

It should be noted that, the description of the class interface in terms of methods is not able to represent all the relationships that objects may have with respect to other objects, especially in a concurrent environment (Bucci, et. al, 1993), (Coleman, Hayes and Bear, 1992), since this does not represent the services that a class of objects *requires* from other objects (Wirsf-Brock and Wilkerson, 1989), (Walker, 1992). In fact, these requests are encapsulated into the methods body and, thus, they are hidden to the outer objects.

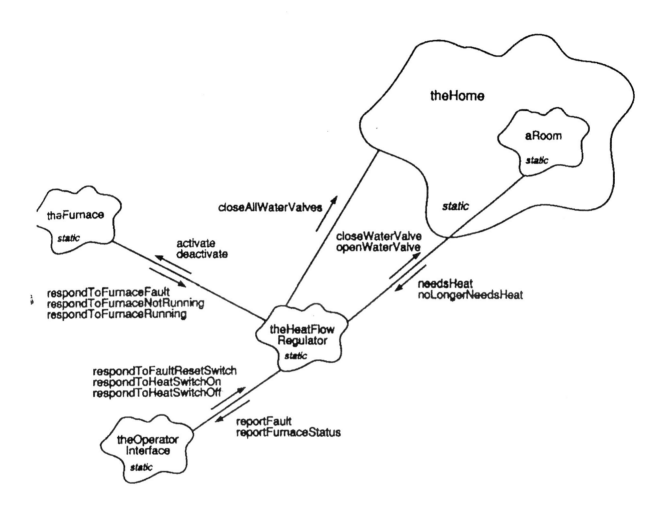

Figure 13. Example of a home heating system, Object Diagram in Booch's notation.

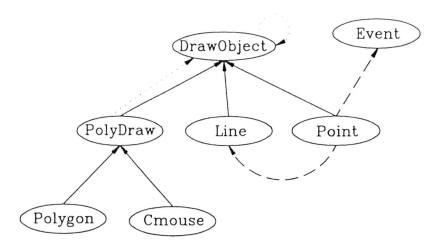

Figure 14. Example of Class Diagram (also called class tree — DrawObject is the root), where continuous lines define relationships of specialization between classes (i.e., inheritance) (*is_a*), dashed lines those of aggregation (*is_part_of*), and dotted lines those of association (*is_referred_by*).

Furthermore, though many of these methodologies are especially defined for the analysis and design of reactive systems, some of them are not completely satisfactory for specifying real-time systems. Usually, these notations only provide support for defining timing constraints of the system under analysis, but unfortunately they are not strongly supported by techniques for verifying the consistency and completeness of time relationships. This derives from the fact that these methods are not enough formal for supporting a formal semantics and for defining an executable model of the system.

In spite of the previous considerations, many CASE tools have been built on the basis of the above mentioned methodologies. In these CASE tools, model limitations have been partially circumvented through specific notations which add formalism and executability — e.g., object-oriented and state machines (e.g., Shlaer and Mellor (Shlaer and Mellor, 1988), Booch (Booch, 1991)), object-oriented.

4. Descriptive Approaches

The use of descriptive languages for program specification has been proposed by several researchers during the 1970s — e.g., (Guttag, 1977), (Liskov, et. al, 1977). Descriptive approaches are based on mathematical notations (axioms, clauses, set theory, etc.) and produce precise, rigorous specifications, giving an abstract view of the system state space. The system is described by specifying its global properties, forcing the analyst to specify *what* must be done by the system rather than *how* it must be done. Descriptive specifications can usually be automatically processed for verifying their completeness and consistency. Moreover, a specification can also be validated by proving that high-level properties are verified by the specification itself. This is performed by means of theorem provers or Prolog engines. Since most of these are not enough efficient and predictable (from the performance point of view), descriptive approaches are not considered adequate for producing executable real-time specifications. Only in the late 1980s, some descriptive languages have been enriched with primitives for dealing with time, making them suitable for specifying real-time systems.

In the following, we have tried to classify descriptive approaches on the basis of their main nature, that is algebraic or logical. Of course, many mixed approaches have been proposed making this classification questionable. A different classification can be found in (Wing, 1990a).

4.1. *Descriptive Approaches Based on Algebraic Methods*

Algebraic methods are based on the concepts of Abstract Data Type (ADT) (Guttag, 1977), (Guttag and Horning, 1978). With these methods of specification the system is described in an abstract manner; however, the description remains quite intuitive and lightly operational to be easily understandable. Most of the algebraic methods allow to specify the system at different levels of abstraction, starting from a coarse description and arriving at the most detailed one. For these methods, the system itself is regarded as an ADT, and its specification consists in describing its syntax and semantics. The syntax definition gives the description of the operator domains of the ADT, while the semantics is given by an implementation of these operators by means of mathematical expressions. Semantics is often defined by writing a set of axioms with a programming language based on first-order logic. Complex abstract data types are defined on the basis of simpler ones; hence, the semantics of complex types is specified by using the axioms of simple types, and thus the behavior of complex types can be again validated by using the axioms of the simple types. This allows to verify the specification correctness at each level of specification detail.

By iterating the ADT implementations the entire system is specified. Iteration ends when the elementary data types of the system are defined. Therefore, the system obtained is specified on the basis of few elementary ADTs, whose operators must be implemented by means of a traditional programming language (e.g., Pascal, C, etc.). The validation process is carried out with respect to high-level system properties. Then, if elementary ADTs are correctly implemented, the overall system will also be correct.

In the 1980s, many interesting specification languages have been proposed, according to the concept of ADT — e.g., ACT ONE (Algebraic Specification Technique (Ehrig and Mahr, 1985), which inspired LOTOS (Bolognesi and Brinksma, 1987), see Section 4.1.2), AFFIRM (Musser, 1980), and the Larch family of languages (Guttag, Horning and Wing, 1985).

Algebraic methods have been used for defining abstract data types in conventional applications (Musser, 1980); later on, they have been employed for specifying reactive systems and communication protocols (Sunshine, et. al, 1982). To give an idea of how these languages are structured, an example of protocol in AFFIRM (Sunshine, et. al, 1982) is reported in Fig.15, while Fig.16 shows the corresponding state machine in the Mealy model (see Section 3.1). As can be noted, state variables are modeled by means of axioms, which in turn are functions of the axioms of other ADTs. For example, in Fig.16 the *SimpleMessageSystem* is defined by using *Message* and *QueueOfMessage* ADTs. For *QueueOfMessage* the operations of *NewQueueOfMessage*, *Add*, and *Remove* are defined. In general, the operators can be classified as constructors (*InitializeService, UserSend, SendComplete, UserReceive*), and selectors (*ReceiveComplete, Buffer, Sent, Received*). *State* is the axiom which models the data type behavior.

The completeness can be verified when it is proven that a defined property is verified by the axioms of the system. This confers a descriptive rather than the operational nature to these approaches, although the ADT behavior can be in many cases translated in state machines. The operational descriptions are distributed among the operators and, therefore, they are not simply executable. The property of liveness can also be verified, for example by proving that a message transmitted will be received in any case by the *SimpleMessageSystem*. In AFFIRM, there is no method for describing timing constraints.

The Larch family of specification languages has been defined on the basis of a common support, the so-called *used traits*. This support describes the common Larch model by means of an algebraic language — i.e., the *Larch Shared Language* (Guttag, Horning and Wing, 1985), (Garland, Guttag and Horning, 1990). By using this language new ADTs can be defined. An interface support must be defined on the Larch Shared Language by using a predicative language (e.g., pre- and post-conditions) (Wing, 1987). This layer plays the role of a support for a host language. For example, the Larch/Pascal provides a support for programming in Larch style by using the conventions of Pascal. On the contrary, each Larch language is based on the same support (i.e., Larch Shared Language). In the literature, there are many other Larch languages: the Larch/CLU (for CLU see (Liskov, et. al, 1977), (Liskov and Guttag, 1986)), Larch/ADA (Guaspari, Marceau and Polak, 1990), Larch/C, and also object-oriented languages such as the Larch/Smalltalk, the Larch/Modula-3 and the Larch/C++ (Wing, 1990b), (Leavens and Cheon, 1992), (Cheon and Leveson, 1993).

The above mentioned languages are enough formal to create specifications that can be easily verified, but unfortunately most of them are not supported by any specific construct for specifying timing constraints such as timeouts, deadlines, etc.

4.1.1. Z

The Z language is based on the theory of sets and predicate calculus (Abrial, 1982), (Sufrin, 1986), and was introduced in 1982. Differently from AFFIRM, the operations on a described data type are given by using the predicate logic (Spivey, 1988). As in other algebraic approaches, in Z the final specification is reached by refinement, starting from the most abstract aspects of the system. In Z, there is also a mechanism for system decomposition known as Schema Calculus. Therefore, a system specification is decomposed in smaller pieces called schemes where both static and dynamic aspects of system behavior are described.

type SimpleMessageSystem;
  needs types Message, QueueOfMessage;
  declare s: SimpleMessageSystem, m: Message;
  interfaces
    State(s): {ReadyToSend,Sending,ReadyToReceive,Acking};
    Sent(s), Received(s), Buffer(s): QueueOfMessage;
    InitializeService(s), UserSend(s,m), SendComplete(s): SimpleMessageSystem;
    UserReceive(s), ReceiveComplete(s): SimpleMessageSystem;
  axioms
    State (UserSend(s,m)) = **if** State(s) = ReadyToSend
                      then Sending
                      else State(s),
    State (SendComplete(s,m)) = **if** State(s) = Sending
                      then ReadyToReceive
                      else State(s),
    State (UserReceive(s)) = **if** State(s) = ReadyToReceive
                      then Acking
                      else State(s),
    State (ReceiveComplete(s)) = **if** State(s) = Acking
                      then ReadyToSend
                      else State(s),
    State (InitializeService) = ReadyToSend,
    Sent (UserSend(s,m)) = **if** State(s) = ReadyToSend
                      then Sent(s) Add m,
                      else Sent(s),
    Sent (InitializeService) = NewQueueOfMessage,
    Receive (UserReceive(s)) = **if** State(s) = ReadyToReceive
                      then Received(s) Add Front(Buffer(s))
                      else Received(s),
    Received (InitializeService) = NewQueueOfMessage,
    Buffer (UserSend(s,m)) = **if** State(s) = ReadyToSend
                      then Buffer(s) Add m
                      else Buffer(s),
    Buffer (ReceiveComplete(s)) = **if** State(s) = Acking
                      then Remove(Buffer(s))
                      else Buffer(s),
    Buffer (InitializeService) = NewQueueOfMessage,
end;

Figure 15. Example of *SimpleMessageSystem* in AFFIRM.

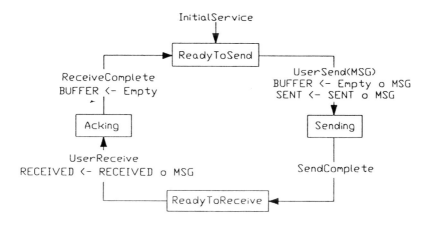

Figure 16. The corresponding state diagram of the *SimpleMessageSystem* as previously defined in AFFIRM.

A well-known specification example of the Z language is the Birthday book (Spivey, 1988), that is a system for recording people's birthday. Each entry contains a NAME and the DATE of birthday. The first step of specification consists in defining the state space of the system by means of the following schema:

```
┌─── BirthdayBook ──────────────────────────────────────
│
│  known : P NAME
│  birthday : NAME ↦ DATE
├──────────────────────────
│  known = dom birthday
└───────────────────────────────────────────────────────
```

specifying that the state space must satisfy the condition that *known* is equal to the domain of birthday and that the NAME is a known domain. It should be noted that in this example one person can have only one birthday, but the same birthday can belong to more than one person. Operations are defined by using other schemes, for example the schema *AddBirthdayBook* for adding a new element is reported in Fig.17.

In the *AddBirthdayBook* scheme, the qualifier Δ defines that the operation described can change the state space of *BirthdayBook*. The two declarations: *name? : NAME* and *date? : DATE* define that these are inputs (outputs are represented by the symbol "!" as in the CSP (Hoare, 1985)), while *name? ∄ known* imposes that the name read must not be already included in the BirthdayBook. The last line simply describes the update operation on the birthday set (*birthday'* is the updated value). Schemes can be combined by means of the Z schema calculus, in which operations of *and*, *or*, etc., are defined. The Z language also includes a mathematical tool-kit allowing the definition of operations on sets and data. It is very useful for describing the mathematical aspects of a problem.

A specification in Z is a mixture of: informal text, definitions, axiomatic descriptions, constraints, type definitions, and schemes. Therefore, it cannot be considered a fully descriptive approach (Zave, 1990).

As regards real-time systems specification, the Z language does not have any support for defining timing constraints. Therefore, in the recent years, several extensions for adding time management have been proposed. In (Richardson, Aha and O'Malley, 1992), the Z language has been integrated with the RTIL (Real-Time Interval Logic) (Razouk and Gorlick, 1989).

Several object-oriented extensions of the Z language have been presented — e.g., OOZE (Alencar and Goguen, 1991), MooZ (Meira and Cavalcanti, 1991), Z++ (Lano,

```
┌─── AddBirthdayBook ───────────────────────────────────
│
│  Δ BirthdayBook
│  name? : NAME
│  date? : DATE
├──────────────────────────
│  name? ∄ known
│  birthday' = birthday ∪ { name? ↦ data? }
└───────────────────────────────────────────────────────
```

Figure 17. Schema of AddBirthdayBook in Z language.

1991), Object-Z (Carrington, et. al, 1990). Most of them provide information hiding, inheritance, polymorphism and instantiation into the Z Schema Calculus. With these extensions, the system state space is defined as a composition of the state spaces of the individual system objects. The object-oriented paradigm has added formalism for modularity and specification reuse. Object-Z integrates also the concepts of temporal logic (Carrington, et. al, 1990), making it suitable for real-time specification. In this language the object status is a sort of event history of object behavior making the language more operational than the early version of Z.

4.1.2. LOTOS

LOTOS (Language Of Temporal Ordering Specification) is a formal technique belonging to the standard FDT defined within ISO (International Organization of Standardization) for the specification of open distributed systems (Bochmann, et. al, 1982). It was defined by ISO/TC97/SC21/WG1 subgroup C in 1981-86 (Bolognesi and Brinksma, 1987), (Bolognesi and Brinksma, 1989). LOTOS is based on the algebraic descriptive technique firstly presented by Milner (CCS) (Milner, 1980) and the abstract data type language ACT ONE (Ehrig and Mahr, 1985). Being based on ADT, LOTOS allows to define new ADTs. LOTOS uses the concepts of ADT for defining also the structural aspects of the system under specification, differently from other FDT which do not address the structural aspects.

LOTOS is strongly based on the concept of process. Structural decomposition is made on the basis of processes, and a distributed system is also regarded as a process with subprocesses. Algebraic operators are used to define relationships among processes — e.g., sequential ($\gg$), and parallel ($\|$) executions. For these reasons, LOTOS can be considered a process-oriented descriptive algebraic language. Processes communicate by means of messages, through gates. Messages can bring data or controls; they are considered events, are assumed to be atomic, and their occurrence is supposed to be instantaneous without time consumption. A system specification consists in the definition of process behavior, by describing how processes communicate, execute, and synchronize. Process definition specifies the temporal ordering in which a process interacts with other processes, by means of its gates. A process definition may include the definition of a set of types which are equivalent to ADTs.

Consistency among descriptions is verified by a syntax checker and by simulation. A compiler translating LOTOS specifications into a machine-oriented language is also available. The LOTOS tool has been produced by the ESPRIT project SEDOS. The G-LOTOS, which is a graphic editor to produce LOTOS specifications by means of a visual language is also present (Bolognesi, Najm and Tilanus, 1993). LOTOSPHERE is an integrated tool environment for defining systems in LOTOS (LOTOSPHERE, 1992). LOTOSPHERE is the result of an ESPRIT project (n.2304). With this tool the user can define process behavior in both descriptive and operational manner. The latter resort to the formalism based on extended finite state machines.

4.1.3. VDM

VDM (Vienna Development Method) dates back to the 1970s and to the work of a reasearch group at the IBM Laboratory in Vienna, attempting to create a formal approach capable of defining the programming language PL/I. Afterwards the original group was dispersed, but the ideas instead of dying spread to a larger community. The final outcome is reported in (Jones, 1986). At present, VDM is very popular and has become a British standard. VDM is mainly a specification language, but it can be profitably used for program designing and developing. Its mathematical support is used to verify the correctness of the resulting program by proving properties (Andrews, 1992).

The mathematical bases of VDM are the theory of sets and the theory of logic predicates. A VDM system specification consists in defining types, functions and operations, in the syntax of the so-called Meta-IV language. Data types can be defined by homogeneous or heterogeneous combinations of VDM basic types (natural numbers, integer, Boolean, etc.). For the new types, a set of operations (i.e., sum, etc.) is automatically available. Functions are defined as procedures which have as arguments, and return as results, elements of primitives or user-defined data types. Functions can also be specified through their pre- and post-conditions. An operation is applicable to a set of states selected on the basis of a pre-condition associated with the operation itself (thus it seems to be very similar to the concept of condition on transition). Operations can contain *read* and *write* of external events. A post-condition is also associated with an operation. The post-condition describes the state domain after the operation execution. The specification of a system is generated by starting from a coarse description, until the final specification is obtained by refinement (Fields and Elvang-Goransson, 1992). Specification consistency is verified by checking if the definitions at different levels of abstractions are consistent. The validation consists in proving if some selected important properties are verified by the given specification.

The VDM model has no mechanism for defining the system structure. Data types are defined in terms of other data types, without partitioning the system into communicating subsystems. However, the formalism is powerful enough to describe (with a certain effort) even these conditions, but the reuse of VDM specification, as for other ADT-based approaches, is very hard. VDM is widely employed for specifying safety critical systems by using specific extensions for managing timing constraints.

Recently, an object-oriented extension of VDM has been presented — e.g., VDM++ (Dürr and vanKatwijk, 1992). This supports inheritance and instantiation without allowing the mechanism related to polymorphism. VDM++ permits the definition of timing constraints which makes it adequate for real-time system specification.

4.2. Descriptive Approaches Based on Logical Methods

These methods describe the system under specification by means of a set of logic rules, specifying how the system must evolve from certain conditions. Differently from the operational methods, the state space described by these specifications is limited and abstract. Rules can be given in the form of first-order clauses of Horn or higher-order logical expressions (Maier and Warren, 1988). These languages are unsuitable for representing the structural aspect of a system, but are very appropriate for describing properties of the system under specification.

Validation consists in proving high-level properties, which are also given in the form of logical expressions, by means of theorem solvers or Prolog engines. Simulation is also based on the same techniques. For this reason, time of execution and time ordering of events during the proof can be unpredictable and thus the real-time execution of logical specifications is almost unfeasible.

Of course logic and temporal logic date back to the ancient Greeks. These have been brought in computer science in the 1970s (Gotzhein, 1992). During the 1980s some papers have been published dealing with the use of temporal logic for program specification (Schwartz and Melliar-Smith, 1982), (Jahanian and Mok, 1986). In the literature, there are many examples of logic languages for the specification of relationships among times and actions. These are often integrated with other techniques addressing also the functional and/or the structural aspects of the system under specification — e.g., RT-ASLAN (Real-Time extension of ASLAN) integrates the first-order logic with the ADT (Auernheimer and Kemmerer, 1986).

4.2.1. RTL

RTL (Real-Time Logic) is a formal language to describe the temporal relationships among events and actions (Jahanian and Mok, 1986). In RTL, the concept of time is absolute and the execution semantics quite independent of the scheduling mechanism, since all the language constructs are defined in terms of the symbol @, which assigns the current value of time to event occurrence.

In RTL, there are three types of constants, that is, actions, events, and integers. Actions can be simple or composite: the latter can be sequential or concurrent. In turn, events are divided in three classes: start/stop, transition, and external. Events and actions are similar to stimuli and responses, respectively, as defined by Dasarathy (Dasarathy, 1985). Periodic events are specified through recursive predicates. Integers can be either time durations or number of events. A system specification in RTL consists in deriving a set of axioms from the event-action model of the system, considering: (a) the relations between events and their 'start' and 'stop' occurrences; (b) periodic or sporadic events; (c) causes of transition; and (d) artificial constraints on the internal behavior. A system property (i.e., an RTL assertion) can be proven by refutation. For example, considering the specification reported in (Jahanian and Mok, 1986): "Upon pressing button #1, action SAMPLE is executed within 30 time units. During each execution of this action, the information is sampled and sequentially transmitted to the display panel. The computation time of action SAMPLE is 20 time units.", its translation in RTL results to be:

$$\forall x :@(\Omega button1, x) \leq @(\uparrow SAMPLE, x) \wedge$$
$$@(\downarrow SAMPLE, x) \leq @(\Omega button1, x) + 30 \tag{1}$$

$$\forall y : @(\uparrow SAMPLE, y) + 20 \leq @(\downarrow SAMPLE, y)$$

where Ω means that the variable corresponds to an external event. The so-called *Constraint Graph* is constructed from the RTL specification and is used to verify the safety of the system. The constraint graph simplification by means of simple rules permits the detection of incongruences among temporal constraints. RTL is supported by an automatic inference procedure to perform reasoning about timing properties. RTL specifications can be generated directly from a description given by using the notation of Modecharts (Jahanian and Stuart, 1988).

4.2.2. TRIO

TRIO (Tempo Reale ImplicitO) is a language based on first-order logic, augmented by temporal operators (Ghezzi, Mandrioli, and Morzenti, 1990). It allows to define logic equations which may include timing relationships. A time-dependent TRIO formula is given with respect to the current time; time is implicit. Temporal relationships between events are expressed on the basis of the operator *Dist(F,t)* (Mandrioli, Morasca and Morzenti, 1992, (Felder, Mandrioli, and Morzenti, 1991), which is satisfied at the current time if and only if the property F holds at an instant which is distant t time units from the current time. Many other operators are defined for describing system behavior in TRIO logical expressions in the past and in the future. For example, the special functions $Futr(F,t) = t \geq 0 \wedge Dist(F,t)$, and $Past(F,t) = t \geq 0 \wedge Dist(F,-t)$ are defined.

Since TRIO is based on a completely formal syntax and semantics, and includes the managing of time, it is intrinsically executable, in the sense that from a TRIO formula a precise model can be generated in which the variables inside the predicates have well-defined values. Expressions are usually given in the implicative forms:

$$A \rightarrow B \overset{def}{=} \neg A \vee B$$

$$A \leftrightarrow B \overset{def}{=} (A \rightarrow B) \wedge (B \rightarrow A)$$

where $\neg$ is the *not*, $\vee$ the *or* and $\wedge$ the *and* Boolean operator. *For all* $\forall$ and the *existence* (i.e., $\exists x A \overset{def}{=} \neg \forall x \neg A$) qualifier can be used.

The following example is quoted from (Mandrioli, Morasca and Morzenti, 1992). Consider a pondage power station where the quantity of water held in the tank is controlled by means of a sluice gate. The gate is controlled by the commands: *up* and *down* which respectively open and close the gate. These are represented by a predicate *go* having a range { *up, down* }. The gate can be in one of the states: *up, down, mvUp, mvDown*. The state is modeled by a time-dependent variable named *position*. The following formula describes that the gate in Δ time units passed from the *down* to the *up* condition after receiving a *go(up)* command:

$$(\text{position=down} \wedge go(up)) \rightarrow (Lasts(position=mvUp, \ \Delta) \wedge Futr(position=up, \Delta))$$

When a *go(up)* command reaches the system and the gate is not yet in the *down* position, but it is moving down for a previous command *go(down)*, then the direction of motion is not changed but the system waits until the *down* position is reached:

$$position=mvDown \land go(up) \rightarrow$$
$$\exists\, t\ (NextTime(position=down,\ t) \land Futr(\ Lasts(position=mvUp, \Delta) \land Futr(position=up, \Delta),\ t\ )\ )$$

where $NextTime(F,d)=Futr(F,t) \land Lasts(\neg F,t)$, and $Lasts(F,t)=\forall t'\ (0 < t' < t \rightarrow Dist$ $(F,t))$. Since the gate behavior can be supposed to be symmetric with respect to its direction of motion, other two similar expressions should be written which describe the commands and their effects.

A TRIO specification can be validated against high-level properties described by means of the same formalism. Moreover, an efficient interpreter is available that makes a TRIO specification executable for real-time systems. Since the time relationships are given implicitly and the time is expressed in time units, the absolute time constraints cannot be specified. On the other hand, it has the capability to guaranteeing system safety by verifying the temporal ordering among events, independently of the underlying hardware.

4.2.3. Other Descriptive Approaches Based on Logical Methods

Many other interesting approaches, which essentially correspond to extensions of temporal logic — e.g., CTL (Computation Tree Logic) (Emerson and Halpern, 1986), RTIL (Real-Time Interval Logic) (Razouk and Gorlick, 1989), TCTL (Timed CTL) (Alur, 1990), TPTL (Timed Propositional Temporal Logic) (Alur and Henzinger, 1990), have been defined. Most of these approaches do not cover the structural and functional aspects of the system under specification.

5. Dual Approaches

In order to obtain the best benefits from the descriptive and the operational approaches, in the late 1980s the so-called "dual approaches" have begun to appear (Ostroff, 1989), (Felder, Mandrioli, and Morzenti, 1991). Dual methods try to integrate in a single approach the formal verifiability of descriptive approaches and the executability of operational approaches, though they are often in contrast, especially as regards the reuse and the verification of software specifications,

In effect, an ideal tool for specifying real-time systems should be:

1. An *easy and intuitable method and tool*. Where, "easy" means "very close" to the analyst mindset. For this reason, the tool must be endowed with a graphic user interface, and it must allow both top-down and bottom-up approaches for software specification, as well as a combination of these. Operational models seem to be suitable for this purpose, since they can be visually represented; in the literature, there are many examples of their use in both top-down and bottom-up approaches for software specification.

2. A model to make easier the *reusing of reactive system specifications*. This means that the model adopted must provide support for software composition by reusing already defined software components. In the specification of reactive systems, both

static (module interface and structure) and dynamic aspects (module behavior with timing constraints) should be reused. In addition, since the system specification must be validated to ensure its correctness, also the process of composition/decomposition must be supported by a validation method technique. For this purpose, descriptive formal methods are strongly preferable with respect to operational methods, since the validation of decomposition cannot be performed through simulation but only by means of proof of properties. This is related to the fact that during the decomposition low-level details are not yet available.

3. A *method for verifying and validating the specified software against critical conditions since the early phases of system specification*. This feature with that of the previous point should allow the verification and validation at each level of abstraction even if the implementation details are not available (such as in the early phases of system specification — i.e., partial specification). It should be noted that the operational models, differently from the descriptive ones, are not suitable to be executed when the model is partially specified. For this reason, descriptive methods seem to be preferable for this purpose, even if with these methods the validation is usually carried out through properties proof.

4. An *executable model to allow the validation of system behavior by means of simulation*. The simulation of an executable model improves the confidence of system validation and, together with the above features, provides support for rapid system prototyping. For this purpose, operational models could be profitably used, while most of the descriptive models are not efficient since they are usually "executable" by means of inferential engines which are typically strongly inefficient.

As has been pointed out, the above objectives are often in contrast, and they cannot be met by a specification approach which is only descriptive or only operational. Recently, several dual methods to overcome these difficulties have been defined (Bucci, et. al, 1993), (Mandrioli, 1992).

To a certain extent, several of the already discussed approaches can be considered dual languages. On the contrary, only those that have both operational and descriptive semantics allowing the specification executability and the verification of properties should be considered really dual. One of the first examples of dual approach can be considered the Transition Axiom Method proposed by Lamport (Lamport, 1993), (Lamport, 1989). In this method, the specification is equivalent to a state machine, on which the proof of high-level properties given by means of axioms can be verified.

5.1. *ESM/RTTL*

ESM/RTTL is a dual approach obtained be the integration of ESM (Extended State Machine) language and RTTL (Real-Time Temporal Logic) (Ostroff and Wonham, 1987), (Ostroff, 1989).

ESM is an operational model based on communicating finite state machines in which variables with arbitrary domains are used (Ostroff and Wonham, 1987). The *operations* allowed are assignments, send or receive. The state machine follows a Mealy model in which conditions on transitions (in ESM, they are called *guards*) between states are equivalent to first-order expressions on state variables, while the output is an assignment to state variables. Each event is represented by an exit activity A_e, a source activity A_s, an *operation* and a *guard*: $(A_e, guard, operation, A_s)$. A system description refers to only a single state domain. The concept of time is enforced by means of a global time variable which can be tested, updated, and increased or not at each state transition. Time is discrete, and a state transition can be formally executed in zero time units. For each state transition the minimum and the maximum time can be specified in which the enabling condition becomes true.

RTTL is a logic language based on the classical operator of temporal logic: *until* ($\sqcap$), and *next* ($\odot$). From these the more useful operators of: eventually ($\diamond$), henceforth ($\square$), etc., are derived. RTTL can be used to describe high-level properties of the system under specification by means of first-order logic formulae.

The integration between RTTL and ESM is obtained by describing the high-level behavior of the system with first-order expressions in which conditions for transitions containing RTTL expressions can be also present. Both RTTL and ESM formulae can refer to the absolute time value.

5.2. TRIO+

TRIO+ (TRIO object-oriented) is a logical language for modular system specification (Mandrioli, 1992), (Mandrioli, 1993) extending TRIO (see Section 4.2.2) with object-oriented capabilities. It is based on a first-order temporal language, providing support for a variety of validation activities, such as testing, simulation and property proof. TRIO+ is considered a dual language since it combines the use of visual notation, hierarchical decomposition (typically of operational approaches), with the rigour of the descriptive logical language. In Fig.18, the example reported in Section 4.2.2 for the TRIO language has been rebuilt in TRIO+. Since TRIO+ is based on logic programming, the object-oriented concept of an instance corresponds to a history of the Prolog interpreter (that is the history of the status of an object).

Differently from TRIO, TRIO+ is endowed with a graphical notation that covers only the declarative part of the language. With this graphic interface the structural aspects can be described, by defining the components of a class and their relationships (see Fig.19). TRIO+ is an executable model which supports the executions of partially defined specifications.

5.3. TROL

TROL (Tempo Reale Object-oriented Language) is an object-oriented dual language for the specification of real-time systems (Bucci, et. al, 1994). TROL adopts a dual model which is able to satisfy the above requirements presenting both descriptive and operational aspects. TROL adopts a modified object-oriented model, and has the capability to

Class sluice_gate
    visible go, position
    temporal domain integer
    TD Items
      Predicates go({up,down})
      vars position: { up, down, mvup, mvdown }
    TI Items
      vars Δ : integer
    axioms
      vars t: integer
      go_down: position=up $\wedge$ go(down) $\rightarrow$ Lasts(position=mvdown,Δ) $\wedge$ Futr(position=down,Δ)
      gp_up: position=down $\wedge$ go(up) $\rightarrow$ Lasts(position=mvup,Δ) $\wedge$ Futr(position=up,Δ)
      move_up: position=mvup $\wedge$ go(down) $\rightarrow$ $\exists$t (NextTime(position=up,t) $\wedge$
            Futr(Lasts(position=mvdown,Δ) $\wedge$ Futr(position=down,Δ),t)
      move_down: position=mvdown $\wedge$ go(up) $\rightarrow$ $\exists$t (NextTime(position=down,t) $\wedge$
            Futr(Lasts(position=mvup,Δ) $\wedge$ Futr(position=up,Δ),t)
end sluice_gate

Figure 18. Textual description of the class *sluice_gate* in TRIO+.

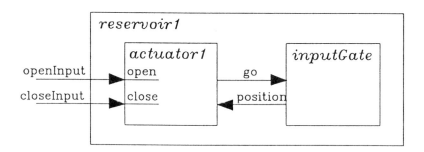

Figure 19. Visual description of class *reservoir1* comprised of *actuator1* and *inputGate* objects in TRIO+.

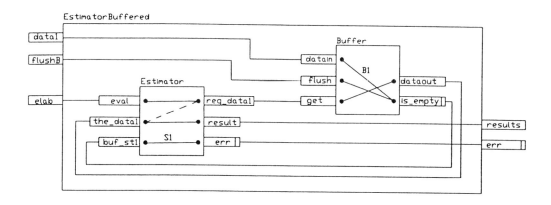

Figure 20. The class EstimatorBuffered as comprised of S1 and B1 sub-objects (i.e., its attributes) in TROL.

describe the system behavior, its functionality and structural aspects. Moreover, differently from other dual models and languages, the TROL model is mainly based on reusing both static and dynamic aspects of specifications. TROL is based on an extension of timed CSP — i.e., the CRSM (Shaw, 1992) (see Section 3.1.5).

In TROL, the system under specification is hierarchically decomposed in objects and sub-objects. For these objects, the behavior can be specified by means of first-order clauses, since the early phases of decomposition (see Fig.20, and Fig.21). Moreover, also timing constraints at the external interface of each object can be defined according to (Dasarathy, 1985). These constraints can be associated with *Provided* and *Required* services of each class, and to *Clauses*. TROL allows to describe the system at different levels of structural abstractions and of specification details without boundaries among the specification steps. The TROL model allows the verification and validation of composition/decomposition mechanisms. At each specification level, TROL helps the user in the verification of consistency, thus allowing the incremental specification and the execution of partially specified systems (i.e., prototyping) (Bucci, et. al, 1993). These features are very useful when a component under reuse can be verified and validated in order to check if it satisfies the requirements.

Objects that cannot be further decomposed are defined as extended state machines (see Fig.22a and 22b). These are internally concurrent, defining in this way a high reactive architecture. The state machine model supports the definition of timing constraints such as timeout, and minimum and maximum time for transition. Moreover, any time failure can be recovered by using special functions.

In TROL, the descriptive aspects of the language are used to help the developer to generate a correct, complete and congruent specification, validating the system composition/decomposition by means of clauses and the reasoning on timing constraints. Also the state machines are validated by using clauses. Thus, the final validated model is executable by using the operational model of state machines. Is should be noted that in TROL the analysts use a descriptive language in the phase of analysis while state machines are used in the phase of design. TROL supports all the aspects of the object-oriented paradigm allowing inheritance, instantiation, etc. In order to guarantee the predictability and, hence, an a-priori real-time schedulability, some assumptions have

Class Estimator **specializing** XSM
    Provided_services:
        eval : **Signal**;
        the_data1 : DataType;
        buf_st1 : **Boolean**;
    Required_services:
        req_data1 : **Signal**;
        result : **Real**;
        err **available** : EstimatorErrType;
    Clauses:
        REQ_DATA1: **New**(eval) $\wedge$ err==OK $\rightarrow$ **Ready** (req_data1);
        WAITDATA1: **reverse Ready**(req_data1) $\rightarrow$ **New**(the_data1);
        RESULT: **New**(the_data1) $\rightarrow$ **Ready**(result);
        BUFEMPTY: buf_st1 $\rightarrow$ err==EMPTY ;
end;

Class EstimatorBuffered **specializing** non_basic_object_class
    Provided_services:
        data1 : DataType;
        flushB : **Signal**;
        elab [4,6] : **Signal**;
    Required_services:
        results : **Real**;
        err **available** : EstimatorErrType;
    Clauses:
        ESTIMATION: **New**(elab) $\wedge$ err==OK $\rightarrow$ **Ready**(results) - - [2, 3.1];
        FLUSH : **New** (flushB) $\rightarrow$ err==EMPTY;
        DATA : **New** (data1) $\wedge$ err==EMPTY $\rightarrow$ err==OK;
    /*** private parts ***/
    Attributes:
        B1 : Buffer;
        S1 : Estimator;
    Connections:
        data1 - - B1.datain;   elab - - S1.eval;
        S1.result - - results;   S1.err - - err;
        S1.req_data1 - - B1.get;   B1.dataout - - S1.the_data1;
        B1.is_empty - - S1.buf_st1;   flushB - - B1.flush;
end;

Figure 21. Description in TROL of class EstimatorBuffered with the external description of class Estimator, where EstimatorErrType is defined as an enumeration: **enum** EstimatorErrType {EMPTY,OK};.

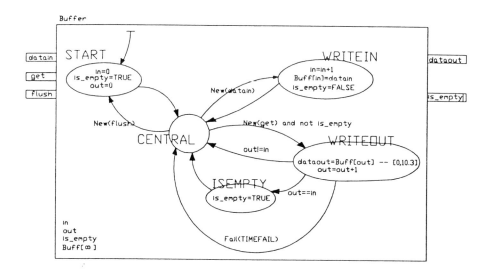

Figure 22a. Textual descriptions of class Buffer in TROL.

been made on the TROL model: no dynamic binding, no dynamic object instantiation (no dynamic sizing of object collections), no direct or indirect recursion in class specifications, no multiple inheritance among classes is allowed.

TROL has its visual representation which is supported by a CASE tool named TOOMS (Bucci, et. al, 1993). TOOMS consists in a set of visual editors, a report generator, a database for collecting and recovering specifications for reuse, a compiler, an analyzer to perform the verification of completeness and consistency, a simulator (that can simulate the system behavior by using both clauses and state machines) and a metricator (Bucci, et. al, 1993), (Campanai and Nesi, 1994). Automatic code generation is also provided through the TROL-compiler which transforms the TROL code in C++ for an *ad-hoc* real-time kernel called TROL-KERNEL working on OS/2 and UNIX.

6. Discussion and Conclusions

The most significative formal methods for the specification of real-time systems have been reviewed, with respect to the power of formalism, the tool capability, and the low-level characteristics, as discussed in the introduction. The presentation has been referred to the historical evolution.

In Tab.1 a summary of the main features of the tools analyzed is reported. The legend of the Table reported in the caption is self-explicative and thus we refrain from commenting on it. However, it is worth to spend a few words on columns labelled as *Sem.* (for semantics) and *Orien.* (for orientation). In the column *Sem.*, the approaches are classified as operational and/or descriptive, considering as dual those which present both these aspects. Column *Orien.*, indicates whether the approach is Process-, State-, Functional-, or sTructure-oriented. Process-oriented approaches are those which consider the system as decomposed in processes; state-oriented approaches are those that are

Class Buffer **specializing** XSM
    Provided_services:
        datain : DataType ;
        get : **Signal** ;
        flush : **Signal** ;
    Required_services:
        dataout : DataType ;
        is_empty **available** : **Boolean**;
    Clauses:
        GET : **New** (get) $\wedge \neg$ is_empty $\rightarrow$ **Ready** (dataout);
        FLUSH : **New** (flush) $\rightarrow$ is_empty;
        DATAIN : **New** (datain) $\wedge$ is_empty $\rightarrow \neg$ is_empty;
    /*** private parts ***/
    Attributes:
        in : **Integer** ;
        out : **Integer** ;
        is_empty : **Boolean** ;
        Buff : DataType [∞];
    States:
        START: { in=0; is_empty=TRUE; out=0; }
        CENTRAL: { }
        WRITEIN: { in=in+1; Buff[in]=datain; is_empty=FALSE; }
        WRITEOUT: { dataout=Buff[out] - - [0,10.3]; out=out+1; }
        ISEMPTY: { is_empty=TRUE; }
    Paths:
        INIT: { START: $\rightarrow$ CENTRAL;
               CENTRAL: **New**(flush) $\rightarrow$ START;}
        PUT: { CENTRAL: **New**(datain) $\rightarrow$ WRITEIN;
               WRITEIN: $\rightarrow$ CENTRAL; }
        GET: { CENTRAL: **New**(get) $\wedge \neg$ is_empty $\rightarrow$ WRITEOUT;
               WRITEOUT: in != out $\rightarrow$ CENTRAL;
               WRITEOUT: in==out $\rightarrow$ ISEMPTY;
               ISEMPTY: $\rightarrow$ CENTRAL;
               WRITEOUT: **Fail**(TIMEFAIL) $\rightarrow$ CENTRAL; }
end;

Figure 22b. Visual descriptions of class Buffer.

focused on describing the system state domain; functional-oriented approaches are those that decompose the system in data transformations; and structure-oriented approaches are those that consider the system as a set of sub-systems (i.e., objects or modules). In this column only the two most relevant aspects are reported.

It can be noted that during the last 20 years most of the early approaches for describing system behavior (e.g., Z, VDM, SDL, etc.) have been integrated by using high-level methods in order to improve their capability in modeling all the system aspects (i.e., structural, behavioral and functional) and providing support for reusability. In many cases, this coverage has been reached by transforming the model from process- or state- or function-oriented to object-oriented (Z++, VDM++, OSDL, etc.). The adoption of the object-oriented paradigm has added to the early formalisms the capability of system structuring (by means of the concept of *class*) and of reusing real-time specifications (by means of the concepts of *inheritance*, *polymorphism*, and *instantiation*). This trend holds for both descriptive, and operational approaches as well as for dual approaches.

For most of the formal methods, facilities for managing timing constraints have also been added. Operational approaches, based on state machines and Petri nets have been extended so as to include the notion of time by augmenting the model with first-order logic. The resulting models are more complex to be verified and validated, but the verification and validation can be performed in the same manner under certain restrictive conditions.

The operational approaches based on other notations (firstly created as methodologies for supporting the analysis and/or design phases of the system under specification, e.g., DFD, JSD, Booch, Wirsf-Brock, etc.) (see Section 3.3) have followed a different path. The early versions of most of these methodologies have been integrated by using low-level methods for supporting the lack of formalities and for covering the design phase of software life-cycle. Currently, methods exist which are based on DFD and state machines (e.g., RT-DFD (Hatley and Pirbhai, 1987)), JSD and state machines (e.g., Entity-Life (Sanden, 1989c), (Sanden, 1989b)), DFD and Petri nets (e.g., IPTES (Pulli, et. al, 1991)), extended Entity-Relationships and VDM (e.g., ATMOSPHERE (Dick and Loubersac, 1991)), object-oriented model and state machines (e.g., Booch (Booch, 1991), Shlaer and Mellor (Shlaer and Mellor, 1991)), object-oriented model and Petri nets (e.g., PROTOB (Baldassari and Bruno, 1991)), etc.. For most of them, the definition and verification of timing constraints and the final validation are still a problem. For example, when the definition of timing constraints is allowed in the early phases of system specification, their consistency is not verified with respect to the low-level description. On the other hand, the definition of timing constraints is allowed only at the low-level — i.e., at the level of state machines or Petri nets, where the consistency can be verified and the validation performed. It should be noted that, in the latter case, timing constraints are specified when the system architecture is already defined and, therefore, their verification can lead to demonstrate that the system structure (e.g., decomposition) is wrong or partially incorrect.

Due to the fact that formal languages are too far from the analysts mindset to be easily adopted for specifying real-time systems (since they need too many details), CASE tools have been implemented including visual editors, compilers, metric support, configuration

Table 1. Summary of formalism evaluation, where: *Sem.* (semantics): Operational and/or Descriptive (Algebraic or Logic); *Orien.* (orientation): Process-, State-, Functional-, sTructure-oriented; *Desc.* (description): Textual (5pt.), Visual (5pt.); *Cov.* (coverage): Structural (3pt.), Behavioral (5pt.), Functional (2pt.); *Comm.* (communications among processes); *Time* (time model): Implicit (3pt.), Explicit (7pt.) (Relative or Absolute), None (0pt.); *Verif.* (verification of consistency and congruence): Yes (10pt.) or No (0pt.); *Valid.* (validation of system behavior): Static (6pt.) (i.e., by proving properties), Dynamic (4pt.) (i.e., by simulation); *Exec.* (executable specification, by means of interpretation or simulation): Yes (10pt.) or No (0pt.); *Prot.* (prototyping — i.e., simulation or execution of partial specifications): Yes (10pt.) or No (0pt.).

	Sem.	Orien.	Desc.	Cov.	Comm.	Time	Verif.	Valid.	Exec.	Prot.
PAISLey	O	P	T	B,F	A	ER	Y	S,D	Y	Y
SDL	O	P	V,T	S,B	A	ER	Y	D	Y	Y
OSDL	O	P	V,T	S,B,F	A	ER	Y	D	Y	Y
Esterel	O	P	T	B,F	S	EA	Y	S,D	Y	N
Statecharts	O	S	V	B	S	ER	Y	D	Y	N
Objectcharts	O	S	V	B,S	S	EA	Y	D	Y	N
RTRL	O	S	T	B	N	ER	Y	S	Y	N
CRSM	O	P,S	V,T	B	S	ER	Y	D	Y	N
PN	O	S	V	B	A	I	Y	D	Y	N
CmPN	O	P,S	V	S,B	A	I	Y	S,D	Y	N
SPN	O	S	V	B	A	ER	Y	S,D	Y	N
PROT nets	O	P,S	V,T	S,B	A	ER	Y	S,D	Y	Y
TPN	O	S	V	B	A	ER	Y	S,D	Y	N
Timed PN	O	S	V	B	A	ER	Y	S,D	Y	N
HMS	O	S	V	B,S	A	ER	Y	S,D	Y	Y
SADT	O	F,S	V	F,S,B	N	EA	Y	N	N	N
DFD	O	F	V	F,S	N	N	Y	N	N	N
RT-DFD	O	F,S	V	F,S,B	N	EA	Y	D	Y	Y
JSD	O	T	V	S	N	N	Y	N	N	N
Entity-Life	O	P,S	V	S,B	A	ER	Y	D	Y	Y
Wirsf-Brock	O	P,F	V	S,F	S	N	N	N	N	N
HOOD	O	T,S	V	S,B	A,S	EA	Y	N	N	N
BOOCH	O	P,S	V	S,B	A,S	EA	N	N	N	N
OMT	O	T,S	V	S,B,F	A	EA	N	N	N	N
Shlaer-Mellor	O	T,S	V	S,B	A	EA	N	N	N	N
Coad-Yourdon	O	T,F	V	S,F	A	EA	N	N	N	Y
AFFIRM	DA	S	T	B	N	N	Y	S	N	Y
Larch	DA	S	T	B	N	N	Y	S	N	Y
Larch/C++	DA	S	T	B	A,S	N	Y	S	N	Y
Z	DA	S	T	S,B	N	N	Y	S	N	Y
Object-Z	DA	S	T	B	S	ER	Y	S	Y	Y
LOTOS	DA	P,S	T	B,S	A	N	Y	S	Y	Y
G-LOTOS	DA	P,S	T,V	B,S	A	N	Y	S	Y	Y
VDM	DA	S	T	B	N	N	Y	S	N	Y
VDM++	DA	S	T	B	N	ER	Y	S	Y	Y
RTL	DL	S	T	B	N	ER	Y	S	N	N
Modecharts	DL	S	V,T	B,S	S	ER	Y	S,D	Y	N
TRIO	DL	S	T	B	N	I	Y	S,D	Y	Y
TCTL	DL	S	T	B	N	ER	Y	S	N	N
CTL	DL	S	T	B	N	N	Y	S	N	N
ESM/RTTL	O,DL	T	T	B	N	ER	Y	S,D	Y	N
TRIO+	O,DL	T,	T,V	B,S	N	I	Y	S,D	Y	Y
TROL	O,DL	T,S	T,V	B,S,F	S,A	ER	Y	S,D	Y	Y

management support, report generators, simulators, test generators, etc. A CASE tool with a visual interface makes easier the work of the designer by representing formal syntax through graphic symbols and, thus, the user is helped by collecting the specification details in a structured manner. Of course, a CASE tool must maintain consistency between the visual representation and the syntax and semantics of the model. As a result, by means of a CASE tool, a specification language improves its power. From this point of view, the operational approaches have an advantage over the descriptive approaches, since they are intrinsically endowed of a visual notation, while the definition of a visual language supporting the syntax of the latter is a more difficult task. In general, the presence of an integrated CASE tool gives a major confidence to the specification quality, improving the fulfilment of requirements, the verification of consistency, the validation of system behavior with respect to temporal constraints, etc.

A graph reporting the trend of the specification tools capability with respect to last 20 years is reported in Fig.23. This graph has been drawn on the basis of tools analysis carried out in this paper, considering a particular score for each feature. Scores have been defined on the basis of their usefulness in specifying real-time systems. Scores associated with the different features are reported in the caption of Tab.1. As is appeared from this graph, the number of positive features is increasing with time. This growth has been obtained in many cases by integrating different approaches, and thus transforming the early nature of a model towards a dual approach. In our opinion, in the next years, we will witness a tangible additional growth of tool capabilities These improvements will be mainly focused on tools integration, so as to help the analyst in all phases of the software life-cycle, without boundaries from one phase to another. The integrated CASE tools will give a major confidence for the specification of *perfect* software (e.g., a software which is safe, congruent, complete, satisfying temporal constraints, etc.).

Acknowledgments

The authors want to thank CESVIT (High-Tech Agency, Italy) which allowed them to test most of the tools mentioned in this paper (StP of Interactive Development Environments, ARTIFEX of ARTIS, GEODE of Verilog, Teamwork of CADRE, EXCELERATOR of Index Technology, etc.). In addition, they wish to thank also A. Corgiatini, R. Mattolini, O. Morales, M. Traversi, and E. Vicario, for their help.

References

Jean-Raymond Abrial. The Specification Language Z: Basic Library. Technical report, Programming Research Group, Oxford University, UK, 1982.

G. A. Agha. *ACTORS: A Model of Concurrent Computation in Distributed Systems*.   The MIT Press, Cambridge, Massachusetts, London, 1986.

A. J. Alencar and J. A. Goguen. OOZE: An Object Oriented Z Environment. In *Proc. of European Conference on Object Oriented Programming, ECOOP'91*, pages 180–199. Springer Verlag, Lecture Notes in Computer Sciences, LNCS n.512, 1991.

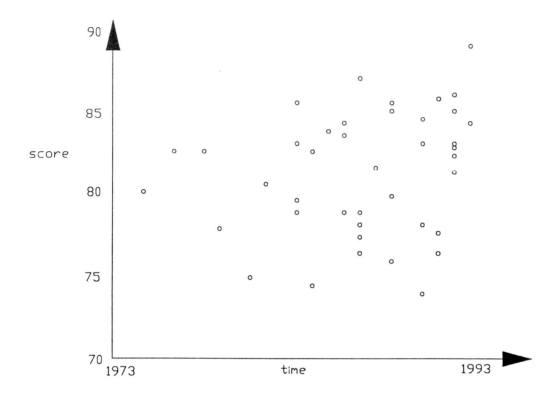

Figure 23. Trend of tool capabilities in modeling specifications for real-time systems in the last 20 years.

M. Alford.   A Requirements Engineering Methodology for Real-Time Processing Requirements.   *IEEE Transactions on Software Engineering*, 3(1), Jan. 1977.

M. Alford. SREM at the Age of Eight; The Distributed Computing Design System. *Computer*, April 1985.

R. Alur, C. Coucorbertis, and D. Dill. Model-Checking for Real-Time Systems. In *Proc. of 5th IEEE LICS 90*, pages 414–425. IEEE, 1990.

R. Alur and T. A. Henzinger. Real Time Logics: complexity and Expressiveness. In *Proc. of 5th IEEE LICS 90*. IEEE, 1990.

D. Andrews.   VDM Specification Language, Proto-Standard.   Technical report, BSI IST/5/50, Leicester University, 1992.

ARTIFEX. ARTIFEX User's Manual, ver.3.0. Technical report, ARTIS, Turin, Italy, 1993.

B. Auernheimer and R. A. Kemmerer. RT-ASLAN: A Specification Language for Real-Time Systems. *IEEE Transactions on Software Engineering*, 12(9):879–889, Sept. 1986.

M. Baldassari and G. Bruno.   PROTOB: an Object Oriented Methodology for Developing Discrete Event Dynamic Systems. *Computer Languages,*, 16(1):39–63, 1991.

H. Barringer. *A Survey of Verification Techniques for Parallel Programs.* Lecture Notes in Computer Science 191, Springer Verlag, New York, 1985.

Z. Bavel.   *Introduction to the Theory of Automata.*   Reston Publishing Company, Prentice-Hall, Reston, Virginia, 1983.

G. Berry and L. Cosserat. *The ESTEREL Synchronous Programming Language and Its Mathematical Semantics.* Springer Verlag, Lecture Notes in Computer Science, LNCS n.197, 1985.

B. Berthomieu and M. Diaz. Modeling and Verification of Time Dependent Systems Using Time Petri Nets. *IEEE Transactions on Software Engineering*, 17(3):259–273, March 1991.

T. E. Bihari and P. Gopinath. Object-Oriented Real-Time Systems: Concepts and Examples. *Computer*, pages 25–32, Dec. 1992.

N. D. Birrel and M. A. Ould. *A practical handbook for software development.* Cambridge University Press, Cambridge U.K., 1985.

G. V. Bochmann, E. Cerny, M. Cagne, C. Jard, A. Leveille, C. Lacaille, M. Maksud, K. S. Raghunathan, and B. Sarikaya. Experience with Formal Specification Using an Extended State Transition Model. *IEEE Transactions on Communications*, 30(12):2505-2513, Dec. 1982.

T. Bolognesi and E. Brinksma. Introduction to the ISO Specification Language LOTOS. In P. H. J. van Eijk and C. A. Vissers, editors, *The Formal Description Technique LOTOS*, pages 23-71. Elsevier Science Publisher, North-Holland, 1989.

T. Bolognesi and E. Brinksma. Introduction to the ISO specification language LOTOS. *Computer Networks and ISDN Systems*, 14(1):25-29, 1987.

T. Bolognesi, E. Najm, and P. A. J. Tilanus. G-LOTOS: a Graphical Language for Concurrent Systems. Technical report, CNR Istituto CNUCE, PISA, Italy, March 15 1993.

G. Booch. Object-Oriented Development. *IEEE Transactions on Software Engineering*, 12(2):211-221, Feb. 1986.

G. Booch. *Object-Oriented Design with Application*. The Benjamin/Cummings Publishing Company, California, USA, 1991.

T. L. Booth. *Sequential Machines and Automata Theory*. John Wiley and Sons, New York, USA, 1967.

R. Braek and O. Haugen. *Engineering Real Time Systems: An object-oriented methodology using SDL*. Prentice hall, New York, London, 1993.

P. Brinch-Hansen. The programming language concurrent Pascal. *IEEE Transactions on Software Engineering*, 1(2):199-207, June 1975.

S. D. Brookes. On The Relationship of CCS and CSP. In J. Diaz, editor, *Automata, Language and Programming, Proc. of 10th Colloquium*, pages 83-96, Barcelona, Spain, July 1983. Springer Verlag, Lecture Notes in Computer Science, LNCS 154.

G. Bruno and G. Marchetto. Process-translatable Petri nets for the rapid Prototyping of process control systems. *IEEE Transactions on Software Engineering*, 12(2):346-357, Feb. 1986.

G. Bucci, M. Campanai, P. Nesi, and M. Traversi. An Object-Oriented CASE Tool for Reactive System Specification. In *Proc. of 6th International Conference on Software Engineering and Its Applications (sponsored by: EC2, CXP, CIGREF, and SEE)*, Le CNIT, Paris la Defense, France, 15-19 Nov. 1993.

G. Bucci, M. Campanai, P. Nesi, and M. Traversi. An Object-Oriented Dual Language for Specifying Reactive Systems. In *Proc. of IEEE International Conference on Requirements Engineering, ICRE'94*, Colorado Spring, Colorado, USA, 18-22 April 1994.

G. Bucci, R. Mattolini, and E. Vicario. A Framework for the Development of Distributed Object-Oriented Systems. In *Proc. of the International Symposium on Automated and Decentralized Systems, ISADS'93*, pages 44-51. IEEE Press., Kawasaky, Japan, March 1993.

S. Budkowski and P. Dembinski. An Introduction to Estelle: A Specification Language for Distributed Systems. *Computer Networks and ISDN Systems*, 14(1):3-23, 1987.

J. R. Cameron. An Overview of JSD. *IEEE Transactions on Software Engineering*, 12(2):222-240, Feb. 1986.

M. Campanai and P. Nesi. Supporting Object-Oriented Design with Metrics. In *Proc. of the International Conference on Technology of Object-Oriented languages and Systems, TOOLS Europe'94*, Versailles, France, 7-11 March 1994.

D. Carrington, D. Duke, R. Duke, P. King, G. Rose, and G. Smith. Object-Z: An Object-Oriented Extension to Z. In S. T. Voung, editor, *Formal Description Techniques*. Elsevier Science, 1990.

P. P. Chen. The Entity Relationship Model – Toward a Unified View of Data. *ACM Transactions on Database Systems*, 1(1):9, March 1976.

Y. Cheon and G. T. Leveson. A Quick Overview of Larch/C++. Technical report, Dept. of Computer Science, Atanasoff Hall Iowa State University, Ames, Iowa 50011-1040, USA, March 1993.

P. Coad and E. Yourdon. *Object-Oriented Analysis*. Yourdon Press, New Jersey, USA, 1991.

D. Coleman, F. Hayes, and S. Bear. Introducing Objectcharts or How to Use Statecharts in Object-Oriented Design. *IEEE Transactions on Software Engineering*, 18(1):9-18, Jan. 1992.

B. Cox. Message/Object Programming: an Evolutionary Change in Programming Technology. *IEEE Software*, 1(1):50-61, 1984.

B. Dasarathy. Timing Constraints of Real-Time Systems: Constructs for Expressing Them, Methods of Validating Them. *IEEE Transactions on Software Engineering*, 11(1):80-86, Jan. 1985.

T. DeMarco. *Structured Analysis and System Specification*. Yourdon Press, Prentice Hall, 1979.

J. Dick and J. Loubersac. Integrating Structured and Formal Methods: A Visual Approach to VDM. In A. vanLamsweerde and A. Fuggetta, editors, *Proc. of 3rd European Software Engineering Conference*,

ESEC91, pages 37–59, Milan, Italy, Oct. 1991. Springer Verlag. Lecture Notes in Computer Sciences, LNCS 550.

J. Diederich and J. Milton. Object, Message, and Rules in Database Design. In W. Kim and F. H. Lochovsky, editors, *Object-Oriented Concepts Databases and Applications*, pages 177–198. Addison-Wesley Publishing Company, ACM Press, New York, USA, 1989.

E. W. Dijkstra. Co-operating sequential processes. In F. Genuys, editor, *Programming Languages*, pages 43–112. Academic Press, NY, USA, 1968.

M. Dorfman. System and Software Requirements Engineering. In H.Thayer and M.Dorfman, editors, *System and Software Requirements Engineering*, pages 4–16. IEEE Compute Society Press, Los Alamitos CA, 1990.

E. H. H. Dürr and J vanKatwijk. VDM++: A Formal Specification Language for Object-Oriented Designs. In G. Heeg, B. Mugnusson, and B. Meyer, editors, *Proc. of the International Conference on Technology of Object-Oriented Languages and Systems, TOOLS 7*, pages 63–78. Prentice-Hall, 1992.

H. Ehrig and B. Mahr. *Fundamentals of Algebraic Specification - 1*. Springer Verlag, Berlin, 1985.

C. A. Ellis and S. J. Gibbs. Active Objects: Realities and Possibilities. In W. Kim and F. H. Lochovsky, editors, *Object-Oriented Concepts Databases and Applications*, pages 561–572. Addison-Wesley Publishing Company, ACM Press, New York, USA, 1989.

E. A. Emerson and J. Y. Halpern. Sometimes and not never revisited: on branching versus linear time temporal logic. *Journal of the ACM*, 33(1), Jan. 1986.

V. Encontre, E. Delboulbe, P. Gabaud, P. Leblanc, and A. Baussalem. Combining Services, Message Sequence Charts and SDL: Formalism Methods and Tools. Technical report, Verilog, 1990.

Excelerator. User Manual, Ver.1.2. Technical report, Index Technology Corporation, Cambridge Massachusetts, USA, 1986.

M. Felder, D. Mandrioli, and A. Morzenti. Proving Properties of Real-Time Systems Through Logical Specifications and Petri Net Models. Technical report, Politecnico di Milano, Dipartimento di Elettronica e Informazione, 91-072, Piazza Leonardo da Vinci 32, Milano, Italy, 1991.

B. Fields and M. Elvang-Goransson. A VDM Case Study in mural. *IEEE Transactions on Software Engineering*, 18(4):279–295, April 1992.

A. Forin. Real-Time, UNIX and Mach. Technical report, School of Computer Science, Carnegie Mellon University, Pittsburg, Pa 15213, USA, 1992.

A. Gabrielian and M. K. Franklin. Multilevel Specification of Real-Time Systems. *Communications of the ACM*, 34(5):50–60, May 1991.

S. J. Garland, J. V. Guttag, and J. J. Horning. Debugging Larch Shared Language Specifications. *IEEE Transactions on Software Engineering*, 16(9):1044–1057, Sept. 1990.

GEODE. AGE/GEODE Editor, User's Manual, ver.1.4. Technical report, Verilog, avenue Artistide Briand, 52, 92220 Bagneaux, France, 1992.

R. Gerber and I. Lee. Communicating Shared Resources: A Model for Distributed Real-Time Systems. In *Proc. of the IEEE Real-Time Systems Symposium*, pages 68–78. IEEE Computer Society Press, Dec. 1989.

C. Ghezzi, D. Mandrioli, S. Morasca, and M. Pezze. A Unified High-Level Petri Net Formalism for Time-Critical Systems. *IEEE Transactions on Software Engineering*, 17(2):160–172, Feb. 1991.

C. Ghezzi, D. Mandrioli, and A. Morzenti. TRIO, a logic language for executable specifications of real-time systems. *Journal of Systems and Software*, 12(2):107–123, May 1990.

H. Gomaa. A Software Design Method for Real-Time Systems. *Communications of the ACM*, 27(9):938–949, Sept. 1984.

H. Gomaa. Software Development of Real-Time System. *Communications of the ACM*, 29(7):657–668, July 1986.

H. Gomaa. A Behavioral Analysis and Modeling Method for Real-Time Systems. In *International Workshop on Real-Time Programming WRTP'92*, pages 43–48, Bruges, Belgium, 23-26 June 1992. International Federation of Automatic Control, IFAC International Federation for Information Processing, IFIP Belgian Federation of Automatic Control, IBRA-BIRA.

R. Gotzhein. Temporal logic and applications – a tutorial. *Computer Networks and ISDN Systems, North-Holland*, 24:203–218, 1992.

D. Guaspari, C. Marceau, and W. Polak. Formal Verification of ADA Programs. *IEEE Transactions on Software Engineering*, 16(9):1058–1075, Sept. 1990.

J. Guttag. Abstract Data Types and Development of Data Structures. *Communications of the ACM*, 20(6):396–404, June 1977.

J. V. Guttag and J. J. Horning. The Algebraic Specification of Abstract Data Types. *ACTA Informatica*, 10, 1978.

J. V. Guttag, J. J. Horning, and J. M. Wing. The Larch Family of Specification Languages. *IEEE Software*, pages 24–36, Sept. 1985.

A. Hall. Seven Myths of Formal Methods. *IEEE Software*, 7(5):11–19, Sept. 1990.

D. Harel. On Visual Formalism. *Communications of the ACM*, 31(5):514–530, May 1988.

D. Harel, H. Lachover, A. Naamad, A. Pnueli, M. Politi, R. Sherman, A. S.-Trauring, and M. Trakhtenbrot. STATEMATE: A Working Environment for the Development of Complex Reactive Systems. *IEEE Transactions on Software Engineering*, 16(4):403–414, April 1990.

D. Harel, A. Pnueli, J. P. Schmidt, and R. Sherman. On the Formal Semantics of Statecharts. In *Proc. 2nd IEEE Symposium on Logic in Computer Science, Ithaca, NY, USA*, pages 54–64, 22-24 June 1987.

D. J. Hatley and I. A. Pirbhai. *Strategies for Real Time System Specification*. Dorset House Publishing, New York, 1987.

C. A. R. Hoare. Towards a Theory of Parallel Programming,. In *Operating Systems Techniques*, pages 61–71. Academic Press, NY, USA, 1972.

C. A. R. Hoare. Communicating Sequential Processes. *Communications of the ACM*, 21(8):666–677, Aug. 1978.

C. A. R. Hoare. A Calculus of Total Correctness for Communicating Processes. *Sci. Comput. Program.*, 1:49–72, 1981.

C. A. R. Hoare. *Communicating Sequential Processes*. Prentice Hall International, NY, USA, 1985.

HOOD. An Overview of the HOOD Toolset. Technical report, Software Sciences, 1988.

Y. Ishikawa, H. Tokuda, and C. W. Mercer. An Object-Oriented Real-Time Programming Language. *Computer*, pages 66–73, Oct. 1992.

M. A. Jackson. *Principle of Program Design*. Academic Press, Inc., New York, USA, 1975.

M. A. Jackson. *System Development*. Prentice Hall International, C. A. R. Hoare Series, New York, USA, 1983.

R. J. K. Jacob. A State Transition Diagram Language for Visual Programming. *Computer*, pages 51–59, Aug. 1985.

M. S. Jaffe, N. G. Leveson, M. P. E. Heimdhal, and B. E. Melhart. Software Requirements Analysis for Real-Time Process-Control Systems. *IEEE Transactions on Software Engineering*, 17(3):241–258, March 1991.

F. Jahanian and A. K.-L. Mok. Safety Analysis of Timing Properties in Real-Time Systems. *IEEE Transactions on Software Engineering*, 12(9):890–904, Sept. 1986.

S. Jahanian and D. A. Stuart. A Method for Verifying Properties of Modechart Specifications. In *Proc. of 9th IEEE Real-Time Systems Symposium*, pages 12–21, Huntsville, Ala., USA, 1988. IEEE Press.

K. Jensen. Coloured Petri nets and the Invariant-Method. *Theoret. Comput. Sci.*, 14:317–336, 1981.

K. Jensen. Coulored Petri nets. In W. Brauer, W. Resig, and G. Rozenberg, editors, *Advanced in Petri Nets 1986*. Springer Verlag, New York, USA, 1987.

C. B. Jones. *Systematic Software Development Using VDM*. Prentice Hall, 1986.

R. Koymans, R. K. Shyamasundar, W. P. deRoever, R. Gerth, and A. Arun-Kumar. Compositional Semantics for Real-Time Distributed Computing. In *Proc. of Logics of Programs Lecture Notes in Computer Sciences, LNCS 193*, New York, 1985. Springer Verlag.

L. Lamport. A Simple Approach to Specifying Concurrent Systems. *Communications of the ACM*, 32(1):32–45, Jan. 1989.

L. Lamport. Specifying concurrent program modules. *ACM Transactions on Programming Languages and Systems*, 5(2):190–222, April 1993.

K. Lano. Z++, An Object-Oriented Extension to Z. In J. E. Nicholls, editor, *Proc. of the 4th Annual Z User Meeting*, pages 151–172, Oxford, UK, 1991. Workshop in Computing, Springer Verlag.

G. T. Leavens and Y. Cheon. Preliminary Design of Larch/C++. In U. Martin and J. Wing, editors, *Proc. of First International Workshop on Larch*. Springer Verlag, Workshop in Computer Science Series, 1992.

N. Leveson and J. L. Stolzy. Safety Analysis Using Petri Nets. *IEEE Transactions on Software Engineering*, 13(3):386–397, March 1987.

S.-T. Levi and A. K. Agrawala. *Real-Time System Design*. McGraw-Hill Publishing Company, New York, USA, 1990.

B. Liskov and J. Guttag. *Abstraction Specification in Program Development*. The MIT Press, Cambridge, MS, USA, 1986.

B. Liskov, A. Snyder, R. Atkinson, and G. Schaffert. Abstraction Mechanisms in CLU. *Communications of the ACM*, 20(8):564–576, Aug. 1977.

C. L. Liu and J. W. Layland. Scheduling Algorithms for Multiprogramming in a Hard Real-Time Environment. *Journal of the ACM*, 20(1):46–61, 1973.

LOTOSPHERE. User Manual, ESPRIT Project n.2304. Technical report, consortium LOTOSPHERE, 1992.

D. Maier and D. S. Warren. *Computing with Logic*. The Benjamin/Cummings, Inc., Menlo Park, CA, USA, 1988.

D. Mandrioli. The Specification of Real-Time Systems: a Logical Object-Oriented Approach. In *Proc. of the International Conference on Technology of Object-Oriented Languages and Systems, TOOLS'92*, 1992.

D. Mandrioli. The Object-Oriented Specification of Real-Time Systems. In *Tutorial Note of the International Conference on Technology of Object-Oriented Languages and Systems, TOOLS Europe '93*, Versailles, France, 8-11 March 1993.

D. Mandrioli, S. Morasca, and A. Morzenti. Functional test case generation for real-time systems. Technical report, Politecnico di Milano, Dipartimento di Elettronica e Informazione, 91-072, Piazza Leonardo da Vinci 32, Milano, Italy, 1992.

M. A. Marsan, G. Balbo, and G. Conte. A class of generalized stochastic Petri nets. In *Proc. of Performance 83, ACM Sigmetrics*, Oct. 1983.

J. Martin and J. Odell. *Object Oriented Analysis and Design*. Prentice-Hall, Englewood Cliffs, New Jersey, USA, 1991.

G. H. Mealy. A Method for Sinthesizing Sequential Circuits. *BST Journal*, 34:1045–1079, 1955.

S. R. L. Meira and A. L. C. Cavalcanti. Modular Object Oriented Z Specifications. In J. E. Nicholls, editor, *Proc. of the 4th Annual Z User Meeting*, pages 173–192, Oxford, UK, 1991. Workshop in Computing, Springer Verlag.

P. M. Merlin and D. J. Faber. Recoverability of Communication Protocols Applications of a Theoretical Study. *IEEE Transactions on Communications*, 24, Sept. 1976.

B. Meyer. On Formalism in Specifications. *IEEE Software*, pages 6–26, Jan. 1985.

B. Meyer. *Object-Oriented Software Construction*. Prentice Hall, C. A. R. Hoare Series, New York, USA, 1988.

R. Milner. *A Calculus of Communicating Systems*. Lecture Notes in Computer Science 92, Springer Verlag, New York, 1980.

J. Misra and K. M. Chandy. Proofs of Networks of Processes. *IEEE Transactions on Software Engineering*, 7:417–426, 1981.

M. K. Molloy. Discrete Time Stochastic Petri Nets. *IEEE Transactions on Software Engineering*, 11(4):417–423, April 1985.

D. E. Monarchi and G. I. Puhr. A Research Typology for Object Oriented Analysis and Design. *Communications of the ACM*, 35(9):35–47, Sept. 1992.

A. P. Moore. The Specification and Verified Decomposition of System Requirements Using CSP. *IEEE Transactions on Software Engineering*, 16(9):932–948, Sept. 1990.

E. F. Moore. Gedanken-Experiments on Sequential Machines. In *Automata Studies, Annals of Mathematical Studies*, pages 129–153, Preston NJ, USA, 1956. Princeton Univesity Press.

T. Murata. Petri Nets: Properties, Analysis and Applications. *Proceedings of the IEEE*, 77(4):541–580, April 1989.

D. R. Musser. Abstract data type specification in the AFFIRM system. *IEEE Transactions on Software Engineering*, 6(1):24–32, Jan 1980.

O. Nierstrasz. A Survey of Object-Oriented Concepts. In W. Kim and F. H. Lochovsky, editors, *Object-Oriented Concepts Databases and Applications*, pages 3–22. Addison-Wesley Publishing Company, ACM Press, New York, USA, 1989.

NorthernTelecom. ObjecTime: Object-Oriented CASE for Real-Time Systems. Technical report, Bell-Northern Telecom, 1993.

E.-R. Olderog and C. A. R. Hoare. Specification-Oriented Semantics for Communicating Processes. In J. Diaz, editor, *Automata, Language and Programming, Proc. of 10th Colloquium*, pages 561–572, Barcelona, Spain, July 1983. Springer Verlag, Lecture Notes in Computer Sciences, LNCS 154.

E. R. Olderog and C. A. R. Hoare. Specification Oriented Semantics for Communicating Sequential Process. *ACTA Informatica*, 23:9–66, 1986.

J. S. Ostroff. *Temporal Logic for Real-Time Systems*. Research Studies Press LTD., Advanced Software Development Series, 1, Taunton, Somerset, England, 1989.

J. S. Ostroff and W. Wonham. Modeling and Verifying Real-Time Embedded Computer Systems. In *Proc. IEEE Real-Time Systems Symp.*, pages 124–132. IEEE Computer Society Press, Dec. 1987.

J. L. Peterson. *Petri Net Theory and the Modeling of Systems*. Engelwood Cliffs, Prentice-Hall, NJ, 1981.

C. Petri. Kommunikation mit atomation. Technical report, Ph.D. Thesis, Schriften des Reinsh-Westfalischen Inst. Fur Instrumentelle Mathematik an der Universitat Bonn, Bonn, West Germany, 1962.

P. Pulli, R. Elmstrom, G. Leon, and J. A. delaPuente. IPTES – Incremental Prototyping Technology for Embedded real-time Systems. In *Proc. of 1991 ESPRIT Conference*, 1991.

C. Ramachandani. Analysis of asynchronous concurrent systems by timed Petri nets. Technical report, Massachusetts Inst. Technol. Project MAC, TR. 120, USA, Feb. 1974.

C. V. Ramamoorthy and G. S. Ho. Performance evaluation of asynchronous concurrent systems using Petri nets. *IEEE Transactions on Software Engineering*, 6(5), Sept. 1980.

R. R. Razouk and M. M. Gorlick. A Real-Time Interval Logic for Reasoning About Execution of Real-Time Programs. In *Proc. of ACM/SIGSOFT'89 (TAV3)*. ACM Press, Dec. 1989.

G. Reed and A. Roscoe. A Timed Model for Communicating Sequential Processes. In *Proc. ICALP'86*, pages 314–323. Springer Verlag, Lecture Notes in Computer Sciences, LNCS 226, 1986.

W. Reisig. *Petri Nets. An introduction*. EATCS Monographs on Theoretical Computer Science, Springer Verlag, New York, 1985.

D. Richardson, S. L. Aha, and T. O. O'Malley. Specification-based Test Oracles for Reactive Systems. In *Proc. of 14th International Conference on Software Engineering*, pages 105–118, Melbourne, Australia, 11-15 May 1992. IEEE press, ACM.

A. Rockstrom and R. Saracco. SDL – CCITT Specification and Description language. *IEEE Transactions on Communications*, 30(6):1310–1318, June 1982.

D. T. Ross and K. E. Schoman. Structured Analysis for Requirements Definition. *IEEE Transactions on Software Engineering*, 3(1):6–15, Jan. 1977.

J. Rumbaugh, M. Blaha, W. Premerlani, F. Eddy, and W. Lorensen. *Object-Oriented Modeling and Design*. Prentice Hall International, Englewood Cliffs, New Jersey, 1991.

B. Sanden. The Case for Eclectic Design of Real-Time Software. *IEEE Transaction on Software Engineering*, 35(3):360–363, March 1989a.

B. Sanden. Entity-Life Modeling and Structured Analysis in Real-Time Software Design — A Comparison. *Communications of the ACM*, 32(12):1458–1466, Dec. 1989b.

B. Sanden. An Entity-Life Modeling Approach to the Design of Concurrent Software. *Communications of the ACM*, 32(3):330–343, March 1989c.

R. Sarraco and P. A. J. Tilanus. CCITT SDL: Overview of the Language and its Applications. *Computer Networks and ISDN Systems*, 13(2):65–74, 1987.

P. A. Scheffer, A. H. StoneIII, and W. E. Rzepka. A Case Study of SREM. *Computer*, pages 47–54, April 1985.

R. L. Schwartz and P. M. Melliar-Smith. From State Machines to Temporal Logic: Specification Methods for Protocol Standards. *IEEE Transactions on Communications*, 30(12):2486–2496, Dec. 1982.

B. Selic. An Efficient Object-Oriented Variation of Statecharts Formalism for Distributed Real-Time Systems. In *Submitted to CHDL'93: IFIP Conference on Hardware Description language and Their Applications*, Ottawa, Canada, 26-28 April 1993.

B. Selic, G. Gullekson J. McGee, and I. Engelberg. ROOM: An Object-Oriented Methodology for Developing Real-Time Systems. In *Proc. of 5th International Workshop on Computer-Aided Software Engineering, CASE'92*, Montreal, Quebec, Canada, 6-10 July 1992.

L. Sha and J. B. Goodenough. Real time Scheduling Theory and Ada. *Computer*, pages 53–62, April 1990.

A. C. Shaw. Communicating Real-Time State Machines. *IEEE Transactions on Software Engineering*, 18(9):805–816, Sept. 1992.

S. Shlaer and S. J. Mellor. *Object Oriented Analysis: Modeling the World in Data*. Prentice Hall, Englewood Cliffs, New Jersey, USA, 1988.

S. Shlaer and S. J. Mellor. *Object Life Cycles: Modeling the World in States*. Prentice Hall, Englewood Cliffs, New Jersey, USA, 1991.

J. Sifakis. *Automatic Verification Methods for Finite State Systems, Proc. of the International Workshop Grenoble, France, June 12-14*. Springer Verlag, Lecture Notes in Computer Science, LNCS n.407, 1989.

J. M. Spivey. *The Z Notation – a Reference manual*. Prentice-Hall, New York, 1988.

J. A. Stankovic. Misconceptions About Real-Time Computing: A Serious Problem for Next-Generation Systems. *IEEE Computer*, pages 10–19, Oct. 1988.

J. A. Stankovic and K. Ramamritham. *Advances in Real-Time Systems*. IEEE Computer Society Press, Washington, 1992.

STATEMATE. STATEMATE: The Languages of Statemate. Technical report, i-Logic, Inc., 22 Third Avenue, Burlington, Mass. 01803, USA, 1987.

A. D. Stoyenko. The Evolution and State-of-the-Art of Real-Time Languages. *Journal of Systems and Software*, pages 61–84, April 1992.

StP. Software through Pictures: Products and Services Overview. Technical report, Interactive Development Environment, 1991.

Bernard A. Sufrin. Formal Methods and the Design of Effective User Interfaces. In M.D. Harrison and A.F. Monk, editors, *People and Computers: Designing for Usability*. Cambridge University Press, UK, 1986.

C. A. Sunshine, D. H. Thompson, R. W. Erickson, S. L. Gerhart, and D. Schwabe. Specification and Verification of Communication Protocols in AFFIRM Using State Transition Models. *IEEE Transactions on Software Engineering*, 8(5):460–489, Sept. 1982.

C. P. Svoboda. Structured Analysis. In H.Thayer and M.Dorfman, editors, *System and Software Requirements Engineering*, pages 218–237. IEEE Compute Society Press, Los Alamitos CA, 1990.

B. Taylor. A Method for Expressing the Functional Requirements of Real-Time Systems. In *Proc. of 9th IFAC/IFIP Conference of Real-Time Programming*, pages 111–120. New-York: Pergamon, 1980.

Teamwork. User Manuals, Ver. 4.0. Technical report, Teamwork Division of CADRE, Providence, R.I., USA, 1992.

H. Thayer and M. Dorfman. *System and Software Requirements Engineering*. IEEE Compute Society Press, Los Alamitos CA, 1990.

H. Tokuda, T. Nakajima, and P. Rao. Real-Time Mach: Towards a Predictable Real-Time System. In *Proc. Usenix Mach Workshop*, pages 1–10, Oct. 1990.

I. J. Walker. Requirements of an Object-Oriented Design Method. *Software Engineering Journal*, pages 102–113, March 1992.

P. T. Ward. The Transformation Schema: An Extension of the Data Flow Diagram to Represent Control and Timing. *IEEE Transactions on Software Engineering*, 12(2):198–210, Feb. 1986.

P. T. Ward and S. J. Mellor. *Structured Development for Real-time Systems*. Prentice Hall, Englewood Cliffs, NJ, USA, 1985.

R. R. Willson and B. H. Krogh. Petri Net Tool for the Specification and Analysis of Discrete Controllers. *IEEE Transactions on Software Engineering*, 16(1):39–50, Jan. 1990.

J. M. Wing. Writing Larch Interface language Specifications. *ACM Transactions on Programming Languages and Systems*, 9(1):1–24, Jan. 1987.

J. M. Wing. A Specifier's Introduction for Formal Methods. *Computer*, pages 8–24, Sept. 1990a.

J. M. Wing. Using Larch to Specify Avalon/C++ Objects. *IEEE Transactions on Software Engineering*, 16(9):1076–1088, Sept. 1990b.

R. J. Wirfs-Brock, B. Wilkerson, and L. Winer. *Designing Object Oriented Software*. Prentice Hall, Englewood Cliffs, N.J., USA, 1990.

R. Wirsf-Brock and B. Wilkerson. Object-Oriented Design: a responsibility-driven approach. In *Proc. OOPSLA'89*, pages 71–75, New Orleans, Louisiana,, Oct. 1989. SIGPLAN NOT, ACM Press.

E. Yourdon and L. L. Constantine. *Structured Design: Fundamentals of a Discipline of Computer Program and Systems Design*. Prentice-Hall, Englewood Cliffs, New Jersey, USA, 1979.

P. Zave. An Operational Approach to Requirements Specification for Embedded Systems. *IEEE Transactions on Software Engineering*, 8(3):250–269, May 1982.

P. Zave. The Operational Versus the Conventional Approach to Software Development. *Communications of the ACM*, 27(2):104–118, Feb. 1984.

P. Zave. A Comparison of the Mayor Approaches to Software Specification and Design. In H.Thayer and M.Dorfman, editors, *System and Software Requirements Engineering*, pages 197–199. IEEE Compute Society Press, Los Alamitos CA, 1990.

P. Zave and W. Schell. Salient Features of an Executable Specification Language and Its Environment. *IEEE Transactions on Software Engineering*, 12(2):312–325, Feb. 1986.

The Highs and Lows of Change Control

James Bach, SmartPatents

Change control. For me, this vital issue in software project management immediately conjures the image of the famous 1984 Macintosh commercial. Remember that one? Gray drudges standing row upon row, staring with numb compliance at a lecturing bureaucrat, set free by a hero who bursts in and hurls a hammer that breaks the spell of Big Bad Brother.

This image depicts my personal struggle with the problem of managing improvements to a product. Although my temperament is that of hammer-throwing hero, my role as quality assurance guy is more like lecturing bureaucrat. Part of me wants to open the flood gates to improvements and better ideas; the other part wants to protect the existing quality of the product by limiting change.

CHANGE CONTROL

Change control is vital. But the forces that make it necessary also make it annoying. We worry about change because a tiny perturbation in the code can create a big failure in the product. But it can also fix a big failure or enable wonderful new capabilities. We worry about change because a single rogue developer could sink the project; yet brilliant ideas also originate in the minds of

Editor: James Bach, SmartPatents, 1975 Landings Dr., Mountain View, CA 94043; j.bach@computer.org

Change control is vital. But the forces that make it necessary also make it annoying.

those rogues, and a burdensome change-control process could effectively discourage them from doing creative work.

My ambivalence about this issue is only deepened by the fact that change-control processes are easily corrupted. Change control means risk analysis, and there's no easy or certain way to do that. Coupled with the amazing capacity we humans have for oversimplifying the complex, change control can become mindless resistance to change and an automatic rejection of all risk, regardless of potential reward.

Or, just as easily, change control may degenerate into a set of empty rituals that allow any change to be made as long as the rituals are honored. Such a process is less a practical device than a sort of gargoyle meant to scare evil spirits or impress clients. Midway between allowing nothing or everything, change control may also become a political filter where change is resisted unless you're in with the in-crowd, regardless of the situation's merits.

At SmartPatents, change control processes are (at least officially) my responsibility. How can I avoid the role of bureaucrat, gargoyle, or political pollster? How can I help the process work *well*? Let me describe the process we've arrived at, then decide for yourself if I deserve the hammer treatment.

PROBLEM AND PROCESS

The only legitimate purpose of defined process is to solve problems. So let's start there. What problem do we have?

SmartPatents is a market-driven software company, not a contract-driven one. We aren't regulated either. We don't need to justify ourselves to an outside client or agency. Our need for change control comes mainly from our desire to minimize the chance that a major problem will be introduced into the product while we're trying to improve it, especially late in the cycle. We want to minimize expensive and time-consuming regression testing. We also want to assure that the change process respects the concerns of each team member who may be impacted by a particular change. At the same time, our process must be flexible enough to let us add product functionality late in the development cycle, because that's how market-driven software companies compete.

When I joined the company last October, it had three change-management processes in place:

- We stored all source code in a source control system.
- we compiled and linked the product according to an official build process executed on a dedicated build machine; and
- we put the project under *code freeze* in the last few weeks of development.

Code freeze doesn't mean that code stops changing. It means that we impose a formal code-change protocol. Originally, following protocol meant that Gordon, our senior tester, had to grant a waiver for each change. Being an easygoing fellow, Gordon waived virtually everything. Since he knew about each change, he theoreti-

Reprinted from IEEE Computer, Vol. 31, No. 8, Aug. 1998, pp. 113-115.

August 1998   113

cally had some inkling of what needed to be retested for each new build.

This protocol was administered through a communal spreadsheet. Anyone requesting a change was supposed to enter the request as a single line in the sheet. Gordon reviewed the spreadsheet periodically and granted waivers. However, if someone, for whatever reason, made a change without going through the spreadsheet, Gordon would never know.

Many waivers were granted in the hallway, off the record. So the process got pretty sloppy. I don't mean people behaved badly or actively subverted the process. The process became sloppy because it was not designed to fit the way technical people work. People get distracted, forget details, and make decisions on the fly, often in hallways. Any robust method of change control must take this into account.

REDUCING THE RISK

To reduce the risk of a dangerous change, I wanted a more visible, reliable process. So we retired the old spreadsheet and installed a bug-tracking system to manage change requests. (A bug report at SmartPatents can be a change request, problem report, or other task assignment that may involve code changes.) For each code change after a code freeze, we required developers to place a check-in comment in the bug database with the change request's ID number. Prior to each build, a QA engineer examines the check-in comments and verifies that each code change corresponds to a waived bug in the database.

This process is a system for tracing code changes back to change requests and approvals. Barring intentional subversion, the system is theoretically airtight. Hallway waivers can slip through the cracks, and developers can still forget to follow the process. However, when that happens, the prebuild comment check detects the problem, and the build stops until each rogue change is justified and documented. This feedback loop allows the process to tolerate human error while gently discouraging it.

For this process to be more than an empty ritual, however, it needs a brain. How do we decide which changes to

approve? We do that mainly via the *waiver meeting*, a systematic, daily review of the bug list by representatives of each major project function: marketing, support, documentation, development, and QA. In this meeting we decide whether to allow a change or postpone it to the next project release. Decisions are made by unanimous consent.

Since December 1997, this has been our official process for change control after code freeze.

> **It is important that change control not become either mindless resistance to change or a set of empty rituals for permitting change.**

Now, any wizened veteran of software process improvement who heard a story like this—perhaps over coffee during a morning break at a software quality conference—might well nod sagely and have another muffin. But behind the pastry, he'd probably wonder: "What part of James' story is real, and what part is fantasy? How does he know that his process is worth following? What are its problems and liabilities?"

HURLING THE HAMMER

Reality versus fantasy? Problems and liabilities? Sit down, this will take a while. There are a lot of problems with this approach. We've had to make a number of changes to our change-control protocol in order to make it more efficient and effective. I'm still not satisfied with it. If I call it a best practice, that's only because I haven't yet become aware of a better one.

Jerry Weinberg once quipped, "We don't manage projects, we manage stories about projects." My change-control story is a simplification of what we actually do, so here are some additional details to give you a better feel for our situation and the struggles we're having.

- It seems that every other waiver meeting is cancelled or postponed. Sometimes I feel too tired or harried to run them. Daily meetings wear everybody down, but

I haven't yet thought of an effective alternative. If we don't grant waivers frequently, we hinder product improvement. Perhaps we are freezing code too soon and staying frozen too long.

- We go through periods where we're so busy that we neglect the prebuild comment check. The truth is, I'm not always very motivated to do it. We've had such good compliance to the protocol that I no longer expect to see unauthorized changes.
- What looks like good compliance to the protocol may actually be the unauthorized reuse of old waivers on new changes. I only have a developer's word that a particular change is genuinely related to the grant of a particular waiver. Even if a developer is absolutely honest, there is a lot of room for creative interpretation.
- Each waiver meeting is designed to handle many issues. We hunch around a monitor and discuss each problem until we reach a consensus. The group gets impatient if a discussion about an item goes more than a few minutes. Since we typically handle 15 to 20 problems per hour, and we never let any single meeting go more than 90 minutes, the pressure is on. I don't think that pressure creates a good environment for carefully considering each issue.
- Sometimes we encounter a problem that requires a detailed explanation and analysis by an expert who is not normally in the waiver meeting. The meeting is then disrupted while someone searches for that expert.
- We often have to hold the waiver meeting without an ideal set of participants. The minimum quorum is one person from QA and one development lead. This allows the meeting to go forward but increases the risk of a poor decision or an unpleasant surprise to support people or technical writers.
- Sometimes the developers are confused about what a waiver means. A waiver is always permission—but usually not a recommendation—to make a change. We rely on the judgment of each developer to determine which changes are too risky. (And what does "risky" mean? Its definition varies with the situation and the developer involved.)
- We rarely check that waived problems are actually being properly resolved. It's

possible for a waived problem to sit on a developer's plate for days (for example, if a developer forgets to check the tracking system) or to be resolved in an unacceptable way. We have occasionally been forced to postpone important changes just because an earlier decision to make the change was not noticed in time.

• Gordon and I still sometimes grant waivers outside of the waiver meeting. Since doing so bypasses the meeting, we try to grant hallway waivers only on noncontroversial matters. But sometimes we're wrong.

• What if a single waiver relates to the work of several developers? There is no easy way to handle that case within our system. It's possible for a problem to bounce around among several developers, none of whom takes full responsibility for it.

• What happens to changes that are mandated by a code review? To cooperate with our change protocol, developers must reduce each issue resulting from a code review to a change request. But the resulting paperwork has discouraged developers from holding code reviews after code freeze.

• Some problems in our system are chronically kicked forward from release to release, and are never resolved. We call these problems *bow wave bugs* because they keep getting driven ahead like dolphins riding the bow wave of a big ship. A bow wave situation develops when a problem is too hard or risky to fix during code freeze of the current release, but not quite important enough to make it into the next release's project plan.

SMACK!

We have refined the code freeze protocol in a number of ways to respond to these experiences and problems. In one case, the project lead proposed and implemented a special change-control board to consider changes that are too complex for waiver meetings. The CCB, as we call it, has the same membership as the waiver meeting, but instead of being held every day to consider a series of issues, it's held at the discretion of a project lead to consider a single issue. The CCB gives us a systematic way to have deeper conversations about changes.

I feel good about our continuing refinement of this process, but I wonder about something that may be a tragic flaw in this grand design. Perhaps you've already spotted it: Our change-control process may indeed work too well.

Good risk management late in the project does indeed compensate for problems with poor requirements analysis and design early in the project. However, if we believe we can clean anything up in the end, we don't have much incentive to learn better problem-prevention methods. Rather, we may feel an incentive to be even more reckless with our early design and coding, in the interests of pumping more features into the product.

In other words, my company may be addicted to change control. And each improvement in change control may deepen that addiction.

I experienced this sort of thing when I worked at Borland, where I first encountered the waiver meeting process, which we called *the bug council*. At first we administered the meeting by writing each approved change on a big whiteboard, which could hold only about 200 changes. As we reached that number we'd begin to murmur and moan about how there were too many changes coming through. Two hundred items on a whiteboard look intimidating. We'd start asking basic questions about the quality of our schedules and processes. When we "improved" the way we managed the meeting by putting the change requests and waivers online, a curious thing happened: We no longer worried about having 200 change requests, or even 2,000. Without the visibility of the whiteboard, we became numb to the psychological impact of all those change requests.

W e have to control our changes. We try to do it well. Yet, unless we keep our eyes and minds wide open to the dynamics of the situation, our tactical success will ensure our strategic failure. Oh, my head hurts to think about it, but that's how it is in the nonlinear world of software processes. Be warned ye bureaucrats. Just when you get all your drudges in a row, reality bursts in and breaks the spell. ❖

CHALLENGES

Many of the technological and ethical problems that remain unresolved in existing smart-card systems are no less prominent in future systems. On the technical side, wireless-network ubiquity, communication channel bandwidth, support for mobility, server interoperability, user authentication, encryption, and system robustness are just a few of the challenges.

Challenges also arise because of the system's ability to collect sensitive and personal user data. Since a highly mobile system like the Smart Badge is more vulnerable to misuse than a stationary system, abuse of such data and user privacy become major ethical issues. To address these concerns, it will be necessary (on the technical side) to provide user authentication, anonymous transactions, and secure tunneling.

Other challenges include design tradeoffs between power, latency, and cost. Sensors and untethered communication increase the power consumption of devices. System latency also becomes a concern if it impedes the application. Finally, any system design must address cost. How will we build these systems, and who will pay for them? Some applications may need more than one service from different providers. How will service, transport, and client providers share revenue?

F uture smart-card and Smart Badge systems represent a large investment in integrated engineering, but the investment can pay off by creating new business opportunities. These systems consume a wide variety of revenue-generating services and promote emerging technologies like wireless networks and biometrics. By conforming to user expectations and thus being easy to use, these systems could potentially attract a large user base and eventually change the way people and technology interact in daily life. ❖

Mark T. Smith is a project manager in the Visual Computing Department at Hewlett-Packard Laboratories, Palo Alto, Calif. Contact him at msmith@ hpl.hp.com.

Capers Jones, Software Productivity Research Inc., 1 New England Executive Park Burlington, MA 01803-5005; phone (617) 273-0140; fax (617) 273-5176; Internet capers@spr.com; CompuServe 75430,231

Software change management

Capers Jones
Software Productivity Research

Software projects change rapidly, which makes efficient change management a major challenge for the software industry. This challenge was poorly met for years because of rudimentary tools. Source code changes, for example, were managed with stand-alone, file-based version control systems. Other changes—in text specification and planning documents, cost estimates, test libraries, graphics and illustrations, and bug inventories—were managed with limited tools that rarely communicated across domains.

It has been recognized since at least 1990 that for many projects, source code isn't the only deliverable that changes. Frequently, the number of words created to deal with a software project significantly exceed the size of the source code, and the words change more rapidly. Bug reports, for example, undergo constant change during software development and maintenance as bugs are reported, tested, fixed, and documented.

Modern change management, or configuration control, tools must encompass changes affecting every kind of software deliverable and artifact: requirements, project plans, project cost estimates, contracts, design, source code, user documents, illustrations and graphics, test materials, and bug reports. Ideally, these tools would use hypertext to handle cross-references among deliverables so that when something changes, corresponding material is modified appropriately.

> **M**odern change management or configuration control, tools must encompass changes affecting every kind of software deliverable and artifact

The cost of changes

Besides acquiring new tools to deal with change, the software world has learned to understand the economics of change. Traditionally, software costs were normalized with the lines-of-code (LOC) metric, which was useless when dealing with the production costs of noncode software artifacts such as text materials, graphics, and test cases. As a result, noncode material's development and modification costs were essentially invisible.

In 1978, IBM's Allan J. Albrecht developed the function-point metric. Function points are synthetic metrics derived from the weighted sum of software projects' external attributes—inputs, outputs, logical files, inquiries, and interfaces. The function-point metric can be applied to source code as well as software plans, estimates, specifications, and test materials, for example. Consequently, this metric has helped enormously in understanding the economic impact of change to all software artifacts.

To assess the rate at which software deliverables change, we need to know roughly how big the deliverables are under normal conditions. With that baseline knowledge, the function-point metric can then be applied to normalize deliverables.

With the function-point metric, fairly accurate costs and values can be assigned to changes. Outsource vendors, for example, are beginning to include "cost per function point" in contracts and to include sliding scales so that features added late in the development phase cost more than function points derived during the requirements phase.

A hypothetical software project

Table 1 shows the nominal sizes associated with a generic systems software project, programmed in C, of 1,000 function points.

It typically takes 18 months, from specification to customer delivery, to develop a systems software application of 1,000 function points. The overall production effort would total about 200 person months, with a productivity rate of five function points per month. Assuming an average burdened salary rate of $6,000 per month, the total cost would be $12,000,000, and the cost per function point would be $1,200.

Volume of noncode deliverables

Most software deliverables are actually noncode material like text and graphics. Table 2 shows the major paper deliverables associated with software and their approximate volumes. Many other ephemeral documents are produced, such as letters, memos, presentations, and progress reports. Large software projects can result in as many as 50 kinds of paper documents. These ephemeral documents may not come under configuration control, however, while the basic specifications, contracts, plans, estimates, and user documents usually do.

Because the source code in our example amounts to 125,000 logical statements, it's clear that more than 184 English words are generated for every source code statement. (A comparable military project would generate more than 400 words per source code statement.)

Noncode deliverables such as graphics and illustrations are more difficult to quantify than text and vary widely. As graphics production tools improve and become more read-

Reprinted from *IEEE Computer*, Vol. 29, No. 2, Feb. 1996, pp. 80-82.

Table 1. Average deliverable sizes for a system software project of 1,000 function points

Deliverable	Size per function point	Basic size	Monthly change rate
Requirements	0.3 pages	300 pages	2%
Plans/estimates	0.2 pages	200 pages	10%
Design	1.5 pages	1,500 pages	5%
Source code	125.0 lines of code	125,000 lines of code	7%
Test cases	5.0 test cases	5,000 cases	10%
User manuals	0.6 pages	600 pages	5%
Defects (bug reports)	5.0 bugs	5,000 reports	15%

Table 2. Volume of text and words produced for a generic system software project of 1,000 function points

Deliverable	Basic size in pages	English words	English words per function point
Requirements	300	120,000	120
Plans/estimates	100	40,000	40
Design	1,500	600,000	400
User manuals	500	240,000	240
Bug reports	5,000	1,350,000	1,350
Total	7,500	2,350,000	2,150

Table 3. Volume of graphic illustrations produced for a generic system software project of 1,000 function points.

Deliverable	Basic size in pages	Number of graphics	Graphics per function point
Requirements	300	100	0.10
Plans/estimates	100	50	0.05
Design	1,500	600	0.60
User manuals	600	300	0.30
Total	2,500	1,050	1.05

ily available, we can expect that significantly more graphics will be created to support software, and they will have to be managed. Table 3 shows the amount of graphical materials that might be produced for our example.

Even in 1996, graphics and illustrations are troublesome for configuration control. They will only become more difficult when dynamic or animated models, simulations, and multimedia approaches for software become common.

Rates of changing requirements

Managing requirements changes is essential, because "creeping requirements" affect all downstream deliverables. Moreover, requirements changes become progressively more problematical after the requirements phase has been completed. During the design phase, the average rate of requirements change can exceed 3 percent per month. This burst of rapid change might last a year for large software systems but only three months on our sample project. The burst of new requirements slows to about 1 percent per month during coding and eventually stops when testing begins. (Requirements changes don't really stop, of course, but the requirements tend to get pushed downstream into follow-on releases.)

For systems software, such as our example, and for commercial software, changes may be due to market needs or pressure from competitive products. The average rate is 2 percent per month from the end of initial requirements until start of testing. If a competitor suddenly announced a new product, however, monthly change rates could exceed 15 percent.

> Managing requirements changes is essential, because "creeping requirements" affect all down stream deliverables

142

Table 4. US averages for software defects and defect removal efficiency (data expressed in terms of defects per function point)

Defect origin	Direct Potentials	Removal efficiency	Delivered defects
Requirements	1.00	77%	0.23
Design	1.25	85%	0.19
Coding	1.75	95%	0.09
Document	0.60	80%	0.12
Bad fixes	0.40	70%	0.12
Total	5.00	82%	0.75

For a company's internal software, requirements changes are driven by user needs and average 1 percent per month from the start of design until well into coding. For military software, the average is 2 percent per month.

Military software requirements call for strict "requirements traceability," which means that downstream deliverables must explicitly identify the requirements they include. This implies, ideally, that software requirements would include hypertext links to other downstream software artifacts.

Costs of changing requirements

Software outsourcers and contractors can now derive the function-point totals of software during the requirements phase, which means that downstream costs of changing requirements can be quantified.

Since cost per function point is now used to price software features, tools such as Function Point Workbench that can assign function-point totals to various application features are increasingly important business tools. These tools are currently standalone, but eventually direct links will be developed so that changes in requirements or design automatically trigger new size and cost estimates. For example, assume that our sample project were performed as a contract development effort. The contract might include items like the following:

- Development costs for requirements derived during months 1 to 3 or the requirements phase of project = $1,500 per function point.
- Development costs for new requirements added during months 4 through 6 = $1,750 per function point.
- Costs for requirements deleted during months 4 through 6 = $150 per function point.
- Development costs for new requirements added during months 6 to 12 = $2,250 per function point.
- Costs for requirements deleted during months 6 through 12 = $500 per function point.
- Development costs for new requirements added during months 12 to 18 = $5,000 per function point.
- Costs for requirements deleted during months 12 to 18 = $1,000 per function point.

> **D**efect tracking is vital to software change management. Defect tracking spans the entire life cycle of a software project: 20 years or more in some cases

As a contractual metric, cost per function point (rather than the primitive LOC) helps everyone understand software economics better—clients, accountants, project managers, contract officers, and attorneys. As a matter of fact, the Internal Revenue Service is even exploring cost per function point to determine software's taxable value.

Bugs are expensive

Normally, many bugs (defects) are inadvertently created during the intellectually rigorous tasks of software development and maintenance, although many are also found and eliminated during these tasks. Defect removal is the most expensive cost component of software, and the information volume associated with software bugs is the largest of any software artifact. Because of this situation, it's mandatory that configuration control tools have powerful capabilities to track and report defects.

Naturally, noncode materials have their share of bugs, too. Table 4 shows US national averages for software defects and the percentages of defect removed prior to initial deployment.

Assuming that our hypothetical project is average, about 1,000 errors would be found in requirements; 1,250 in design; 1,750 in the source code; and 600 in the user manuals. Another 400 bugs would be secondary errors or "bad fixes" introduced when a bug repair itself contained a new error. Roughly 5,000 bugs, then, would have to be found and eliminated in this average project.

Defect tracking is crucial

Because of the costs and importance of quality control, it's clear that defect tracking is vital to software change management. Defect tracking spans the entire life cycle of a software project: 20 years or more in some cases.

Change management is one of the most important aspects of successful software development. Evidence of this fact are the new companies building integrated change management tools that handle much more than source code revisions. Certainly, function-point metrics, which quantify the costs of change with a previously impossible precision, are partly behind the emergence of these companies.

The nature of software change may not yet be fully understood, but progress is steady and ongoing. Incorporating the costs of change in contracts is a solid start.

Chapter 4

REUSE AND REENGINEERING

Due to its increasing importance from engineering and an economic standpoint, software reuse and reengineering needed to be covered in depth. Because of the rich diversity of viewpoints (both pro and con) there are more than a few papers in this section. These papers cover research directions (e.g. the papers by Mili et al) and the more practical side (e.g. Jacobson et al and Myers).

The approaches to reuse vary widely, but the objectives are always the same—cost savings, reliability, and flexibility.

Finally, the paper by Chikofsky et al provides an excellent overview of the various types of reengineering that are encountered by the software project manager.

Identifying and Qualifying Reusable Software Components

Gianluigi Caldiera and Victor R. Basili

University of Maryland

Effective reuse of knowledge, processes, and products from previous software developments can increase productivity and quality in software projects by an order of magnitude. In fact, software production using reusable components will probably be crucial to the software industry's evolution to higher levels of maturity.

Software reuse is not new. McIlroy[1] proposed using modular software units in 1969, and reuse has been behind many software developments. However, the method has never acquired real momentum in industrial environments and software projects, despite its informal presence there.

The first problem we encounter in reusing software arises from the nature of the object to be reused. The concept is simple — use the same object more than once. But with software it is difficult to define what an object is apart from its context.[2] We have programs, parts of programs, specifications, requirements, architectures, test cases, and plans, all related to each other. The reuse of each software object implies the concurrent reuse of the objects associated with it, and informal information traveling with the objects. Thus, we must reuse more than code. Software objects and their relationships incorporate a large amount of experience from past development. We need to reuse this experience in the production of new software. The experience makes it possible to reuse software objects.[3]

A second major problem in code reuse is the lack of a set of reusable components,

---

Software metrics provide a way to automate the extraction of reusable software components from existing systems, reducing the amount of code that experts must analyze.

---

despite the large amount of software that already exists in the portfolios of many software producers. Reuse efficiency and cost effectiveness require a large catalog of available reusable objects.

In this article, we outline a way to reuse development experience along with the software objects it produces. Then, we focus on a problem in the development of a catalog of reusable components: how to analyze existing components and identify ones suitable for reuse. After they are identified, the parts could be extracted, packaged in a way appropriate for reuse, and stored in a component repository. This catalog of heterogeneous objects would

have to be designed for efficient retrieval of individual components, but that topic is beyond our scope.

Our model for reusing software components splits the traditional life-cycle models into two parts: one part, the project, delivers software systems, while the other part, the factory, supplies reusable software objects to the project. The factory's primary concerns are the extraction and packaging of reusable components, but it must, of course, work with a detailed knowledge of the application domain from which a component is extracted.

Our approach to identification and qualification of reusable software is based on software models and metrics. Because software metrics take into account the large volume of source code that must be analyzed to find reusable parts, they provide a way to automate the first steps of the analysis. Besides, models and metrics permit feedback and improvement to make the extraction process fit a variety of environments.

The extracted candidates are analyzed more carefully in the context of the semantics of the source application in a process we call "qualification."

In this article, we describe some case studies to validate our experimental approach. They deal with only the identification phase and use a very simple model of a reusable code component, but our results show that automated techniques can reduce the amount of code that a domain expert needs to evaluate to identify reusable parts.

February 1991

0018-9162/91/0200-0061$01.00 © 1991 IEEE

61

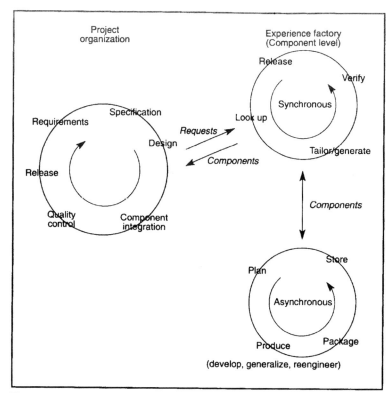

Figure 1. The reuse process model.

Reuse framework and organization

In many software engineering projects, reuse is as common as in everyday life: It is an informal sharing of techniques and products among people working on the same or similar projects. Transforming informal reuse concepts into a technology of reuse would provide the basis for the future software factory, improving quality and increasing productivity, as well as making production more manageable. To achieve higher levels of reuse, we must recognize the experience appropriate for reuse, package experience in a readily available way, and formally integrate reuse into software development.

Currently, all reuse occurs in the project development, where reuse is difficult because a project's focus is system delivery. Packaging reusable experience is at best a secondary concern. Besides, project personnel cannot recognize the pieces of experience appropriate for other projects.

Existing process models, which tend to be rigidly deterministic, are not defined to take advantage of reuse, much less to create reusable experience. To create packaged experience and then reuse it, multiple process models are necessary.

Figure 1 shows an organizational framework that separates project-specific activities from the reuse-packaging activities, with process models that support each activity.[4] The framework defines two separate organizations: a project organization and an experience factory.

The project organization develops the product, taking advantage of all forms of packaged experience from prior and current developments. In turn, the project offers its own experiences to be packaged for other projects. The experience factory recognizes potentially reusable experience and packages it so it is easy for the project organization to use.

Within the experience factory, an organization we call the component factory develops and packages software components. It supplies code components to the project upon demand, and creates and maintains a repository of components for future use. As a subdivision of the experience factory, the experience that the component factory manipulates is programming and application experience as embodied in programs and their documentation. Because the experience factory gathers all kinds of experience from the project, the component factory understands the project context and can deliver components that fit.

The project organization performs activities specific to implementation of the system to which it is dedicated. It analyzes the requirements and produces the specifications and the high-level system design. Its process models are like those used by today's software engineering projects (for instance, it may use the waterfall model or iterative enhancement model). Software engineers generate specifications from requirements and design a system to satisfy those requirements. However, when the engineers have identified the system components, usually after the so-called preliminary design, they request components from the component factory and integrate them into the programs and the system they have designed. The project organization engineers may also request a list of components that satisfy a given specification. Then, from several design options, they can choose the one for which more reusable components are already available.

After component integration, the project organization process model continues as usual with product quality control (system test, reliability analysis) and release.

The component factory's process model is twofold:[3] it satisfies requests for components coming from the project organization, but it also prepares itself for answering those requests. This mix of synchronous and asynchronous activities is typical of the process model of the experience factory in general.[4]

Synchronous activity. When the component factory receives a request from the project organization, it searches its catalog of components to find a software component that satisfies that request with or without tailoring. Two kinds of tailoring can be applied to a software component: instantiation and modification. To an extent, the component's designer has anticipated instantiation by associating with the component some parameters to make it suit different contexts. A generic unit in Ada is an example of such a parametric component and of the instantiation process. Modification is an unanticipated tailoring process in which statements are changed, added, or deleted to adapt the component to a request.

If no component that approximates the

request can be found in the catalog of the available components or if the necessary modification is too expensive, the component factory develops the requested component from scratch or generates it from more elementary components. After verification, the component is released to the project organization that requested it.

Asynchronous activity. The component factory's ability to efficiently answer requests from the project organization is critical for the successful application of the reuse technology. Therefore, the factory's catalog must contain enough components to reduce the chances that the factory will have to develop a component from scratch. Moreover, looking up components must be easy. This is why the component factory's process model has an asynchronous part.

To produce some software components without specific requests from the project organization, the component factory develops a component production plan — it extracts reusable components from existing systems or generalizes components previously produced on request from the project organization. The Booch components[5] are an example of a component production plan: The most common data structures and the main operations on them have been implemented as Ada packages.

A component factory can develop an application-oriented component production plan by analyzing an application domain to identify the most common functions. Then it can implement these functions into reusable components to be used by the developers. Or the factory can generalize a preexisting component into a new one by adding more functionality or parameterizing it.

To ensure that the generated components are well packaged and easily retrieved, a process called component qualification provides components with functional specifications and test cases, and classifies them according to a component taxonomy.[6] Software components are then stored in a repository.

Extracting components

In the short term, developing reusable components is generally more expensive than developing specialized code, because of the overhead of maintaining the component factory. A rich and well-organized catalog of reusable components is the key to a successful component factory and a long-term economic gain. But at first such a catalog will not be available to an organiza-

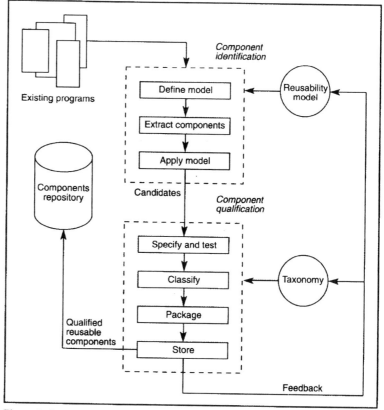

Figure 2. Component extraction.

tion, unless it can reuse code that it developed in the past without reuse in mind.

Mature application domains, where most of the functions that need to be used already exist in some form in earlier systems, should provide enough components for code reuse. In such cases, the earlier systems were probably designed and implemented by reusing code informally. For example, Lanergan and Grasso found rates of reuse of about 60 percent in business applications.[7]

To package such code for reuse, the component factory analyzes existing programs in the two phases shown in Figure 2. First, it chooses some candidates and packages them for possible independent use. Next, an engineer with knowledge of the application domain where the component was developed analyzes each component to determine the service it can provide. Then, components are stored in the repository with all information that has been obtained about them.

The first phase can be fully automated. The necessary human intervention in the

second phase is the main reason for splitting the process in two steps, instead of searching through existing programs looking for "useful" components first. The first phase reduces the amount of expensive human analysis needed in the second phase by limiting analysis to components that really look worth considering.

In the component identification phase, program units are automatically extracted, made independent, and measured according to observable properties related to their potential for reuse. There has been much discussion about these properties. According to Prieto-Diaz and Freeman,[6] a software component is reusable if the effort required to reuse it is remarkably smaller than the effort required to implement a component with the same functions. Thus, we need a quantitative measure of the distance of the component from its potential reuse. In the section below on component identification, we give details about a family of such measures that we call the reusability attributes model.

The identification phase consists of three steps:

(1) *Definition (or refinement) of the reusability attributes model.* Using our current understanding of the characteristics of a potentially reusable component in our environment, we define a set of automatable measures that capture these characteristics and an acceptable range of values for these metrics. We verify the metrics and their value ranges using the outcomes in the next steps and continually modify them until we have a reusability attributes model that maximizes our chances of selecting candidate components for reuse.

(2) *Extraction of components.* We extract modular units from existing systems, and complete them so they have all the external references needed to reuse them independently (for example, to compile them). By "modular unit" we mean a syntactic unit such as a C function, an Ada subprogram or block, or a Fortran subroutine.

(3) *Application of the model.* The current reusability attributes model is applied to the extracted, completed components. Components whose measurements are within the model's range of acceptable values become candidate reusable components to be analyzed by the domain expert in the qualification phase.

During the component qualification phase, a domain expert analyzes the candidate reusable components to understand and record each component's meaning while evaluating its potential for reuse in future systems. The expert also repackages the component by associating with it a reuse specification,[8] a significant set of test cases, a set of attributes based on a reuse classification schema, and a set of procedures for reusing the component.

The reuse classification schema, called a taxonomy, is very important for storing and retrieving reusable components efficiently. The definition and the domain of the attributes that implement the taxonomy can be improved each time an expert performs component qualification and analyzes the problems encountered.

The qualification phase consists of six steps:

(1) *Generation of the functional specification.* A domain expert extracts the functional specification of each candidate reusable component from its source code and documentation. This step provides insight into the correctness of the component in relationship to the new specification.

Components that are not relevant or not correct, or whose functional specification is not easy to extract, are discarded. The expert reports reasons for discarding candidates and other insights so they can be used to improve the reusability attributes model.

(2) *Generation of the test cases.* Using the functional specification, the expert generates, executes, and associates with the component a set of test cases. Components that do not satisfy the tests are discarded. Again, the reasons for discarding candidates are recorded and used to improve the reusability attributes model, and possibly the process for extracting the functional specification and assessing its correctness (step 1). This is most likely the last step at which a component will be discarded.

(3) *Classification of the component.* To distinguish it from the other components and assist in its identification and retrieval, the expert associates each reusable component with a classification according to a set of attributes identified in the domain analysis. Problems with the taxonomy are recorded for further analysis.

(4) *Development of the reuser's manual.* Information for the future reuser is provided in a manual that contains a description of the component's functions and interfaces as identified during generation of its functional specification (step 1), directions on how to install and use it, information about its procurement and support, and an appendix with structure diagrams and information for component maintenance.

(5) *Storage.* Reusable software components are stored in the repository together with their functional specifications, test cases, classification attributes, and reuser's manuals.

(6) *Feedback.* The reusability attributes model is updated by drawing on information from the qualification phase to add more measures, modify and remove measures that proved ineffective, or alter the ranges of acceptable values. This step requires analysis and possibly even further experimentation. The taxonomy is updated by adding new attributes or modifying the existing ones according to problems reported by the experts who classified the components (step 3).

This sketch illustrates the main concepts behind our approach: the use of a quantitative model for identification of components and a qualitative, partially subjective model for their qualification, with continuous improvement of both models using

feedback from their application. The reusability attributes model is the key to automating the first phase.

Component identification

According to Booch, a software component "is simply a container for expressing abstractions of data structures and algorithms."[5] The attributes that make a component reusable as a building block of other, maybe radically different, systems are functional usefulness in the context of the application domain, low reuse cost, and quality.

The reusability attributes model attempts to characterize those attributes directly through measures of an attribute, or indirectly through measures of evidence of an attribute's existence. These measures must be automatable.

We define a set of acceptable values for each of the metrics. These values can be either simple ranges of values (measure α is acceptable between α_1 and α_2) or more sophisticated relationships among different metrics (measure α is acceptable between α_1 and α_2, provided that measure β is less than β_0).

Figure 3 shows a "fishbone diagram" that represents the reusability factors. With each factor in the diagram, we associate metrics directly measuring the factor or indirectly predicting the likelihood of its presence.

Costs. Reuse costs include the costs of extracting the component from the old system, packaging it into a reusable component, finding and modifying the component, and integrating it into the new system. We can measure these costs directly during the process or use metrics to predict them.

To define the *basic reusability attributes model*, the entry-level model that the component factory starts with and later improves through feedback from the qualification phase, we divide reuse costs into two groups: costs to perform the extraction and costs to use the component in a new context. To minimize the costs of finding the component and extracting it, we need code fragments that are small and simple. Measures of volume and complexity also provide a partial indication of how easy qualification will be. The costs to reuse the component can be influenced by the readability of a code fragment, a characteristic that can again be partially evaluated using volume and complexity measures, as well as measures of the nonredundancy and structuredness of the component's implementation.

Usefulness. Functional usefulness is affected by both the commonality and the variety of the functions performed by the component. The commonality of a component for reuse can be divided into three parts: its commonality within a system or a single application, its commonality across different systems in the same application domain, and its overall commonality. It is hard to associate metrics with these factors. Experience with the application domain might provide subjective insight into whether the function is primitive to the domain and occurs commonly. An indirect automatable measure of functional usefulness might be the number of times the function occurs within the analyzed system (if we assume that an often-reused component is probably highly reusable). The variety of functions performed by the component is even more difficult to measure: An indirect metric could be component complexity. However, for a component's complexity to reflect its ability to perform more functions, we would have to assume that the component was developed in a nonredundant way.

The basic reusability attributes model measures a component's functional usefulness, derived from the commonality of the functions performed by the component, by comparing the number of times the component is invoked in the system with the number of times a component known to be useful is invoked. Components known to be useful can usually be found in the standard libraries of a programming environment. The basic reusability attributes model measures the commonality of a function by the ratio between the number of its invocations and the invocations of standard components.

The basic reusability attributes model assesses functional usefulness derived from the number and the variety of functions incorporated in a component by measuring its complexity and the nonredundancy of its implementation. This last feature can be translated into volume measures comparing the component's actual volume with its expected volume, which is computed from the number of tokens (operators and operands) that the component processes. When these values are close, we say the implementation of the component is regular. High regularity suggests that the component's complexity indicates the "amount" of function it performs.

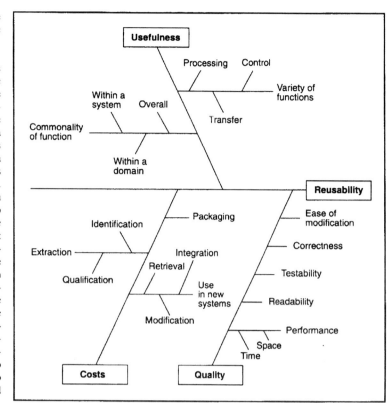

Figure 3. Factors affecting reusability.

Quality. Several qualities important for component reuse are correctness, readability, testability, ease of modification, and performance. Most are impossible to measure or predict directly. The domain expert who extracts the functional specification handles correctness and testing (steps 1 and 2 of the qualification phase). For the reusability attributes model, we are interested in qualities we can predict based upon automated measures. Therefore, we might consider such indirect metrics as small size and readability as predictors of correctness, and the number of independent paths as a measure of testability.

The basic reusability attributes model attempts to predict a component's correctness and testability using volume and complexity measures. It assumes that a large and complex component is more error prone and harder to test. Ease of modification is reflected in a component's readability.

Four metrics. Synthesizing these considerations, the basic reusability attributes model for identifying candidate reusable components characterizes a component's reusability using the four metrics shown in Figure 4.

Volume. A component's volume can be measured using the Halstead Software Science Indicators,[9] which are based on the way a program uses the programming language. First, we define the operators and the operands.

The *operators* represent the active elements of the program: arithmetic operators, decisional operators, assignment operators, functions, etc. Some operators are provided by the programming language, and some are defined by the user according to the rules of the language. The total number of these operators used in the program is denoted by η_1, and the total count of all usage of operators is denoted by N_1.

The *operands* represent the passive elements of the program: constants, variables, etc. The total number of unique operands defined and used in the program is denoted by η_2, and the total count of all usage of operands is denoted by N_2.

151

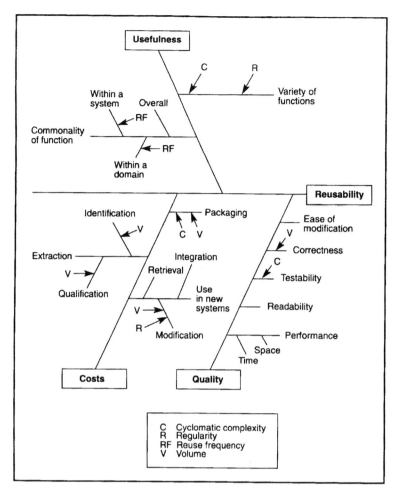

Figure 4. The basic reusability attributes model.

Legend within figure:
```
C    Cyclomatic complexity
R    Regularity
RF   Reuse frequency
V    Volume
```

Using the operators and operands, we define the Halstead volume by the formula

$$V = (N_1 + N_2) \log_2 (\eta_1 + \eta_2)$$

The component volume affects both reuse cost and quality. If a component is too small, the combined costs of extraction, retrieval, and integration exceed its intrinsic value, making reuse very impractical. If it is too large, the component is more error prone and has lower quality. Therefore, in the basic reusability attributes model, we need both an upper and a lower bound for this measure.

Cyclomatic complexity. We can measure the complexity of a program's control organization with the McCabe measure,[9] defined as the cyclomatic number of the control-flow graph of the program:

$$v(G) = e - n + 2$$

where e is the number of edges in the graph G, and n is the number of nodes.

The component complexity affects reuse cost and quality, taking into account the characteristics of the component's control flow. As with volume, reuse of a component with very low complexity may not repay the cost, whereas high component complexity may indicate poor quality — low readability, poor testability, and a higher possibility of errors. On the other hand, high complexity with high regularity of implementation suggests high functional usefulness. Therefore, for this measure we need both an upper and a lower bound in the basic model.

Regularity. We can measure the economy of a component's implementation, or

the use of correct programming practices, by seeing how well we can predict its length based on some regularity assumptions. Again using the Halstead Software Science Indicators, we have the actual length of the component

$$N = N_1 + N_2$$

and the estimated length

$$\dot{N} = \eta_1 \log_2 \eta_1 + \eta_2 \log_2 \eta_2$$

The closeness of the estimate is a measure of the regularity of the component's coding:

$$r = 1 - \frac{N - \dot{N}}{N} = \frac{\dot{N}}{N}$$

Component regularity measures the readability and the nonredundancy of a component's implementation. Therefore, we select components whose regularity is in the neighborhood of 1.

Reuse frequency. If we compare the number of static calls addressed to a component with the number of calls addressed to a class of components that we assume are reusable, we can estimate a given component's frequency of reuse. Let's suppose our system is composed of user-defined components $X_1,..., X_N$ and of components $S_1,..., S_M$ defined in the standard environment (such as printf in C or text_io.put in Ada). For a given component X, let $n(X)$ be the number of calls addressed to X in the system. We associate with each user-defined component a static measure of its reuse throughout the system: the ratio between the number of calls addressed to the component C and the average number of calls addressed to a standard component:

$$v_\sigma (C) = \frac{n(C)}{\frac{1}{M} \sum_{i=0}^{M} n(S_i)}$$

The reuse-specific frequency is an indirect measure of the functional usefulness of a component, if we assume that the application domain uses some naming convention, so components with different names are not functionally the same and vice versa. Therefore, in the basic model we have only a lower limit for this metric.

Criteria. To complete the basic model we need some criteria to select the candidate reusable components on the basis of the values of the four measures we have defined. The extremes of each measure depend on the application, the environment, the programming and design method, the programming language, and many other factors not easily quantified. We determine therefore the ranges of acceptability for the measures in the basic reusability attributes model experimentally, through a series of case studies described in the section titled "Case studies."

The basic model is elementary, but it is a reasonable starting point that captures important characteristics affecting software component reusability. Moreover, it probably contains features that will be common to every other reusability attributes model.

Care system

To support component factory activities, we have designed a computer-based system that performs static and dynamic analysis on existing code and helps a domain expert extract and qualify reusable components. We call the system Care, for computer-aided reuse engineering.

Figure 5 shows the parts of the Care system.

Component identifier. The component identifier supports source code analysis to extract the candidate reusable components according to a given reusability attributes model. The system stores candidates in the components repository for processing in the qualification phase. The identifier has two segments:

- *Model editor.* The user either defines a model, selecting metrics from a metrics library and assigning to each metric a range of acceptable values, or updates an old model from a models library, adding and deleting metrics or changing the adopted ranges of values.
- *Component extractor.* Once a reusability attributes model has been defined, the user can apply it to a family of programs to extract the candidate reusable components. The user can work interactively or extraction can be fully automated, provided that the system can automatically solve problems associated with the naming of the components.

Component qualifier. The component qualifier supports interactive qualification of the candidate reusable components according to the process model outlined earlier. For the qualifier to be effective, the candidate components must be small and simple. The qualifier has three segments:

- *Specifier.* The specifier supports the construction — through code reading and program analysis — of a formal specification to be associated with the component. The interactive tool controls as much as possible the correctness of the specification a domain expert extracts from a component. If the domain expert generates specifications, they are stored in the component repository together with the expert's measure (a subjective evaluation) of the component's practical usefulness.
- *Tester.* The tester uses the formal specification produced by the specifier to generate or to support user generation of a set of test cases for a component. If, as is likely, the component needs a "wrapping" to be executed, the tester supports the generation of this wrapping. It then executes the generated tests, reporting their outcomes and coverages. Test cases, wrapping, and coverage data are stored in the component repository with the expert's test report recommending retention or rejection of the component.
- *Classifier.* The classifier directs the user across the taxonomy of an application domain to find an appropriate classification for the component. Users with special authorization can modify the taxonomy, adding or deleting facets or altering the range of values available for each facet. The classifier and the taxonomy are directly related to the query used to retrieve the components from the repository.[6]

The current version of the Care system supports ANSI C and Ada on a Sun workstation with Unix and 8 Mbytes of memory. In the prototype, we have implemented three parts of the system:

- A component extractor for C programs based on the basic reusability attributes model described earlier. We used this part of the Care system for the case studies described in the next section. We have enriched the basic model with the data bindings metric[10] to take into account a static analysis of the flow of information between components of the same program. We have also developed a measurement tool and a data bindings analyzer for Ada programs.

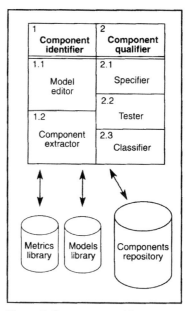

Figure 5. Care system architecture.

- A coverage analyzer for C programs (part of the tester in the component qualifier). An equivalent analyzer for Ada programs is under development.
- A prototype specifier to help the user build the Mills specification for programs written in a subset of Pascal. We plan to develop a version to process components written in C.

Case studies

In this section, we describe experiments with the current version of the Care system and the basic reusability attributes model, analyzing existing systems to identify reusable components. Some goals of the case studies were to

- evaluate the concept of extracting reusable candidates from existing programs using a model based on software metrics,
- complete the basic reusability attributes model with experimentally determined extremes for the metrics given earlier,
- study the application of the basic reusability attributes model to different environments and observe its selective power,
- analyze the interdependence of the metrics used in the basic model, and

Table 1. Characteristics of the analyzed systems.

Case	Application	Lines of Code (in thousands)	User-Defined Components
A	Data processing	4.04	83
B	File management	17.41	349
C	Communication	67.02	730
D	Data processing	17.63	156
E	Data processing	6.50	53
F	Language processing	58.55	1,235
G	File management	3.32	57
H	Communication	7.70	232
I	Language processing	4.63	87

Table 2. Average values for measures of the basic reusability attributes model.

Case	Volume	Complexity	Regularity	Reuse-Specific Frequency
A	8,967	21.1	0.76	0.05
B	7,856	23.6	0.74	0.08
C	45,707	153.7	0.66	0.10
D	11,877	32.1	0.64	0.11
E	4,054	16.8	0.76	0.18
F	82,671	198.7	0.33	0.13
G	7,277	25.5	0.65	0.24
H	12,044	40.7	0.77	0.23
I	20,131	44.7	0.79	0.41

Table 3. Measurement data for components whose reuse-specific frequency is greater than 5.0.

Case	Average Volume	Average Complexity	Average Regularity	Reuse-Specific Frequency
A	2,249	7.0	0.89	>0.50
B	2,831	4.8	0.77	>0.50
C	13,476	43.8	0.68	>0.50
D	4,444	8.5	0.80	>0.50
E	1,980	10.7	0.87	>0.50
F	156,199	384.3	0.40	>0.50
G	1,904	5.4	0.70	>0.50
H	8,884	31.1	0.75	>0.50
I	6,237	9.6	0.85	>0.50

• identify candidate reusable components to use with research and experimentation on the qualification phase.

The data we discuss here originated from the analysis of nine systems totalling 187,000 lines of ANSI C. The systems analyzed ranged from file management to communication applications, including data processing and system software. Table 1 outlines their characteristics.

Because of the characteristics of C, the natural "component" is the C function. But a function is not self-contained: It references variables, data types, and functions that are not part of its definition. To have an independent component, we had to complete the definition of the function with all the necessary external references. Therefore, in the context of the case studies, a component is the smallest translation unit containing a function. We performed each case study according to these steps:

(1) Acquire and install the system, making sure all the necessary sources are available.

(2) Build the components from the functions, adding to each function its external references and making it independently compilable.

(3) Compute the four metrics of the basic reusability attributes model for the components.

(4) Analyze the results.

Table 2 shows the average values for the measures of the basic model obtained from the case studies.

The case studies show volume, regularity, and reuse-specific frequency to have a high degree of independence. Volume and complexity show some correlation related to the "size" of the component, but it is not significant enough to make the two measures equivalent. Thus, the basic reusability attributes model is not redundant.

The data in the last column of Table 2 are below 0.5. Therefore, we can assume that a component whose specific reuse frequency is higher than 0.5 is a highly reused one. This choice is rather arbitrary, but it is useful for setting a reference point for the case studies. Accordingly, Table 3 presents the measurement data for high-reuse components whose reuse-specific frequency is more than 0.5.

Comparing Tables 2 and 3 we see, with a few exceptions, a very regular pattern. The highly reused components have volume and complexity lower than the average — about one fourth of the average. Their regularity is slightly higher than the average, generally above 0.70. The only exception is case F, a compiler with a very peculiar design, where the function calls are mostly addressed to high-level and complex modules. These results confirm, in different environments, the results obtained for Fortran programs in NASA's Software Engineering Laboratory.[11]

The regularity result is very important by itself. Because the length equation used in the regularity measure has such a good fix on the reusable components, we can use it to estimate the size of the components. Recall that the Halstead length equation ($\dot{N} = \eta_1 \log_2 \eta_1 + \eta_2 \log_2 \eta_2$) is a function of the two indicators η_1 and η_2. The first, the number of operators, is more or less fixed in the programming environment. The second, the number of operands, corresponds to the number of data items the system deals with. The value of η_2 can be rather precisely estimated in the detailed design phase of a project. The high regularity of the reusable components implies, therefore, that we can estimate the total effort for their development with an accuracy often higher than 80 percent. This is better than the estimate we get from components that are not as reusable.

The case studies show that, in most cases, we can obtain satisfactory results using the values in Table 4 as extremes for the ranges of acceptable values. Table 5 compares the number of user-defined functions in each system with the number of candidate reusable components extracted with the settings of Table 4.

Table 5 shows that, in general, 5 to 10 percent of the existing code should be analyzed for possible reuse. This is a cost-effective rate of reduction of the amount of code needing human analysis in the qualification phase. It is also a satisfactory figure for future reuse. In absolute terms, this 5 to 10 percent of the existing code accounts for a large part of a system's functionality.

The number of those candidates that the qualification phase will actually find to be reusable is hard to determine without a series of controlled experiments. On the basis of a cursory analysis, we think that the extracted components perform useful functions in the context of the application domain they come from. A complete and rigorous evaluation of the model is an immediate goal of our project.

These case studies show that reusable components have measurable properties that can be synthesized in a simple quantitative model. Now, we need to bring experimentation to the qualification activities, to verify how good the basic model is in practice, and to study how we can process the feedback from the qualification phase to improve the reusability attributes model. A possibility is a mechanism associated with the model editor for manipulating the reusability attributes model. We also need to broaden our analysis to different programming environments for broader verification of our hypotheses.

We foresee two major developments in the architecture of the Care system. The first is the design of a prototype for the components repository, supporting component retrieval both by queries to the classification system and by browsing on the basis of the specification.

Table 4. Extremes for ranges of acceptable values in the basic reusability attributes model.

Measure	Minimum	Maximum
Volume	2,000	10,000
Complexity	5.00	15.00
Regularity	0.70	1.30
Reuse frequency	0.30	

Table 5. User-defined system components compared with extracted candidates for reuse.

Case	User-Defined Components	Extracted Candidates	Percentage of User-Defined Components Extracted
A	83	4	5
B	349	17	5
C	730	36	5
D	156	16	10
E	53	4	8
F	1,235	81	7
G	57	10	18
H	232	24	10
I	87	11	13

The second development will be an integration with the Tame system for tailoring a measurement environment.[12] In the version of Care we outlined here, the metrics library is a static object from which users can only retrieve measures. The Tame system allows users to create a measurement environment tailored to the goals of their activities and to their model. This environment will provide a more elastic metrics library for defining measures in the reusability attributes model. ∎

Acknowledgments

We are indebted to Daniele Fantasia, Bruno Macchini, and Daniela Scalabrin of Italsiel S.p.A., Rome, for developing the programs that made possible the case studies, and for many useful discussions.

This work was supported by Italsiel S.p.A. with a grant given to the Industrial Associates Program of the Department of Computer Science at the University of Maryland. Computer support was provided in part through the facilities of the Computer Science Center at the University of Maryland.

References

1. M. McIlroy, "Mass Produced Software Components," *Proc. NATO Conf. Software Eng.*, Petrocelli/Charter, New York, 1969, pp. 88-98.

2. P. Freeman, "Reusable Software Engineering Concepts and Research Directions," *ITT Proc. Workshop on Reusability in Programming*, ITT, Stamford, Conn., 1983, pp. 129-137.

3. V.R. Basili and H.D. Rombach, "Towards a Comprehensive Framework for Reuse: A Reuse-Enabling Software Evolution Environment," Tech. Report CS-TR-2158 (UMIACS-TR-88-92), Computer Science Dept., Univ. of Maryland, College Park, Md., 1988.

4. V.R. Basili, "Software Development: A Paradigm for the Future," *Proc. Compsac 89*, IEEE Computer Soc. Press, Los Alamitos, Calif., Order No. 1964, pp. 471-485.

5. G. Booch, *Software Components with Ada*, Benjamin/Cummings, Menlo Park, Calif., 1987.

6. R. Prieto-Diaz and P. Freeman, "Classifying Software for Reusability," *IEEE Software*, Vol. 4, No. 1, Jan. 1987, pp. 6-16.

7. R.G. Lanergan and C.A. Grasso, "Software Engineering with Reusable Designs and Code," *IEEE Trans. Software Eng.*, Vol. SE-10, No. 5, Sept. 1984, pp. 498-501.

8. V.R. Basili and H.D. Mills, "Understanding and Documenting Programs," *IEEE Trans. Software Eng.*, Vol. SE-8, No. 3, May 1982, pp. 270-283.

9. S.D. Conte, H.E. Dunsmore, and V.Y. Shen, *Software Engineering: Metrics and Models*, Benjamin/Cummings, Menlo Park, Calif., 1986.

10. D. Hutchens and V.R. Basili, "System Structure Analysis: Clustering with Data Bindings," *IEEE Trans. Software Eng.*, Vol. SE-11, No. 8, Aug. 1985, pp. 749-757.

11. R.W. Selby, "Empirically Analyzing Software Reuse in a Production Environment," in *Software Reuse: Emerging Technology*, W. Tracz, ed., IEEE Computer Soc. Press, Los Alamitos, Calif., 1988, pp. 176-189.

12. V.R. Basili and H.D. Rombach, "The Tame Project: Towards Improvement-Oriented Software Environments," *IEEE Trans. Software Eng.*, Vol. SE-14, No. 6, June 1988, pp. 758-773.

Gianluigi Caldiera is on the faculty of the Institute for Advanced Computer Studies and coordinates projects on software quality and reusability in the Computer Science Department at the University of Maryland. His research interests are in software engineering, focusing on reusability, productivity, measurement, and quality management. Previously, he was an assistant professor of mathematics at the University of Rome and a lecturer in the Graduate School for Systems Engineering.

Caldiera has worked for the Finsiel Group and has been involved in the ESPRIT program as a project leader and a project reviewer. He received a Laurea degree in mathematics from the University of Rome and is a member of the IEEE Computer Society and the American Society for Quality Control.

Victor R. Basili is a professor in the Institute for Advanced Computer Studies and the Computer Science Department at the University of Maryland, where he served as chairman for six years. His research involves measuring and evaluating software development in industrial and government settings. He has consulted with many agencies and organizations, including IBM, GE, GTE, AT&T, Motorola, Boeing, and NASA.

In 1976, Basili cofounded and was a principal investigator in the Software Engineering Laboratory, a joint venture of NASA Goddard Space Flight Center, the University of Maryland, and Computer Sciences Corp. He received the *IEEE Transactions on Software Engineering*'s Outstanding Paper Award in 1982 and the NASA Group Achievement Award in 1989. Basili is an IEEE fellow, a former member of the IEEE Computer Society Board of Governors, and a present Computer Society member.

The authors can be contacted at the Computer Science Department, University of Maryland, College Park, MD 20742, fax (301) 405-6707.

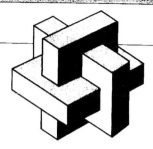

Reverse Engineering and Design Recovery: A Taxonomy

Elliot J. Chikofsky, *Index Technology Corp. and Northeastern University*
James H. Cross II, *Auburn University*

Reverse engineering is evolving as a major link in the software life cycle, but its growth is hampered by confusion over terminology. This article defines key terms.

The availability of computer-aided systems-engineering environments has redefined how many organizations approach system development. To meet their true potential, CASE environments are being applied to the problems of maintaining and enhancing existing systems. The key lies in applying reverse-engineering approaches to software systems. However, an impediment to success is the considerable confusion over the terminology used in both technical and marketplace discussions.

It is in the reverse-engineering arena, where the software maintenance and development communities meet, that various terms for technologies to analyze and understand existing systems have been frequently misused or applied in conflicting ways.

In this article, we define and relate six terms: forward engineering, reverse engineering, redocumentation, design recovery, restructuring, and reengineering. Our objective is not to create new terms but to rationalize the terms already in use. The resulting definitions apply to the underlying engineering processes, regardless of the degree of automation applied.

Hardware origins

The term "reverse engineering" has its origin in the analysis of hardware — where the practice of deciphering designs from finished products is commonplace. Reverse engineering is regularly applied to improve your own products, as well as to analyze a competitor's products or those of an adversary in a military or national-security situation.

In a landmark paper on the topic, M.G. Rekoff defines reverse engineering as "the process of developing a set of specifications for a complex hardware system by an orderly examination of specimens of that system."[1] He describes such a process

0740-7459/90/0100/0013/$01.00 © 1990 IEEE

Reprinted from *IEEE Software*, January 1990, pp. 13-17.

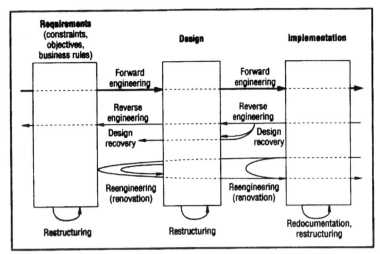

Figure 1. Relationship between terms. Reverse engineering and related processes are transformations between or within abstraction levels, represented here in terms of life-cycle phases.

as being conducted by someone other than the developer, "without the benefit of any of the original drawings ... for the purpose of making a clone of the original hardware system...."

In applying these concepts to software systems, we find that many of these approaches apply to gaining a basic understanding of a system and its structure. However, while the hardware objective traditionally is to duplicate the system, the software objective is most often to gain a sufficient design-level understanding to aid maintenance, strengthen enhancement, or support replacement.

Software maintenance

The ANSI definition of software maintenance is the "modification of a software product after delivery to correct faults, to improve performance or other attributes, or to adapt the product to a changed environment," according to ANSI/IEEE Std 729-1983.

Usually, the system's maintainers were not its designers, so they must expend many resources to examine and learn about the system. Reverse-engineering tools can facilitate this practice. In this context, reverse engineering is the part of the maintenance process that helps you understand the system so you can make appropriate changes. Restructuring and reverse engineering also fall within the global definition of software maintenance. However, each of these three processes also has a place within the contexts of building new systems and evolutionary development.

Life cycles and abstractions

To adequately describe the notion of software forward and reverse engineering, we must first clarify three dependent concepts: the existence of a life-cycle model, the presence of a subject system, and the identification of abstraction levels.

We assume that an orderly life-cycle model exists for the software-development process. The model may be represented as the traditional waterfall, as a spiral, or in some other form that generally can be represented as a directed graph. While we expect there to be iteration within stages of the life cycle, and perhaps even recursion, its general directed-graph nature lets us sensibly define forward (downward) and backward (upward) activities.

The subject system may be a single program or code fragment, or it may be a complex set of interacting programs, job-control instructions, signal interfaces, and data files. In forward engineering, the subject system is the result of the development process. It may not yet exist, or its existing components may not yet be united to form a system. In reverse engineering, the subject system is generally the starting point of the exercise.

In a life-cycle model, the early stages deal with more general, implementation-independent concepts; later stages emphasize implementation details. The transition of increasing detail through the forward progress of the life cycle maps

well to the concept of abstraction levels. Earlier stages of systems planning and requirements definition involve expressing higher level abstractions of the system being designed when compared to the implementation itself.

These abstractions are more closely related to the business rules of the enterprise. They are often expressed in user terminology that has a one-to-many relationship to specific features of the finished system. In the same sense, a blueprint is a higher level abstraction of the building it represents, and it may document only one of the many models (electrical, water, heating/ventilation/air conditioning, and egress) that must come together.

It is important to distinguish between *levels* of abstraction, a concept that crosses conceptual stages of design, and *degrees* of abstraction within a single stage. Spanning life-cycle phases involves a transition from higher abstraction levels in early stages to lower abstraction levels in later stages. While you can represent information in any life-cycle stage in detailed form (lower degree of abstraction) or in more summarized or global forms (higher degree of abstraction), these definitions emphasize the concept of *levels* of abstraction between life-cycle phases.

Definitions

For simplicity, we describe key terms using only three identified life-cycle stages with clearly different abstraction levels, as Figure 1 shows:

• requirements (specification of the problem being solved, including objectives, constraints, and business rules),

• design (specification of the solution), and

• implementation (coding, testing, and delivery of the operational system).

Forward engineering. Forward engineering is the traditional process of moving from high-level abstractions and logical, implementation-independent designs to the physical implementation of a system.

While it may seem unnecessary — in view of the long-standing use of design and development terminology — to introduce a new term, the adjective "forward"

14

has come to be used where it is necessary to distinguish this process from reverse engineering. Forward engineering follows a sequence of going from requirements through designing its implementation.

Reverse engineering. Reverse engineering is the process of analyzing a subject system to
- identify the system's components and their interrelationships and
- create representations of the system in another form or at a higher level of abstraction.

Reverse engineering generally involves extracting design artifacts and building or synthesizing abstractions that are less implementation-dependent. While reverse engineering often involves an existing functional system as its subject, this is *not* a requirement. You can perform reverse engineering starting from any level of abstraction or at any stage of the life cycle.

Reverse engineering in and of itself does *not* involve changing the subject system or creating a new system based on the reverse-engineered subject system. It is a process of *examination*, not a process of change or replication.

In spanning the life-cycle stages, reverse engineering covers a broad range starting from the existing implementation, recapturing or recreating the design, and deciphering the requirements actually implemented by the subject system.

There are many subareas of reverse engineering. Two subareas that are widely referred to are redocumentation and design recovery.

Redocumentation. Redocumentation is the creation or revision of a semantically equivalent representation within the same relative abstraction level. The resulting forms of representation are usually considered alternate views (for example, dataflow, data structure, and control flow) intended for a human audience.

Redocumentation is the simplest and oldest form of reverse engineering, and many consider it to be an unintrusive, weak form of restructuring. The "re-" prefix implies that the intent is to recover documentation about the subject system that existed or should have existed.

Some common tools used to perform redocumentation are pretty printers (which display a code listing in an improved form), diagram generators (which create diagrams directly from code, reflecting control flow or code structure), and cross-reference listing generators. A key goal of these tools is to provide easier ways to visualize relationships among program components so you can recognize and follow paths clearly.

Design recovery. Design recovery is a subset of reverse engineering in which do-

---

Reverse engineering in and of itself does not involve changing the subject system. It is a process of examination, not change or replication.

---

main knowledge, external information, and deduction or fuzzy reasoning are added to the observations of the subject system to identify meaningful higher level abstractions beyond those obtained directly by examining the system itself.

Design recovery is distinguished by the sources and span of information it should handle. According to Ted Biggerstaff: "Design recovery recreates design abstractions from a combination of code, existing design documentation (if available), personal experience, and general knowledge about problem and application domains ... Design recovery must reproduce all of the information required for a person to fully understand what a program does, how it does it, why it does it, and so forth. Thus, it deals with a far wider range of information than found in conventional software-engineering representations or code."[2]

Restructuring. Restructuring is the transformation from one representation form to another at the same relative abstraction level, while preserving the sub-

ject system's external behavior (functionality and semantics).

A restructuring transformation is often one of appearance, such as altering code to improve its structure in the traditional sense of structured design. The term "restructuring" came into popular use from the code-to-code transform that recasts a program from an unstructured ("spaghetti") form to a structured (goto-less) form. However, the term has a broader meaning that recognizes the application of similar transformations and recasting techniques in reshaping data models, design plans, and requirements structures. Data normalization, for example, is a data-to-data restructuring transform to improve a logical data model in the database design process.

Many types of restructuring can be performed with a knowledge of structural form but without an understanding of meaning. For example, you can convert a set of If statements into a Case structure, or vice versa, without knowing the program's purpose or anything about its problem domain.

While restructuring creates new versions that implement or propose change to the subject system, it does not normally involve modifications because of new requirements. However, it may lead to better observations of the subject system that suggest changes that would improve aspects of the system. Restructuring is often used as a form of preventive maintenance to improve the physical state of the subject system with respect to some preferred standard. It may also involve adjusting the subject system to meet new environmental constraints that do not involve reassessment at higher abstraction levels.

Reengineering. Reengineering, also known as both renovation and reclamation, is the examination and alteration of a subject system to reconstitute it in a new form and the subsequent implementation of the new form.

Reengineering generally includes some form of reverse engineering (to achieve a more abstract description) followed by some form of forward engineering or restructuring. This may include modifications with respect to new requirements not met by the original system. For exam-

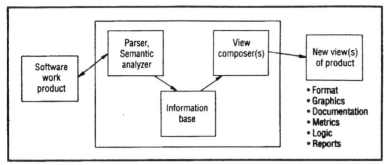

Figure 2. Model of tools architecture. Most tools for reverse engineering, restructuring, and reengineering use the same basic architecture. The new views on the right may themselves be software work products, which are shown on the left. (Model provided by Robert Arnold of the Software Productivity Consortium.)

ple, during the reengineering of information-management systems, an organization generally reassesses how the system implements high-level business rules and makes modifications to conform to changes in the business for the future.

There is some confusion of terms, particularly between reengineering and restructuring. The IBM user group Guide, for example, defines "application reengineering" as "the process of modifying the internal mechanisms of a system or program or the data structures of a system without changing the functionality (system capabilities as perceived by the user). In other words, it is altering the *how* without affecting the *what.*"[3] This is closest to our definition of restructuring. How-

ever, two paragraphs later, the same publication says, "It is rare that an application is reengineered without additional functionality being added." This supports our more general definition of reengineering.

While reengineering involves both forward engineering and reverse engineering, it is *not* a supertype of the two. Reengineering uses the forward- and reverse-engineering technologies available, but to date it has not been the principal driver of their progress. Both technologies are evolving rapidly, independent of their application within reengineering.

Objectives

What are we trying to accomplish with reverse engineering? The primary purpose of reverse engineering a software system is to increase the overall comprehensibility of the system for both maintenance and new development. Beyond the definitions above, there are six key objectives that will guide its direction as the technology matures:

• Cope with complexity. We must develop methods to better deal with the shear volume and complexity of systems. A key to controlling these attributes is automated support. Reverse-engineering methods and tools, combined with CASE environments, will provide a way to extract relevant information so decision makers can control the process and the product in systems evolution. Figure 2 shows a model of the structure of most tools for reverse engineering, reengineering, and restructuring.

• Generate alternate views. Graphical representations have long been accepted as comprehension aids. However, creating and maintaining them continues to be a bottleneck in the process. Reverse-engi-

neering tools facilitate the generation or regeneration of graphical representations from other forms. While many designers work from a single, primary perspective (like dataflow diagrams), reverse-engineering tools can generate additional views from other perspectives (like control-flow diagrams, structure charts, and entity-relationship diagrams) to aid the review and verification process. You can also create alternate forms of nongraphical representations with reverse-engineering tools to form an important part of system documentation.

• Recover lost information. The continuing evolution of large, long-lived systems leads to lost information about the system design. Modifications are frequently not reflected in documentation, particularly at a higher level than the code itself. While it is no substitute for preserving design history in the first place, reverse engineering — particularly design recovery — is our way to salvage whatever we can from the existing systems. It lets us get a handle on systems when we don't understand what they do or how their individual programs interact as a system.

• Detect side effects. Both haphazard initial design and successive modifications can lead to unintended ramifications and side effects that impede a system's performance in subtle ways. As Figure 3 shows, reverse engineering can provide observations beyond those we can obtain with a forward-engineering perspective, and it can help detect anomalies and problems before users report them as bugs.

• Synthesize higher abstractions. Reverse engineering requires methods and techniques for creating alternate views that transcend to higher abstraction levels. There is debate in the software community as to how completely the process can be automated. Clearly, expert-system technology will play a major role in achieving the full potential of generating high-level abstractions.

• Facilitate reuse. A significant issue in the movement toward software reusability is the large body of existing software assets. Reverse engineering can help detect candidates for reusable software components from present systems.

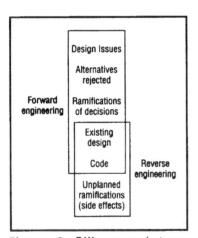

Figure 3. Differences between viewpoints. Although reverse engineering can help capture lost information, some types of information are not shared between forward- and reverse-engineering processes. However, reverse engineering can provide observations that are unobtainable in forward engineering.

Economics

The cost of understanding software, while rarely seen as a direct cost, is nonetheless very real. It is manifested in the time required to comprehend software, which includes the time lost to misunderstanding. By reducing the time required to grasp the essence of software artifacts in each life-cycle phase, reverse engineering may greatly reduce the overall cost of software.

In commenting on this article, Walt Scacchi of the University of Southern California made the following important observations: "Many claim that conventional software maintenance practices account for 50 to 90 percent of total life-cycle costs. Software reverse-engineering techniques are targeted to the problems that give rise to such a disproportionate distribution of software costs. Thus, if reverse engineering succeeds, the total system expense may be reduced/mitigated, or greater value may be added to current efforts, both of which represent desirable outcomes, especially if one quantifies the level of dollars spent. Reverse engineering may need to only realize a small impact to generate sizable savings."

Scacchi also pointed out that "software forward engineering and reverse engineering are *not* separate concerns, and thus should be viewed as opportunity for convergence and complement, as well as an expansion of the repertoire of tools and techniques that should be available to the modern software engineer. I, for one, believe that the next generation of software-engineering technologies will be applicable in both the forward and reverse directions. Such a view also may therefore imply yet another channel for getting advanced software-environment/CASE technologies into more people's hands — sell them on reverse engineering (based on current software-maintenance cost patterns) as a way to then introduce better forward engineering tools and techniques."

We have tried to provide a framework for examining reverse-engineering technologies by synthesizing the basic definitions of related terms and identifying common objectives.

Reverse engineering is rapidly becoming a recognized and important component of future CASE environments. Because the entire life cycle is naturally an iterative activity, reverse-engineering tools can provide a major link in the overall process of development and maintenance. As these tools mature, they will be applied to artifacts in all phases of the life cycle. They will be a permanent part of the process, ultimately used to verify all completed systems against their intended designs, even with fully automated generation.

Reverse engineering, used with evolving software development technologies, will provide significant incremental enhancements to our productivity. ❖

Acknowledgments

We acknowledge the special contributions of these individuals to the synthesis of this taxonomy and the rationalization of conflicting terminology: Walt Scacchi of the University of Southern California, Norm Schneidewind of the Naval Postgraduate School, Jim Fulton of Boeing Computer Services, Bob Arnold of the Software Productivity Consortium, Shawn Bohner of Contel Technology Center, Philip Hausler and Mark Pleszkoch of IBM and the University of Maryland at Baltimore County, Linore Cleveland of IBM, Diane Mularz of Mitre, Paul Oman of University of Idaho, John Munson and Norman Wilde of the University of West Florida, and the participants in directed discussions at the 1989 Conference on Software Maintenance and the 1988 and 1989 International Workshops on CASE.

References

1. M.G. Rekoff Jr., "On Reverse Engineering," *IEEE Trans. Systems, Man, and Cybernetics*, March-April 1985, pp. 244-252.
2. T.J. Biggerstaff, "Design Recovery for Maintenance and Reuse," *Computer*, July 1989, pp. 36-49.
3. "Application Reengineering," Guide Pub. GPP-208, Guide Int'l Corp., Chicago, 1989.

Elliot J. Chikofsky is director of research and technology at Index Technology Corp. and a lecturer in industrial engineering and information systems at Northeastern University.

Chikofsky is an associate editor-in-chief of *IEEE Software*, vice chairman for membership of the Computer Society's Technical Committee on Software Engineering, president of the International Workshop on CASE, and author of a book on CASE in the Technology Series for IEEE Computer Society Press. He is a senior member of the IEEE.

James H. Cross II is an assistant professor of computer science and engineering at Auburn University. His research interests include design methodology, development environments, reverse engineering, visualization, and testing. He is secretary of the IEEE Computer Society Publications Board.

Cross received a BS in mathematics from the University of Houston, an MS in mathematics from Sam Houston State University, and a PhD in computer science from Texas A&M University. He is a member of the ACM and IEEE Computer Society.

Address questions about this article to Chikofsky at Index Technology, 1 Main St., Cambridge, MA 02142 or to Cross at Computer Science and Engineering Dept., 107 Dunstan Hall, Auburn University, Auburn, AL 36849.

Quality Improvement Using A Software Reuse Failure Modes Model

William B. Frakes and Christopher J. Fox

Abstract—This paper presents a failure modes model of parts-based software reuse, and shows how this model can be used to evaluate and improve software reuse processes. The model and the technique are illustrated using survey data about software reuse gathered from 113 people from 29 organizations.

Index Terms—Software reuse, quality, improvement, failure modes, analysis, Pareto, probability, model, survey, Deming PDCA cycle.

———————————— ✦ ————————————

1 INTRODUCTION

SOFTWARE REUSE may be broadly defined as the use of existing engineering knowledge or artifacts to build new software systems. Software reuse can significantly improve software quality and productivity [1], so many organizations are now trying to implement systematic reuse programs that will allow them to derive maximum leverage from their existing software assets. Implementing systematic reuse has proven to be a difficult process, however, involving many factors both technical and nontechnical.

Reuse can be either generative or parts-based. *Generative reuse* relies on tools and methods that automatically create applications or parts of applications from specifications. *Parts-based reuse* assumes a programmer integrating existing software components to build applications. This paper presents an overall approach to measuring and improving a parts-based reuse process using a model of the ways the reuse process can fail. The model can be used by managers and software quality specialists to evaluate a systematic reuse program, to identify reuse impediments in an organization, and to devise an improvement strategy for a systematic reuse program.

1.1 Problems Implementing Systematic Reuse

There are many issues an organization must face in implementing systematic reuse. These issues fall into four categories:

1) *Managerial.* How can a software engineering organization promote and reward reuse? An example of a managerial variable influencing reuse might be economic incentives to create reusable parts, expressed in dollars.
2) *Economic.* How can software reuse be made economical? An example economic variable influencing reuse might be payment to creators of reusable components.
3) *Legal.* How can the rights of creators and consumers of reusable software be legally protected? A legal variable affecting reuse might be whether there is a law limiting part-supplier liability.
4) *Technical.* As mentioned above, there are two basic technical approaches to reuse: parts-based reuse and generative reuse. The parts-based approach assumes a human programmer integrating software components into an application. The generative approach assumes that domain knowledge is

• *W.B. Frakes is with the Department of Computer Science, Virginia Tech, Falls Church, VA 22042. E-mail: wfrakes@vt.edu.*
• *C.J. Fox is with the Computer Science Department, James Madison University, Harrisonburg, VA 22807. E-mail: fox@cs.jmu.edu.*

Manuscript received Aug. 26, 1994; revised Dec. 13, 1995.
Recommended for acceptance by J. Knight.
For information on obtaining reprints of this article, please send e-mail to: transactions@computer.org, and reference IEEECS Log Number S95606.

Reprinted from *IEEE Transactions on Software Engineering*, Vol. 22, No. 4, Apr. 1996, pp. 274-279.

encoded into an application generator or a programming language so that components are selected and integrated automatically. Lex and yacc in the UNIX environment are examples of application generators. APL and SAS are examples of domain specific programming languages that have mathematical and statistical domain knowledge encoded in their operators. A technical variable affecting reuse is whether parts-based or generative methods are used. There are many other technical variables that may affect reuse, including design method, coding standards and practices, and reuse library indexing method. The model we present in this paper assumes a parts-based approach to systematic reuse. It may be adapted to a generative approach, but we do not discuss this here.

In quality improvement terms, these factors are the potential independent variables of experiments aimed at improving the quality of software reuse processes [2]. The problem is that it is not clear which variables have the greatest impact on reuse in a given organization, and should therefore be the focus of evaluation and improvement efforts in the organization.

In this paper we propose an approach to evaluating and improving a software reuse effort based on an analysis of the ways that a software reuse process can *fail*. This approach is effective because it is simple and easy to apply, and because it concentrates on the bottom line outcome of a software reuse process, namely its ability to get reusable parts into an application.

1.2 Failure Mode Analysis

Failure mode analysis is a standard engineering technique for process and product improvement [3], providing a systematic procedure for determining and classifying the ways that a product or process can fail. A failure mode analysis of the reuse process can identify the ways that an effort to reuse an asset can fail. By collecting data about the frequency of reuse failure modes, an overall measure of the likelihood of reuse failure can be produced. This value is a measure of the overall quality of a reuse effort.

A *Pareto analysis* [4], [5] is an examination of frequency or relative frequency category data to determine the most important categories. Pareto analysis is a salient quality improvement tool because it helps direct improvement efforts to those categories that contribute most to quality problems. Effort is most effective when it is directed to solving the most important problems first; Pareto analysis is a tool for identifying the most important problems.

Pareto analysis can be done by ordering data in a table, but is usually done using a graphical tool called a Pareto diagram. A *Pareto diagram* is a bar chart of data categories against frequency or relative frequency of occurrence in each category, with the categories ordered from greatest to least frequently occurring. Typically the first, or first several, categories in a Pareto diagram will have markedly higher bars than the rest—these are the categories that contribute the most to quality problems, and those to which quality improvement efforts should be directed.

Pareto analysis is used in failure mode analysis to study failure mode frequency data. Pareto analysis identifies the failure modes that contribute most to overall product or process failure, thus identifying the failure modes where improvement efforts should be directed. These failure modes, or *key impediments to reuse*, should then be the target of investigation aimed at finding the root causes of the failure mode(s), and removing these root causes.

Data about failure modes from a reuse improvement effort can be combined with other failure mode data to generate a new overall measure of the likelihood of reuse failure for process evaluation and improvement tracking. Another Pareto analysis can then identify new key impediments to reuse as the basis of the next improvement effort. In this way continuous improvement of reuse processes is achieved.

The next section of this paper presents a reuse failure modes model that can be applied to any parts-based reuse process. The third section illustrates the model and the method using data from a survey of industry reuse practices. The outcomes of this analysis are an estimate of current industry reuse process quality, and an identification of key impediments to reuse in the industry.

2 REUSE FAILURE MODES MODEL

Given the many factors that may affect reuse, how can the important ones for a given organization be chosen? One way to answer this question for a given organization is to find out why reuse is not taking place in that organization. This can be done by considering reuse failure modes—that is, the ways that reuse can fail. Every software life cycle object that is created from scratch or is modified is, in a sense, a reuse failure if it expends resources that might otherwise have been saved through reuse.

2.1 General Description of the Model

The model we present in this section is general enough to apply to both *ad hoc* and *systematic* parts-based reuse [6]. In all cases, successful reuse depends on the satisfaction of seven main conditions. In our model these conditions form a temporal sequence, called the *reuse success chain*, as depicted in Fig. 1.

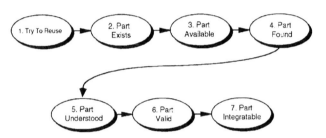

Fig. 1. Reuse success chain.

Failure of any of these conditions will cause reuse to fail. For reuse to take place, a software engineer must first try to reuse. This requires that the engineer know about reuse, and that his or her environment supports reuse attempts. Then, the needed part must exist, and further must be available in the local environment. The engineer must be able to find it and understand it. Once found and understood, the part must meet local quality standards, and must be in a form that can be integrated into the target application. A failure mode is associated with each of these conditions, leading to seven reuse failure modes that form the reuse failure modes model. These failure modes are called *no attempt to reuse, part does not exist, part not available, part not found, part not understood, part not valid,* and *part not integratable*.

Each of the failure modes in the model have failure causes associated with them. A failure cause, or root cause, is ultimately what must be corrected to alleviate reuse failures. Failure causes will vary from organization to organization, but many common failure causes can be identified. For example, a common cause of the reuse failure mode *no attempt to reuse* is that there is no incentive to reuse. Investigation and correction of reuse failure root causes should be the goal of efforts to improve reuse.

2.2 Probabilistic Interpretation

Insight into the reuse implementation problem can be had by considering the probabilistic aspects of the reuse failure modes model. Each failure mode in the model can be assigned a probability. When this is done, an overall probability of reuse failure (or success) can be calculated. Although this is a simplifying assumption, the easiest way of calculating an overall probability is by assuming independence of the failure modes. Assumptions of independence are common in applying probabilistic models in engineering problems [3]. The overall probability of reuse success is given by the equation:

$$P(reuse\ success) = \Pi(1 - f_i)$$

where f_i is the probability of failure mode i. The probability of reuse failure is:

$$P(reuse\ failure) = 1 - P(reuse\ success).$$

This model emphasizes that even if a reuse program is quite good, and the probability of reuse failure at any step is low, the overall probability of successful reuse can still be relatively low. Assume, for example, that each failure mode has a 10% probability. The probability of successful reuse will then be only 0.48.

Probabilities of reuse failure modes may be assigned either *subjectively* or *objectively*. A subjectively assigned failure mode probability is simply a guess about the likelihood of a particular sort of reuse failure. An objectively assigned probability is based on the observed relative frequency of the failure modes in an organization.

3 CURRENT REUSE FAILURE MODES

The failure mode analysis method can be applied to analyze the state of reuse practice in particular organizations, or across the software industry. As a case study, we have applied the model in analyzing failure modes in the software industry using data from a survey of developers, researchers, and managers in software engineering.

3.1 The Survey and Survey Respondents

A survey of individual and organizational software reuse practices was circulated through the software engineering community in 1991 and 1992 [7], [8]. One hundred thirteen people responded to the survey. Most of the survey respondents are software engineers (43%) or managers (35%) with an average of 12.2 years of experience on 9.2 projects in 3.3 organizations. Sixty-two percent of the respondents have advanced degrees, mostly in computer and information science (51%), electrical engineering (20%), or mathematics (11%).

The survey respondents are from 29 organizations, all but one in the US. Respondents work for companies in software development (34%), aerospace (25%), manufacturing (14%), and telecommunications (6%). The remaining 21% work in a variety of industries including universities, electronic instrumentation and equipment manufacturing, and telemetry collection and management. Respondent companies run the gamut from those with a few employees to one with over 350,000; the median number of employees in respondents' companies is 25,000.

Respondents were also asked the following open-ended question about software reuse failures: "What problems have you had when trying to reuse software?" Replies to this question were classified by the authors using the failure modes model and are the basis for the analysis below. A stronger methodology might use independent classifiers, and some way of resolving classification conflicts. Although survey respondents were asked questions about reusing assets from all phases of the life cycle, the phrasing of this question probably elicited responses primarily about code reuse.

3.2 Reuse Failures In the Software Industry

Respondents' replies to the question "What problems have you had when trying to reuse software?" were analyzed to generate data about failure modes and failure causes. Responses were first analyzed to determine which of the seven failure modes characterized each reply; a reply might mention more than one failure

mode, and all mentioned failure modes were counted. The numbers accompanying the major entries in Table 1 are the results of this analysis.

Next, replies were analyzed to determine failure causes. This analysis used a predefined list of causes for each failure mode. Some causes were not mentioned by any respondents, and some respondents mentioned several causes for a single failure mode. For example, the *part does not exist* failure mode occurred 18 times, with two causes for this failure mode (*part not designed for reuse*, and *no economic incentive*) mentioned by respondents 16 times. All causes mentioned were counted, and appear with the causes as the subentries in Table 1.

TABLE 1
REASONS FOR REUSE FAILURE

No Attempt to Reuse	32
Resource constraints	8
No incentive	6
Time constraints	5
Utility of reuse unclear	5
Lack of education	5
Communication problems	3
Legal problems	3
No management support	2
No reuse support organization	2
No customer support	1
NIH syndrome	1
Nonegoless programming	1
Reuse technology immature	1
No success model	0
More fun to write than to reuse	0

Part Not Integratable	22
Environment incompatibilities	11
Improper form	7
Hardware incompatibilities	4
Too much modification required	3
Nonfunctional specifications	0
Linkage to extraneous software	0

Part Not Understood	21
Inadequate documentation	18
Part too complex	2

Part Not Valid	19
Poor inspection, testing, verification	6
Poor support from producer	5
Inadequate performance	5
Lack of standards	2
Insufficient information	0

Part Does Not Exist	18
Part not designed for reuse	14
No economic incentive	2
Novel techology	0

Part Not Found	12
Insufficient representation	4
Poor or no search tools	4
Inability to specify search	0

Part Not Available	7
No reuse repository	4
Part is proprietary/classified	1
No import organization	0
Part can't be scavenged	0
Part can't be found	0
Source code missing	0

Fig. 2 is the Pareto diagram of the failure modes. By far the most common failure mode is no *attempt to reuse*, which is half again as frequent as the next most important failure mode. Based on our survey, we may immediately conclude that the most important reuse failure mode in the software industry, and the problem on which reuse improvement efforts should be focused, is to get software engineers to attempt to reuse.

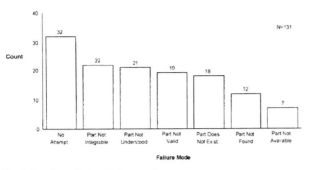

Fig. 2. Pareto analysis of failure modes.

3.3 Causes of Reuse Failures

Failure to try to reuse assets is primarily a management problem. According to the survey respondents, (and again applying the Pareto principle to order the responses) the most common root cause of this failure mode is resource constraints, followed by lack of incentive to reuse, time constraints, lack of clarity on reuse utility, and lack of education. This conclusion is consistent with analysis of other data in the survey [8]. This demonstrates the size and complexity of tasks management must undertake to implement reuse, including clear directives for more reuse backed up with education, resources, and incentives. Until these things are done, technical aids to reuse are not likely to have much effect.

After *no attempt to reuse*, the next four failure modes have very similar frequencies, and the sixth and seventh have considerably lower frequencies. In this case, effort should be concentrated on the single dominant failure mode. If data were collected from a single organization, it would likely show a different single failure mode as dominant, or perhaps two or three failure modes as dominant. Improvement efforts would then of course be different. The following paragraphs discuss some of the aspects of the observed failure modes, their causes, and how to respond to them.

The second most common failure mode in Table 1 is *part not integratable*. The primary causes were incompatible environments and improper form. The 3 C's model of reuse design [9] identifies three aspects of making a component reusable:

1) *Concept*. The abstract semantics of the component, e.g., what might be specified with an abstract data type.
2) *Content*. How the component is implemented
3) *Context*. The environment needed to use the component.

The *part not integratable* failure mode is concerned primarily with content and context. A component might have the right concept, but not the right content or context. For example, it might be in the wrong language, use the wrong version of the compiler, have the wrong parameter list, etc. One way for an organization to address this problem is to institute standards and practices for designing reusable components. There is currently much effort directed toward creating and promulgating such standards and practices; see, for example, Hollingsworth [10] for Ada, and McGregor and Sykes [11] for C++.

Part not understood, the next most frequent failure mode in our survey, means that reuse failed because the engineer could not understand the component well enough to use it (or perhaps to trust it). By far the most common reason for this failure mode is inadequate documentation. This observation agrees with a recent study that found that none of the methods currently used for indexing reusable components does more than moderately well in

helping users understand components [12]. This problem might be addressed by implementing component documentation standards, and possibly through the use of formal specifications of components (see for example [13]), though this technique has not been experimentally verified.

The next most common failure mode in our survey is *part not valid*. This refers to whether a part met quality standards, i.e., did it possess the attributes required of it by the potential user? The most common causes for this failure among our respondents are:

- poor inspection, testing, and verification
- poor support from the part producer
- inadequate performance

The first two of these problems might be addressed by establishing a set of properties that components accepted by an organization must have. Such a set might include the requirements that all components be regression tested and receive 90% branch testing coverage. Producers would be required to adhere to these standards. Some reuse repositories do require their assets to meet certification standards [14].

Inadequate performance can be a serious obstacle to reuse. Designers of reusable collections have observed that if reusable components are more than about 10% slower than their single use equivalents, engineers tend to avoid using them. This can be addressed by establishing standards for performance, and by using tools and techniques for software optimization [15].

The failure mode *part does not exist* means that there is no component that satisfies the reuse need of the engineer. The primary cause in our survey is that components were not designed for reuse. This problem might be addressed by analyzing the domains in which the organization does business, and developing or reengineering components as appropriate.

The failure mode *part not found* means that the component exists and is available in the organization, but the engineer could not find it. The primary causes for this are insufficient representation and inadequate search tools. Insufficient representation might be addressed by indexing components using more that one indexing method. Research has shown that each indexing method will find different components, and that no single method is preferred by all engineers [12]. Various search tools are now commercially available, the Internet can be used, and search tools can also be built easily using standard text processing tools such as those found in the UNIX environment.

The failure mode *part not available* means that a suitable component exists, but is not available in the organization. The primary cause for this failure mode is lack of a repository. The obvious fix for this problem is to establish an organizational reuse repository, or to use one of the public repositories such as ASSET or MountainNet. The Internet has also become a source of many valuable assets.

Removing the most common causes for the majority of failure modes depends on developing and enforcing standards for design, documentation, and performance. The recent history of the software industry demonstrates the difficulty of this effort. Nevertheless, the importance of standards for reuse in other engineering disciplines shows that standards are necessary, and that standardization efforts must continue.

4 How To Use The Reuse Failure Modes Model

The reuse failure modes model is a tool for continuously improving software reuse in an organization. To place this tool in context, consider the Deming model for continuous improvement, the Plan-Do-Check-Act (PDCA) Cycle [5]:

1) *Plan* improvement efforts by collecting data and analyzing it to find improvement opportunities;

2) *Do* what was planned by making a change to improve quality and productivity;

3) *Check* that the change is really an improvement by collecting data and analyzing it in comparison with the original data;

4) *Act* to propagate the improvement throughout the organization, establishing a new standard of performance.

These steps form a cycle: after step 4, return to step 1 and repeat the cycle to generate a new round of improvements. The reuse failure modes model is a tool for *planning* and *checking*. It is used to direct the collection and analysis of data, to guide the direction of quality improvement efforts, and to check that improvement efforts are succeeding.

Using the failure modes model (or any effective quality improvement tool) requires that data be collected from software engineers and managers in the organization. This can be done with a survey form. (Survey design is beyond the scope of this paper, but there are many books on the subject e.g., [16].) The survey should provide information on the frequency of reuse failure modes in the organization. Another example of a way to gather such data is from design reviews and inspections. Here, failures to reuse would be identified and recorded during the review sessions.

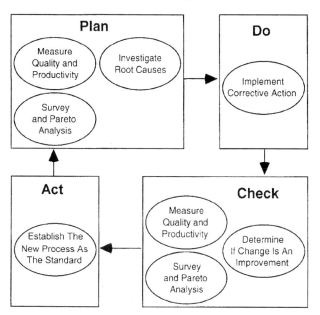

Fig. 3. Using the reuse failure modes model in the PDCA cycle.

Fig. 3 illustrates how to incorporate the failure modes model into the PDCA cycle. Data is first collected in the *Plan* phase of the PDCA cycle. This data should include measurements of quality and productivity levels as well as data about reuse failure modes. Once the data is collected, the failure mode data should be analyzed using the Pareto technique described above. This will identify the key reuse impediments in the organization. Further investigation will likely be necessary to identify the root causes of these key reuse impediments. Corrective measures for the impediments can then be identified. In the *Do* phase of the PDCA cycle, the corrective measures are implemented. Data must then be collected again for the *Check* phase of the PDCA cycle. The data on quality and productivity should show improvement, and the failure modes data should show a decrease in targeted failure modes, if the improvement effort is succeeding. If not, the change may not be working, and something else should be tried. If the data shows improvement, then the change should be propagated to other engineers or systems; this is the *Act* phase of the PDCA cycle. The

cycle may then begin again, either by using the data collected for the checking phase, or by collecting further data.

Say, for example, that an organization is interested in reuse to improve software product quality as measured by the number of defects observed during system test per thousand lines of code. Reuse will be measured using *reuse level*, which provides ratios of reused to total components in a system [17]. This data is collected for products at the beginning of the reuse improvement process giving a set of baseline figures.

Next, the organization surveys employees and does a failure modes analysis. They discover that failure to try to reuse is the primary failure mode, and that lack of education is the primary cause of this failure. The organization decides to implement a pilot reuse education program to reduce occurrence of this failure mode. At this point the organization has completed the *Plan* stage of the PDCA cycle. The organization implements a reuse education pilot program for several projects, completing the *Do* stage of the cycle. After some period of time, say one year, measures of reuse levels and defect densities for the targeted projects are taken, and the survey is redone to gather further failure mode and cause data. The data is analyzed to see if progress has been made, thus realizing the *Check* phase of the cycle. If the pilot education program is shown to be a success, it is expanded to include all engineers, thus spreading the improvement throughout the organization and establishing a new standard of behavior. This constitutes the *Act* phase of the PDCA cycle. The organization now reenters the cycle at the *Plan* phase, thus continuing improvement efforts.

5 SUMMARY

This paper presents a failure modes model of reuse as a tool for improving the level of reuse in organizations. This model consists of seven reuse failure modes. Each of these failure modes has causes, many of which are also discussed. A process for using the model is described.

The model is used to analyze data on reuse failures collected from 113 subjects in 29 organizations. We find the primary reuse failure mode for these organizations is *no attempt to reuse* and that the primary cause is resource constraints, such as too little money and personnel allotted for reuse. This is, of course, primarily a management problem and underscores the observation that management support is necessary for reuse.

REFERENCES

[1] W. Frakes, "Software Reuse: Is it Delivering?" *Proc. 13th Int'l Conf. Software Engineering*, Austin, Texas: IEEE CS Press, 1991.

[2] W. Frakes, "Software Reuse as Industrial Experiment," *American Programmer*, vol. 6, no. 9, pp. 27-33, 1993.

[3] R. Billington and R. Allen, *Reliability Evaluation of Engineering Systems: Concepts and Techniques*. London: Pitman Books, Ltd. 1983.

[4] H. Wadsworth, K. Stevens, and A.B. Godfrey, *Modern Methods for Quality Control and Improvement*. New York: John Wiley & Sons, 1986.

[5] L.J. Arthur, *Improving Software Quality: An Insiders Guide to TQM*. New York: John Wiley & Sons. 1993.

[6] W. Frakes and S. Isoda. "Success Factors of Systematic Reuse," *IEEE Software*, vol. 11, no. 5, pp. 14-19, 1994.

[7] W. Frakes and C. Fox, *Software Reuse Survey Report*. Sterling, Va: Software Engineering Guild, 1993.

[8] W. Frakes and C. Fox, "Sixteen Questions about Software Reuse," *Comm. ACM*, vol. 38, no. 6, pp. 75-87, 1995.

[9] W. Tracz, "The 3 Cons of Software Reuse," *Third Ann. Conf. Software Reuse*, Syracuse, N.Y., 1990.

[10] J. Hollingsworth, "Software Component Design for Reuse," PhD dissertation, Ohio State Univ., Columbus, 1992.

[11] J.D. McGregor and D. A. Sykes, *Object-Oriented Software Development: Engineering Software for Reuse*. New York: Van Nostrand Reinhold, 1992.

[12] W. Frakes and T. Pole, "An Empirical Study of Representation Methods for Reusable Software Components," *IEEE Trans. Software Engineering*, vol. 20, no. 8, pp. 617-630, Aug. 1994.

[13] B.W. Weide, W.F. Ogden, and S.H. Zweben. "Reusable Software Components," *Advances in Computers*, M. Yovits, ed., 1991.

[14] J. Poore and C. Trammell, "Component Certification, Validation, and Qualification." *Proc. Second Ann. West Virginia Education and Training Workshop*, Morgantown, W. Va., pp. 57-72. 1993.

[15] J. Bentley, *Writing Efficient Programs*. Englewood Cliffs, NJ: Prentice Hall, 1982.

[16] C. Backstrom and G. Hursh, *Survey Research*. Evanston, Ill.: Northwestern Press, 1963.

[17] W. Frakes and C. Terry. "Software Reuse: Metrics and Models," *ACM Computing Surveys*, 1996, to appear.

Reusing Software: Issues and Research Directions

Hafedh Mili, Fatma Mili, and Ali Mili

Abstract—Software productivity has been steadily increasing over the past 30 years, but not enough to close the gap between the demands placed on the software industry and what the state of the practice can deliver [22], [39]; nothing short of an order of magnitude increase in productivity will extricate the software industry from its perennial crisis [39], [67]. Several decades of intensive research in software engineering and artificial intelligence left few alternatives but software reuse as the (only) realistic approach to bring about the gains of productivity and quality that the software industry needs. In this paper, we discuss the implications of reuse on the production, with an emphasis on the technical challenges. Software reuse involves building software that is reusable by design and building *with* reusable software. Software reuse includes reusing both the products of previous software projects and the processes deployed to produce them, leading to a wide spectrum of reuse approaches, from the building *blocks* (reusing products) approach, on one hand, to the *generative* or reusable *processor* (reusing processes), on the other [68]. We discuss the implication of such approaches on the organization, control, and method of software development and discuss proposed models for their economic analysis.

Software reuse benefits from methodologies and tools to:

1) build more readily reusable software and

2) locate, evaluate, and tailor reusable software, the last being critical for the building blocks approach.

Both sets of issues are discussed in this paper, with a focus on application generators and OO development for the first and a thorough discussion of retrieval techniques for software components, component composition (or bottom-up design), and transformational systems for the second. We conclude by highlighting areas that, in our opinion, are worthy of further investigation.

Index Terms—Software reuse, managerial aspects of software reuse, software reuse measurements, building reusable components, OO software development, software component retrieval, adapting reusable components.

I. INTRODUCTION

DESPITE several decades of intensive research, the routine production of software under acceptable conditions of quality and productivity remains an unfulfilled promise. While a great deal of progress has been achieved in understanding the mechanics of constructing a program from a specification, little progress has been achieved in improving the practice of software development accordingly. This predicament stems, in our opinion, from two premises:

- First, a problem of scale: most of our current knowledge

Manuscript received April 1992; revised August 1993.

H. Mili is with the Département d'Informatique, université du Québec à Montréal, Boite Postale 8888, Succ "A", Montréal, Québec, H3C 3P8 Canada.

F. Mili is with the School of Engineering and Computer Science, Oakland University, Rochester, MI 48309-4401.

A. Mili is with the Department of Computer Science, University of Ottawa, Ottawa, Ontario K1N 6N5 Canada.

IEEECS Log Number S95009.

in program construction deals with minute details about semantics of programming languages and correctness formulas; while this knowledge is enlightening and instructive, it is rather inadequate to deal with the current pressures on the software industry (in terms of productivity and quality).

- Second, a problem of emphasis: the problem of scale could in principle be tackled with automated tools if it were not for the fact that the most crucial decisions that must be taken in a program construction process, such as the choice of algorithms, control structures, and data structures, are also the most difficult to formalize—hence to automate.

As a result, a wide gap exists nowadays between the demands placed on the software industry (by a society that is increasingly dependent on software and increasingly intolerant of software failure) and what the state of the practice in the industry can deliver; also the brief history of the field abounds with instances of failure [19], [38], [67].

Software reuse offers a great deal of potential in terms of software productivity and software quality, because it tackles the above issues adequately: By dealing with software products at the component level and by focusing on arbitrarily abstract descriptions of software components, it addresses the question of scale; on the other hand, by dealing with software design at the architectural level, rather than the coding level, it addresses the question of emphasis. However, several factors hinder reuse, including the infancy of software development as a scientific [44] or engineering discipline [144], inadequate training in software development in general and software reuse in particular [159], inadequate management structures and practices [59], and the lack of methodologies and tools to support software reuse or software development in general [47]. In this paper, we discuss the most important of these issues and focus on the methodological and technical aspects.

It is customary to categorize software reuse work based on what is being reused (the *object of reuse*) or on the method of reuse (see, e.g., [83] and [68]), the two being closely related. It is customary to distinguish between two general categories of reuse approaches, the *building blocks* approach, which is based on reusing software development *products*, and the *generative* or *reusable processor* approach, which is based on reusing the *process* of previous software development efforts, often embodied in computer tools (processor) that automate part of the development life cycle [68]; these are but two extreme approaches on a continuum involving different mixes of product and process reuse [148]. We refer to both products and processes as *reusable assets*. Reuse approaches raise a number of issues that may be divided into issues related to developing *reusable assets* and issues related to *developing* with *reusable assets*. Under the former set of issues, we focus on

Reprinted from *IEEE Transactions on Software Engineering*, Vol. 21, No. 6, June 1995, pp. 528-562.

169

OO software development, as an enabling technology for developing reusable building blocks, and application generators as an example of a commercially successful application of the generative approach. Developing with reusable assets raises issues related to providing methodological and computer support for:

1) locating reusable assets,
2) assessing their relevance to the current needs and
3) adapting them to those needs.

Such issues are anywhere from secondary to irrelevant to the reusable processor end of the spectrum, but are central to the building blocks end of the spectrum. Under adaptation, we discuss a number of techniques for automating the integration and maintenance of reusable components, with an emphasis on techniques other than those offered by object orientation, which are discussed separately, along with other OO principles.

In the next section, we attempt to motivate and define software reuse, and provide a typology of software reuse research, to be used throughout the paper. In Section III, we discuss the overall impact of software reuse on the production of software, starting with the organizational and methodological impact of reuse on the development of software, and then discuss cost/benefit models of software reuse. Sections IV and V focus on the technical challenges and research solutions involved in building reusable software assets and building *with* reusable software assets, respectively. We conclude in Section VI by outlining areas and issues that, in our view, deserve further attention in the research community.

II. A FRAMEWORK FOR SOFTWARE REUSE

A. Motivations

Software productivity has been steadily rising for the past 30 years [160]. However, even with the steady rise in the number of computer professionals [22], it has not kept up with the rising demand for developing new ever more complex software systems and for maintaining existing software [22], [103]. While current software production management practices leave room for improvement [15], nothing short of an order of magnitude increase in programmer productivity will extricate the software industry from the current crisis [67]. According to Boehm, the only factor that can yield that kind of productivity leverage is the number of software source instructions that have to be developed to deliver a given functionality [22]: Instead of searching for ways of writing code faster, we have to look for ways of writing less of it. Automatic programming, whereby a computer system is capable of producing executable code based on informal, incomplete, and incoherent user requirements, is decades away, if ever possible [136]. That leaves us with software reuse as the only realistic, technically feasible solution: We could reuse the processes and products of previous development efforts in order to develop new applications.

Intuitively, savings occur with software product reuse because reused components do not have to be built from scratch.

Further, overall product quality improves if quality components are reused. With software process reuse, productivity increases to the extent that the reused processes are automated, and quality improves to the extent that quality-enhancing processes are systematized. Further, there is plenty of duplication in the applications being developed and maintained nowadays, and hence plenty of room for reuse. In 1984, for example, the U.S. software market offered some 500 accounting programs, 300 payroll programs, 150 communication programs, 125 word-processing packages, etc. [77]; the figures are probably higher today. In the early eighties, Lanergan and Grasso estimated that 60% of business applications can be standardized and reused [85]. Generally, potential (estimated) and actual reuse rates range from 15% to 85% (see, e.g., [59], [103]). Existing experience reports suggest that indeed good— sometimes impressive—reuse rates, productivity and quality increases can be achieved (see, e.g., [12], [13], [73], [100]). However, successes have not been systematic (see, e.g., [59], [133]), and a lot of work remains to be done both in terms of "institutionalizing" reuse practice in organizations and in terms of addressing the myriad of technical challenges that make reuse difficult [83].

B. The Object of Reuse

The idea of formal software reuse, as first introduced by McIlroy in his 1968 seminal paper [104], entailed the development of an industry of reusable source-code software components and the industrialization of the production of application software from off-the-shelf components. Software reuse is now understood to encompass all the resources used and produced during the development of software (see, e.g., [43], [50], [133]). Different researchers proposed different categorizations of reusable knowledge, but by and large, most classifications rely on one of three factors or a combination thereof:

1) stage of development at which the knowledge is produced and/or used,
2) level of abstraction (e.g., abstract versus concrete/implemented) and
3) nature of knowledge (e.g., artifacts versus skills).

Jones identified four types of reusable artifacts [77]:

1) *data reuse*, involving a standardization of data formats,
2) *architectures reuse*, which consists of standardizing a set of design and programming conventions dealing with the logical organization of software,
3) (detailed) *design reuse*, for some common business applications and
4) *program reuse*, which deals with reusing executable code. In addition to product/artifact reuse, Horowitz considered various kinds of reuse based on the utilization of very high-level program-producing systems [68].

Three general classes of systems that have been commonly recognized by researchers are:

1) reusable program patterns [19], [68], whereby code or design patterns are used to instantiate specific code fragments or designs, as in application generators or the Programmer Apprentice's clichés [137],

2) *reusable processors* [68], which are interpreters for executable high-level specifications and

3) *reusable transformation systems* [19], [68], whereby some development activities have been embodied in more or less formal transformations (see, e.g., [17], [118], [123]).

Krueger proposed a multilevel categorization of reusable information based on levels of abstraction, where reusable items of level i are, by and large, abstractions of reusable items of level $i-1$, and thus managed to account, more or less easily, for reuse approaches as diverse as source code-scavenging and very high-level languages within the same "abstraction hierarchy" [83].

The above categorizations account for application domain knowledge only to the extent that such a knowledge is embedded in the artifacts (e.g., code and designs) or processes (e.g., application generators). Freeman proposed a five-level hierarchy of reusable *software development knowledge* in which domain knowledge is represented explicitly:

1) environmental knowledge,
2) external knowledge,
3) functional architectures,
4) logical structures and
5) code fragments [50].

The classification corresponds somewhat to the software life cycle, where the last three levels map to the products of system design, detailed design, and coding. The first two (environmental and external) are typically used to derive a particular system's specifications from the user requirements. Freeman distinguished between user- (consumer-) related domain-dependent requirements and developer- (supplier-) related, technology-dependent requirements and characterized the needed knowledge as shown in Table I.

TABLE I
A BREAKDOWN OF ENVIRONMENTAL AND
EXTERNAL SOFTWARE DEVELOPMENT KNOWLEDGE [50]

Level	Supplier-Related Knowledge	Customer-Related Knowledge
Environmental	**Technology transfer knowledge**: consists of knowledge about such things as the organizational impact of software technology, personnel training, computer literacy, and so forth.	**Utilization knowledge**: describes the business context in which the software product will be used.
External	**Development knowledge**: deals with the planning and management of software projects such as cost and schedule estimation, test plans, benchmarking, and others.	**Application-area knowledge**: deals with the underlying models for the application domain.

It is the environmental level of software development knowledge that is explicitly lacking from similar life cycle-based categorizations of reusable information. In his 1987 paper, Freeman identified the reuse of environmental knowledge as one of the long-term research goals in software reuse [50]. We know of no research effort that has attempted or is attempting to formalize the reuse of such knowledge since. One area that has been getting considerable attention recently, however, is the reuse of application domain knowledge under the form of *domain models* (see, e.g., [5], [50], [91], [132], [148]). Domain models serve three major purposes:

1) helping developers *understand* an application domain,
2) serving as the starting point for systems analysis (e.g., by specializing the domain model) and
3) providing an application-dependent categorization/classification of existing reusable components (of later development stages) so that opportunities for reuse can be identified as early in the development process as possible [5], [130], [132].

Domain models should identify:

- the entities and operations on those entities that are common to the application domain,
- relationships and constraints between the entities and
- "retrieval cues," i.e., properties of objects that are likely to be used by developers in the process of searching for reusable components [5], [132].

We know of few research efforts that include *declarative* domain models that support all three functions described above (see, e.g., [5], [91]). Neighbors's DRACO system [121] and Simos's work on ASLs [148] achieve much of the same goals by developing domain-dependent specification languages that embody an application domain's common objects and operations

In the next section, we propose our own ontological categorization of reusable knowledge. Our categorization is geared toward highlighting the *paradigmatic* differences between the various reuse methods and abstracting what we consider to be inessential differences between various reusable assets (e.g., code reuse versus design reuse).

C. The Method of Reuse

We adopt the transformational systems' view of software development as a sequence of transformations and/or translations of the description of the desired system from one language (level i description) to another (level $i + 1$ description) as shown in Fig. 1. Three levels of knowledge are used in this translation:

1) knowledge about the source domain (level i),
2) knowledge about the target domain (level $i + 1$), and
3) knowledge about how objects (entities, relations, structures) from the source domain map to objects in the target domain.

For a given level, the knowledge can be seen in linguistic terms, as consisting of a domain language, and a set of expressions known to be valid. The domain language consists of domain entities (or classes) and domain structures. The description of the various entities and structures can be based on an enumeration of legal entities and structures, or based on a set of properties that must be satisfied by either (e.g., consistency checks, composition rules), or a mix of the two. We refer to the description methods as enumerated and compositional, respectively. The descriptions of past problem instances constitute the expressions that are known to be valid.

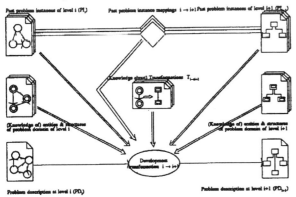

Figure 1. A categorization of reusable knowledge

The mapping knowledge consists of a set of transformation rules, from level i to level $i + 1$, and a set of known mappings between problem instances of level i and problem instances of level $i + 1$. The transformation rules[1] embody what is usually referred to as process reuse or *skill reuse* (see, e.g., [133]). We shall refer to them as the transformation grammar. Note that this formalism does not distinguish between declarative knowledge and procedural knowledge as we feel the distinction to be mainly a representation issue.

Typically, development consists of, first, describing (specifying) the problem at hand in the language of level i to obtain a description PD_i and, second, transforming that description into one at level $i + 1$ (PD_{i+1}), supposed to be the target description language (e.g., executable code). With reuse, one would want to avoid having to *manually*:

1) specify *completely* the problem at hand and/or
2) transform the entire specification of level i into level $i + 1$.

Thus, reusable assets include all the kinds of knowledge involved in the development transformation (DT_{i_i+1}), which can be thought of as the result of applying a generic level-independent problem-solving method on the relevant knowledge sources. The various reuse approaches can be categorized based on:

1) the extent to which the language of level i covers the problem domain of level i and
2) the extent to which the mapping knowledge (T_{i_i+1}) covers all the entities and structures (i.e., all the valid expressions) of the domain of level i.

1. These rules do not only ensure syntactic correctness of the result description of level $i + 1$, but also the preservation of some properties and the satisfaction of some "development constraints."

Finer characterizations may be based on the kind of language description used, along the enumerated versus compositional dimension. Table II shows the characteristics of some of the approaches commonly referred to in the literature. As we go down the rows of Table II, we move from what is generally referred to as the *building blocks* approach to increasingly automated *generative* approaches. Automation requires the complete "cover" of the source domain language (level i) *and* the completeness of the mapping knowledge $i \rightarrow i + 1$. In other words, automation is possible if we can express all new problems in terms of problems, or combinations of problems, that have already been solved. We comment below on the various approaches separately.

With source code components, a new problem is solved by composing solutions to subproblems. A complete cover of level i domain would mean that all the components that one may need have been developed, or, more astutely—but equally unrealistic—a set of components has been developed such that every problem can be reduced to subproblems that these components can solve. Notwithstanding the issue of finding such a decomposition/reduction, which can be as challenging as solving the original problem analytically from scratch (see Section V.B), the number of required components is most probably prohibitive [83]. That number depends on:

1) the breadth of the application domain and
2) the composition technique used.

With source code components, composition often takes place "too late" in the software life cycle,[2] limiting the range of behaviors that can be obtained from a set of components to variations on functional composition, as supported by traditional module interconnection languages (see, e.g., [129]) or programming languages. Source code components approaches that support composition of components at a higher level of abstraction yield a greater range of behaviors (see, e.g., [78], [149]). Software schemas are similar to source code components, except that the reusable artifacts are defined at a higher level of abstraction, allowing for a greater range of instantiations (through partial generation) and compositions. Further, the added parameterization makes it possible to build complex, yet generally useful structures (see, e.g., [16]). However, the artifacts are still not meant to cover all the needs of the application domain, and finding and expressing the right compositions are still challenging design problems.

With the remaining three approaches, the source domain language covers the application domain. Transformational systems fall short of automation because the mapping knowledge is incomplete or non-deterministic: A transformational system needs developer assistance in selecting among applicable—and perhaps *objectively* equivalent—transformations [123]. The transformational approach can be used in conjunction with source code components to assist in the modification and integration of such components in new applications [113]. Full

2. Booch's C++ components include 18 implementations of dequeues corresponding to all the possible combinations of choices of
• the concurrency control algorithm,
• the memory allocation algorithm, and
• the ordering algorithm [149].

TABLE II
A CATEGORIZATION OF COMMON REUSE APPROACHES

Approach	Language Level I			Mapping Knowledge		Spectrum	Examples
	Life Cycle Stage	Covering	Description Type	Covering	Description Type		
Source code components (see [50], [83])	mostly design	partial	compositional (mostly)	partial	composition al (mostly)	wide spectrum	RSL [27], REBOOT [116], and a number of other "nameless" tools and approaches (e.g. [85], [131], [161]). Object-orientation, seen as a development methodology for reusable components, is discussed in §IV.C. Problems related to the use of such components are discussed in various subsections §V.
Software schemas (see e.g. [83], or referred to as *reusable program patterns* in [77])	mostly design	partial	compositional (mostly)	partial (mostly)	compositional (mostly)	wide spectrum	The programmer's apprentice [137], the PARIS system [80], and Basset's *frame-based software engineering*, in which an application could be *completely* specified and generated using frames [16]. Software schemas are briefly discussed in the context of OO technology §IV.C).
Reusable transformation systems (see e.g. [19], [50])	Software specifications	complete	compositional	partial	compositional	wide-spectrum	A somewhat outdated survey of transformational systems is given in [123]; their potential for quality-preserving maintenance and reuse has been recognized by a number of researchers, including Feather [45], Arango et al. [4], and Baxter [17]. They are discussed in more detail in §V.C.
Application generators (see e.g. [83])	User requirements complete	complete	enumerated (mostly)	complete	narrow, domain-specific	narrow, domain-specific	Unix's Yacc, a number of commercial tools in business information processing (see e.g.[69] for a survey), a number of user interface building frameworks (see e.g. [119] for a survey), etc. Discussed in more detail in §V.B.
Very high-level languages [83], reusable processor [77], etc	Software specifications	complete	*Emphatically* compositional	complete	compositional	depends on the system	Simos' ASL are application-specific languages [148], PAISLey [162] SETL [82] and others are based on application-independent mathematical and computational abstractions. T}.TE.LP.ls 2.cc Table 2. A categorization of common reuse approaches..LP.sp.PP

automation is achieved with application generators and very high-level languages. With very high-level languages, automation is possible at the cost of code efficiency and design quality; very high-level languages are not intended to implement production quality software. Automation is possible with application generators because of a restriction of the application domain.[3] The restriction has the added advantage of making it practical to enumerate a set of template software specifications (or the corresponding software "solutions") parameterized directly with user requirements

It is fair to say that as we go down Table II, the focus shifts from components to composition, and the language for expressing compositions moves up in terms of abstraction. This corresponds closely to Simos's "reuse life cycle," which prescribes an evolution of reuse approaches within organizations, following the maturing of both the application domain *and* the expertise of developers within that domain [148].

The next section deals with the non-technical effects of software reuse on the production of software, including,

1) its effects on the organizational structure of software producing organizations and on the software life cycle,
2) measuring reuse effectiveness, both in technical and economic terms and
3) some reported case studies.

Section IV deals with issues related to building reusable knowledge, with a focus on source code components and application generators. Section V deals with issues related to building new applications *with* reusable knowledge. Such issues are, for the most part, trivial or irrelevant to the application generators and very high-level languages approaches. The discussion will thus be geared toward the building blocks end of the spectrum, and we address issues related to component retrieval, composition, and adaptation. Transformational systems will be discussed to the extent that they help adapt reusable components in a time-saving, quality-preserving way.

---

3. No application generator available today can build a corporate information system. However, big chunks of such systems (e.g., report generators) can be generated using application generators [34].

III. SOFTWARE REUSE AND THE PRODUCTION OF SOFTWARE

Software reuse provides some feasible remedies to the current software crisis, but many questioned the suitability of existing management practices, organizational structures, and technologies to support software reuse. There is a general agreement that a rethinking of software manufacturing is needed. There is also agreement that the required changes are managerial, cultural, and technical in nature, as was the case for other engineering disciplines [15], [39], [144]. There is no consensus, however, as to the nature and scope of changes, both because the changes involve some yet to be proven management techniques and structures and because the proposed technological answers are different. In this section, we first discuss the effect of software reuse on the organization of software development processes (Section III.A); these changes depend on the reuse paradigm used, along the building blocks versus generative spectrum. Next (Section III.B), we discuss ways to measure software reuse and its impact on productivity and quality. We conclude in Section III.C by discussing the relation between the qualitative effects and measurable effects of software reuse and the challenges that stand in the way of comparing the effectiveness of the various reuse approaches.

A. Software Reuse and Software Engineering

It is fair to say that technological innovations in software development contributed to enhancing software reusability, starting with high-level programming languages, up to structured and modular programming, up to design and analysis notations and methodologies. The same cannot be said about the organization and management of software organizations, which are at best reuse-neutral when they do not hinder reuse practice. We organize our discussion of the changes required and implied by reuse practice into,

1) new organizational structures (e.g., staffing structure),
2) new process models (life cycles) and
3) punctual methodological changes.

A.1. New Organizational Structures

Software reuse relies on the availability of a base of reusable software in all forms (Section IV). Wegner argues that software companies should treat software as capital goods and their organization, including team structures and cost imputations, should reflect that [155]. This is true whether we are dealing with the building blocks approach or with the generative approach: in both cases we have to divert resources, both human and financial, into building a common base of reusable software assets to be amortized over several uses, be they application generators or source code components. It is widely accepted that, in addition to the typical project team structure of software organizations, a team responsible for building and maintaining a base of reuse capital is needed. Different authors proposed different divisions of labor between project teams and "reuse capital" teams. Within the building blocks approach, the component library team would, minimally, be responsible for packaging (e.g., documenting) and controlling

the quality of what gets added to the reuse base [131]. The library team could also play an active role in *creating* reusable software of all forms. Barnes studied the economic models for two such arrangements [10]:

1) a pure producer-consumer relationship between the library team and project teams, where the library team is solely responsible for producing reusable components, and
2) a shared arrangement where project teams contribute to and consume what is in the library.

Caldieri and Basili [28] proposed a more software factory-like approach [40]. In their model, project teams do no programming (see Fig. 2). They are responsible for requirements and design specifications—which they submit to the *experience factory*—and for integration and integration testing [28]. The experience factory's activities can be divided into:

1) *Synchronous activities,* which are activities initiated following requests from project teams, and can range from a simple look-up to building the required components from scratch. Such activities are subjected to project teams' schedules.
2) *Asynchronous activities,* consisting of creating components that are likely to be requested (anticipating future demands), or reengineering components generated by the synchronous activities to enhance their reusability.

In [12], Basili et al. report on experiences at the Software Engineering Laboratory (SEL), funded and operated by the University of Maryland, NASA, and the Computer Sciences Corp., in which the above structure has evolved over the years.

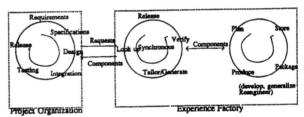

Figure 2. Reuse framework and organization. From [28].

The experience factory was responsible mainly for *process* (vs. *product*) development and reuse [12], [13]. Over a period of five years, reuse rates increased from 26% to 96%, the cost per delivered statement decreased by 58%, a 138% increase in productivity[4]—and the number of errors decreased by a factor of four [12]. It is not clear how a pure producer-consumer relationship between the experience factory and the project teams would have worked. With the building blocks approach, there are a number of motivational and managerial challenges to putting into place such a structure, including putting the

---

4. The experiments reported in [12] used a project implemented in Fortran as a baseline for errors and cost. Subsequent projects were implemented in Ada. The numbers mentioned here used the first year data with Ada projects as a baseline, instead of the Fortran project. When the Fortran project is used as a baseline, we obtain smaller decrease of cost of delivered statement (35% instead of 58%), but a greater decrease in error rates (a factor of eight, instead of a factor of four), which is to be expected.

most qualified developers[5] in the least satisfying tasks (experience factory) [28] and redistributing responsibility and control of individual projects in a way that may diffuse accountability. Such a division of labor is less problematic with the application generators approach where the skills required from *application developers* are markedly different from those required of *application generator developers*: The former have to be versed in the application domain, possibly end users, while the latter have to be both domain experts *and* software development experts [89]. Less revolutionary divisions of labor exist in more traditional organizations where the job of system administrators and support staff often evolves into building and supporting custom-tailored development tools— embodying reusable processes—or at Japanese software factories, based essentially on a tighter management and measurement of software activities and products (see, e.g., [99], [100]).

A.2. New Process Models

A software life cycle is a model for organizing, planning, and controlling the activities associated with software development and maintenance [124]. For the most part, a life cycle identifies development tasks and identifies and standardizes intermediary work products (deliverables) and review and evaluation criteria. The known life cycles may be classified based on the kind of development tasks and work products involved, and the organization of such tasks. For example, the waterfall life cycle, the spiral model [21], and to some extent prototyping, all involve some measure of analysis, design, coding, and testing. However, while the waterfall life cycle implies that an entire system is analyzed before any part of it is designed or implemented, both the spiral model and prototyping prescribe the analysis $\longleftrightarrow$ testing cycle on system increments [1]. Newer development paradigms usually shorten the analysis $\longleftrightarrow$ testing cycle by automating one or more steps along the cycle [2]. When we talk about software reuse, there are two life cycles to consider

1) the life cycle for developing reusable assets and
2) the life cycle for developing *with* reusable assets.

Issues to consider include whether the two life cycles are different and whether the availability of a base of reusable assets modifies the underlying life cycle. This depends on both the reuse approach used—along the building blocks $\longleftrightarrow$ generative dimension—and on the development methodology used.

With the building blocks approach, both the reusable assets and the products developed with them are software components. Reusable components may be developed either concurrently or separately from specific product development, corresponding closely to the synchronous and asynchronous activities, respectively, of the experience factory in Caldieri and Basili's model (see above). When they are developed concurrently, they follow the same life cycle as non reusable components, except that greater care may go into building and pack-

aging them. When a separate activity is set aside for developing them, we talk about *domain analysis* and *domain engineering*. One of the major inputs of domain analysis is a set of already developed systems within the domain, whose common features are identified, abstracted, implemented, and then packaged [132]. The identification and abstraction of common features can take place at the earliest development stage for which there is adequate documentation. For example, if good quality analysis documents for the existing systems are available, the common features can be recognized at the analysis level. If not, one needs to look at existing designs or even code fragments, perform some measure of reverse-engineering to recover requirements of individual systems/components, identify common features, abstract them, and forward-engineer them

Building new applications with reusable components need not follow a radically different life cycle from building new applications without reusable components (see, e.g., [6], [27], [76], [131]). One of the criticisms leveled at the waterfall life cycle is that each life cycle stage is mainly influenced by the previous stages (top-down), while the existence of reusable components requires some sort of a look-ahead procedure to identify opportunities for reuse and take advantage of them [66], [148]. We believe this to be mainly a documentation issue: Reuse has traditionally meant reuse of small code fragments that have little or no life cycle documentation; if analysis information were stored in components libraries, for example, analysts could identify opportunities for reuse at the analysis level without looking at the actual code of reusable components. The point has been made, though, that OO software development, the reuse methodology par excellence, requires a mix of top-down and bottom-up approaches[6] [66]. This is explained by the premise that an OO development life cycle needs to combine application and domain engineering in order to attain reuse objectives [66]. The application engineering part of the life cycle proceeds in a top-down fashion from requirements gathering to high-level system design. Domain engineering consists of building "clusters" (libraries or layers [107]) of classes, starting with the lowest level (building blocks) which would most likely be needed no matter what the final system design is like, and moving up to application-specific classes, looping back on system design or even analysis [66]. Other OO-induced life cycle changes have been proposed in the literature that are motivated by considerations other than reuse, such as managing the risks inherent in switching to a new development technology [125].

The situation is markedly different with the generative approach. Application generators, which experienced some commercial success, have been studied in the literature (see, e.g., [89], [98]). However, by and large, the process of build-

---

5. In the SEL at the Univ. of Maryland, the experience factory was mainly staffed by researchers [12]. However, they spent their time mainly collecting and analyzing data and proposing process enhancements, rather than developing variants of sort algorithms or stack structures!

6. The terms top-down and bottom-up are used in software engineering to mean two things. They may refer to the direction used to go through the stages of a life cycle. For the waterfall life cycle, top-down means going from requirements to testing/integration. The terms are also used to refer to construction paradigms, the analytical (top-down) versus synthetic (bottom-up). Things get confused because synthesizing systems from components suggests that detailed design is done before system design, e.g., and the two meanings overlap.

ing "reusable processors" has not earned a lot of attention, perhaps because most of the executable specification languages are research prototypes. A notable exception is Simos's work on application-specific specification languages (ASL), and what he calls *domain life cycle* [148]. He sees ASLs as the culmination of the maturation of an application domain, or of an organization's expertise in that domain. The maturation starts with small reusable code components and moves toward more abstract representations and more complex constructs until an entire application domain is "covered" (Section II.C) [148]. The effect of using the generative approach for software development is much easier to assess: The generative approach shortens traditional life cycles through automation (see, e.g., [98]). Application generators, for example, obviate the need for specifying the software requirements, designing, coding, and testing, of big chunks of applications [89]. Executable specification languages and transformational systems obviate the need for designing, coding, and testing, but developers still need to produce precise formal specifications of the desired system [1].

A.3. Effects on Development Methods

Software development can be considered as a problem-solving activity, the problem being that of finding a software implementation that satisfies a set of user requirements. Cognitive scientists and AI theorists alike consider recall as an essential part of human problem-solving (see, e.g., [88], [141]). Broadly speaking, when faced with a problem, we first perform a "rote recall" to see if we haven't solved the problem before [88]. When that fails, we start looking for *analogical* (similar) problems that we might have already solved and adapt their solution to the problem at hand [29]. When that fails, we fall back on general analytic problem-solving knowledge and skills [88]. Traditional development methodologies (e.g., SA/SD [124]) are analytical in nature and fall back immediately on general problem-solving knowledge and heuristics such as divide and conquer and successive refinements. Researchers recognize that "informal reuse" (i.e., in developer's head) has always been taking place, whereby the base of reusable knowledge is "acquired" individually by developers through experience (see, e.g., [11]). To some extent, "formal" software reuse in general and the building blocks approach in particular recognize the earlier recall-based phases of problem-solving and aim at formalizing them and providing computer support for them.

Challenges to supporting reuse within development methodologies include:

1) identifying reuse tasks and the skills required to perform those tasks (see, e.g., [95]),
2) providing methodological and tool support for these tasks (see, e.g., [113], [116]), and
3) integrating reuse activities into the normal workflow of developers (see, e.g., [47] and [113]).

The reuse tasks depend heavily on the reuse approach used along the building blocks vs. generative axis. With the generative approach, the reuse tasks consist of specifying the desired application in a high-level language (executable specification

language, 4GL, etc.), and the required cognitive skills need not be different from those required of traditional development methods. With the building blocks approach, developers try to build a system that satisfies a set of requirements by using as many existing components (or developing as little code) as possible. For any part of the target system, developers must (see, e.g., [47], [95], [113], [135]):

1) formulate the requirements of the part in a way that supports retrieval of potentially useful reusable components,
2) understand the retrieved components and
3) if the retrieved components are sufficiently "close" to the needs at hand and are of sufficient quality, then adapt them.

If no component is found that matches perfectly or closely the given requirements, developers may fall back on general-purpose analytical heuristics to decompose the system (or part thereof) into smaller parts for which steps 1 to 3 may be reiterated [135].

The search and retrieval problem benefits from a large body of work in the area of document retrieval and will be discussed in more detail in Section V.A. For the time being, we note that in the context of reuse, we need more than an algorithm that tries to match a requirement to a *single* component; we need a retrieval system that is capable of *synthesizing* a set of building blocks into a single component that satisfies the developer's requirement. This is what is commonly referred to as bottom-up development. This is perhaps the most challenging problem in the building blocks approach, and where computer assistance is much needed. Yet, there have been few concrete proposals (see, e.g., [62], [79]). Component synthesis and aggregation is discussed in more detail in Section V.B.

Component/program understanding represents an important part of both the mental effort and the cost factor, in reuse [47], [95] and maintenance[7] [103]. Component understanding can mean three things:

1) understanding what it does,
2) understanding how it does it and
3) understanding how to modify it in such a way that it does something a little different.

In a reuse—and maintenance—context, some abstract (implementation independent) component documentation should accommodate step 1, obviating the need for reusers to browse through actual code—i.e., obviating the need for step 2. For components whose evolution/adaptation and extension has been properly planned, the amount of knowledge needed for step 3 can be very small, compared to what it would take to explain how the component works, i.e., step 2; the knowledge required for step 3 corresponds to documenting what Krueger called the *variable part* of component abstractions [83]. It is reasonable to assume that if a component is to be modified in an unanticipated (or not properly parameterized) fashion, one might need to delve into the minute details of the component, and the knowledge required for step 3 may be comparable to that required for step 2. However, studies have shown that reusers are able to edit and adapt components

---

7. A 1979 study done at IBM revealed that "maintainers" spend at least 30% of their time trying to understand the code to be modified [103].

with only a sketchy understanding of how they work [95]; whether that is desirable or not is another issue.[8]

Program understanding involves the recognition of high-level abstract patterns amid complex and detailed structures. Studies have shown that experts and novices use different approaches to program understanding[9] suggesting that reusers and maintainers may need training in program understanding or the support of tools that help them understand programs [47], [95], [103].

Component understanding is the first step toward component adaptation. Unplanned component adaptation constitutes a textbook case in *analogical problem-solving* [29]. Analogical problem-solving is used when the mapping from problem to solution cannot be characterized intensionally, but such that some <problem,solution> pairs are known for which elements in the solution space (software artifacts) can be traced to elements in the problem space (requirements). A new problem NP is solved by first matching it to a known problem-solution pair <KP, KS>, and then using the difference between NP and KP to infer the difference between KS and the actual solution of NP (NS). Analogical problem-solving is unsound in the sense that a problem solution NS is not guaranteed to solve the problem NP; if we modify a component using this kind of reasoning, we lose any assurances that the modified version does what it says (verification), and what we want it to do (validation). It is *inherently* unsound because it relies on an incomplete knowledge (partial *extension*) of the problem → solution mapping. This kind of technique is only used in the constrained context of transformational systems (see, e.g., [17] and Section V.C) or for informal software artifacts for which there is not much else that can be done (see, e.g., [94]).

In terms of tool support and integration, there is a fairly wide consensus that tools for reuse tasks should integrate seamlessly into CASE environments (see, e.g., [47], [94], [113], [116]). Typical reuse functionalities such as search, copy, and edit should be available to developers in a modeless fashion, and should not distract them from their normal workflow (see, e.g., [113]). Broadly speaking, reuse-oriented CASE environments should be viewed as problem-solving aids, to be used as extensions of developer's mental workspace, rather than a rigid formalism requiring constant translation back and forth to that mental workspace. This entails, among other things, enabling developers to custom-tailor their development environments and providing them with *proactive* development aids/tools [47]. The former is made possible by offering fine-grained development functionalities which developers may combine and sequence at will [116]. The latter remains a research goal, although some knowledge-based systems made some headway in that direction (see, e.g., [147]).

---

8. Such reuse does away with the quality incentive, and may cost resources for debugging and testing.
9. It was found that experts classify program segments along functional lines, while novices classify program segments along syntactical/superficial similarities. Also, experts use a mix of a bottom-up phase, collecting enough clues to formulate a hypothesis (a pattern), followed by a top-down predictive/verification phase during which they check whether the remaining clues fit in the pattern, while novices use a straight bottom-up strategy, trying to understand programs one line at a time [95].

B. Measuring Software Reuse

Economic considerations are at the center of any discussion of software reuse. Indeed, the most vaunted advantages of software reuse are:

1) an increase of the productivity of software development, which translates directly into monetary terms and
2) an improvement of the quality of the products, which may mean less corrective maintenance, easier perfective maintenance, greater user satisfaction, and so forth, all of which translate into monetary gains.

There are also different costs associated with software reuse, both capital setup (up-front) costs and proportional costs (cost-per-use). Further, different technical approaches to reuse have different investment and return on investment profiles (see, e.g., [42], [148]). Economic models and software metrics are needed that quantify the costs and benefits of reuse. Only recently have researchers started to tackle this problem (see, e.g., [7], [10], [11]). Such studies will not only help convince management of the advantages of software reuse—in case there are any—but will also guide the choice of the technical approaches, and improve the management of the introduction of reuse work methods within organizations [12], [15].

Traditional software metrics that estimate (predict) or measure (after the fact) effort, size, and the relation between them (productivity) need to be amended to account for software reuse. For example, reusable components that accommodate several uses tend to be bigger in size than a version that accommodates a single use, and more complex (see, e.g., [7], [97]). Further, reuse practice presents managers and developers with choices whose implications have to be measured at the organization, project, and task levels. We recognize three such decisions:

1) the decision to launch an organization-wide software reuse program (a long-term, capital investment-like decision [11], [52], [128]),
2) the decision to develop a reusable asset (a *domain engineering decision* [52]) and
3) the decision to (re)use a reusable asset in an application currently under development (an *application engineering decision* [52]).

In the next three sections, we discuss the work relevant to these decisions. Because of the dependencies between some of the metrics and models, we proceed in reverse order. We conclude in Section III.D by discussing the weaknesses of the existing methods and suggesting areas for research.

B.1. Reuse Instance Costs

A reuse instance means different things whether we are talking about the building blocks approach or the generative approach. In the context of the building blocks approach, a reuse instance is a point in the development where a developer has the option of building a component from scratch, but chooses instead to *try* to reuse a component from the library. With the generative approach, a reuse instance corresponds to an entire project life cycle, or a significant part thereof, as the decision to reuse—in this case, generate—modifies the life cycle in significant ways (see Section III.A). Models appropriate for the generative technology are needed that estimate (or measure) the cost of generative development (see, e.g., [98], [154]) and that compare it to the cost of more traditional development (see, e.g., [114]). In this section, we focus on studies that dealt with the building blocks approach.

Barnes and Bollinger recognized the existence of two kinds of building blocks reuse, namely, *black box reuse*, whereby the component is integrated in its host environment without modifications, and *white box reuse*, whereby the component is adapted and integrated into its host environment [11]. The average cost of attempting reuse can be formulated as follows:

$$[Search + (1-p) \times Development]$$

where *Search* is the cost of performing a search operation on the database, *Development* is the cost of developing the component from scratch, and *p* is the probability that the component is found in the database. The reuse option is attractive only if:

$$[Search + (1-p) \times Development]$$
$$< Development,$$
$$\text{or } Search < p \times Development.$$

To favor reuse, we must have an adequate coverage of the library (large *p*) and make sure that developers can, quickly, either find the component they need or be fairly confident that it does not exist. Obviously, the more complex the reusable component, the more worthwhile it is for a developer to keep searching.

In the context of white box reuse, the developer must weigh the cost of producing a component from scratch against the cost of attempting to reuse one, possibly after modifying it. The average cost of developing with intent to reuse can be formulated as follows:

$$[Search + (1-p) \times (ApproxSearch$$
$$+ q \times Adaptation$$
$$+ (1-q) \times Development)]$$

where *p* is the probability that the component is found in the database, *q* is the probability that a satisfactory approximation of the component can be found, *ApproxSearch* is the cost of performing the approximate search, *Search* is the cost of performing an exact search operation on the database, *Development* is the cost of developing the component from scratch, and *Adaptation* is the cost of adapting the component to its host environment [11]. The reuse option is attractive if:

$$Search + (1-p) ApproxSearch$$
$$+ (1-p) q Adaptation \leq$$
$$(p + (1-p) q) Development \qquad (1)$$

If we consider that the fact that a satisfactory approximation of the component is found means that *Adaptation* ≤ *Development*,[10] then a sufficient (but not necessary) condition for reuse to be attractive is given by:

---

10. A study by Woodfield and Embley suggested that developers would not consider reusing if they estimate the cost of adaptation to be 70% or higher than the cost of developing from scratch [159]. They also found that developers systematically underestimate adaptation effort by about 15%, which means that what they perceive to be 70% may actually be 85%. Thus, all in all, developers are reasonably trustworthy as far as ensuring that they don't adapt reusable components in cases where they should develop from scratch.

$$Search + (1-p) ApproxSearch \leq p \: Development \qquad (2)$$

which means the overall cost of search, whether a satisfactory component is found or not, is less than the savings that actually result from those (100 × p) % cases where a satisfactory component is found.

This inequality has to be understood in the context of experimental evidence to the effect that the cost of adapting a component for the purpose of software reuse jumps very fast as the portion of code to be modified goes up [23]; e.g., the cost of modifying 20% of the code of a component is estimated at near 90% the cost of developing the component from scratch [23]. Margono and Rhoads argued that adaptation costs depended on whether a component was reused within or across application domains and on whether a component was developed in-house or acquired externally [97]. It is fair to say that, in general, white box reuse is cost-effective if it is restricted to those cases where modifications are very minor or already planned and/or parameterized. That being said, inequality (2) can be used as a baseline for developing component libraries and retrieval systems, where we should replace *p* above by *p* × recall,[11] which represents the probability that a component exists that satisfies the needs *and* that is found by the retrieval system. Putting more components in the library increases its coverage (*p*), but may increase search time (*Search* and *ApproxSearch*) by returning more irrelevant components that need to be studied by developers. Putting in bigger components (higher development costs) increases also the cost effectiveness of the library. We discuss the marginal costs of adding a component to a library in the next section.

We conclude our discussion by pointing out that a developer who is fairly familiar with the contents of a component library can locate what she/he needs more quickly and knows when not to bother even looking. This has the effect of reducing the cost of individual searches (*Search* and *ApproxSearch*) and their relative frequency, which in case of perfect knowledge about the contents of the library, go down from 1 to *p* for exact search and from 1−*p* to *q* for approximate search.

B.2. Building a Reusable Asset

Building a reusable asset represents a more or less major investment, depending on the reuse approach used. With the building blocks approach, building components is a regular, recurring activity, whose implications, positive or negative, are minor. By contrast, building a generator is an extraordinary and *costly* decision, on which the success or failure of a reuse program may depend. For the case of application generators, the biggest challenge is to recognize opportunity: When is a generator appropriate [98]. This depends on both the stability of the application domain and the number of systems that need to be developed and maintained within that domain (see, e.g., [34], [89]). The second question has to do with the extent of application development that should be automated. Levy argued that deciding the coverage of the generator should be

---

11. Simply put, the *recall* of a search on a retrieval system is the probability that a relevant item to the search is retrieved by the system. The recall of a retrieval system is the statistical average over a sample of representative searches/queries.

based on rational economic decisions, namely, on the marginal costs of automating an extra ε % of applications, relative to the marginal benefits expected from automating that extra ε % [89]. In particular, he noted that the 20/80 rule holds, namely, incrementally automating the development of applications gets much harder as we come close to full automation [89]. The cost increments have to be measured against (amortized over) the number of systems to be developed and maintained during the "life expectancy" of the generator, which depends on the stability of the application domain.

With the building blocks approach, the decision to build a reusable component should take into account several cost factors:

1) the initial cost of development,
2) the direct and indirect costs of including the component into a library of reusable components,
3) the cost of integrating and/or adapting the component and
4) the expected usage frequency of the component.

Barnes argued that organizations should consider acquiring reusable components from other vendors, and the decision should be purely economical. As a rule of thumb, build reusable components in-house for local expertise, and purchase reusable parts[12] in external expertise. But how to estimate the cost of developing a reusable component? There is a wide consensus that reusable components cost more to develop than nonreusable components with comparable functionality, but estimates range from 50% more [128] to twice the cost or more [97]. The extra cost could be due to a more demanding requirements identification stage (*domain analysis*), lengthier or more complex code[13] (see, e.g., [7]), or more demanding testing and packaging. Balda and Gustafson explored a CO-COMO-like empirical cost model for software projects that accounts for both reusing reusable components and developing reusable components [7]. They argued that reusable components tend to be longer and more complex than their nonreusable counterparts, and that the differences depend on the application domain, but offered no detailed breakdown of the extra costs [7]. Rhoads and Margano tracked software projects in which reuse—mainly *within* project—was a priority and found that 60% of overhead costs for building reusable components were incurred during the detailed design of the components [97]. In their study, reusable components were built as a byproduct of application development, and not in the context of a stand-alone domain engineering activity, for which different cost profiles may hold.

Once a reusable component is built, it needs to be included in a repository/library of reusable components. In addition to the obvious (and negligible) costs associated with storage and degraded time performance, there are a number of insidious retrieval costs that are more significant and harder to measure. For a thorough assessment of the result of adding a reusable component to an existing library, we have to see the effects on the reuse instance cost equation:

$$[Search + (1-p) \times (ApproxSearch$$
$$+ q \times Adaptation$$
$$+ (1-q) \times Development)]$$

In principle, adding a component increases the coverage of the component library and thus increases both probabilities p and q and modifies the averages *Adaptation* and *Development* (depending on the new component size relative to the average component size in the library and the average component size "outside the library"). It will also probably increase the costs *Search* and *ApproxSearch*. For instance, with document retrieval systems, there is a three-way trade-off between *recall*, *precision*,[14] and simplicity of the encoding and search strategies [142]. Increasing the size of the document collection degrades the performance of the retrieval system both in absolute terms (e.g., for the same precision level, the user has more irrelevant items to examine) and in relative terms (e.g., "higher resolution" encoding is required to describe components, and thus more complex queries are required to retrieve them with equal precision[15]). It is widely recognized in the literature that bigger libraries are not necessarily better (see, e.g., [73]). Thus, components should be added only after very careful consideration (see, e.g., [28]) and should be taken out of the library, if they have poor reuse record; in [73], Isoda reports on an experimental reuse program at NTT where components were withdrawn from libraries if they haven't been used in three years. In that same experiment, where the components in the library ranged in size from 50 lines or fewer to several thousand lines, it was found that modules of 50 lines or fewer accounted for 48% of the reuse instances and 6% of the reuse volume, while modules 1,000 lines or larger accounted for only 6% of the reuse instances, but of 56% of the reuse volume [73]. Unfortunately, no statistical distribution of module size is provided in [73], but we would not be surprised if pulling those small components out of the library would have actually increased its effectiveness, whereby the loss of coverage is more than offset by enhanced search performance.

B.3. Setting Up a Reuse Program

The question is not so much whether to set up a reuse program or not, but how. There are a number of intertwined organizational and technological choices to be considered, with different cost/benefit characteristics, and managers must have the tools to evaluate and compare them. In this section, we discuss the most salient choices, and any reuse-specific measurables (or measures) proposed in the literature that are relevant to these choices. As shown in Section III.A, reuse practice benefits from new organizational structures and managerial practices. Accounting for such changes in the cost/benefit analysis would be no different from that in any business process re-engineering effort, and won't be discussed below. We organize our discussion around the steps of a reuse adoption process proposed by Davis [42]:

---

12. This explains in part why mathematical and statistical packages have gained wide acceptance in the software market: Few companies have an in-house mathematician or statistician.

13. E.g., using conditional compilation (extra code) or more parameterization (more complex) to offer several variants of the same functionality.

14. Precision is the average ratio of retrieved and relevant items out of the retrieved items.

15. The readers can convince themselves of the above using intuitive information-theoretic arguments: to encode *and* distinguish between (*precision*) n items, we need codes of length Log(n). The more items we have, the longer the codes.

Initiate reuse program development: This step includes identifying organizational objectives (e.g., productivity and quality objectives) and reuse opportunities [42]. An organization may be active in different application domains, and the reuse potential in each of these domains must be estimated. It is widely recognized that MIS applications are fairly stable and high reuse rates are possible, while systems software and programming environments, e.g., offer few opportunities for reuse (see, e.g., [85], [100]). However, there is no easy way of finding out how much reuse is possible within an application domain without actually doing it over a period of years or performing some extent of domain analysis.

Define reuse program: This step includes:

1) defining the scope/coverage of the reuse program,
2) establishing "reasonable" reuse targets and
3) identifying alternative reuse adoption strategies.

Scoping the reuse program consists of choosing an application domain, or a subdomain thereof, that offers the most reuse potential, the lowest risks, the fastest returns on investment, etc. Once the scope is identified, organizations must establish reuse objectives that they can attain with reasonable effort, depending on a self-assessment of their managerial and technical processes [42]. Davis proposed a *reuse capability model* which defines reuse objectives in terms of three measures:

1) *reuse proficiency,* which is the ratio of the value of the actual reuse opportunities exploited to the value of potential reuse opportunities,
2) *reuse efficiency,* which measures how much of the reuse opportunities targeted by the organization have actually been exploited and
3) *reuse effectiveness,* which is the ratio of reuse benefits to reuse costs [42].

Note that all three measures assume that a reuse program is already in place. Davis pointed out that these measures are not metrics that organizations must be able to calculate at the outset, but are objectives to be attained once a program has started [42].

As mentioned above, it is difficult to precisely quantify the reuse potential of an application domain, and thus, reuse proficiency is only an indicative measure. There has been some interest in the literature for measures of reuse *efficiency,* although mostly as target reuse rates, i.e., as a target percentage of reused code in new projects (see, e.g., [12], [99], [100]). However, there are a number of problems in measuring reuse rates by comparing code sizes, as reflected by the sometimes surprisingly low productivity increases that resulted from impressive reuse rates (see, e.g., [59]). First, there are difficulties in applying such measures for the generative approaches to reuse, where the generated code does not necessarily correspond to what a developer might write, either in style or in size [34]. Second, as shown earlier, reusable components tend to be larger than their nonreusable counterparts, inflating the percentage of reused code within projects. This is exacerbated in the case of the black-box reuse of modules that offer several functionalities: One cannot separate the needed features from those that are not needed (e.g., with OO components) and

count them separately. Third, there are also difficulties with defining what constitutes an instance of reuse (see, e.g., [128]): A reusable component that is imported (used) in several client modules should be counted only once. To alleviate these problems, functional (versus size) metrics, such as *function points,* could be used instead. For each project developed under the reuse program, let fp_{tot} and fp_{new} be the function points of the entire project, and of the *new code* developed *for* the project, respectively; the *functionality reuse rate* may be defined as: $\dfrac{fp_{tot} - fp_{new}}{fp_{tot}}$. The trouble with such a measure is that a function points count cannot be entirely automated. Further, while function points are additive for coarse-grained modules,[16] they may lose significance when we are dealing with low-level components.

Finally, *reuse effectiveness* can be measured directly—and globally—from observables. A naive approach would consist of measuring productivity levels before and after the introduction of reuse. Productivity can be measured as the time average of the ratio of delivered functionality per expended resources. Because reuse involves both proportional recurring costs and one-time fixed costs, productivity studies must necessarily account for different amortizing schedules and account, implicitly or explicitly, for various product line life expectancies. Most of the work on metrics and economic models for software reuse takes into account the time-varying aspects of productivity and explores different return on investment scenarios (see, e.g., [11], [52], [89], [128]).

Analyze reuse adoption strategies: The identification of reuse objectives (in the previous step) suggests a number of candidate reuse adoption strategies, whose costs and benefits are analyzed at this step. An adoption strategy may be seen as a combination of a technical approach and a deployment strategy (e.g., starting at the project level vs. department level, pace of introduction of the technology, etc.). For example, the building-blocks approach may be suited to a low-investment and low-risk, incremental reuse adoption strategy. It also has some inherent limitations in terms of attainable reuse efficiency and effectiveness. A generative approach, on the other hand, supports a high-risk, high-payoff strategy.

Plan reuse adoption strategy: Based on the comparative analysis of the various adoption strategies, one or a combination of strategies may be chosen. At this stage, a detailed deployment plan is produced. Decisions such as how much of the reusable domain to cover the first year, the pace of acquiring the reusable assets, etc. are made here. Detailed cost models such as those discussed in Section III.B.1 and Section III.B.2 are needed.

Implement and monitor reuse program: Monitoring involves collecting data to support the various metrics.

In summary, setting up a reuse program is a major capital investment decision and has been recognized as such by a number of researchers. The economic models proposed in the

---

16. I.e., are such that for a given two modules $M1$ and $M2$, $FP(M1 + M2) = FP(M1) + FP(M2)$.

literature address fairly adequately the economics of reuse at the organization level and at the project level, by integrating a set of *elementary* cost variables in an encompassing model (see, e.g., [11], [52], [128]). However, it is often those elementary cost variables, or the observables used to derive them, that are hard to measure or interpret, undermining the forecasting or explanatory abilities of these models.

B.4. Discussion

A lot of progress has been achieved on the analysis of the software reuse processes and the derivation of cost estimation models for these processes, and a great deal more is needed. We feel that future efforts should be concentrated on addressing the following aspects:

In relation to reuse instance costs: We need more precise effort and cost models for adapting reusable software. Existing empirical evidence suggests that small changes—which defeat the quality advantage—require substantial efforts [23]—defeating the productivity advantage. We need a better breakdown of those efforts (e.g., trying to understand the code versus implementing the actual change) to focus technical research on those aspects that are most costly. We also need a better characterization of which adaptation efforts are costly and which are not. For example, changing the type of a parameter of a procedure is probably less costly than changing the outcome of a control sequence. Such knowledge may help us develop better techniques for modularizing and parameterizing reusable components and computer tools to support the adaptation process (see, e.g., [94]). We also need a finer characterization and a better integration of retrieval costs in the cost equation (Sections III.B.1 and III.B.2).

In relation to the cost of building reusable assets: It is widely recognized that reusable components are costlier to develop than their nonreusable counterparts. However, there is no agreement over how much more, and there are very few studies about the distribution of "reusability overhead" (see, e.g., [7]); more are needed. There is already recognition in the literature that the extra cost depends on the domain (see, e.g., [7], [97]). Other factors could include the parameterization range, the implementation technique, and associated adaptation/instantiation techniques, etc.

In relation to project-level and organization-level measures: This is perhaps the area where most work is needed. First, we need more accurate and *practical* measures of reuse rates. As shown above, code reuse rates are difficult to measure accurately and do not reflect either effort or savings. Further, they apply only to code reuse and cannot be used to measure design reuse, e.g. We showed that functional metrics are useful, but impractical. We could ignore reuse rates (a means) altogether and look directly at productivity gains (an end). But then, how much of the productivity gains are due to reuse, how much are due to process improvement? How much are due to enhanced communication between developers because teams get smaller? For example, the greatest productivity gains with 4GL tools occur for those projects that become small enough to handle for a single developer [98]. These are

not moot questions because we need precise indicators to help us improve those aspects of the reuse plan that can (or should) be improved.

Until (most of) these concerns are properly addressed, there can be no objective basis for comparing different reuse approaches, especially those that fall on different segments of the building blocks ←→ generative axis. The various approaches discussed in the remainder of this paper will only be compared for the extent to which they address specific issues. Where appropriate, we will guesstimate their likely relative effectiveness, but we will not, and cannot, go any further.

IV. ACQUIRING REUSABLE ASSETS

We saw in Section II.B that all the artifacts, both used and produced, and the processes of past software development activities are reusable. We choose the word "acquire" to encompass purchasing, building, and various degrees of re-engineering or otherwise transforming existing assets. We discussed the economics of acquiring reusable assets in Section III.B.2. In this chapter, we deal with the technical aspects of acquiring reusable assets. We first discuss general issues related to the acquisition and packaging of reusable assets, with a focus on building blocks. In Section IV.B, we discuss application generators as an example of a commercially successful application of the generative approach. In Section IV.C, we discuss OO software development, as an enabling technology for developing reusable blocks.

A. Overview

What makes a software component reusable? We see reusability as a combination of two attributes, *(re)usefulness*, which means that the component addresses a common need, or provides an often requested service, and *usability*, which means that the component is of good enough quality and easy enough to understand and use for new software developments. The two are often at odds because the generality of a component (its usefulness) entails abstracting the details specific to its individual uses, which often means that these details have to be somehow put back in to use the component, making it less usable. New abstraction techniques in programming and design enable us to reach new optimums but do not change the basics of the trade-off (see, e.g., [72], [83]). This is part of what makes the development of reusable assets more challenging than that of custom-made components.

Acquiring reusable components involves various mixes of new developments and use of existing assets/raw resources, depending on their usability, reusefulness, and desired level of computer support for *unit reuse* tasks (search, understanding, and adaptation/integration). Approaches that rely on existing resources include:

- providing access to existing "assets," which could be as simple as grouping existing computer files in publicly accessible directories, or providing indexing and search tools, browsers, etc. (see, e.g., [113]),
- re-engineering and preemptive maintenance (enhancing the maintainability and the reuse worth of components),

- reverse engineering (recovering "implicit" development knowledge).

or, more generally, transforming available software knowledge that is otherwise too specific (usable but not reuseful) or too diffuse (reuseful but not usable) into a level of abstraction that makes it (re)useful and usable.

Domain analysis and *engineering* may involve any or a combination of the above approaches to identify the basic entities, relations, and operations of the application domain (see, e.g., [132]). Domain analysis is a relatively new activity, and there is some disagreement as to what it involves, both in terms of process/activities and in terms of outputs/work products. However, most researchers agree that a critical (and notoriously difficult) step in domain analysis is the identification of the boundaries of the domain [5], [101], [130]. Lest we oversimplify, domain analysis follows a process similar to that in developing specific software systems. Namely, it involves requirements, analysis, and the production of domain-wide reusable components [5], [101], [130]. The outputs, however, differ from traditional system development in that reusable components typically include standards and guidelines (i.e., *semantic knowledge*), as well as generic, but concrete components such as domain models (i.e., generic functional architectures), generic design architectures and templates, and even generic code fragments [130]. For the case of DRACO [121] and ASLs [148]), however, the output of domain analysis is a domain-dependent executable specification language that embodies the domain objects and operations on those objects.

One of the limitations of "recycling" existing components is that the quality requirements for reusable artifacts exceed those for custom-developed components, and few of the existing components will qualify to be included in a base of reusable assets or will be worth expending effort on. Thus "recycling" is only cost-effective if it can be automated, fully, or to a large extent [28]. Indexing, searching and browsing tools play an important role by organizing existing software knowledge for the purposes of (as an input to) domain engineering (see, e.g., [113]), but do not provide/generate components that are directly usable. In our own work, we built a set of tools that extract a structured representation of software components suited for a reuse-driven CASE tool from diverse and disconnected sources of documentation [113]. However, the added value provided by such tools remains to be proven in a practical setting [113].

In the remainder of this section, we will focus on methods for building new reusable assets, namely, application generators and OO components. Some of the issues related to indexing, retrieval, and browsing, as they relate to software components, will be discussed in various subsections of Section V.A. The interested reader can consult the literature on reverse-engineering; a good starting point is the Jan. 1990 issue of *IEEE Software*.

B. Building Application Generators

Generally speaking, an application generator may be defined as *a tool or a set of integrated tool, that inputs a set of specifications and generates the code of an application within an implementation language*. What distinguishes application generators from compilers of high-level and very high-level languages or automatic programming systems are the "specifications" or "programs" input by the developer, which are:

1) partial—the tool completes them by a set of domain-dependent reasonable defaults and
2) partially or totally nonprocedural—declarative, graphical, etc. [98].

Martin enumerated a number of mostly behavioral properties that application generators should exhibit, including

1) user-friendliness,
2) usable by nonprofessional programmers,
3) support for fast-prototyping,
4) applications take an order of magnitude less time to develop than with traditional development, etc. [98].

It is next to impossible to give a more precise operational definition of what constitutes an application generator without excluding known classes of application generators. This is due to the fact that the specification language used—and hence the generation technique—depends very heavily on the application domain. For the same reasons, it is difficult to design a development methodology for application generators that is appropriate for all application generators, and the development of application generators *in general* received little attention in the literature; by contrast developing *with* application generators has received a fair amount of attention (see, e.g., [114], [154]). The material presented below is based mostly on the work of Levy [89] and Cleaveland [34], describing work at AT&T Bell Labs.

Viewed as translators, applications generators have a fairly standard architecture (system design). Further, the programming techniques for implementing translators (detailed design) are well-understood and fairly standardized. In fact, the design and implementation of translators are so well-understood and standardized that application generators themselves can be built using application generators [34]! The major difficulties in building generators reside in:

1) recognizing cases when they are appropriate [34], [89],
2) defining their requirements, in terms of defining the input language, the output language, and the "transformation grammar" [34], [89] and
3) validating their outputs, i.e., verifying that the code generated does what it is supposed to do [72].

The first two difficulties are methodological in nature. Defining the input language involves striking the proper balance between a language that is sufficiently abstract to be usable by noncomputer experts, but also concrete enough so that executable code can be efficiently generated. Validating the generated code poses a number of technical—and theoretical—challenges [72].

Levy identified a coarse three-step methodology for developing with application generators (what he calls *metaprogramming* [89]):

1) identifying the requirements of the generator,
2) building the generator and
3) using the generator.

Cleaveland proposed a breakdown of the requirements phase into six subphases briefly summarized below [34]:

Recognizing domains: This step consists of assessing whether an application generator approach is appropriate or not. According to Levy, applications generators are appropriate for applications that embody a "complex synthetic set of rules" [89]; complex in the sense that no notation is known within which they can be described succinctly, and synthetic in the sense that they are man-made. This entails that the rules cannot be had right the first time, and they will keep evolving. This makes it appropriate for prototyping. Or, if we look at the full half of the cup instead, application generators are needed when several similar systems have to be built and maintained. This makes it suitable for stable and well-understood application domains. Cleaveland proposed a number of "appropriateness heuristics" including [34]:

1) recognizing recurring patterns between applications (code, design, architecture),
2) a "natural" or "emergent" separation between the functional (declarative) requirements and the implementation (procedural) of applications, or
3) a fairly systematic procedure to go from one to the other.

Defining domain boundaries: This consists of identifying the parts of applications that will be generated, the parts that will have to be built by hand, and the interfaces between the two [34]. There is a trade-off between the range of applications that can be built with the generator (breadth) and how much of these applications will be automated (depth); the decision should be based on economic considerations [34], [89].

Defining an underlying model: This step consists of defining an abstract computational model for the application domain. It is abstract in the sense that it does not depend on a particular implementation technique. Different computational models are appropriate for different application domains [89]. For example, a computational model appropriate for reactive systems could be finite state machines, while one appropriate for database applications could be relational calculus or algebra. Computational models are important for consistency, understandability, and validation [34]. They also make it easier to systematize the implementation of a generator and the generation of a family of generators.

Defining the variant and the invariant parts: the invariant part of an application family consists of the implementation details of the application and all of the defaults assumed by the generator; the variant part consists of those aspects that the developer has to specify. The variant part includes input specifications as well as *code escapes* [34]. Code escapes are used when a part of the application cannot be captured—concisely or at all—within the computational model; they defeat some of the advantages of generators (maintainability at the specification level, traceability, testability, etc.) and should be avoided whenever technically possible [34] and economically justifiable [89].

Defining the specification input method: The input method is essentially the user(developer)-interface of the generator. Input methods depend on the underlying computational model and the target user (developer) community. Input methods include:

1) textual inputs (expressions),
2) graphical inputs (e.g., for user-interface builders [119]),
3) interactive template-filling, etc. [34].

Defining the products: Generators can generate programs, documentation, tests programs or data, and even input to other generators [34]. Issues such as packaging for readability and/or integration and performance, e.g., are important for code fragments [34].

A major concern with application generators is their testing: checking that they do generate the correct code. One of the ways programs are usually tested is by comparing their actual outputs to expected outputs. With program generators, we are not certain that the expected output is correct: it, itself, has to be tested. This additional level of indirection makes it that much harder to validate generators [72]. The problem is more acute than with traditional high-level language compilers which translate imperative code into imperative code, and where there is an easier correspondence between source code and—nonoptimized—target code.

C. Object Oriented Programming

In the past decade, object oriented programming has come to be considered a panacea to all computing aches. Software engineers view object orientation (OO) as the answer to their numerous and intractable problems: enhancing software quality, reusability, and providing a seamless development methodology (see, e.g., [35], [38], [106]). Database researchers recognize that OO allows modeling the semantic *behavior* of data by encapsulating data with the procedures that manipulate them [25]. In the knowledge-based systems arena, OO reincarnates old ideas such as procedural knowledge representation, inheritance, and distributed control [141]. While researchers may not agree on the specifics of the tenets of object orientation, there is a fairly wide consensus that it is an enabling technology for creating interchangeable and reusable software components. We first provide a brief tutorial on OO. Next, we discuss reusability issues across the OO life cycle, i.e., analysis, design, and programming. This is by no means a survey of OO research; our focus is on those aspects of OO that make reuse inevitable, possible, or difficult.

C.1. Object Orientation 101

The concept of "object" in programming was introduced by Dahl and Nygaard in their language SIMULA [41]. SIMULA was designed as a language for simulating dynamic physical systems. Physical objects were modeled by structures containing state variables and procedures used to manipulate them. Using today's jargon, we would say that objects are compilation units that encapsulate data with the procedures that manipulate them. One of the advantages of such structures, from a programming language point of view, was to separate the visibility of variables from their lifetime, i.e., a variable could be active outside the scope of its visibility. This is the basic idea behind *information hiding*. Information hiding enables us to build modules that are easier to understand and more reusable. Because of information hiding, "objects" can only be manipulated through *public interfaces*—sometimes called *protocols* or simply *interfaces*—i.e., a set of procedures that are "publicly" visible. This makes it possible to change the implementation details of an object without affecting its clients.

Intuitively, a *class* is (the description of) a collection of objects that share the same data structure and support the same operations. The description of a class includes a data template and a definition of the operations supported by the objects—called *instances*—of the class. In some OO languages and modular languages (e.g., Modula and Ada), a distinction is made between the *specification* of a class (e.g., *package specification* in Ada) and its *implementation* (e.g., *implementation module* in Modula). Typically, the specification of a class corresponds to its public interface.[17] An *abstract class* is a class that has a specification but no implementation. *Overloading* makes it possible for several classes to offer/implement the same operations; the compiler disambiguates operation references using the parameter/operand types. *Polymorphism* makes it possible for a variable to hold objects belonging to different classes. *Dynamic binding* delays the resolution of operation references until run-time when the actual type of the variable is known; this allows for greater flexibility in programming [106]. Overloading and polymorphism make it possible to develop general-purpose client code that is indifferent to the *reimplementation and extension* of server code. Classes can be organized along *hierarchies* supporting different kinds of "inheritance." The parallel with natural taxonomies, whereby a natural category "inherits" a number of properties from its ancestors, is tempting, sometimes useful, and often misleading [72]. For the time being, let us just say that inheritance in programming languages is a built-in code-sharing mechanism that, without polymorphism and dynamic binding, would not be much different from various module import mechanisms in traditional languages.

In addition to its programming significance, OO is also a modeling paradigm. As a computational model, OO represents a significant departure from traditional process-oriented modeling approaches in which there is a clear divide between process and data. In process-oriented approaches, data are viewed as static entities, whose *domain-dependent* dynamic semantics are buried into processes which embody *application-dependent* tasks. Complexity in modeled systems is then reflected in the procedures. By contrast, OO encapsulates data with their *domain-wide* dynamic semantics, and complexity in the modeled systems is reflected in the data instead. Presumably, this makes for partial models (components) that are reusable across various applications within the same domain [106]. Further, because procedures evolve faster than data in domains, OO models tend to be more resilient to change [106].

---

17. This is the case in the Modula and Ada families of languages. In C++, however, the specification must list the procedures and data variables that are not visible outside, but say so.

The modeling potential of OO found its way into analysis and design (see, e.g., [140], [146], [157]). OO proponents argue that OO models, in addition to their reusability and resilience to change, are easier to understand and to communicate to end-users (see, e.g., [35]). Typically, OO analysis is concerned with the derivation of two views of a system:

1) a *static* or *structural* model, describing the objects of the domain and their relationships and
2) a *dynamic* or *behavioral* model, describing the functional and control aspects of the system as embodied in individual object operations and interobject interactions (see, e.g., partial surveys in [46], [158]).

Objects that have the same properties and exhibit the same behavior are grouped in classes. Class hierarchies start taking shape where classes that share *application-significant* data and *application-meaningful external behavior* are grouped under more *general* classes. Identifying generalizations of classes at this level has several advantages, including:

1) enhancing the understandability of the models by reducing the number of *independent* concepts that an analyst/user has to deal with,
2) providing a cross-check with data dictionaries to enforce consistency within the model and
3) identifying opportunities for code reuse [35], [140], [157].

The last is justified by the intuitive realization that similar requirements in terms of external behaviors—an analysis-level product—generally lead to similar implementations.

Object oriented design binds domain-level classes—a requirement—into computational structures that, in addition to "implementing" the required functionality, maximize code sharing and satisfy environmental and performance constraints (see, e.g., [31], [70], [140]). *System* (architectural) design includes partitioning a system into subsystems and/or layers, choosing an overall control paradigm (e.g., event-driven versus hierarchical), and distributing data and processing (see, e.g., [140]). *Class* (detailed) design includes:

1) representation issues (e.g., of attributes, associations, and collections),
2) algorithms, which are tightly coupled into representation issues, and
3) object control paradigm [31], [140], [146].

There are a number of advantages to keeping design (and implementation) class hierarchies close to analysis-level hierarchies, including:

1) traceability [36],
2) conceptual clarity (see, e.g., [39]),
3) reuse of interfaces (see, e.g., [37]) and
4) potential for reusing *application-meaningful computations*—by contrast to structure-manipulation operations which are *inherently* representation/implementation dependent.

Methodologists recognize that in some cases, environmental considerations may dictate different representations for behaviorally similar classes, leading to either suboptimal code reuse/sharing or, if we insist, unsavory class hierarchies (lots of cancellations, unsafe inheritance, methods having awkward names, etc. [37]). They also suggest looking into alternatives to inheritance (e.g., *delegation*) that achieve the same goals [140]. In general, the transition from design to implementation is fairly straightforward. For the case of control-intensive (e.g., real-time) applications, the transformation can even be automated (see, e.g., [105]).

C.2. Reusability Issues in Object Oriented Analysis

The proponents of OO attribute a number of qualities to OO analysis and to the resulting models, most of which are supposed to favor reuse. We will discuss these as well as other tenets of OO analysis that may impact reuse positively or negatively.

An often-cited advantage of OO analysis and OO models is what Hoydalsvik and Sindre called *problem orientation* [70], i.e., the models are cast into terms of the problem domain. This makes models easily communicable to the target user community and favors greater user involvement in development and hence greater satisfaction with the final product (see, e.g., [35], [36]). We share the view that this is only true in data-rich, processing-poor application domains where objects are intuitive and easy to identify [3] and where most of the processing consists of associative data access; these are domains where more traditional data modeling techniques are already known to be more appropriate than process-oriented techniques [46]. In control-intensive applications, objects are synthetic (artificial) service providers rather than natural data holders, and most of the complexity is embedded in the dynamic model, which uses the same notations as those used in process-oriented techniques.

A second related advantage of OO models is their—presumed—resilience to evolution. Presumably, in application domains, processes change more often and faster than the entities of the domain, and hence a model structured around the data of the problem domain will be more stable [106]. To this, we add the fact that:

1) information hiding minimizes the impact of data structure changes and
2) hierarchical classification enables us to handle data specialization and extension quite handily.

Lubars et al. set out to test the claim that OO models are stable [90]. They define model stability in terms of three properties:

1) *localization*, i.e., changes should be localized in the model, even if they require considerable rework in a localized area,
2) *conservative extension*, meaning that the effect of a change on the work *already done* should be minimal, i.e., we should, as much as possible, extend existing work but not redo it and
3) *model independence*, in the sense that changes to structural (data) models have little impact on behavioral models, and vice-versa.

The authors modeled the ATM application using Rumbaugh et

al.'s object modeling technique (OMT [140]) and considered two "small change" scenarios to assess the stability properties. They observed that the structural model—called object *model* in OMT—was well-behaved, but that the behavioral models[18] were not. They also observed that the models were somewhat interdependent because in one scenario, changes to the behavioral models led to revising the object model [90]. The authors recognized that theirs was not a controlled experiment and that no definitive conclusions could be drawn. We believe that some of the difficulties were specific to OMT, and to data-driven methods in general,[19] but concur with their observation that ease of evolution may conflict with ease of description. The authors mentioned two modeling "tricks" that would have stabilized the models:

1) the use of abstract classes to leave room for future specialization or factoring of existing classes and
2) the use of "mixins"[20] to separate concerns and reuse them independently;

both techniques have no meaning to the end user [90].

A third advantage of OO analysis is that it lends itself naturally to *domain analysis* (versus single application analysis) and thus leads to more widely reusable components. This is attributed as much to the notation as it is to the process. For example, once it has been recognized that the class **CheckingAccount** is part of an application, it is difficult not to think of operations to deposit, withdraw, and give balance, even when the application at hand requires only one or two operations. Further, data-driven methodologies (e.g., OMT [140]) explicitly prescribe that analysts should rely on their knowledge of an application domain to complement the statement of the problem as a source for identifying the relevant objects/classes. However, this approach has been criticized for being open-ended, i.e., analysts do not know when to stop adding objects and classes that may be relevant to the domain, but could be irrelevant to the application at hand, and thus unduly burdening the project at hand (see, e.g., [74], [125]). *Use-case driven* or *scenario-driven* methodologies are supposed to alleviate this problem by focusing on the objects that participate in useful system behavior (see, e.g., [74], [138]). And finally, generalization enables developers to factor out the shared data and behavior between classes in (abstract) classes which are even more reusable than the actual (concrete) classes. We find it surprising that, despite the importance of the analysis-level hierarchical organization of classes on the OO development life cycle, and the long-established research tradition in classification in artificial intelligence, there have been relatively few efforts to provide automated or semi-automated tools for building or maintaining class hierarchies

---

18. OMT uses several complementary notations to represent behavior, including *event flow diagrams* to represent messages exchanged between objects, and *Harel statecharts* for individual objects to represent objects' individual behaviors.

19. A method is considered to be data-driven if modeling starts by identifying the *objects* of the domain/application, before analyzing any desirable behavior the system has to have.

20. Broadly speaking, *mixins* correspond to "mixing in" the features inherited from two different superclasses (multiple inheritance), each representing a view of the class.

(see, e.g., [18], [37], [55], and [56] for a brief literature survey on classification techniques in OO analysis). Notable weaknesses of existing hierarchical classification methods include the fact that most methods do not take into account behavior [56]. Further, nearly all classification methods are limited to "naive" factorizations in the sense that they assume that every attribute or operation is defined in only one place, ignoring redefinition (extension or specialization) at lower levels; this leads to factorizations that are either oversimplifications (unsound) or suboptimal (incomplete) [56].

Some aspects of OO analysis have also been criticized for *hindering* reuse or for underusing the potential of OO for reusability. One of the thorniest problems resides in the specification of interobject behavior (see, e.g., [3], [46], [158]). An unspoken corollary of OO is that any behavior that an object system may exhibit must be attached to an object/class within the system. This forces us to specify—and implement—the interaction between two objects as an operation on one of the two, i.e., it forces us to assign responsibility for a behavior involving two objects to one of the two objects. If that behavior (or the interaction underlying it) is contextual (specific to) a given application, the object made responsible for the joint behavior is not reusable across applications [109]. This led a number of researchers to propose dynamic entities, other than state-bearing application objects, that embody interobject behavior (e.g., *relationships* [139], *constraints* [109], *contracts* [65], etc.). Recognizing the need for such constructs has not made the identification of "behavioral boundaries" between objects any easier (see, e.g., [3], [109], [158]).

A second set of problems deals with the related issues of view modeling and multiple inheritance. Multiple inheritance occurs when a class has two or more *nonhierarchically related* ancestor classes. Multiple inheritance may occur in natural taxonomies and has been supported by a number of knowledge representation languages (e.g., KL-ONE [24] and its derivatives). Further, automatic hierarchical classification (class factoring) algorithms that avoid redundancy may generate *lattices* rather than trees (see, e.g., [37], [56]). Multiple inheritance, which is a powerful modeling concept, becomes a programming language nightmare when the transition is made to implementation. Further, it often results from integrating different *roles* that objects may play within the same application. Forcing all the roles on the same class definition has a number of disadvantages [63]. First, the models tend to be hard to read and understand. For instance, generalization relationships become hard to understand as a class may descend from two unrelated superclasses, each representing a different role. Further, a unified nomenclature must be found for all the roles, inevitably losing meaning and significance. Second, this leads to suboptimal reuse as the individual roles cannot be reused (extended and/or specialized) independently [63]. The problem of providing different views of objects has been addressed in OO programming languages for some time (see, e.g., [145], and C++'s three visibility/access modes for class features [152]). Views as a modeling concept have been getting more attention recently (see, e.g., [63], [122]).

C.3. Reusability Issues in Object Oriented Design

In OO software development the same basic set of concepts is used to describe the products of analysis, design, and implementation [66]. Presumably, this helps make a seamless transition between analysis and design (see, e.g., [31], [35]). The advantages of such a seamless transition are numerous and have been thoroughly documented[21] (see, e.g., [35] and Section IV.B.1). It has been known for some time that the mere use of an object notation is not sufficient to ensure a seamless transition from analysis to design, and that additional care must be taken to ensure that it is (see, e.g., [31], [81]). For instance, it is widely recognized that OO design involves more than adding detail to analysis-level models, and analysis-level class hierarchies may need to be reorganized to take into account environmental and performance factors (see, e.g., [66], [111], [140]). This may lead to design models where classes that have the same external (application-meaningful) behavior are no longer hierarchically related, leading to suboptimal code reuse [111]. Worse yet, if we insist on maximizing code reuse, we may end up with two hierarchically related classes that do not share application semantics. This may lead to unsavory class hierarchies, with lots of cancellations, unsafe inheritance, awkward method names, unpredictable behavior, et. [37], [81]. Most methodologies recognize the problem, but don't do much about it beyond suggesting aggregation/delegation as an alternative to inheritance for code sharing (see, e.g., [140]).

We believe that concerns for reusability and safety need not be contradictory if we view class design as consisting of two *distinct* and possibly *asynchronous* activities:

1) the development of computational structures that support generic, application-independent *structure* manipulations with given performance characteristics and
2) choosing, for a given application-meaningful analysis-level class, the *structure* that best matches its requirements.

To some extent, the above problems are due to the fact that computational structures are essentially designed one application class at a time and are, in a sense, *prematurely* bound to the semantics of application classes by both data types and names, i.e., before they can be refined and reused. Shlaer and Mellor recognize this problem, and the design phase of their methodology includes three steps:

1) building a system-wide design policy,
2) building mechanisms and code templates to support this policy and
3) populate the templates with analysis-level models [105], [146].

However, while they insist that code templates are highly reusable, they provide no formal mechanisms for their reuse.[22]

---

21. Hoydalsvik argued that because analysis models should be problem/application-oriented and design models should be solution-oriented, then any methodology that claims to bridge the two is not doing analysis correctly [70].

22. The CASE tools that support Shlaer and Mellor may offer specific functionalities that support editing existing templates.

In [111], we proposed a design framework that makes it possible to:

1) reuse interfaces and application-meaningful behavior between design-level classes that do not share the same representation and
2) reuse representation and structure manipulation code to the fullest, without jeopardizing the interface conformance of two hierarchically related design-level classes.

Our solution to the first challenge relies on:

1) defining a flavor of inheritance restricted to *method* inheritance, excluding memory structure[23] and
2) enforcing a strict discipline in designing/coding application-meaningful logic in a way that does not bind it to the representation.[24]

Our solution to the second challenge relies on:

1) defining reusable design templates, including data structure definition and *manipulation* and
2) developing a mechanical procedure for "instantiating" a design-level class by mapping an analysis-level class over a design template [111].

Our design templates may be seen as generic data structures parameterized by both data component types and data component (field) names. A design template may be *extended* by adding new data components and/or operations. Because data component names are meaningless parameters, developers need to specify parameter mappings in case of ambiguity or multiple inheritance/extension [111].

We have not had reliable practical experience with our methodology to ascertain its effectiveness. For example, it is not clear how much of an application's logic can be coded (in an object-flavored PDL [111]) without referring to an internal representation. Further, from a theoretical point of view, thorny subtyping issues with generic types are made even worse by the name parameterization [111]. It does build, however, on the proven principle that greater reuse can be achieved by delaying binding component specification to component realization/implementation and exemplifies the progressive move from a pure building-blocks approach, to one that includes some generation (see, e.g., [149] and Section II.C).

C.4. Reusability and Object Oriented Programming

Naturally, any impediments to reuse that may appear during analysis and design persist when the components are actually implemented. Implementation further binds components to a particular programming language and style, inevitably reducing their applicability. There is disagreement among methodologists whether language considerations should come into play during design or not (see, e.g., [140] vs. [31]). This is an important question because different languages support different sets of OO features (e.g., typed vs. untyped polymorphism,

single versus multiple inheritance), with different reusability characteristics that may tip design trade-offs. For example, if we want to maximize code-sharing in a language that does not support multiple inheritance, it is not enough to "linearize" a lattice that maximizes code-sharing; in order to keep the same class hierarchy at design and implementation, we have to consider language features at the design level [37], [56].

In addition to the loss of reusability due to language power, some of the very basic tenets of OO programming go against reusability. First, encapsulation and information hiding replace the traditional stamp coupling between modules, by common coupling[25] *within* modules [156]: All the methods within a class are common-coupled via the structure of the class. Further, inheritance in OO programming languages violates encapsulation and information hiding [150]. For instance, in most OO languages, a class has access to all the implementation details of its superclasses. Thus, methods can be—and often are—written in such a way that they depend on the implementation details of their superclasses: When those change, the entire class hierarchy beneath them may be affected. The C++ language addresses this problem by providing three access levels for attributes and methods:

1) *private* attributes and methods are accessible only to the methods of the defining class,
2) *protected* attributes and methods are accessible to the methods of the defining class and its subclasses and
3) *public* attributes and methods which are accessible to all objects/methods [152].

These access levels are further modulated through the accessibility/visibility of the subclass relationship itself: A client object A may be prevented from using knowledge that server B is a subclass of C, thereby preventing him from using facilities (e.g., operations) that B inherited from C [152]. Meyer argued that inheritance in class libraries is a mechanism that is useful only to the component builder, but that the component user (client) need not and should not be aware of inheritance relationships [107]. When the programming language does not have the built-in mechanisms to discipline the use of inheritance, programmer discipline ("*always* use access functions to read/write objects' attributes") or language preprocessors are needed [111].

C.5. Current Trends

As object technology matures, the distinction between what it *guarantees*—no matter what—what it *enables*—if additional guidelines are used—and what it cannot *deliver*, becomes clearer. Object oriented *programming* guarantees very little, in and of itself. It is mostly an adequate packaging technology for reusable components. The major obstacles and opportunities for building reusable components remain at the analysis and

---

23. Theoretically, this flavor is nothing but subtyping. From a programming language point of view, it is a mix of class inheritance and delegation.

24. Roughly speaking, we use a stricter version of the *private* mechanism as used in C++. Our version makes sure that data fields/structures are private to the methods used to access them; no other method, even ones belonging to the same *class*, can access them [111].

25. Two modules are *stamp-coupled* if they interact through a *visible* complex data structure, as when a procedure invokes another one whose parameters include a record. Two modules are *common-coupled* if they interact through a *hidden* complex data structure, as when two procedures access the same "global" complex data structure. Common-coupling is less desirable than stamp-coupling because the dependency between the modules is hidden, making changes to the modules error-prone.

design level. Research efforts in analysis and design shift from notations to processes. There are marked weaknesses in analysis and design heuristics and increasing demands for more formal processes, with verifiable properties (see, e.g., [3], [31], [70]). One of the still open, yet fundamental issues that have a direct bearing on the reusability of components has to do with the identification of object's behavioral boundaries and the elicitation and representation of interobject behavior (see, e.g., [3], [157], [158]). Succinctly put, given a high-level specification of the behavior of an object system (whose component objects may be known or not), how to distribute the behavior among component objects in a way that maximizes a given quality criterion—in this case, reusability. The answer to this and related questions may build on existing work on formal specification techniques for reactive systems [64]. It is also becoming clear that not all global behaviors can be effectively distributed among objects (see, e.g., [70]) and there is increasing interest in multi-paradigm programming, e.g., combining logic and OO programming (see, e.g., [96]).

A second major thrust in OO research was motivated by practical experience, as it quickly became clear that classes and methods are too fine-grained reuse units to provide any substantive leverage and bigger reusable units need to be considered. For instance, objects seldom offer any interesting behavior on their own and it is often in combination (interaction) with other objects that any useful functionality is achieved [75]. The idea of object *frameworks* [43], as design-level collections of interacting and *interchangeable* objects, captured significant attention recently.[26] The idea of reusable software (micro-)architectures is not new. However, object orientation's abstraction, parameterization and code-sharing mechanisms support elegant ways for developing and using *frameworks* (see, e.g., [72]). OO frameworks have been developed and used successfully in the area of graphical user interfaces (see, e.g., [43], [58], [110]). A lot of attention has been devoted recently to the documentation of frameworks, both formally, in terms of specifying interobject interactions (see, e.g., [65]), and informally, to describe their applicability and illustrate their use (see, e.g., discussions about *pattern languages* [51], [75], [87]). It is interesting to note that, according to Krueger's classification of reuse approaches [83], the emphasis on OO frameworks moves the reuse of OO software from a pure component-oriented approach to a combination of "software schemas" and "software architectures" approach, i.e., occurring at a higher level of abstraction and providing much greater reuse leverage [83].

V. BUILDING WITH REUSABLE SOFTWARE

In this section, we discuss issues related to developing *with* reusable software. We focus on issues related to the building-blocks approach because, as mentioned in Section III.A.2 and Section III.A.3, the generative approach does not affect much

26. For example, IEEE's *Computer* started a new department called *Frameworks* in the March 1994 issue. An entire conference is devoted to the documentation of frameworks. The seven-year-old Software Frameworks Association is a self-help nonprofit organization. For info, e-mail to info@frameworks.org.

the steps that it does not automate. We will discuss in turn component retrieval, component composition and component adaptation. In component retrieval, we look at the problem of matching a set of requirements for a component to a database of component descriptions. The matching seeks a *monolithic* component that satisfies the requirements. With component composition, the matching seeks a *combination* of components (such as functional composition) that satisfies the requirements. Finally, we shall discuss component adaptation from the perspective of transformational systems.

A. Software Component Retrieval

Given a set of requirements, the first step in building with reusable components consists of finding a component that satisfies the requirements, either in its present form, or modulo minor modifications. When the number of components in the library is large, developers can no longer afford to examine and inspect each component individually to check its appropriateness. We need an automated method to perform at least a first-cut search that retrieves an initial set of potentially useful components. Such a method would match an encoded description of the requirements against encoded descriptions of the components in the library. The choice of the encoding methods, for both the requirements and the components, and of the matching algorithms involves a number of trade-offs between cost, complexity, and retrieval quality. We start by formulating the retrieval problem from a software reuse perspective. Next, we discuss some of the trade-offs involved in the choices mentioned above. Finally, we briefly describe a representative subset of related work in the literature.

A.1. The Component Retrieval Problem

We can formalize the component retrieval problem as follows. We make the distinction between a problem space and a solution space, where the problem consists of the developer's needs. We can further divide the problem space into:

1) *actual problem space*, as opposed to,
2) problem space as understood by the *developer* and
3) *query space*, which consists of the developer's perceived need's translation into a "query" that the component retrieval system can understand (see Fig. 3).

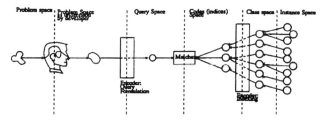

Fig. 3. A model of component retrieval.

We use the term *query* to mean an expression of the developer's need. It can be as simple as a string fed into a string search command or as complex as a Z specification of the component. Depending on the level of expertise of the developer, his/her understanding of the need can be as close to the actual need as possible. Also, depending on the expressiveness of the language used to formulate queries, the developer (or some other agent) can translate those needs as accurately as possible.

From the solution space end, we can identify three sub-spaces:

1) component instances space,
2) component classes space and
3) codes/indices space.

The component instances space consists of components some of which may be equivalent in some respect. For example, two stable in-situ sorting algorithms are *functionally equivalent*. Two quicksort programs coded in *exactly* the same way, but such that variable names differ are *functionally equivalent* and *performance equivalent*—they generate the same machine code. Within the class space, these two components will be represented by the same class. The class space is the space of equivalence classes. The equivalence relationship may include functional equivalence (same input-output relation), performance equivalence (same time and space requirements), etc. The codes space consists of the descriptions of the component classes using an encoding or *indexing* language. In practice, the encoding step inevitably results in a loss of information. In the best case, "indexing" encodes only a subset of the properties of a component class, as when the encoded description of a program module does not state *all* the potential uses of the program. Depending on the relative size of that subset, indexing would project more or fewer distinct component classes into the same codes (or indices). Worse yet, the encoding can assign properties to classes that don't have them.

Matchers compare an encoded description of the developer's needs (query) to the encoded descriptions of the components in the library. The languages for describing queries and components should be identical or homomorphic. Given the number of translations and their complexity, there are ample opportunities for inaccuracy and ambiguity, and it is a wonder any needs get satisfied! Any one of the above steps have kept information retrieval (IR) researchers busy for years. A full survey of IR research is beyond the scope of this paper. We explore below the relation between encoding languages and methods and the corresponding matching algorithms, in general, and from a software reuse perspective.

A developer query may be seen as a predicate Q(.) that retrieves software components X such that Q(X) is true. Each class C in the class space is characterized by a description represented as a predicate $D_C(.)$ such that *all* (and *only*) instances Y of the class C are such that $D_C(Y)$ is true. As mentioned above, encoding generally results into a loss of information by replacing the actual description D_C of a class C by a "simpler" description $\overline{D}_c(\cdot)$. Accordingly, retrieval takes place by comparing Q(.) (the developer query) to the *approximate descriptions* of component classes ($\overline{D}_c(\cdot)$ s). We distinguish between two basic matching approaches:

1) *partial-order-based retrieval*: The retrieval algorithm returns classes of items such that $D_C(.)$ **LT** Q(.), for some

partial-order relation **LT**. Notice that in practice $\overline{D}_c(\cdot)$ will be used for comparison. If **LT** is a logical implication, the algorithm returns classes C such that $D_C(.) \rightarrow Q(.)$. In this case, for all X such that $D_C(X)$ ($\overline{D}_c(X)$) is true, we are assured that Q(X) is true.

2) *distance-based retrieval*: The retrieval algorithm returns classes of items such that Dist($D_C(.)$, Q(.)) (Dist $\overline{D}_c(\cdot)$, Q(.))) is smallest, where Dist is generally a metric that satisfies the following property:

$$[D(.) \text{ } \mathbf{LT} \text{ } Q(.)] \rightarrow [\text{Dist}(D(.), Q(.)) = 0]$$

Intuitively, Dist. measures the extent by which $D_c(\cdot)$ ($\overline{D}_c(\cdot)$) fails the partial-order relation. Needless to say, in either case, the quality of retrieval depends on the quality of indexing, i.e., the relation between $D_c(\cdot)$ and $\overline{D}_c(\cdot)$.

Independently of the retrieval used, queries seldom return software components that fit the needs exactly, especially when those needs are not very precise in the beginning. Thus, most likely, the components retrieved will have to be adapted, and the assessment stage consists of evaluating the retrieved components for the efforts required to modify them. We consider assessment to be an integral part of retrieval. For instance, developer queries should be seen from the following perspective:

> Find components that satisfy the functional requirements Q(.) *OR are easy to modify so that they satisfy Q(.)*.

In other words, a binary predicate IsEasyToAdaptTo(., Q(.)) should be appended, implicitly or explicitly, to any developer query. What makes a component Y easy to adapt to the set of requirements Q(.)? There are two kinds of criteria that make a component easy to adapt:

1) some general criteria related to the intrinsic quality of the component to be adapted and
2) differences between the retrieved component and the requirements Q(.).

In other words, the predicate IsEasyToAdaptTo(., Q(.)) can be seen as the conjunction of two predicates:

$IsEasyToAdaptTo(X, Q(.)) \equiv EasyToModifyInGeneral(X) \wedge$
[CostOfImplementingDifference($D_{class of X}(.)$, Q(.))
on X is small]

where $D_{class of X}(.)$, or $D_X(.)$ for short, is the description of X's properties.

Criteria that make a component easy to understand and adapt include the complexity of the component (size, cyclomatic complexity, number of inputs and outputs, etc.) and the quality of its documentation [28], [131], [159]. Estimating the cost of implementing the difference between $D_X(.)$ and Q(.) on X poses two major difficulties. First and foremost, we have to develop a procedure that, based on the difference between two descriptions $D_X(.)$ and Q(.), tells what kind of changes need to be incurred to components with description $D_X(.)$ so that they fit in (satisfy) the description Q(.). In fact, *distance-based retrieval is fairly useless if the measure Dist doesn't correlate somehow to the amount of effort required to adapt the component*; this issue is discussed in more detail in the next section. Second, we need a way to estimate the costs of making various kinds of changes to a program. Changing a program may involve modifying its interface, its (internal) structure, or both. Clearly, the cost of adaptation depends on the scope of change (interface alone, versus internal logic) and extent of the change. As mentioned in Section III.B.4, more work is needed in this area.

A.2. Evaluating Retrieval Performance

Traditionally, retrieval quality is measured by recall and precision. Recall measures the ratio of number of *retrieved* and *relevant* items to the total number of *relevant* items in the information/knowledge base. Precision measures the ratio of the number of *retrieved* and *relevant* items to the number of *retrieved* documents. Such measures are only adequate for partial-order-based retrieval, which assumes that relevance is a Boolean function, and have been widely criticized for this reason. We add to this the concern for estimating the effort required to adapt a component that doesn't match the developer's requirements. In this section, we study the properties that the encoding schemes and retrieval algorithms need to have to address these problems.

First, it is interesting to discuss the conditions under which we can achieve 100% recall and 100% precision. With partial-order-based retrieval, perfect precision (only items that *truly* satisfy the query are returned) implies that indexing/encoding should be such that:

$$(\forall C)\left[\left(\overline{D}_c(\cdot) \text{ LT } Q(\cdot)\right) \to \left(D_c(\cdot) \text{ LT } Q(\cdot)\right)\right] \quad \text{(A1)}$$

The reader can check that condition (A1) is satisfied if for all C, $D_c(\cdot) \text{ LT } \overline{D}_c(\cdot)$. If the partial order is logical implication, the condition $\left[D_c \to \overline{D}_c\right]$ means *that all that have been encoded ("said") about classes is accurate.* We say that the encoding is *sound*. For perfect recall, encoding should be such that:

$$(\forall C)\left[\left(D_c(\cdot) \text{ LT } Q(\cdot)\right) \to \left(\overline{D}_c(\cdot) \text{ LT } Q(\cdot)\right)\right] \quad \text{(A2)}$$

Condition (A2) is satisfied if for all C, $\overline{D}_c(\cdot) \text{ LT } D_c(\cdot)$. If LT stands for logical implication, this says that *all that is true (and functionally significant) about a class C, and possibly more (erroneously), has been encoded in $\overline{D}_c(\cdot)$.* Not surprisingly, to achieve perfect recall and precision, we need equivalence between the actual intension of classes ($D_C(\cdot)$) and their encoding ($\overline{D}_c(\cdot)$); *logical* equivalence if LT is logical implication. In practice, neither is possible, as mentioned in the previous section. With distance-based retrieval, we don't need logical equivalence but the encoding process should be such that the ranking produced by *Dist* using $\overline{D}_c(\cdot)$ is similar to that which would have been produced using the actual $D_C(\cdot)$. The following must hold:

$$(\forall C_1, C_2)$$
$$\left[\left(Dist\left(\overline{D}_{c_1}(\cdot), Q(\cdot)\right) < \right.\right.$$
$$Dist\left(\overline{D}_{c_2}(\cdot), Q(\cdot)\right)\right) \to \quad \text{(B1)}$$
$$\left(Dist\left(D_{c_1}(\cdot), Q(\cdot)\right) \leq Dist\left(D_{c_2}(\cdot), Q(\cdot)\right)\right)$$

$$(\forall C_1, C_2)$$
$$\left[\left(Dist\left(D_{c_1}(\cdot), Q(\cdot)\right) \leq \right.\right.$$
$$Dist\left(D_{c_2}(\cdot), Q(\cdot)\right)\right) \to \quad \text{(B2)}$$
$$\left(Dist\left(\overline{D}_{c_1}(\cdot), Q(\cdot)\right) \leq Dist\left(\overline{D}_{c_2}(\cdot), Q(\cdot)\right)\right).$$

Condition (B1) means that if an item C_1 is presented to the developer before item C_2, then it is truly more relevant[27] than C_2. Condition (B2) means that if C_1 is more relevant than C_2, then it will be presented to the developer before C_2. The reader can check that because, for a given query, *Dist* defines a total order on the class space, the two conditions are actually equivalent.

Another way of interpreting condition (B1) (or (B2)) is to say that encoding is monotonic, or, introduces a consistent bias. A cautionary note is, however, in order:

In a reuse context, the thoroughness of component encoding is limited by the developer's willingness to formulate long and precise queries; there is no point in encoding every bit of relevant information about a component if a developer barely has the patience for typing string search regular expressions!

We now look at the issue of estimating the cost of adapting a component that does not match exactly the needs of the developer. Notwithstanding cases where a component fails to match the query on nonessential (nonfunctional) properties, distance-based retrieval implicitly assumes that the measure *Dist* somehow correlates to the effort required to adapt the component to match the query. It is fair to assume that the effort is related to the extent of structural changes needed to change the component. A component may be described by either its function (input-output relation, the "what") or its structure (the "how"). Typically, a developer queries the library for a component that fulfills a given purpose ("what"), i.e., by specifying its functional properties rather than by specifying or sketching its structure; the former being, supposedly, easier than the latter. Hence, for matching purposes, component classes are described by their functional properties. Therefore, *in order to estimate the structural changes needed to apply to a component that fails a developer query, we need to have a model of the relation between functional requirements (function, types of inputs/outputs, etc.) and component structure.*

---

27. The left-hand side of (B1) has strict inequality (<) because we don't care what happens for cases where $Dist\left(\overline{D}_{c_i}(\cdot), Q(\cdot)\right) = Dist\left(\overline{D}_{c_j}(\cdot), q(\cdot)\right)$, since encoding naturally maps distinct classes to equivalent codes.

The kind of knowledge needed to model a structure-function relationship is not much different from that needed in automatic programming. For instance, if we can characterize the structures that implement a given function, we are only one step away from generating those structures automatically based on the specification of the function! It is extremely difficult to characterize such structures, in no small measure because several algorithms, e.g., can implement the same function, and the same algorithm can implement several "functions," depending on the data it manipulates. However, we should mention that automatic programming systems do not generate *all the possible programs* that can satisfy a given set of requirements; one that does suffices. Further, we do not need to characterize the full range of (function, structure) pairs, but rather the structural modifications associated with "small" functional differences. In other words, if FS is the mapping that associates to a function f a set of structures $\{s_i\}_i = FS(f)$, we do not need a characterization of FS, but rather of $FS(f + \Delta f) - FS(f)$. This reduces the problem to finding types of functional differences that can be accommodated by (measurably) small structural differences,[28] knowing that several kinds of structural differences can accommodate a given functional change. In the next section, we will comment on the extent to which the encoding and retrieval methods discussed address this problem in one form or another.

A.3. A Survey of Existing Approaches

Existing approaches to software component retrieval cover a wide spectrum of component encoding methods and search or matching algorithms. The encoding methods differ with respect to their soundness, completeness, and the extent to which they support an estimate of the effort it takes to modify a component. Striving for any of these qualities makes encoding more complex and costlier. It also makes it possible to support more sophisticated retrieval, provided queries of equal richness and expressiveness to that of the encoding scheme are used. In practice, there is a limit to how complex queries can be for component search and reuse to be worthwhile (Section III.B.1). Accordingly, overly complex encoding schemes are wasteful unless reusers are provided computer assistance in formulating equally complex queries. The approaches discussed below strike different balances between complexity and cost on one hand and retrieval quality on the other. Further, some are immediately practicable and have been used in a production setting, while others are mere theoretical explorations. We discuss three major classes of encoding and retrieval approaches, by increasing order of complexity:

1) *text-based* "encoding" and retrieval,
2) *lexical descriptor-based* encoding and retrieval and
3) *specification-based* encoding and retrieval.

With text-based encoding and retrieval, the textual representation of a component is used as an implicit functional descriptor: Arbitrarily complex string search expressions supplied by the reuser are matched against the textual representa-

tion (see, e.g., [113]). The main advantage of such an approach is related to cost: No encoding is required, and queries are fairly easy to formulate. Its disadvantages have been thoroughly investigated in the information retrieval literature [20]. Simply put, plain-text encoding is neither sound nor complete. Short of a full-fledged language understanding system that takes into account the context, the presence of a concept (term or phrase) in the text does not imply that the component is about that concept (e.g., "Unlike quicksort, this procedure..."). Conversely, the absence of a concept from the text does not mean that the component is *not* about that concept, as different developers and documenters may use a different terminology.

Plain text encoding and search, and variants thereof, have been used in a number of software libraries (e.g., [48], [93], [113]), alone or in conjunction with other search methods, and had fairly good recall and precision rates. In a controlled experiment performed at the Software Productivity Consortium, Frakes and Pole found that more sophisticated methods (see below) had no provable advantage over plain text retrieval in terms of recall and precision [49]. However, they found that developers took 60% more time than with the best method to be satisfied that they had retrieved all the items relevant to their queries. This accounts for both the speed with which individual search statements/expressions can be formulated and the number of *distinct* search statements that had to be submitted to answer the same query. With traditional document retrieval systems such as library systems, longer search times are a mere annoyance. *In a reuse context, bigger search times can make the difference between reusing and not reusing* (Section III.B.1).

With lexical descriptor-based encoding, each component is assigned a set of *key phrases* that tell what the component "is about." We could define a two-place predicate *IsAbout* $(.,.)$, where key phrase K is assigned to a component (or component class) C iff *IsAbout*(K, C). If C is assigned a set of phrases $\{K_1, ..., K_n\}$, then *IsAbout*$(C, K_1) \wedge ... \wedge$ *IsAbout*(C, K_n) is true, and the one-place predicate *IsAbout*$(., K_1) \wedge ... \wedge$ *IsAbout*$(., K_n)$ may be considered as the description of the component (class) C (Section V.A.2). Typically, subject experts inspect the components and assign to them key phrases taken from a *predefined vocabulary* that reflects the important concepts in the domain of discourse (see, e.g., [6], [27], [113], [131]). Notwithstanding the possibility of human error and the coarseness of the indexing vocabulary, such encoding is sound, as opposed to plain-text encoding. Further, because a key phrase need not occur in a component's textual representation to be assigned to it, it is also *more* complete[29] than plain text encoding. Reusers formulate their queries as Boolean expressions of key phrases. Let $Q = E(K'_1, ..., K'_m)$, a Boolean expression with terms $K'_1, ..., K'_m$. A component C with key phrases $K_1, ..., K_n$ is considered relevant to the Boolean expression (query) Q iff *IsAbout*$(., K_1) \wedge ... \wedge$ *IsAbout*$(., K_n) \rightarrow E(IsAbout(., K'_1), ..., [sAbout(., K'_m))$, or, equivalently, if $K_1 \wedge ... \wedge K_n \rightarrow Q = E(K'_1, ..., K'_m)$. *Boolean retrieval*, as it is called, corresponds to what we called partial-order-based retrieval.

---

28 For example, we can compare graphical representations of programs obtained through data and control flow analysis, see, e.g., [86].

29 An encoding scheme can be considered complete only if it says everything of consequence about the component; that is hard to define.

In practice, the method presented above is refined in many ways. In one refinement, instead of using the one generic relation $IsAbout(.,.)$ between components and descriptors, several specific relations are used such as $HasFunction(.,.)$, $ApplicableToDomain(.,.)$, $OperatesOn(.,.)$, etc. [27], [112], [131]; this is commonly referred to as *multifaceted classification* in the information retrieval literature, where each facet corresponds to a relation, and the descriptions for each facet are logically ANDed. For example, if we use the facets *HasFunction* and *OperatesOn*, a routine that sorts both arrays and linked lists may be described by the one-place predicate [$HasFunction(.,\ Sorting)$] $\wedge$ [$OperatesOn\ (.,\ Array)\ \wedge\ OperatesOn(.,\ LinkedList)$]. Similarly, reuser queries are now formulated using a conjunction of Boolean expressions, one for each facet on which the reuser wishes to search.

A second set of refinements amend the retrieval algorithm itself to handle approximate matches. We illustrate them for simple (single-facet) indexing; extending them to multifaceted indexing is fairly straightforward. First, if there is a partial order between key phrases themselves, the partial order may be used to extend queries. Assume for example that the key phrases are organized in a taxonomy. Let K_1 and K_2 be two phrases such that K_1 has an "is-a" relation with K_2. By definition, any component C that is about K_1 ($IsAbout(C, K_1)$), by default, is also about K_2 ($IsAbout(C, K_2)$). However, the reverse is not true. Thus, in the process of looking for components that are about K_2, the ones that are about K_1—and K_2's descendants in general—would also do. This approach is used in MEDLINE [102], an on-line medical literature retrieval system operated and maintained by the (U.S.) National Library of Medicine. Two additional refinements turn Boolean retrieval—which is partial-order-based—into distance-based retrieval. The first ranks components by decreasing number of key phrases that match phrases from the query [142]. The second method is used when key phrases are organized in a taxonomy (see, e.g., [134]) or a weighed semantic net in general (see, e.g., [131]). The former has been used in the European ESPRIT Practitioner (software reuse) project (see, e.g., [113]). The latter has been more widely used in software libraries (see, e.g., [27], [48], [131]). In SoftClass, a prototype CASE tool with integrated support for reuse, we implemented three classes of lexical descriptor-based component retrieval algorithms that combine the above features with weighed facets and a number of fuzzy bells and whistles [112]. We are currently setting up a series of experiments to compare the different methods. However, we don't expect significant improvements to result from some of the refinements mentioned above.

Lexical descriptor-based encoding and retrieval suffers from a number of problems. First, an agreed (or agreeable) vocabulary has to be developed. That is both labor-intensive and conceptually challenging. Sorumgard et al. reported a number of problems developing and using a classification vocabulary [151]. They experienced known problems in building indexing vocabularies for document retrieval, including trade-offs between precision and size of the vocabulary and the choice between what is referred to as precoordinated or post-

coordinated *indexing*,[30] with the confusion that may result from mixing the two [151]. Software-specific challenges include the fact that one-word or one-phrase abstractions are hard to come by in the software domain [83], [151].

Further, it is not clear whether indexing should describe the computational semantics of a component, as in "this procedure returns the record that has the highest value for a float field, among an array of records," or its application *semantics*[31] as in "this procedure finds the highest paid employee within the employees file" [151]. Characterizing computational semantics is important for reuse across application domains. However, reusers may have the tendency to formulate their queries in application-meaningful terms. Formal specification methods suffer from the same problem, but to a lesser extent, since application semantics show up specifically as terminal symbols in the specification language. Finally, neither the encoding mechanism nor the retrieval algorithm lend themselves to assessing the effort required to modify a component that does not match the query perfectly. This is so because the descriptors have externally assigned (linguistic) meanings and bear no relationship to the structure of the components. For example, what does it mean for a component C to have the function *Sort*, i.e., what does it mean to have $HasFunction(C, Sort)$? it only means what we wish the symbol "Sort" to mean to us, and any relation between two symbols has to be posited by us, rather than proven by a formal proof system.

From the reuser's point of view, a familiarity with the vocabulary is needed in order to use a component retrieval system effectively [142]; a hierarchical (e.g., taxonomical) organization of the key phrases and proper browsing tools can alleviate the problem significantly [113]. Further, queries tend to be fairly tedious to enter, especially for the case of multifaceted encoding. In SoftClass, where software components are grouped into component categories, each with its own facets, queries are entered by filling out a simplified component template that stands for the prototypical component the developer wishes to retrieve [113]; the filled out template is then internally translated into a Boolean query and matched against the component base. While this format does not handle all kinds of queries efficiently, we believe that it handles the most common queries efficiently [113].

Specification-based encoding and retrieval comes closest to achieving full equivalence between what a component is and does and how it is encoded. With text and lexical descriptor-based methods, retrieval algorithms treat queries and codes as mere symbols, and any meaning assigned to queries, component codes, or the extent of match between them is external to the encoding language. Further, being natural language-based, the codes are inherently ambiguous and imprecise. By contrast, specification languages have their own semantics within which

---

30. (Very) roughly speaking, with precoordinated indexing, several phrases for the same facet are to be interpreted *disjunctively*, while with postcoordinated indexing, they should be interpreted *conjunctively*; see [112].

31. Using our approach to object-oriented design (seec Section IV.C.3 and [111]), generic design *templates* would be described by their computational semantics. Application data *structures* would be characterized *explicitly* by their application semantics, and implicitly, through the generic design template to which they map, by their computational semantics.

the fitness of a component to a query can be formally established [32], [108], [161], and "mismatches" between the two can be formally interpreted [108], [161]. Typically, the formal specification-based methods correspond to what we called partial order-based retrieval, using a partial-order relationship between specifications. This partial order is often used to pre-organize the components of the library to reduce the number of comparisons between specifications—an often prohibitively costly operation [108], [115]. The methods discussed in the literature differ in the expressiveness of the specification language. Also, different retrieval algorithms take advantage more or less fully of the power of the specification language. The subset of the language used for retrieval *often* has no effect on recall, but degrades precision, as in using operations' signatures instead of using signatures *and* pre- and post-conditions.

In [108], A. Mili et al. describe a method for organizing and retrieving software components that uses relational specifications of programs and refinement (contravariance) ordering between them. Any given program is correct with respect to (satisfies) the specification to which it is attached, as well as the specifications that are "above" it. Hence, a specification retrieves the programs attached to it, as well as those attached to specifications that are "below" it. A theorem prover is used to establish a refinement ordering between two specifications. Two forms of retrieval are defined: *exact retrieval*, which fetches all the specifications that are more refined than a re-user-supplied specification, say K, and *approximate retrieval*, which is invoked whenever the exact retrieval fails, and which retrieves specifications that have the biggest "overlap"[32] with K [108]. One nice property about approximate retrieval is that, while it does not directly assess the effort required to modify a component, the difference actually means something (e.g., a program is found that gives the desired outputs for a subset of the inputs) and may suggest a way of modifying the returned programs to make them satisfy the requirements or use several of them in combination [108].

Chen et al. proposed a similar approach that uses algebraic specifications for abstract data types and an *implementation* partial ordering between them [32]. Reusable components, which may be seen as abstract data types, are specified by both their signature and their *behavioral axioms*. However, while the *implementation* relationship takes into account the behavioral axioms, the retrieval algorithm uses only signatures, modulo a renaming of the "types" of the components to match those of the query [32]; the authors did envision using an "interactive system [read semiautomatic] for algebraic implementation proofs" [32]. Moorman-Zaremski and Wing propose an approach based exclusively on signature matching [161]. The major advantage of their approach is that the information required for matching can be extracted directly from the code. They first define *exact matches* between function signatures, to within parameter names, and then define module signatures and partial matches between modules using various generalization and subtyping relationships [161]. They too

envision taking into account behavioral specifications in future versions, using LARCH (cf. [60]) specifications—which would then have to be encoded manually.

None of the formal specification-based methods we know about addresses directly (or successfully) the issue of assessing the effort required to modify a component returned by approximate retrieval (inexact match). Further specification-based methods that include *behavioral* specifications (and not just signatures) suffer from considerable costs. First, there is the cost of deriving and validating formal specifications for the components of the library (see also [115]). This cost is recoverable because it could be amortized over several *trouble-free* uses of the components and is minimal if specifications are written *before* the components are implemented, which is the way it should be (and seldom is) done. The second cost has to do with the computational complexity, if not outright undecidability, of proof procedures. This cost can be reduced if actual proofs are performed only for those components that match a simplified form of the specifications, e.g., the signature; not much else can be done about the inherent complexity of proof procedures or their undecidability without sacrificing specification power. Last but not least, there is the cost for the reuser to write full-fledged specifications for the desired components. Because there is no evidence that specifications are either easier or shorter to write than programs, reusers need motivations other than time-savings, or computer assistance, to write specifications for the components they need. We believe that formal specification-based matching will remain a theoretical curiosity for the time being and will integrate only in the more formal development methods that address application domains such as reactive and real-time systems.

B. Component Composition

Under component composition, we address two dual sets of issues:

1) Given a set of components, and a schema for composing them, check that the proposed composition is feasible (*verification*) *and* satisfies a given set of requirements (*validation*); we refer to this as the composition verification and validation problem and

2) given a set of requirements, find a set of components within a component library whose combined behavior satisfies the requirements; we refer to this as the bottom-up design problem.

The first problem benefits from a large body of work that is not often associated with reuse. A thorough coverage of this problem is beyond the scope of this paper. We will be content to highlight the general issues and describe a representative sample of work in this area (Section V.B.1). The second problem, discussed in Section V.B.2, benefits from work on verification and validation of compositions, but presents challenging search problems of its own.

---

32. The overlap between two specifications is determined using the "meet" lattice operation [108].

B.1. Composition Verification and Validation

Component composition verification and validation poses three challenges:

1) designing a language for describing compositions of components that lends itself to verification and validation,
2) performing verification and
3) performing validation.

There are two general methods for describing compositions of components. If we think of a component as consisting of a specification and a realization (or a set of realizations, see, e.g., [83]), then composition may occur either at the specification level or at the realization (implementation) level (see also Section V.B.3). Specification languages usually provide built-in composition operators with well-defined semantics. For example, with relational specifications, any of the set theoretic and relational operations may be seen as a composition. In this case, we might say that the set of specifications is closed under composition, and verifying or validating a composition of specifications or validating it against a target specification is not different from verifying any individual specification or validating it against another specification. With regard to validation, we can expect the same challenges discussed for specification-based component encoding and retrieval (Section V.A.3). The problem with specification-level composition is that it is often difficult to characterize specification-level manipulations by manipulations on the actual realizations (programs) of these specifications [108].

When composition takes place at the component realization level, we obtain a (much) smaller range of behavioral compositions, but we are assured that these compositions are feasible without additional development. Component compositions are usually described using the so-called *module interconnection languages* [61], [129]. A module may be seen as having an *internal structure*, consisting of a set of data structures and a set of procedures that reference them, and an *external interface* specifying the external entities the module depends on and the internal entities the module exports. Module interconnection languages describe component (module) compositions by specifying:

1) the *obligations* of the individual participants and
2) the *interactions* between the components.

The specification of the obligations of the individual components consists, minimally, of the signatures of the operations they need to support; this is similar to Ada's constrained generics, where generic packages list the operations that type parameters have to support [106]. It could also include the specification of the *behavior* of the operations. This is the approach followed in Helm et al.'s *contracts* [65] and a number of algebraic specification-based interconnection languages such as Goguen's library interconnection language (LIL [57]) and other derivatives of OBJ or LILEANNA [153], e.g., an application of LIL's concepts to *ANN*otated Ada packages. One of the interesting features of LIL is that obligations are specified in terms of *theories*, and a given module (in this case, an abstract data type) may satisfy a theory in different ways,

called *views* [57]. This has the advantage of ignoring operation names during verification, by focusing on their behavioral semantics instead.

The specification of the interactions between the components varies from simple call dependencies [61] to a full-fledged behavioral specification including interaction logic, aggregate-wide preconditions, postconditions, invariants, etc. (see, e.g., [61], [65], [109]). Behavioral interactions between components can also be specified *implicitly* in logic-based (or logic-flavored) languages. One such language is MELD, an OO language developed by Kaiser and Garlan [78]. In MELD, classes are represented by *features*. Methods are represented by semideclarative[33] constructs called *action equations*. When the same methods are implemented by two features, their action equations are merged. In case the merge creates dependencies, a topological sort determines which action equations are to be executed first [78]. This constitutes, in our opinion, MELD's most interesting feature for reuse by composition as it automates code-level integration. Validating the behavior of a composition of modules against a desired behavioral specification is generally a difficult problem [84], [163]. One of the major difficulties is due to the fact that it is difficult to get a closed form expression for the behavior of the aggregate. This is due to the fact that the language used for describing compositions is different from that used for specifying individual components (see, e.g., [163]).

B.2. Bottom-Up Development

Top-down development consists of decomposing the requirements for a module into requirements for a set of (simpler, more reusable, etc.) submodules and patterns of interactions between them. Informal requirements analysis and specification methods use informal heuristics to guide the decomposition process. Formal methods use various reduction and factoring mechanisms to decompose specifications (see, e.g., [30], [33]). In both cases, the decomposition is guided by properties that the component submodules and their patterns of interactions have to have. For non-trivial requirements, a virtually limitless number of solutions of equal quality could be found. With bottom-up development, the major requirement is that the decomposition yields specifications for which components have already been developed. This is generally a very difficult problem.

Enumerating compositions of components within a library "until one is found that has the desired behavior" seems unthinkable at first. In practice, a number of practical and theoretical considerations can make the number of compositions to explore manageable. In [62], Hall describes a component retrieval method that explores combinations of components when none of the individual components matches the user query. Users specify the desired behavior by giving an example input-output pair $<I, O>$. The idea of retrieving components based on the output they *actually* produce when executed on a user-supplied input was first proposed by Podgurski and Pierce [127]. Hall extends Podgurski and Pierce's work by

---

33. Action equations are essentially predicates. However, they do contain some control information such as iteration and sequencing.

exploring compositions of components when no single component is found that returns O given I. For example, if all the components in the library are single-parameter functions $f_1, ..., f_n$, then if for all i, $f_i(I) \neq O$, we try out $f_j(f_i(I))$, for all $1 \leq i, j \leq n$, and if none is found that returns O, we try three levels deep function compositions, etc. [62]. Hall showed that, in general, the number of compositions of components of depth d or less is doubly exponential in d, i.e., of the form $O(n^{(n^d)})$. However, a number of techniques help reduce that number considerably, without missing any potential solutions. Type-compatibility requirements considerably restrict the range of possible compositions. More dramatic results are obtained by dynamic programming: When generating compositions of depth d $(f_{i_1}o \ ... \ of_{i_d})$, apply new components to all the combinations of distinct return *values* of depth $d - 1$, rather than all combinations of distinct *programs* of depth $d - 1$.

Hall tested his algorithm on a library of 161 Lisp functions. The retrieval system itself is written in Common Lisp. He limited the depth of compositions to three, with the level three functions limited to those that have a single input. Fifteen queries took an average of 20 seconds, and a maximum of 40 seconds, running on a SUN SPARC II. In one example, a query provoked 2,400 component executions instead of a potential 10^{16} executions [62]. While more testing is needed to assess the efficiency of the algorithm, the processing times remain reasonable for a reasonably large library and show that the method could indeed be computationally practical. However, as Hall pointed out, this method could not be applied to retrieving nonexecutable reusable components [62]. A less serious engineering difficulty has to do with multiplatform libraries, components that raise exception while being tested out or loop endlessly, and components with side-effects, all of which pose challenging but tractable engineering problems [62].

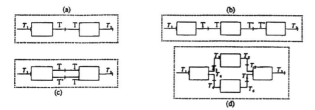

Fig. 4. Alternative compositions that could be considered by the composition retrieval algorithm.

We have started work on a combination of Hall's work and Moorman-Zaremski and Wing's work on signature matching [161]. Assume that a developer is looking for a component that takes an input variable of type T_1 and produces an output variable of type T_2. Failing to find such a component, an algorithm could find any of the compositions shown in Fig. 4, that "concatenates" components based on type compatibility between their inputs and outputs. The *function realization problem*, as we called it, consists of finding all the compositions of functions (signatures) that consume no more than the inputs specified by the developer's query and produce at least the outputs specified by the developer's query [112]. We showed in [112] that the *set cover problem*, which is known to

be NP-complete [54], could be reduced to the function realization problem. Worse, we know of no heuristic that guarantees a solution value within a constant factor of the optimum cover of a set [54], which suggests that none could be found for the function realization problem either. Fortunately, finding out whether a function signature has a realization or not can be done in polynomial time [112]; bear in mind, though, that a realization does not necessarily exhibit the desired behavior. Because several realizations could be equivalent, we defined a "minimal" form for realizations called *normal realization*, where each function is needed (i.e., without it the composition would not be a realization), and where each function has the minimal possible depth, i.e., is "called as soon as all its inputs are available." We developed an algorithm for finding normal realizations and implemented it in Lisp [112].

Our method has the advantage of not requiring component execution, and like Moorman-Zaremski and Wing's method [161], the information required for search can be extracted from components themselves. However, programming language types alone can be hopelessly nondiscriminatory. A library written in a weakly typed language (e.g., C) is likely to have a handful of types, and the algorithm will have a dismal precision. Application-oriented definitions of types can sharpen the search but may miss out on some valid realizations [62]. We are currently testing the algorithm on a library of data manipulation functions (string manipulation, data conversion, etc.). While we do not expect a good precision, we are hoping that an inspection of the results will help us recognize classes of realizations or subrealizations that should be pruned out of the search, thereby increasing the efficiency of the algorithm. However, we expect most of the gains to come from using richer semantics for types and type compatibility, and we are pursuing work in that direction as well.

C. Adapting Reusable Components

We use the term adaptation to refer to what happens to a component between the time a decision is made to reuse it and the time it has become part of the product. We recognize three potential subtasks,

1) what Krueger called *selection* [83]: if a reusable component has a variable part or explicitly enumerated alternative implementations, select (the) one that is appropriate for the problem at hand,

2) *modification*: in case the component or any of its variants cannot be used as is and

3) *integration*, which is essentially a verification step that checks whether the component is compatible with its environment.

One of the major differences between selection and modification is that with selection, the changes to the component have been planned ahead of time. This is generally done using various parameterization and abstraction techniques and will be discussed briefly below. With *modification*, the changes are often unanticipated or poorly planned. As mentioned in Sections III.A.3 and III.B.1, modifying reusable components may defeat both the quality and the productivity advantages of reuse. Hence, it should be automated as much as possible to save time and ensure that the modifications are quality-preserving. We discuss modification in the context of transformational systems. As for the integration of reusable components, what is not addressed by module interconnection languages discussed in Section V.B.1 is not specific to the reusability of the components and will not be discussed further here.

C.1. Selection

Two commonly used selection mechanisms are specialization and instantiation of abstract software components. Abstraction has been supported by programming language constructs for some time [143]. At the most basic level, declaring program constants or using variable-dimension arrays is a form of parameterized programming. Conditional compilation is another more sophisticated form of parameterized software, whereby different code sequences are compiled based on a number of system and environmental parameters. In this case, adaptation consists simply of setting the right environmental parameters. In general the mechanisms involved depend on the nature and complexity of the parameters, ranging from a simple compile or linkage-time binding (e.g., of an unresolved reference to a type T to a specific type), to a mix of substitutions, conditional compilation and code generation as in [16], and template-based approaches in general (see, e.g., [85], [137]).

Object oriented languages support a number of abstraction and selection mechanisms, including generic classes, abstract classes, and metaclasses with metaprogramming [72]. *Genericity* supports the development of complex data structures with parameterized component types. For example, one could define a generic list structure LIST[T] whose node values (or "data" fields) are of a generic type T that supports comparison operators. In this case, selection consists of using the (e.g., declaring a variable of) data type LIST[< >] by specifying an actual type instead of the parameter T. The obligations of the type T may be specified explicitly in the specification of the generic type (called constrained *genericity* [106]) or implicitly based on what types will actually compile or execute. With *abstract classes* (Section IV.B.1), selection consists of choosing among several concrete subclasses that *conform* to the behavior of the abstract class, or creating a subclass of our own, to address the specific needs of the application at hand [72]. Note that subclassing alone does not guarantee that a class conforms to its superclasses, i.e., that the types they implement are in a subtype relationship. We showed in Section IV.B.3 how design-level considerations may lead to situations where subclasses do not implement subtypes, and vice-versa. Unfortunately, few programming languages (e.g., Eiffel [106]) ensure that subclasses implement types that are in a subtype relationship, and subclassing remains essentially a code-sharing mechanism, with the problems we discussed in Sections IV.B.3 and IV.B.4. Finally, the use of *metaclasses with metaprogramming* may be seen as an OO packaging (design) for program generators (Section IV.2) and will not be discussed further here; the reader is referred to [72] for a more thorough discussion.

C.2. Modification

Modification is required when a retrieved component has to be *reworked* to accommodate the needs of the application at hand. The need for modification may become clear during retrieval: The *encoded description* of the component does not match perfectly the query. Alternatively, a closer inspection of a component whose encoded description did match the query may reveal inadequacies. The latter case is possible because encoding is often incomplete: The encoded description leaves out some functional properties of the component. We saw in Section V.A.2 that the mismatch between a query and the encoding of a component may be more or less revealing as to the (extent of the) changes that need to be incurred to the component, depending on the completeness of the encoding. For the purposes of presentation, we consider the two situations as instances of the same problem: Given the specification of a desired component S_D, the "closely matching" specification S_C of an existing component C, and its realization R_C (i.e., implementation), find the realization for the desired component—call it R_D; the additional problem of working our way back from differences between encoded (partial) description used for retrieval to actual functional specifications raises similar issues because in both cases we have to walk our way back, upstream of an information-losing mapping (see Fig. 5).

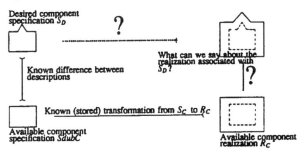

Fig. 5. The component modification problem.

This problem is best understood in the context of a transformational view of software development. Software development is seen as a (possibly long) sequence of transformations, starting with more or less formal specifications, leading eventually to executable code [1]. Fig. 6 shows the typical software life cycle for transformational systems. In such systems, software development consists of two major steps:

1) deriving *formal* specifications from user requirements—if the transformations to be applied are to do any substantive work and
2) applying a set of transformations on the formal specifications, gradually building a computer program, in either a target programming language or in a readily translatable language [123].

An important characteristic of transformational systems is the potential for maintaining software systems at the specifications level [8]. According to this view, the complexity of software development lies not in the individual transformations, but in applying the "right" transformation when several alternatives are possible. Existing transformational systems provide varying levels of support for selecting the "right" transformations, ranging from simply enacting/executing transformations chosen by the developer to full automation [8], [123].

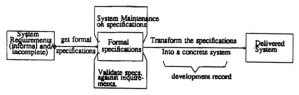

Fig. 6. Typical software life cycle in transformational systems. Adapted from [1].

Regardless of the "intelligence" of the transformations (e.g., their knowledge about their own appropriateness), the transformational approach has the following advantages:

1) relieving developers from labor-intensive, knowledge-poor tasks,
2) virtually eliminating clerical errors,
3) ensuring correctness of the resulting programs by construction and
4) maintaining a record of development choices, their rationale, or both for maintenance purposes.

It is this last characteristic of transformational systems that concerns us most in this paper, namely, the potential for software reuse. Maintenance has been recognized by a number of researchers as a particular form of reuse (see, e.g., [14]). Balzer et al. recognized transformational systems' potential for enhancing software reuse, whereby reusable components are maintained and modified at the specification level rather than at the implementation level [8]. While a number of researchers have recognized the importance of recording development decisions for reuse purposes, the transformational approach to software development makes *explicit computer-supported* use of those decisions to maintain/reuse existing software.

The transformational approach makes maintenance and reuse easier, not only because it makes development easier in general, but also because "similar" inputs (e.g., formal specifications or any other intermediary form) *often* call for the same transformations to be applied. Cases where the same sequence of transformations cannot be replayed, e.g., the preconditions of one of the transformations fail to hold as a result of a modification, developer intervention is only needed from that point onward. Baxter studied the commutativity and dependencies between transformations to minimize the scope of modifications [17]. Take the example of a program P that was derived from a specification S using the chain of transformations $T_n \ o \ ... \ o \ T_i \ o \ ... \ o \ T_1$ and assume that S was modified into S′ such that all transformations up to, not including, T_i (i.e., $T_1, ..., T_{i-1}$) were applied successfully. Normally, a developer would have to intervene to choose an alternative transformation to T_i and proceed from that point to the end. However, if it is known that some transformation T_j, for $i < j \le n$, commutes with (thus, independent of) T_i, then it could be moved (applied) ahead of T_i, and the developer would have fewer transformations to consider. Generally speaking, replaying de-

sign histories is not foolproof. The level of confidence in the replayed process depends on the knowledge embodied/used in selecting transformations (e.g., completeness and soundness of preconditions) and the responsiveness of the transformation selection algorithm to specification changes. One can easily imagine a case where an innocuous change in specifications might require a significant change in program structure to maintain a similar level of performance.

Transformational systems have been criticized by some researchers for their limited range of applicability [123]. The programs generated with this approach were mostly toy examples, as was the case with other AI-oriented automatic programming systems [9]. While, in principle, the transformational approach is not limited to small programs, the amount of knowledge that needs to be encoded to handle large software systems is prohibitively large. Most of the earlier transformational systems embody basic, domain-independent, *programming knowledge*. More recent efforts such as the DRACO system [121] support domain-specific specification languages, and transformations embody some form of domain knowledge. Software reuse research may well benefit from relaxing the formal correctness-preserving nature of transformations and fromusing more heuristic rules such as analogical reasoning [29], especially when we deal with informal or poorly structured software products (see, e.g., [94]). Alternatively, we could settle for localized or partial transformational approaches, as opposed to ones covering the entire specification → program cycle.

To the extent that software reuse benefits from automatically propagating software changes across development stages, work on configuration management systems and program dependencies is eminently relevant. Configuration management systems are concerned primarily with maintaining the integrity of software systems and the interoperability of components as they undergo change [120]. Minimally, such systems help localize the effects of changes [92]. On a different scale, work on program dependencies is concerned primarily with the *local* effects of change, typically within a procedure. Typically, data and control flows within a program are analyzed, thereby identifying the parts that depend on a particular datum/control statement. Such analyses support reuse in many ways:

1) localizing the effects of changes [117], [126], thus guiding reusers in the process of adapting retrieved components to their needs,
2) simplifying program structures [71], which enhances program readability and understandability and
3) "slicing" programs to extract specific functionalities [53], [71], in case the retrieved component does more than what is required.

The latter is an interesting dual to reuse by composition (see Section V.B). We should mention, however, that reliable flow analysis depends on a number of restrictive assumptions, such as the absence of side-effects and "global variables" (see, e.g., [117], [126]). On the positive side, they help increase the reuse worth of code fragments by automating some of the code modification tasks and do not require the availability of design or analysis information. A combination of *macroscopic* configuration management and *microscopic* program flow analysis can help reduce the cost of maintaining and reusing software.

VI. SUMMARY AND DISCUSSION

Reuse is the default problem-solving strategy in most human activities [88], and software development is no exception. Software reuse means reusing the inputs, the processes, and the outputs of previous software development efforts. Software reuse is a means toward an end: improving software development productivity and software product quality. Reuse is based on the premise that *educing* a solution from the statement of a problem involves more effort (labor, computation, etc.) than *inducing* a solution from that to a similar problem, one for which such efforts have already been expended. While the inherent complexities in software development [26] make it a good candidate for explorations in reuse, it is far from obvious that actual gains will occur. The challenges are structural, organizational, managerial, and technical. In this paper, we discussed some of the most important issues, with an emphasis on the technical ones.

Economic considerations, and cost/benefit analyses in general, must be at the center of any discussion of software reuse. Notwithstanding differences between reuse approaches along the building blocks—generative dimension, it is useful to think of software reuse research in terms of attempts to minimize the average cost of a reuse occurrence (see Section III.B.1):

$$[Search + (1 - p) \times (ApproxSearch + q \\ \times Adaptation_{old} + (1 - q) \times Development_{new})]$$

where *Search(ApproxSearch)* is the average cost of formulating a search statement to a library of reusable components, and either finding one that matches exactly (approximatively) the requirements, or be convinced that none exists, *Adaptation*$_{old}$ is the average cost of adapting a component returned by approximate retrieval, and *Development*$_{new}$ the average cost of developing a component that has no match, exact or approximate, in the library. For reuse to be cost-effective, the above must be smaller than:

$$p \times Development_{exact} + (1-p) \times q \\ \times Development_{approx} + (1 - p) \\ \times (1 - q) \times Development_{new})$$

where *Development*$_{exact}$ and *Development*$_{approx}$ represent the average cost of developing custom-tailored versions of components in the library that could have been used as is or adapted, respectively. Note that all these averages are time averages and not averages on individual components, i.e., a reusable component will be counted as many times as it is used.

Work on developing reusable software aims at maximizing *p* (probability of finding an exact match) and *q* (probability of finding an approximate match)—i.e., maximizing the coverage of the application domain—and minimizing *Adaptation*$_{old}$ for a set of common mismatches, i.e., packaging components in such a way that the most common mismatches are handled easily. Increasing *p* and *q* does not necessarily mean putting more components in the library; it could also mean putting

components that are more frequently needed. Because adding components increases search costs (see Section III.B.1), we could use a two-pronged approach:

1) identify components that are generally useful and
2) try to cover the same set of needs with fewer components.

Identifying the components that are generally useful is sometimes called *domain analysis* and is an important activity for both application generator development (Section IV.B) and OO software development (Section IV.C). Covering the same set of needs using fewer components involves two paradigms:

1) *abstraction*, essential to application generators, and very important to OO software development and
2) *composition*, which is central to OO software development.

Composition supports the creation of a virtually unlimited number of aggregates from the same set of components and reduces the risk of combinatorial explosion that would result from enumerating all the possible configurations (cf. Section II.C and [149]). In general, the higher the level of abstraction at which composition takes place, the wider the range of systems (and behaviors) that can be obtained (see Section V.B). The combination of abstraction and composition provides a powerful paradigm for constructing systems from reusable components and constitutes the major thrust behind research in OO frameworks. It also exemplifies the ways in which software reuse addresses the scalability and focus issues in software engineering (see Section I).

Work on developing *with* reusable software aims at minimizing the cost of search (exact and approximate) and the cost of adaptation. Minimizing the cost of searches involves a number of trade-offs between the cost of formulating searches (*Search* and *ApproxSearch*) and the quality of the retrieval. For instance, the coverage probabilities *p* and *q* above should be replaced by smaller probabilities to take into account the less than perfect recall of search methods (see Section V.A). Further, a search method that is not precise (i.e., returns irrelevant components) increases the cost of finding a component by forcing the developer to examine irrelevant components. As a rule of thumb, given a fixed amount of effort to be spent on formulating queries, we can achieve higher recall values only at the expense of lower precision, and vice-versa. To enhance both recall and precision, more effort should be spent formulating queries. We discussed a range of approaches that strike different balances between query complexity and retrieval quality (c.f. Section V.A.3). However, there is an inherent practical limit to how complex queries can be, beyond which developers will not bother searching. As for adaptation, empirical evidence showed that the cost of modifying components in non-anticipated ways goes up very quickly with the scope and extent of the modifications [23]. The two major cost factors are:

1) understanding what changes need to be made and
2) verifying and validating the component after the change.

198

Transformational systems reduce the first cost by enabling developers to make changes directly at the requirements level and reduce the second cost by propagating such changes in a—mostly—correctness-preserving way [17] (cf. Section V.C).

How far can we reduce the cost of reuse occurrences? If we achieve full coverage ($p = 1$) and develop a query language that is perfectly precise and that has perfect recall—that is called a specification language!—then we have achieved wide-spectrum automatic programming! The generative approach and the building blocks approach to software reuse approach full coverage from two different, but complementary directions. The generative approaches often have a perfect coverage within a subarea of the application domain and need to be extended "horizontally" to cover the entire domain. In order to maintain performance characteristics (e.g., code optimality), different models/generators may be needed to cover a given domain. Conversely, the building blocks approach has the potential to cover an entire domain, but only sparsely so. To fill in the gaps, so to speak, abstract language constructs (e.g., module interconnection languages) are often added, yielding a coarse application-specific specification language whose atoms are *concrete* application components. As language constructs are added and increasingly abstract representations of components are used, we move progressively toward generative approaches based on very high-level languages [148]. Finally, it is interesting to note that in the context of the building blocks approach, perfect retrieval and effortless adaptation are only possible if the relation between specifications and implementations has been completely formalized. To some extent, software reuse turns the automatic programming problem into several optimization subproblems, allowing us to tackle software automation piecewise.

ACKNOWLEDGMENTS

Some of the material in Sections III.A.3 and IV.C benefited from discussions and joint work with Robert Godin (professor of computer science, University of Québec at Montréal), Gregor Bochmann (professor of computer science, University of Montréal), and Piero Colagrosso (Bell Northern Research).

Some of the background material for Section V.B was collected and compiled by Hassan Alaoui, a PhD student; the complexity results and algorithms for finding function realizations based on types are due to Odile Marcotte (professor of computer science, University of Québec at Montréal).

H. Mili was supported by grants from the Centre de Technologie Tandem de Montréal (CTTM), a division of Tandem Computers Inc., Cupertino, Calif, the Natural Sciences and Engineering Research Council (NSERC) of Canada, and the Fonds pour la Création et l'Aide á la Recherche (FCAR) of Québec, and Centre de Recherche en Informatique de Montréal (CRIM) through the *MACROSCOPE* initiative and the Québec Ministry of Higher Education's *SYNERGIE* programme (IGLOO Project).

F. Mili was supported by grants from the National Science Foundation, and the School of Engineering and Computer Science, Oakland University.

A. Mili was supported by grants from NSERC and the School of Graduate Studies and Research of the University of Ottawa (Ottawa, Canada).

REFERENCES

[1] W.W. Agresti, "What are the new paradigms?," *New Paradigms for Software Development*. ed. W.W. Agresti, pp. 6-10, IEEE, 1986.

[2] William W. Agresti, "Framework for a flexible development process," *New Paradigms for Software Development*, William W. Agresti, ed., pp. 11-14, IEEE, 1986.

[3] M. Aksit, and L. Bergmans, "Obstacles in OO software development," *Proc. OOPSLA '92*, Vancouver, B.C., Canada, Oct. 18-22, 1992.

[4] G. Arango, Ira Baxter, P. Freeman and C. Pidgeon, "Software maintenance by transformation," *IEEE Software*, pp. 27-39, May 1986.

[5] G. Arango, "Domain engineering for software reuse," PhD thesis, Dept. Information and Computer Science, Univ. of California, 1988.

[6] S.P. Arnold and S.L. Stepoway, "The reuse system: Cataloguing and retrieval of reusable software," *Proc. COMPCON S'87*, IEEE CS Press, pp. 376-379. 1987.

[7] D.M. Balda and D.A. Gustafson, "Cost-estimation models for the reuse and prototype software development," *ACM SIGSOFT*, pp. 42-50, July 1990

[8] R. Balzer, T. Cheatham Jr., and C. Green, "Software technology in the 1990s: Using a new paradigm," *Computer*, Nov. 1983, pp. 39-45

[9] R. Balzer, "A 15 year perspective on automatic programming, *IEEE Trans. Software Engineering*, pp. 1,257-1,268, Nov. 1985.

[10] B. Barnes, T. Durek, J. Gaffney, and A. Pyster, "A framework and economic foundation for software reuse," *Proc. Workshop Software Reusability and Maintainability*, 1987.

[11] B.H. Barnes and T.B. Bollinger, "Making reuse cost-effective," *IEEE Software*, vol. 8, no. 1, pp. 13-24, Jan. 1991.

[12] V.R Basili, G. Caldiera, F. McGarry, R. Pajerski, G. Page, and S. Waligora, "The software engineering laboratory—an operational software experience," *Proc. 14th Int'l Conf. Software Engineering*, Melbourne, Australia, pp. 370-381, May 11-15, 1992.

[13] V.R. Basili and S. Green, "Software process evolution at the SEL," *IEEE Software*, pp 58-66, July 1994.

[14] V.R. Basili, "Viewing maintenance as reuse-oriented software development," *IEEE Software*, vol. 7, no. 1, pp. 19-25, Jan. 1990.

[15] V. R. Basili, and J.D. Musa, "The future engineering of software: A management perspective," *IEEE Computer*, , vol. 24, no. 9, pp. 90-96, Sept. 1991.

[16] P.G. Bassett, "Frame-based software engineering," *IEEE Software*, pp. 9-16, July 1987.

[17] I.D. Baxter, "Design maintenance dystems," *Comm. ACM*, vol. 35, no. 4, pp. 73-89, Apr. 1992.

[18] P. Bergstein and K.J. Lieberherr, "Incremental class dictionary learning and optimization," *Proc. ECOOP '91*, Geneva, Switzerland, pp. 377-395.

[19] T.J. Biggerstaff, and C. Richter, "Reusability framework, assessment, and directions," *IEEE Software*, pp. 41-49, July 1987.

[20] D. Blair and M.E. Maron, "An evaluation of retrieval effectiveness for a full-text," *Document-Retrieval System Comm. ACM*, vol. 28, no. 3, pp. 289-299, Mar. 1985.

[21] B. Boehm, "A spiral model of software development and enhancement." *Computer*, vol. 21, no. 5, pp. 61-72, May 1988.

[22] B. Boehm,, "Improving software productivity," *IEEE Software*, pp. 43-57, Sept. 1987.

[23] B.W. Boehm, "Megaprogramming," *Keynote speech, ACM Computer Science Conf.*, Phoenix, Ariz., Feb. 1994,

[24] R.J. Brachman and J.G. Schmolze, "An overview of the KL-ONE knowledge representation system," *Cognitive Science*, vol. 9, pp. 171-216, 1985.

[25] R. Bretl, D. Maier, A. Otis, J. Penney, B. Schuchardt, J. Stein, E.H. Williams, and M. Williams, "The GemStone data management system," *Object Oriented Concepts, Databases, and Applications*. pp. 283-308, W. Kim, ed., Addison Wesley 1989.

[26] F. Brooks, "No silver bullet: Essence and accidents of software engineering," *Computer*, , pp. 10-19, Apr. 1987.

[27] B.A. Burton, R.W. Aragon, S.A. Bailey, K.D. Koehler, and L.A. Mayes, "The reusable software library," *IEEE Software*, pp. 25-33, July 1987.

[28] G. Caldiera, and V.R. Basili, "Identifying and qualifying reusable software components," *Computer*, vol. 24, no. 2, pp. 61-70, Feb. 1991.

[29] J. Carbonell, "Derivational analogy in problem solving and knowledge acquisition," *Proc. Int'l Machine Learning Workshop*, Monticello, Ill., June 1983.

[30] D. Carrington, D. Duke, I. Hayes, and J. Welsh, "Deriving modular designs from formal specifications," *Software Engineering Notes, Proc. First ACM SIGSOFT Symp. Foundations of Software Engineering*, vol. 18, no. 5, pp. 89-98, Los Angeles, Calif., Dec. 7-10, 1993.

[31] D. de Champeaux, D. Lea, and P. Faure, "The process of OO design," *Proc. OOPSLA '92*, Vancouver, B.C., Canada Oct. 18-22, 1992

[32] P.S. Shicheng Chen, R. Hennicker, and M. Jarke, "On the retrieval of reusable components," *Selected Papers from the Second Int'l Workshop on Software, Reusability Advances in Software*, ReuseLucca, Italy Mar. 24-26, 1993.

[33] S.C. Cheung, and J. Kramer, "Enhancing compositional reachability analysis with context constraints," *Software Engineering Notes, Proc. First ACM SIGSOFT Symp. on the Foundations of Software Engineering*, vol. 18, pp. 115-125, Los Angeles, Calif., Dec. 7-10, 1993.

[34] C.T. Cleaveland, "Building application generators," *IEEE Software*, July 1988, pp. 25-33.

[35] P. Coad and E. Yourdon, *Object Oriented Analysis*. Prentice Hall, 1991, second edition.

[36] P. Coad, "RE: On the purpose of OO analysis," *Proc. OOPSLA'93*, Washington, D.C. Sept. 26 - Oct. 1, 1993.

[37] W.R. Cook, "Interfaces and specifications for the Smalltalk-80 collection classes," *Proc. OOPSLA'92*, 1992, Vancouver, B.C., Canada, Oct. 18-22.

[38] B.J. Cox, *Object Oriented Programming: An Evolutionary Approach*. Reading, Mass..: Addison Wesley, 1987.

[39] B.J. Cox, "Planning the software revolution," *IEEE Software*, vol. 7 , no. 6, pp. 25-35, Nov. 1990.

[40] M.A. Cusumano, "The software factory: A historical interpretation," *IEEE Software*, pp. 23-30, Mar. 1989.

[41] M.B. Dahl and K. Nygaard, "Simula common base language," Technical report S-22, Norvegian Computing Center, 1970.

[42] T. Davis, "The reuse capability model: A basis for improving an organization's reuse capability," *Advances in Software Reuse, Selected Papers from the Second Int'l Workshop on Software Reusability Advances in Software Reuse*, pp. 126-133, Lucca, Italy Mar. 24-26, 1993.

[43] L.P. Deutsch, "Design reuse and frameworks in the Smalltalk-80 programming system," *Software Reusability*, vol. II , A.J. Perlis, ed., ACM Press, 1989.

[44] E.W. Dijkstra, "On the cruelty of really teaching computer science," *Comm. ACM*, vol. 32, no. 12, pp. 1,398-1,404, Dec. 1989.

[45] M.S. Feather, "Reuse in the context of a transformation-based methodology," *ITT Proc. Workshop on Reusability in Programming*, pp. 50-58, 1983.

[46] R.G. Fichman and C.F. Kemerer, "Object oriented and conventional analysis and design methodologies: Comparison and critique," *Computer*, vol. 25, pp. 22-39, Oct. 1992.

[47] G. Fischer, "Cognitive view of reuse and design," *IEEE Software*, pp. 60-72, July 1987.

[48] W.B. Frakes and B. A. Nejmeh, "An information system for software reuse," *Software Reuse: Emerging Technology*, IEEE CS Press, 1990, pp. 142-151.

[49] W. B. Frakes and T. Pole, "An empirical study of representation methods for reusable software components," Tech. Report, Software Productivity Consortium, Herndon, Va. May, 1992.

[50] P. Freeman, "Reusable software engineering: Concepts and research directions," *Tutorial: Software Reusability*, P. Freeman, ed., pp. 10-23, 1987.

[51] R.P. Gabriel, "The failure of pattern languages," *J. Object Orientedriented Programming*, pp. 84-88, Feb. 1994.

[52] J. E. Gaffney and R.D. Cruickshank, "A general economics model of software reuse," *Proc. 14th Int'l Conf. Software Eng.*, pp. 327-337, ACM Press , Melbourne, Australia, May 11-15, 1992.

[53] K.B. Gallagher and J.R. Lyle, "Using program slicing in software maintenance, *IEEE Trans. Software Engineering*, vol. 17, no. 8, pp. 751-761, Aug. 1991.

[54] M. Garey and D Johnson, *Computers and Intractability*. San Francisco: Freeman, 1979.

[55] S. Gibbs, D Tsichritzis, E. Casais, O. Nierstrasz, and X. Pintado, "Class management for software communities," *Comm. ACM*, vol. 33, no. 9, pp. 90-103, 1990.

[56] R. Godin and H. Mili, "Building and maintaining analysis-level class hierarchies using galois lattices," *ACM SIGPLAN Notices, OOPSLA '93 Proc.*, vol. 28, pp. 394-410, Washington, D.C. Sept. 26 - Oct. 1, 1993,.

[57] J.A. Goguen, "Reusing and interconnecting software components," *Computer*, pp. 16-28, Feb. 1986,.

[58] A. Goldberg, "Information models, views, and controllers," *Dr. Dobb's*, July 1990.

[59] G. Gruman, "Early reuse practice lives up to its promise," *IEEE Software*, pp. 87-91, Nov. 1988.

[60] J.V. Guttag, J.J. Horning, and J.M. Wing, "An overview of the Larch family of specification languages," *IEEE Software*, vol. 2, no. 5, pp. 24-36, Sept. 1985.

[61] P. Hall and R. Weedon, "Object oriented module interconnection languages,"*Selected Papers from the Second Int'l Workshop on Software Reusability Advances in Software Reuse*, IEEE C S Press, pp. 29-38, Lucca, Italy, Mar. 24-26, 1993.

[62] R.J. Hall, "Generalized behavior-based retrieval," *Proc. 15th Int'l Conf. Software Eng.*, ACM Press, pp. 371-380, Baltimore, Md., May 17-21, 1993.

[63] W. Harrison and H. Ossher, "Subject-oriented programming: A critique of pure objects," *SIGPLAN Notices Proc. OOPSLA '93*, vol. 28, no. 10, pp. 411-428, Washington D.C., Sept. 26 - Oct. 1, 1993.

[64] B. Harvey, H. Kilov, and H. Mili, "Specification of behavioral semantics in OO information modeling: Workshop report," *OOPS Messenger Addendum to the OOPSLA '93 Proc.*, ACM Press.

[65] R. Helm, I. Holland, and D. Gangopadhyay, "Contracts: Specifying behavioral compositions in OO systems," *Proc. OOPSLA '90*, ACM Press, Ottawa, Canada, Oct. 22-25, 1990. ,

[66] B. Henderson-Sellers and J.M. Edwards, "The OO systems life cycle," *Comm. ACM*, vol. 33, no. 9, pp. 143-159, Sept. 1990.

[67] R.C. Holt, T. Stanhope, and G. Lausman, "Object oriented computing: Looking ahead to the year 2000," ITRC TR-9101, Apr. 1991, Information Technology Research Center, Univ. of Toronto.

[68] E. Horowitz and J.B. Munson, "An expansive view of reusable software," *IEEE Trans. Software Engineering*, vol. 10 , no. 5, pp. 477-487, 1984.

[69] E. Horowitz, A. Kemper, and B. Narasimhan, "A survey of application generators," *IEEE Software*, vol. 2, no. 1, Jan. 1985.

[70] G. M. Hoydalsvik and G. Sindre, "On the purpose of OO analysis," *Proc. OOPSLA '93*, ACM Press, pp. 240-255, Washington, D.C., Sept. 26-Oct. 1, 1993.

[71] J. C. Huang, "State constraints and pathwise decomposition of programs," *IEEE Trans. Software Engineering*, vol. 16 , no. 8, pp. 880-898, Aug. 1990.

[72] Y. Intrator and H. Mili, "Getting more out of your classes: Building families of programs in OOP," Tech report no. 234, Dept. Maths and Computer Science, Univ. of Quebec at Montreal, May 13, 1994.

[73] S. Isoda, "Experience report on a software reuse project: Its structure, activities, and statistical results," *Proc. 14th Int'l Conf. Software Engineering*, pp. 320-326, Melbourne, Australia, May 11-15, 1992.

[74] I. Jacobson, *Object Oriented Software Engineering: A Use Case Driven Approach*. ACP Press, 1992. ,

[75] R.E. Johnson, "Documenting frameworks using patterns," *Proc. OOPSLA '92* , ACM Press, pp. 63-76, Vancouver, B.C., Oct. 18-22, 1992.

[76] G. Jones, "Methodology/Environment Support for Reusability," *Software Reuse: Emerging Technology*, Will Tracz, ed., IEEE CS Press, pp. 190-193, 1990.

[77] T. Capers Jones, "Reusability in programming: A survey of the state of the art," *IEEE Trans. Software Engineering*, vol. 10, no. 5, pp. 488-494, Sept. 1984.

[78] G.E. Kaiser and D. Garlan, "Melding software systems from reusable building blocks," *IEEE Software*, pp. 17-24, July 1987.

[79] K.C. Kang, "A reuse-based software development methodology," *Software Reuse: Emerging Technology*, Will Tracz, ed. , pp. 194-196, IEEE CS Press 1990.

[80] S. Katz, C. Richter, and K.-S. The, "PARIS: A system for reusing partially interpreted schemas," *Proc. Ninth Int'l Conf. on Software Eng.*, pp. 377-385, 1987.

[81] G. Kiczales and J. Lamping, "Issues in the design and documentation of class libraries," *Proc. OOPSLA '92 SIGPLAN Notices*, ACM Press, vol. 27, no. 10, pp. 435-451, Vancouver, B.C, Oct. 18-22, 1992.

[82] P. Kruchten, E. Schonberg, and J. Schwartz, "Software prototyping using the SETL programming language," *IEEE Software*, vol. 1, no. 4, pp. 66-75, Oct. 1984.

[83] C.W. Krueger, "Software reuse," *ACM Computing Surveys*, ACM Press, vol. 24, no. 2, pp. 131-183, June 1992.

[84] S.S. Lam and A.U. Shankar, "Specifying modules to satisfy interfaces: A state transition system approach," *Distributed Computing*, vol. 6, pp. 39-63,1992.

[85] R.G. Lanergan and C.A. Grasso, "Software engineering with reusable designs and code," *IEEE Trans. Software Engineering*, vol. 10, no. 5, pp. 498-501, Sept. 1984.

[86] J. Laski and W. Szermer, "Regression analysis of reusable program components," *Selected Papers from the Second Int'l Workshop on Software Reusability Advances in Software Reuse*, IEEE CS Press, pp. 134-141, Lucca, Italy, Mar. 24-26, 1993.

[87] D. Lea, "Christopher Alexander: An introduction for OO designers," *Software Engineering Notes*, vol. 19, no. 1, pp. 39-46, Jan. 1994.

[88] D.B. Lenat, R.V. Guha, K. Pittman, D. Pratt, and M. Shepherd, "CYC: Toward programs with common sense," *Comm. ACM*, special issue on Natural Language Processing, vol. 33 , no. 8, pp. 30-49, Aug. 1990.

[89] L.S. Levy, "A metaprogramming method and its economic justification," *IEEE Trans. Software Engineering*, vol. 12, no. 2, pp. 272-277, Feb. 1986.

[90] M. Lubars, G. Meredith, C. Potts, and C. Richter, "Object oriented analysis for evolving systems," *Proc. 14th Int'l Conference on Software Engineering*, pp. 173-185, May 11-15, 1992 Melbourne, Australia, ACM Press.

[91] M.D. Lubars, "Wide-spectrum support for software reusability software reuse: Emerging technology," pp. 275-281, ed. W. Tracz, IEEE CS Press, 1990.

[92] Luqi, "A Graph Model for Software Evolution," *IEEE Trans. Software Engineering*, vol. 16 , no. 8, pp. 917-927, Aug. 1990.

[93] Y.S. Yoelle S. Maarek, D.M. Berry, and G.E. Kaiser, "An information retrieval approach for automatically constructing software libraries," *IEEE Trans. Software Engineering*, vol. 17, no. 8, pp. 800-813, Aug. 1991.

[94] N.A. Maiden and A.G. Sutcliffe, "Exploiting reusable specifications through analogy," Special issue on CASE, *Communications of the ACM*, vol. 35 no. 4, pp. 55-64, Apr. 1992.

[95] N.A. Maiden and A. Sutcliffe, "People-oriented software reuse: the very thought," *Proc. Second Int'l Workshop on Software Reuse, Computer*, pp. 176-185, PressLucca, Italy March 24-26, 1993.

[96] J.H. Maloney, A. Borning, and B.N. Freeman-Benson, "Constraint technology for user-interface construction in ThingLab II," pp. 381-388, *Proc. OOPSLA '89*, ACM Press, Oct. 1989.

[97] J. Margono and T.E. Rhoads, "Software reuse economics: cost-benefit analysis on a large-scale ada project," *Proc. 14th Int'l Conference on Software Engineering*, pp. 338-348, May 11-15, Melbourne, Australia.

[98] J Martin, "Fourth Generation Languages—Volume I: Principles," Prentice-Hall 1985.

[99] Y. Matsumoto, "A Software Factory: An Overall Approach to Software Production Tutorial: Software Reusability," pp. 155-178, ed. P. Freeman, IEEE Press, 1987.

[100] Y. Matsumoto, "Experiences from software reuse in industrial process control applications," *Selected Papers from the Second Int'l Workshop on Software Reusability Advances in Software Reuse*, pp. 186-195, Lucca, Italy, March 24-26, 1993 IEEE CS Press.

[101] R. McCain, "A software development methodology for reusable components *Proc. 18th Hawaii Conference on Systems* Sciences, Hawaii, Jan. 1985.

[102] D.B. McCarn, "MEDLINE: an introduction to on-line searching," *J. American Society for Information Science*, vol. 31 , no. 3, pp. 181-192, May 1980.

[103] C. McClure, "The three R's of software automation: re-engineering, repository, *Reusability.*" Prentice-Hall, 1992.

[104] D. McIlroy, "Mass produced software components," *Software Engineering Concepts and Techniques, 1968 NATO Conference on Software Engineering*, pp. 88-98, eds. J. M. Buxton, P. Naur, and B. Randell, Petrocelli/Charter, New York 1969.

[105] S. Mellor, "The Shlaer-Mellor Method," *Tutorial notes*, OOPSLA'93, Washington, D.C. Sept. 26 - Oct. 1, 1993 ACM Press.

[106] B. Meyer, "Object oriented software construction," ed. Prentice-Hall Int'l, 1988. ,

[107] B. Meyer, "Lessons from the design of the eiffel libraries," *Communications of the ACM,*. vol. 33, no. 9, pp. 69-88, Sept. 1990.

[108] A. Mili, R. Mili, and R. Mittermeir, "Storing and retrieving software components: a refinement-based approach," *Proc. 16th Int'l Conf. on Software Engineering*, Sorrento, Italy, May 1994.

[109] H. Mili, J. Sibert, and Y. Intrator, "An OO model based on relations," *J. Systems and Software*, vol. 12, pp. 139-155, 1990.

[110] H. Mili, A. E. El Wahidi, and Y. Intrator, "Building a graphical interface for an OO tool for software reuse," *Proc. TOOLS USA '92*, ed. B. Meyer, Aug. 2-6, 1992, Santa Barbara, Calif.

[111] H. Mili and H. Li, "Data abstraction in softclass, an OO case tool for software reuse," *Proc. TOOLS '93*, pp. 133-149, Santa-Barbara, CA Aug. 2-5, ed. B. Meyer, Prentice-Hall.

[112] H. Mili, O. Marcotte, and A. Kabbaj, "Intelligent component retrieval for software reuse," *Proc. 3rd Maghrebian Conf. on Artificial Intelligence, and Software Engineering*, pp. 101-114, Apr. 11-14, 1994, Rabat, Morocco.

[113] H. Mili, R. Rada, W. Wang, K. Strickland, C. Boldyreff, L. Olsen, J. Witt, J. Heger, W. Scherr, and P. Elzer, "Practitioner and SoftClass: A Comparative Study of Two Software Reuse Research Projects," *J. Systems and Software*, vol. 27, May 1994.

[114] S.K. Misra and P.J. Jalics, "Third-generation versus fourth-generation development," *Software*, vol. 5, no. 4, pp. 8-14, July 1988.

[115] Th. Moineau, and M.C. Gaudel, "Software reusability through formal specifications, *Proc. 1st Int'l Workshop on Software Reusability*, Universitaet Dortmund 1991.

[116] J.M. Morel and Jean Faget, "The REBOOT environment," *Selected Papers from the 2nd Int'l Workshop on Software Reusability Advances in Software*, pp. 80-88, ReuseLucca, Italy, March 24-26, 1993, IEEE CS Press.

[117] M. Moriconi, and T.C. Winkler, "Approximate reasoning about the semantic effects of program changes," *IEEE Trans. Software Engineering*, vol. 16, no. 9, pp. 980-992, Sept. 1990.

[118] J. Mostow, M. Barley, "Automated reuse of design plans," *Proc. Int'l Conf. on Engineering* Design, Boston, MA 1987.

[119] B.A. Myers, "User-Interface Tools: Introduction and Survey," *Software*, pp. 15-23, Jan. 1989, Special issue on user interfaces.

[120] K. Narayanaswamy, W. Scacchi, "Maintaining configurations of evolving software systems," *IEEE Trans. Software Engineering*, vol. 13, no. 3, pp. 324-334, March 1987.

[121] J.M. Neighbors, "The DRACO approach to constructing software from reusable components," *IEEE Trans. Software Engineering*, pp. 564-574, Sept. 1984.

[122] H. Ossher and W. Harrison, "Combination of inheritance hierarchies," *SIGPLAN Notices, Proc. OOPSLA' 92.*, vol. 27 no. 10, pp. 25-40, Oct. 18-22, 1992, Vancouver, B.C., Canada,

[123] H. Partsch and R. Steinbruggen, "Program transformation systems," *Computing Surveys*, vol. 15 no. 3, pp. 399-236, Sept. 198.

[124]L. Peters, "Advanced Structured Analysis and Design," ed. R.W. Jensen, Prentice Hall, 1987.

[125]M. Pittman, "Lessons learned in managing OO development," *Software*, pp. 43-53, Jan. 1993.

[126]A. Podgurski and L.A. Clarke, "A formal model of program dependences and its implications for software testing, debugging, and maintenance," *IEEE Trans. Software Engineering*, vol. 16, no. 9, pp. 965-979, Sept. 1990.

[127]A. Podgurski and L. Pierce, "Retrieving reusable software by sampling behavior," *ACM Transactions Software Engineering and Methodology*, vol. 2 no. 3, pp. 286-303, July 1993.

[128]J.S. Poulin and J.M. Caruso, "A reuse metrics and return on investment model," *selected papers from the 2nd. int'l workshop on software reusability advances in software*, pp. 52-166, ReuseLucca, Italy, March 24-26, 1993, IEEE CS Press.

[129]R. Prieto-Diaz and J.M. Neighbors, "Module interconnection languages, *J. Systems and Software*, vol. 6, no. 4, pp. 307-334, Nov. 1986.

[130]R. Prieto-Diaz, "Domain analysis for reusability," *Proc. COMPSAC '87*, pp. 23-29, 1987, IEEE Press.

[131]R. Prieto-Diaz and P. Freeman, "Classifying software for reusability *Software*, pp. 6-16, Jan. 1987.

[132]R. Prieto-Diaz, "Integrating domain analysis and reuse in the software development process *Proc. 3rd Annual Workshop on Methods and Tools for Reuse*, CASE Center, Syracuse University, Syracuse, N.Y. June 13-15, 1990.

[133]R. Prieto-Diaz, "Status Report: Software Reusability," *Software*, vol. 10 no. 3, pp. 61-66, May 1993.

[134]R. Rada, H. Mili, E. Bicknell, and M. Blettner, "Development and application of a metric on semantic nets *IEEE Trans. Systems, Man, and Cybernetics*, Jan./Feb. 1989, vol. 19 , no. 1, pp. 7-30.

[135]C.V. Ramamoorthy, V. Garg, and A. Prakash, "Support for reusability in Genesis," *IEEE Trans. Software Engineering*, vol. 14 , no. 8, pp. 145-1154, Aug. 1988.

[136]C. Rich and R. Waters, "Automatic programming: myths and prospects *Computer*, pp. 40-51, Aug. 1988.

[137]C. Rich and R. Waters, "The programmer's apprentice: A research overview," *Computer*, pp. 1-25, Nov. 1988.

[138]K.S. Rubin A. Goldberg, "Object behavior analysis," *Communications of the ACM*, vol. 35, no. 9, pp. 48-62, Sept. 1992.

[139]J. Rumbaugh, "Relations as semantic constructs in an OO language," *Proc. OOPSLA '87*, pp. 466-481, Oct. 4-8, 1987, ACM Press.

[140]J. Rumbaugh, M. Blaha, W. Premerlani, F. Eddy, and W. Lorensen, "Object oriented modeling and design," Prentice Hall, 1991.

[141]D. Rumelhart and D. Norman, "Representation in memory," Center for Human Information Processing, La Jolla, Calif.

[142]G. Salton and M. McGill, "Introduction to Modern Information Retrieval," McGraw-Hill, New York, 1983.

[143]M. Shaw, "Abstraction techniques in modern programming languages," *Software*, pp. 10-26 Oct. 1984.

[144]M. Shaw, "Prospects for an Engineering Discipline of Software," *Software*, vol. 7 , no. 6, pp. 5-24, Nov. 1990.

[145]J.J. Shilling and P.F. Sweeny, "Three steps to views: Extending the OO paradigm," *Proc. ACM Conf. on Object Oriented Programming, Systems, Languages, and Applications*, pp. 353-361, New Orleans, Louisiana, Oct. 1989, ACM.

[146]S. Shlaer and S. Mellor, "*Object Oriented* systems analysis: Modeling the world in data," Yourdon Press: Englewood Cliffs, N.J. 1992.

[147]B.G. Silverman, "Survey of expert critiquing systems: practical and theoretical frontiers," *Communications of the ACM*, vol. 35, no. 4, pp. 06-127, Apr. 1992.

[148]M.A. Simos, "The domain-oriented software life cycle: Toward an extended process model for reusability software reuse: emerging technology," pp. 354-363, ed. Will Tracz, IEEE CS Press, 1990.

[149]M. Sirkin, D. Batory, and V. Singhal, "Software components in a data structure precompiler, *Proc. 15th Int'l Conf. on Software Engineering*, pp. 437-446, Baltimore, Maryland, May 17-21, 1993, ACM Press.

[150]A. Snyder, "Encapsulation and inheritance in OO programming languages," *Proc. OOPSLA '86*, pp. 38-45, Sept. 1986, Portland, Oregon.

[151]L.S. Sorumgard, G. Sindre, and F. Stokke, "Experiences from application of a faceted classification scheme," *Selected papers from the 2nd Int'l Workshop on Software Reusability Advances in Software*, pp. 116-124, ReuseLucca, Italy, March 24-26, 1993, IEEE CS Press.

[152]B. Stroustrup, "The C++ programming languages," Addison-Wesley 1986.

[153]W. Tracz, "LILEANNA: A parameterized programming language," *Selected Papers from the 2nd Int'l Workshop on Software Reusability Advances in Software*, pp. 66-78, ReuseLucca, Italy, March 24-26, 1993 IEEE CS Press.

[154]J. Verner and G. Tate, "Estimating size and effort in fourth-generation development," *Software*, vol. 5, no. 4, pp. 5-22, July 1988.

[155]P. Wegner, "Varieties of reusability tutorial: Software reusability, ed. Peter Freeman , pp. 24-38, 1987.

[156]P. Wegner, "Dimensions of OO modeling, OO computing," *Computer*, CS Press, vol. 25 no. 10, pp. 2-20, Oct. 1992.

[157]R. Wirfs-Brock, B. Wilkerson, and L. Wiener, "Designing OO software," Prentice-Hall: 1990.

[158]R. Wirfs-Brock and R.E. Johnson, "Surveying current research in OO design," *Communications of the ACM*, vol. 33, no. 9, pp. 105-124. , Sept. 1990.

[159]S.N. Woodfield, D.W. Embley, and D.T. Scott, "Can programmers reuse software," *Software*, July 1987, pp. 52-59.

[160]E. Yourdon, "Decline & fall of the american programmer," Prentice-Hall: Englewood Cliffs, N.J, 1992.

[161]A.M. Zaremski and J.M. Wing, "Signature matching: A key to reuse software engineering, *Notes, 1st ACM SIGSOFT Symp. on the Foundations of Software Engineering*, vol. 18, pp. 582-190, 1993.

[162]P. Zave, W. Schell, "Salient features of an executable specification language and its environment," *IEEE Trans. Software Engineering*, vol. 12, no 2, pp. 312-325, Feb. 1986.

[163]P. Zave and M. Jackson, "Conjunction as composition," *ACM Transactions on Software Engineering and Methodology*, vol. 2, no. 4, pp. 379-411, Oct. 1993.

Hafedh Milli is an associate professor of computer science at the University of Quebec in Motreal, Canada. He holds an engineering diploma from the Ecole Central de Paris, Paris, France, which was awarded in 1984, and a PhD in computer science from George Washington University, Washington, DC, which he earned in 1988.

His research interests include object orientation, software reuse, information retrieval, and knowledge representation. He has been leading or participating in a number of government- and industry-sponsored (BNR, IBM, DEC, Tandem Computers, CAE Electronics, DMR Group, National Bank of Canada, etc.) R&D projects in the area of object orientation and software reuse.

He is founder and president of INFORMILI, Inc., a computer services company that specializes in training and consulting in OO and software reuse.

Fatma Mili is an associate professor at Oakland University, Rochester, Michigan. Her research interests are in software engineering, formal methods, and scientific databases. She holds a doctorate degree from the University Pierre et Marie Curie in France.

Prof. Mili is a member of the ACM and the IEEE Computer Society.

Ali Mili holds a PhD from the University of Illinois at Urbana-Champaign (earned in 1981). He earned a doctorat es science d'etat from the University of Grenoble, France, in 1985.

His research interests are in software engineering, ranging from the technical to the managerial aspects of the discipline.

His latest book, coauthored by J. Desharnais and F. Mili, deals with the mathematics of program construction. It is published by Oxford University Press, New York.

Repository Evaluation of Software Reuse

Rajiv D. Banker, Robert J. Kauffman, and Dani Zweig

Abstract— The traditional unit of analysis and control for software managers is the software project, and subsequently the resulting application system. Today, with the emerging capabilities of computer-aided software engineering (CASE) and corresponding changes in the development process, productivity gains can be realized by reusing portions of the organization's inventory of existing application designs and code. With this opportunity, however, comes the need to monitor software reuse at the corporate level, as well as at the level of the individual software development project. Integrated CASE environments can support such monitoring. We illustrate the use and benefits of repository evaluation of software reuse through an analysis of the evolving repositories of two large firms that recently implemented integrated CASE development tools. The analysis shows that these tools have supported high levels of software reuse, but it also suggests that there remains considerable unexploited reuse potential. Our findings indicate that organizational changes will be required before the full potential of the new technology can be realized.

Index Terms— CASE, computer-aided software engineering, domain analysis, organizational learning, repositories, software metrics, software reuse.

I. INTRODUCTION

TRADITIONALLY, the management of software development has focused upon the individual software project. Managers are evaluated, in turn, on the basis of their projects' success in meeting cost and quality targets. Some organizations are devoting resources to process improvement, so that projects may be held to increasingly high standards, but even here, in all but the most mature organizations, the emphasis is on project-level monitoring [25]. Yet there is a range of insights that can only be attained through the monitoring and management of the software inventory at the level of the entire firm.

The example upon which this paper focuses is that of software reuse in an integrated computer-aided software engineering (CASE) environment built around an object repository. Software reuse, the incorporation of previously developed software elements into a system under development, has shown itself to yield substantial productivity benefits, even in traditional development environments.[1] CASE technology can provide considerable support for software reuse.

A number of industry observers have pointed to the special potential for development productivity and software quality improvements, when development occurs using CASE tools [8], [9], [16], [34]–[36], [40], [27]. The emergence of CASE tools that emphasize software reuse can mean that much of the real value of modular software will be derived from the extent to which it can:

- defray the costs of the construction and testing, and raise the overall level of perceived quality and reliability of systems that are delivered;
- speed the implementation of new systems while opportunities for competitive advantage still exist in the business areas that the software is meant to support; and
- be leveraged across projects and areas of the firm in support of multiple businesses.

Meanwhile, recent empirical research has begun to uncover the extent of those gains [2]–[4].

The time-worn epithet that "you can't manage what you can't measure" clearly applies here. Reuse, by its nature, is an activity that spans multiple projects and application systems enterprisewide. To manage such reuse requires monitoring the firm's software at the level of the organization or enterprise. Even relatively simple metrics, collected at that level, can answer key questions for senior managers that traditional monitoring does not address.

Repository-based integrated CASE environments make the collection of such metrics practical. A repository maintains all of a corporation's software and, more importantly, all relevant information about that software, including its design, its history, and its interactions with other system elements. By analyzing software reuse at the repository level—what we call *repository evaluation*—we can cut across multiple projects to ask questions such as:

- What kinds of objects are most likely to be reused?
- Under what conditions is reuse most likely to occur?

This can lead, in turn, to a shift away from single or isolated software product-oriented questions to a new focus on more development process-oriented questions, such as:

Manuscript received October 23, 1991; revised December 9, 1992. This work was supported in part by the Nippon Electric Corporation and by the U.S.–Japan Business and Economics Research Center, Stern School of Business, New York University. Recommended by R. Selby and K. Torii.

R. D. Banker is with the Department of Accounting and Information Systems, Carlson School of Management, University of Minnesota, Minneapolis, MN 55455.

J. J. Kauffman is with the Department of Information Systems, Stern School of Business, New York University, New York, NY 10012.

D. Zweig is with the Department of Administrative Sciences, Naval Postgraduate School, Monterey, CA 93943.

IEEE Log Number 9207593.

[1] See, for example, Cavaliere's [15] report on the software reuse program at the Hartford Insurance Group, Lanergan and Grasso's [26] review of Raytheon's achievement of 50% productivity gains through software reuse and elimination of redundant software, and Cusamano's [18] discussion of efforts to reuse software among major Japanese electronics firms. For an overview of the key references in the software reuse literature, see the books by Biggerstaff and Perlis [11], [12], Freeman [22], and Tracz [46], and the articles published in two special issues of IEEE TRANSACTIONS ON SOFTWARE ENGINEERING (vol. SE-10, Sept. 1984) and *IEEE Software* (July 1987); Hooper and Chester [24] offer a useful update.

0098-5589/93$03.00 © 1993 IEEE

- Do technical advances in the development methods increase reuse to the same extent in different environments?
- Do differences in organizational structure lead to different levels of success in managing software reuse?
- What can be done to encourage more software reuse?

In this paper we will use automated repository evaluation to explore and interpret the experiences of two firms, the First Boston Corporation, a large New York City-based investment bank, and Carter Hawley Hale Information Services, the information systems organization of a large California-based retailing firm. A repository-based integrated CASE tool called High Productivity Systems (HPS) was deployed at both sites. Both firms believed that productivity increases in software development would only become possible through significant changes to their software development processes, and both firms considered software reuse to be a key element of the process improvement they sought. But, as the discussion will show, the firms took contrasting approaches to its tactical implementation.

II. SOFTWARE REUSE AND REUSE MEASUREMENT

Most of the attempts to implement formal programs of software reuse have been initiated within the past decade. Such programs rely heavily upon technological (CASE) support and high levels of process maturity.

A. Software Reuse

Extensive reuse in the construction phase has been shown to increase productivity by 20% or more [30], [3], [4], through the use and invocation of previously developed software modules. Greater productivity gains may be achieved by extending reuse to other phases of the software life cycle.

Reuse Throughout the Life Cycle: As modern software development practices increasingly emphasize phases of the life cycle other than programming, it becomes increasingly profitable to extend reuse efforts to those phases. Early in the life cycle, it is possible to reuse system architecture, and data structure and data model elements [19], [26], as well as the abstract representations of systems that are provided to the people who do the coding work [30]. When the opportunity arises, it may even be appropriate to reuse application prototypes and partial systems [37]. Later in the life cycle, it is possible to reuse existing code, particularly where prior development efforts have left behind well-documented code. For example, see the discussions of the Reusable Software Library (RSL) at Intermetrics Inc. in [13], and Westinghouse Electric's Reusability Search Expert (REUSE) in [33]. Even later, there is potential for the reuse of test routines and test data [43].

The benefits of reuse are enhanced when the software development methodology focuses on the reuse of entire modules [32] and software objects [31]. These may embody analysis and design efforts, as well as code, and prior testing and documentation, as well. When the activities involving reuse spread throughout the life cycle are linked by a methodology (for example, SSADM, information engineering or object-oriented design and construction) or an integrated tool set (as is the case with integrated CASE tools such as Texas Instru-

ments' IEF, Andersen's FOUNDATION or Seer Technologies' HPS), software reuse offers the potential to create even greater long-term benefits [29], [41], [42].

Horizontal and Vertical Reuse, and Domain Analysis: The success of a program of software reuse depends upon the degree of commonality among the applications across which software is shared. Prior research distinguishes between reuse across vertical and horizontal domains [45]. *Vertical reuse* can occur when the majority of the applications built by software developers are representative of a single kind of data processing activity, and many software objects that are employed by one can be shared among the others. *Horizontal reuse* , by contrast, occurs across a broad range of application areas.

According to [24], horizontal reuse is more often employed and better understood than vertical reuse. Organizations that operate across different, highly technical domains, where little knowledge is readily transferred across businesses are likely to emphasize horizontal reuse. The software reuse programs undertaken by Raytheon [26], Hitachi [18], and the National Aeronautics and Space Administration [33], and the hypertext reuse search interface to unrestricted software at the Jet Propulsion Laboratory [10] are good examples.

Vertical reuse occurs less frequently. Such reuse offers greater potential benefits, but requires developers to first carry out a relatively thorough domain analysis, in order to design systems with the greatest possible commonalities. Prieto-Diaz [39] offers a useful introduction to domain analysis, and indicates that its use to date has tended to be ad hoc; the analysis process itself, in his view, is more an art than a science, and only with time can appropriate design decisions be made so as to optimize design for the purposes of reuse. Still there is a growing number of examples of vertical reuse. Examples that have been reported in the literature include the reusable software development program pursued by the Hartford Insurance Group [15] and McNicholl *et al.*'s [28] software reuse project in the domain of missile guidance systems.

We expect that vertical reuse will increase over time with the increasing sophistication of the CASE tools that support the functional and technical design activities. Although horizontal reuse is likely to offer more easily implemented reuse opportunities, vertical reuse offers higher payoffs, since it takes place across systems with higher degrees of potential commonality. In the absence of careful domain analysis, though, one expects vertical reuse to fall short of its potential.

Reuse Search, Adaptation, and Incorporation Costs: A major element that will determine the success of a software reuse program is the relative magnitude of two costs:

- the cumulative cost of locating, adapting and incorporating an appropriate existing software object or 3GL module into a new application, and
- the cost of building the same function from scratch and incorporating it into the new software, thereby eliminating the search and adaptation costs.

Search and adaptation can represent a significant cost to a well-meaning developer who is interested in reusing software [22]. The research suggests that search costs alone may often be too high, causing a developer to end a search prior to locating the appropriate reusable software. One response to these findings has been an effort to develop classification methods for potentially reusable software. (See, for example, [38] or [14].) A second has been the creation of tools and techniques to assist the developer in her search. The approaches include facet classification analysis [38], rule-based retrieval [21], and hypertext search [10], among others.

Gaffney and Durek [23] presented an economic model of software reuse that reflects the costs of porting, adapting, and incorporating reusable software. The authors argue that the value that reuse can deliver must be weighted by the costs that developers experience as they sort out these problems, relative to the total proportion of the application that results from reuse. Bullard *et al.* point to varying component quality when horizontal reuse occurs, and indicate that the major reuse costs come in verifying and validating their performance.

Templating, Mining, and Refining: It is common knowledge among software development researchers that there is widespread, often informal, application of partial reuse approaches, such as templating new functions from similar old ones, mining existing code to pull out just the relevant pieces and refining existing code to serve a different purpose [1]. The benefits of these techniques, however, are largely restricted to the coding phase of the software life cycle.

B. Measurement of Software Reuse

Software reuse is commonly measured as a ratio of reused code to the total amount of code in a given system. Such measures focus upon code to the exclusion of the products of other development phases, but they have the virtue of objectivity.

For example, Toshiba computes the percent of the lines of debugged and delivered *equivalent assembler source lines* (EASL) that were incorporated into an application from elsewhere with little or no modification [18]. The Software Productivity Metrics Working Group of the IEEE (1992) has proposed that reuse be measured as the number of source lines of code (SLOC) incorporated in a system without modification, divided by the total number of SLOC in the system. Note that these metrics consider only instances of reuse in which adaptation costs can be ignored.

We have been engaged in a program of research on productivity in object-based CASE environments. Our findings suggest that for such environments it is appropriate and meaningful to measure reuse in terms of entire objects, rather than SLOC [3]–[5]. In related work, [6], showed that "object counts" were found to be more useful than SLOC as a basis for software cost estimation at such sites (they yielded post hoc estimates that were as accurate, and they were available far earlier in the life cycle) and were far more meaningful to programmers and project managers. Objects have the added advantage that they embody analysis and design efforts as well as the product of the coding phase.

III. THE RESEARCH SITES

In this research, reuse levels were tracked over the first two years of application systems development with the newly deployed CASE tool, HPS, as two research sites: The First

Boston Corporation (FBC) and Carter Hawley Hale Information Services (CHH).

Both FBC and CHH exhibited strong managerial support for software reuse. Both sites believed themselves to have application systems with high degrees of commonality, and considerable scope for reuse, and programmers at both sites were encouraged to take advantage of HPS's support of reuse. Although the two sites followed different philosophies of reuse management, their experiences turned out to be remarkably similar.

A. The First Boston Corporation

This investment bank faced two key problems in the mid-1980's. It foresaw itself losing the ability to control its development costs and to produce the increasingly complex systems it needed in order to remain competitive. Efforts to engineer software costs were hamstrung by application complexity, which required expensive developer expertise, and the development of applications running cooperatively on multiple hardware platforms. Senior management believed that the bank would be unable to control the costs of software development five years into the future. At the same time, strategic analysis indicated that the bank's competitiveness depended upon its ability to bring software-based trading products to market ahead of, or at least in synch with, the competition.

To senior management's dismay, a 1986 survey determined that there would be no commercially available software development tools within five years which would support cost-effective expansion of the firm's systems. Without substantial changes in the firm's software development methodology, it was just a matter of time before the bank's systems would be unable to meet the demand for increased financial market trades processing in a 24-hour a day, global market. At this time, First Boston employed over 700 person-years of full-time-equivalent software labor (in-house or contracted), an expense that was growing more rapidly than any other cost category.

The firm's solution was to develop its own integrated CASE tool, and to emphasize software reuse. The bank began the development of HPS in 1987. When HPS was first deployed, software developers reported that it took about two to three months to travel about 70% of the way down the learning curve. In addition to learning how to work with the CASE tool set, developers and project managers reported that they were simultaneously learning how to reuse software in that environment. Part of that process involved learning the extent to which it was necessary to concentrate on application design, in lieu of technical design or construction. Most developers whom we interviewed reported that development under HPS encouraged the substitution of design labor for construction labor.

B. Carter Hawley Hale Information Services (CHH)

The complexity of the data processing requirements of multibusiness, multiunit retailing firms also grew dramatically during the 1980's. CHH's Information Services unit was under pressure to deliver a new generation of retailing applications that would improve the flow of store and product performance data to senior managers, enabling them to improve inventory management and refine product pricing. These systems had to support extremely high transaction volumes, at acceptable costs, at a time when slowing economic growth and increasing competition were intensifying cost pressures in the retailing industry.

Beginning in mid-1989, CHH carried out what it called its "benchmark project," to determine the extent to which the application design and software construction philosophies embodied in HPS were workable for its own software development. With technical challenges akin to those of FBC, CHH investigated the extent to which HPS might enable the development of complex transaction processing and multilevel management reporting systems operating cooperatively across multiple platforms. In addition, management hoped to evaluate HPS in terms of its ability to support rapid prototyping of applications that later would be deployed to the buying and store organizations, where the usability of a system was of paramount concern.

In the process of evaluating the results of the "benchmark project," CHH's software development managers identified software reuse as a key to improved productivity. They came to believe that software products could be produced most efficiently using HPS if there were many opportunities to reuse software objects built for other projects. For this reason, and with the benefit of FBC's experiences, CHH chose to establish a project whose sole purpose was to produce software objects representing the core functions of its retailing domain, when it adopted HPS in late 1989.

IV. SOFTWARE REUSE IN HPS

HPS was designed to support the development of widely distributed application systems cooperatively processed on a range of platforms. Developers are shielded from the technical complexities entailed by such systems. They do not have to develop platform-dependent code, and the programming of communications between platforms is largely automated by what the developers call "middleware." The design of HPS emphasizes productivity improvement through object-based development, software reuse, and an integrated family of CASE tools.

A. HPS: An Integrated CASE Environment

HPS is an integrated CASE environment of object-based design. Its first applications were in the investment banking industry, where it had to support the development of trading systems, which required global distribution and 24 hour availability. Further, performance requirements demanded that these systems run cooperatively on several different platforms: High-function workstations programmed in C++ had to communicate with central DB2 databases residing on mainframes programmed in COBOL. Minicomputers programmed in PL/I linked the workstations and mainframes with each other and with the market, providing real-time communication and pricing information. The challenge was to create and maintain such systems without having to support and interface three sets of programmers, as had previously been the case.

```
map SCG_CUST_ID of SCG_CTRCT_BOX_LST_X to
    SCG_CUST_ID of SCG_CTRCT_BOX_SQL_FET_X
map SCG_FIRST_NM of SCG_CTRCT_BOX_LST_X to
    SCG_FIRST_NM of SCG_CTRCT_BOX_LST
map SCG_LAST_NM of SCG_CTRCT_BOX_LST_X to
    SCG_LAST_NM of SCG_CTRCT_BOX_LST
use rule SCG_CTRCT_BOX_SQL_FET
converse window SCG_CTRCT_BOX_LST
caseof WINDOW_RETCODE
case 'BOXLST.BOXFLD' 'OK'
        map 'SCG_CTRCT_BOX_FET_OCC' to
                VIEW_LONG_NAME of GET_SELECTED_FIELD_X
        use component GET_SELECTED_FIELD
        map SCG_CTRCT_...............
        ..............
        return
endcase
```

Fig. 1. An HPS rule set.

HPS supports a number of predefined object types, including Screen Definitions, Report Definitions, Files, Data Domains, Fields, Database Views, and Rule Sets, each class having its own procedures and semantics. The Rule Sets are the backbone of an HPS application system. Most of the procedural logic of HPS applications is embodied in the Rule Sets (see Fig. 1 for an example), which are written in a fourth-generation programming language. Rule Sets are the most labor-intensive HPS objects to create, and our discussion of reuse in HPS will focus upon the reuse of Rule Sets.

Other object types have more specialized functions. For example, Screen Definitions are created by a screen-painting utility to define a window's format, input and output fields, and front-end data validation. Report Definitions are created by a report-generating utility to define a report's output field and format. All interactions between objects are mediated by Database Views: if a Rule Set invokes a Screen Definition, for example, it will typically use one output View to send data to the terminal and one input View to receive data from the terminal. A Rule Set may also call an existing 3GL module.[2] For example, FBC was able to make considerable use of a library of optimized 3GL routines for specialized financial computations.

Third-generation code (PL/I, COBOL, or C++, depending on the designers' decisions as to which platforms would be most appropriate) is generated automatically from the HPS objects, and later compiled for the target machines.

All the objects of the application systems are stored in a single repository. All calling relationships between objects are also maintained in this repository, in the form of entries to DB2 database tables. All such relationships are of the form Object1-uses-Object2.[3]

Once an object has been created, it may be incorporated into an application system by adding a calling relationship between that object and one which is part of the target application system. Similarly, HPS implements software reuse by adding a calling relationship between a previously-created object and

---

[2] It should be noted that the HPS object types described here are objects of the CASE environment, rather than objects of the application environment. The 4GL is not an object-oriented programming language, though HPS can, and does, support object-based design. For more information about the design of HPS, see [7].

[3] To be more precise, "uses" is restricted to a Rule Set calling another Rule Set. A Rule Set calling a Screen Definition, for example, would have a different operator, and somewhat different semantics.

one that is already in the repository. Beyond the obvious role this capability plays in facilitating reuse, it also makes it practical to monitor reuse, without having to examine system documentation or program code, by analyzing the repository's database of calling relationships.

B. Reuse Measurement

The structure of the repository makes it practical to automate reuse analysis. An application system consists of a high-level Rule Set, designated as the root of that system, all the objects which it calls, and all the objects which they call, etc. Collectively, these objects are structured as a hierarchy that defines the application. (Note that it is imprecise to speak of an object as "belonging" to any one application system. An object is part of any system which calls it.)

Once we have identified the objects of an application system, the information in the repository allows us to identify the application system for which each object was originally created, and to count the number of times each object is called within the current system.

A number of measures of software reuse may be computed, depending on the purpose of the analysis. For the discussion that follows, reuse will be measured in terms of *REUSE PERCENTAGE*, which is defined as the proportion of object calls that represent the reuse of unmodified, previously created objects, rather than the initial creation of new objects:

$$REUSE\ PERCENTAGE = \left(1 - \frac{NUMBER\ OF\ NEW\ OBJECTS\ BUILT}{TOTAL\ NUMBER\ OF\ OBJECTS\ USED}\right) * 100$$

where

1) *NUMBER OF NEW OBJECTS BUILT = the number of new objects that had to be created from scratch for the application system* and

2) *TOTAL NUMBER OF OBJECTS USED = the number of objects the application system would contain in the absence of reuse, i.e., if a new objects had to be written for every cell.*

Note that objects that are reused multiple times are considered to represent multiple instances of reuse; this metric focuses on the total benefit attributable to reuse [3], [4]. Fig. 2 illustrates the measurement of software reuse.

In the example in Fig. 2, there are four unique objects: A, B, C, and D. But there are five object calls (counting the original invocation of A), since B and C both call D. This subsystem, then, has five calls for four unique objects: *Reuse_Percentage* is 100*(1 − 4/5), or 20%. In the absence of reuse, object D would be replaced by two unique objects, D1 and D2. The subsystem would have five object calls and five unique objects, for a Reuse_Percentage of 0%.

A further distinction may be made between internal reuse and external reuse. *Internal reuse* is the multiple use of an object (or, in other environments, a subroutine, procedure, or module) within the application system for which it was originally written. *External reuse*, the use of an object originally written for another application system,[4] is more difficult to

[4] External reuse can be vertical or horizontal, depending on whether or not the systems belong to a common domain.

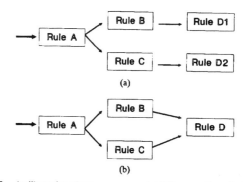

Fig. 2. An illustration of reuse measurement. (a) No reuse: five calls for five unique objects. Reuse percentage is $100 * (1 - 5/5)$ or 0%. (b) Rule D is reused: five calls for four unique objects. Reuse percentage is $100 * (1 - 4/5)$ for 20%.

achieve, since it requires compatibility (planned or accidental) of design [1], [17]. HPS programmers need not distinguish between the two forms of reuse, but the distinction may be important to the management of reuse. Some organizations only reward external reuse.

C. Repository Evaluation in HPS

HPS stores all the objects of all its application systems, the calling relationships linking those objects, and a considerable amount of information *about* the objects, in the same easily-accessible repository, an architecture that makes it highly practical to automate repository evaluation. A suite of database access routines has been created to monitor and analyze the repository: we can determine when each object was created, by whom, and for which application system. We can identify the objects that call any given object, the objects it calls, and the application systems in which it is used. We can also analyze individual objects in greater detail, determining, for example, what data is passed between any pair of objects. This has made it possible to develop automated function point and software reuse analyzers.

By analyzing the entire repository over time, we can assess the success of the research sites in implementing a software reuse strategy through the adoption of HPS. We can also begin to open the black box of software reuse and identify the factors—technological and otherwise—that determine the success of the reuse effort.

V. REUSE PREDICTIONS AND OBSERVATIONS

Our earlier discussion of the software reuse literature reflected the primarily technical focus of the research in this field: application domains are more or less conducive to reuse, cataloging schemes are more or less successful in guiding the search for reuse opportunities, and reuse is constrained by search and adaptation costs. The initial reuse efforts at FBC and CHH reflected a similar technical focus.

A. Simple Model of Reuse

Fig. 3 presents a simple model of reuse. In this model, the chance that a programmer will reuse an existing object,

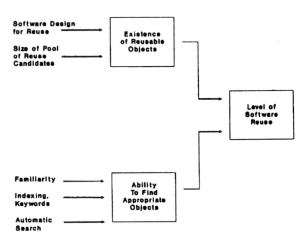

Fig. 3. A preliminary model of reuse.

TABLE I
AN OVERVIEW OF THE HPS REPOSITORIES

Object Type	FBC	CHH
Rule Sets	8892	1775
Screens	7230	662
Domains	4200	97
Files	4236	170
3GL Modules	6062	92
Fields	6266	5823
Views	6755	3861

rather than write a new one, depends upon the availability of potentially reusable software, and upon the programmer's ability to find it. We can increase reuse levels by making more reuse candidates available and by reducing programmers' search costs. This is the *software library* theory of reuse—that the keys to reuse are a large stock of objects within the application domain, and a catalog to help locate them as needed. HPS supports reuse by maintaining a growing pool of reuse candidates within a single repository, by providing a keyword search mechanism for locating appropriate objects, and by automating the incorporation of reused objects into the application system. From the perspective of the model in Fig. 3, this represents a strong foundation for a program of reuse.

Managers were aware of many of the limitations of these mechanisms, and of the relevance of organizational factors. They believed, correctly, that HPS's technical support of reuse could still allow them to realize far higher reuse levels than they had with traditional software development tools. The discussion that follows will seek to assess the utility of this approach, and to identify factors which will enable the achievement of yet higher levels of reuse.

The view of the reuse process depicted above suggests a number of predictions:

1) As the pool of reusable objects increases over time with the size of the repository, so will the level of reuse.

2) Objects belonging to the system currently being programmed are more likely to be known to the programmers, so they will exhibit comparatively low search costs, and there will be a relatively high level of internal reuse.

2a) By a similar token, we expect programmers to exhibit high levels of reuse of objects that they wrote themselves. Both these familiarity effects may be mitigated by the presence of a good search mechanism.

3) Given a high level of reuse of familiar objects, we may expect reuse levels to be higher for larger systems, since they represent a larger pool of salient reusable objects and familiar reuse opportunities.

4) Programmers with more HPS experience at the site will be familiar with more of the software, and will therefore experience higher levels of reuse.

B. Repository Evaluation Findings

Automated repository analysis was used to assess each site's repository after about two years of HPS software developed. The two sites had very different startup experiences. CHH began using HPS two years later than FBC, when the tool was more mature. The analyses that follow skip the initial learning periods, and cover the 20 months following the first development successes. Table I gives an overview of the contents of the two repositories at the end of this time. The repositories reflect differences in the application domains. The retailer's systems, for example, may be seen to be far more data intensive.

Repository Growth and Software Reuse: Fig. 4 presents the growth in Rule Set population and reuse during the periods under analysis.[5] It is immediately clear that our first prediction, that reuse levels would grow over time as the repository grew, was incorrect: the repositories grew steadily during this period. (So did the experience of the programmers, since this was their first experience with HPS.) Reuse percentage, however, achieved a strong initial value and never bettered it. The level of reuse didn't grow as the pool of reuse candidates grew.

Reuse of Familiar Objects: Our second prediction, which was based on the belief that familiar objects were more likely to be reused, was borne out strongly. We predicted that programmers would tend to reuse objects from the system upon which they were currently working, as those would be the most easily identified as being appropriate for the task at hand. We also predicted, on the basis of the belief that familiarity was an important reuse factor, that programmers would exhibit a strong propensity to reuse software written by themselves.

Fig. 5(a) shows the relationship between internal and external reuse: 85% of all observed instances of reuse were internal. That is, if use was made of a previously written rule, that rule was almost always one that had been written for the same system.

This offers a partial explanation of the leveling off of reuse over time. Reuse appears to be driven by the pool of a familiar code, rather than by the entire pool of reuse candidates. Each project is largely a self-contained universe (we assume that programmers will be most familiar with the code with which they are currently working than with

---

[5] Recall that Rule Sets are the most labor-intensive objects in these systems. 3GL modules might be more significant, except that they are typically used in cases where special-purpose routines are already "on the shelf."

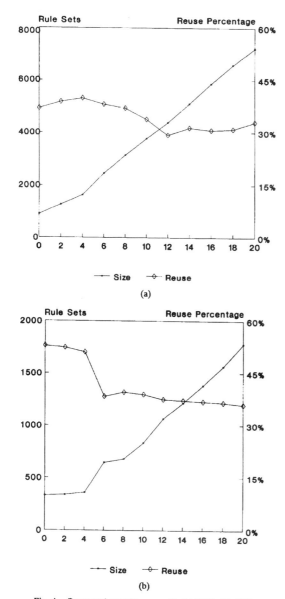

Fig. 4. Reuse and repository growth. (a) FBC. (b) CHH.

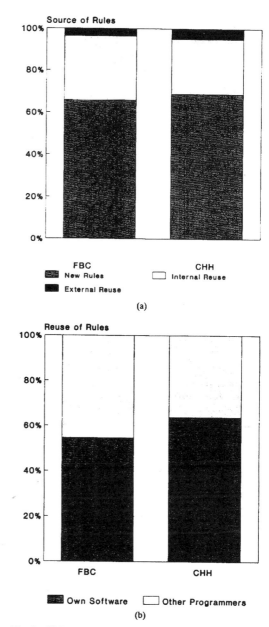

Fig. 5. (a) Internal and external reuse. (b) Reuse of own software.

that upon which other programming teams are working) and new projects derive little benefit from previous projects. The importance of familiarity suggests that the search mechanisms available are either inadequate or underutilized. As we explain below, we believe both to be the case.

Fig. 5(b) shows the prevalence of self-reuse. Despite the presence of over 250 programmers at FBC and over 100 programmers at CHH, more than 60% of the reuse consisted of programmers reusing their own software.

If reuse is driven by the availability of familiar objects, we would expect to find, as we also predicted, that larger projects exhibit higher levels of reuse—since they provide larger pools of familiar reuse candidates. This prediction was moderately supported. Fig. 6 shows the relationship between system size

and reuse. The correlation between these two factors was 37% ($p = 0.09$) for 22 application systems at FBC and 58% ($p = 0.04$) for 13 application systems at CHH.[6]

The strong tendency of programmers to reuse objects of their own development is further evidence of the importance of familiarity. We are not able to estimate the degree to which the prevalence of internal reuse is also driven by two other

[6] Fig. 6 uses a logarithmic scale to display system size, because order-of-magnitude differences between systems make a linear display difficult to interpret. In fact, though, the correlations between reuse and the *log* of system size at the two sites is exactly the same as that between reuse and system size: 37% and 58%, respectively.

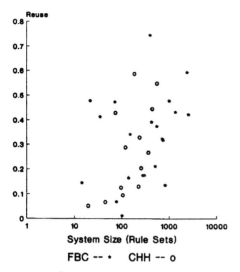

Fig. 6. Reuse and system size.

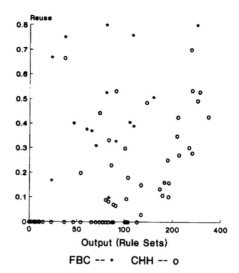

Fig. 7. Reuse and programmer output.

factors—the better "fit" an application system's own objects might be expected to have, and the efforts of the developers to design for internal reuse. We note, however, that the provision of a pool of generally reusable objects did not enable CHH to achieve higher levels of external reuse than FBC. This suggests that familiarity is at least as important a factor as fit.

Individual Programmer Differences: As with so many software-related activities, a small number of outstanding programmers appear to account for a disproportionate amount of the reuse achieved. Fig. 7 shows the distribution of programmer output and reuse. The top 5% of the programmers accounted for the creation of over 20% of the Rule Sets and for over 50% of the reuse, with the top reusers achieving average reuse percentages as high as 75%. Reuse levels were consistently higher for programmers with larger total outputs. The correlation between these factors is 50% ($p = 0.03$) for ($n = 19$) at FBC and 60% ($p = 0.0001$) for ($n = 76$) at CHH.[7]

There are three possible explanations for these observations. One is that the same skills that make some programmers extraordinarily productive also make them extraordinarily good reusers of software. A second is that these programmers have a larger pool of familiar objects (i.e., objects of their own making) to reuse. A third is that we are observing an attitude change over time, with the high-reuse programmers simply being the ones who had been using HPS the longest, and had absorbed the reuse "message." The data did not bear this last hypothesis out: the partial correlations, controlling for months of HPS experience, were within 1% of the raw correlations.

In summary, it appears that HPS provides capabilities which allow programmers to achieve high levels of reuse. However, the pattern of reuse—with most reuse attributable to a small number of enthusiastic software reusers—suggests

that there remains considerable unexploited reuse potential. Programmers are writing new objects rather than searching for reuse opportunities. It is of considerable interest to determine whether the high reuse levels achieved by the most productive programmers represent a skill that can be taught.

VI. ORGANIZATIONAL FACTORS AFFECTING SOFTWARE REUSE

In addition to analyzing the repositories, we interviewed developers to learn about the practice of software reuse from the perspective of the users of the CASE tools. These interviews revealed some technical barriers to the realization of software reuse opportunities. Most serious, however, were the organizational barriers and disincentives to reusing software.

A. Search and Organizational Incentives

HPS makes the invocation of a previously written object trivial. All objects reside in the same repository, and are available for reuse. The main formal mechanism for identifying such an object, however, is a keyword search mechanism, the use of which often turns out to require more effort than programmers are willing to expend. We found no indication that developers are failing to enter keywords into the index. It appears to be the case, however, that such keywords do not provide an efficient search mechanism. Given the relative ease of writing any single object, programmers are often reluctant to bother with an extended search.

The primary unexploited opportunity that we identified at FBC and CHH revolves around the lack of formal incentives to reuse objects. Managers believed that it was premature to enforce reuse benchmarks while they were still learning the best ways to use and to manage HPS and software reuse.[8] While formal incentives to reuse software were not

---

[7] Of the 110 programmers at CHH, only the 76 who wrote at least one Rule Set were included in this analysis. Our data for FBC represents a sample of 19 programmers out of 250. A log scale is used, for display purposes only, because order-of-magnitude differences in programmer outputs make a linear display difficult to interpret.

[8] In follow-up interviews at the sites, we learned that managers now believe that higher levels of reuse can result from a maturing managerial process based on formal productivity and reuse measurement. A study conducted at CHH by an independent outside consultant, subsequent to our study, disclosed that

a primary focus of management, informal incentives existed for a programmer to *prevent* others from reusing her objects. The creator of an object is its "owner," and every reuse of that object is a potential call upon that owner to maintain the object in case of trouble—often trouble arising from its use within an application for which it was not originally tuned and tested. Every reuse is also a constraint on the owner's subsequent ability to modify that object, since any modification must meet the requirements of all users of the object. Stronger change control mechanisms might have mitigated this problem, at the cost of interfering with the learning and experimentation that management was trying to encourage in its HPS programmers.

In practice, programmers who wish to use an object from another application are encouraged (by the other programmers, not by management) to copy the object in question, to rename it, and to use it as though it were a new object. We refer to this practice as "hidden reuse," a form of reuse which is not captured by the monitoring mechanism. (The related practice of "templating" is a dominant form of reuse in traditional application environments.) Hidden reuse achieves only some of the goals of software reuse: coding effort and unit testing are reduced, but adaptation costs are higher, and subsequent life cycle savings, particularly in maintenance, are not realized.

B. Preliminary Conclusions about Reusable Software

The initial drive for reuse at FBC and CHH was premised upon the assumption that the primary determinants of reuse were technical—that reuse could be achieved to the extent that we had a large pool of reusable objects, and that we had good tools for locating and using them. These expectations were correct, as far as they went, but they did not go far enough. In particular, they did not sufficiently stresses the organizational prerequisites for successful reuse. The repository-level analysis illustrated above heightened management awareness of organizational issues, and motivated a more complex model of software reuse.

The managers continue to believe that there are high degrees of commonality among the application systems at each site, but the relatively low levels of external reuse reinforce the importance of domain analysis, and formally designing for reuse, in achieving the full benefits of vertical reuse.

Fig. 8 presents a revised model of software reuse, in light of the repository evaluation results presented in Section V. The mostly technical factors that the earlier model presented as drivers of software reuse are still in place: the research sites did achieve strong initial levels of software reuse, with reuse percentages of about 35% at both sites, with the aid of the technical support provided by HPS. At the time this study was conducted, however, reuse appeared to have reached a plateau.

The immediate barriers to higher reuse levels appear to have been organizational. Software reuse was encouraged, but not mandated. Programmers were not rewarded for reuse while HPS use was still in the learning and innovation stage.

CHH now produces about 30% more function points per person-year at 30% less cost per function point, compared to a reference sample of over 25 other Fortune 500 companies. Management attributed this in part to its program of software reuse.

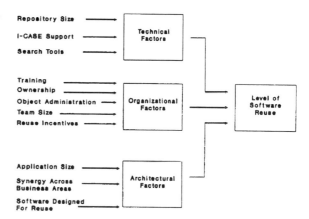

Fig. 8. A revised model of reuse.

The weakest technical aspect of HPS with respect to software reuse is the keyword search mechanism, which appears to be unequal to its task. Since most objects are relatively small, and since HPS is successful in making individual objects very easy to develop, programmers are willing to bear extremely low search costs before choosing to just write their own objects—in the absence of managerial incentives to search longer.

The findings reflected in our repository evaluation and in our model suggest that integrated CASE technology can indeed contribute to high levels of software reuse, but that the realization of their full benefits requires corresponding changes in the software development process.

VII. CONCLUSION

Integrated CASE tools support not only the implementation of advanced software development processes, but also their monitoring and control. In this paper, we have used repository evaluation to study software reuse at two sites that are pursuing reuse by means of the same CASE tool. Repository evaluation allowed us to assess the success of these efforts. It enabled us to critique a simple model of software reuse, and to suggest a richer one.

We investigated the extent to which the CASE technology supported reuse, and found that it enabled both sites to achieve steady-state reuse percentages of approximately 35%, but that higher levels probably depended on nontechnical factors. We are now attempting to estimate the degree of unexploited reuse potential, and the costs of achieving it.

We asked whether expert programmers were also better at reuse, and found that the highest levels of reuse were achieved by the programmers with the highest outputs of objects. We are investigating the question of whether this is a familiarity effect or a skill effect, as this would determine the best way to teach reuse.

We investigated the relative success of internal reuse, compared to that of external reuse. Our findings reinforced the messages of prior researchers, that success in external reuse cannot be achieved informally. It relies upon formal domain analysis and effective cataloguing and search mechanisms.

Repository evaluation allowed us to put numbers to aspects of reuse of which we previously had only a qualitative understanding—and it allowed senior management to assess the strengths and weaknesses of their software reuse efforts, and to decide how to improve them.

ACKNOWLEDGMENT

We wish to acknowledge M. Baric, G. Bedell, T. Lewis, and V. Wadhwa for the access they provided us to the software development activities and staff at The First Boston Corporation and Seer Technologies in New York City. B. Menar, N. Liebson, J. Yent, and D. Christy at Carter Hawley Hale Information Services, in Anaheim, CA, provided similar support. We also appreciated the research assistance of L. Erlihk, R. Kumar, and M. Oara, whose efforts to automate repository queries made this research possible. Finally, R. J. Kauffman thanks the Nippon Electric Corporation and the U.S.–Japan Business and Economics Research Center, Stern School of Business, New York University, for partial funding of data collection.

REFERENCES

[1] K. Allen, W. Krutz, and D. Olivier, "Software reuse: Mining, refining, and designing," in *TRI-Ada '90 Proc.*, Dec. 1990, pp. 222–226.
[2] U. Apte, C. S. Sankar, M. Thakur, and J. Turner, "Reusability strategy for development of information systems: Implementation experience of a bank," *MIS Quart.*, vol. 14, no. 4, pp. 421–431, Dec. 1990.
[3] R. D. Banker and R. J. Kauffman, "Reuse and productivity: An empirical study of integrated computer-aided software engineering (ICASE) at the First Boston Corporation," *MIS Quart.*, vol. 15, no. 3, pp. 375–401, Sept. 1991.
[4] ——, "Automated software metrics, repository evaluation and the software asset management perspective," Center Inform. Syst., Stern School of Business, New York Univ., Working Paper, 1991.
[5] ——, "Measuring the development performance of integrated computer-aided software engineering: A synthesis of field study results from the First Boston Corporation," in *Software Engineering Economics*, T. Gulledge, Ed. New York: Springer-Verlag, 1993, to be published.
[6] R. D. Banker, R. J. Kauffman, and Kumar, "An empirical study of object-based output metrics in a computer-aided software engineering environment," *J. Management Inform. Systems.*, vol. 6, no. 3, Winter 1992.
[7] R. D. Banker, R. J. Kauffman, C. Wright, and D. Zweig, "Automating output size and reuse metrics in a repository-based computer-aided software engineering environment," Stern School of Business, New York Univ., Working Paper, 1991.
[8] H. B. Barnes and T. Bollinger, "Making software reuse cost effective," *IEEE Software*, vol. 8, no. 1, Jan. 1991.
[9] V. Basili, "Viewing maintenance as reuse-oriented software development," *IEEE Software*, vol. 7, no. 1, pp. 19–25, Jan. 1990.
[10] B. Beckman, W. Van Snyder, S. Shen, J. Jupin, L. Van Warren, B. Boyd, and R. Tausworthe, "The ESC: A hypermedia encyclopedia of reusable software components," Jet Propulsion Lab., California Inst. Technol., Pasadena, CA, Sept. 1991.
[11] T. J. Biggerstaff and A. J. Perlis, Eds., *Software Reusability: Volume I—Concepts and Models.* New York: Addison-Wesley/ACM Press, 1989.
[12] ——, Eds., *Software Reusability: Volume II—Applications Experience.* New York: Addison-Wesley/ACM Press, 1989.
[13] B. A. Burton, R. W. Aragon, S. A. Bailey, K. D. Koehler, and L. A. Mayes, "The reusable software library," *IEEE Software*, vol. 4, no. 4, pp. 25–33, July 1987.
[14] G. Caldiera and V. R. Basili, "Identifying and qualifying reusable software components," *IEEE Computer*, pp. 61–70, Feb. 1991.
[15] M. J. Cavaliere, "Reusable code at the Hartford insurance group," in *ITT Proc. Workshop Reusability in Programming*, Newport, RI, 1983; reprinted in *Software Reusability: Volume II—Applications Experience*, T. J. Biggerstaff and A. J. Perlis, Eds. New York: Addison-Wesley/ACM Press, 1989.

[16] M. Chen and E. H. Sibley, "Using a CASE-based repository for systems integration," in *Proc. 1991 Hawaii Int. Conf. Systems Sciences*, IEEE, Jan. 1991, pp. 578–587.
[17] S. Cohen, "Process and products for software reuse in Ada," in *TRI-Ada '90 Proc.*, Dec. 1990, pp. 227–239.
[18] M. Cusamano, *Japan's Software Factories: A Challenge to U.S. Management.* Oxford, England: Oxford University Press, 1991.
[19] E. M. Dusink, "Towards a design philosophy for reuse," in *Proc. Reuse in Practice Workshop*, J. Baldo and C. Braun, Eds. Pittsburgh, PA: Software Eng. Inst., 1989.
[20] J. B. Frakes, T. J. Biggerstaff, R. Prieto-Diaz, K. Matsumura, and W. Shaefer, "Software reuse: Is it delivering?" in *Proc. 13th Int. Conf. Software Eng.*, Austin, TX, IEEE Comput. Soc. Press, May 13–17, 1991, pp. 52–59.
[21] J. B. Frakes and Nejmeh, "Software reuse through information retrieval," in *Proc. 20th Hawaii Int. Conf. Syst. Sci.*, B. D. Shriver and R. H. Sprague, Jr., Eds., Kailua-Kona, HI, 1987, pp. 530–535.
[22] P. Freeman, Ed. *Tutorial on Software Reusability* . Washington, DC: IEEE Comput. Soc. Press, 1987.
[23] J. E. Gaffney, Jr. and T. A. Durek "Software reuse—Key to enhanced productivity: some quantitative models," *Inform. Software Technol.*, vol. 31, no. 5, pp. 258–267, June 1989.
[24] J. W. Hooper and R. O. Chester, *Software Reuse: Guidelines and Methods.* New York: Plenum, 1991.
[25] W. S. Humphrey, *Managing the Software Process.* Reading, MA: Addison-Wesley, 1989.
[26] R. G. Lanergan and C. A. Grasso, "Software engineering with reusable designs and code," *IEEE Trans. Software Eng.*, vol. SE-10, no. 5, pp. 498–501, Sept. 1984.
[27] M. Lenz, H. A. Schmid, and P. F. Wolfe, "Software reuse through building blocks," *IEEE Software*, vol. 4, no. 4, pp. 34–42, July 1987.
[28] D. G. McNichol, C. Palmer, S. G. Cohen, W. H. Whitford, and G. O. Goeke, "Common Ada missile packages—CAMP, Vol. I: Overview and commonality study results," McDonnell Douglas, St. Louis, MO, Tech. Rep. AFATL-TR-85-93, 1986.
[29] B. McNurlin, "Building more flexible systems," *I/S Analyzer*, Oct. 1989.
[30] Y. Matusmoto, "Some experiences in promoting reusable software: Presentation in higher abstract levels," *IEEE Trans. Software Eng.*, vol. SE-10, no. 5, pp. 502–512, Sept. 1984.
[31] B. Meyer, *Object-Oriented Software Construction.* Englewood Cliffs, NJ: Prentice-Hall, 1987.
[32] J. M. Neighbors, "The DRACO approach to constructing software from reusable components," *IEEE Trans. Software Eng.*, vol. SE-10, no. 5, pp. 564–574, Sept. 1984.
[33] W. E. Novak, "U.S. Army SDS CRWG reuse committee technical requirements document: Technical guidance section," draft version, 1990.
[34] J. F. Nunamaker, Jr. and M. Chen, "Software productivity: A framework of study and an approach to reusable components," in *Proc. 22nd Hawaii Int. Conf. Syst. Sci.*, IEEE, Jan. 1989, pp. 959–968.
[35] ——, "Software productivity: Gaining competitive edges in an information society," in *Proc. 22nd Hawaii Int. Conf. Syst. Sci.*, IEEE, Jan. 1989, pp. 957–958.
[36] A. Pollack, "The move to modular software," *New York Times*, pp. D1–D2, Apr. 23, 1990.
[37] Polster, "Reuse of software through generation of partial systems," *IEEE Trans. Software Eng.*, vol. SE-10, no. 5, pp. 402–416, Sept. 1984.
[38] R. Prieto-Diaz, "Classifying software for reusability," *IEEE Software*, vol. 4, no. 1, pp. 6–16, Jan. 1987.
[39] ——, "Domain analysis: An introduction," *ACM Software Eng. Notes*, vol. 15, no. 2, pp. 47–54, Apr. 1990.
[40] H. D. Rombach, "Software reuse: A key to the maintenance problem," *Inform. Software Technol.*, vol. 33, no. 1, Jan./Feb. 1991.
[41] J. A. Senn and J. L. Wynekoop, "computer-aided software engineering (CASE) in perspective," Inform. Technol. Management Center, College Business Administration, Georgia State Univ., Working Paper, 1990.
[42] *CASE Research Report*, Sentry Market Research, Westborough, MA, 1990.
[43] V. Sepannen, "Reusability in software engineering," in *Tutorial: Software Reusability*, P. Freeman, Ed. Austin, TX: IEEE Comput. Soc. Press, 1987, pp. 286–297.
[44] "Software productivity metrics working group of the software engineering standards subcommittee, standards for software productivity metrics," IEEE Comput. Soc. P1045/D5.0 (draft), Mar. 8, 1992.
[45] W. Tracz, "RECIPE: A reusable software paradigm," in *Proc. 20th Hawaii Int. Conf. Syst. Sci.*, B. D. Shriver and R. H. Sprague, Jr., Eds., Kailua-Kona, HI, 1987, pp. 546–555.
[46] ——, *Tutorial: Software Reuse—Emerging Technology.* Austin, TX: IEEE Comput. Soc. Press, 1988.

Rajiv D. Banker received the Doctorate in business administration from Harvard University, Cambridge, MA, in 1980, with a concentration in planning and control systems.

He is the Arthur Andersen & Co./Duane R. Kullberg Chair in Accounting and Information Systems at the Carlson School of Management, University of Minnesota, Minneapolis. He has published numerous articles and serves on the editorial boards of several prominent research journals. His research on information systems development and maintenance is field-based and empirical, involving collection and analysis of data on software complexity, project characteristics, systems environment and programmer experience, and ability and effort, to estimate the impact of managerial and technological factors on productivity and quality of commercial software. Of particular interest is the study of integrated CASE technologies and the management of reusable software.

Robert J. Kauffman received the Doctorate in industrial administration from Carnegie Mellon University, Pittsburgh, PA.

He is an Associate Professor of Information Systems at the Stern School of Business, New York University (on leave in 1992–1993 at the Federal Reserve Bank of Philadelphia and the Simon Graduate School of Management, University of Rochester), where he specializes in information technology in the financial services sector. Previously an international bank lending and strategic planning officer, he is currently Nippon Electric Corporation (NEC) Faculty Fellow of the U.S.–Japan Business and Economics Research Center. He has published articles in *MIS Quarterly, Journal of Management Information Systems*, IEEE TRANSACTIONS ON SOFTWARE ENGINEERING, *Information and Software Technologies, Information and Management*, and elsewhere. His current research focuses on developing new methods for measuring the business value of information technology investments (including CASE), using techniques from finance and economics.

Dani Zweig received the Doctorate in industrial administerial administration from Carnegie Mellon University, Pittsburgh, PA.

He is an Assistant Professor of Information Systems in the Department of Administrative Sciences at the Naval Postgraduate School, Monterey, CA. Prior to this he was a consultant for Peat Marwick. His research focuses on software reuse and on cost implications of software complexity. He is also currently working on an analysis of the Department of Defense's software inventory, its rate of obsolescence, and expected replacement costs.

Making the Reuse Business Work

Ivar Jacobson
Rational
Software Corp.

Martin
Griss
Hewlett-Packard
Laboratories

Patrik
Jonsson
Rational
Software Corp.

Reuse technology is ready now. In fact, enough companies have demonstrated substantial improvement, often as much as 90 percent reuse, to assure us that it can be achieved.[1] If we take 15 percent as an approximation of the current rate of "passive" reuse that individual engineers achieve anyway and 90 percent as the figure that more than a few organizations are achieving, that is a gain of six times. With this level of reuse, the overall cost savings are dramatic. Moreover, these organizations are achieving comparable gains in development time. They are getting a system into operation in months, instead of years.

The third great component of software system development (after cost of development and time to market) is quality. "Quality" implies a host of factors. Many of them are hard to quantify or, at least, have not been quantified by most organizations. However, participants in successful reuse invariably believe that "quality," however they define it, has improved. Certainly, freedom from defects, flexibility, and robustness in the face of system evolution are important aspects of quality to many organizations.

REUSE IMPROVES THE PERFORMANCE OF YOUR BUSINESS PROCESSES

Increasing the productivity of your software development, shortening the time to market, and reducing the number of defects in the software product are all very nice. They are certainly worth seeking, but they are only the first installment of the prospective gains. The second installment is the improvement of the business processes that this software supports. Even though you are not consciously applying the methods of business engineering, the act of redoing the software that operates your business processes will result in some incremental improvement of those processes.

The third installment is the gain that the conscious application of business engineering offers. Instead of automating the business model that the business currently follows, business engineering straightens out these processes and takes advantage of the coordina-

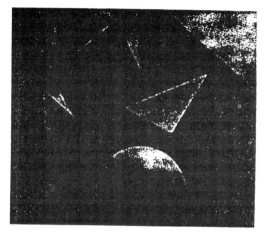

tion capabilities that information systems provide.

First, let's clear the decks. A number of misconceptions stand in the way of achieving these gains.

COMMON MISCONCEPTIONS

Software reuse is a field replete with misunderstandings. We list some of the common misconceptions and our responses:

- *Instituting software reuse is primarily a matter of introducing the appropriate technology.* It is not. It is that and everything else—management, organization, architecture, processes, investment, and persistence.
- *Reuse does not work.* Put that in the past tense. Some companies have failed to make it work. Many companies are making it work.
- *It may work, but it is too expensive.* True, it does cost money up front, but it coins money down the trail. How far do you want to follow the trail?
- *The changes reuse asks us to make are too risky.* Take out the "too." Change is "risky" in the near term, but failure to change is "too" risky in the long term.
- *You should defer a systematic reuse program until your organization reaches SEI Capability Maturity Level 3.* You should not. Start one now. Achieving reuse takes the same kind of steps that bettering your maturity level does.
- *Architecture does not have to be addressed as a*

This article excerpts Chapter 15 of *Software Reuse: Architecture, Process and Organization for Business Success*; ISBN 0-201-92476-5; published by Addison Wesley, 1997; ©1997, ACM Press. Reprinted with permission.

36

Reprinted from *IEEE Computer*, Vol. 30, No. 4, Oct. 1997, pp. 36-42.

217

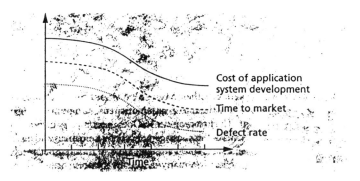

specific task. Oh, yes, it does. It is the technical plan that leads to effective reuse across an application family.

- *Adopting object-oriented languages will lead to systematic reuse.* No, it won't. Not all by itself. There are all those factors listed under the first misconception. Moreover, most successful reuse has been in Cobol, Fortran, C, and even Ada, because that is where much of the existing code is.
- *Limit reuse to code components.* Don't. Just writing code is usually down in the 10-20 percent range of total development costs.
- *Developers will select the components they will reuse from tens of thousands of small components.* No, they won't. They are human; their brains are adapted by evolution to hold in contemplation only seven, plus or minus two, items at a time. (And those seven have to include lunch and a few other pressing matters.)
- *Reused code components are too slow.* They may be, but then that is a design flaw. Components should be developed under even more rigorous requirements than "ordinary" classes, which includes requirements on performance, size, and quality.
- *Setting up a library of reusable components will itself induce developers to reuse them.* It does not work. There is the little matter of trust, for instance.
- *Paying application developers to contribute components to the repository will build up the library.* This sortie has not worked in practice.
- *Paying application developers to use components from the repository will encourage reuse.* This bribe, too, has been ineffectual.

Have we missed your favorite misconception? Possibly, just possibly, we have been a bit more blunt than the history of reuse efforts justifies. Still, suffice it to say that all these misconceptions together have blinded management and greatly delayed the coming of systematic reuse and the reuse business.

DOING REUSE IS DIFFICULT

In addition to the role that misconceptions have played in delaying the arrival of systematic reuse, the plain fact is that it is hard. It is hard primarily because at least five factors have to be interwoven and mastered:

- Vision
- Architecture
- Organization and the management of it
- Financing
- Software engineering process

In addition, if a company chooses to employ object-oriented requirements capture, analysis, design, and implementation, that is a new technology for its people to master. Furthermore, if an organization decides to reengineer its business processes, that effort is another complicating factor to integrate into the entire picture.

A single developer can reuse a little of what he or she has done before—on the order of 10-20 percent. If the manager of a single project can establish some machinery to encourage sharing within the project, he or she can add another 10-20 percent. At the level of a group of similar projects, such as a line of instruments, systematic reuse can get under way. At this level, of course, the five factors appear and the reuse task becomes complicated.

Systematic reuse cannot be adopted piecemeal. An occasional forward-looking developer can keep some experience and some code in his hip pocket, but he is not in an organizational position to carry through a systematic reuse program. At best, he is in a position to talk about the need for reuse, providing the organizational culture does not choke him off. In fact, such a person can sometimes become the champion a systematic program needs.

The integration that a systematic reuse program involves means that only management can lead it, which means that the upper management (division head and department directors) of a division has to understand what reuse can accomplish and how to go about it. They also have to be in a position to back a fairly expensive and long-running effort. It takes several years for the funds invested in reuse to begin coming back.

Typical reductions are diagrammed in Figure 1. A marginal company may not be able to afford the several-year-long initial investment.

WITHOUT VISION, THE PEOPLE PERISH

Wolves hunt in packs. They seem to have a vision of what cooperative hunting can do for the pack—in spite of lacking language in which to communicate that vision. We humans do have language; we have also abused that facility to the point where we hardly know any more whom to trust to set out a common vision. The problem in business organizations is how to carry it out in an atmosphere that may be laden with mistrust.

The past generation has seen a score of promising initiatives held forth. Their number, probably, is limited only by the number of three-letter combinations the alphabet provides. Only a few succeed. What char-

Figure 1. Cost or effort, time to market, and defect rate all start at a fairly high level. At first, as the reuse effort is in the planning stage, they remain steady. As reuse begins to make a difference, they drop rapidly. Eventually, when reuse reaches 80 or 90 percent, the rate of decline flattens out.

acterizes them? Can we pick out those features and apply them to a systematic reuse program?

The first requisite is: Does the company have a problem that its management (both executives and middle management) can agree on and that reuse can solve, such as too many defects in the software? Is there a family of applications in which there are exploitable reuse opportunities?

Second: Is the company prepared to make a long-term commitment? Can it commit the investment funds necessary? Is it prepared to change its organization structure to meet the needs of reuse? Can it finance the training that underlies a complex effort?

Third: Will the company have some sort of measure of the degree to which the program is working? This measure may be established based on the obtained return on investment, the reduction in product cycle time, or even something as simple as a count of the number of component systems reused in each new project. Having a metric to measure success is both an indication of seriousness and a guide to whether the program is on the right track.

Fourth is the promise of persistence. Executives often have to multiplex between many issues each day. Appointments may be scheduled at 15-minute intervals. Can component management spend the time and provide the focus a program takes? This short-run pattern sometimes makes it difficult to pay attention to such a major change effort.

The fact of persistence has to show up in more than posters on the walls. Rather, it is better to maintain a continuing interest in the reuse metrics. Get them every week or every month and comment on them. Even more important, take the actions that they suggest. The words in companywide communications—or on those wall posters—matter little. It is action appropriate to the situation that people rack up on their mental scorecards.

Fifth comes feedback. Of course, the taking of action is a form of feedback. Here, however, we refer to letting people immersed in the bowels of some activity know how it turned out. There is specific feedback to the group involved—a particular detail worked out. There is general feedback, perhaps to the entire division—the program flew. Everyone is interested in word of how the program first worked out in the field. Software development success stories need to be shared in a graphic form with all participants.

REUSE DEPENDS ON ARCHITECTURE

As recently as one hundred years ago in rural United States, farm neighbors used to get together and raise a barn. They all knew what a barn looked like. It was simple enough to build without architectural plans. About the same time in US cities, large contractors were building the first skyscrapers. They worked from architectural plans. There appeared to be a difference between small, well-understood buildings on the plentiful acres of a farm and tall steel-framed structures on city lots.

Similarly, there is a difference between a small, well-understood software application being coded by one or two programmers and a system of hundreds of thousands of source lines of code being attacked by groups of teams. There is another step-up in complexity when we go from a single system, however large, to a family of application systems. There is a further step-up when we make component systems that are reusable throughout the family. And again, complexity increases when we add variability mechanisms to the components to enable them to be employed satisfactorily within a greater family range. Finally, a time frame extending into the future increases complexity still further.

This ever-increasing complexity is inherent in large-scale reusable systems. It cannot be sidestepped. It requires a plan. This plan is called the architecture. The software architecture, first of all, defines a structure. Software components have to fit into some kind of design. The lowest layer of components, for example, rests on the operating system. Successively more specialized layers build on it, up to the application systems themselves.

Second, the architecture defines the interfaces between components. It defines the patterns by which information is passed back and forth through these interfaces. With this kind of architectural plan, component engineers can develop components that work for application systems developed by different groups or at different locations.

Frankly, we have encountered some resistance to the concept of software architecture. This resistance may arise from lack of experience with architecture. In the past, architecture was not recognized as a separate function. When an organization plans a family of large systems and expects substantial software reuse, it will need component systems reusable in dozens of systems for years to come. This requires coming to terms with significant planning, and specifically, with architecture.

Coming to terms implies a string of obligations. It requires a separate team headed by a broadly experienced developer, assisted by the best people available. The reason: Developing architecture for a family is more difficult than developing it for a single system.

It requires time. The application-family engineering team has to gather information not just on a single system's requirements, but on the requirements of a whole group of systems, now and into the future, preferably by looking at a business model of the organization to support with information systems. It has to analyze this information as a basis for defining a layered architecture. In the course of preparing this architecture, the team will often find that its analysis is incomplete. It will have to gather and analyze additional information. That takes more time. The time frame can be speeded up only at the expense of an incomplete or incorrect architecture. A weak architecture would lead to poor application systems later on. That, of course, would take time (and cost money) at that point. Getting the architecture right is one of the reasons it takes several years to move a reuse business into the black.

On the plus side, however, the main part of the architectural task is a one-time-only assignment. Once completed, it is good for a period of years. Of course, during its lifetime, a smaller team has to monitor its relevance and make such modifications as experience and changing circumstances dictate.

Getting the architecture right provides many advantages. It ensures that many organization units, scattered in space and time, can work on different components and rest assured that they will come together successfully. It ensures that a system put together in this manner will have integrity and a robust structure. It enables maintainers later to modify local parts of it without disrupting other parts. This ability to modify the system successfully enables it to evolve, as its environment changes. In turn, successful evolution extends the life of the system.

Perhaps not the least of the merits of a good architecture is that the underlying design of the scores of component and application systems based on it can be understood. An architecture, explained with use cases and an analysis model, can be understood not only by the original developers but also by new recruits and the later maintainers. A layered architecture is furthermore intuitive enough to be relevant to several layers of management, customers, and end users. This understanding enhances everyone's ability to manage the work.

MANAGEMENT WORKS THROUGH ORGANIZATION

Up until recently there has been a tendency to assume that the existing organization structure, given a few statistics on the benefits of reuse to motivate it and given some technical training on the mechanics of it, could go forth and practice reuse.

This approach has not been successful. One of the reasons is that existing software development is organized on a project basis. Projects focus on getting out a "good enough" product within the time and cost budgeted. Producing reusable components takes longer and costs more, as those parts of the industry practicing reuse have found by experience. This experience runs counter to project motivation. Systematic reuse rests on an organization structure adapted to its needs.

What are these needs? There are four principal func-

tions. First is an organization unit to capture the requirements of a family of applications and to construct an architecture, as we outlined in the preceding section. This architecture leads to an indication of what components and component systems are reusable. Creating these reusable components is the province of the second function: component system engineering. The third function is application system engineering, roughly comparable to the older project engineering groups. People in these groups capture the requirements on their particular application and then combine reusable component systems with new work to meet the requirements. The fourth function is a component support group under a support manager. Its function is to relieve the component system engineering team of housekeeping chores and project support activities, so that it can concentrate on its creative tasks.

These four functions report to a single manager, the software engineering business manager. This overall structure then becomes a Reuse-Driven Software Engineering Business. We call it a "business" because it exists in an economic environment. It has to make its way in this environment, a subject to which we turn next.

THE REUSE BUSINESS MUST EARN A RETURN ON ITS INVESTMENT

Setting up a reuse business costs money. Over a period of time, it should more than return that money and also meet the strategic business goals that motivate establishing the reuse business.

However, cost recovery is not necessarily the most important reason to mount a large-scale, architected reuse effort. In many cases, without an architected reuse effort it would not be possible to meet the business objectives at all. For example, in the case of Ericsson, the telecommunications company, it was critical to invest in architected reuse for its AXE telecommunications switching systems—without architected reuse it would simply not have been feasible to develop the thousands of customized AXE installations.[2,3]

In the case of the reuse business, the company has to provide funds—partly investment and partly operational—to

- analyze the family of applications to build with reuse,
- define an architecture,
- create components and component systems,
- reorganize,
- communicate the use of component systems through the support group to reusers, and
- train all types of teams in the pertinent technology.

The pattern that this flow of investment funds follows is charted in Figure 2. In the early years, as the

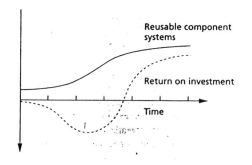

Figure 2. In the first months of the reuse program the investment is small, as only a few people are working on the planning stage. Then, for several years the investment is heavy as architects develop architecture and component engineers generate component systems. When component systems become available in quantity, as the reusable component systems curve shows, the reuse business begins to return its investment. Eventually, when reuse reaches 90 percent or so, ROI, too, approaches a ceiling. In time, it may decline as competition erodes the advantages of reuse.

reuse program is getting under way, the outgo is negative. In later years, when application engineers can draw component systems from a substantial stock, the investment pays off.

A rather lackadaisical reuse program in which a few indifferent creators provide a few components that developers don't much care for is not going to pay off. Reuse is not a "faith" that one wishes to spread to the benighted. It is a business in which the company wishes to make money. Financial people who have tried to place money values on the factors involved in ROI (return on investment) programs know that it is difficult to evaluate all these factors. For example, how do you place a monetary value on seizing the market window a few months sooner? How do you place a value on the increased competitiveness and new opportunities that the reduced time to market and flexible architecture enable? Nevertheless, making a return on investment is what keeps the reuse business in business.

Without this financial feedback, the reuse program has to depend on enthusiasm, plus the general view that reuse is a good thing. In the competition within the company for scarce funds, this view is a thin reed.

In addition to ROI, Jeffrey S. Poulin has enumerated six sources of reuse data that the reuse business itself can collect:[4]

- Source lines of code
- Number of lines, not written, but reused, included in a source file
- Number of lines reused by other products
- Software development cost
- Software development error rate
- Error repair cost

From these observable data elements, he derives three further metrics:

- Percentage of reuse in a product
- Cost avoidance resulting from reuse
- Reuse value added—a productivity ratio comparing a reusing organization with one that is not

The cost-avoidance metric reflects the reduction in product costs resulting from reuse. The reuse value-added productivity ratio measures the leverage provided by practicing reuse and contributing to the reuse practiced by others.

In general, metrics derived directly from reuse mea-

sures are available sooner than cost or ROI figures provided by accounting. Often they act as early indicators of specific process problems, and can do so more precisely than overall accounting results can. For example, these detailed metrics can help determine if problems are due to an inadequate supply of components, if application engineers are not reusing enough components, or if some other process problem is the source of difficulty. These measures enable management to investigate troublesome projects and processes more quickly and to take action more pointedly.

OBJECT TECHNOLOGY AIDS PROCESS

Object-oriented analysis and design, followed by the use of an object-oriented programming language at the implementation stage, do not, by themselves, guarantee a high level of reuse. The fact that some characteristics of object-oriented languages, such as inheritance, make it possible to reuse code have been emphasized far too much. There is much more to reuse than object orientation, as our earlier discussion of vision, architecture, organization, financing, and software engineering processes suggest.

At the same time, object-oriented ways of thinking can be a great aid to carrying through the software engineering processes that enable reuse to take place. The reason lies all the way back in the physical world and in the way that human beings have evolved to view that world. The world consists of objects that (1) have properties and (2) can act. For instance, a dog has four movable feet and runs.

The first step in requirements capture, the creation of use cases, focuses on value added. After that, object orientation is often an aid in thinking through the analysis model, the design model, and the remaining development stages. The object concept represents the elements in this series, enabling engineers to move smoothly from high-level abstractions in the early stages to concrete code in the construction phase.

BUSINESS ENGINEERING: OVERHAULING THE BUSINESS MODEL

Software engineering is, at its core, model building. Changing a business also requires building models— be it traditional hierarchical organization charts or process-oriented diagrams. A business, however, is not a model; it is a rather woolly slice of reality. The people down in the ranks who make it work may have to twist its formal procedures (that is, the business models) almost beyond recognition to make things come out. When software engineers implement support for a business's procedures in code, they often find, as the code operates, that the implemented support does not support the true business needs. The reason, of course, is undocumented twisting of the formal procedures. This twisting leads to complications, and complications spell inefficiency. As a result of this gap between formal procedures and twisted operations, a current model of the existing business is difficult to lay hands on. Then when the existing business is being reengineered, the complications mount.

Still, improving processes is not new. Businessmen have been engineering processes at least since the days of Adam Smith's pin factory. Then they took the labor of making a pin from one worker and divided it into many steps, each performed by a different worker. It was the principle of division of labor. Put that way, it sounds very efficient.

As work became ever more finely divided into hundreds of operations in factories or service operations employing thousands of workers, the information content of keeping all these jobs in play became formidably large. We know it under such names as receiving, receiving inspection, stockroom, material control, production control, maintenance, and many more. We also know it—and decry it—as overhead.

Moreover, all these people in overhead, as well as the direct labor force, the purchasing people extending out to suppliers, and the marketing force reaching out into the world, have to be kept on track by a substantial structure of supervisors, managers, executives, and their clerical assistants. Some observers have characterized this administrative structure as a series of stovepipes. Each stovepipe works fairly well within its stack. Needed information passes up and down through supervisory levels within a stovepipe, that is, a department. One stovepipe, however, doesn't pass information very well to and from the other stovepipes.

Keeping track of the information needed to control the flow of work through a series of stovepipe departments is something that computer programs can do. By now it is evident that forward-looking businesses can substitute information systems for at least part of the information coordination formerly done in the stovepipe structure and make some coordination obsolete by instead reorganizing to perform the business processes directly.

That is business engineering. It is the use of information systems, rather than an administrative (stovepipe) structure, to coordinate a business process. The point for us to note especially is that the creation of this coordinating information system is an integral part of business engineering. Without it, you have to have the stovepipes.

It has taken about 40 years to build up the 100 billion lines of code that now operate the stovepipe structure of business. If we were to redo that code in the same way to operate the business-process approach, it might take another 40 years. If we could reduce cycle time by 70 percent through reuse, as Netron's sample projects did,[5] we might reengineer business processes in a decade or so. That is a goal that is within reach

with presently known methods.

These gains sound wonderful! No doubt everyone is getting into business engineering. No doubt they are gearing up to support it with high levels of reuse. Well, if you look around a bit, you see that they are not. In fact, 50-70 percent of business engineering attempts fail, largely due to insufficient attention to the "soft" factors. In our approach we try to address these risks with a systematic transition process that emphasizes vision, organization building focused on competence units, and suitable models of financing.

Despite the many challenges, business engineering, software modeling, and systematic reuse mark the path business is to follow in the future. In fact, the pioneers are already following it. Their success establishes that it can be done.

As we have seen earlier in this chapter, as well as in the book as a whole, inaugurating a reuse business requires integrating

- an overall vision of where the company is heading;
- an architecture that sets the pattern for sorting out components, grouping them in component systems, and fitting them into application systems;
- a compatible organization with distinct processes and teams for application-family engineering, component system engineering, application system engineering, a unit for component support, and reuse management;
- the financing arrangements that, first, make the up-front investments and, second, make the measurements that show the reuse business to be operating in the black; and
- the software engineering processes—the five-stage modeling sequence—that enables engineers in both component and application system engineering teams to think through development in communicable steps from requirements to code.

Further, the software engineering processes have to be carried out under some guiding principles. It is possible to do so with the structured-design approach, but it is preferable to use object-oriented technology.

Finally, software reuse makes business engineering feasible, particularly in terms of three factors:

By reducing the time to complete the software that supports reengineered business processes, reuse brings the software online in the same time frame as the reengineering takes, and increases market agility.

By reducing the cost of this software, reuse makes a major contribution to the execution of business reengineering.

By improving the quality and reliability of this software, reuse makes the business process run more

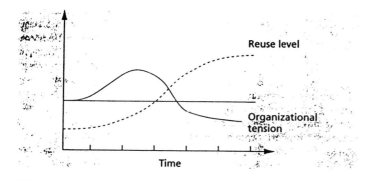

Reuse level

Organizational tension

Time

Figure 3. During the transition to a reuse business, tension among the people may rise and stay high during the period of change. As the reuse business becomes fully established, tension drops, eventually to a level lower than that at the start.

smoothly. As a result, customers are happy. They get quality and reliability sooner at less cost.

Now, we have just gone through quite a string of new activities of which your people will not exactly be masters. We'll just list education, training, in-house conferences, consultants, mentors, and so on. Getting these aids to the right people at the time they need them is another factor to be integrated into the mix.

Without these aids and, in particular, without being continuously filled in on what is going on, people become edgy. With the issuance of the reengineering directive, they begin to wonder "How does this new stuff affect me?" As Figure 3 indicates, tension tends to rise as the reuse business gets under way. Some rise is probably inevitable, but good communication can hold it within bounds. As the reuse business demonstrates its effectiveness, tension falls off. If the reuse business is fully successful, the tension falls to a level below that at the start.

There is one "little" issue yet to consider. How do we get to the point where a senior executive (a chief executive officer, chief operating officer, division head) is ready to kick off the steps leading to a reuse business? We might cast that question in slightly different terms. What help does a senior executive need to get to that point?

How does a valid idea get into practice? Well, it has to get to an executive with the organizational position necessary to take action. In the case of reuse, the professional [advocating reuse] is probably several levels below that executive. That means the idea has to move through several levels. Those levels exist because the senior executive is already overburdened. The intervening executives try, quite rightly, to reduce that burden.

Many companies have become aware of the need for good ideas to move up. Several arrangements are in use. One is that the less senior executives also look for what Andrew Grove, Intel's CEO, calls "10x" factors, that is, developments that may have a significant effect on the company. Another is that the senior executives reach out to senior professionals in such events as all-day retreats.

A third is practiced by Bill Gates of Microsoft. He goes off to his mountain cabin for a week at a time, several times a year, to "think." He carries with him books and reports with which he believes he ought to be familiar. It takes time to "think," when you put it in quotation marks. It also takes material to "think" with.

A fourth arrangement is the divisional organization structure. It was probably instituted for reasons other than the nourishing of new ideas, but one or another division often has an idea and makes it work. The challenge then is for other divisions or the company as a whole to notice the step forward.

We hope you enjoyed the journey through this book. We hope that you "enjoy" the journey to a reuse business, and we put it in quotation marks because at times you might not feel that way. You will find that the end result is worth the effort. ❖

References
1. I. Jacobson, M. Griss, and P. Jonsson, *Software Reuse: Architecture, Process, and Organization for Business Success*, Addison Wesley, Reading, Mass., 1997.
2. I. Jacobson, "A Large Commercial Success Story Based on Objects," *Object Magazine*, May 1996.
3. I. Jacobson, "Succeeding With Objects: Reuse in Reality," *Object Magazine*, July 1996.
4. J.S. Poulin, "Measuring Reuse," *Proc. 5ᵗʰ Int'l Worksop Software Reuse*, Palo Alto, Calif., 1992.
5. P.G. Bassett, *Framing Software Reuse: Lessons from the Real World*, Prentice Hall, Upper Saddle River, N.J., 1996.

Ivar Jacobson is vice president of business engineering at Rational Software Corp., where he is intimately involved with the development of the Unified Modeling Language and a leader in the OO community. He is principal author of two influential books, Object-Oriented Software Engineering—A Use Case Driven Approach (Addison Wesley, 1993) and The Object Advantage: Business Process Reengineering with Object Technology (Addison Wesley, 1994).

Martin Griss is a senior laboratory scientist at Hewlett-Packard Laboratories. As HP's "Reuse Rabbi," he created the Corporate Reuse Program and led the systematic introduction of software reuse into HP's divisions. He led HP's technical contribution as co-submittor of UML to the Object Management Group. He also writes a reuse column for Object Magazine and is active on several reuse program and steering committees.

Patrik Jonsson is a senior consultant for Rational Software Corp. in Sweden. He has been involved in specifying the requirements for Objectory's CASE tool and has been developing the architecture and method of the Objectory process with a current focus on reuse and user interface development. He is a coauthor of Object-Oriented Software Engineering—A Use Case Driven Approach.

Contact Jacobson at ivar@rational.com, Griss at griss@hpl.hp.com, and Jonsson at patrik@rational.com.

Guest Critic: Ware Myers, 1271 N. College, Claremont, CA 91711; 73153.1762@compuserve.com

Software Reuse: Ostriches Beware

Ware Myers

When it comes to reuse, many software executives, like ostriches, are pushing their heads deeper into the sand. Rather, they should study an idea Andrew Grove talks about in his new book (*Only the Paranoid Survive: How to Exploit the Crisis Points That Challenge Every Company and Career*, Doubleday, 1996): *strategic inflection points.* Grove defines a SIP as a time in the life of a business when its fundamentals are about to change. Both Grove and Intel have been through several of them; for example, the geometric increase in the number of transistors on a chip and Intel's mid-1980s move from memory chips to microprocessors.

Grove's not talking about day-to-day changes—he's after the ones that are 10 times larger. At the moment, he's considering whether the Internet will be Intel's next 10X change. Software people should consider whether reuse is our industry's next 10X change.

A strategic inflection point doesn't come in a package labeled "SIP." It tiptoes in, enveloped in a black scarf, sealed in a black box, wrapped in black paper, tied with black string. Those who fail to inspect the package immediately will later find a black card under the string with the inscription "Don't open until it's over."

Martin A. Goetz seems to echo the black card's sentiment. In a recent *Computerworld* column (Jan. 20, 1997) Goetz, the holder of possibly the first software patent, called the search for the fountain of reuse "futile." There are not just "hurdles to overcome," he writes.

"Reusability will *never* become widespread."

Reading this, those with their heads in the sand can take comfort. Yet Goetz seems not to have noticed that software reuse of a sort has been around since the first programmer reused a program coded in 0s and 1s. Today many developers take code from their hip pockets that amounts to 10 to 20 percent of their projects. Ed Yourdon calls this *passive reuse.* These developers work for companies that have no active reuse program. Evidently Goetz has noticed that even now this describes most software organizations.

> Why should executives turn their organizations upside down for slowly developing results?

But why would software executives want to turn their development organizations upside down for results that develop slowly and can be difficult to quantify? Because others are already doing it and reaping huge rewards.

ACTIVE REUSE PROGRAMS

Those of us who read north woods stories as teenagers remember Hudson's Bay Company. Founded by fur trappers in 1670 as a trading post, Hudson's Bay has not only survived but thrived: It is Canada's largest department store chain. Over the past 300 years, it has surmounted a lot of SIPs—one may be software reuse. The company's latest achievement is 85 to 90 percent reuse on six applications ranging in size from 100,000 to 4 million lines of code (*Computerworld*, Oct. 14, 1996). Hudson's Bay used Paul Bassett's frame technology (*Framing Software Reuse: Lessons from the Real World*, Prentice Hall, 1996).

In his book, Bassett cites the case of a $12 billion global company that attained 95 to 99 percent reuse. One of its tactics, Bassett says, is to buy weaker companies, eviscerate their information systems, and substitute its own frame-based systems. The company does this with 40 frame engineers instead of the several thousand programmers typical in companies of its size.

Ivar Jacobson, Martin Griss, and Patrik Jonsson list half a dozen projects in the 90-percent range in an upcoming book from Addison Wesley. And Griss has also outlined some reuse programs in operations (*Object*, Feb. 1995):

- bus-based operation support systems at AT&T in C,
- scientific and spacecraft software at NASA in Fortran,
- instrument and printer firmware at Hewlett-Packard in C,
- financial and insurance software in Cobol, and
- experience with Visual Basic and object-oriented reuse at Verilog SA, Brooklyn Union Gas, and Ascent Logic.

THE CARROT

In an analysis of 15 projects from nine companies employing frame technology, QSM Associates documented cost reductions averaging 84 percent and time-to-market gains of 70 percent, compared to the average of the 4,000-project database maintained by Quantitative Software Management Inc. (Although I've written articles and books with Lawrence H. Putnam of the latter company, I was not involved in the QSM Associates' study.) At the CEO level, gains of this magnitude are the stuff of strategic-plan breakthroughs.

Over time, no status quo can compete with productivity improvements like

Continued on page 119

Reprinted from *IEEE Computer*, Vol. 30, No. 4, Apr. 1997, pp. 119-120.

these. Achievements of this magnitude warrant the suspicion that something big is in the wind. The number of companies employing active reuse is high enough to establish that reuse on this scale is possible at the current state of the software art.

THE CATCH

Reuse at the 90-percent level sounds at first blush like Grove's 10X factor. If a company reuses 90 percent and develops only 10 percent, it appears to do only 10 percent as much new work. The catch is that the work is not split 90-10—at least not at first. Reused software has to come from somewhere; it takes effort to develop, time to prepare, and money to store. More time and effort go into convincing application developers to use the code that's there. As a result, the net cost curve looks something like Figure 1.

Considering these factors alone, early returns fall far short of Grove's 10X mark. In addition, other factors influence returns. For example, Hudson's Bay director of development support, Mary-Jane Jarvis, points out one cost factor: Not every developer conceptualizes reuse well. Such skill is different from writing code. To overcome this mind-set, Hudson's Bay enlisted consulting help in applying frame technology. This help cost "in the low seven figures" over three years, according to *Computerworld*.

MAKING REUSE HAPPEN

It is easy to see why Goetz can believe that "The simple truth is that trying to find and maintain reusable code for enterprise applications just isn't cost effective or practical." Early on, the facts are fuzzy.

What must software executives do to overcome this fuzz? A very senior executive has to start the ball rolling. Only a high-level executive can champion the multiyear investment that reuse requires.

However, mid-level executives, people who deal with the outside world, "are often the first to realize that what worked before doesn't quite work any more; that the rules are changing," Grove tells us. Unfortunately, they often ". . . don't have

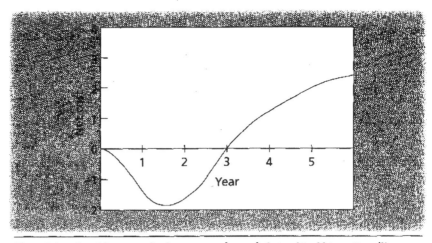

Figure 1. Investment in reuse extends over several years before net cost becomes positive. Initially, a company invests in planning, domain analysis, architecture evolution, and developing reusable components. Only after several years do the savings from reused components begin to offset initial investments.

an easy time explaining it to senior management." Many companies stall here. They don't have a plan for dealing with order-of-magnitude change.

Suppose a senior executive does see the opportunity. The next step is to appoint a small planning group, first to figure out the advantages in more detail and second to develop an implementation plan. In general, a senior executive can't just order reuse—the planning group has to sell the rest of the management team. They will all have a long, tough slog, made easier if they see the reuse path and are convinced the end result will be worth the effort. Then management has to lay out a future-with-reuse vision to every employee.

What has to change? The project-centric structure of most software organizations, that's all. Traditionally, the project had full responsibility for capturing and analyzing requirements, establishing architecture, designing, implementing, testing, and installing the software. Projects have not tried actively to reuse in any of these stages.

Reuse lifts development focus to a domain level above the project. The domain covers a score or more of related systems, and someone has to analyze the requirements it imposes. They must also construct a general architecture that covers all the domain systems—a more complicated task than analyzing a single project. Moreover, how does a company accustomed to charging activities to a project allocate costs for a domain architecture?

Parts of a domain architecture will include components that are candidates for reuse. Who should develop these components? How should a company

allocate development costs? Stockpile components? Who alerts the application engineers to their availability?

"In almost all cases, a simple architecture, a separate component group, a stable application domain, standards, and organizational support are the keys to success," Griss wrote in his *Object* article. "Correct handling of these (largely nontechnical) issues is almost always more critical to successful reuse than the choice of specific language or design method."

Issues like these can require significant time to analyze. Here, I emphasize only a simple point: Creating an organization that reuses software is *difficult*. That is why many companies have failed in their attempts. This is the current reality that occupies Goetz.

It is unclear how rapidly companies will move toward reuse. Perhaps we need to know much more about how to do it. Perhaps software development has yet to pass the SIP labeled reuse. I believe it is on the curve racing toward it.

It seems certain that the move to software reuse is well under way, though, as usual, the wind blows dust in the eyes of those bold enough to raise their heads above the sand. If you are a senior executive, it is time to listen to the sounds the SIP wind carries. If you are a software professional, contribute your ideas to that wind—it may blow in the face of your senior executive. ❖

Ware Myers is a freelance writer and contributing editor for IEEE Software *magazine.*

William B. Frakes, *Virginia Polytechnic Institute and State University*
Sadahiro Isoda, *Toyohashi University of Technology*

◆ *Implementing system-atic reuse is risky. Not doing it is also risky. Trying systematic reuse unsuccessfully can cost precious time and resources and may make management skeptical of trying it again. But if your competitors do it successfully and you do not, you may lose market share and possibly an entire market.*

Software reuse — broadly defined as the use of engineering knowledge or artifacts from existing systems to build new ones — is a technology for improving software quality and productivity. Individuals and small groups have always practiced ad hoc software reuse. Now many organizations want to achieve systematic reuse, which is domain focused, based on a repeatable process, and concerned primarily with the reuse of higher level life-cycle artifacts, such as requirements, designs, and subsystems.

A key concept in systematic reuse is the domain, which may be defined as an application area or, more formally, a set of systems that share design decisions. Systematic software reuse thus is a paradigm shift in soft-ware engineering from building single systems to building families of related systems. The goal of software-reuse research is to discover systematic procedures for engineering new systems from existing assets.

COMPETITIVE ADVANTAGE

The potential effect of systematic reuse on competitiveness is profound. Companies compete within domains, and — as Barry Boehm's well-known analysis shows — software accounts for most of the cost of many systems, a trend that is accelerating rapidly.[1] Companies that do a better job of understanding their domains and implementing systematic reuse will have a powerful competitive advantage.

Success Factors of SYSTEMATIC REUSE

0740-7459/94/$04.00 © 1994 IEEE

Reprinted from *IEEE Software*, Vol. 11, No. 5, Sept. 1994, pp. 14-19.

SIGNPOSTS AND LANDMARKS: A REUSE READING LIST

I selected these references to give you quick access to various reuse technologies, not for their historical importance. They also provide pointers to other sources. The reuse literature is skewed towards reporting successes; failures are largely unreported. This is unfortunate, because failures can often be at least as instructive as successes.

Domain analysis:

♦ G. Arango, "Domain Analysis Methods," in *Software Reusability*, W. Schaefer, R. Prieto-Díaz, and M. Matsumoto, eds., Ellis Horwood, New York, 1994.

♦ *Domain Analysis and Software Systems Modeling*, R. Prieto-Díaz and G. Arango, eds., IEEE CS Press, Los Alamitos, Calif., 1991.

Reusable component design:

♦ J.E. Hollingsworth, *Software Component Design for Reuse: A Language Independent Discipline Applied to Ada*, doctoral dissertation, Ohio State University, Columbus, 1992.

♦ B.W. Weide, W.F. Ogden, and S.H. Zweben, "Reusable Software Components," in *Advances in Computers, Vol. 33*, M. Yovits, ed., Academic Press, New York, 1991, pp. 1-65.

Reuse libraries:

♦ W.B. Frakes and P. Gandel, "Representing Reusable Software," *Information and Software Tech.*, Oct. 1990, pp. 47-54.

♦ W.B. Frakes and T. Pole, "An Empirical Study of Representation Methods for Reusable Software Components," *IEEE Trans. Software Eng.*, Aug. 1994.

Software factories:

♦ M. Cusumano, *Japan's Software Factories — A Challenge to U.S. Management*, Oxford University Press, New York, 1991.

Generative methods:

♦ J.C. Cleaveland, "Building Application Generators," *IEEE Software* July 1988, pp. 25-33.

♦ C. Krueger, "Software Reuse," *ACM Computing Surveys*, Feb. 1992.

Reengineering:

♦ *Software Reengineering*, R. Arnold, ed., IEEE CS Press, Los Alamitos, Calif., 1993.

Legal Issues:

♦ W. Tracz, "Legal Obligations for Software Reuse: A Repository Scenario," *American Programmer*, April 1991, pp. 12-17.

Management:

♦ M. Griss, J. Favaro, and P. Walton, "Managerial and Organizational Issues: Starting and Running a Software Reuse Program," in *Software Reusability*, W. Schaefer, R. Prieto-Díaz, and M. Matsumoto, eds., Ellis Horwood, New York, 1994.

Measurement:

♦ W.B. Frakes and C. Terry, "Software Reuse Models and Metrics: A Survey," Tech. Report 94-27, CS Dept., Virginia Tech, Falls Church, Va, 1994.

Surveys of Industry Reuse Practices:

♦ W.B. Frakes and C.J. Fox, *Software Reuse Survey Report*, Software Engineering Guild, Sterling, Va., 1993.

♦ J. Morrison et al., *Software Reuse in Japan*, Technology Transfer Int'l, Colorado Springs, Colo., 1992.

Edited collections:

♦ *Software Reusability, Vol 1. and Vol. 2*, T.J. Biggerstaff and A. J. Perlis, eds., ACM Press, New York, 1989.

♦ *Tutorial: Software Reusability*, P. Freeman, ed., IEEE CS Press, Los Alamitos, Calif., 1987.

♦ *Software Reusability*, W. Schaefer, R. Prieto-Díaz, and M. Matsumoto, eds., Ellis Horwood, New York, 1994.

♦ *Software Reuse: Emerging Technology*, W. Tracz, ed., IEEE Press, New York, 1988.

Conferences and workshops:

Conferences and workshops are also good sources of information and inspiration. The International Conference on Software Reuse and the Annual Workshops on Software Reuse have been very helpful.

The first two international meetings on reuse (in Dortmund, Germany, in 1991 and Lucca, Italy, in 1993) were actually workshops (IEEE CS Press, Los Alamitos, Calif., published the proceedings of the Italy workshop).

The next meeting is the International Conference on Software Reuse in Rio de Janeiro in November (IEEE CS Press, Los Alamitos, Calif.).

The Annual Workshops on Software Reuse (also known as the WISR workshops) began in the late 1980s. Proceedings of the workshops are available via anonymous ftp from the University of Maine at gandalf.umcs. maine.edu, in library pub/WISR.

Electronic newsletter:

ReNews, an electronic software reuse newsletter, provides software reuse information, including component sources, tool and database descriptions, articles, announcements and summaries of workshops and conferences, experience reports, bibliographies, and reviews of books and articles. ReNews is affiliated with the IEEE Computer Society's Technical Council on Software Engineering, Subcommittee on Software Reuse. Back issues are available via anonymous ftp at ftp.vt.edu in pub/reuse.

— *William Frakes, Virginia Tech*

Worldwide, many commercial, academic, and governmental organizations are devoting significant resources to software reuse.

♦ In the US, reuse programs are underway at commercial organizations like AT&T, Digital, Hewlett-Packard, IBM, Microsoft, and Motorola and at governmental organizations like the US Department of Defense's Advanced Research Projects Agency, Software Technology for Adaptable, Reliable Systems, and the Defense Information Systems Agency/Center for Information Management. The federal government is attempting to build large national software-asset repositories, such as ASSET (Asset Source for Software-Engineering Technology) and Mountainnet. And at least one standards group, the Reuse

Interoperability Group, is attempting to develop integration standards for the myriad libraries that are emerging.[2]

♦ In Europe, the European Space Agency, Siemens, and the European Strategic Program for Research in Information Technology report major efforts.

♦ Japanese companies have been exploring reuse for years, some for more than a decade. Many people believe the software factory concept has given Japan the leadership in reuse; the box on p. 18 gives some details about their efforts.

There is also rapid growth in the commercial marketplace for reuse-related products and services, such as consulting, components, library tools, and tools that support the design and generation of reusable software.

CRITICAL FACTORS

Despite all this work, implementing a successful systematic reuse program is difficult and risky. An organization that attempts it must successfully address a wide range of problems, both technical and nontechnical. There is no cookbook solution — each organization must analyze its own needs, implement reuse measurements, define the key benefits it expects, identify and remove impediments, and manage risk.[3] Reliable data on how much this costs and the benefits an organization will derive is insufficient.

The articles in this issue reflect this diversity, addressing issues from management, measurement, law, economics, libraries, and the design of reusable software.

Management. Systematic reuse requires long-term, top-down management support because

♦ it may require years of investment before it pays off, and

♦ it involves changes in organizational funding and management structures that can only be implemented with upper management support.

Without such long-term support and guidance, none of the other reuse activities is likely to be successful. There are many management tasks to implement a systematic reuse program, including educating personnel, creating and managing incentives, and leading a change in culture. Two articles in this issue discuss some of these management issues. Danielle Fafchamps describes four ways to organize a reuse program along producer-consumer models and, based on a study done at HP Labs, offers some advice to managers about each model. Rebecca Joos reports on Motorola's experiences, good and bad, in implementing systematic software reuse and provides some guidance on reuse implementation and technology transfer.

Measurement. As with any engineering activity, measurement is vital for systematic reuse. In general, reuse benefits (improved productivity and quality) are a function of the reuse level achieved.[4] The *reuse level* — the ratio of reused to total components — may involve the reuse of components developed outside the system (*external reuse level*) or for the system (*internal reuse level*). The reuse level, in turn, is a function of reuse factors. *Reuse factors* are the things that can be manipulated to increase reuse, and they fall into four categories: managerial, legal, economic, and technical.[3]

Many kinds of reuse measures have been reported, from the amount of code reused to the economic effect of reuse. The first article, by Wayne Lim, discusses some of these economic issues and reports various measures of improved quality and productivity observed at Hewlett-Packard.

Legal. Legal issues, many of them unresolved, are also important. What are the rights and responsibilities of providers and consumers of reusable assets? Should a purchaser of reusable assets be able to recover damages from a provider if the component fails in a critical application? Legal issues are less of an impediment for reuse within an organization, but will increase as reusable assets cross organizational boundaries.

> ### THERE IS INSUFFICIENT RELIABLE DATA ON THE BENEFITS AND COSTS OF REUSE.

Economics. Systematic reuse requires a change in economics. Costs incurred by a project that creates reusable assets must be recovered from the users of those assets. One study has found that some assets must be reused more than 13 times to recover development costs.[5] An organization must be able to do a cost-benefit analysis to determine if systematic reuse is feasible. The article by Lim reports on various measures of improved quality and productivity observed at HP.

Design for reuse. Designing for systematic reuse requires domain engineering. Domain engineering has two phases, domain analysis and domain implementation. *Domain analysis* is the process of discovering and recording the commonalties and variabilities of the systems in a domain.[6] Several domain-analysis methods have been proposed; Steven Wartik and Rubén Prieto-Díaz have published a brief survey and comparison of them.[7] *Domain implementation* is the use of the information uncovered in domain analysis to create reusable assets and new systems. There are two main approaches to domain implementation, one based on parts and the other on formal languages. Parts-based reuse is familiar to most programmers, who routinely combine reusable functions, packages, and objects with new components to construct new systems. The article by Werner Staringer

PROGRESS IN REUSE IN JAPAN

In Japan, software development is done mainly by mainframers and their subsidiaries, and their major products are customized. This differs from the package market in the US, and has greatly influenced reuse. By the end of the 1980s, each of the Japanese mainframers — NEC, Hitachi, Fujitsu, and Toshiba — had developed their own integrated software-development environments and all of them support reuse.

REUSE TECHNOLOGY. Hitachi's Eagle environment[1] lets software engineers reuse standard program patterns (or "skeletons") and functional procedures (about 1,600 data items and routines for I/O data conversion and validation) to write business applications in Cobol or PL/I. Eagle provides two sets of program patterns, one for batch programs and the other for on-line programs. The former consists of 31 types, including file conversion, editing, updating, and report generation, and the latter consists of 45 types, including inquiry, database updating, and data entry.

Eagle's capability is limited in the sense that software engineers must add their own coding to the Eagle-generated programs or modify them. Nevertheless, at Hitachi the *generation rate* — the ratio of generated to total lines of code is now between 60 and 98 percent.

As Japanese mainframers have succeeded in reusing code and design, they are now trying to extend their coverage to application architectures. Fujitsu reports that systems analysis of business applications can be greatly improved by the reuse of application architectures.[2] To define an application architecture, they analyzed an existing business package, a production-management package for medium-size manufacturers that ran on PCs and small mainframes. The application consists of 500 Cobol programs.

Fujitsu had been selling the package together with a customization service. However, it was taking 30 person-months to customize each package. This large cost caused the company to think about reusing application architectures, which in this case is essentially the same as systems analysis.

To analyze the package, Fujitsu got information from the developers and the system engineers who customized it. They then modeled the architecture using 14 different representations, including business-function structure graphs, transaction flows, and transaction file tables. The final documentation amounted to several hundred pages. They experimented reusing the architecture for the systems analysis of a typical application system. This time, the customization took only four person-days.[2]

Encouraged by these favorable results, Fujitsu is developing a standardized methodology, AA/BR (Application Architecture/Business Rule Modeling) Modeling and a supporting CASE tool, AA/BR Modeler, to accumulate reusable models. And its System Engineering Group now assigns development teams to specific industries. Currently, 65 projects are creating business models using the AA/BR methodology and CASE tool. They expect the number of such projects will increase to 200 by March 1995.

SUCCESS FACTORS. The importance of managerial aspects in fostering reuse is now becoming better understood. At NTT, the Software Laboratories' reuse project lasted four years and involved as many as 600 engineers. NTT learned that the critical success factors are senior-management commitment, selection of appropriate target domains, systematic development of reusable modules based on domain analysis, and several years' continuous effort.[3]

Technology transfer is a major issue in managing for reuse. Japanese mainframers are generally believed to be advanced in software reuse, but it is rather unlikely that every one of their software-developing departments enjoys high reusability. It is more likely that some are successful, but most are reluctant to apply it, for various reasons.

Toshiba's Fuchu Factory had great success in applying library-based software reuse to its process-control software in the early 1980s.[4] However, Toshiba develops everything from large information-processing systems to electrical appliances, so not every department applied these lessons.

Now the company's System and Software Engineering Laboratory, which is responsible for developing reuse methods and tools, has developed a reuse course for managers and senior engineers that it hopes will facilitate the transfer of reuse technology. The two-day course consists of lectures, hands-on exercises, and discussion. Sample topics are reuse fundamentals, reuse-oriented software development, domain analysis, and managerial aspects. Classes are held at the central location and at local development sites.

INDEPENDENTS. Independent Japanese software houses are at a disadvantage because they work in various domains and on several platforms. Yet several companies have been persistent about reuse. Nippon Novel employs about 100 software engineers developing software for measurement, process control, CAD/CAM, communications, and factory automation. Their reuse program, began in 1987, uses a cash-incentive system: Nippon Novel pays software engineers five cents per line of code when they register and when they reuse a module. The developer of the reused module gets another one cent per line of code when it is reused. Last year, the program cost about $10,000.

In addition to these activities, universities and industry labs are pursuing advanced research. For example, ATR Communication Systems Research Laboratories is researching design-history reuse.

REFERENCES

1. M. Tsuda et al., "Productivity Analysis of Software Development with an Integrated CASE Tool," *Proc. Int'l Conf. Software Eng.*, CS Press, Los Alamitos, Calif., 1992.
2. A. Yoshioka and K. Hashimoto, "A Practice in Reuse of Business Model," *Proc. Symp. Software Reusability*, Information Processing Society of Japan, Tokyo, 1992 (in Japanese).
3. S. Isoda, "Experience Report of Software Reuse Project: Its Structure, Activities, and Statistical Results," *Proc. Int'l Conf. Software Eng.*, IEEE CS Press, Los Alamitos, Calif., 1992.
4. Y. Matsumoto, "Some Experiences in Promoting Reusable Software Presentation in Higher Abstract Level," *IEEE Trans. Software Eng.*, May 1984, pp. 502-513.

— Sadahiro Isoda, Toyohashi University of Technology

in this issue describes how his project used commercial components to build a financial application.

However, although some general principles have been identified,[8] there is still no complete method for designing reusable components. Making components reusable often means adding functionality to the component and complexity to the interface, while minimizing the negative effect on execution time and program size. Important software-engineering principles such as data abstraction, encapsulation, and controlled optimization are critical to the design of good reusable components. This issue includes an article by Bruce Weide, William Ogden, and Murali Sitaraman that describes how to look at algorithms as reusable objects.

Domain implementation approaches based on a formal language capture domain knowledge in a programming language or generator that can be used to create part or all of a new system. This type of reuse requires a more formal knowledge of the domain, but may also have greater payoffs. In this issue, Don Batory and colleagues describe a productive research program to build application generators that has identified interesting commonalties in the generator domain. The article by James O'Connor, Catharine Mansour, Jerri Turner-Harris, and Grady Campbell describes domain implementation in a case study of an industrial command-and-control system. Finally, a short case study by Ernesto Guerrieri describes the development of an application generator at Digital.

Libraries. Once an organization acquires reusable assets, it must have a way to store them, search for them, and retrieve them — a reuse library. There is an extensive body of literature on methods and tools for creating reuse libraries. Many representation methods from library science, artificial intelligence, and other disciplines have been tried, at least experimentally. An article in this issue, by Scott Henninger, describes both a tool — Code-Finder — and an empirical study of its effectiveness versus other methods in helping users form queries.

In this issue, we aimed to provide a summary of the basic concepts, potential, and risks of systematic software reuse, data on reuse costs and benefits, a summary of reuse activities in various software organizations, and some key research results. We hope this information encourages you to begin the process of systematic reuse in your organizations, or at least to begin studying it in greater detail.

Implementing systematic reuse involves risk. Not doing it is also risky. Trying systematic reuse unsuccessfully can cost an organization precious time and resources and may make management skeptical of trying it again. On the other hand, if your competitors do it successfully and you do not, it may mean the loss of market share and possibly the loss of an entire market. ◆

REFERENCES

1. B. Boehm, *Software-Engineering Economics*, Prentice-Hall, Englewood Cliffs, N.J., 1981.
2. J. Moore et al., "Reuse Library Interoperability Group (RIG): Purpose and Progress," *Proc. Tri-Ada*, ACM Press, New York, 1993.
3. W. Frakes, "Software Reuse as Industrial Experiment," *American Programmer*, Nov. 1993, pp. 27-33.
4. W. Frakes, "An Empirical Framework for Software Reuse Research," *Proc. Third Annual Reuse Workshop*, Syracuse University CASE Center Tech. Report 9014, Syracuse University, Syracuse, N.Y., 1990.
5. J. Favaro, "What Price Reusability? A Case Study," *Ada Letters*, Mar. 1991, pp. 115-124.
6. *Domain Analysis and Software Systems Modeling*, R. Prieto-Díaz and G. Arango, eds., IEEE CS Press, Los Alamitos, Calif., 1991.
7. S. Wartik and R. Prieto-Díaz, "Criteria for Comparing Reuse-Oriented Domain Analysis Approaches," *Int'l J. Software Eng. and Knowledge Eng.*, Oct. 1992.
8. W. Tracz, "The 3 Cons of Software Reuse," *Proc. Third Annual Reuse Workshop*, CASE Center tech. report, Syracuse University, Syracuse, N.Y., 1990.

William Frakes is an associate professor and director of the computer science program at Virginia Polytechnic Institute and State University in Falls Church. He has written many technical papers and books including *Software Engineering in the UNIX/C Environment* (Prentice-Hall, 1991) and *Information Retrieval: Data Structures and Algorithms* (Prentice-Hall, 1992). He edits *ReNews*, an electronic software reuse newsletter.

Frakes received an MS from the University of Illinois at Champaign-Urbana and an MS and a PhD, both from Syracuse University. He chairs the IEEE Technical Council on Software Engineering subcommittee on software reuse, and is general chair of the Third International Conference on Software Reuse.

Sadahiro Isoda is a professor at Toyohashi University of Technology. He recently left NTT after 23 years in the Software Laboratories. He has authored many technical papers. His research interests include CASE, design methodologies, software reusability, metrics, project management, and human factors.

Isoda received a BS, an MS, and a PhD, all from the University of Tokyo. He is a member of the IEEE TCSE subcommittee on software reuse, chair of the Information Processing Society of Japan's special-interest group for software engineering, and general chair of the First Asia-Pacific Conference on Software Engineering.

Address questions about this issue to Frakes at Computer Science Dept., Virginia Polytechnic Institute and State University, Falls Church, VA 22042; frakes@sarvis.cs.vt.edu or to Isoda at Toyohashi University of Technology, Tenpaku-cho, Toyo-hashi-shi, 441 Japan; isoda@tutkie.tut.ac.jp.

Chapter 5

RELIABILITY

The papers in this section focus on predicting, measuring and assessing software reliability (whatever that means). In fact, each paper takes great care in defining just what software reliability is, because software reliability is often such a fuzzy notion. Most importantly, reliability must be a measurable quantity (see the paper by Everett) and not just a heuristic notion of some customer. Without a measure of reliability, software project managers are doomed to ever-unreliable software—at least in the customers' eyes.

The paper by Everett and Musa is very important because they are among the founders of the science of software reliability.

Measuring software reliability

*Code must be reliable
from the surprisingly
divergent viewpoints
of software developers,
testers, and users*

Software reliability can mean different things to different people in different situations. A software developer, who views code as instructions to hardware, may judge them reliable if each software requirement is executed properly by a related set of those instructions. A user sees the same software as a set of functions and deems it reliable if nothing malfunctions.

The two viewpoints may yield contradictory estimates of the same software's reliability. For example, someone placing a telephone call at a time when all circuits are busy may be dropped mid-call by a system seeking to balance the load on the overall system and keep as many people as possible on the line. To the caller, the system looks unreliable; to the developer, it is working exactly as required.

Conversely, the same person calling from New York City to San Francisco is happy to find that calls always go through. But because of a fault in the system, all calls between those two points are routed through Chicago. The user thinks the system is reliable, but the phone company staff who maintain the system see the unusually high volume of traffic through Chicago and know something is wrong.

Examining the component concepts of that vague term "reliability" should clarify why its measurement is difficult. It should also reveal what issues require further exploration and definition before reliability measurement becomes as straightforward for software as for hardware.

MANY PRODUCTS. The notion of software reliability borrows heavily from its counterpart in hardware: a reliable system is one that works correctly over a long period of time. But in hardware, the final product—say, an automobile—is not the only product of development. There are many intermediate products: the requirements that specify

Shari Lawrence Pfleeger   Mitre Corp.

the automobile's characteristics and functions, the architectural layout of its parts and wiring, and the prototype built to test the reliability of the design before it enters manufacture. The final car will not be reliable unless the requirements, the design, and the individual parts are all reliable.

Similarly, computer code—1s and 0s—is only the final product of software development. The intermediate products are the requirements specifying the functions the software must perform; the design drawn from the requirements and used by the programmers to generate code; and even the plans for testing the software.

All those intermediate products of development can and should be considered when evaluating a software system's reliability. The requirements specify how reliable the code must be. The design must implement the requirements in such a way that the specified reliability is likely to be achieved. The test plans measure how well the code meets the requirements.

FINDING THE SOURCE. But testing may uncover not just mistakes in the code but also problems with the design and the requirements. Since correcting a problem in the requirements costs only 1 percent as much as fixing code, early reliability prediction can save money and time.

> Fixing a problem in
> the requirements costs
> 1% as much as fixing
> the resulting code

To describe problems in software, the IEEE/American National Standards Institute (ANSI) Standard 982.2 distinguishes among errors, faults, defects, and failures. While all the definitions are related, differentiating among them assists software developers in pinpointing the source of a problem.

According to the IEEE/ANSI standard, an *error* is a human mistake that results in incorrect software. For example, a user may have omitted a critical requirement in the software specification, so that the software developers design an inappropriate product. Similarly, the developers may have misinterpreted a requirement, or translated incorrectly from design to code.

The resulting *fault* is an accidental condition that causes a unit of the system to fail

to function as required. Thus, the fault is a manifestation of an error in the software. Sometimes, faults are called bugs—parts of the software needing to be fixed.

Faults often lead to a *defect*—an anomaly in a product. Defects include problems not only with the code (the final product) but also with the design and requirements (intermediate products). Defects include an ambiguous requirement, an omission in a design document, a fault in code mature enough for test or operation, an incorrectly specified set of test data, an incorrect entry in the user documentation, and more. And it is defects that lead to failures.

A *failure* occurs when a functional unit of the software-related system (including the software-driven hardware) either can no longer perform its required function, or cannot perform it within specified limits.

CAUSE AND EFFECT. Human errors, software faults, and product defects describe the causes of problems, whereas functional failures describe the effects.

The cause of each problem must be traced to its root, because that determines the problem's impact on system reliability. A design flaw is often more serious than a simple software fault. Consider an analogous situation in automobile production, where testing has shown that a new car is likely to explode when hit from behind. If the root cause is that the gasoline tank is made from inferior metal, then the solution may simply be to find a new metal supplier. However, if the root cause is faulty design—the placement of the gasoline tank—then the automobile may need total redesign.

In the same way, an intermediate product may be ultimately responsible for unreliable software. A human may misinterpret a critical requirement, leading to a bad design, resulting in bad code. Such a chain of events is often harder to remedy than a misplaced comma in code.

Note that faults, defects, and failures represent dissimilar points of view. Faults and defects are what the developer and maintainer see: they view the system from the inside out, tracking faults and defects to find the cause of problems. On the other hand, failures represent a user's view of the system: the concern is how the system functions (or fails to), regardless of cause.

An error can occur from either point of view. The user may err in specifying the requirements for a system or in using the system. Alternatively, the developer may code

0018-9235/92/$3.00©1992 IEEE

incorrectly or misinterpret a requirement. Either error can lead to faults and/or failures. **TOUGH TO MEASURE.** The distinctions among errors, faults, defects, and failures are important because reliability, often viewed in terms of software faults (the developer's view), is officially defined in terms of functional failures (the user's view).

As defined by IEEE/ANSI Standard 982.2, software reliability is "the probability that software will not cause the failure of a system for a specified time under specified conditions." This definition parallels that of the hardware world. But any attempt to measure software reliability quantitatively, according to the standard IEEE/ANSI definition, runs into several problems.

First, the standard IEEE/ANSI definition is not accepted by everyone who writes reliability requirements. The interpretations of the term as expressed in user requirements are many and varied. Some indeed follow the IEEE/ANSI definition and deal with the user's view of the system (looking at failure information). Others focus on characteristics of the code as seen by the developer (looking at faults). Different measures may be needed to capture each.

Second, the standard requires tracking the use of the system over time while noting the number of failures. But when reliability requirements are strict, it may be impossible to test the system for long enough to verify a very low probability of failure. Or the system may be untestable in the field, as are several of the systems proposed for the U.S. Strategic Defense Initiative.

Perhaps most serious, the standard IEEE/ANSI definition requires the system to be completely designed, developed, and operational before reliability can be measured. That leaves developers with no direct, preliminary measures of reliability while the software is being written—even though software is harder and more costly to fix when complete than while still in development. **REAL WORLD.** Broadly speaking, there are two approaches to measuring the reliability of finished code. The first, a developer-based view, focuses on software faults; if the developer has grounds for believing that the

1. Some existing software reliability indicators

Measure	Purpose	Definition	When to use
(obscured) *reliability*	*(obscured)* *reliability*	*(obscured) very* *(obscured) high, based on* *Cocomo cost driver[a]*	*For the requirements* *specification*
Run reliability	Predicts final software reliability	Given k randomly selected runs during a specified time, probability that all k runs give correct results	Whenever set of possible discrete input patterns and states is well-defined
Fault density	Predicts remaining faults	Number of faults divided by thousands of lines of code (reported by severity level[b])	During testing
Mean time to discover next k faults	Predicts time to reach reliability goal	Based on certain reliability models, observed times until last failure divided by number of failures from start of test to now, plus observed time between the two failures	During testing
Independent process reliability	Measures service reliability	Sum of correctness delta function weighted by user profile[c]	During testing, when processes are still logically independent and can be tested separately
Failure rate	Indicates growth in reliability as a function of test time	Cumulative probability distributions based on certain reliability models	In acceptance testing
Mean time to failure	Predicts stability of system	Mean observed times to next failure (either clock time or execution time)	In acceptance testing

a Cocomo stands for Constructive Cost Model, a cost-estimation technique.
b Severity level is how much impact a failure may have on a system ranging from, for example loss of income through loss of subsystem function or of total system to loss of life.
c The correctness delta function maps a correct response as 1, an incorrect one as 0, weights the results by the likely use of each function, and adds them to yield a figure of merit.

system is relatively fault-free, then the system is assumed to be reliable. The second, a user-based view more in keeping with the standard IEEE/ANSI definition, emphasizes the functions of the system and how often they fail.

In the first approach, the developer may collect information about fault density: the number of those faults discovered per 1000 lines of code. The developer then tracks the total number of unique faults in a given time interval. This number of faults divided by the total number of lines of code in the final product yields the fault density. By comparing fault density numbers for similar systems, the developer can judge whether the current system has been tested thoroughly. In

addition, the developer can infer the likely reliability of the software once it is installed in the field.

Alternatively, the developer may use a technique called fault seeding to estimate the number of faults remaining in the existing software. The quality-control team deliberately inserts into the software faults representative of the kinds observed to have occurred in the past (such as transposed 1s and 0s, or an incorrect exponent, or a branch to a wrong place in the code). The distribution of the faults matches the probability distribution previously observed on similar projects.

Then, the test team searches the code for all faults. In theory, if they discover all the seeded faults, the testing has been thorough enough to uncover all the accidental unseeded faults as well. The ratio of discovered non-seeded to seeded faults is taken to indicate the number of faults remaining in the code, the thoroughness of testing, and—indirectly—the system's reliability.

THE FAULT WITH FAULTS. The problem with the fault-seeding approach is that it does not look at failures in any context. Faults may exist in the code but not affect user function (for example, in income-tax-computation software, a fault may cause certain programmed equations not to work in the case of someone having negative income—but since no one has negative income, the fault does not matter). The system is thus faulty but reliable, according to the standard IEEE/ANSI definition.

Defining terms

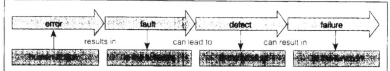

Error: any human mistake that results in incorrect software; errors include an omission of a critical requirement in a software specification, a developer's misinterpretation of the requirement, or an incorrect translation from design to code.
Fault: an error's manifestation in software that causes a functional unit of the software system to fail in performing its required function; sometimes called a "bug," a fault is a part of the code that needs to be fixed.
Defect: an anomaly in any intermediate or final software product resulting from an error or fault, ranging from an incorrectly specified set of test data to an incorrect entry in user documentation.
Failure: inability of a functional unit of the system depending on the software to perform its required function, or to perform the function within required limits.

Moreover, all the fault-based techniques can be misleading: the fact that many faults are discovered can mean that testing is thorough; but it can also mean that many more faults remain in the code.

For this reason, John Musa, supervisor of software quality at AT&T Bell Laboratories in Whippany, N.J., and others have concentrated on a failure-based approach to reliability. Musa broke new ground in 1975 by defining software reliability as how closely user requirements are met by a computer program in actual operation. His definition incorporates the profile of the user's probable usage of the various system functions (an "operational profile") and counts in only the time the system is running, rather than clock time. Musa suggested that reliability be considered as the probability of failure-free operation of a computer program for a specified time—for example, software reliability of 0.92 for 8 hours of execution.

One technique uses failure profiles, tracking failures in several categories of severity level. That is, failures can be classified in terms of the severity of their effect(s) on the system. For example, developers of a telecommunications system may use three levels of severity. Level 1 is minor, resulting at most in loss of income (example: system consistently underreports connection time by one minute when billing). Level 2 is major, producing partial loss of function (example: system cannot forward calls for all exchanges). Level 3 is critical, entailing total loss of a key function (example: no calls can be made to the East Coast). Cumulative failures may be tracked over time, where time may be measured in a variety of ways, including execution time, clock time, and usage time. The failure profile may be viewed for the overall system, for subsystems, and even for modules. The shape of the resulting curve is then used to project when testing will be complete, assuming sufficient test coverage.

Another technique is the analysis of time between failures. A model of failure rate is chosen (based on which models have been most accurate for similar software applications), and estimates are made of initial fault content (number of faults), normalizing constants (distribution of faults throughout the code), and initial mean time to failure. The model is then used to estimate the number of remaining faults, the ultimate mean time to failure, and hence the system's overall reliability.

Many such failure-rate models exist, including some based on mathematical models of a non-homogenous Poisson process and on a Bayesian model. As might be expected, choosing the correct model is a challenge with failure-based approaches.

All those approaches, however, depend on

2. Levels of reliability of code

Type of testing	What is tracked	Reliability measured			
		Modules	Subsystems	System	Functions
Unit	Faults	X			
Integration	Faults	X	X		
System	Faults	X	X	X	.
Acceptance	Failures	X	X	X	X

the software system's being nearly complete and look primarily for mistakes in the code. Ideally, well before the system is cast into code, there should be some way of evaluating the reliability of all the early and intermediate products, including the requirements and the design, so as to predict the reliability of the code.

As of now, no proven ways exist of evaluating the reliability of a system's requirements or design. At best, the probability that the design will result in reliable code can be assessed only in terms of measurements that may indicate the likely reliability. Examples are design complexity, the number of defects discovered in a design review, or the density of defects relative to some measure of the design's size [Table 1].

Note that none of these indicators is a direct measurement of reliability, nor is any of them a foolproof, accurate predictor of the required reliability. Neither do developers always have methods to examine intermediate code products to reassure them that the final code will meet the system's reliability requirements. At best, intermediate indicators suggest trends.

Thus, although reliability can be expressed in quantitative terms when defining the system's requirements, there are only indirect ways of controlling this feature during the system's development. Furthermore, although it may be possible to measure the completed system's reliability, it may not be possible to change the system at that point if it is found to be unacceptable.

THEORY VS. PRACTICE. This gap between theory and practice—between predictions of reliability from indirect indicators (such as the number of design defects) and actual measurements of reliability (such as the number of failures over time)—is quite wide and narrowing very slowly. Several circumstances contribute to this situation.

First, regardless of whether reliability is defined in terms of software faults or functional failures, it is difficult to generalize from measurements of the reliability of software subsystems to the likely reliability of the system as a whole. There are a host of reasons, among them the fact that the reliability of the individual units indicates nothing about the reliability of the connections and sequencing among units.

More fundamentally, Maria Teresa Mainini of Esacontrol, Genoa, Italy, and Luc Billot of CISI Ingénierie, Rungis, France, point out that testing various subsets of the system actually conveys different views of reliability and different test results [Table 2]. Unit testing, integration testing, and system testing, for example, which each focus on identifying software faults, say something about the reliability of individual modules, of subsystems (that is, collections of reliable modules) and of the system, respectively. But it is not until acceptance testing that the test team looks directly at functional failures to evaluate the system's actual operational reliability and to verify its functionality is as specified in the requirements.

To be sure, in some cases the earlier measures (of faults) can be linked to predict what later measures (of failures) are likely to be. But as pointed out earlier, faults in the code are not the only causes of failure. For example, users may misuse the system because of a poor design. Thus, the indicators of software reliability should be viewed in the context of what question is being asked. Otherwise an inference about ultimate reliability from earlier indicators could be inappropriate.

Finally, even when there is agreement on a definition of reliability and it is measured in the correct context, a simple measure may not be enough to capture the measurer's intent. If so, it is better to view reliability as a composite of measures of the various products of development in the context of the reliability goals. In fact, in many cases, the reliability of the earlier products sets an upper limit to the reliability of the final product. For example, an inherently unreliable design may never yield reliable code.

A composite approach to reliability is timely. For years, software engineering researchers have defined simple one-dimensional metrics to measure complex things: usability, design complexity, maintainability, and more. Only now are researchers acknowledging that a broader perspective is needed. The simple measures must be combined to form a multidimensional composite, and for complete understanding, each measure must be interpreted in context.

THREE LEVELS OF MEASUREMENT. At least three steps are needed to implement this composite approach for reliability indicators at the early stages in software development, as well as help developers choose which set of mathematical models is appropriate in the

> Ideally, there should be some way of evaluating the reliability of the requirements and design

evaluation of software faults or functional failures at later stages. The steps involve defining reliability, identifying what about it needs to be known, and then measuring a variety of characteristics that help answer critical questions [Table 3].

Step one is crucial, since reliability presents a different aspect to developer, maintainer, and user. Each definition must be placed in the context of an overall system view of someone who understands the need for reliability.

The importance of this top level cannot be underestimated. Consider what happens when an error occurs in an airplane's software. Usually, the supporting system tries to compensate so as to maintain system integrity. No general, systemwide failure occurs; the plane must keep flying no matter what, so each contributing subsystem must keep working.

In a telephone system, though, a similar error is usually handled by restarting an entire system or subsystem: the problem call is dropped, and the remaining system is intact. Such an approach is appropriate for communications but is out of the question for aerospace applications. Each system's needs dictate opposite interpretations of reliability.

Next, at the middle level of the reliability measurement framework, the overall definition of reliability is used to develop a model of the system from a given viewpoint. The model should show how and when the viewer must predict or verify the current reliability of the system. To illustrate, a system model can show how reliability is assessed from the design, is predicted from design and code characteristics, and improves during testing. This model makes it possible to determine the reliability goals of the system and to pose questions about those goals that measurement can answer.

To revert to the phone system and airplane: the model for the first reflects the definition that a failure may be counted only when the entire system ceases to work,

3. Three levels of reliability measurement

Beholder	View	Model	Definition
User	Pilot	Airplane is a collection of interdependent key subsystems	Total system works properly
	Telephone caller	Network is a collection of independent but connected subsystems	A chain of subsystems works properly
Developer	Airplane control software developer	Software controls a collection of interdependent key subsystems	All key subsystems work properly
	Switch software developer	Software connects available independent subsystems	At least one chain of key subsystems works properly
Maintainer	Airplane control software maintainer	Software enhancement at the least maintains system reliability by maintaining or increasing the reliability of each key subsystem	Same as for airplane control software developer
	Switch software maintainer	Software enhancement at the least maintains system reliability by maintaining or increasing the number and reliability of connections	Same as for switch software developer

Beholder	Reliability view	Reliability goal	Reliability questions	Reliability indicators/measures
Pilot	Sees airplane as the sum of its subsystems	Maintain flight	Can plane maintain flight at all times?	Number of failures of total system over time Number of failures of key subsystems over time
Telephone caller	Sees telephone system as a connection between self and called party	Obtain and maintain connection	Can caller be connected with called party? Can caller and called party stay connected for duration of call?	Number of disconnects (failures) over time
Airplane control software developer/ maintainer	Sees airplane as a sequence of interdependent subsystems (sequential reliability)	Maintain flight	Can overall system maintain flight? Can key subsystems meet required reliability?	Number of failures of total system of time Number of failures of key subsystems over time Number of faults discovered per subsystem Depending on goals, reliability of system can be the minimum, maximum, or product of subsystem reliabilities
Switch software developer/ maintainer	Sees telephone system as a multitude of parallel connections (parallel reliabilities)	Maintain maximum number of connections	Does any new connection lower system reliability? What is the minimum acceptable system reliability?	Number of failures (fewer than acceptable connections) over time Number of individual connections dropped over time Depending on goals, reliability of system can be the minimum, maximum, or product of 1 minus subsystem reliabilities

Set initial goals for software reliability
→ Collect data on early software products (e.g., design defects)
→ Analyze data for indicators of reliability of final system
→ Predict reliability of actual system
→ Develop final code
→ Collect faults/failures data
→ Analyze data for actual reliability
→ Revise reliability goals, if necessary
→ Answer reliability questions
→ Correct code
→ Meet reliability goals

How much testing is enough?

When is software deemed to be reliable enough to release to the customer? Software developers vary in how they combine software-reliability measures and models to make that decision. One decision technique is the zero-failure method of Motorola Inc., headquartered in Schaumburg, Ill., outlined by Ralph Brettschneider in the July 1989 issue of *IEEE Software*.

The zero-failure method specifies the number of hours of testing needed without a failure before the software is deemed ready for release to the customer. If even one failure is detected during this target test time, then the request for release to the customer is denied and testing must be continued.

According to Brettschneider, the zero-failure method—like other reliability models—is based on several key assumptions, of which two are particularly important.

First, the longer that testing proceeds without a failure, the more likely it is that the number of failures remaining is very small. Specifically, the zero-failure method assumes that the rate at which failures are discovered decreases exponentially as testing progresses.

Second, the zero-failure method assumes that testing is representative of the actual use of the software in the field, and that the probability of discovering failures is constant and equal for all kinds of failures.

To apply the method, Motorola sets a reliability goal in terms of an average number of failures per thousand lines of code. To calculate the number of failure-free test hours required, three inputs are need-ed: the permissible average number of failures due to faults embedded in the code sent to the customer; the total number of test failures detected so far; and the total number of hours the software has been tested up to the discovery of the last failure.

The Motorola zero-failure method sets forth a formula for calculating the number of hours needed to test without failure before the software can be deemed reliable.

As an example, Brettschneider considered a 33 000-line revision to a program. Up to now, 500 hours of execution time have revealed 15 repairable failures. No failures have been discovered in the past 50 hours since the last repair. If the goal is to deliver a product with no more than one failure (1 out of 33 000 lines or 0.03 failure per thousand lines of code), has the software now been tested enough?

Using the formula, Brettschneider showed that Motorola's test organization must test the 33 000 lines of code for another 27 hours with no failure discovered before the software is deemed ready to ship to the customer. If a failure occurs, however, the clock must be reset and testing must continue until there are 77 continuous hours without a failure.

Brettschneider's example shows that while measurement cannot ensure reliability, it can guide the development process and minimize the probability of unreliable software. Just as Motorola has done, other software developers can build or borrow a reliability model based on past experience and use it to increase confidence in the effectiveness of their testing. —*S.L.P.*

---

whereas the model for the airplane deems it a failure when any key function stops working correctly.

Finally, the bottom level addresses the actual measurement values. During data collection and analysis, where information is gathered to instantiate the model, questions are answered, the answers viewed in the context of the overall system, and decisions made accordingly. At this lowest level, the measures of reliability may support quite contrary decisions for seemingly comparable failures. In the extreme, a telephone system with 100 dropped calls (partial failures) and zero complete system failures may be considered reliable, while an airplane with the same track record may be a dead loss.

Approaching reliability in this way provides a three-level framework for the process of reliability measurement: build a process or system model to depict the relevant issues, decide what questions are to be answered and define measures that address the questions, and gather information to help find the answers.

BURNING ISSUES. Models and measures of hardware reliability have been invaluable in assuring users that their hardware will function properly over time. So it is encouraging that the same notions are being applied to software reliability in the hope of generating similar assurances—especially when software has become a key part of almost all systems that are in use today.

But current efforts have a long way to go. Close to home, the telephone system is still subject to embarrassing failures due to unreliable software: a widespread telephone outage in June and July 1991 was caused by one line of a subcontractor's code that had not been tested thoroughly ["Faults & failures," *Spectrum*, May 1992, p. 52].

Clearly, several issues must be addressed, or addressed more completely, before complete confidence can be reposed in the ability to predict and measure software reliability. At a minimum, researchers must:
• Build a family of traditional and non-traditional models of reliability, including parameters to determine which model is best for a given situation.
• Generate indicators of reliability early in the development process.
• Define the reliability of artifacts other than code.
• Determine composite measures of reliability that reflect the reliabilities of related artifacts.
• Suggest additional techniques for using reliability information to guide software development and maintenance.

This blueprint for the future suggests areas for researchers to investigate.

TO PROBE FURTHER. The 1988 *IEEE Guide for the Use of IEEE Standard Dictionary of Measures to Produce Reliable Software*, *IEEE Standard 982.2*, discusses almost three dozen commonly used indicators of reliability, summarizing the underlying theory and giving examples of how the indicators can be used.

Bev Littlewood, in his article "Theories of Software Reliability: How Good Are They and How Can They Be Improved?," discusses the pros and cons of several popular models of software reliability. The paper was published in *IEEE Transactions on Software Engineering*, Vol. SE-6, no. 5, September 1980, pp. 489–500.

Ralph Brettschneider, in "Is Your Software Ready for Release?," published in the July 1989 issue of *IEEE Software*, pp. 100, 102, and 108, gives a concrete, mathematical example of how a tailored reliability model is used to decide when testing is complete at Motorola Inc.

In the January 1990 issue of *Software Engineering Journal*, Vol. 5, no. 1, pp. 27–32, Maria Teresa Mainini and Luc Billot in their paper "PERFIDE: An Environment for Evaluation and Monitoring of Software Reliability Metrics During the Test Phase" supply an example of the actual tools and techniques used to evaluate reliability on a large project.

John D. Musa's seminal paper on defining reliability as a measure of how closely user requirements are met is "A Theory of Software Reliability and its Application," published in the *IEEE Transactions on Software Engineering*, September 1975, Vol. SE-1, no. 3, pp. 312–27.

Musa, Anthony Iannino, and Kazuhira Okumoto, in their textbook *Software Reliability: Measurement, Prediction, Application* (McGraw-Hill, New York, 1987), survey numerous leading approaches to the subject, including the development of an operational profile, choice of a reliability model, and use of the profile and model to guide software testing.

Musa summarized some of his approaches in "Tools for measuring software reliability," published in *IEEE Spectrum*, February 1989, pp. 39–42.

The second edition of *Software Engineering: The Production of Quality Software* (Macmillan, New York, 1991) by the author of this article discusses reliability in the context of the overall software development process.

ABOUT THE AUTHOR. Shari Lawrence Pfleeger (M) is a principal scientist at Mitre Corp.'s Software Engineering Center in McLean, Va., whose current research focuses on software metrics and the software development process. The author of two textbooks and more than two dozen journal articles in mathematics and computer science, Pfleeger's numerous IEEE activities include being a member of IEEE Software's Industrial Advisory Board. She also is a member of the Association for Computing Machinery, where she chairs the Committee on the Status of Women and Minorities in Computing. ◆

Predicting Software Reliability

Alan Wood
Tandem Computers

Critical business applications require reliable software, but developing reliable software is one of the most difficult problems facing the software industry. After the software is shipped, software vendors receive customer feedback about software reliability. However, by then it is too late; software vendors need to know whether their products are reliable before they are delivered to customers. *Software reliability growth models* help provide that information. Unfortunately, very little real data and models from commercial applications have been published, possibly because of the proprietary nature of the data.

Over the past few years, my colleagues and I at Tandem have experimented with software reliability growth models. At Tandem, a major software release consists of substantial modifications to many products and may contain several million lines of code. Major software releases follow a well-defined development process and involve a coordinated quality-assurance effort. We applied software reliability modeling to a subset of products for four major releases. This article reports on what we have learned.

We collected defect occurrence times during system test and statistically correlated the test data with known mathematical functions, called software reliability growth models. If the correlation is good, then the function can be used to predict future failure rates, or the number of *residual defects* in the code. We found that the correlation with a simple exponential model was good and that this model can reasonably predict the number of residual defects in our delivered software.

Table 1 shows the predicted number of residual defects versus the number of defects actually found in the first year of product use. The predictions are excellent except for Release 2. Although Release 2 was a major release, it received very little customer use because it was quickly followed by Release 3, so we cannot accurately compare our predictions with field use. To compensate for this lack of field data, we developed a model that combined the system test data from Releases 2 and 3. As Table 1 shows, the combined model prediction does correlate well with field use.

The defect data used in creating our models is considered proprietary,

Experiments with software reliability growth models show that simple models of execution time and cumulative defects predict a number of defects that is close to the number reported in the field.

Table 1. Model predictions versus field experience.		
Release	**Predicted residual defects**	**Defects in first year**
1	33	34
2	65	8
3	24	20
4	10	9
2/3	33	28

Reprinted from *IEEE Computer*, Vol. 29, No. 11, Nov. 1996, pp. 69-77.

241

but we have developed a way to transform the data so it can be published. We hope its publication will stimulate other software reliability practitioners to provide similarly transformed data for use in future model development and testing.

A tutorial of software reliability modeling is outside the scope of this article. For a very brief overview of how these models work and the models we evaluated, see the "Software reliability growth models" sidebar.

SUMMARY OF FINDINGS

The predicted number of defects is a software reliability growth model parameter that is statistically estimated from test time and defect data. There are many different software reliability growth models in the literature and many different types of data and statistical techniques that can be used in combination with these models. We experimented with different models, data, and statistical techniques with the following results:

- *Test time.* This can be measured using calendar time, the number of tests run, or execution time. We found that execution time is the only option that works in our environment.
- *Defect data.* At Tandem, potential defects are recorded as Tandem Problem Reports. Analyzing the TPRs to establish which ones are *truly* new defects takes time. We found that we can use TPR data as a surrogate for defect data, which enhances our ability to make real-time decisions during the test phase.
- *Grouped data.* TPRs and test logs are gathered weekly and grouped. We thought we might need to collect data more often, but we found that the weekly grouped data works fine.
- *Growth model.* We first established our evaluation criteria (See the sidebar "What makes a model useful?" for more information about how we evaluated these models.) and then evaluated the eight models. We found that a simple exponential function outperformed more complex models in terms of both stability and predictive ability.
- *Statistical technique.* Fitting a mathematical function to data involves estimating the function's parameters from the data. The two most popular estimation techniques are *maximum likelihood* and *least squares.* We found that least squares provides the best point estimates and that maximum likelihood is better for deriving confidence intervals.

Software reliability growth models

Reliability—usually defined as the probability that a system will operate without failure for a specified time under specified operating conditions—is concerned with the *time between failures* or its reciprocal, the *failure rate.* The data in this article comes from a test environment, so here I use *defect-detection rate* instead of failure rate.

A defect detection is usually a failure during a test, but test software may also detect a defect even though the test continues to operate. Defects can also be detected during design reviews or code inspections, but I do not consider those activities in this article.

Each defect is fixed when it is discovered. This decreases the number of defects in the code (excepting defects introduced by repair), so the defect-discovery rate should decrease. In other words, the length of time between defect discoveries should increase. When the defect-discovery rate reaches an acceptably [...] he software is deemed suitable to ship. However, it [...] extrapolate from defect-discovery rate in a test environment to failure rate during system operation, primarily because it is hard to extrapolate from test time to system operation time. Instead, the expected number of remaining defects—*residual defects*—provide an upper limit on the number of unique failures customers could encounter in field use.

Knowing the number of residual defects helps determine whether or not the code is suitable for customer use and how much more testing is required if it is not. It also provides an estimate of the number of failures that customers will encounter when operating the software. This estimate helps define the appropriate levels of support that will be required for defect correction after the software has shipped.

Two types. Software reliability growth models are mathematical functions that describe defect-detection rates. There are two major classes: *concave* and *S-shaped* models, illustrated in Figure A. Concave models are so-called because they bend downward. S-shaped models, on the other hand, are first convex and then concave. This reflects their underlying assumption that early testing is not as efficient as later testing, so there is a "ramp-up" period during which the defect-detection rate increases. This period terminates at the inflection point in the S-shaped curve.

The most important thing about both models is that they have the same *asymptotic behavior:* The defect-detection rate decreases as the number of defects detected increases, and the total number of defects detected asymptotically approaches a finite value. (A third, less-common class of models, called *infinite failure models,* assumes the code has an infinite number of failures.)

Of course, defect repair can introduce new defects. Some models explicitly account for new defect introduction during test by modify-

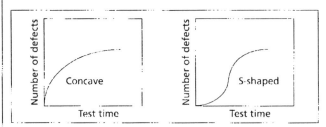

Figure A. Most software reliability growth models fall into two classes: concave and S-shaped.

ing the mathematical form of the model, while others assume new defects are accounted for by the statistical fit of the model to the data. In practice, either method works as long as the model does a good job of fitting the data.

Prediction formula. Software reliability growth models predict the expected number of defects, μ, at test time, t, or $\mu(t)$. For example, the Goel-Okumoto exponential model expresses this as

$$\mu(t) = a(1 - e^{-bt})$$

where a is the expected total number of defects and b is the *shape factor*, or the rate at which the defect-detection rate decreases. The Goel-Okumoto model has two parameters; other models can have three or more parameters. Table A summarizes the eight models we evaluated.

Table A. Software reliability growth models.

Model name	Model type	$\mu(t)$	Comments
Goel-Okumoto (G-O)[1]	Concave	$a(1-e^{-bt})$ $a \geq 0, b > 0$	Also called the Musa model or exponential model.
G-O S-Shaped[2]	S-shaped	$a(1-(1+bt)e^{-bt})$ $a \geq, b > 0$	Modification of G-O model to make it S-shaped.
Hossain-Dahiya/G-O[3]	Concave	$a(1-e^{-bt})/(1+ce^{-bt})$ $a \geq, b > 0, c > 0$	Solves a technical condition with the G-O model. Becomes same as G-O as c approaches 0.
Gompertz[4]	S-shaped	$a(b^{c^t})$ $a \geq 0, 0 \leq b \leq 1, 0 < c < 1$	Used by Fujitsu, Numazu Works.
Pareto[5]	Concave	$a(1-(1+t/\beta)^{1-\alpha})$ $a \geq 0, \beta > 0, 0 \leq \alpha \leq 1$	Assumes failures have different failure rates and failures with highest rates removed first.
Weibull[6]	Concave	$a(1-e^{-bt^c})$ $a \geq, b > 0, c > 0$	Same as G-O for $c=1$.
Yamada Exponential[7]	Concave	$a(1-e^{-r\alpha(1-e^{-\beta t})})$ $a \geq 0, r\alpha > 0, \beta > 0$	Attempts to account for testing effort.
Yamada Raleigh[7]	S-shaped	$a(1-e^{-r\alpha(1-e^{-\beta t^2/2})})$ $a \geq 0, r\alpha > 0, \beta > 0$	Attempts to account for testing effort.

1. A.L. Goel and K. Okumoto, "A Time Dependent Error Detection Model for Software Reliability and Other Performance Measures," *IEEE Trans. Reliability*, Aug. 1979, pp. 206-211.

2. S. Yamada, M. Ohba, and S. Osaki, "S-Shaped Reliability Growth Modeling for Software Error Detection," *IEEE Trans. Reliability*, Dec. 1983, pp. 475-484.

3. S. Hossain and R. Dahiya, "Estimating the Parameters of a Non-Homogeneous Poisson-Process Model of Software Reliability," *IEEE Trans. Reliability*, Dec. 1993, pp. 604-612.

4. D. Kececioglu, *Reliability Engineering Handbook, Vol. 2*, Prentice-Hall, Englewood Cliffs, N.J., 1991.

5. B. Littlewood, "Stochastic Reliability Growth: A Model for Fault Removal in Computer Programs and Hardware Design," *IEEE Trans. Reliability*, Dec. 1981, pp. 313-320.

6. J. Musa, A. Iannino, and K. Okumoto, *Software Reliability*, McGraw-Hill, New York, 1987.

7. S. Yamada, H. Ohtera, and H. Narihisa, "Software Reliability Growth Models with Testing Effort," *IEEE Trans. Reliability*, Apr. 1986, pp. 19-23.

Table 2. Transformed data and predicted total number of defects for four releases

| | Release 1 | | | | | Release 2 | | |
| | CPU hours | Percent CPU hours | Defects found | Predicted total defects | | CPU hours | Percent CPU hours | Defects found | Predicted total defects |
Test week									
1	519	—	16	—		384	—	13	—
2	968	—	24	—		1,186	—	18	—
3	1,430	—	27	—		1,471	—	26	—
4	1,893	—	33	—		2,236	—	34	—
5	2,490	—	41	—		2,772	—	40	—
6	3,058	—	49	—		2,967	—	48	—
7	3,625	—	54	—		3,812	—	61	—
8	4,422	—	58	—		4,880	—	75	—
9	5,218	—	69	—		6,104	—	84	—
10	5,823	58	75	98		6,634	65	89	203
11	6,539	65	81	107		7,229	70	95	192
12	7,083	71	86	116		8,072	79	100	179
13	7,487	75	90	123		8,484	83	104	178
14	7,846	78	93	129		8,847	86	110	184
15	8,205	82	96	129		9,253	90	112	184
16	8,564	86	98	134		9,712	95	114	183
17	8,923	89	99	139		10,083	98	117	182
18	9,282	93	100	138		10,174	99	118	183
19	9,641	96	100	135		10,272	100	120	184
20	10,000	100	100	133		—	—	—	—

TRANSFORMATION TECHNIQUE

As I have mentioned, I applied software reliability growth models to a subset of products of four major software releases. To avoid confidentiality issues, I do not identify specific products and releases, and I have suitably transformed the test data. "Suitably transformed" means that we reach the same conclusions from models of the transformed data and models of the original data.

The transformation technique consists of multiplying

What makes a model useful?

We wanted to know how useful software reliability growth models are for commercial applications. Since none of them will match a company's development and test process exactly, what makes a model useful? During system test, we would like the model to predict the additional test effort required to achieve a suitable quality level (as measured by number of remaining defects). At the end of system test, we would like the model to predict the number of remaining defects that could be experienced as failures in the field.

This leads to two criteria for a useful model:

- *It must become and remain stable.* If a model says there are 50 remaining defects one week and 200 the next, no one is going to believe either prediction. For a model to be accepted by management, its prediction should not vary significantly. Stability is subjective, but in our experience a good rule of thumb is that the pre-

diction should vary by no more than 10 percent from week to week. It would be nice if the model was immediately stable, but stability requires a reasonable amount of data. The literature[3,4] and our experience indicate that the model will not become stable until about 60 percent of testing is complete. Fortunately, this is sufficient, because management will not be closely monitoring the model until near the end of testing.

- *It must be reasonably accurate at predicting the number of defects left at delivery.* A model is reasonably accurate if the number of defects discovered after delivery is within the 90 percent confidence interval developed from the model. Unfortunately, the range defined by the 90 percent confidence interval may be much larger than managers would like. In our experience, 90 percent confidence intervals are often larger than twice the predicted remaining defects.

Release 3				Release 4			
CPU hours	Percent CPU hours	Defects found	Predicted total defects	CPU hours	Percent CPU hours	Defects found	Predicted total defects
162	—	6	—	254	—	1	—
499	—	9	—	788	—	3	—
715	—	13	—	1,054	—	8	—
1,137	—	20	—	1,393	—	9	—
1,799	—	28	—	2,216	—	11	—
2,438	—	40	—	2,880	—	16	—
2,818	—	48	—	3,593	—	19	—
3,574	71	54	163	4,281	—	25	—
4,234	84	57	107	5,180	—	27	—
4,680	93	59	93	6,003	53	29	84
4,955	98	60	87	7,621	67	32	53
5,053	100	61	84	8,783	78	32	44
—	—	—	—	9,604	85	36	45
—	—	—	—	10,064	89	38	46
—	—	—	—	10,560	93	39	48
—	—	—	—	11,008	97	39	48
—	—	—	—	11,237	99	41	50
—	—	—	—	11,243	99	42	51
—	—	—	—	11,305	100	42	52
—	—	—	—	—	—	—	—

the test time by an arbitrary (but convenient) constant and multiplying the number of defects observed by a different arbitrary constant. For this technique to provide the same results as the original data, the predicted number of total defects must be unaffected by the test-time scaling and must scale by the same amount as the defect data.

For example, if we experience 50 total defects and want to scale that to 100, we simply multiply the number of defects reported each week by 2. Now the total number of defects predicted from the scaled data must also increase by a factor of 2. For example, if 75 total defects were predicted by a model based on the unscaled data, then the total defects predicted from the scaled data must be 150. Fortunately, both the maximum likelihood and least squares statistical techniques provide this linear scaling property.[2]

Table 2 shows the data from four separate releases. To transform the data, we first artificially set the total test execution time in Release 1 to 10,000 hours and created a ratio by dividing 10,000 by the the real Release 1 test hours. We then multiplied the test execution time in other releases by this ratio. Similarly, we set the total number of defects discovered in Releases 1 to 100 and then ratioed the number of defects discovered in the other releases appropriately. As the table shows, the four

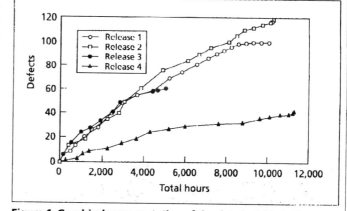

Figure 1. Graphical representation of the data in Table 2. The test data for four releases shows a concave curve.

releases were tested for different lengths of time. Figure 1 depicts the cumulative defect occurrence times.

As Table 2 shows, the *predicted total number of defects* becomes stable at around week 11 or 12 for Releases 1, 2, and 4, which is after approximately 60 percent of calendar test time and 70 percent of execution time. It took longer (percentage wise) for the Release 3 predicted total number of defects to stabilize, probably because there is less total data.

November 1996

73

TEST TIME

The predicted number of total defects in Table 2 have been calculated using execution time to represent the amount of testing. However, you can also measure test time as calender time, particularly if you have a dedicated test group that continuously runs the machines. Although we use our test machines asynchronously, we wanted to see if the amount of testing could be represented by calendar time in our environment.

Table 3 shows the results of fitting Release 4 defects to calendar time. We were unable to get a prediction until week 15 because the curve fit did not converge. After week 15, the prediction was very unstable, especially in comparison to execution time results. Similar results with the other releases indicates that in our environment, execution time is a much better measure of amount of testing.

We also attempted to represent test time using number of tests instead of execution time. This would be a good measure if all tests had a similar probability of detecting a defect, but often that is not the case in our environment. We have some test suites that execute 100 tests an hour and more sophisticated tests that execute one test every 24 hours. More sophisticated test cases usually stress the software more and thus have a higher probability of finding a defect per test case run.

Table 4 shows the results of fitting the Release 3 defects to test cases. Note that the number of test cases increases faster than execution hours. This occurs because many simple automated tests that do not take much execution time are run early in the test phase. Again, the prediction was unstable and did not match the field results in Table 1. Similar results with the other releases indicate that in our environment, execution time is a much better measure of test time than is number of test cases.

DEFECT DATA

At Tandem, potential defects are recorded as Tandem Problem Reports. TPRs are not always defects: They may reflect confusion about how to use the software or what the software is supposed to produce. In addition, due to parallel testing several people may report the same defect, which we call duplicates or rediscoveries. Rediscoveries are not included in the count of unique defects. The amount of nondefects and rediscoveries generated during system test varies over time and by release, but a good estimate is that only 60 to 70 percent of all TPRs are unique defects.

The number of rediscoveries after the software is shipped usually climbs because many customers may encounter the same defect.

The appropriate data to use in software reliability growth models is the number of unique defects—the defect only TPRs. However, it takes time to analyze a TPR and determine if it is a unique defect. We estimate that about 50 percent of TPRs are analyzed within one week and 90 percent are ana-

Table 3. Comparing predictions using execution time versus calendar time for Release 4.

Test week	Execution hours	Percent execution hours	Defects found	Predicted total defects, execution time	Predicted total defects, calendar time
10	6,003	53	29	84	—
11	7,621	67	32	53	—
12	8,783	78	32	44	—
13	9,604	85	36	45	—
14	10,064	89	38	46	No prediction
15	10,560	93	39	48	457
16	11,008	97	39	48	178
17	11,237	99	41	50	125
18	11,243	99	42	51	101
19	11,305	100	42	52	85

Table 4. Comparing predictions using execution time versus number of test cases for Release 3.

Test week	Execution hours	Percent execution hours	Test cases	Percent test cases	Defects found	Predicted total defects, execution time	Predicted total defects, test cases
1	162	3	671	7	6	—	—
2	499	10	1,920	19	9	—	—
3	715	14	2,150	22	13	—	—
4	1,137	23	3,112	31	20	—	—
5	1,799	36	3,802	38	28	—	—
6	2,438	48	5,009	50	40	—	—
7	2,818	56	6,443	64	48	—	—
8	3,574	71	7,630	76	54	163	No prediction
9	4,234	84	9,263	93	57	107	204
10	4,680	93	9,690	97	59	93	152
11	4,955	98	9,934	99	60	87	137
12	5,053	100	10,000	100	61	84	132

Table 5. Comparing predictions using defects versus Tandem Problem Reports for Release 3.

Test week	TPRs reported	Predicted total TPRs	Defects found	Predicted total defects based on defects	Predicted total defects based on TPRs
1	8	—	6	—	—
2	12	—	9	—	—
3	22	—	13	—	—
4	35	—	20	—	—
5	47	—	28	—	—
6	62	—	40	—	—
7	75	—	48	—	—
8	84	213	54	163	127
9	89	159	57	107	95
10	94	143	59	93	86
11	100	145	60	87	87
12	101	147	61	84	88

Table 6. Comparing predictions based on grouped and ungrouped data for Release 4.

Test week	Execution hours	Defects found	Predicted total defects, grouped data	Predicted total defects, ungrouped data (random times)	Predicted total defects, ungrouped data (fixed spacing)
10	6,003	29	84	149	116
11	7,621	32	53	60	61
12	8,783	32	44	57	54
13	9,604	36	45	46	46
14	10,064	38	46	47	47
15	10,560	39	48	47	48
16	11,008	39	48	48	48
17	11,237	41	50	49	49
18	11,243	42	51	49	49
19	11,305	42	52	50	50

lyzed within two weeks, so models based on defect data lag models based on TPRs by about two weeks. Therefore, defect-based predictions lag TPR-based predictions by about two weeks. When you are trying to make a real-time decision about releasing software to customers, models based on current TPR data are more useful than models based on two-week old defect data.

We found that TPRs are an excellent surrogate for defects. As Table 5 shows, the predictions based on TPRs become stable earlier than predictions based on defects because there is more data. The ratio of TPRs to defects (column 2 versus column 4) was used to predict a total number of defects from the TPR model. This ratio is usually about 60 percent.

During system test, we used the TPRs and defects from a few weeks preceding the current test week to predict a ratio of defects to TPRs. We then used this ratio and the current test week TPR prediction to predict expected defects. The results for Release 3 show that, despite a change in the defect-to-TPR ratio from 64 percent in Week 9 to 60 percent in Week 12, this technique still provides a good prediction of total defects.

GROUPED DATA

The best possible data is a list of the exact failure occurrence times and the amount of execution time between each failure. However, our current data-collection process provides only weekly test logs. Therefore, currently we are able to gather only *grouped data*—the number of failures and amount of test time accumulated during a week of system test.

We wanted to determine if having the exact failure occurrence times and test hours would provide better results. To simulate exact data, we took the data for Release 4 and distributed the defects throughout the week in which they were detected, using a random number generator and a fixed pattern. For example, we placed defects at two failure occurrence times during the week, distributing them either randomly or at fixed intervals (2.3 and 4.7 days).

Table 6 shows the results. We had hypothesized that the extra data might cause the prediction to stabilize sooner, but this was not the case. The predictions from the simulated exact data and the weekly grouped data are essentially identical. We conclude that the weekly grouped data works fine for our system test environment. This is useful

Table 7. Comparing predictions from using various models for Release 1.

| Model | Total defects predicted several weeks after the start of system test | | | | |
	10 weeks	12 weeks	14 weeks	17 weeks	20 weeks
Goel-Okumoto	98	116	129	139	133
G-O S-Shaped	71	82	91	99	102
Hossain-Dahiya/G-O	All results same as G-O model				
Gompertz	96	110	107	114	112
Pareto	757	833	735	631	462
Weibull	All results same as G-O model				
Yamada Exponential	152	181	204	220	213
Yamada Raleigh	77	89	98	107	111

There were 134 total defects found for Release 1: 100 in system test, 34 in the field

because it means that we do not have to try to change the data input and collection processes.

GROWTH MODELS

We fit the data in Table 2 to the eight software reliability growth models listed in the "Software reliability growth models" sidebar. Table 7 shows the results for Release 1. The table shows the predicted number of total defects for each model at various times in the test process. Note that most of the models become reasonably stable at about the same time as the Goel-Okumoto model, but their predictions are significantly different from the Goel-Okumoto model.

The S-shaped models (G-O S-shaped, Gompertz, and Yamada Raleigh) all tended to underpredict the residual defects. This is expected because, as Figure 1 shows, the data has the shape of a concave model rather than an S-shaped model. The models that are variants of the Goel-Okumoto model (Hossain-Dahiya/G-O and Weibull) both predicted exactly the same parameters as the Goel-Okumoto model. The other concave model variants (Pareto, Yamada Exponential) both tended to overpredict the number of residual defects.

We conclude that, in our environment, the Goel-Okumoto model was significantly better than the other models at predicting the number of residual defects.

Two-stage models

All of these models assume that the code being tested does not change during test, except for defect repair, and they assume that the effects of defect repair are minimal.

There is a technique that will allow us to account for significant amounts of new code added during the test period, called a *two-stage reliability model*. Theoretically, adding a significant amount of code should increase the defect detection rate. Therefore, the overall curve will look something like Figure 2, in which D_1 defects are found in T_1 time prior to the addition of the new code and an additional D_2-D_1 defects are found in T_2-T_1 time after that code addition. The problem is to translate the data to a result that would have been obtained if the new code had been part of the software at the beginning of the test.[3]

This is the situation we encountered in Release 2. Release 2 was a preliminary release used by very few customers. Release 3 was very similar to Release 2 with some functionality and performance enhancements, and the testing of Release 2 and Release 3 overlapped (Release 2 test week 17 was the same as Release 3 test week 1).

Therefore, Releases 2 and 3 can really be treated as a single release, and Release 3 can be considered as the addition of functionality into the test process. This is the classic setup for a two-stage software reliability model.

Figure 3 shows that the Release 2 and Release 3 data has the shape of the two-stage model shown in Figure 2. Note that the data has an inflection point at about 9,700 hours, which was the start of Release 3 test. When we evaluate this data using the two-stage model techniques, the predicted

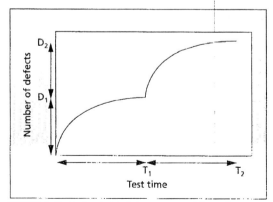

Figure 2. Two-stage model curve, used for releases that add significant functionality during test.

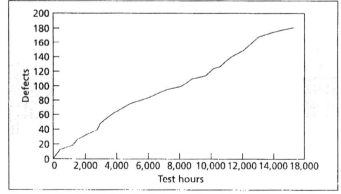

Figure 3. Combined data for Releases 2 and 3, showing an inflection point at 9,700 hours when Release 3 began test.

Table 8. Comparing predictions from maximum likelihood versus least squares for Release 4.

Test Week	Defects	Maximum likelihood				Least squares		
		ML pred.	Lower 5% conf. level	Upper 95% conf. level		LS pred.	Lower 5% conf. level	Upper 95% conf. level
10	29	65	—	—		84	—	—
11	32	43	36	68		53	46	60
12	32	38	35	46		44	39	50
13	36	46	40	65		45	40	50
14	38	51	44	78		46	42	51
15	39	54	46	82		48	43	52
16	39	52	45	74		48	44	53
17	41	57	48	88		50	46	54
18	42	63	51	111		51	47	55
19	42	62	51	106		52	48	56

number of residual defects is 33, which compares favorably with the actual number of 28 field defects (in Table 1) in the first year for Releases 2 and 3 combined.

STATISTICAL TECHNIQUE

The two most common techniques for estimating a mathematical function's parameters from test data are *maximum likelihood* and *least squares*. The maximum likelihood technique estimates parameters by solving a set of simultaneous equations that maximize the likelihood that the observed data came from a function with those parameter values. Maximum likelihood satisfies a number of important statistical conditions for an optimal estimator and is generally considered to be the best statistical estimator for large sample sizes. Unfortunately, the set of equations it defines are very complex and must usually be solved numerically.[3,5]

The least squares approach is to fit the curve described by the function to the data and estimate the parameters from the best fit to the curve. The theory of least squares curve-fitting[3] is that the parameter values must minimize the difference between the data and the function fitting the data. The difference is defined as the sum of the squared errors. This technique is generally considered to be the best for small to medium sample sizes. In this article, the parameter estimates have been calculated using least squares.

Both statistical techniques can be used to derive *confidence intervals*. Since no prediction is expected to match exactly the results from field use, a confidence interval provides a range in which the field results are expected to fall. Table 8 compares the results for Release 4 obtained from the least squares and maximum likelihood techniques (see my technical report for more details[5]). The least squares predictions are more stable and correlate slightly better with field data, but the maximum likelihood results are reasonable.

Table 8 also shows the confidence intervals. The confidence intervals derived from the least squares technique are very small. In fact, they are too small—the confidence intervals for weeks 12-14 do not even include the final total defect estimate. For our data, the confidence interval results obtained with the least squares technique are not very satisfactory. The confidence intervals provided by the maximum likelihood technique are more realistic because they are wider and asymmetric (the upper limit is farther

away from the prediction than the lower limit, which does a better job taking into account the discovered defects). Unfortunately, these confidence intervals are very wide—almost three times larger than the predicted residual defects. Note the range at week 19: The predicted residual defects are 20 (62 predicted minus 42 discovered) while the confidence interval range is 55 (106-51).

ALTHOUGH THEY ARE STILL IN THE EXPERIMENTAL stage, software reliability growth models can be used to provide reasonable predictions of the number of defects remaining, which is an indication of whether the software is ready to release to customers. Our experience has shown that predictions from simple models of defect occurrence times correlate reasonably well with field data. However, the many choices for data representation and model type must be evaluated across multiple software releases to determine the appropriate models and obtain confidence in the results. ∎

References

1. J. Tian, P. Lu, and J. Palma, "Test-Execution-Based Reliability Measurement and Modeling for Large Commercial Software," *IEEE Trans. Software Eng.*, May 1995, pp. 405-414.
2. A. Wood, "Software Reliability Growth Models," Tandem Tech. Report 96-1, Tandem Computers Inc., Corporate Information Center, Cupertino, Calif., 1996.
3. J. Musa, A. Iannino, and K. Okumoto, *Software Reliability*, McGraw-Hill, New York, 1987.
4. W. Ehrlich, S.K. Lee, and R. Molisani, "Applying Reliability Measurement: A Case Study," *IEEE Software*, Mar. 1990, pp. 56-64.
5. A. Mood, F. Graybill, and D. Boes, *Introduction to the Theory of Statistics*, McGraw-Hill, New York, 1974.

Alan Wood is a senior engineer in the Reliability Engineering Department at Tandem Computers. He has 15 years' experience in reliability engineering for nuclear energy, defense, and commercial environments. His current primary research interests are software reliability and client-server availability. He has published more than 20 papers on these topics. Wood received a PhD in operations research from Stanford University. He is a member of IEEE and INFORMS.

Contact Wood at Tandem, 10300 N. Tantau Ave., LOC 55-52, Cupertino, CA 95014-0725; wood_alan @tandem.com.

Software Reliability Measurement

WILLIAM W. EVERETT, MEMBER, IEEE

Abstract—There has been a good deal of interest recently in the emerging discipline of software reliability engineering. This interest can be attributable to the growing amount that software reliability contributes to the overall reliability of products being built. This paper describes the measurement and analysis aspects of software reliability and is intended to provide software engineers and managers a feeling of where and how software reliability measurement can be applied to their projects. It first provides some background for understanding software reliability measurement, and then discusses activities associated with measuring and analyzing software reliability in the context of the software product life cycle.

INTRODUCTION AND BACKGROUND

UNLIKE the field of hardware reliability engineering, software reliability engineering is a relatively new discipline. Because of its newness, there are many aspects of software reliability engineering that are still in a state of flux. However, techniques for measuring and analyzing the reliability of software have reached a stage where they can and should be more widely used during product development.

You might ask, "Why all this concern with software reliability?" In the past, reliability has been equated to hardware reliability. However, the amount that software failures contribute to overall product reliability has been increasing. For example, a survey of customers of one AT&T operations support system product indicated that as many as 4 of 5 failures at customer sites were software related. In addition, the ratio of software to hardware failures is growing to the point where software failures are beginning to predominate. One study summarizing digital switch reported problems between 1984 and 1988 indicated the number of software and hardware problems being nearly equal. Yet a more recent update of such reported problems covering the period March 1988 to March 1989 shows the proportion of software reported problems increasing to two and one-half times the number of hardware reported problems.[1]

The intent of this paper is to describe the measurement and analysis aspects of software reliability engineering. It is intended for those software engineers and managers who may be interested in such questions as: "What are the key notions of software reliability? How can the measurement and analysis of software reliability fit into my product de-

velopment? What can I expect from such measurement and analysis?" The focus of this paper is on developing an appreciation of where and how measurement and analysis of software reliability fit into product development. The specifics on measurement and analysis techniques which would require much more space and time to cover are left to other references such as [4] and [5, ch. 5].

The remainder of this paper is divided into two sections. The first section provides some background on software reliability measurement. First, the notions of failures and faults are contrasted. Then some basic software reliability concepts are described. A brief description of software reliability modeling is provided. And finally, the analysis of hardware reliability is contrasted with that of software reliability.

The second section of the paper discusses activities associated with measuring, analyzing, and modeling software reliability. These activities are discussed in the context of the phases of the software product life cycle. The focus in this section is on failures (what the customer sees) and the rate at which they occur. The thrust of reliability measurement and analysis is to specify what the customer needs in terms of reliability before a software product is built, to validate that these needs are met before delivery of the product to the customer, and to track and monitor that the customer's needs continue to be met after delivery.

Failure versus Fault

Keeping the distinction between failures and faults is important in applying software reliability. Since software reliability is integrally associated with software failures, any discussion of software reliability must start with a definition of software failure. A formal definition of a *software failure* is a departure of the operation of a software system from its requirements. Generally, the requirements are assumed to be explicitly stated in a Requirements Specification. However, in applying software reliability, the notion of requirements may be extended to cover anything relating to the customer's satisfaction with the product. Examples of software failures might be simply the absence of a field in a generated output report. A more serious software failure might result in the system being completely inoperable but recoverable by reinitializing the system software.

On the other hand, a *fault* is an underlying defect in the software. Examples of a fault might simply be an uninitialized variable or an incorrectly coded program statement. Other examples of faults would be an incorrect im-

Manuscript received May 22, 1989; revised September 22, 1989.
The author is with AT&T Bell Laboratories, Middletown, NJ 07748.
IEEE Log Number 8932099.

[1]Some license is taken here in using reported problems as a measure of number of failures (not all failures result in reported problems). However, the intent is to illustrate the increasing importance of software reliability.

Reprinted from *IEEE Journal on Selected Areas in Communications*, Vol. 8, No. 2, Feb. 1990, pp. 247-252.

plementation of a design or requirement specification. Software failures are an external manifestation of the presence of a fault. However, there is not necessarily a one-to-one correspondence between fault and failure. A fault may result in many failures (if the fault is not removed after the first failure is encountered). Also, different faults may cause failures to occur at different rates. On the other hand, a fault may cause no failure at all. This would be the situation if the customer uses the software product in a way that the fault is never encountered under the right conditions to cause a failure.

Customers are not concerned per se with how many faults there are in a software product. They are concerned with how often the software will fail for their intended use and how costly each failure will be to them.

Measures related to faults and fault density (i.e., the number of faults per thousand lines) have been and will continue to be an important in-process metric for software development. In fact, striving to reduce the number of faults introduced in software during a particular stage of development and seeking ways of isolating and removing faults as software moves from development stage to stage can go a long way in improving its reliability. However, to measure reliability of the software from the customer's perspective requires measures related to failures and rates at which failures occur.

Some Basic Concepts

There are two important concepts in measuring software reliability. First, the rate at which software fails is a function of execution time. *Execution time* is a measure of software processing time or CPU time and is generally expressed in terms of CPU-seconds or CPU-hours. To understand this relationship between failures and execution time, consider an extreme situation where a software product is loaded on a computer system but is not processing. No matter how much elapsed time (what we refer to as calendar time) transpires, no failures will occur because the software is doing no processing (and hence the execution time is zero). As the software processes more and more (and hence the execution time increases), the probability increases of first traversing a path in the code that contains a fault and, second, just the right conditions prevail for the fault to cause a failure. There are times when CPU time (and hence execution time) cannot be measured directly. However, under appropriate conditions, execution time can be approximated in other ways. For example, if the utilization of the CPU is relatively constant, then elapsed (or calendar) time multiplied by average utilization is a good approximation to execution time. In another instance, if the mix of types of items (e.g., transactions, jobs, commands) being processed is relatively constant, then execution time is relatively proportional to the number of items processed. The important point to make here is the modeling and analysis of software reliability is done in the execution time domain.

Second, the operational profile plays a large role in how frequently the software fails. An *operational profile* is the set of all the input states to the software together with the frequency with which they will occur in normal operation by the customer. In essence, the operational profile specifies how a customer will use the software product in his or her operating environment ([3] describes an operational profile for one software product).

Software Reliability Modeling

Models play an important role in estimating and analyzing software reliability. Software reliability models generally have the following two components.

• The *execution time component*, which relates the failure of software to execution time, properties of the software being developed, properties of the development environment, and properties of the operating environment. With regard to the execution time component, there are two general classes of models:

—*reliability growth models* (so named because reliability improves with execution time)—these models are particularly applicable during system test because the removal of faults reduces the rate at which failures occur; and

—*constant reliability models* (so named because reliability does not change with execution time)—these models are suitable after the product is introduced in the field when no fault removal is generally occurring.

• The *calendar time component*, which relates the passage of calendar time to execution time and the number of failures that have occurred.

The passage of calendar time depends on the consumption of resources such as processing cycles on a computer system as a function of execution time and number of failures. During system test, other resources such as testers' time in detecting failures, and developers' time in locating and fixing the underlying faults, come into play in relating calendar time to execution time and number of failures. Reference [4] provides a review of existing models and illustrates the use of one set of models in analyzing the reliability of software in a number of situations.

Software versus Hardware Reliability

There are some fundamental differences between hardware and software failures that impact the analysis of hardware versus software reliability. The primary difference is in the underlying mechanisms causing failures. With hardware, failures are generally caused by physical processes related to stresses imposed by the operating environment. Specifically, failures are due to components degrading, deteriorating, or being subjected to environmental shocks.

With software, there is nothing to "wear out." The primary mechanism for failures are the latent faults within the software. These faults may be the result of errors in coding or implementation of design or requirements specifications. However, just the presence of a fault is not enough to cause a failure. First the software must be executing, and second the input being processed during execution must be such that the fault will be encountered under just the right set of conditions that result in a failure.[2]

Just as there are differences in the mechanisms for failures, there are some major aspects in which the analysis of software reliability differs from the analysis of hardware reliability. An example would be the notion that adding redundancy of components improves reliability. Whereas duplicating hardware components will generally improve reliability, duplicating software components will not generally improve reliability. This phenomenon in software is due to the fact that encountering a fault under a given set of conditions that result in a failure of one of the software components will result in the same failure in the duplicate component. The only time this may not occur is when the software components are "independently" developed and thus are not exactly duplicated.

On the other hand, there are a number of similarities in the analysis of hardware and software reliability. These similarities allow the two reliabilities to be combined using reliability block diagram analysis to compute an overall system reliability for a product. More complicated models may be needed if there is significant hardware-software dependence. Chapter 4 of [4] illustrates how hardware and software reliability can be combined to determine system reliability.

SOFTWARE PRODUCT LIFE CYCLE ACTIVITIES

The remainder of this paper will discuss software reliability measurement activities that should be carried out during product development. These activities will be discussed in the context of the various phases of the product life cycle. This paper divides the product life cycle into four phases: *product definition*, *product design and implementation*, *product validation*, and *product operation and maintenance*. Following is a brief description of the primary purpose of each of the life cycle phases. The product definition phase focuses on defining what the customer needs and developing a requirements specification for the product that addresses those needs. In the design and implementation phases, designs are rendered using the product requirements, and these in turn are implemented into the software product. In the validation phase, the software product is certified that it meets the requirements through system testing and field trials. Finally, during the operation and maintenance phase, the product is delivered to and used by the customer. Problems reported by the customer may lead to "software fixes" being developed by the maintenance staff and delivered back to the customer.

Activities During the Definition Phase

Proper product definition is essential for having a successful product on the market. The primary output of the definition phase is a requirement specification for the product.

Reliability objectives should be included as an explicit part of the requirements specification. The first step in setting reliability objectives is to define what a failure is from the customer's perspective. Next, failures should be categorized by the impact they have on customers. A key step is understanding customers' tolerance to failures of different categories and customers' willingness to pay for reduced failure rates in each failure category. Looking at customers' experiences with past and existing products will help in determining these tolerance levels. Another step is assessing the reliability capabilities of products developed by competitors. The information developed in each of these steps can then be used to develop reliability objectives for the product. After such objectives are established for the product as a whole, they must be allocated among the hardware and software components within the product. In effect, a reliability budget is being established for each of the components within the product.

Once reliability objectives are established for software components, the following two important items are needed to proceed.

- *An Operational Profile that Reflects How the Customer Will Use the Product:*[3] An indicated earlier, the reliability of the product will in general depend on the operational profile and therefore must be included as part of the reliability specification. The operational profile in effect defines a "field of use"[4] for the product being developed. This involves a tradeoff. Establishing a wide "field of use" for the product may require multiple operational profiles to fully cover the field of use of the product. This in turn will increase the cost of developing the product. For example, the costs for testing the product will increase, as reliability objectives must now be certified under more than one set of operating conditions.

- *Estimates Relating Calendar Time to Execution Time:* Because the rate at which software failures occur is a function of execution time, such estimates are needed to translate calendar time to execution time. Specifically, these estimates will allow reliability objectives expressed in terms of calendar time (in a form customers can relate to) to be translated into reliability objectives expressed in terms of execution time (in a form that can be measured and analyzed).

Another activity in setting reliability objectives is trading off product reliability, product cost, and product delivery time frame (see [4, ch. 7] for examples). Increased

---

[2]Some hardware failures may also be caused by latent design faults which would be analogous to the underlying mechanism causing software failures.

[3]One approach in characterizing the operational profile is to analyze the frequency that desired features will be used by the customer. In employing the techniques of Quality Function Deployment, one should get customers to quantify how often they anticipate a desired feature will be used in their environment. Getting customers to estimate the "frequency of use" of features is not only useful in characterizing the operational profile, but it is also useful in helping customers to rank the features they desire.

[4]The term "field of use" as used here is borrowed from hardware products. It effectively indicates the operating environments in which the product was intended to be used.

reliability generally means increased development costs and time. It also means increased costs and time for testing the product. An interesting note here is that the cost and time for testing products is becoming a major, if not dominant, component in the overall development cost and time. Some estimates of the development costs devoted to testing and field trials run as high as 40%. Additionally, the testability of the reliability requirements should be reviewed during product definition, as this may have a large impact on the cost of testing the product.

Increases in development costs and times equate to similar increases in the price of the product to the customer and to delays in when the customer will receive the product. The point here is customers will be making tradeoffs among reliability, price, and when the product will be available in selecting the products they will buy. Models can help in making tradeoffs with regard to cost, reliability, and delivery time frame.

Models applied at this stage of development should have strong "descriptive validity,"[5] as the parameters of the model must be estimated from the characteristics of the development and system test environment and the software being developed. Chapters 5 and 7 in [4] describe how certain models can be calibrated and applied prior to system test.

Two questions often asked about applying models during this phase are:

• How accurate are reliability predictions made at this point of product development?

• Is the effort to model reliability at this point worth it?

With regard to the first question, there is not enough information to give a definitive answer. However, the accuracy of predictions is most likely what can be expected for predictions of hardware reliability models and software development effort models (for example, the CO-COMO model discussed in [1]) applied during this phase. For these latter models, errors of 100% order of magnitude have been experienced. In answer to the second question, if the modeling were carried no further than just "predicting software reliability," then the effort would probably not be worth it. However, the modeling should continue into the *design, implementation, validation, operations*, and *maintenance* phases of the software product life cycle. Especially during the *validation* and *operations* phases, modeling will help in structuring a plan for collecting reliability measurement data. The collected data can be used not only to track that reliability objectives are being met, but also can be used to refine the models for subsequent releases of software products. The real utility of modeling is to get into this cycle of model, measure, and refine. Moreover, applying models in this point of the life cycle forces projects to focus up front on issues related to reliability and to baseline assumptions about the reliability of the product before development begins.

<hr>

[5] The "descriptive validity" of a model is its ability to be "explained" by the underlying process being modeled.

Activities During the Design and Implementation Phases

The primary purpose of the design and implementation phases is to turn a requirement specification for a product into a design specification, and then to implement the design into the product. One activity during the design phase is allocating and budgeting software reliability objectives among software components. An analysis should be conducted to ascertain whether the reliability budget can be attained within the proposed design.

Another important activity should be to certify the reliability of "reused" software (not only application software but also system software such as operating system software and communication interface software). There is a strong push to reuse software developed for one product within another product. However, the reliability of the reused software may not be sufficient to satisfy the needs of the new product. Before reusing software in a new product, its reliability should be established through reliability testing under the operating conditions intended for the new product. It is important to use the operational profile for the new product in reliability testing. The reliability of the software using the operational profile for the original product may be significantly different from the reliability using the operational profile for the new product. Once the reliability of the reused software components is established under operating conditions intended for the new product, then software reliability objectives can be allocated among the new software components in a way that overall reliability objectives are met.

The operational profile itself provides an indirect benefit during the design phase. Developers can use information on the frequency of use of different features to weigh alternatives. In addition, because the operational profile limits the field of use for the product, developers can produce simpler designs to satisfy reliability requirements. For example, a designer might opt for a simpler manual recovery design for an operating condition that occurs very infrequently rather than a more complex automated recovery design. In general, simpler designs lead in turn to a more reliable product. In addition, the operational profile indicates "high usage" features that designers can focus their energies on to maximize customer satisfaction.

There are many verification activities that should be going on during the implementation phase. Verification activities such as inspections, unit testing, and integration testing are intended to "verify" that what was *actually* produced within a development stage is the same as what was *intended* to be produced. Verification activities, such as inspections, can be applied to such development stages as specifying requirements, design, and coding (unit implementation). The intention of verification activities is to minimize the propagation of the number of faults introduced in one development stage to another stage. At this time, there is little that can be done to estimate software reliability using measures from such product verification activities as unit test, integration test, or inspections. This is due in large part to the processing frequency of input states during unit and integration testing or the pseudo-processing frequency of input states during inspections. In both cases, the processing frequencies do not match those in the operational profile.

Activities During the Validation Phase

The primary thrust of validation activities is to certify the product is suitable for customer use. Product validation is associated with evaluating a software product at the end of development to ensure it complies with the initial requirements for the product. Product validation activities for software products generally include system test and field trial activities.

Software reliability measurements are particularly useful in this phase in conjunction with reliability testing to monitor the progress of testing and to help in making product release decisions. Reliability testing (also referred to as longevity or stability testing) is conducted to ensure that reliability objectives are met. During reliability testing, input states are generally executed with a frequency that matches what is specified in the operational profile. This type of testing provides a nice alternative way of doing regression testing, particularly when the number of regression test cases becomes large. In a way, this amounts to using statistical sampling to select regression test cases based on the frequency with which they would occur in field use.

The sequence of activities during testing typically proceeds as follows.
- Failures and the corresponding execution time (from the start of testing) are recorded during testing.
- Statistical techniques are used to estimate the parameters of software reliability execution time model components based on the recorded failure data.[6]
- Using the execution time component with the estimated parameters, such useful quantities as present failure intensity and the remaining execution time can be estimated.
- Finally, the calendar time component of the models can then be applied to estimate remaining calendar time needed for testing to achieve a desired failure intensity objective.

Activities During the Operations and Maintenance Phases

The primary thrust of the operations and maintenance phases is to move the product into the customers' day-to-day operations, to support the customer in the use of the product, and to repair or fix faults within the software that are impacting the customers' use of the product.

For those organizations that have operations responsibility for software products, software reliability measurements can be useful to monitor the reliability of the operating software. The results can be used to determine if there is any degradation in reliability that is occurring over time (for example, degradation caused by the introduction of software fixes into the operating environment). Software reliability measurements can also be used in deciding on when to incorporate new software releases into the operating environment. The reliability of the currently operating software should be great enough so that introducing the new software release will not reduce the reliability below a "tolerable" level for the end user of the software product.

Software reliability measures are useful to those who have field support responsibilities for the released product. Failure data collected in the customer's operating environment can be used to verify the customer's perceived level of reliability to the measured reliability of the product. A number of items could be contributing factors to differences in customers' perceived level of reliability and the measured reliability of the product.
- The definition of what the customer perceives as failures is different from the definition used in testing the product.
- The operational profile for the customer environment is significantly different from the operational profile used in testing the product.
- The test environment does not reflect the customer environment in one or more key areas.[7]
- The original reliability objectives set for the product do not truly reflect what the customer originally desired or the customer's desires have changed.

Determining what factors contribute to the differences and feeding information back to the appropriate development phase is an important task.

Software reliability measurement and modeling are also useful for maintenance activities. One prime example is using the frequency and cost of failures to rank the order for repairing underlying faults. Software reliability models can also be used to size maintenance staff for "repairing" faults reported from field sites (see [2]). However, the most important activity that can be conducted at this time is to conduct a "Root Cause Analysis" of field-reported faults.[8] The intent of such an analysis is to determine what stages of the development process such faults are introduced and what changes should be made to the development process to reduce the probability of similar faults being introduced in that stage or propagating to later stages.

---

[6]These are discussed in [4, ch. 12].

[7]For example, simulators may have been used in a test environment to replace actual hardware components that a product is to interface with. This may have been done because of the high cost of including the actual hardware components in the test environment. However, the simulators may not faithfully reflect the operation of the component that is being replaced.

[8]Strictly speaking, faults uncovered during product validation activities such as system test and field trials should also be included.

REFERENCES

[1] B. W. Boehm, *Software Engineering Economics*. Englewood Cliffs, NJ: Prentice-Hall, 1981.

[2] D. A. Christenson, "Using software reliability models to predict field failure rates in electronic switching systems," in *Proc. Annu. Nat. Joint Conf. Software Quality and Productivity*, Washington, DC, Mar. 1-3, 1988.

[3] W. W. Everett, "Experiences in applying software reliability to network operations systems," in *Proc. 4th Annu. Nat. Joint Conf. Software Quality and Productivity*, Washington, DC, Mar. 1-3, 1988.

[4] J.D. Musa, A. Iannino, and K. Okumoto, *Software Reliability—Measurement, Prediction, Application*. New York: McGraw-Hill, 1987.

[5] M. L. Shooman, *Software Engineering—Design, Reliability and Management*. New York: McGraw-Hill, 1983.

William W. Everett (M'88) received the Engineer's degree from the Colorado School of Mines in 1965 and the Ph.D. degree in applied mathematics from the California Institute of Technology in 1970.

He is a Distinguished Member of Technical Staff at AT&T Bell Laboratories. His areas of interest include software engineering, software reliability, and computer systems performance analysis.

Dr. Everett is a member of the Society of Industrial and Applied Mathematics (SIAM).

Qualitative and Quantitative Reliability Assessment

KARAMA KANOUN, MOHAMED KAÂNICHE, *and* JEAN-CLAUDE LAPRIE
French National Organization for Scientific Research

Traditional system reliability efforts have failed to focus on software reliability. To remedy this, the authors propose a method that uses descriptive analyses, trend analyses, and reliability models to control testing activities, evaluate software reliability, and plan maintenance.

During the development of a software system, the supplier must efficiently monitor the development activities; comply with the delivery schedule; predict when a specified level of reliability will be reached, or at least check how well the software will satisfy the customer's requirements; and reduce maintenance efforts. On the other hand, the customer needs a reliable product, delivered on time and at the lowest price. Our method helps reach these goals. It is based on the analysis and evaluation of software reliability by processing failure data collected on a software product during its development and operation.

Traditionally, system reliability efforts have not focused on software reliability. We believe that failure prediction can be improved if software reliability modeling is integrated into an overall approach. The method we propose is based on the combined use of descriptive analyses, trend analyses, and reliability models to control testing activities, evaluate software reliability, and plan maintenance.

0740-7459/97/$10.00 © 1997 IEEE

Reprinted from *IEEE Software*, Vol. 14, No. 2, Mar/Apr 1997, pp. 77-87.

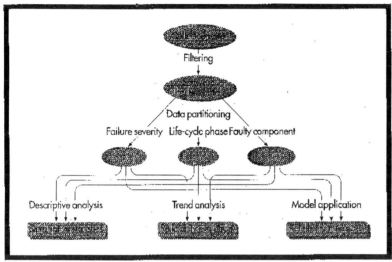

Figure 1. *The various steps of reliability analysis and evaluation.*

Even though each reliability evaluation can be considered a special case due to the diversity of several factors, including

♦ the software's nature and the corresponding failure data,

♦ the development and validation methods adopted,

♦ the organization of data collection, and

♦ the aims of the analysis,
our experience let us define a general method for software reliability analysis that covers the entire life cycle, from development to operational use. This method emphasizes real-time data processing within a controlled environment that allows efficient, real-time feedback. Doing so helps control the development process and quantify software reliability. To facilitate the processing of failure data, we developed the Sorel tool, which allows automatic data processing. The box on page 79 gives a more detailed description of Sorel.

OVERVIEW

The objectives of a reliability study are directly related to the point of view considered—whether supplier or customer—and the life-cycle phase concerned. Generally, the main objectives of development—follow-up, maintenance planning, and reliability evaluation—are expressed as measures.

During software development, important measures to track include

♦ the evolution of the trend—whether reliability increases or decreases—in response to the testing and debugging effort to monitor these activities, and

♦ the number of failures expected to occur over several subsequent time periods so as to plan the test effort and thus the testing time and the size of the test team.

Once the software is implemented and operating, two types of measures become useful.

♦ From the customer's perspective, the failure intensity, mean time to failure, or failure rate are important because they help evaluate whole-system reliability, including hardware and software.

♦ From the supplier's perspective, the expected number of failures among all installations, or the number of corrections to be performed, are important because they help estimate the

maintenance effort still needed.

These measures determine the nature of data to be collected and the kind of data processing to be done. Two categories of data can be recorded:

♦ data characterizing the product itself, the production process, and the use environment, such as the software size, language, functions, current version, verification and validation methods, tools used, workload, and so on; and

♦ data associated with failures and corrections, such as date of occurrence, nature of failures, consequences, fault types, fault location, and so on.

Usually, data is collected through use of failure and correction reports. Figure 1 summarizes the various operations you can perform on the collected data set and the results you may expect from these operations, which include descriptive statistics, reliability evolution, and reliability measures. The collected data may include foreign data, which requires filtering to keep only the data related to software. Depending on your study's objectives, you may perform reliability analysis using the whole data set or subsets of it obtained through data partitioning. The latter approach enables more detailed analyses yielding more elaborate results.

Three types of analysis may be performed on the whole data set and on the derived subsets.

♦ Descriptive analyses are based on statistics that address fault density, the number of faults per release, or combined analyses such as fault location and failure severity. They are not directly related to software reliability evaluation; they enhance knowledge about the software and the corresponding failure data.

♦ Trend analyses concern the time evolution of reliability measures, such as the time to failure or the number of failures, which help gauge the effectiveness of the testing activities to be assessed. Trend analyses also lead to better estimations when using reliabili-

MARCH/APRIL 1997

ty growth models, because those models can be applied directly to subsets of the data that display trends that confirm the underlying assumptions, rather than blindly.

♦ Application of one or several reliability growth models lets you predict the reliability measures based on the observed behavior of the software.

Trend analysis and reliability evaluation are performed on data in the form of time to failure or number of failures per unit of time. The latter are also called grouped data. These values are extracted from the failure and correction reports. The choice between the two forms is governed by the objective of the study and the life cycle phase being analyzed. Grouped data can be collected easily and helps mitigate the impact of local fluctuations on software reliability evaluation. The unit of time used for grouped data is a function of the system usage type and the number of failures occurring during the period analyzed, and may differ for different phases.

FILTERING, PARTITIONING, ANALYSIS

Operations on data filtering, partitioning, and descriptive analysis are specific to the system under study, the way data has been collected, the purpose and structure of the software, and the objectives of the analysis.

You may not need all these successive operations in every reliability study. For example, if you enter the collected data into a database and check it on entry, filtering is not needed. You would perform data partitioning and analysis depending on the level of detail sought.

Collected data may include, in addition to the reports related to actual software failures, extraneous data such as false trouble reports or duplicate data, which must be discarded.

SOREL

Sorel is a software reliability analysis and evaluation tool composed of two modules, for testing trends and modeling the growth of reliability (see Figure A). It can operate on two types of failure data: interfailure times and number of failures per time unit. The two modules operate on the same input-data files, which can be created and changed by any word processing or graphics editor. Numerical results are displayed automatically on the screen during execution; the user can also ask for the corresponding curves. The results are recorded as ASCII files that can serve as input to other applications, allowing for instance comparison of results issued from different models.

Sorel runs on the Macintosh II-xx with an arithmetical coprocessor. We gave the interface special attention, making it interactive, menu-driven, and ensuring that it takes advantage of the Macintosh's multiple-window management facilities. Sorel is modular, so new reliability growth tests and models can be added easily. Written in 5,000 lines of Pascal, it requires about 300 Kbytes of memory.

Figure A. Sorel overview.

REFERENCE

1. K. Kanoun et al., "Sorel: A Tool for Reliability Growth Analysis and Prediction from Statistical Failure Data," *23rd Int'l Symp. Fault-Tolerant Computing*, IEEE Computer Soc. Press, Los Alamitos, Calif., 1993, pp. 654-659.

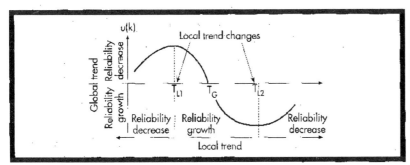

Figure 2. Laplace factor and trend changes.

Rediscoveries—such as multiple activation of the same fault—must be kept when adopting the customer's viewpoint, because they correspond to different failures occurring on the same or a different installation and as such affect observed reliability. Data filtering—also known as data validation—though time-consuming and cumbersome, accomplishes this. It requires precise knowledge of the system and software and you must interview those involved in software testing and data collection. When you enter the trouble reports into a database, you can partly automate the filtering. From our experience[1] and that of others,[2,3] we have found that about half the failure reports generated by a supposed software failure are either unusable or, after a detailed examination, reveal problems that cannot be attributed to software.[4] Thus, data filtering is essential because accurate reliability analysis can only be conducted on filtered data.

You must partition your data into subsets whenever you require a detailed analysis. The most common partitions concern failure severity and faulty software components.

Applying reliability growth models to the most severe failures allows for example evaluation of the software failure rate corresponding to the most critical behavior. This failure rate is generally more significant than that for the whole software product, which may also incorporate failures with no major impact on the system's behavior. Partitioning according to fault location and evaluation of the failure rate of various components allows measurement of each component's influence on the whole failure rate and identification of the most and least reliable components.

Descriptive analysis relies on synthesis of the observed phenomena in the form of control charts or tables that identify the most significant phenomena. The description may consist of simple analyses such as fault density, fault typology, and fault distribution among new, modified, and reused software components. Alternatively, it could derive from a combined analysis, such as the relationship between failure occurrence conditions and criticality; fault location and failure criticality; or the number of faults in the components and the component size. Such statistics are commonly used by some companies.[4,5] The accumulation and analysis of information about several projects, products, and releases provides a company with better insights into its products and the impact of the development process on them.

TREND ANALYSIS

You can analyze reliability evolution with trend indicators. Three simple graphical tests can help determine whether the system becomes more or less reliable:

♦ time to failure,
♦ the cumulative number of failures, and
♦ the number of failures per unit of time (failure intensity).

You derive the trend empirically, using eyeball analysis, from the evolution of the plotted measures. While these plots provide a quick and useful indication of the trend, they may be ambiguous and even misleading in some situations because they fail to offer quantifiable means. Therefore, you need formal statistical tests to enhance confidence in the results. Such tests allow for trend quantification. Various statistical tests such as the Laplace, Kendall, and Spearman tests are available for identifying trends in time-series or grouped data. Previous studies have shown the Laplace test to be optimal within the framework of the most famous software reliability models.[6] This test consists of calculating the Laplace factor, u(T), for the observation period [0, T]. When expressed in terms of time to failure, the Laplace factor is

$$u(T) = \frac{\frac{1}{N(T)} \sum_{i=1}^{N(T)} \sum_{j=1}^{i} \theta_j - \frac{T}{2}}{T \sqrt{\frac{1}{12 N(T)}}}$$

where θ_j is the time to failure j counted from system restart after failure $j - 1$, and N[T] is the number of failures in [0,T]. In terms of $n(i)$, the number of failures during unit of time i, the expression of the Laplace factor is

$$u(k) = \frac{\sum_{i=1}^{k} (i-1)n(i) - \frac{(k-1)}{2} \sum_{i=1}^{k} n(i)}{\sqrt{\frac{k^2-1}{12} \sum_{i=1}^{k} n(i)}}$$

Significance levels are associated with

these statistics. For example, for a significance level of 5 percent, values of $u(k)$ such as $-1.96 \leq u(k) \leq +1.96$ indicate stable reliability over $[1, k]$. In practice, in the context of reliability growth,

♦ negative values indicate a decreasing failure intensity and thus a reliability increase,

♦ positive values suggest an increasing failure intensity and thus a reliability decrease, and

♦ values oscillating between -2 and $+2$ indicate stable reliability.

In its classical form, the Laplace test gives the trend over a given interval of time—the global trend—and identifies the regions of global trend change as indicated by point T_G of Figure 2. The work we have performed[7] allows extension of the Laplace factor to detect the regions of local trend changes as indicated by points T_{L1} and T_{L2} of Figure 2. If you change the origin of the considered interval, and let the observation interval start at T_{L1}, $u(k)$ becomes negative over the whole (remaining) interval. The change in the time origin does not result in a simple translation: removal of failure data from 0 to T_{L1} underlines the local variations and thus amplifies the Laplace factor variation. However, the points of local trend change are preserved.

From a pragmatic viewpoint, using the Laplace factor as a trend indicator, the procedure we've described lets global and local trends be defined as follows:

♦ negative or positive Laplace factor values over an interval indicate a global reliability increase or decrease, respectively, for that interval; and

♦ decreasing or increasing values of the Laplace factor over a subinterval indicate local reliability increase or decrease, respectively, for that subinterval.

In real situations, we use the Laplace factor to analyze the trend, considering its sign (plus or minus) along with its evolution. Doing so lets both global and local trends be identified "at a glance."

Using trend analysis results. Trend analysis is intended only to draw attention to problems that might otherwise pass unnoticed until too late, thus providing an early warning that will likely shorten the search for a solution. It can be used to enrich the interpretation of someone who knows the software from which the data is derived, the development process, and the user environment. Typically, we analyze three trends: decreasing reliability, increasing reliability, and stable reliability.

Decreasing reliability is generally expected and considered normal at the start of a new activity, such as a new life cycle phase, changing test sets within the same phase, adding new users, or activating the system with a different user profile. Decreasing reliability may also result from regression faults. Trend analysis reveals this kind of behavior. If the duration of the decrease seems long, you must pay attention to it. Those situations in which reliability continues to decrease can point to problems in the software: analyzing the reasons for the decrease and the nature of the activated faults is of prime importance in such a situation. This analysis may influence the decision to re-examine the corresponding software part.

Reliability growth that follows a reliability decline is usually welcome because it indicates that, after removal of the first faults, the corresponding activity reveals fewer and fewer faults. When calendar time is used, sudden reliability growth may result from a period during which the system is used less or not at all; it may also be caused by unrecorded failures. When you notice a reliability growth trend, you must take particular care and analyze the reasons for the sudden increase.

Stable reliability indicates that either the software is not receiving corrective maintenance, or the corrective actions have no visible effect on reliability. When the software is being validated, stable reliability with almost no failures means that the corresponding activity has reached "saturation": the application of the corresponding test sets reveals no new faults. At this point, you must either stop testing and introduce new test sets or proceed to the next phase. More generally, we recommend that you continue a test phase as long as reliability keeps growing and end it only when you reach stable reliability with almost no failures. Thus, in practice, if you have not reached stable reliability, your validation team (and its manager) may decide to continue testing before software delivery because it will be more efficient and cost-effective to remove faults during validation than during operation.

For the debugger, however, identifying the region in which the local trend changes is of prime importance: these regions herald the beginning of new trend periods. If the debugger enters a period of reliability decrease, he must be vigilant; he need not wait for the moment when the global trend changes to undertake corrective action. Conversely, if he enters a period of reliability growth, he becomes confident earlier.

As stated earlier, it is more efficient to exploit the results in combination with other criteria such as test coverage and development activities, and with information emerging from the descriptive analyses such as the nature

> **Trend analysis only draws attention to problems that might otherwise pass unnoticed.**

of activated faults, failure consequences, or affected components. An example of applying trend analysis to monitor the development of a real-world software product can be found elsewhere.[4]

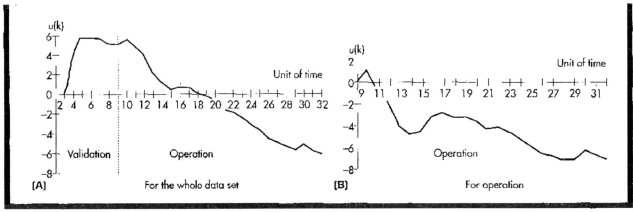

Figure 3. Laplace factors for all the installed systems in operation: (A) for the whole data set; (B) only during the operational phase.

TABLE 1 COMPONENT-SIZE AND NUMBER OF CORRECTIONS IN OPERATION		
Application	**Size (Kbytes)**	**Number of corrections**
Telephony	75	40
Defense	103	47
Interface	115	41
Management	42	18
Total	335	146

MODEL APPLICATION

Trend tests give information about trend evolution. However, if you want to evaluate the reliability of a particular piece of real-world software, you should apply reliability growth models. This lets you do the evaluation during validation. You are thus able to handle the delays and ensure that the software meets its reliability requirements. Growth models also let you assess the software's reliability in operation and thus estimate overall system dependability. Estimating the number of failures that will occur over a future time period is useful when planning the software maintenance effort. During development, frequent changes in the use environment restrict you to very short-term estimations. The relevance of the measures obtained from applying a reliability growth model varies with the considered life-cycle phase:

♦ Applying reliability growth models during the early stages of validation is not convincing—when the observed times to failure are of the order of magnitude of minutes or hours, the mean time to failure predictions obtained from such data can hardly exceed minutes or hours, which is distant from any expected reasonable reliability. In this case, software validation should be guided by trend analyses, as shown in the previous section.

♦ When the software being validated becomes more reliable, the time to failure may be large and the application of reliability growth models is more convincing, particularly when the software is activated under an operational profile.

♦ When the software is in operation, on multiple installations, the results are usually highly relevant since you have a larger sample of failure data.[8,9]

Models and trend analysis. Blindly applying a reliability growth model may lead to nonrealistic results when the trend displayed by the data differs from the one assumed by the model. However, if the model is applied to data displaying a trend that behaves according to its assumptions, results may improve dramatically.[9,10] This is because the already existing reliability growth models only allow two types of behavior to be modeled: decreasing failure intensity, or increasing failure intensity prior to undergoing decreasing failure intensity. Thanks to trend analyses, failure data can be partitioned according to trend, and reliability growth models can be selected as follows:

♦ In the case of reliability growth, most existing reliability growth models can be applied.

♦ When the failure data exhibits decreasing reliability followed by reliability growth, we recommend an S-shaped model.

♦ When the system displays stable reliability, you can apply a constant failure intensity model; reliability growth models are not needed in this case.

Models in real time. To predict the software's future behavior based on the information available at a given time, you must carry out a trend test on the available data. This helps you choose the reliability growth model or models to be applied and the subset of data to which they should be applied. The models are applied as long as the environmental conditions remain significantly unchanged, showing no major changes in the testing strategy or specifications and no new system installation with different operational profiles. Even in these situations, declining reliability may be noticed. Initially, you can consider this to result from a local, random fluctuation and assume that reliability will increase sometime in the near future. Thus, you can still rely on the predictions without partitioning data. If reliability continues to decline, you must find the reasons why. Meanwhile, new predictions may be made by partitioning data into subsets according to the new trend displayed by the data.

If a significant change in the devel-

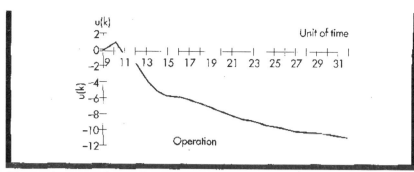

Figure 4. Laplace factors for an average system produce a smooth curve, in contrast to Figure 3.

opment or operational conditions occurs, you must be aware that local reliability trend changes may result, leading to erroneous predictions. If there is insufficient evidence that a different phase in the program's reliability evolution has been reached, you can trust the results of reliability growth models. If there is an obvious reliability decrease, you must wait until a new reliability growth period is reached, at which time the data must be partitioned according to the new trend.

We developed Sorel to make it easier to process failure data and to apply trend analysis and growth models in combination.

CASE STUDY

To explore the application of our Sorel tool, we consider the failure data collected on an electronic switching system (ESS) that was installed at 42 different sites during the collection period. The software faults detected and removed were recorded in appropriate failure reports, known as FRs. Raw data were filtered before being entered into the database: the 210 FRs correspond to genuine software faults removed and recorded over 32 time units, including the end of validation (8 time units, 73 FRs) and the beginning of operation (24 time units, 137 FRs). The ESS software consists of four components corresponding to the system's four main functions: telephony (all modules that provide switching), defense (all online testing and reconfiguration mechanisms), interfaces (all those with local devices, including memories, terminals, alarms, and so on), and management (programs that allow communication with external devices). Table 1 gives the size of the various components and the number of corrections carried out on each during the system's operational life. The sum of the corrections made on different components during operation, 146, is

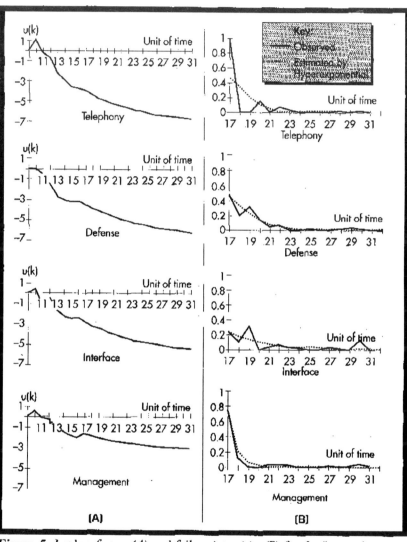

Figure 5. Laplace factors (A) and failure intensities (B) for the four main components of the electronic switching system we studied.

higher than the number of corrections performed on the software as a whole during operation, 137. This is because 11 failures led to the modification of more than one component.

To plan for the ongoing mainte-

nance effort, we analyzed the trend, evaluated the operational reliability for the whole software and its various components, then estimated the number of failures that would occur over a future period.

263

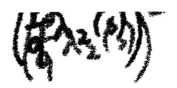

TABLE 2		
RESIDUAL FAILURE RATES AND AVERAGE FAILURE RATE OVER THE LAST 10 MONTHS		
	Estimated residual failure rate	**Observed average (last 10 units of time)**
Telephony	1.2×10^{-6}/h	1.0×10^{-5}/h
Defense	1.4×10^{-5}/h	1.6×10^{-5}/h
Interface	2.9×10^{-5}/h	3.7×10^{-5}/h
Management	8.5×10^{-6}/h	2.0×10^{-5}/h

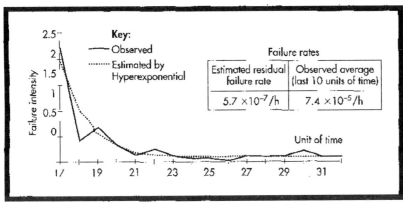

Figure 6. Failure rate and failure intensity observed and estimated by the hyperexponential (HE) model for the whole software.

Trend analysis. Figure 3A plots the Laplace factor for the whole data set when considering all the installed ESSs. Between time units 4 and 6, declining reliability occurred as a result of changes in the nature of the validation phase tests because new parts of the programs were activated. The software was put into operation before observing a noticeable reliability growth. Reliability growth took place only during the system's operational life.

Evaluating the Laplace factor for FRs recorded during system operation leads to Figure 3B, which shows reliability fluctuation from time units 14 to 24, which was not obvious when considering the whole data set. This fluctuation confirms that removal of a part of the data corresponding to declining reliability leads to negative Laplace factor values and amplifies the variation in the trend. This fluctuation is due mainly to the installation of 40 ESSs during this period.

Analyzing an average system by dividing the failure intensity by the number of installations in service leads to Figure 4: the curve obtained is smooth compared to that of Figure 3. Reliability fluctuation between time units 14 and 17 corresponds to the introduction of six ESSs. Reliability growth tends to be regular from time unit 17 onwards. This behavior is also apparent in the four components, as shown by the Laplace factor displayed in Figure 5A: all the components exer-

cised reliability fluctuation between time units 14 and 16, with the management component most sensitive to change.

Reliability growth models. We first adopt the customer's perspective: evaluation of the software's reliability in operation. Then, we consider the supplier's perspective: to plan the maintenance effort, we estimate the number of failures expected to occur during the subsequent time period.

Software and component reliability evaluation. When the software is in operation, one of the main measures of interest is the residual failure rate corresponding to the steady behavior of the software. The hyperexponential (HE) model[11] is the only one that lets us estimate this measure, so we will use this model to evaluate the residual failure rate and the failure intensity.

The results of the trend analyses in Figures 4 and 5A show regularity from time unit 17 on. These results guide the model application: the failure intensity and residual failure rate are evaluated using failure data from time unit 17. Figure 5B shows the results of applying HE to each component separately, which gives the observed and estimated failure intensities. Table 2 gives the residual failure rates obtained from applying HE.

To check the validity of the results, we evaluated the average failure rate observed during the last 10 time units of operation, as shown in the last column of Table 2. As expected, this average is higher than the residual for all components. However, it is very close to the latter for the defense and interface components. This means that these components had almost reached a steady behavior during the last 10 time units, whereas the telephony and management components were still evolving. Figure 6 gives the results obtained from applying HE to the whole software.

If we review figures 5B and 6 and

Table 2, we can conclude the following:

• The evolution of the whole-failure intensity masks the real evolution of the component intensities.

• The failure rate obtained by summing over the component residual failure rates (5.3×10^{-5}/h) is close to the residual failure rate of the software (5.7×10^{-5}/h), which means that even though the components are not totally independent, the residual failure rate of the software is almost equal to the sum of the failure rates of its components.

• The residual failure rate may be regarded as high when compared to those of other systems. However, this failure rate must be moderated by acknowledging that the severity of failures is not distinguished and the estimated value includes failures with minor consequences as well. Unfortunately, the FRs do not record failure severity.

Maintenance planning. We adopt here the supplier's and maintainer's perspective: the maintenance effort is a function of the average effort to make a correction and the number of corrections to be performed. To do this, we consider data collected from all the installed systems.

Figure 3B indicates global reliability growth over the operational life and suggests the application of models with decreasing failure intensity: we use HE and the exponential model[12] (EXP) for data pertaining to operation. However, we also present the results of an S-shaped model[13] (SS) to allow for comparison and highlight the advantage of analyzing trends before applying models. We use failure data observed during time units 9 to 19 to predict the number of failures that will occur during the rest of the observation period. Figure 7 shows the results. As expected, HE and EXP give good results, whereas SS is overly optimistic. Compared to the 34 observed failures for this period, HE predicted 37, EXP predicted 33, and SS predicted only 9.

Nevertheless, Figure 3A suggests

applying the SS model from the beginning, to include the trend change around time units 5 to 9. This is more in line with the model's assumptions. Doing so gives the results shown in Figure 8, including a significant improvement in the model's prediction accuracy.

The results show how much the use of trend test results can improve predictions when we apply the models to data exhibiting behavior according to the

models' assumptions. Moreover, we can obtain equivalent and good results for maintenance planning over the next year if the models we use are applied to subsets of data displaying a trend in accordance with the models' assumptions.

Software reliability now faces a paradox: although software is the current bottleneck to achieving dependable computer systems, current

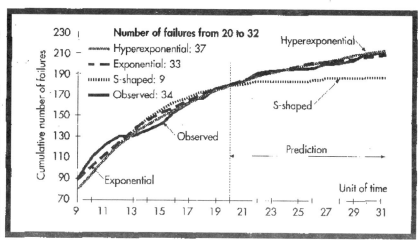

Figure 7. Cumulative number of failures observed and estimated by the models using the operational data set.

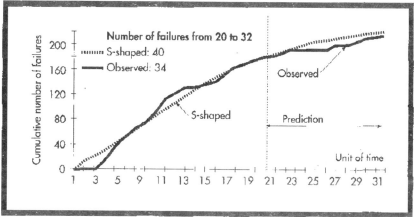

Figure 8. Cumulative number of failures estimated by the SS model using the whole data set.

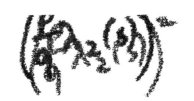

reliability practice does not generally take software reliability into account. In part this is because reliability evaluation has often been restricted to the application of reliability models to failure data and in many cases those applications failed to give accurate predictions.

Our method has successfully helped analyze the software reliability of several real systems. We believe it is mature enough to be integrated into a more general approach to software reliability engineering and to be used in real time to manage software development. The approach we propose provides some solutions to the current software reliability evaluation paradox. However, some limits in the current state of the art must still be overcome to allow efficient application of software evaluation in the development process. We must tie software reliability more strongly to the earlier part of the development process and correlate the observed reliability with some characteristics of this process to identify significant areas for reliability improvement. ◆

ACKNOWLEDGMENT

We thank the company that provided the data analyzed in this article and, especially, the engineers who participated in that analysis. We also thank Sylvain Metge for his contribution to the development of Sorel. Our work was partially supported by the European ESPRIT Long Term Research Project 20072: Deva (Design for Validation).

REFERENCES

1. M. Kaâniche, K. Kanoun, and S. Metge, "Failure Analysis and Validation Monitoring of a Telecommunication Equipment Software System," *Annales des Telecommunications*, Vol. 45, Nos. 11-12, 1990, pp. 657-70.
2. V.R. Basili and D.M. Weiss, "A Methodology for Collecting Valid Software Engineering Data," *IEEE Trans. Software Eng.*, Vol. 10, No. 6, 1984, pp. 728-38.
3. Y. Levendel, "Reliability Analysis of Large Software Systems: Defects Data Modeling," *IEEE Trans. Software Eng.*, Vol. 16, No. 2, 1990, pp. 141-52.
4. R. Chillarege and S. Biyani, "Identifying Risk Using ODC Based Growth Models," *5th Int'l Symp. Software Reliability Eng.*, IEEE CS Press, Los Alamitos, Calif., 1994, pp. 282-288.
5. R.B. Grady and D.L. Caswell, *Software Metrics: Establishing a Company-Wide Program*, Prentice Hall, Englewood Cliffs, N.J., 1987.
6. O. Gaudoin, "Optimal Properties of the Laplace Test for Software-Reliability Models," *IEEE Trans. Reliability*, Vol. 41, No. 4, 1992, pp. 525-32.
7. K. Kanoun and J.-C. Laprie, "Software Reliability Trend Analyses: From Theoretical To Practical Considerations," *IEEE Trans. Software Eng.*, Vol. 20, No. 9, 1994, pp. 740-747.
8. N. Adams, "Optimizing Preventive Service of Software Products," *IBM J. Research and Development*, Vol. 28, No. 1, 1984, pp. 2-14.
9. K. Kanoun and T. Sabourin, "Software Dependability of a Telephone Switching System," *17th IEEE Int'l Symp. Fault-Tolerant Computing*, IEEE, Pittsburgh, 1987, pp. 236-41.
10. K. Kanoun, M. Kaâniche, and J.-C. Laprie, "Experience in Software Reliability: From Data Collection to Quantitative Evaluation," *4th Int'l Symp. Software Reliability Eng.*, IEEE CS Press, Los Alamitos, Calif., 1993, pp. 234-245.
11. J.-C. Laprie et al., "The KAT (Knowledge-Action-Transformation) Approach to the Modeling and Evaluation of Reliability and Availability Growth," *IEEE Trans. Soft. Eng.*, Vol. 17, No. 4, 1991, pp. 370-82.
12. A. L. Goel and K. Okumoto, "Time-Dependent Error Detection Rate Model for Software and Other Performance Measures," *IEEE Trans. on Reliability*, R-28, 1979, pp. 206-11.
13. S. Yamada, "Software Quality/Reliability Measurement and Assessment: Software Reliability Growth Models and Data Analysis," *J. Information Processing*, Vol. 14, No. 3, 1991, pp. 254-66.

Karama Kanoun is chargee de recherche of CNRS, the French National Organization for Scientific Research. She joined LAAS CNRS in 1977 as a member of the Fault Tolerance and Dependable Computing group. Her current research interests include modeling and evaluation of computer system dependability, including hardware and software. Kanoun has completed several research contracts and has been consultant for several French companies and for the International Union of Telecommunications. She also served as a program committee cochair of the International Symposium on Software Reliability Engineering, as vice-chair of the Second International Conference on Reliability, Maintainability, and Safety, and as general chair of ISSRE '95. She is a member of the working group of the European Workshop on Industrial Computer Systems, Technical Committee 7: Reliability, Safety, and Security, and a member of the Dependability of Computing Systems AFCET working group.

Kanoun received a CE from the French National School of Civil Aviation and PhDs in engineering and science from the National Institute Polytechnique of Toulouse. Her doctorate of science thesis dealt with the theoretical and practical aspects of software dependability growth characterization, modeling, and evaluation. She is a member of the IEEE Computer Society, ACM, and AFCET.

Mohamed Kaâniche is charge de recherche at CNRS. He joined the LAAS-CNRS's Fault Tolerance and Dependable Computing group in 1988. His current research interests include dependability modeling and computing systems evaluation with a focus on software reliability growth evaluation and operational systems' security assessment. He also works on the definition of process models for the development of dependable systems.

Kaâniche received a CE from the French National School of Civil Aviation and a PhD in computer science and automation from the University of Toulouse. He is a member of AFCET.

Jean-Claude Laprie is directeur de recherche of CNRS, the French National Organization for Scientific Research. He joined LAAS-CNRS in 1968 and directed the research group on Fault Tolerance and Dependable Computing from 1975 to 1996. His research has focused on dependable computing since 1973, and especially on fault tolerance and on dependability evaluations, subjects on which he has authored and coauthored more than 100 papers, as well as coauthored or edited several books. He also founded and directed, from 1992 to 1996, the Laboratory for Dependability Engineering, a joint academia-industry laboratory. In 1984 and 1985, Laprie was chairman of the IEEE Computer Society Technical Committee on Fault-Tolerant Computing, and he was chairman of IFIP WG 10.4 on Dependable Computing and Fault Tolerance from 1986 to 1995.

Laprie received a CE from the Higher National School for Aeronautical Constructions, Toulouse, a PhD in engineering in automatic control, and a PhD in computer science from the University of Toulouse. He is a member of the IEEE Computer Society, ACM, and AFCET.

Address questions about this article to Kanoun at Centre National De La Recherche Scientifique, Laboratoire d'Analyse et d'Architecture des Systemes, 7, avenue du Colonel Roche, 31077 Toulouse Cedex 4, France, kanoun@laas.fr.

Editor: Norman F. Schneidewind, Naval Postgraduate School, Code AS/Ss, Monterey, CA 93943, fax (408) 656-3407, e-mail 0442p@vm1.cc.nps.navy.mil

A software reliability engineering practice

William W. Everett and John D. Musa, AT&T Bell Laboratories

In 1989, AT&T launched initiatives to improve its product development processes. One initiative was identifying and documenting proven best-in-class product-development practices and providing companywide support to projects to implement them.

Expert practitioners define these best current practices (BCPs) as the best currently known way to accomplish a set of tasks. The BCP itself is documented in a handbook and is supported by training and consulting services to help projects in implementation. A recently adopted BCP at AT&T involves performing software reliability engineering (SRE) tasks over the software life cycle.

Work on the SRE BCP handbook began in mid-1991, and 16 months later, a council of senior AT&T Bell Laboratories managers approved it. Mary Donnelly, William Everett, John Musa, and Geoff Wilson teamed to do the writing and editing, drawing on the experiences of 85 other contributors and reviewers.

The handbook outlines the attainable benefits and implementation costs for doing SRE, recommends a sequence of implementation steps, and provides a list of conformance questions to help project managers assess how well they are following the practice. A seminar, training, and "jump start" consulting services have been put in place to assist projects in implementing SRE.

Eight case studies. Eight projects submitted case studies for inclusion in the handbook. The case studies describe how the projects implemented SRE, the benefits and costs the projects realized, and the key factors that contributed to their successful implementation. The basic practice describes 20 SRE activities that should be performed over the software product life cycle and recommends who should perform them. The activities

(1) quantify product usage in its environmental context by specifying

how often customers will use the various features of a product and how frequently environmental factors will influence processing;

(2) set reliability objectives by defining failures and failure severities from a customer's perspective and balancing customer needs for high reliability, timely delivery, and low price;

(3) employ product usage data and reliability objectives to guide product design and implementation and to manage development resources to achieve the reliability the customer wants at a cost and within a delivery time frame the customer desires;

(4) certify that the software components outside suppliers provide meet reliability needs for the product being developed;

(5) track reliability during test and field trials, and use this information to guide decisions on releasing products; and

(6) monitor reliability after product release to insure that reliability objectives and customer needs are satisfied, to guide new feature introduction, and to improve development processes and future product releases.

The life-cycle approach to managing software product reliability is described in the literature.[1,2]

Software reliability defined. Software reliability is the capability of a software product to operate failure-free for a given period under specified operating conditions. This definition is consistent with the definition for hardware reliability; hence, we can combine software and hardware reliability measures to derive system reliability measures.

Failure intensity, a measure of the frequency at which failures occur, is a related reliability indicator commonly used with software. Failure intensity complements fault-density-based metrics like faults per thousand lines of code. Fault-based metrics provide a developer-oriented view of product quality, while failure-based metrics

provide a customer-oriented view. Software product customers and users are not concerned with faults per se, but rather with the failures the faults cause, how often failures occur, and how much is lost because they occur.

Failures are what the customer or product user experiences. This is consistent with the way the term is used for hardware. However, although the primary underlying cause of hardware failures is deterioration or overstressing of materials, software failures are most often due to faults inserted during software product development.

Operating conditions affect product reliability. With electronic hardware, the operating conditions commonly affecting reliability include such factors as temperature and humidity. With software, the way the customer uses the product affects reliability. Such usage determines which software paths are followed, and that determines which faults are encountered and result in failures. This usage is specified by a profile that shows the operations invoked and their frequency. The operational profile also accounts for how often environmental factors occur that significantly affect processing. Musa describes an operational profile and how to develop one for a software product.[3]

Failure measurement, modeling, and analysis is done in processing- or execution-time terms because failures can occur only when the software is executed. The more processing done, the more likely a fault will occur under certain, precise conditions. Execution time is measured in CPU time (for example, CPU seconds or CPU hours). If CPU time cannot be measured directly, it often can be approximated by other means (such as calendar time or number of items processed).

A classical application of software reliability modeling occurs during reliability growth testing. Figures 1 and 2 show how such models are applied. In Figure 1, asterisks plot failures as they occur versus cumulative execution time. The solid line plots one of sever-

Reprinted from *IEEE Computer*, Vol. 26, No. 3, Mar. 1993, pp. 77-79.

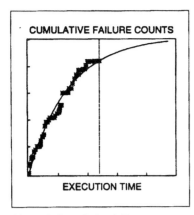

Figure 1. Cumulative failures versus execution time showing individual failures and a fitted reliability growth model.

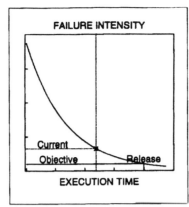

Figure 2. Failure intensity versus execution time showing how to read current failure intensity and the time to reach the failure-intensity objective.

al possible reliability growth models fitted to the failure data. The slope of the curve at any point represents the estimated instantaneous failure intensity, as plotted in Figure 2. Using Figure 2, we can locate the estimated current failure intensity on the plot line, along with an estimate of how much execution time is needed to reach a specified failure intensity objective.

What is the SRE BCP? Figure 3 shows 20 SRE activities and the product life-cycle phase each activity falls into.

Feasibility and requirements. In the feasibility and requirements phase, activities focus on defining product-reliability requirements. Since software product usage influences its reliability, activities start by establishing what this usage is. This is done by specifying what "functions" the product will perform for each user and how frequently the functions will be performed. We will use this "functional profile" later in forming the operational profile.

Next, failures are defined from the product-user perspective. A failure can be defined as the inability to meet a user's need or perform a user function. Many failure types will generally result. Failures should be grouped into a manageable number of categories by cost or impact on product users.

Next, a systems engineer develops an understanding of what product users need in terms of reliability. The customers' (users') desire for reliability, the price they are willing to pay for

the product, and the urgency with which they need it must be balanced. Striking such a balance provides a way of setting product reliability objectives. These objectives, along with the operating conditions under which the objectives are to be met (that is, as specified by the functional profile), should be made part of the requirements specification.

Design and implementation. During the design and implementation phase, developers allocate the reliability objectives between software and hardware components as high-level and low-level design proceeds. As the design evolves and the definition of the software product components and their properties improves, they can make better estimates of component reliabilities. These component reliabilities in turn can be used to identify "hot spots" for special attention during development. Developers weigh design and implementation alternatives to engineer the software product to meet objectives. The functional profile helps focus development resources because it shows which parts of the software will be used most frequently.

Many development activities can influence the number of faults introduced into the software and the number that will propagate undetected between development stages. Controlling the number introduced and their propagation between stages influences the reliability of the end product.

Finally, most software applications are built on software "acquired" from other sources. Acquired software can

range from operating and database management system software to "reused" software from other applications or earlier releases of the same software application. Since the reliability of acquired software components may have been certified under usage that differs from the current application, their reliability may have to be recertified under usage that conforms to the intended product.

System test and field trial. During the system-test and field-trial phase, the focus is on ensuring that the completed software product meets its reliability objectives as specified in the requirements. The first step is to refine the functional profile into an operational profile. Operations represent the implementation of functions. This operational profile is used to select test cases for reliability growth testing.

The primary purposes of this testing are to utilize the product as the customer/user will utilize it, collect failure data so that reliability growth can be estimated, and use the reliability growth model output to assess current product reliability and determine how much additional testing is needed to reach reliability objectives. This use of SRE has received the most attention on projects because it provides a way to assess a major customer-perceived quality attribute versus the amount of testing performed.

Post delivery and maintenance. The practice of SRE doesn't stop with product delivery. Field reliability is monitored against established product objectives. However, this is not enough. Efforts must be undertaken to track customer satisfaction (the reliability objectives established during the feasibility and requirements phase may not have been enough to satisfy customer needs).

This information, along with root-cause-analysis techniques, can be used to improve the reliability of future product releases and identify parts of the development process that can be improved. Predicted reliability levels can be used to estimate the rate of customer-reported failures. This, in turn, can be used to project staff needs for software maintenance and field-support activities. Software product customers can use SRE data to time introducing new software releases into their operations, while maintaining a specified customer-service level.

As stated above, the handbook describes in detail what goes into each

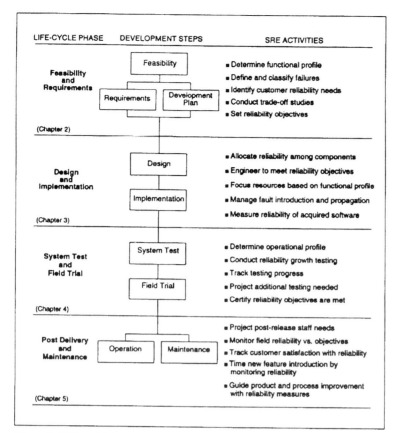

LIFE-CYCLE PHASE	DEVELOPMENT STEPS	SRE ACTIVITIES

Feasibility and Requirements (Chapter 2)
- Feasibility
- Requirements
- Development Plan

SRE Activities:
- Determine functional profile
- Define and classify failures
- Identify customer reliability needs
- Conduct trade-off studies
- Set reliability objectives

Design and Implementation (Chapter 3)
- Design
- Implementation

SRE Activities:
- Allocate reliability among components
- Engineer to meet reliability objectives
- Focus resources based on functional profile
- Manage fault introduction and propagation
- Measure reliability of acquired software

System Test and Field Trial (Chapter 4)
- System Test
- Field Trial

SRE Activities:
- Determine operational profile
- Conduct reliability growth testing
- Track testing progress
- Project additional testing needed
- Certify reliability objectives are met

Post Delivery and Maintenance (Chapter 5)
- Operation
- Maintenance

SRE Activities:
- Project post-release staff needs
- Monitor field reliability vs. objectives
- Track customer satisfaction with reliability
- Time new feature introduction by monitoring reliability
- Guide product and process improvement with reliability measures

Figure 3. SRE activities over the software product life-cycle phases.

activity (including the people involved). Activities in the system-test and field-trial phase are the most mature in terms of both supporting technology and project numbers. Although activities in the other phases are less mature, project experience accrues from applying them. SRE emphasizes involvement in all life-cycle phases before a project can be truly effective in managing product reliability.

Support mechanisms. Because the handbook does not provide everything needed to implement SRE, supplemental support mechanisms are needed. A three-day "SRE Applications" course provides much of the technology training behind SRE. In addition, a one-day management course provides information for decision makers who evaluate the technology. Another course provides an overview for those not directly performing SRE but who may be affected by it.

Finally, consultants work hand-in-hand with project managers to plan how to integrate SRE into their development environments and get them off to effective starts. Another major support mechanism is an SRE users' group, which publishes a newsletter about three times a year and sponsors a yearly workshop that gives practitioners an opportunity to exchange information.

Conclusions. Several AT&T projects have implemented elements of SRE and have reported substantial savings with modest investment. Musa[3] reports a cost reduction of 56 percent in system test activities for typical projects, leading to an 11 percent savings in overall project cost. This is supported in Abramson et al.[4] for the AT&T Definity system project.

References

1. W.W. Everett, "Software Reliability Measurement," *IEEE J. Selected Areas in Comm.*, Vol. 8, No. 2, Feb. 1990, pp. 247-252.

2. J.D. Musa and W.W. Everett, "Software Reliability Engineering: Technology for the 1990s," *IEEE Software*, Vol. 7, No. 6, Nov. 1990, pp. 36-43.

3. J.D. Musa, "Operational Profiles in Software Reliability Engineering," *IEEE Software*, Vol. 10, No. 2, Mar. 1993, pp. 14-32.

4. S.R. Abramson et al., "Customer Satisfaction-Based Product Development," *Proc. 14th Int'l Switching Symp.*, Vol. 2, Inst. of Electronics, Information, and Communications Engineers, 1992, pp. 65-69.

William W. Everett is a distinguished member of the technical staff at AT&T Bell Laboratories, Rm. 2L-503, Holmdel, NJ 07733-3030, phone (908) 949-2334, e-mail w.w.everett@att.com.

John D. Musa is supervisor of software reliability engineering at AT&T Bell Laboratories, Rm. 2C-535, Murray Hill, NJ 07974-0636, phone (908) 582-4993, e-mail j.d. musa@att.com.

March 1993

271

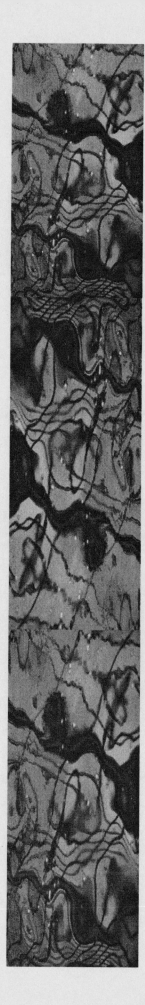

Chapter 6

USING METRICS

The use of metrics as an important weapon in the arsenal of the software project manager cannot be overemphasized. Metrics provide the only objective means whereby project progress can be tracked, trouble spots identified and credit can be given.

While I may not agree with all of the papers in this section, I feel a wonderful diversity of thought is presented here. In particular, the last paper by Fenton provides a very rigorous framework for the use of metrics.

Software metrics:

Capers Jones,
Software Productivity Research

The software industry is an embarrassment when it comes to measurement and metrics. Many software managers and practitioners, including tenured academics in software engineering and computer science, seem to know little or nothing about these topics. Many of the measurements found in the software literature are not used with enough precision to replicate the author's findings — a canon of scientific writing in other fields. Several of the most widely used software metrics have been proved unworkable, yet they continue to show up in books,

> **Several widely used software metrics do not work, yet they continue to show up in books, encyclopedias, and refereed journals.**

encyclopedias, and refereed journals. So long as these invalid metrics are used carelessly, there can be no true "software engineering," only a kind of amateurish craft that uses rough approximations instead of precise measurement.

Software metrics that don't work. Three significant and widely used software metrics are invalid under various conditions: lines of code or LOC metrics, software science or Halstead metrics, and the cost-per-defect metric. The first two metrics are not invalid under all conditions, but they are when used to compare productivity or quality data across different programming languages. The third metric requires a

COMPUTER

Reprinted from *IEEE Computer*, Vol. 27, No. 9, Sept. 1994, pp. 98-100.

Capers Jones, Software Productivity Research Inc., 1 New England Executive Park, Burlington, MA 01803-5005;
(617) 273-0140; fax (617) 273-5176; Internet capers@spr.com; Compuserve 75430,231

Good, bad, and missing

careful separation of fixed and variable costs to produce valid information.

Lines of code. The widely used LOC metric is one of the most imprecise metrics ever used in scientific or engineering writing. After more than 50 years of use, it lacks a standard definition for any major programming language, and there are more than 400 programming languages in use.

The software literature, and even draft LOC counting standards, are about equally divided between those using physical lines and those using logical statements as the basis for the LOC metric. This difference alone can cause variations of 500 percent for some programming languages that allow multiple statements per physical line. Even worse, when used as a normalizing metric, LOC has been proven to penalize high-level languages, object-oriented languages, program generators, and every useful modern programming language.

If a manufacturing process includes substantial fixed costs, reducing the number of units manufactured increases the cost per unit. For software, more than half the effort is usually devoted to noncoding work such as requirements, design, user documentation, and management. If you define a line of code as a manufacturing unit, and then move from a low-level language to a high-level language, the paperwork costs tend to act like fixed costs and hence drive up the cost per line of code.

Here is an example. Suppose you're doing a project in assembly language that takes 10,000 lines of code. The requirements, design, documentation, and paperwork activities take five months, and the coding and testing take 10 months. So total project time is 15 months. The productivity of the entire project is 10,000 LOC divided by 15 months, or 666 lines of code per month.

At $5,000 per staff month, the project costs $75,000 or $7.50 per LOC.

Now suppose you're doing the same project in Ada83. Since Ada is a much more powerful language, you'll need only 2,000 lines of code. The paperwork activities still take five months, but coding requires only two months. Now the total project amounts to seven months of effort, which is more than a 50 percent reduction compared to assembly language. Yet the apparent productivity of the project using the LOC metric is reduced: 2,000 LOC divided by seven months is only 285 lines of code per month. At $5,000 per staff month, the project costs only $35,000, but the cost per LOC has ballooned to $17.50.

It is hazardous to use a metric that gets worse as real economic productivity gets better.

Obviously, if used carelessly, LOC metrics penalize high-level languages, and the magnitude of the penalty is directly proportional to the level or power of the language. Only if all data is converted into "equivalent lines" in the same language can the LOC metric produce valid results across different languages. It is hazardous to use a metric that gets worse as real economic productivity gets better.

Halstead and cost per defect. The software science or Halstead metrics (invented by the late Maurice Halstead of Purdue University) are essentially a more convoluted way of dealing with code, by dividing it into operator and operand portions. These metrics share the same mathematical anomaly of lines

of code and are equally unreliable.

The cost-per-defect metric is also misleading because of the impact of fixed costs. It actually penalizes quality and gets worse as quality gets better.

Suppose you are unit testing the assembly language example and find 100 bugs. Creating the test cases takes a week, running them takes another week, and fixing the 100 bugs takes one month. At a labor cost of $5,000 per month, unit test costs $7,500 or $75.00 for each bug found.

Now suppose the Ada version of the same project has only 10 bugs, an order-of-magnitude improvement in quality. Creating the test cases still takes a week, and running them still takes a week. Assume the bugs are fixed on the fly, with essentially no extra effort. Now unit testing takes only two weeks and costs only $2,500, for a savings of $5,000 compared to assembly language. But the cost per defect for the Ada version has jumped to $250. A 66 percent reduction in unit testing costs is a significant improvement, but it becomes invisible when using the cost-per-defect metric. Also, if only one bug were found instead of 10, then the cost per defect would explode to $2,500 because the entire cost of creating and running the test suite would be charged to that single bug.

It can easily be seen that careless use of the cost-per-defect metric penalizes quality and approaches infinity as quality approaches zero defects.

Metrics that do work. Fortunately, two metrics that actually generate useful information — complexity metrics and function-point metrics — are growing in use and importance.

Complexity metrics. We've known since the 1960s that excessive complexity in software usually raises defect potentials and reduces productivity of both development and maintenance.

This general statement can be quantified by cyclomatic complexity and essential complexity metrics, although there are other complexity metrics as well.

Of course, there are some exceptions to the "excessive complexity" rule. However, my own and my company's observations of several thousand projects over the past 15 years indicate that excessive complexity is often associated with lower than average quality and higher than average maintenance expenses. Surprisingly, much of the observed complexity appears to be technically unnecessary. In interviews with the programmers themselves, we find that excessive schedule pressure and hasty design tend to be a common root cause.

Various complexity metrics have been discussed and popularized by many researchers. Among those widely known are cyclomatic and essential complexity. Cyclomatic complexity is essentially the measure of the branches in the control flow of a program. Perfectly structured code that has no branching has a cyclomatic complexity of 1. If the control flow is graphed, cyclomatic complexity captures the basic branching structure. As the branching becomes more convoluted, this metric can indicate areas that may need simplification or restructuring, such as modules with a cyclomatic complexity above 20.

Essential complexity is derived from cyclomatic complexity and is a similar concept, except that it uses special graph-theoretic techniques to eliminate redundancy.

While it's possible to calculate cyclomatic and essential complexity manually, there's also no shortage of commercial tools to automate the work. Tools that directly scan source code are now available for most programming languages, and they operate on various platforms such as DOS, Windows, and Unix.

Function points. The function point metric, developed within IBM by A.J. Albrecht, has been in the public domain since 1979. It's not perfect, but it is free of the economic distortions of the LOC metric.

Function points are the weighted sum of five external attributes of software projects — inputs, outputs, inquires, logical files, and interfaces — that have been adjusted for complexity. The actual counting rules are quite complex, but they are logical and consistent enough to have been encoded in scores of automatic function-point counting tools.

It's easy to see why function points are now so widely used. The function point total for an application does not change with the programming language. For example, both the assembly example and the Ada example would contain the same function point total, since both versions actually perform the same functions.

Assuming that both versions contain 50 function points, productivity is 3.3 function points per month for the assembly language version and 7.14 for the Ada83 version. Economic costs can also be calculated with function points. The assembly language cost per function point is $1,500, while the Ada version is only $700 per function point. Now it's possible to see the economic advantages of the Ada version. For once, the industry has a metric that moves in the right direction when used with high-level languages.

Use of function points and associated tools has been exploding throughout the software industry. At least 30 com-

---

For once, the industry has a metric that moves in the right direction when used with high-level languages.

---

mercial software-estimating tools now support function points. Indeed, 1994 will probably mark the first time in software history that every major commercial software-cost-estimating tool in the United States supports the function point metric. Some of the software estimating tools that already support functional metrics include (in alphabetic order) AEM, Asset-R, Bridge, BYL, Checkpoint, Cocomo II, Gecomo, Estimacs, Microman, Price-S, SEER, SLIM, SoftCost, and SPQR/20. Also, many upper CASE tools can now create function point totals automatically during the design phase. There are now probably more commercial tools supporting function point automation than for all other metrics combined.

Many of the commercial software-estimating tools also support a technique called "backfiring," a mathematical conversion of data between lines of code and function points. About 400 programming languages, and many combinations of mixed languages, can now be normalized using both LOC metrics and functional metrics by means of the backfiring approach. Using both metrics can clarify the problems with LOC metrics.

Missing metrics. One very important software domain — the data or information associated with software — lacks any metrics whatsoever. As of 1994, there are no known metrics for quantifying or normalizing the volume of data contained in a database or repository or used by a corporation. There are no metrics for dealing with the costs of creating, using, or removing data. There is no way to explore the volume of active data versus archival data, nor the costs of moving data back and forth between active and inactive status. There are no metrics for measuring data quality, although everyone who has ever worked with a database realizes that poor data quality is a critical problem.

Database consultants suspect that the costs of data creation and use in large companies are roughly equivalent to the costs of creating software. The value of the data may be even higher than the value of the software, but no one can explore these hypotheses until useful data metrics are invented.

Another domain with a severe shortage of useful metrics is that of hybrid applications that include hardware, microcode, and software. There are no metrics that can cross the hardware/software boundary and allow unified economic analysis at the complete system level.

Metrics and measurement are the basic underpinnings of science and engineering. Software has suffered through most of its 50-year history with inaccurate metrics and inadequate measurements. But as the 20th century draws to a close, improvements are rapidly occurring.

Recent developments in functional and complexity metrics and measurement are steps in the right direction, but the software community still has far to go before the phrase "software engineering" can be taken seriously.

The Role of Object-Oriented Metrics

Bertrand Meyer, EiffelSoft

Perhaps the most common concern of project managers who use or who are about to use object technology is for more measurement tools. I suspect that some of these people would kill for anything that could give them some kind of quantitative grasp on the software development process.

There is, in fact, an extensive literature on software metrics, including much that pertains to object-oriented development. But surprisingly little of it is of direct use to actual projects. The publications that directly address object-oriented metrics often go back quite a while. An example is Barry Boehm's *Software Engineering Economics* (Prentice Hall, 1981), with its Cocomo cost-prediction model. Despite the existence of more recent works on the subject, Boehm's is still among the most practical sources of quantitative information and methodology.

Metrics are not everything, of course. Lord Kelvin's famous observation is exaggerated:

> When you cannot measure, when you cannot express [what you are speaking about] in numbers, your knowledge is of a meager and unsatisfactory kind: You have scarcely, in your thoughts, advanced to the stage of a science.

Editor: Bertrand Meyer, EiffelSoft, ISE Bldg., 2nd Fl., 270 Storke Rd., Goleta, CA 93117; voice (805) 685-6869; ot-column@eiffel.com

Much of math—and most of logic—is not quantitative, but we don't dismiss those elements of science as nonscientific.

Much of math—and most of logic—is not quantitative, but we don't dismiss those elements of science as nonscientific.

These considerations also put in perspective some of the comments published recently in *Computer* by Walter Tichy ("Should Computer Scientists Experiment More?" May 1998, pp. 32-40) on the need for more experimentation; his article was largely a plea for more quantitative data. I agree with Tichy's central argument: We need to submit our hypotheses to the test of experience. But when Tichy writes

> Zelkowitz and Wallace also surveyed journals in physics, psychology, and anthropology and again found much smaller percentages of unvalidated

papers [that is, papers not supported by quantitative evaluation] than in computer science...

I cannot help but think, "Physics, OK, but do we really want to take *psychology* as the paragon of how scientific computer science should be?" I don't think so. In an engineering discipline, we cannot tolerate the fuzziness that is almost inevitable in social sciences, in spite of all their numbers. If we are looking for rigor, the tools of mathematical logic and formal reasoning are crucial, even though they are not quantitative.

Still, we need better quantitative tools. In this column I present a classification of software metrics and five basic rules for their application.

TYPES OF METRICS

The first rule of quantitative software evaluation is that if we collect or compute numbers we must have a specific intent related to understanding, controlling, or improving software and its production. This implies that there are two broad kinds of metrics: *product metrics*, which measure properties of the software products, and *process metrics*, which measure properties of the process used to obtain these products.

Product metrics include two categories: External product metrics cover properties visible to the users of a product; internal product metrics cover properties visible only to the development team.

External product metrics include

- *Product nonreliability metrics*, which assess the number of remaining defects.
- *Functionality metrics*, which assess how much useful functionality the product provides.
- *Performance metrics*, which assess a product's use of available resources, including computation speed, space, and occupancy.
- *Usability metrics*, which assess a product's ease of learning and ease of use.
- *Cost metrics*, which assess the cost of purchasing and using a product.

Internal product metrics include

Reprinted from *IEEE Computer*, Vol. 31, No. 11, Nov. 1998, pp. 123-127.

November 1998   123

279

- *Size metrics*, which provide measures of how big a product is internally.
- *Complexity metrics*, which are closely related to size metrics and assess how complex a product is.
- *Style metrics*, which assess adherence to writing guidelines for product components like programs and documents.

Process metrics include

- *Cost metrics*, which measure the cost of a project or of some project activities such as original development, maintenance, and documentation.
- *Effort metrics*, which are a subcategory of cost metrics and estimate the human part of the cost, typically measured in person-days or person-months.
- *Advancement metrics*, which estimate the degree of completion of a product under construction.
- *Process nonreliability metrics*, which assess the number of defects uncovered so far.
- *Reuse metrics*, which assess how much of a development benefits from earlier developments.

INTERNAL AND EXTERNAL METRICS

The second rule is that internal and product metrics should be designed to mirror relevant external metrics as closely as possible. Clearly, the only metrics of interest in the long run are external metrics, which assess the result of our work as perceived by our market. Internal metrics and product metrics help us improve this product and the process of producing it. These metrics should always be designed so as to be eventually relevant to external metrics.

Object technology is particularly useful here because of its seamlessness properties, which reduce the gap between problem structure and program structure—the *direct mapping property*. In an object-oriented context the notion of function point—a widely accepted measure of functionality—can be replaced by a much more objective measure: the number of exported features (or operations) of relevant classes that require no

human intervention and can be measured trivially by a simple parsing tool.

DESIGNING METRICS

The third rule is that any metric applied to a product or project should be justified by a clear theory of what property the metric is intended to help estimate. The set of things we can measure is infinite, but most of them are not interesting. For example, I can write a tool to compute the sum of all ASCII character codes in a program, but this is unlikely to yield anything of interest to product developers, product users, or project managers.

> *The set of things we can measure is infinite, but most of them are not interesting.*

A simple example is a set of measurements that we performed some time ago on the public-domain EiffelBase library of fundamental data structures and algorithms, reported in my book *Reusable Software* (Prentice Hall, 1994). One of the things we counted was the number of arguments to a feature (attribute or routine) over 150 classes and 1,850 features; we found an average of 0.4 and a maximum of three, with 97 percent of the features having two or less.

We were not measuring this particular property blindly: It was connected to a very precise hypothesis that the simplicity of such interfaces is a key component of the ease of use (and hence the potential success) of a reusable component library. These figures show a huge decrease in arguments compared to the average number for typical non-OO-subroutine libraries, which often contain five or more and sometimes as much as 10. (Note that a C or Fortran subroutine has one more argument than the corresponding OO feature.)

Sometimes people are skeptical of the reuse claims of object technology; after all, their argument goes, the idea of reuse has been around for a long time, so what's so special with objects? But quantitative arguments like those derived from EiffelBase measurements provide

some concrete evidence to back the OO claims.

A THEORY OF METRICS

The third rule requires a theory and implies that the measurements will only be as good as the theory. Indeed, the correlation between a small number of feature arguments and how easy a library is to use is only a hypothesis. Authors such as Tichy might argue that the hypothesis must be validated through experimental correlation that measures ease of use.

They would have a point, but the first step is to have a theory and make it explicit. Experimental validation is seldom easy anyway, given the setup of many experiments that often use students under the sometimes dubious assumption that their reactions can be used to predict the behavior of professional programmers.

In addition, as Tichy suggests, it is very hard to control all the variables. For example, I recently found out, by going back to the source, that a 1970s study often used to support the use of semicolons as terminators rather than separators in programming languages seemed to rely on an unrealistic assumption that casts doubt on the results.

Two PhD dissertations at Monash University—by Jon Avotins and Glenn Maughan under the supervision of Christine Mingins—have applied these ideas further by producing a guide called a "Quality Suite for Reusable Software" (http://www.sd.monash.edu.au). Starting from several hundred informal methodological rules in the book *Reusable Software* and others, they identified the elements of the rules that could be subject to quantitative evaluation, defined the corresponding metrics, and produced tools that evaluate these metrics on submitted software. Project managers or developers using these tools can assess the values of these measurements on their products.

In particular, you can compare the resulting values to industry-wide standards or to averages measured over your previous projects. This brings us to the fourth rule, which states that measurements are usually most useful in relative terms.

CALIBRATING METRICS

The fourth rule is that most measurements are only meaningful after calibration and comparison to earlier results. This is particularly true of cost and reliability metrics. A sophisticated cost model such as Cocomo will become more and more useful as you apply it to successive projects and use the results to calibrate the model's parameters to your own context. As you move on to new projects, you can use the model with more and more confidence because of comparisons with other projects.

Similarly, many internal product metrics are particularly useful when taken relatively. Presented with an average argument count measure of four for your newest library, you will not necessarily know what it means. Is this good, bad, or irrelevant? Assessed against published measures of goodness, or against measures for previous projects in your team, the figures will become more meaningful.

Particularly significant are outlying points: If the average value for a certain property is five with a standard deviation of two, and you measure ten for a new development, it's probably worth checking further, assuming of course—see rule two—that there is some theory to support the assumption that the measure is relevant. This is where tools such as the Monash suite can be particularly useful.

METRICS AND THE MEASURING PROCESS

The fifth rule is that the benefits of a metrics program lie in the measuring process as well as in its results. The software metrics literature often describes complex models purporting to help predict various properties of software products and processes by measuring other properties. It also contains lots of controversy about the value of the models and their predictions.

But even if we remain theoretically skeptical about some of the models, we shouldn't throw away the corresponding measurements. The very process of collecting these measurements leads—as long as we confine ourselves to measurements that are meaningful, at least by some informal criteria—to a better organization of the software process and a better understanding of what we are doing.

This idea explains the attraction and usefulness of process guidelines such as the Software Engineering Institute's Capability Maturity Model that encourage organizations to monitor their processes and make them repeatable, in part through measurement.

To quote Emmanuel Girard, a software metrics expert, in his advice for software managers: "Before you take any measures, take measurements." ❖

Implementing Effective Software Metrics Programs

TRACY HALL, *University of Westminster*
NORMAN FENTON, *City University*

Increasingly, organizations are foregoing an ad hoc approach to metrics in favor of complete metrics programs. The authors identify consensus requirements for metric program success and examine how programs in two organizations measured up.

Until relatively recently, software measurement in the Western world has been a rather *ad hoc* affair focused on measuring individual, product-based software attributes. This rather one-dimensional approach to software measurement is now changing. Increasingly, organizations are integrating complete software metrics programs into their software development processes. That is, they are habitually using a balanced range of product and process measures in their micro and macro decision making systems.

There are several reasons that partially explain the recent move toward complete metrics programs. Not only has the process improvement bandwagon raised a general awareness of metrics, but to reach higher Capability Maturity Model levels, organizations must incorporate metrics into their development process. Moreover, there now appears to be consensus about the need for

55

Reprinted from *IEEE Software*, Vol. 14, No. 2, Mar/Apr 1997, pp. 55-65.

TABLE 1
ORGANIZATIONAL DETAIL

Characteristic	Embedded Systems	Information Systems
General profile	Engineering company	Large public-sector organization (in the process of transferring into the private sector)
Applications	Defense-related Embedded control software 90% of applications are safety-critical	Online data processing systems
Development environment	Variety of advanced approaches, including formal methods and code, analyzing tools	State-of-art in using new methods Keen on using project-management methods and tools
Quality framework	Strong (on the surface), but suboptimal use of reviews and inspections AQAP certified (defense quality certificate)	Well-used framework Consistent use of basic quality controls In the process of seeking software quality certification
Management framework	Very complex staff structure Steep hierarchy Low morale score Two-year pay freeze High staff attrition rate	Simple staff structure Flattish hierarchy Average morale score Stable staff group

metrics programs within improvement initiatives.[1] However, perhaps the most important positive push for metrics programs was the publication of Robert Grady and Deborah Caswell's 1987 book, *Software Metrics: Establishing a Company Wide Program*.[2] The book—and its 1992 revision[3]—describes the Hewlett-Packard software metrics program. Grady and Caswell identify many important, and usually neglected, organizational issues surrounding software measurement. In particular, they proposed, along with other commentators,[3-5] various criteria for achieving a successful metrics program. After studying this and other research, we identified a consensus on requirements for metric program success.

♦ *Incremental implementation.* Implementing a metrics program over time holds significantly less risk than a "big bang" approach.

♦ *Transparency.* The metrics program must be obvious to practitioners. Practitioners must understand what data is being collected, why it is being collected, and how it is being used.

♦ *Usefulness.* The usefulness of metrics data should be obvious to all practitioners. If usefulness is not transparent (or, worse, if the data is not actually useful), practitioners will collect data

without enthusiasm and the data will probably lack validity.

♦ *Developer participation.* Developers should participate in designing the metrics program. With high levels of developer participation, buy-in is more likely, as is the implementation of a more incisive metrics program.

♦ *Metrics integrity.* Practitioners should have confidence in the collected data. They should believe it is sensible to collect, accurately collected, and not being "fiddled."

♦ *Feedback.* When practitioners get feedback on the data they collect, it gives them a clear indication that the data is being used rather than going into a black hole. This makes practitioners more likely to view the program positively. Commentators suggest several feedback mechanisms including newsletters, newsgroups, and graphical posters.

♦ *Automated data collection.* This should be done wherever possible. Minimizing extra work for developers also minimizes developer resistance to metrics. It also means that the data collected is more likely to be valid.

♦ *Practitioner training.* Case studies show that a metrics program that has a base of trained practitioners is more likely to be successful. Appropriate training must be targeted at all levels in

a company and should range from awareness raising to training in statistical analysis techniques.

♦ *Gurus and champions.* Organizations can increase practitioners' initial enthusiasm by bringing in an external metrics guru (Hewlett-Packard, for example, brought in Barry Boehm; Contel brought in Dieter Rombach). Organizations should also appoint internal metrics champions to help with the difficult and arduous task of sustaining a metrics program.[6]

♦ *Dedicated metrics team.* Responsibility for the metrics program should be assigned to specific individuals.

♦ *Goal-oriented approach.* It is very important that companies collect data for a specific purpose. Usually the data will be for monitoring the attainment of an improvement goal. Unsuccessful or ineffective programs collect data for no specific reason and find they have no use for the data they have collected. The Goal-Question-Metric model[7] has been highly popular among companies implementing a goal-oriented approach to measurement.

On the last two factors, the broader software engineering community does not entirely agree. Although there is consensus on the need for some kind of dedicated metrics team, there is no clear agreement on how

Organization	Staff Directly Affected by Metrics Program	Number Responding to Questionnaire			Response Rate (%)
		Total	Manager	Developer	
Embedded systems	24	20	10	10	83
Information systems	125	103	48	55	82

TABLE 2: RELEVANT STAFF AND RESPONSE RATE

centralized it should be, nor whether metrics should be the team's sole activity. Questions have also been raised about the GQM approach.[8] For example, Hetzel highlights the fact that GQM encourages organizations to use data that is likely to be difficult to collect.[9] This directly contradicts other advice on metrics programs, which encourages organizations to use available or easily collected data.

Notwithstanding these minor doubts, the factors above appear to be commonsense advice on implementing a metrics program. However, these factors are apparently proposed on the basis of either anecdotal evidence or single program experiences.

We spent six months conducting an independent study of these factors at work in two organizations. Here, we present quantitative data that describes practitioner experiences of metrication. This data generally supports—but occasionally contradicts—existing anecdotal evidence about metrics programs.

Although both of our case study programs were structurally similar, one was judged to be successful (by the organization and by us), and the other was judged as not yet successful (by the organization's metrics group and by us). Despite the fact that anecdotal evidence suggests that most metrics programs are unsuccessful, with a few notable exceptions (such as a 1993 study by Ross Jeffery and Mike Berry[10]), only successful programs are typically reported.

Our ultimate aim in this article,

which follows on our earlier work,[11] is to present the critical success and failure factors associated with the two metrics programs. In particular, we report on each organization's metrics implementation strategy, quantify the extent to which they implemented various metrics, and detail the ongoing management of the metrics programs.

THE STUDY

Our case study involved two organizations which, for reasons of commercial confidentiality, we refer to as Embedded Systems (ES) and Information Systems (IS). Both organizations

♦ have more than 10,000 employees, are more than 20 years old, and have complex internal bureaucracies;

♦ have a large software development function, with more than 400 software staff;

♦ are fully dependent on in-house software systems to support or enhance their main (nonsoftware) products;

♦ have a progressive approach toward new development methods and tools;

♦ have mature quality programs and usually consider the software they produce to be high quality; and

♦ have had a metrics program for between two and three years.

Some metricating success or failure factors may result from organization-specific issues; Table 1 gives the organizational context of each metrics program.

Phase one: fact finding. At each organi-

zation, we started with a few fact-finding interviews with middle managers who had a high level of corporate responsibility for the metrics program. We designed this fact-finding phase to identify the context, framework, and content of the "officially" implemented metrics program. Managers commonly have an inaccurate picture of what is really happening "on the ground." Thus, we designed this phase to establish what state the organization believed its metrics program to be in. In particular, we found out about the organization (such as number of employees in various activities), applications developed, development environment, metrics collected and how they were used, and implementation and management of metrics. We used the results of phase one as a baseline for phase two.

Phase two: data collection. In phase two we wanted to find out what was really happening in the metrics program. We managed to get serious input from nearly all the relevant staff by distributing detailed questionnaires to all managers and developers affected by metrics.

The aims of the questionnaire were to

♦ identify which metrics were really being collected (as opposed to the ones managers believed were being collected),

♦ find out how the metrics program was initially implemented and subsequently managed,

♦ establish the contributions that individuals and groups made to metrics, and

TABLE 3
IMPLEMENTATION FACTORS

Implementation Factors	ES	IS
Consensus recommendations		
Incremental implementation	✓	✗
Well-planned metrics framework	✓	✗
Use of existing metrics materials	✓	✗
Involvement of developers during implementation	✓	✗
Measurement process transparent to developers	✓	✗
Usefulness of metrics data	✓	✗
Feedback to developers	✓	✗
Ensure that the data is seen to have integrity	✓	✗
Measurement data is used and seen to be used	✓	✗
Commitment from project managers secured	✓	✗
Use automated data collection tools	✓	✗
Constantly improving the measurement program	✓	✗
Internal metrics champions used to manage the program	✓	✗
Use of external metrics gurus	✗	✗
Provision of training for practitioner	✗	✗
Other Recommendations		
Implement at a level local to the developers	✓	✗
Implement a central metrics function	✗	✓
Metrics responsibility devolved to the development teams	✓	✗
Incremental determination of the metrics set	✓	✗
Collecting data that is easy to collect	✗	✗

Key: ✓ shows that the recommendation is followed; ✗ shows that it is not

♦ solicit views and experiences of the success and value of metrics.

As Table 2 shows, we had an overall response rate of 83 percent. Thus, almost everyone affected by the metrics programs at both organizations contributed to this study: 24 practitioners at ES and 125 at IS. (ES implemented metrics in only one critical department whereas IS implemented metrics throughout software development.)

Our high response rate can likely be attributed to several factors.

♦ *Topicality.* Although both metrics programs were maturing, neither was long established. Thus, metrics was still a hot issue in both organizations, and practitioners had a lot they wanted to say about it.

♦ *Desire for evaluation and improvement:* In both organizations, metrics program managers fully and publicly supported our study. Because they had not formally evaluated the metrics programs themselves, they were keen to find out their practitioners' views. Developers also seemed keen to contribute, perhaps thinking their contribution might improve the metrics program.

♦ *Independence of the study:* Practitioners were confident that their views could not be used against them by management, and, thus, we suspect, were more open and honest in their contributions.

Because of our high response rate, we're confident that our results are an accurate representation of each organization's metrics program. However, this was not a controlled experiment and does not assess each factor's impact on metrics program success. Moreover, although it would be wrong to generalize results from a case study to the industry as a whole,[12] we believe our results offer many interesting insights that are relevant and applicable to other metricating organizations.

STUDY RESULTS

At both organizations, metric program managers agreed that good metrics implementation was important. Still, as Table 3 shows, they ignored experts' key recommendations discussed above, although ES adhered to more of the proposed success factors than IS did. And, indeed, ES's metrics program was the successful one. Now the details.

Introducing metrics. No comprehensive international survey has quantified the industrial penetration of metrics since the Drummond-Tyler study.[13] Indeed, influential software commentators disagree about the extent to which metrics have penetrated the software industry. For example, Capers Jones claims an encouraging industry-wide use of measures such as function points,[14] while Bill Hetzel is much less optimistic.[9]

Measurement was initially introduced at ES only because they were given external funding to field test the Application of Metrics in Industry (ami) approach to metrication.[1] Ami combines CMM with the Goal-Question-Metric method. With it, you use the SEI CMM questionnaire to establish process maturity, then use GQM to identify metrics that are appropriate for your organization's maturity level.

Although not particularly motivated at the start, ES quickly discovered the value of metrics and implemented the

program reasonably well. Metrics were implemented initially only in one development team, which meant that the metrics program was very close to the developers and could be tightly controlled by the managers.

Metrics implementation at IS was weak. The initial motivation for implementing metrics was that senior managers wanted to monitor productivity. Other studies have shown that weak motivations like this are commonplace, although the relationship between weak motivations and program failure is not clear.

IS set up a centralized metrics group to introduce metrics across the whole development function. There was no discernible use of metrication aids, nor was metrics use piloted. The implementation strategy seemed to consist solely of the metrics group instructing

the development departments to start collecting specified metrics.

Developer involvement. Although managers were very involved in metrics design in both organizations, IS had little developer input into the design process. Interestingly, managers at both organizations thought developers were more involved in metrics design than developers said they were: 60 percent of managers—compared to 20 percent of developers—thought metrics design at ES was a joint effort, while 27 percent of managers and 4 percent of developers at IS thought the same.

Goal clarity. We asked practitioners to rank five software development goals according to their organization's priorities and their own. A score of 1 was awarded for the most important goal

and 5 for the least important goal. Table 4 shows practitioner perception of the organization's goals. Clearly, neither ES nor IS was good at communicating development goals to their employees.

These poor results are surprising considering that ES was actively using GQM (though the model does not address the method of identifying and disseminating goals). There was, however, much less disagreement when practitioners were asked to rank their own personal goals (and not everyone ranked low costs as their least important goal).

Usefulness. As Table 5 shows, practitioners were generally positive about the usefulness of metrics, although the practitioners at ES were more positive than those at IS (90 percent of ES practitioners and 59 percent of IS prac-

TABLE 4
RANKING SOFTWARE GOALS

| Perceived Organizational Goals | Embedded Systems | | | Perceived Organizational Goals | Information Systems | | |
| | Mean Scores | | | | Mean Scores | | |
	Overall	Managers	Developers		Overall	Managers	Developers
Low costs	2.5	2.2	2.8	User satisfaction	2.6	2.6	2.6
Conformance	2.9	2.6	3.2	Speed	2.9	2.9	2.8
Speed	3.0	3.0	3.0	Reliability	3.0	3.0	3.0
Reliability	3.1	3.6	2.6	Conformance	3.1	3.2	3.1
User satisfaction	3.5	3.6	3.4	Low costs	3.4	3.3	3.5

TABLE 5
USEFULNESS OF METRICS

| Metrics Usefulness | Embedded Systems | | | Information Systems | | |
	Overall	Managers	Developers	Overall	Managers	Developers
Very useful	30	40	20	15	22	9
Quite useful	60	60	60	44	50	41
Not very useful	10	0	20	25	18	30
Not useful at all	0	0	0	10	9	11
Don't know	0	0	0	7	1	10

287

TABLE 6
METRICS EFFICACY AND INTEGRITY

| | Embedded Systems | | | Information Systems | | |
	Overall (%)	Managers (%)	Developers (%)	Overall (%)	Managers (%)	Developers (%)
1. Is the data collected accurately?						
Accurate	40	60	20	18	31	8
Not accurate	10	10	10	41	39	43
Don't know	50	30	70	41	29	50
2. Metrics feedback?						
Feedback is provided	30	50	10	18	25	11
Feedback is not provided	15	20	10	53	56	50
Don't know	55	30	80	29	19	39
3. Is the right data collected?						
Yes	40	60	20	11	13	10
No	10	0	20	46	48	44
Don't know	50	40	60	43	39	44
4. Is the data manipulated?						
Often	20	20	20	27	29	26
Occasionally	40	30	50	50	58	41
Never	5	10	0	1	0	2
Don't know	35	40	30	22	13	31
5. Who manipulates the data?						
Developers	5	0	10	15	21	9
Managers	35	40	30	40	42	39
Neither	5	10	0	2	2	2
Both	20	20	20	22	24	20
Don't know	35	30	40	20	10	30

titioners thought metrics were very useful or quite useful).

Table 6 shows practitioner confidence in each organization's metrics program. Once again, the metrics program at ES was received much more positively than the metrics program at IS. However, as the table also shows, most practitioners at both organizations were convinced that the metrics data was manipulated. Follow-up research suggests the practitioners were convinced that data was "massaged" (usually by managers) to make a situation look better than it actually was.

We also found a clear difference in metrics feedback between ES and IS. At ES, 30 percent of practitioners said feedback was provided, compared with only 18 percent at IS. Still, uncertainty reigned: 55 percent of ES practitioners and 29 percent of those at IS said they didn't know if their organization provided feedback or not.

Overall results. The approach adopted by each organization gives us a particu-lar insight into GQM, which forces an incremental approach to identifying a metrics set. GQM thus complimented ES's incremental implementation strategy and helped it avoid problems, such as lack of transparency and devel-oper buy-in.

IS used neither GQM nor data that was easily available. They had many problems with their metrics program. IS's approach to identifying a metrics set lacked a clear strategy. Whether GQM is being used or not, an organization must provide its practitioners a clear use for the data they collect. IS did not do this. Further, there must be a clear link between the metrics and improvement goals. If this relationship is not obvious, practitioners lack moti-vation to put effort into metrics collec-tion. The validity of the data collected is thus compromised.

Our results also gave us interesting insight into the nature of metrics feed-back. Practitioners at ES were reason-ably satisfied with metrics feedback whereas practitioners at IS were not at all satisfied. At ES, only 15 percent said they did not get feedback, as opposed to 53 percent of IS respondents. This surprised program managers at both organizations.

Before our study, IS managers felt confident that formal feedback mecha-nisms were in place (although they had not properly evaluated the effective-ness of these mechanisms). Since the study, managers at IS have taken steps to improve metrics feedback.

Managers at ES were surprised at how relatively satisfied practitioners seemed to be with feedback, as they had few formal feedback mechanisms. They did, however, use metrics on a day-to-day basis and regularly discussed results informally. ES also operated an open-house policy for metrics data. Thus, although metrics results were not for-mally distributed or displayed, practi-tioners did have access to the data. On the other hand, the program may have been an even greater success if ES had provided more formal feedback.

Finally, many practitioners marked

"Don't Know" when asked about aspects of metrication. Even at ES, where the metrics program was well established and apparently successful, many practitioners did not know, for example, whether metrics data was accurate or if the right data was collected. Practitioner ignorance was a weak spot in both programs. However, practitioners had strong views on some aspects of metrication, indicating better communication and higher practitioner interest. On metric usefulness, for example, few practitioners responded with "don't know."

EMERGING CRITERIA

In addition to the expert recommendations discussed so far, there are other, broader ways to assess a metrics program. Among the most important we identified were metrics collection effort, metrics selection, practitioner awareness, and practitioner attitude.

Choosing metrics. Table 7 quantifies the extent to which each organization collected various metrics data. The table lists a subset of the measures con-

tained in the official metrics programs. IS's metrics list included several other measures and was considerably longer than the ES list.

We determined the most frequently used metrics in each organization based upon the activity levels in Table 7. For ES, the core metrics were
♦ resource estimates,
♦ lines of code,
♦ design review data, and
♦ code complexity data.
For IS, the core metrics were
♦ resource estimates,

	Total				Manager				Developer			
	Question One		Question Two		Question One		Question Two		Question One		Question Two	
	ES	IS	ES	IS	ES	IS	ES	IS	ES	IS	ES	IS
Function points[†]	–	86	–	15	–	87	–	19	–	85	–	11
Metrics for size estimates[*]	85	50	40	11	90	57	60	13	80	44	20	9
Metrics for cost estimates[*]	90	80	30	26	90	85	50	56	90	76	10	7
Metrics for effort estimates[*]	70	65	35	27	90	77	60	42	50	54	10	13
Analysis inspection data	40	35	10	8	50	41	20	13	30	30	0	4
Design review data	75	39	25	8	80	44	50	10	70	34	0	6
Design effort data	40	31	20	9	50	40	30	11	30	23	10	7
Code interface data	65	16	20	5	60	13	30	4	70	19	10	6
Code complexity data	70	7	20	0	90	8	30	0	50	6	10	0
Lines of code data	80	43	25	12	100	52	40	19	60	35	10	7
Coding effort data	45	20	10	12	70	49	20	19	20	26	0	6
Code inspection data	30	29	15	7	40	38	20	10	20	22	10	4
Fault rates	25	14	10	2	20	15	10	4	30	13	10	0
Defect densities	20	15	10	3	30	23	20	4	10	9	0	2
Change data	60	28	20	5	70	32	30	6	50	24	10	4
Testing effort data	40	31	10	7	60	49	20	13	20	15	0	2
Test review data	65	25	20	6	70	34	30	11	60	17	10	2

Key: Each entry represents the percentage of respondents answering "yes" to the following questions:
Question One: *Does your organization collect the following metrics data?*
Question Two: *Do you know, from personal involvement, that the following metrics data is collected?*

[†] = IS practitioners were very keen on function points, so we asked them separately about function point penetration.
[*] = We asked only about fairly general metrics in order to avoid fragmenting the results.

- function points, and
- lines of code.

Although ES was generally more active in its metrics activity, both orga-

> **Data cannot be used to motivate productivity if people do not know it is being collected.**

nizations favored a typical set of core metrics, dominated by size and effort metrics—primarily used for resource estimation and productivity measurement—rather than quality metrics. This result supports other research and runs contrary to the advice of all commentators. Overemphasis on cost-oriented data is probably another common fault of many metrics programs.

Collection effort. There is little explicit discussion in the literature about what constitutes a reasonable overhead for a metrics program, although 7 percent overall has been suggested as an average effort overhead.[15] In our study, neither program appeared to have a large effort overhead. At ES, 90 percent of practitioners said they spent less than 3 percent of their time on metrics-related activity, with the remaining 10 percent spending between 3 and 14 percent. At IS, 79 percent spent less than 3 percent, 16 percent spent between 3 and 14 percent, and 4 percent spent between 14 and 29 percent of their time on metrics activities. The fact that practitioners at ES spent less time collecting metrics data than practitioners at IS was probably because ES used automated tools.

Ironically, IS was not as effective at metricating as ES, and yet spent more effort on its metrics program. Part of this was because IS was collecting more metrics data. It is also likely that some of the IS metrics were not needed or used.

As Table 7 shows, managers at both organizations were more personally involved in metrics collection than developers, although ES had a higher overall participation level than IS. Also, while ES had a successful metrics program, there was minimal developer involvement in data collection. This is because the ES program was deliberately driven by managers and used automated data collection. The metrics program at IS seemed generally inactive, with few managers or developers directly participating in metrics collection. Indeed only 19 percent of IS managers and 7 percent of its developers said they knew from personal involvement that LOC data was collected. (IS's program did not use any special-purpose automated metrics collection tools and was largely paper-based.)

These results suggest that it is important for practitioners to know what is going on in the metrics program, but that personal involvement in collection is not very important. This finding supports other experiential reports[4,16] in which using automated tools and keeping practitioners informed seem like necessary prerequisites to metrics success.

Table 7 also shows that although ES had the most active metrics program, it lacked clarity and goal orientation in two areas.

- *Poor transparency.* Although 70 percent of ES managers said that coding effort data was collected, only 20 percent of developers knew this and no developers claimed to be involved in collecting this data. It is difficult to understand how accurate data can be collected over the life cycle without developer participation (although they may not have realized that time sheets are used for collecting coding effort data). It is also difficult to understand the purpose of collecting such data if developers do not know that it is required. It cannot be used to motivate productivity if people do not know it is being collected.

- *Poor goal-metric coupling.* Although 90 percent of managers said code complexity data was collected, only 50 percent of developers realized this and very few managers or developers were involved in collecting it. The main purpose of collecting complexity data is to control complexity. If developers do not know that complexity data is being collected, they are unlikely to take reducing complexity seriously. It also makes collecting complexity data ineffective.

Practitioner awareness. We analyzed metrics activity in terms of what practitioners knew about the measurement and how involved they were in collecting the data. Our rationale was that, although there may be an *official* metrics program in place, unless practitioners are aware of that program and see themselves as involved in it, the organization has not created the necessary measurement culture and the program is likely to be ineffective. Indeed, many of the metrics cited by both organizations as part of their "official" metrics program were so little known about and used that it is difficult to accept that they were an actual part of the metrics programs.

As Table 7 shows, ES had consistently more metrics activity than IS among both managers and developers. Although the official metrics program at IS contained many measures, awareness of these measures was generally low. Although there was a higher general level of awareness at ES, the awareness gap between managers and developers was lower at IS (an average 13-percent difference between managers' and developers' metrics awareness levels at IS and a 20 percent difference at ES). LOC metrics are a good illustration of this awareness gap: 100 percent of managers and 60 percent of developers at ES knew that lines of code data was collected (an awareness gap of 40 percentage points) compared with 52 percent of managers and 35 percent of developers at IS (an awareness gap of

17 percentage points).

Generally, practitioners at both organizations exhibited poor awareness of what was happening to review and inspection data. Both organizations used reviews and inspections regularly; the review process can be a rich source of metrics data. As Table 7 shows, the use of this data was not obvious to managers or developers at either organization, thus suggesting that the data was being used suboptimally. This is probably a common metrication weakness and is another example of organizations not heeding the published experiential advice.

Practitioner attitude. One of the most important factors in metrics program success is practitioner attitude: If you fail to generate positive feelings toward the program, you seriously undermine your likelihood of success. As Table 5 shows, in general, ES practitioners were more positive about metrics use than those at IS.

A significant influence on attitude towards metrics was job seniority. In both organizations, managers were much more positive than developers about metrics use, introduction, and management. Furthermore, the more senior managers were, the more enthusiastic they were about using metrics. At IS, for example, 87 percent of senior managers were positive about metrics compared to 72 percent of middle managers and 45 percent of junior analysts and programmers.

However, we also found that developers were more positive about metrics than conventional wisdom has led us to believe (Tom DeMarco suspected this was this case.[5]) It is generally thought, especially by managers, that developers are unenthusiastic about quality mechanisms like metrics and cannot see their value. Our results actually show that 80 percent of ES developers and 50 percent of IS developers were positive about metrics use.

It has been said that when developers are asked their opinion about software quality mechanisms, they say such things are useful, but when they're asked to participate they find many reasons why their work must be exempt. This could explain the positive attitudes toward metrics that we found in this study. If this is the case—and developers are only positive about metrics in the abstract—then organizations need to work toward realizing this positive potential. In any case, the relationship between positive perceptions and negative action warrants more research.

Table 5 supports our view that practitioners' perceptions of metrics are strongly influenced by the reality of their metrics program rather than vice versa. If this were not the case, we would expect a stronger alignment between developer and manager views between the organizations. In fact, the table shows that practitioner perceptions varied significantly, even though within each organization the perception patterns of managers and developers were very similar. This has important implications for managers: it means that what practitioners think about metrics and how they respond to them is within managers' control. Too frequently, managers assume that developers will be negative about metrics *per se*. Our results suggest that developer attitudes are built upon experience.

The integrity of metrics data also seems to have a powerful influence on practitioner attitudes, as Table 6 shows. Managers at both organizations were significantly more convinced than developers that

♦ the data collected was accurate,
♦ enough metrics feedback was provided, and
♦ the right metrics data was collected.

Such a manager/developer perception gap is troublesome. For an effective metrics program, it is important that the metrics data not only has integrity, but that developers believe that it has. Our study has not yet examined the integrity of the ES and IS metrics data, so we do not know whether the data has integrity or not. We do know, however, that many practitioners affected by metrics do not believe that the data has integrity. This perception will probably do more damage than if the data has no integrity but practitioners believe that it does. As Tables 5 and 6 show, ES developers were less negative overall about the integrity of metrics data and more positive about using metrics.

There are two probable explanations for the manager/developer perception gap that we observed. First, managers probably have more access to metrics information and data. So, for example, they probably have more feedback and are probably in a better position to judge data accuracy. Second, managers in both organizations were more actively involved in setting up and managing the metrics programs. Consequently, they are less likely to criticize something they were instrumental in setting up. This gap may be compounded by the fact that no metrics evaluations had taken place at either organization and so managers may have been unaware of the problems our study uncovered.

> ## What practitioners think about metrics and how they respond to them is within the managers' control.

EPILOGUE

These case studies form part of a continuing longitudinal study into the quality and measurement programs in several major UK organizations. As

such, we continue to monitor the ES and IS metrics programs.

Our results were taken very seriously by the metrics managers at IS. Since we conducted the study two years ago, IS has either rectified, or is in the process of rectifying, many of the weaknesses we identified in its metrics programs. The program has radically improved, both because of our findings and because IS has since been taken over by a company with a more established quality and measurement regime. In particular, the IS program has been improved in the following ways:

♦ Metrics responsibility has been devolved to individual development teams and is thus much more local to developers.

♦ The centralized metrics group now acts in a more advisory rather than managerial role.

♦ Managers have made a big effort to improve transparency and feedback within the program.

♦ The actual metrics set has also been revised and is now smaller and more goal-focused, addressing the basic areas of effort, size, change, defects, and duration.

The metrics program at ES continues to be carefully managed and improved in an incremental way. The metrics set has been refined and some metrics are no longer collected. The program is viewed by ES senior managers as so successful that it is now in the process of being rolled out to all other software teams in the organization.

Neither organization has divulged to us metrics data about software quality. Thus, even at this stage, it is impossible for us to report on how the quality of software produced by ES compares to that produced by IS.

Our study confirmed that the success of a metrics program depends upon a carefully planned implementation strategy. We also found that the consensus "success" factors in the literature are generally correct, but that the advice is not always heeded. Success seems particularly linked to an organization's willingness to

♦ do background research on other metrics programs and use advice given in the published experiential reports,

♦ involve developers in metrics program design and inform them on the program's development and progress,

♦ use an incremental approach to implementation and run a pilot of the metrics program, and

♦ acknowledge developer concerns about metrics data use.

Also, in our study both metrics programs could have benefited from earlier and regular evaluations.

In contemplating the two programs, we suspect that one of the most important but intangible success factors is the approach and attitude of metrics program managers. The successful program was managed with a tenacious commitment to see metrics work. In contrast, the unsuccessful program seemed half-hearted, despite the fact that it was ambitious and expensive to implement. Indeed, at the outset, the odds were probably stacked against the successful organization: it had a weaker quality framework and lower staff morale. This suggests that organizations implementing metrics not only need to make use of the good practices, but must manage those programs with a certain amount of gusto. ♦

REFERENCES

1. *Metric Users Handbook*, ami Consortium, South Bank Univ., London, 1992.
2. R.B. Grady and D.L. Caswell, *Software Metrics: Establishing a Company-Wide Program*, Prentice Hall, Englewood Cliffs, N.J., 1987.
3. R.B. Grady, *Practical Software Metrics for Project Management and Process Improvement*, Prentice Hall, Englewood Cliffs, N.J., 1992.
4. S.L. Pfleeger, "Lessons Learned in Building a Corporate Metrics Program," *IEEE Software*, May 1993, pp. 67-74.
5. T. DeMarco, *Controlling Software Projects*, Prentice Hall, Englewood Cliffs, N.J., 1982.
6. C. Cox, "Sustaining a Metrics Program in Industry," *Software Reliability and Metrics*, N.E. Fenton and B. Littlewood, eds., Elsevier, New York, 1991, pp. 1-15.
7. V.R. Basili and H.D. Rombach, "The TAME Project: Towards Improvement-Oriented Software Environments," *IEEE Trans. Software Eng.*, Vol. 14, No. 6, 1988, pp. 758-773.
8. R. Bache and M. Neil, "Introducing Metrics into Industry: A Perspective on GQM," *Software Quality, Assurance and Measurement: A Worldwide Perspective*, N.E. Fenton et al., eds., Int'l Thompson Computer Press, London, 1995.
9. W.C. Hetzel, *Making Software Measurement Work: Building an Effective Software Measurement Programme*, QED, Wellesley, Mass., 1993.
10. R. Jeffery and M. Berry, "A Framework for Evaluation and Prediction of Metrics Program Success," *1st Int'l Software Metrics Symp.*, IEEE Computer Soc. Press, Los Alamitos, Calif., 1993, pp. 28-39.
11. T. Hall and N.E. Fenton, "Implementing Software Metrics—The Critical Success Factors," *Software Quality J.*, Jan. 1994, pp. 195-208.
12. B. Kitchenham, L. Pickard, and S.L. Pfleeger, "Case Studies for Method and Tool Evaluation," *IEEE Software*, July 1995, pp. 52-63.
13. E. Drummond-Tyler, *Software Metrics: An International Survey of Industrial Practice*, Esprit 2 Project Metkit Sema Group, South Bank Univ., London, 1989.
14. C. Jones, *Applied Software Measurement*, McGraw-Hill, New York, 1991.
15. D.H. Rombach, V.R. Basili, and R.W. Selby, *Experimental Software Engineering Issues*, Springer Verlag, Berlin, 1993.
16. M.K. Daskalantonakis, "A Practical View of Software Management and Implementation Experiences within Motorola," *IEEE Trans. Software Eng.*, Vol. 18, No. 11, 1992, pp. 998-1009.

Tracy Hall is a senior lecturer in software engineering at the University of Westminster, UK. Her research interests center around quality and measurement in software engineering.

Hall received a BA and MSc from Teesside University and is studying for a doctorate at City University, London.

Norman Fenton is a chartered engineer and a professor of computing science at the Centre for Software Reliability, City University, London. His research interests are in software metrics, safety-critical systems, and formal development methods.

Address questions about this article to Hall at the School of Computer Science, University of Wesuninster, 115 New Cavendish St., London W1M 8JS, UK, hallt@westminster.ac.uk.

Software Measurement: A Necessary Scientific Basis

Norman Fenton

Abstract— Software measurement, like measurement in any other discipline, must adhere to the science of measurement if it is to gain widespread acceptance and validity. The observation of some very simple, but fundamental, principles of measurement can have an extremely beneficial effect on the subject. Measurement theory is used to highlight both weaknesses and strengths of software metrics work, including work on metrics validation. We identify a problem with the well-known Weyuker properties, but also show that a criticism of these properties by Cherniavsky and Smith is invalid. We show that the search for general software complexity measures is doomed to failure. However, the theory does help us to define and validate measures of specific complexity attributes. Above all, we are able to view software measurement in a very wide perspective, rationalising and relating its many diverse activities.

Index Terms—Software measurement, empirical studies, metrics, measurement theory, complexity, validation.

I. INTRODUCTION

IT IS over eleven years since DeMillo and Lipton outlined the relevance of measurement theory to software metrics [10]. More recent work by the author and others [4], [11], [46] has taken the measurement theory basis for software metrics considerably further. However, despite the important message in this work, and related material (such as [31], [34], [43], [38]), it has been largely ignored by both practitioners and researchers. The result is that much published work in software metrics is theoretically flawed. This paper therefore provides a timely summary and enhancement of measurement theory approaches, which enables us to expose problems in software metrics work and show how they can be avoided.

In Section II, we provide a concise summary of measurement theory. In Section III, we use the theory to show that the search for general-purpose, real-valued software 'complexity' measures is doomed to failure. The assumption that fundamentally different views of complexity can be characterised by a single number is counter to the fundamental concepts of measurement theory. This leads us to re-examine critically the much cited Weyuker properties [45]. We explain how the most promising approach is to identify specific attributes of complexity and measure these separately. In Section IV, we use basic notions of measurement to describe a framework which enables us to view apparently diverse software measurement activities in a unified way. We look at some well-known approaches to software measurement within this framework, exposing both the good points and bad points.

Manuscript received August 1992; revised September 1993. This work was supported in part by IED project SMARTIE and ESPRIT project PDCS2.

The author is with the Centre for Software Reliability, City University, London, EC1V OHB, UK.

IEEE Log Number 9215569.

II. MEASUREMENT FUNDAMENTALS

In this section, we provide a summary of the key concepts from the science of measurement which are relevant to software metrics. First, we define the fundamental notions (which are generally not well understood) and then we summarise the representational theory of measurement. Finally, we explain how this leads inevitably to a goal-oriented approach.

A. What is Measurement?

Measurement is defined as the process by which numbers or symbols are assigned to attributes of entities in the real world in such a way as to describe them according to clearly defined rules [13], [36]. An *entity* may be an object, such as a person or a software specification, or an event, such as a journey or the testing phase of a software project. An *attribute* is a feature or property of the entity, such as the height or blood pressure (of a person), the length or functionality (of a specification), the cost (of a journey), or the duration (of the testing phase).

Just what is meant by the numerical assignment "describing" the attribute is made precise within the representational theory of measurement presented below. Informally, the assignment of numbers or symbols must preserve any intuitive and empirical observations about the attributes and entities. Thus, for example, when measuring the height of humans bigger numbers must be assigned to the taller humans, although the numbers themselves will differ according to whether we use metres, inches, or feet. In most situations an attribute, even one as well understood as height of humans, may have a different intuitive meaning to different people. The normal way to get round this problem is to define a *model* for the entities being measured. The model reflects a specific viewpoint. Thus, for example, our model of a human might specify a particular type of posture and whether or not to include hair height or allow shoes to be worn. Once the model is fixed there is a reasonable consensus about relations which hold for humans with respect to height (these are the empirical relations). The need for good models is particularly relevant in software engineering measurement. For example, even as simple a measure of length of programs as lines of code (LOC) requires a well defined model of programs which enables us to identify unique lines unambiguously. Similarly, to measure the effort spent on, say, the unit testing process we would need an agreed "model" of the process which at least makes clear when the process begins and ends.

There are two broad types of measurement: direct and indirect. *Direct measurement* of an attribute is measurement which does not depend on the measurement of any other attribute. *Indirect measurement* of an attribute is measurement which involves the measurement of one or more other attributes. It

Reprinted from *IEEE Transactions on Software Engineering*, Vol. 20, No. 3, Mar. 1994, pp. 199-206.

turns out that while some attributes can be measured directly, we normally get more sophisticated measurement (meaning a more sophisticated scale, see below) if we measure indirectly. For a good discussion of these issues, see [25], [27].

Uses of Measurement: Assessment and Prediction: There are two broad uses of measurement: for *assessment* and for *prediction*. Predictive measurement of an attribute A will generally depend on a mathematical model relating A to some existing measures of attributes $A_1, \cdots, A_n$. Accurate predictive measurement is inevitably dependent on careful (assessment type) measurement of the attributes $A_1, \cdots, A_n$. For example, accurate estimates of project resources are *not* obtained by simply "applying" a cost estimation model with fixed parameters [26]. However, careful measurement of key attributes of completed projects can lead to accurate resource predictions for future projects [22] Similarly, it is possible to get accurate predictions of the reliability of software in operation, but these are dependent on careful data collection relating to failure times during alpha-testing [5].

For predictive measurement the model alone is not sufficient. Additionally, we need to define the procedures for a) determining model parameters and b) interpreting the results. For example, in the case of software reliability prediction we might use maximum likelihood estimation for a) and Bayesian statistics for b). The model, together with procedures a) and b), is called a *prediction system* [29]. Using the same model will generally yield different results if we use different prediction procedures.

It must be stressed that, for all but the most trivial attributes, proposed predictive measures in software engineering are invariably stochastic rather than deterministic. The same is true of proposed indirect measures [14].

Measurement Activities must have Clear Objectives: The basic definitions of measurement suggest that any measurement activity must proceed with very clear objectives or goals. First you need to know whether you want to measure for assessment or for prediction. Next, you need to know exactly which entities are the subject of interest. Then you need to decide which attributes of the chosen entities are the significant ones. The definition of measurement makes clear the need to specify both an entity and an attribute before any measurement can be undertaken (a simple fact which has been ignored in much software metrics activity). Clearly, there are no definitive measures which can be prescribed for every objective in any application area. Yet for many years software practitioners expected precisely that: 'what software metric should we be using?' was, and still is, a commonly asked question. It says something about the previous ignorance of scientific measurement in software engineering that the Goal/Question/Metric paradigm of Basili and Rombach [7] has been hailed as a revolutionary step forward. GQM spells out the above necessary obligations for setting objectives before embarking on any software measurement activity.

B. Representational Theory of Measurement

The Issues Addressed: Although there is no *universally* agreed theory of measurement, most approaches are devoted to resolving the following issues: what is and what is not measurement; which types of attributes can and cannot be measured and on what kind of scales; how do we know if we have really measured an attribute; how to define measurement scales; when is an error margin acceptable or not; which statements about measurement are meaningful. The texts [13], [25], [27], [36], [40] all deal with these issues. Here we present a brief overview of the *representational* theory of measurement [13], [25].

Empirical Relation Systems: Direct measurement of a particular attribute possessed by a set of entities must be preceded by intuitive understanding of that attribute. This intuitive understanding leads to the identification of empirical relations between entities. The set of entities C, together with the set of empirical relations R, is called an *empirical relation system* (C, R) for the attribute in question. Thus the attribute of "height" of people gives rise to empirical relations like "is tall", "taller than", and "much taller than".

Representation Condition: To measure the attribute that is characterised by an empirical relation system (C, R) requires a mapping M into a *numerical relation system* (N, P). Specifically, M maps entities in C to numbers (or symbols) in N, and empirical relations in R are mapped to numerical relations in P, in such a way that all empirical relations are preserved. This is the so-called *representation condition,* and the mapping M is called a *representation.* The representation condition asserts that the correspondence between empirical and numerical relations is two way. Suppose, for example, that the binary relation $\prec$ is mapped by M to the numerical relation $<$. Then, formally, we have the following instance:

Representation Condition: $x \prec y \Longleftrightarrow M(x) < M(y)$

Thus, suppose, C is the set of all people and R contains the relation "taller than". A measure M of height would map C into the set of real numbers $\Re$ and 'taller than' to the relation ">". The representation condition asserts that person A is taller than person B, if and only if $M(A) > M(B)$.

By having to identify empirical relations for an attribute in advance, the representational approach to measurement avoids the temptation to *define* a poorly understood, but intuitively recognisable, attribute in terms of some numerical assignment. This is one of the most common failings in software metrics work. Classic examples are where attributes such as "complexity" or "quality" are equated with proposed numbers; for example, complexity with a "measure" like McCabe's cyclomatic number [30], or Halstead's E [18], and "quality" with Kafura and Henry's fan-in/fan-out equation [23].

Scale Types and Meaningfulness: Suppose that an attribute of some set of entities has been characterised by an empirical relation system (C, R). There may in general be many ways of assigning numbers which satisfy the representation condition. For example, if person A is taller than person B, then $M(A) > M(B)$ irrespective of whether the measure M is in inches, feet, centimetres metres, etc. Thus, there are many different measurement representations for the normal empirical relation system for the attribute of height of people. However, any two representations M and M' are related in a very specific way: there is always some constant $c > 0$ such that $M = cM'$

(so where M is the representation of height in inches and M' in centimetres, $c = 2.54$). This transformation from one valid representation into another is called an *admissible transformation*.

It is the class of admissible transformations which determines the *scale type* for an attribute (with respect to some fixed empirical relation system). For example, where every admissible transformation is a scalar multiplication (as for height) the scale type is called *ratio*. The ratio scale is a sophisticated scale of measurement which reflects a very rich empirical relation system. An attribute is never of ratio type *a priori*; we normally start with a crude understanding of an attribute and a means of measuring it. Accumulating data and analysing the results leads to the clarification and re-evaluation of the attribute. This in turn leads to refined and new empirical relations and improvements in the accuracy of the measurement; specifically this is an improved scale.

For many software attributes we are still at the stage of having very crude empirical relation systems. In the case of an attribute like "criticality" of software failures an empirical relation system would at best only identify different classes of failures and a binary relation "is more critical than". In this case, any two representations are related by a monotonically increasing transformation. With this class of admissible transformations, we have an *ordinal* scale type. In increasing order of sophistication, the best known scale types are: *nominal, ordinal, interval, ratio*, and *absolute*. For full details about the defining classes of admissible transformations, see [36].

This formal definition of scale type based on admissible transformations enables us to determine rigorously what kind of statements about measurement are meaningful. Formally, a statement involving measurement is *meaningful* if its truth or falsity remains unchanged under any admissible transformation of the measures involved. Thus, for example, it is meaningful to say that "Hermann is twice as tall as Peter"; if the statement is true (false) when we measure height in inches, it will remain true (false) when we measure height in any constant multiple of inches. On the other hand the statement "Failure x is twice as critical as failure y" is not meaningful if we only have an ordinal scale empirical relation system for failure criticality. This is because a valid ordinal scale measure M could define $M(x) = 6$, $M(y) = 3$, while another valid ordinal scale measure M' could define $M'(x) = 10$, $M'(y) = 9$. In this case the statement is true under M but false under M'.

The notion of meaningfulness also enables us to determine what kind of operations we can perform on different measures. For example, it is meaningful to use *means* for computing the average of a set of data measured on a ratio scale but not on an ordinal scale. *Medians* are meaningful for an ordinal scale but not for a nominal scale. Again, these basic observations have been ignored in many software measurement studies, where a common mistake is to use the mean (rather than median) as measure of average for data which is only ordinal. Good examples of practical applications of meaningfulness ideas may be found in [3] FW86, [37], [39]. An alternative definition of meaningfulness is given in [16].

Representation Theorems: The serious mathematical aspects of measurement theory are largely concerned with theorems which assert conditions under which certain scales of direct measurement are possible for certain relation systems. A typical example of such a theorem, due to Cantor, gives conditions for real-valued ordinal-scale measurement when we have a countable set of entities C and a binary relation b on C:

Cantor's Theorem: The empirical relation system (C, b) has a representation in $(\Re, <)$ if and only if b is a strict weak order. The scale type is ordinal when such a representation exists.

The relation b being a "strict weak order" means that it is:
1) *asymmetric* (xRy implies that it is not the case yRx), and
2) *negatively transitive* (xRy implies that for every $z \in C$, either xRz or zRy).

III. Measuring Software "Complexity"

The representational theory of measurement is especially relevant to the study of software complexity measures. In this section we show that the search for a general-purpose real-valued complexity measure is doomed to failure, but that there are promising axiomatic approaches which help us to measure specific complexity attributes. However, one well-known axiomatic approach [45] has serious weaknesses because it attempts to characterise incompatible views of complexity.

A. General Complexity Measures: The Impossible Holy Grail

For many years researchers have sought to characterise general notions of "complexity" by a single real number. To simplify matters, we first restrict our attention to those measures which attempt only to characterise control-flow complexity. If we can show that it is impossible to define a general measure of control-flow complexity, then the impossibility of even more general complexity measures is certain.

Zuse cites dozens of proposed control-flow complexity measures in [46]. There seems to be a minimum assumption that the empirical relation system for complexity of programs leads to (at least) an ordinal scale. This is because of the following hypotheses which are implicit in much of the work.

Hypothesis 1: Let C be the class of programs. Then the attribute control-flow "complexity" is characterised by an empirical relation system which includes a binary relation b "less complex than"; specifically $(x, y) \in b$ if there is a consensus that x is less complex than y.

Hypothesis 2: The proposed measure $M: C \rightarrow \Re$ is a representation of complexity in which the relation b is mapped to $<$.

Hypothesis 1 seems plausible. It does not state that C is totally ordered with respect to b; only that there is some *general* view of complexity for which there would be a reasonable consensus that certain pairs of programs are in b. For example, in Fig. 1, it seems plausible that $(x, y) \in b$ (from the measurement theory viewpoint it would be good enough if most programmers agreed this). Some pairs appear to be

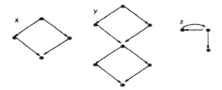

Fig. 1.   Complexity relation not negatively transitive?

incomparable, such as x and z or y and z; if people were asked to "rank" these for complexity they would inevitably end up asking questions like "what is meant by complexity" before attempting to answer. Since b is supposed to capture a general view of complexity, this would be enough to deduce that $(x, z) \notin b$ and $(z, x) \notin b$ and also that $(z, y) \notin b$ and $(y, z) \notin b$. The idea of the inevitable incomparability of some programs, even for some specific views of complexity, has also been noted in [43].

Unfortunately, while Hypothesis 1 is plausible, Hypothesis 2 can be dismissed because of the Representation Condition. The problem is the "incomparable" programs. While b is not a total order in C, the relation $<$ is a total order in $\Re$. The measurement mapping M might force an order which has to be reflected back in C. Thus, if for example $M(z) < M(y)$ (as in the case of McCabe's cyclomatic complexity measure in Fig. 1 where $M(z) = 2$ and $M(y) = 3$) then, if M is really a measure of complexity, the Representation Condition asserts that we must also have $z < y$ for which there is no consensus.

Formally we can prove the following theorem.

Theorem 1: Assuming Hypothesis 1, there is no general notion of control-flow complexity of programs which can be measured on an ordinal scale in $(\Re, <)$

To prove this, the previous argument is made formal by appealing to Cantor's Theorem. It is enough to show that the relation b is not a strict weak order. This follows since (according to our definition of b) it is reasonable to deduce that $(x, y) \in b$ but $(x, z) \notin b$ and $(z, y) \notin b$ (since it is not clear that any consensus exists about the relative complexities of x and z and y and z).

The theorem should put an end to the search for the holy grail of a general complexity measure. However, it does not rule out the search for measures that characterise specific views of complexity (which is the true measurement theory approach). For example, a specific program complexity attribute is "the number of independent paths." McCabe's cyclomatic complexity is an absolute scale measure of this attribute. It might even be a ratio scale measure of the attribute of 'testability' with respect to independent path testing. Other specific attributes of complexity, such as the maximum depth of nesting, distribution of primes in the decomposition tree, and the number of paths of various types, can all be measured rigorously and automatically [11], [34].

This idea of looking at measures with respect to particular viewpoints of complexity is taken much further by Zuse [46]. Zuse uses measurement theory to analyse the many complexity measures in the literature; he shows which viewpoint and assumptions are necessary to use the measures on different scales. The beauty and relevance of measurement theory is

such that it clearly underlies some of the most promising work in software measurement even where the authors have not made the explicit link. Notable in this respect are the innovative approaches of Melton *et al.* [31] and Tian and Zelkowitz [43]. In both of these works, the authors seek to characterise specific views of complexity. In [43], the authors do this by proposing a number of axioms reflecting viewpoints of complexity; in the context of measurement theory, the axioms correspond to particular empirical relations. This means that the representation condition can be used to determine the acceptability of potential measures.

Melton *et al.* [31] characterise a specific view of program complexity by specifying precisely an order relation $\preceq$ on program flowgraphs; in other words they *define* the binary relation b (of Hypothesis 1) as $\preceq$. The benefit of this approach is that the view of complexity is explicit and the search for representations (i.e., measures of this view of complexity) becomes purely analytical. The only weakness in [31] is the assertion that a measure M is "any real-valued mapping for which $M(x) \leq M(y)$ whenever $x \preceq y$." This ignores the sufficiency condition of the Representation Condition. Thus, while McCabe's cyclomatic complexity [30] satisfies necessity, (and is therefore a "measure" according to Melton *et al.* [31]), it is not a measure in the representational sense (since in Fig. 1 $M(z) < M(y)$ but it is not the case that $z \preceq y$). Interestingly, Tian and Zelkowitz also use the same weakened form of representation, but acknowledge that they "would like the relationship" to be necessary and sufficient.

It follows from Cantor's theorem that there is no representation of Melton's $(F, \prec)$ in $(\Re, <)$. However, it is still possible to get ordinal measurement in a number system which is not $(\Re, <)$ (and hence, for which it is not required that $\prec$ is a strict weak order), although the resulting measure is of purely theoretical interest. It is shown in [12] that there is a representation in $(Nat, |)$ where Nat is the set of natural numbers and $|$ is the divides relation. The construction of the measurement mapping M is based on ensuring incomparable flowgraphs are mapped to mutually prime numbers. For the flowgraphs of Fig. 1, $M(z) = 2$, $M(x)$ is a fairly large multiple of 3, and $M(y)$ is a very large multiple of 3.

B. The Weyuker Properties

Despite the above evidence, researchers have continued to search for single real-valued complexity measures which are *expected* to have the magical properties of being key indicators of such diverse attributes as *comprehensibility, correctness, maintainability, reliability, testability,* and *ease of implementation* [30], [32]. A high value for a "complexity" measure is supposed to be indicative of low comprehensibility, low reliability, etc. Sometimes these measures are also called "quality" measures [23]. In this case, high values of the measure actually indicate low values of the quality attributes.

The danger of attempting to find measures which characterise so many different attributes is that inevitably the measures have to satisfy *conflicting* aims. This is counter to the representational theory of measurement. Nobody would expect a single number M to characterise every notion of "quality" of people, which might include the very different notions of a) physical strength, and b) intelligence. If such a measure M existed it would have to satisfy a) $M(A) > M(B)$ whenever A is stronger than B and b) $M(A) > M(B)$ whenever A is more intelligent than B. The fact that some highly intelligent people are very weak physically ensures that no M can satisfy both these properties. Nevertheless, Weyuker's list of properties [45] seems to suggest the need for analogous software "complexity" measures. For example, two of the properties that Weyuker proposes any complexity measure M should satisfy are the following properties.

Property A: For any program bodies P, Q, $M(P) \leq M(P; Q)$ and $M(Q) \leq M(P; Q)$.

Property B: There exist program bodies P, Q, and R such that $M(P) = M(Q)$ and $M(P; R) \neq M(Q; R)$.

Property A asserts that adding code to a program cannot decrease its complexity. This reflects the view that program *size* is a key factor in its complexity. We can also conclude from Property A that low comprehensibility is *not* a key factor in complexity. This is because it is widely believed that in certain cases we can understand a program *more* easily as we see more of it [43]. Thus, while a "size" type complexity measure M should satisfy property A, a "comprehensability" type complexity measure M cannot satisfy property A.

Property B asserts that we can find two program bodies of equal complexity which when separately concatenated to a same third program yield programs of different complexity. Clearly, this property has much to do with comprehensibility and little to do with size.

Thus, properties A and B are relevant for very different, and incompatible, views of complexity. They cannot both be satisfied by a single measure which captures notions of size *and* low comprehensibility. Although the above argument is not formal, Zuse has recently proved [47] that, within the representational theory of measurement, Weyuker's axioms are contradictory. Formally, he shows that while Property A explicitly requires the ratio scale for M, Property B explicitly excludes the ratio scale.

The general misunderstanding of scientific measurement in software engineering is illustrated further in a recent paper [9], which was itself a critique of the Weyuker's axiom. Cherniavsky and Smith define a code based "metric" which satisfies all of Weyuker's axioms but, which they rightly claim, is not a sensible measure of complexity. They conclude that axiomatic approaches may not work. There is no justification for their conclusion. On the one hand, as they readily accept, there was no suggestion that Weyuker's axioms were complete. More importantly, what they fail to observe, is that Weyuker did not propose that the axioms were *sufficient*; she only proposed that they were necessary. Since the Cherniavsky/Smith "metric" is clearly not a measure (in our sense) of any specific attribute, then showing that it satisfies any set of necessary axioms for any measure is of no interest at all.

These problems would have been avoided by a simple lesson from measurement theory: the definition of a numerical mapping does not in itself constitute measurement. It is popular in software engineering to use the word "metric" for any number extracted from a software entity. Thus while every measure is a "metric", the converse is certainly not true. The confusion in [9], and also in [45], arises from wrongly equating these two concepts, and ignoring the theory of measurement completely.

IV. UNIFYING FRAMEWORK FOR SOFTWARE MEASUREMENT

A. A Classification of Software Measures

In software measurement activity, there are three classes of entities of interest [11].

Processes: are any software related activities which take place over time.

Products: are any artefacts, deliverables or documents which arise out of the processes.

Resources: are the items which are inputs to processes.

We make a distinction between attributes of these which are *internal* and *external*.

Internal attributes of a product, process, or resource are those which can be measured purely in terms of the product, process, or resource itself. For example, length is an internal attribute of any software document, while elapsed time is an internal attribute of any software process.

External attributes of a product, process, or resource are those which can only be measured with respect to how the product, process, or resource relates to other entities in its environment. For example, *reliability* of a program (a product attribute) is dependent not just on the program itself, but on the compiler, machine, and user. *Productivity* is an external attribute of a resource, namely people (either as individuals or groups); it is clearly dependent on many aspects of the process and the quality of products delivered.

Software managers and software users would most like to measure and predict external attributes. Unfortunately, they are necessarily only measurable indirectly. For example, productivity of personnel is most commonly measured as a ratio of: *size* of code delivered (an internal product attribute); and *effort* (an internal process attribute). The problems with this oversimplistic measure of productivity have been well documented. Similarly, "quality" of a software system (a very high level external product attribute) is often defined as the ratio of: *faults discovered during formal testing* (an internal process attribute); and *size measured by KLOC)* [19]. While reasonable for developers, this measure of quality cannot be said to be a valid measure from the viewpoint of the user. Empirical studies have suggested there may be little real correlation between faults and actual failures of the software in operation. For example, Adams [1] made a significant study of a number of large software systems being used on many sites around the world; he discovered that a large proportion of faults almost never lead to failures, while less than 2% of the known faults caused most of the common failures.

It is rare for a genuine consensus to be reached about the contrived definitions of external attributes. An exception is the definition of reliability of code in terms of probability of failure free-operation within a given usage environment [21], [29]. In this case, we need to measure internal process attributes. The processes are each of the periods of software operation between observed failures; the key attribute is the duration of the process.

B. Software Metrics Activities Within the Framework

The many, apparently diverse, topics within "software metrics" all fit easily into the conceptual framework described above [14]. Here, we pick out just three examples.

1) Cost Modeling: is generally concerned with *predicting* the attributes of *effort* or *time* required for the *process* of development (normally from detailed specification through to implementation). Most approaches involve a prediction system in which the underlying model has the form $E = f(S)$ where E is effort in person months and S is a measure of system size. The function f may involve other product attributes (such as complexity or required reliability), as well as process and resource attributes (such as programmer experience). In the case of Boehm's COCOMO [6], size is defined as the number of delivered source statements, which is an attribute of the final implemented system. Since the prediction system is used at the specification phase, we have to *predict* the product attribute size in order to plug it into the model. This means that we are replacing one difficult prediction problem (effort prediction) with another prediction problem which may be no easier (size prediction). This is avoided in Albrecht's approach [2], where system "size" is measured by the number of function points (FP's). This is computed directly from the specification.

2) Software Quality Models and Reliability Models: The popular quality models break down quality into "factors," "criteria," and "metrics" and propose relationships between them. Quality factors generally correspond to *external* product attributes. The criteria generally correspond to *internal* product or process attributes. The metrics generally correspond to proposed measures of the internal attributes. In most cases the proposed relationships are based on purely subjective opinions. Reliability is one of the high-level, external product attributes which appears in all quality models. The only type of products for which this attribute is relevant is executable software. Reliability modelling is concerned with *predicting* reliability of software on the basis of observing times between failures during operation or testing. Thus internal attributes of processes are used to predict an external product attribute. The prediction systems [29] used in reliability modelling typically consist of a probability distribution model together with a statistical inference procedure (such as maximum likelihood estimation) for determining the model parameters, and a prediction procedure for combining the model and the parameter estimates to make statements about future reliability.

3) Halstead's Software Science: Halstead proposed measures of three internal program attributes which reflect different views of size, namely *length, vocabulary,* and *volume* [18] (all are defined in terms of μ_1, the number of operators, μ_2 the number of operands, N_1 the number of operators, and N_2 the number of operands). For example, length $N = N_1 + N_2$. Although these seem reasonable measures of the specific attributes from the measurement theory perspective, they have been interpreted by many as being measures of program *complexity*, a totally different attribute. Other Halstead

"measures" such as E effort, and T time for a program P are genuinely problematic from the measurement theory perspective. Specifically, these are given by:

$$E = \frac{\mu_1 N_2 \log \mu}{2\mu_2} \text{ and } T = E/18.$$

E is supposed to represent 'the number of mental discriminations required to understand P', and T represents the actual time in seconds to write P. It should now be clear that these are crude prediction systems. For example, E is a predicted measure of an attribute of the process of *understanding the program*. However, as discussed in Section II-A, a prediction system requires a means of both determining the model parameters and interpreting the results. Neither of these is provided in Halstead's work. More worryingly, it is possible to show that using E leads to contradictions involving meaningful statements about effort (the attribute being measured) [11].

C. The Importance of Internal Attributes

The discussion in Section IV-B confirms that invariably we need to measure internal attributes to support the measurement of external attributes. This point has also been noted in [43]. Even the best understood external product attribute, *reliability* requires inter-failure time data to be collected during testing or operation. In many situations, we may need to make a prediction about an external product attribute before the product even exists. For example, given the detailed designs of a set of untested software modules, which ones, when implemented, are likely to be the most difficult to test or maintain? This is a major motivation for studying measures of *internal* attributes of products, and was the driving force behind much work on complexity measures.

Consider, for example, the product attribute *modularity*. Many modern software engineering methods and techniques are based on the premise that a modular structure for software is a "good thing." What this assumption means formally is that modularity, an internal software product attribute, has a significant impact on external software product attributes such as maintainability and reliability. Although a number of studies such as [42] and [44] have investigated this relationship there is no strong evidence to support the widely held beliefs about the benefits of modularity. While the study in [42] sought evidence that modularity was related to maintainability, it presumed a *linear* relationship, whereas Pressman and others [35] believe that neither excessively high nor excessively low modularity are acceptable. However, the main problem with all the studies is the lack of a previously validated measure of modularity.

Using the representational approach, we need to identify the intuitive notions which lead to a consensus view of modularity before we can measure it. Some empirical relations were identified in [15]. Others can be picked up be reading the general software engineering literature. For example, it is widely believed that the average module size alone does not determine a system's modularity. It is affected by the whole structure of the module calling hierarchy. Thus, the number of levels and the distribution of modules at each level have to be considered; module calling structures with widely varying widths are not considered to be very modular because of ideas of chunking from cognitive psychology.

D. Validating Software Measures

Validating a software measure in the assessment sense is equivalent to demonstrating empirically that the representation condition is satisfied for the attribute being measured. For a measure in the predictive sense, all the components of the prediction system must be clearly specified and a proper hypothesis proposed, before experimental design for validation can begin.

Despite these simple obligations for measurement validation, the software engineering literature abounds with so-called validation studies which have ignored them totally. This phenomenon has been examined thoroughly in [14] and [33], and fortunately there is some recent work addressing the problem [38]. Typically a measure (in the assessment sense) is proposed. For example, this might be a measure of an internal structural attribute of source code. The measure is "validated" by showing that it correlates with some other existing measure. What this really means is that the proposed measure is the main independent variable in a prediction system. Unfortunately, these studies commonly fail to specify the required prediction system and experimental hypothesis. Worse still, they do not specify, in advance, what is the dependent variable being predicted. The result is often an attempt to find fortuitous correlations with any data which happens to be available. In many cases, the only such data happens to be some other structural measure. For example, in [28], structural type measures are "validated" by showing that they correlate with "established" measures like LOC and McCabe's cyclomatic complexity number. In such cases, the validation study tells us nothing of interest. The general dangers of the "shotgun" approach to correlations of software measures have been highlighted in [8].

The search for rigorous software measures has not been helped by a commonly held viewpoint that no measure is "valid" unless it is a good predictor of effort. An analogy would be to reject the usefulness of measuring a person's height on the grounds that it tells us nothing about that person's intelligence. The result is that potentially valid measures of important internal attributes become distorted. Consider, for example, Albrecht's function points [2]. In this approach, the *unadjusted function count* UFC seems to be a reasonable measure of the important attribute of *functionality* in specification documents. However, the intention was to define a single size measure as the main independent variable in prediction systems for effort. Because of this, a *technical complexity factor* (TCF), is applied to UFC to arrive at the number of function points FP which is the model in the prediction system for effort. The TCF takes account of 14 product and process attributes in Albrecht's approach, and even more in Symons' approach [41]. This kind of adjustment (to a measure of system functionality) is analogous to redefining measures of height of people in such a way that the measures correlate more closely with intelligence. Interestingly, Jeffery [20] has shown

that the complexity adjustments do not even improve effort predictions; there was no significant differences between UFC and FP as effort predictors in his studies. Similar results have been reported by Kitchenham and Kansala [24].

V. SUMMARY

Contrary to popular opinion, software measurement, like measurement in any other discipline, must adhere to the science of measurement if it is to gain widespread acceptance and validity. The representational theory of measurement asserts that measurement is the process of assigning numbers or symbols to attributes of entities in such a way that all empirical relations are preserved. The entities of interest in software can be classified as processes, products, or resources. Anything we may wish to measure or predict is an identifiable attribute of these. Attributes are either internal or external. Although external attributes like reliability of products, stability of processes, or productivity of resources tend to be the ones we are most interested in measuring, we cannot do so directly. We are generally forced to measure indirectly in terms of internal attributes. Predictive measurement requires a *prediction system*. This means not just a model but also a set of prediction procedures for determining the model parameters and applying the results. These in turn are dependent on accurate measurements in the assessment sense.

We have used measurement theory to highlight both weaknesses and strengths of software metrics work, including work on metrics validation. Invariably, it seems that the most promising theoretical work has been using the key components of measurement theory. We showed that the search for general software complexity measures is doomed to failure. However, the theory does help us to define and validate measures of specific complexity attributes.

ACKNOWLEDGMENT

I would like to thank B. Littlewood and M. Neil for providing comments on an earlier draft of this paper, and P. Mellor, S. Page, and R. Whitty for sharing views and information that have influenced its contents. Finally, I would like to thank four anonymous referees who made suggestions that clearly improved the paper.

REFERENCES

[1] E. Adams, "Optimizing preventive service of software products." *IBM Res. J.*, vol. 28, no. 1, pp. 2–14, 1984.
[2] A. J. Albrecht, "Measuring application development productivity," in *IBM Applic. Dev. Joint SHARE/GUIDE Symp.*, Monterey, CA, 1979, pp. 83–92.
[3] J. Aczel, F. S. Roberts, and Z. Rosenbaum, "On scientific laws without dimensional constants," *J. Math. Anal. Applicat.*, vol. 119, no. 389–416, 1986.
[4] A. Baker, J. Bieman, N. E. Fenton, D. Gustafson, A. Melton, and R. W. Whitty, "A philosophy for software measurement," *J. Syst. Software*, vol. 12, pp. 277–281, July 1990.
[5] S. Brocklehurst, P. Y. Chan, B. Littlewood, and J. Snell, "Recalibrating software reliability models," *IEEE Trans. Software Eng.*, vol. 16, no. 4, pp. 458–470, Apr. 1990.
[6] B. Boehm, *Software Engineering Economics.* Englewood Cliffs, NJ: Prentice Hall, 1981.
[7] V. Basili and D. Rombach, "The tame project: Towards improvement-orientated software environments." *IEEE Trans. Software Eng.*, vol. 14, no. 6, pp. 758–773, June 1988.

[8] R. E. Courtney and D. A. Gustafson, "Shotgun correlations in software measures," *IEE Software Eng. J.*, vol. 8, no. 1, pp. 5–13, 1993.

[9] J. C. Cherniavsky and C. H. Smith, "On weyuker's axioms for software complexity measures," *IEEE Trans. Software Eng.*, vol. 17, no. 6, pp. 636–638, June 1991.

[10] R. A. DeMillo and R. J. Lipton, "Software project forecasting," in *Software Metrics*, A. J. Perlis, F. G. Sayward, and M. Shaw, Eds. Cambridge, MA: MIT Press, 1981, pp. 77–89.

[11] N. E. Fenton, *Software Metrics: A Rigorous Approach*. London: Chapman & Hall, 1991.

[12] _____, "When a software measure is not a measure," *IEE Software Eng. J.*, vol. 7, no. 5, pp. 357–362, May 1992.

[13] L. Finkelstein, "A review of the fundamental concepts of measurement," *Measurement*, vol. 2, no. 1, pp. 25–34, 1984.

[14] N. E. Fenton and B. A. Kitchenham, "Validating software measures," *J. Software Testing, Verification & Reliability*, vol. 1, no. 2, pp. 27–42, 1991.

[15] N. E. Fenton and A. Melton, "Deriving structurally based software measures," *J. Syst. Software*, vol. 12, pp. 177–187, July 1990.

[16] J.-C. Falmagne and L. Narens, "Scales and meaningfulness of quantitative laws," *Synthese*, vol. 55, pp. 287–325, 1983.

[17] P. J. Fleming and J. J. Wallace, "How not to lie with statistics," *Commun. ACM*, vol. 29, pp. 218–221, 1986.

[18] M. H. Halstead. *Elements of Software Science*. Amsterdam: Elsevier North Holland, 1975.

[19] J. Inglis, "Standard software quality metrics," *AT&T Tech. J.*, vol. 65, no. 2, pp. 113–118, Feb. 1985.

[20] D. R. Jeffery, G. C. Low, and M. Barnes, "A comparison of function point counting techniques," *IEEE Trans. Software Eng.*, vol. 19, no. 5, pp. 529–532, Mar. 1993.

[21] Z. Jelinski and P. B. Moranda, "Software reliability research," in *Statistical Computer Performance Evaluation*, W. Freiberger, Ed. New York: Academic Press, 1972, pp. 465–484.

[22] B. A. Kitchenham and B. de Neumann, "Cost modelling and estimation," in *Software Reliability Handbook*, P. Rook, Ed. New York: Elsevier Applied Science, 1990, pp. 333–376.

[23] D. Kafura and S. Henry, "Software quality metrics based on interconnectivity," *J. Syst. & Software*, vol. 2, pp. 121–131, 1981.

[24] B. A. Kitchenham and K. Kansala, "Inter-item correlations among function points," in *IEEE Software Metrics Symp.*, Baltimore, MD, 1993, pp. 11–15.

[25] D. H. Krantz, R. D. Luce, P. Suppes, and A. Tversky, *Foundations of Measurement*, vol. 1. New York: Academic Press, 1971.

[26] B. A. Kitchenham and N. R. Taylor, "Software project development cost estimation," *J. Syst. Software*, vol. 5, pp. 67–278, 1985.

[27] H. E. Kyburg, *Theory and Measurement*. Cambridge: Cambridge Univ. Press, 1984.

[28] H. F. Li and W. K. Cheung, "An empirical study of software metrics," *IEEE Trans. Software Eng.*, vol. 13, no. 6, June 1987.

[29] B. Littlewood, "Forecasting software reliability," in *Software Reliability, Modelling and Identification*, S. Bittanti, Ed. (*Lecture Notes in Computer Science*, vol. 341). New York: Springer-Verlag, 1988, pp. 141–209.

[30] T. J. McCabe, "A complexity measure," *IEEE Trans. Software Eng.*, vol. SE-2, no. 4, pp. 308–320, Apr. 1976.

[31] A. C. Melton, D. A. Gustafson, J. M. Bieman, and A. A. Baker, "Mathematical perspective of software measures research," *IEE Software Eng. J.*, vol. 5, no. 5, pp. 246–254, 1990.

[32] J. C. Munson and Khoshgoftaar, "The detection of fault prone modules," *IEEE Trans. Software Eng.*, vol. 18, no. 5, pp. 423–433, May 1992.

[33] M. Neil, "Multivariate assessment of software products," *J. Software Testing Verification and Reliability*, to appear 1992.

[34] R. E. Prather and S. G. Giulieri, "Decomposition of flowchart schemata," *Comput. J.*, vol. 24, no. 3, pp. 258–262, 1981.

[35] R. S. Pressman, *Software Engineering: A Practitioner's Approach.*, 2nd ed. New York: McGraw-Hill Int., 1987.

[36] F. S. Roberts, *Measurement Theory with Applications to Decision Making, Utility, and the Social Sciences*. Reading, MA: Addison Wesley, 1979.

[37] _____, "Applications of the theory of meaningfulness to psychology," *J. Math. Psychol.*, vol. 29, pp. 311–332, 1985.

[38] N. F. Schneidewind, "Methodology for validating software metrics," *IEEE Trans. Software Eng.*, vol. 18, no. 5, pp. 410–422, May 1992.

[39] J. E. Smith, "Characterizing computer performance with a single number," *Commun. ACM*, vol. 31, pp. 1202–1206, 1988.

[40] P. H. Sydenham, Ed., *Handbook of Measurement Science*, vol. 1. New York: J. Wiley, 1982.

[41] C. R. Symons, "Function point analysis: Difficulties and improvements," *IEEE Trans. Software Eng.*, vol. 14, no. 1, pp. 2–11, Jan. 1988.

[42] D. A. Troy and S. H. Zweben, "Measuring the quality of structured design," *J. Syst. Software*, vol. 2, pp. 113–120, 1981.

[43] J. Tian and M. V. Zelkowitz, "A formal program complexity model and its applications," *J. Syst. Software*, vol. 17, pp. 253–266, 1992.

[44] S. N. Woodfield, H. E. Dunsmore, and V. Y. Shen, "The effects of modularisation and comments on program comprehension," in *Proc. 5th Int. Conf. Software Eng.*, 1979, pp. 213–223.

[45] E. J. Weyuker, "Evaluating software complexity measures," *IEEE Trans. Software Eng.*, vol. 14, no. 9, pp. 1357–1365, Sept. 1988.

[46] H. Zuse, *Software Complexity: Measures and Methods*. Amsterdam: de Gruyter, 1990.

[47] _____, "Support of experimentation by measurement theory," in *Experimental Software Engineering Issues (Lecture Notes in Computer Science*, vol. 706), H. D. Rombach, V. R. Basili, and R. W. Selby, Eds. New York: Springer-Verlag, 1993, pp. 137–140.

Norman Fenton is a Professor of Computing Science in the Centre for Software Reliability at City University, London, UK. He was previously the Director of the Centre for Systems and Software Engineering (CSSE) at South Bank University and a Post-Doctoral Research Fellow at Oxford University (Mathematical Institute).

He has consulted widely to industry about metrics programs, and has also led numerous collaborative projects. One such current project is developing a measurement based framework for the assessment of software engineering standards and methods. His research interests are in software measurement and formal methods of software development. He has written three books on these subjects and published many papers.

Prof. Fenton is Editor of Chapman and Hall's *Computer Science Research and Practice Series* and is on the Editorial Board of the *Software Quality Journal*. He has chaired several international conferences on software metrics. Prof. Fenton is Secretary of the (National) Centre for Software Reliability. He is a Chartered Engineer (Member of the IEE), and Associate Fellow of the Institute of Mathematics and its Applications, and is a member of the IEEE Computer Society.

Chapter 7

PROCESS MEASUREMENT AND COST ESTIMATION

This final set of papers focuses on formal project tracking and cost estimation. Project tracking and costing is inseparably linked to metrics because without the latter, the former is soft and fuzzy. In particular the papers by Matson et al, and Low and Jeffery link the use of function points to project tracking.

Impact of Schedule Estimation on Software Project Behavior

Tare K. Abdel-Hamid, SRI International
Stuart E. Madnick. Massachusetts Institute of Technology

Efforts to develop better estimation tools must address two issues: First, are more accurate tools necessarily better? Second, how can we measure a new estimation method's accuracy?

Schedule estimation has historically been, and continues to be, a major difficulty in managing software development projects.[1] Farquhar articulated this problem's significance:

> Unable to estimate accurately, the manager can know with certainty neither what resources to commit to an effort nor, In retrospect, how well then resources were used. The lack of a firm foundation for then two judgments can reduce programming management to a random process in that positive control is next to impossible. This situation often results in the budget overruns and schedule slippages that are all too common.[2]

Over the last decade, a number of quantitative software estimation models have been proposed. They range from theoretical models to empirical ones. An empirical model uses data from previous projects to evaluate the current project and derives basic formulas from analyses of available historical databases. In contrast, a theoretical model uses formulas based on global assumptions, such as the rate at which people solve problems and the number of problems awaiting solution at a given point.

Still, software cost and schedule estimation continue to be major difficulties. As noted by Mohanty:

> Even today almost no model can estimate the true cost of software with any degree of accuracy.[3]

Research efforts attempting to develop 'better " estimation tools need to address two important issues: first, whether a more accurate estimation tool is necessarily a better tool; second, how can we adequat measure the accuracy of a new estimat method. Our objective in this article is address these two issues.

An ongoing research effort to study dynamics of software developm resulted in our system dynamics model software development proj management. This model served as laboratory vehicle for simulating impact of schedule estimation on softwa project behavior. Our study revealed t interesting facts: (1) different estima create different projects, implying that n software estimation tools cannot adequately judged by how accurately th estimate historical projects; and (2) mc accurate estimates are not necessari better estimates.

Different estimates create different projects

In this section we am concerned abo the Impact of alternative schedu estimations rather than the methodolog used to arrive at estimates. In later section we will give actual examples methodologies used. For now, the reader merely asked to assume that two differe methods exist (a simplistic method could be "man-days needed = number pages of specifications x 10 man-days pe page" and a simplistic method B could b "man-days needed = number of words i specifications x 0.1 man-days per word").

Consider the following scenario: 64,000--delivered-source-instructions (DSI) software project that had bee estimated at its initiation to take 235 man-days (using estimation method A ends up actually consuming 379 man-days. The project's specifications are then fed into estimation method B (that i

Reprinted from *IEEE Software*, July 1986, pp. 70-75.

1

being considered by management to replace method A) and its results compared to the project's actual performance. Let us assume that method B produces a 5900-man-day estimate. If we define "percent of relative absolute error" in estimating man-days (MD) as

$$\% \text{ Error} = 100 * \text{ABS}[MD_{Actual} - MD_{Estimate}] / MD_{Actual}$$

then, for estimation method A,

$$\% \text{ Error}_A = 100 * \text{ABS}[3795 - 2359] / 3795 = 38\%$$

and for method B,

$$\% \text{ Error}_B = 100 * \text{ABS}[3795 - 5900] / 3795 = 55\%$$

Can one conclude from this that method B would have provided a less accurate estimate of the project's man-days had it been used instead of method A? The answer is No; we cannot draw such a conclusion. Had the project been initiated with B's 590 man-day estimate instead of A's 2359-man-day estimate, we cannot assume it would have still consumed 3795 actual man-days. In fact, the project could end up consuming much more or much less than 1795 man-days. And before such a determination can be made, no accurate assessment of A's versus B's relative accuracy can be made.

Different estimates create different projects. Koolhass states the principle as follows:

> When experimenting with the system about which we are trying to obtain knowledge, we create a new system.[4]

Koolhass goes on to illustrate the principle with an anecdote: A man inquires through the bedroom, door of his sick friend: "How are you?"—whereupon his friend replies "Fine!" and the effort kills him.

This phenomenon is somewhat analogous to Heisenberg's uncertainty principle in experimentation. By Imposing different estimates on a software project we would, in a red sense, be creating different projects. The next section explains how.

The feedback Impact of project estimates

Research findings indicate that decisions people make in project situations, and actions they choose to take, are significantly influenced by pressures and perceptions the project schedule produces.[5] Figure 1's causal loop diagram, excerpted from Abdel-Hamid,[6] depicts such schedule influences.

Schedules have a direct influence on hiring and firing decisions throughout a software project's life. In TRW's COCOMO model,[7] for example, the project's average staff size would be determined by dividing the man-day estimate by the development time estimate (TDEV). Thus, a tight time schedule (that is, a low TDEV value) means a larger work force. Also scheduling can dramatically change manpower loading throughout the life of a project. For example, the work force level in some environments shoots upwards towards the and of a late project when there are strict constraints on the extent to which the project's schedule is allowed to slip.

Through its effects on the work force level, a project's schedule also affects productivity (as illustrated In Figure 1). A higher work force level means more communication and training overhead, affecting productivity negatively.

Productivity is also influenced by the presence of any man-day shortages. If a project is considered behind schedule (that is, when the total effort needed to complete the project is seen as greater than the total effort actually remaining in the project's budget), software developers tend to work harder; they allocate more man-hours to the project In an attempt to compensate for the perceived shortage and bring the project back on schedule.

Obviously, such man-day shortages are more prone to occur when projects are initially underestimated. Conversely, man-day "excesses" could arise if project management initially overestimates a project; as a result, the project would be perceived ahead of schedule (that is, the total man-days remaining in the project's budget would exceed what the project members perceive is needed to complete the project). When such a situation occurs,

> Parkinson's law indicates that people will use the extra time for. . . personal activities, catching up on the mail, etc.[7]

Of course this means that they become less productive.

Having identified how software project estimation can Influence project behavior, are we now in a position to return to the scenario presented earlier and answer the still unanswered question—namely, whether estimation method A is truly more accurate than method B?

Identifying feedback relationships through which project estimation influences project behavior is one thing; discerning dynamic implications of such interactions on the total system is another. Paraphrasing Richardson and Pugh:[8] The behavior of interconnected feedback loop systems often confounds intuition and analysis, even though the dynamic implications of isolated loops may be reasonably obvious.

One option is to effect a controlled experiment conducting the 64,000-DSI software project twice under exactly the same conditions—except that in one case it would be initiated with a 2359-man-day estimate (the method A basis), and in the second case a 5900-man-day estimate would be used (the Method B basis).

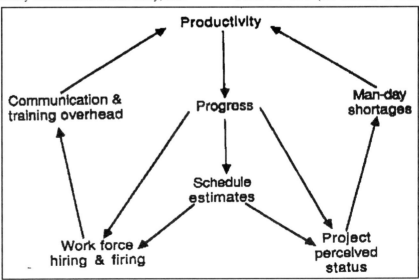

Figure 1. The feedback impact of schedule estimates.

While theoretically possible, such an option Is usually infeasible from a practical point of view because of its high cost in terms of both money and time.

Simulation experimentation provides a more attractive alternative. In addition to permitting less costly and less time-consuming experimentation, simulation makes perfectly controlled experiments possible. Of course such simulations can only capture elements of the model and not reality, but this type of simulation has been found helpful in understanding the behavior of complex social systems.[8]

A software management system dynamics computer model

Research findings reported in this article are based on a doctoral research effort at MIT's Sloan School of Management studying software development dynarnics[6] Culininatins in the development of system dynamics simulation model of software development project management. This structural model achieved several research objectives, one of which was to serve as a laboratory vehicle for conducting experimentation in software estimation. A major advantage of such a structural model is that it can be used to predict the effect of changes to the development process.[1]

This section provides an overview of the model.

Figure 2 depicts the model's four subsystems, namely,

(1) the human resource management subsystem;

(2) the software production subsystem;

(3) the controlling subsystem; and

(4) the planning subsystem

Figure 2 *also* illustrates some interrelationships of the four subsystems.

The human resource management subsystem captures hiring, training, assimilation, and transfer of the project's human resources. Such actions are not carried out in a vacuum; as Figure 2 suggests, they affect and are affected by the other sub-systems. For example, the project's hiring rate is a function of the work force needed to complete the project on its planned completion date. Similarly, the work form available has direct bearing on the allocation of manpower among the different software production activities in the soft. were production subsystem

The four primary software production activities are development, quality assurance, rework, and testing. Development comprises both design and coding of the software. As the software is developed, it is also reviewed; for example, structured walk-throughs are used to detect any design/coding errors. Errors detected through such quality assurance activities are then reworked. Not all errors are detected and reworked, however. Some escape detection until the end of development (that is, until the testing phase).

Progress is reported as it is made. A comparison of the project's actual status (versus where it should be according to plan) is a control-type activity captured within the controlling subsystem. Once project status is assessed using available information, it becomes an important input to the planning function.

In the planning subsystem, initial project estimates are made to start the project. Those estimates are revised, when necessary, throughout the project's life. For example, to handle a project that is considered behind schedule, plans can be revised to hire more people, extend the schedule, or do a little of both.

The preceding overview highlights the structure of the model used. other reports[6,9] provide a full description of the model and of the validation experiments performed on it.

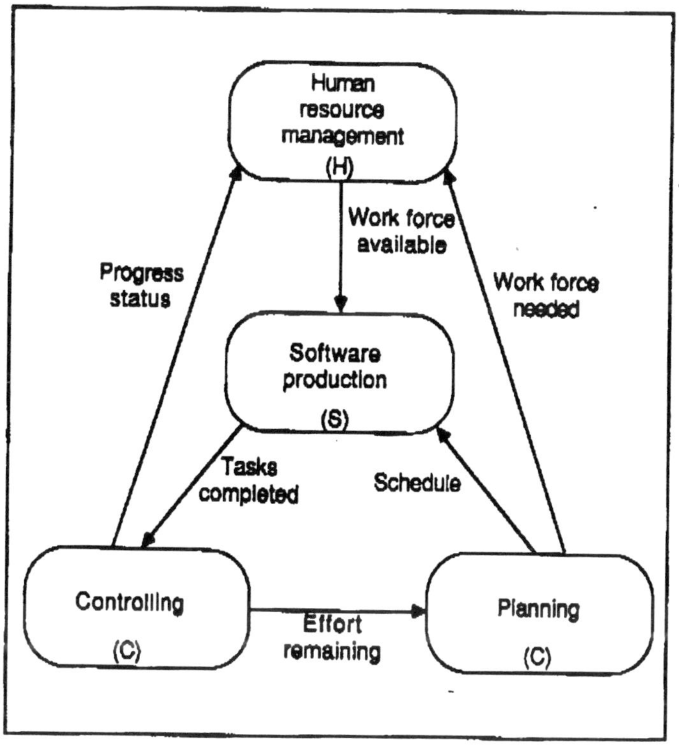

Simulation experiment

The scenario for our simulation experiment is a real-life software development environment—that of a major minicomputer manufacturer involved in our research effort. In this organization, project managers were rewarded based upon how closely their project estimates matched actual project results. The estimation procedure that they informally used follows:

(1) Use basic COCOMO to estimate the number of man-days; that is, use

$$MD = 2.4 * 19 * (KDSI)^{1.05} \text{ man-days.}$$

where KDSI is the perceived project size in thousands of delivered source instructions.

(2) Multiply this estimate by a safety factor (the safety factor ranged from 25 to 56 percent) and add it to MD; that is,

$$MD' = (1 + \text{safety factor}) * MD$$

(3) UN the new value of man-days (MD') to calculate the development time (MEV), using COCOMO; that is. use

$$TDEV = 47.5 * (MD' / 19)^{0.38} \text{ days.}$$

Notice that the primary input to COCOMO is the perceived (not the real) size of the project in KDSI—since at the beginning of development when estimates

Figure 2. Overview of a software development system dynamics model.

307

3

made, the real size of the project is [...]en not known.[7] For our purposes, it is [...]o important to note that COCOMO is [...]d only to exemplify a schedule [...]imation tool; the structural model [...]veloped is not tied to any particular [...]edule estimation technique.

[...]he safety factor philosophy is in no way [...]ique to our scenario organization. For [...]ample, in his study of software cost [...]imation at the Air Force Systems [...]mmand Electronics Systems Division. [...]venny[10] found that most program [...]anagers budget additional funds for [...]ftware as a "management reserve." He [...]o found that these management reserves [...]nged in size (as a percentage of the [...]imated software cost) from 5 to 50 [...]rcent, with a mean of 18 percent. And as [...]as the case with the organization we [...]died, the policy was informal:

... frequently the reserve was created by the program office with funds not placed on any particular contract. Most of the respondents indicated that the reserve was not identified as such to prevent Its loss during a budget cut.[10]

To test the efficacy of various safety [...]ctor policies, we ran a number of [...]mulations on a prototypical software [...]roject that we will call project Example. [...]roject Example's actual size is 64,000 [...]SI. At its initiation, however, it was [...]correctly considered 42.88 KDS1 in size [...]hat is, 33 percent smaller than 64 KDSI). [...]his incorrectly perceived project size of [...]2-88 KDSI was the input used in [...]OCOMO's estimation equations. The [...]asic COCOMO estimate for man-days [...]with no safety factor) was

$$MD = 2.4 * 19 * (42.98)^{1.05} = 2359$$
man-days.

[...]his estimate corresponds to the method A [...]stimate presumed at the beginning of this [...]rticle.

We experimented with safety factor [...]values ranging from 0 (the base run) to 100 percent. For a 50-percent safety factor, the following estimates would be [...]used:
(1) Calculate MD' from MD

$$MD' = MD * (1 + \text{safety factor} / 100)$$
$$= MD * 1.5 = 3538.5 \text{ man-days.}$$

(2) Calculate TDEV

$$TDEV = 47.5 * (MD' / 19)^{0.38} = 34$$
days.

Figures 3 through 6 exhibit the results of these simulations.

In Figure 3, the "percent relative error" in estimating man-days is plotted against different values of the safety factor. Notice that the safety factor policy seems to be working—the larger the safety factor. the smaller the estimation error In the 25- to 50-percent range in particular (the same as was used in the scenario organization),the estimation error drops from approximately 40 percent in the base run to values in the upper 20's. In fact, Figure 3 suggests that

project managers might not be going far enough by using a 25- to 50-percent safety factor since a 100-percent safety factor would drop the estimation error down to a more rewarding 12 percent.

The rationale for using a safety factor is based on the following assumptions:
(1) Past experience indicates a strong bias among software developers to underestimate the scope of software projects. [10, 11]
(2) One might think biases are the easiest of estimating problems to correct since they involve errors moving always in the same direction. But as DeMarco suggests,[11] "biases are almost by definition invisible the same psychological

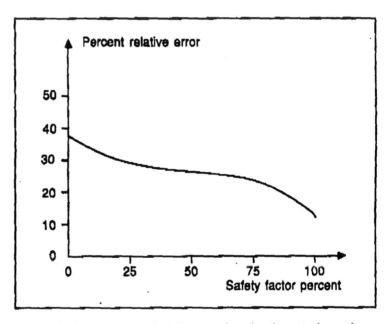

Figure 3. The percentage of relative error in estimating actual man-days.

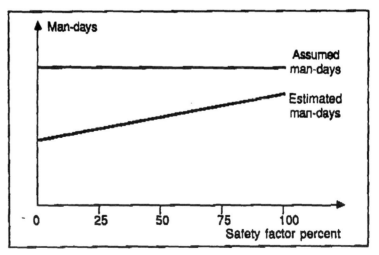

Figure 4. A comparison of assumed man-days with estimated man-days.

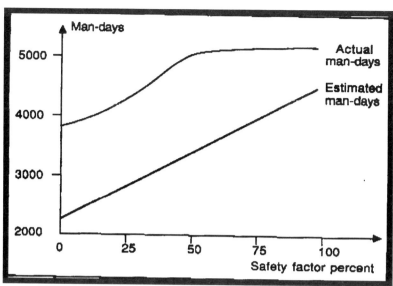

Figure 5. A comparison of actual man-days with estimated man-days.

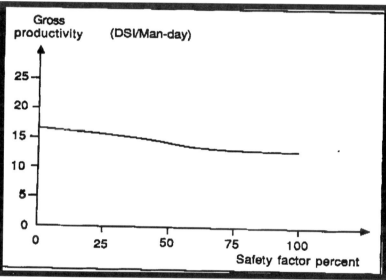

Figure 6. Gross productivity.

mechanism that creates the bias (for example the optimism of software developers) works to conceal it.

(3) To rectify such bias, project management uses a safety factor. Pletrasanta[12] observes that when project managers add contingency factors (ranging, say, from 25 to 100 percent), they are saying in essence; I don't know all that is going to happen so I'll estimate what I don't know as a percentage of what I do know.

In other words, the assumption is that safety factors are simply mechanisms to bring initial man-day estimates closer to true project size in man-days (see Figure 4). Such an assumption cannot be contested solely on the basis of Figure 3,

which provides only part of the story. Figure 5 presents a more complete picture; here, we used the model to calculate the actual man-days consumed by the project. Example when different safety factors were applied to its initial estimate. The Figure 4 assumption is obviously invalidated. As we use higher safety factors, leading to increasingly generous initial man-day allocations, the actual amount of man-days consumed does not remain at some inherently defined value. In the base run, for example, project Example would be initiated with a man-day estimate of 2359 man-days and would consume 3795 man-days. When a 50-percent safety factor is used, leading to a 3538-man-day initial estimate, Example

ends up consuming not 3795 man-days b 5080 man-days.

To reiterate a point made earlie Different estimates create differe projects. Initial project estimates crea pressures and perceptions affecting ho people behave on the project. In particula overestimates of project am-days can lea to a larger work force buildup and high communication and training overhea ultimately reducing productivit Furthermore, over-estimating a proje often invites the expansion discretionary activity (such as non-proje communication, or personal pursuit leading to further productivity reductions

Figure 6 illustrates a plot of gro productivity, defined as the project size i DSI (that is, 64,000 DSI) divided by th actual number of man-days expended fc the different safety factor situations. Gros productivity drop from a value of 16. DSI/man-day In the base run to as low i 12 DSI/man-day when we use a 10C percent safety factor. The drop i productivity is initially significant, an then levels off for higher safety factor: The reason for this is that, when the safet factor increases from 0 (in the base run) t a relatively small value (perhaps 2 percent), most resulting man-day excesse will be absorbed by employees in the forn of less overworking (that is, less days tha employees work longer-than-usual hours and/or more discretionary time.

In the base case, using no safety factor backlogs are experienced as projec Example consumes more man-days (3795 than budgeted (2359). Using a small safety factor, though, project Example's backlog will decrease—leading to less overwork durations. As the safety factor is increased further, man-day excesses rather than backlog reductions will result. When these excesses are reasonable, they tend to be absorbed in the form of reasonably expanded discretionary activities; consequently, the project team becomes less productive.

However, there are limits on how much "fat" employees would be willing (or allowed) to absorb. Beyond these limits, man-day excesses would be translated not into less productivity but into cuts in the project's work force, its schedule, or both.[6] As safety factors increase to larger and larger values, productivity losses due to expanded slack time activity decrease, leading to lower drops in gross productivity.

Methods A and B recompared

We can now answer the question posed the beginning of this article. Our opening scenario concerned a 64,000-DSI project—our own project Example, in fact—and a comparison of two estimation methods, Method A, the estimate used in the base run, produced a 2359 man-day estimate. Since project Example actually consumed 3795 man-days, method A's relative absolute error in estimating man-days is 38 percent. We wondered whether method B, producing a 5900-man-day estimate for project Example (55 percent higher than base-run Example's 3795-man-day expenditure), would have provided a less accurate project estimate had it been used instead of Method A.

Method B's estimate of 5900 man-days 150 percent higher than A's 2359 estimate; indeed, method B is equivalent a 150-percent safety factor. To check the behavior of project Example had it been estimated using method B, we reran the model with a 5900 man-day estimate.

Using this estimate, project Example consumed 5412 man-days—for a nine-percent error factor. Since method A had a 38-percent error factor, method B proves to be a more accurate estimator. However, method B's improved accuracy is costly—the project consumes 43 percent more man-days!

In terms of the minicomputer manufacturer we studied, the message is clear. While the safety factor policy does achieve its intended objective (namely, producing more accurate estimates), the organization is paying dearly for this accuracy. In terms of man-days, as Figure 5 indicates, a 25- to 50-percent safety factor results in a 15- to 35-percent increase in project cost. Taking an extreme case, method B's 150-percent safety factor would be appropriate for a development manager required to complete a project within 10 percent of estimate. Unfortunately, this would not necessarily be economical for the company since costs would be significantly higher than with method A.

The primary purpose of our research effort was to gain a better understanding of software project management dynamics. We gained two basic insights from the work described in this Article:

(1) Different estimates create different projects—implying that project managers as well as students of software estimation should reject the notion that a software estimation tool can be adequately judged based on how accurately it estimates historical projects.

(2) More accurate estimates an not necessarily better estimates—an estimation method should not be judged only on how accurate it is; it should also be judged on how costly are the projects it creates. ⊐

Acknowledgments

We appreciate the contribution of each and every individual in the organizations providing perspectives and data to this research effort. We thank the reviewers, whose suggestions have Improved this article's readability. Work described herein was supported, in part, by NASA research grant NAGW-448.

References

1. M. R. Barbacci, A. N. Haberman, and M. Shaw. "The Software Engineering Institute: Bridging Practice and Potential." *IEEE Software,* Vol. 2. No. 6, Nov. 1985, pp. 4-21.

2. J. A. Farquhar, "A Preliminary Inquiry Into the Software Estimation Process," Tech. Report, AD F12 052, Defense Documentation Center, Alexandria, VL, Aug, 1970.

3. S. N. Mohanty, "Software Cost Estimation: Present and Future," *Software Practice and Experience*, Vol, 11, 1981. pp, 103-121.

4. Z. Koolhass, *Organization Dissonance and Change*, John Wiley & Sons, Now York, N.Y., 1982.

5. F. P. Brooks. *The Mythical Man-Month*, Addison-Wesley, Reading, Mass,. 1979.

6. T. K. Abdel-Hamid, "The Dynamics of Software Development Project Management: An Integrative System Dynamics Perspective," Ph.D. dissertation NTIS N64 16824, MIT, Cambridge, Mass., 1984.

7. B. W. Boehm. Software Engineering Economics, Prentice-Hall, Englewood Cliffs, NJ, 1981.

8. G. P. Richardson and G. L. Pugh III, *Introduction to System Dynamics Modelling with Dynamo*, The MIT Press, Cambridge Mass., 1981.

9. T.K, Abdel-Hamid and SE. Madnick, Software Project Management. Prentice-Hall, Englewood Cliffs, N.J., 1986.

10. T.J. Devenny. "An Exploration Study of Software Cost Estimating at the Electronics Systems Division, NTIS, US, Department of Commerce, Washington, DC, July 1976.

11. T. Demarco, *Controlling Software Projects*, Yourdon Press, New York, NY. 1962.

12. A.M. Pietrasanta. "Managing the Economics of Computer Programming, *Proc. ACM Nat'l Conf.* 1968. Pp. 341-346.

Tarek K. Abdel-Hamid has been a senior management systems consultant at SRI International since January, 1984. His primary research interests are in software engineering project management. particularly computer-based tools for managing large software projects. He received his BSc in aeronautical engineering from Cairo University in 1972, and his Ph.D. in management information system from MIT in 1984. Abdel-Hamid is a member of the ACM, the IEEE-CS. and the SIM.

His address Is 19 Trillium La., San Carlos, CA 94070.

Stuart Madnick is an associate professor of management at the Massachusetts Institute of Technology. His research interests focus on advanced information systems, database computers, computer architecture, operating systems, and software project management. He is author or co-author of four books and mom than 100 papers and technical reports on these subjects.

Madnick has served as chairman of the IEEE Technical Committee on Database Engineering and as a member of the IEEE Computer Society Board of Governors. He is currently associate editor of the ACM *Transactions on Database Systems*. He received his BS In electrical engineering, his MS in management, and his Ph.D. in computer science from MIT.

His address is MIT Sloan School of Management, E53-317, 50 Memorial Dr., Cambridge, MA 02139

Software Development Cost Estimation Using Function Points

Jack E. Matson, Bruce E. Barrett, and Joseph M. Mellichamp

*Abstract—*This paper presents an assessment of several published statistical regression models that relate software development effort to software size measured in function points. The principal concern with published models has to do with the number of observations upon which the models were based and inattention to the assumptions inherent in regression analysis. The research describes appropriate statistical procedures in the context of a case study based on function point data for 104 software development projects and discusses limitations of the resulting model in estimating development effort. The paper also focuses on a problem with the current method for measuring function points that constrains the effective use of function points in regression models and suggests a modification to the approach that should enhance the accuracy of prediction models based on function points in the future.

Index Terms— Function points, regression analysis, cost estimation

I. INTRODUCTION

AN increasingly important facet of software development is the ability to estimate the associated cost of development early in the development life cycle. The primary factor affecting software cost estimation is the size of the project; however, estimating software size is a difficult problem that requires specific knowledge of the system functions in terms of scope, complexity, and interactions [14]. A number of software size metrics are identified in the literature; the most frequently cited measures are lines of code and function point analysis.

A. Lines of Code

The traditional size metric for estimating software development effort and for measuring productivity has been lines of code (LOC). A large number of cost estimation models have been proposed, most of which are a function of lines of code, or thousands of lines of code (KLOC). Generally, the effort estimation model consists of two parts. One part provides a base estimate as a function of software size and is of the following form:

$$E = A + B \times (KLOC)^C.$$

where E is the estimated effort in man-months; $A, B,$ and C are constants; and KLOC is the estimated number of

thousands of line of code in the final system. The second part modifies the base estimate to account for the influence of environmental factors [15]. Examples of environmental factors include the use of such practices as structured code, top-down design, structured walk-throughs, and chief programmer teams; personnel ability; and hardware constraints [5]. As an example, Boehm's [4] COCOMO model uses lines of code raised to a power between 1.05 and 1.20 to determine the base estimate. The specific exponent depends on whether the project is simple, average, or complex. The model then uses 15 cost influence factors as independent multipliers to adjust the base estimate. Conte, Dunsmore, and Shen [7] identified some typical models including the following:

$E = 5.2 \times (KLOC)^{0.91}$	(Walston-Felix model)
$E = 5.5 + 0.73 \times (KLOC)^{1.16}$	(Bailey-Basili model)
$E = 3.2 \times (KLOC)^{1.05}$	(Boehm simple model)
$E = 3.0 \times (KLOC)^{1.12}$	(Boehm average model)
$E = 2.8 \times (KLOC)^{1.20}$	(Boehm complex model)
$E = 5.288 \times (KLOC)^{1.047}$	(Doty model).
for KLOC > 9	

The definition of KLOC is important when comparing these models. Some models include comment lines, and others do not. Similarly, the definition of what effort (E) is being estimated is equally important. Effort may represent only coding at one extreme or the total analysis, design, coding, and testing effort at the other extreme. As a result, it is difficult to compare these models.

There are a number of problems with using LOC as the unit of measure for software size. The primary problem is the lack of a universally accepted definition for exactly what a line of code really is. Jones [10] identified 11 major variations of line counting methods. Since few authors state the line-counting rules they used, much of the literature has an "uncertainty of perhaps 500% attributable to line counting variations." The variations make it very difficult to compare studies using lines of code as a measure of software size.

Another difficulty with lines of code as a measure of system size is its language dependence. It is not possible to directly compare projects developed by using different languages [16]. For example, the time per line for a high-level language may be greater than for a lower-level language. There is no way to accommodate the fact that fewer lines of code may be required for a higher-level language to provide the same function.

Still another problem with the lines of code measure is the fact that it is difficult to estimate the number of lines of code that will be needed to develop a system from the information

Manuscript received April 21, 1993; revised November 1993. Recommended by R. DeMillo.

J. E. Matson is with the Department of Industrial Engineering, University of Alabama, Tuscaloosa, AL 35487.

B. E. Barrett and J. M. Mellichamp are with the Department of Management Science and Statistics, University of Alabama, Tuscaloosa, AL 35487.

IEEE Log Number 9216525.

Reprinted from *IEEE Transactions on Software Engineering*, Vol. 20, No. 4, Apr. 1994, pp. 275-287.

311

available at requirements or design phases of development [8]. If cost models based on size are to be useful, it is necessary to be able to predict the size of the final product as early and accurately as possible. Unfortunately, estimating software size using the lines of code metric depends so much on previous experience with similar projects that different experts can make radically different estimates [7]. Finally, the lines of code measure places undue emphasis on coding, which is only one part of the implementation phase of a software development project. Emrick [8] stated that coding accounts only for 10% to 15% of the total effort on a large development system and questioned whether the total effort is really linearly dependent on the amount of code.

B. Function Point Analysis

Function point analysis is a method of quantifying the size and complexity of a software system in terms of the functions that the system delivers to the user. The function delivered is unrelated to the language or tools used to develop a software project [2]. Function point analysis is designed to measure business-type applications; it is not appropriate for other types of applications such as technical or scientific applications. These applications generally deal with complex algorithms that the function point method is not designed to handle [24].

The function point approach has features that overcome the major problems with using lines of code as a measure of system size. First, function points are independent of the language, tools, or methodologies used for implementation; i.e., they do not take into consideration programming languages, data base management systems, processing hardware, or any other data processing technology [16], [24]. Second, function points can be estimated from requirements specifications or design specifications, thus making it possible to estimate development effort in the early phases of development [16]. Since function points are directly linked to the statement of requirements, any change of requirements can easily be followed by a reestimate [9]. Third, since function points are based on the system user's external view of the system, nontechnical users of the software system have a better understanding of what function points are measuring [12]. The method resolves many of the inconsistencies that arise when using lines of code as a software size measure.

Function points have been incorporated as an option in two commercially available software packages, SPQR/20 [11] and ESTIMACS[TM] [12], [22]. SPQR/20 (software productivity, quality, reliability) is based on a modified function point method; ESTIMACS[TM] contains a module which estimates function points. The primary difference in the SPQR/20 model and the traditional function point method is in the way complexity is handled. Whereas traditional function point analysis is based on evaluating 14 factors, SPQR/20 separates complexity into three categories: complexity of algorithms, complexity of code, and complexity of data structures. The SPQR/20 method makes it easier to evaluate the complexity factors (three questions as opposed to the detail of 14 factors). According to Porter [20], the SPQR/20 method did not seem to differ from function point analysis. The method is available

in a commercial system, but documentation of the counting practices is not available in the public domain. Traditional function point analysis remains the industry standard, however, and is the method of choice of the International Function Point Users Group.

ESTIMACS[TM] [22] is a proprietary system designed to give development effort estimates at the conception stage of a project. At this early phase, the full details of the system are not known, and normally only gross estimates are needed to make "go" and "no-go" decisions. In addition to estimated work effort, the system contains a module which will project the expected function points. This also is a very high-level estimate and generally is not very accurate [21].

In summary, function point analysis appears to have advantages over lines of code as a measure of software size for use in estimating software development cost, and there is widespread industry support for this method. Unfortunately, there are few published cost estimation models that use function points as the key input parameter.

Counting Function Points: Briefly, raw function counts are arrived at by considering a linear combination of five basic software components (inputs, outputs, master files, interfaces, and inquiries), each at one of three levels: low, average or high. We may express this as follows:

$$\text{Function Count} = \sum_{i=1}^{5} \sum_{j=1}^{3} w_{ij} z_{ij},$$

where z_{ij} is the count for component i at level j (e.g., outputs at high complexity) and w_{ij} is the fixed weight assigned by the Albrecht procedure. These function counts are also known as unadjusted function points (UFP). The final number of function points is arrived at by multiplying the UFP by an adjustment factor that is determined by considering 14 aspects of processing complexity. This adjustment factor allows the UFP count to be modified by at most ±35%. The final, adjusted, FP count for the k_{th} project is then the following:

$$\text{FP}_k = c_k \sum_{i=1}^{5} \sum_{j=1}^{3} w_{ij} z_{ij}, \qquad (1)$$

where c_k is between 0.65 and 1.35. (For a summary of the mechanics of function point counting, see [12]. For a more detailed account, see [23].)

Uses of Function Points: The collection of function point data has two primary motivations. One is the desire by managers to monitor levels of productivity, for example, number of function points achieved per work hour expended. From this perspective, the manager is not concerned with when the function point counts are made, but only that the function points accurately describe the "size" of the final software project. In this instance, function points have an advantage over LOC in that they provide a more objective measure of software size by which to assess productivity.

Another use of function points, which is the focus of this article, is in the *estimation* of software development cost. There are only a few previous studies that address this issue, though it is arguably the most important potential use of function point data. In Section II, we briefly review the goals and methodology of model selection and then examine two data sets and associated cost estimation models from the literature, pointing out some of the pitfalls of improper model selection that may arise primarily as a result of too few data points. In Section III we develop two cost estimation models utilizing a comparatively large data set ($n = 104$) and examine the predictive properties of each. Finally, in Section IV, we point out the limitations attendant with using function points to predict software size and propose a new direction for future efforts in the development of function point cost estimation models.

II. ESTIMATION MODELS FROM THE LITERATURE

In developing a useful regression model, a number of concerns must be addressed. The first is model adequacy, or explanatory power of the independent variable(s) in accounting for the variability of the dependent variable. This is typically measured by the coefficient of multiple determination, R^2. However, a large value of R^2 is not the only measure of a good model. In some regard, it is not even the most important. Estimation theory for linear regression is tied to certain assumptions about the distribution of the residual or error terms. If these are seriously violated, a large R^2 may be of little importance.

These concerns come under the heading of model aptness, which refers to the conformity of the behavior of the residuals to the underlying assumptions about the errors in the model. Specifically, the usual assumptions for the error values in linear regression models are that these terms are distributed as independent, normal random variables with mean zero and identical variances. These assumptions are typically verified with the aid of diagnostic plots. Most common are the normal probability plot for verifying the normality of the residuals and a scatter plot of the residuals versus the fitted values to confirm the independence and homoscedasticity (*i.e.*, constant variance) of the residuals. When one or more of these assumptions is violated, transformation of variables is often attempted as a remedy.

A further concern is model stability, which refers to the resistance to change in the fitted model under small perturbations of the data. It is now generally recognized that residual analysis alone is inadequate in answering the questions of stability. This effect can be summarized by saying that the ordinary least-squares criterion gives disproportionately large weights to cases which are extreme in the predictor variables in determining the fit, often resulting in small residuals for those extreme or high leverage cases. Regression diagnostics, then, is generally understood to be the class of methods used to validate the probability assumptions about the errors, as well as the assessment of the stability of the fitted model, distinct from the probabilistic behavior of the errors.

By far, the most common approach for assessing model stability is case deletion. Each case (or data point) is removed in turn from the data and the various regression statistics, such as the estimated regression coefficients, the fitted values and the coefficient covariances, are recalculated. Cases whose removal substantially alter the results obtained using the full set of data are said to be influential. The most widely used influence measure is Cook's Distance [6], which measures changes in the estimated coefficients. This is the measure used in this study.

In assessing the influence of specific cases, we rely on a technique suggested by McCulloch and Meeter [18] and Barrett and Ling [3] to examine Cook's Distance. When investigating cases for their degree of influence, two components are of interest: a leverage component and a residual component. Since the influence may be expressed as a product of the leverage component and the residual component, cases which are large in one or both of these are candidates for high influence. For ease of display, the *logs* of the leverage and residual components are plotted. The contours of constant influence are straight lines with slope of -1, and the sum of the coordinates is the log of the influence.

A. The Albrecht and Gaffney Model

Albrecht and Gaffney [2] collected data on 24 applications developed by IBM Data Processing Services. Using a somewhat less refined counting method than that described in (1), they give the function point counts and the resulting work-hours, which we call effort, for each project. Ordinary least-squares regression was used to determine the fitted line for the dependent variable, E (effort), expressed as a function of the independent variable, FP. A scatter-plot of this data and the resulting regression function are shown in Fig. 1(a).

The explanatory power of the model is relatively high at $R^2 = 87.4\%$. However, the residuals are troublesome in several respects. From Fig. 1(b) we note serious autocorrelation; the first eight residuals are positive while eleven of the next fifteen are negative. There is also some evidence that the variability of the residuals is increasing as the number of function points increases. Four of the five largest residuals belong to the four observations with the largest function point counts: {1}, {2}, {19}, and {20}. The normal probability plot in Fig. 1(c) also suggests that normality of the residuals is suspect. In Fig. 1(d), the influence plot shows that cases {1} and {2} are highly influential, due in large part to their high leverage or extremeness in the independent variable. The Albrecht and Gaffney model also has the unfortunate property that function point counts of less than 245 result in the prediction of negative work-hours for completion.

The basic problem with fitting a model to this data is the relatively few cases with function point counts greater than 1200. For example, if the four cases with function point counts exceeding 1200 are removed, a very different fitted line will result. There are two possibilities to consider here: (1) the relationship between FP and E is not linear; and (2) the relationship is linear but the error variance increases with the number of function points. In the latter situation, cases with large values of FP should be down-weighted in the regression. In either event, the model as suggested by Albrecht and Gaffney is inappropriate.

The plot of residuals in Fig. 1(b) suggests that the relationship may involve a quadratic term. We might, for example, fit E versus FP^2 or $\sqrt{E}$ versus FP. The deficient normal probability plot suggests that transformation of the dependent variable, E, is the better choice.

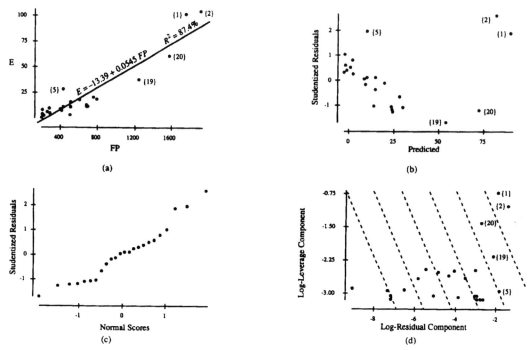

Fig. 1. Regression diagnostics for the Albrecht and Gaffney model using the IBM data. (a) Regression of Developmental Effort (E) versus Function Points (FP) Effort is measured in thousands of work-hours. (b) Studentized Residuals versus Predicted Values for the model in (a). The error terms appear nonrandom and show a strong quadratic component. (c) Normal Probability Plot of residuals for the model in (a). (d) Leverage-Residual plot of Cook's Distance. Cases that lie along the same dashed contour have the same influence. Moving from one contour line to an adjacent line represents an increase or decrease in influence by a factor to 4.

The summary analyses for this transformation are given in Fig. 2. The value of R^2 is about the same at 89.9% while the residual plot (Fig. 2(b)) supports the independence and homoscedastiscity of the error terms. The normal probability plot (Fig. 2(c)) is much improved with only case $\{5\}$ showing as unusual and in need of further investigation. The influence plot (Fig. 2(d)) shows that the influence of cases $\{1\}$ and $\{2\}$ is substantially mitigated. Of greater interest for our purposes we note that the prediction intervals for the transformed model are substantially narrower. For example, suppose we are interested in prediction of a new observation at the mean value of FP (i.e., $FP = 647.625$). The original model (Albrecht and Gaffney) yields a 90% prediction interval of 3.81 to 39.93 thousands of work-hours while that of the transformed model is from 6.76 to 29.92. Of course, neither interval is especially tight due in part to the small number of observations. However, even if the Albrecht and Gaffney model produced a narrower confidence interval we would still prefer the transformed model because probability statements concerning the intervals are predicated on the model assumptions. The degree to which these are violated determines the validity of the prediction interval.

B. The Kemerer Model

Kemmerer [12] also developed a cost estimation model using function points and linear regression. The data set consists of observations from 15 software projects undertaken by a national consulting and development firm identified only as the ABC company. A scatter-plot of the data and the resulting least-squares line are shown in Fig. 3(a). The dependent variable, *Effort*, is measured in man-months where one man-month is 152 work-hours. We use this scale for ease of reference with Kemmerer [12]. Rescaling the units of the dependent variable does not impact on the analysis of the model. We also note that Kemerer reports the *adjusted* R^2 while we have used the unadjusted R^2 throughout this article. These are largely comparable measures related by the expression $1 - R_a^2 = (1 - R^2)(n-1)/(n-p)$, where $p - 1$ is the number of predictors. The adjustment factor compensates for adding variables whose marginal contribution is small. Preference for either measure is inconsequential in practice.

It is clear from Fig. 3(a) that model fit is inappropriate in several respects. The greatest anomaly is case $\{3\}$ which is a very high leverage point and tends to pull the regression line towards itself. If case $\{3\}$ were removed, a vastly different fitted equation would result. Also, the predicted values for the smallest two projects are negative. Another shortcoming of the model is the large mean-squared-error (mse) which results in wide prediction intervals. (See the Appendix section for details.) This large mse, along with the gross violation of model assumptions renders the resulting inferences virtually meaningless.

As was the case with the Albrecht and Gaffney model, the small number of data points make it impossible to determine whether the true relationship is nonlinear, or linear but with

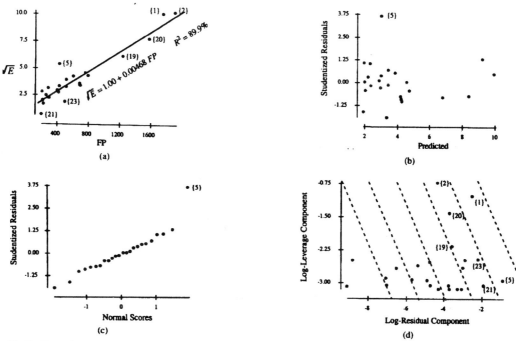

Fig. 2. Regression diagnostics for the transformed IBM data. (a) Regression of Sqrt (Developmental Effort), (E) versus Function Points (FP). Effort is measured in thousands of work-hours. (b) Studentized Residuals versus Predicted Values for the model in (a). (c) Normal Probability Plot of residuals for the model in (a). (d) Leverage-Residual plot of Cook's Distance. Cases that lie along the same dashed contour have the same influence. Moving from one contour line to an adjacent line represents an increase or decrease in influence by a factor of 4.

error variance increasing with project size. In the latter instance, case {3} may be a rather ordinary observation. Fig. 3(b) presents two alternative polynomial models which certainly are a better fit to the data. We do not mean to suggest that either of these is the "correct" functional form of the true relationship, but rather that there are some fairly simple alternatives which provide a much better fit. Without further information about case {3} and possibly additional data points, the relationship is most uncertain.

We also take the opportunity with this data set to point out certain common misconceptions about the importance of R^2 in model assessment. Briefly, in developing a linear model for the purpose of prediction, we are interested in a point estimate and some measure of the uncertainty of the point estimate. This is typically assessed by a confidence interval on a future value, also known as a prediction interval. (For additional details on prediction intervals as well as alternative methods of assessing predictive power, see the Appendix.) All of the usual inferential statistics are based on the assumptions of normality, independence, and homoscedasticity of the residuals. If these are seriously violated, the prediction intervals are invalid.

A regression model may be fit (that is, the least-squares estimates calculated) for *any* set of data, even if the functional form of model is entirely misspecified or there is nonconformity of the residuals to the model assumptions. Such inappropriate models may sometimes have very impressive values of R^2. As an illustration, Fig. 4 presents three regression models associated with Kemerer's ABC data. Equation (a) is

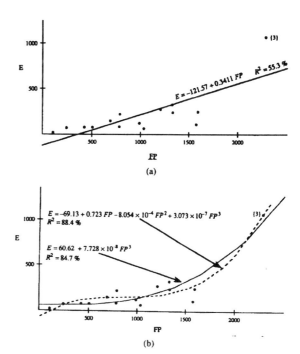

Fig. 3. Kemerer's ABC data: Effort (man-months) versus Function Points. (a) Kemerer's model for ABC data set: Effort in man-months versus Functionpoints. One man-month equals 152 hours. (b) Alternative modelsfor the ABC data: A simple cubic term model and a polynomial model of order 3.

315

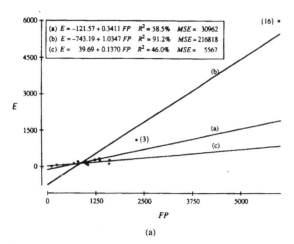

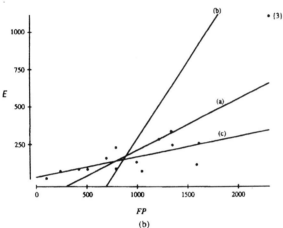

Fig. 4. Kemerer's ABC Data: Examining the Multiple Correlation Coefficient and Mean Squared Error. (a) Kemerer's ABC Data: Effort in man months (E) versus Function Points (FP). Equation (a) is the regression line for the original 15 cases. Equation (b) is the line with case {3} deleted and the artificial case {16} included. Equation (c) is the line for the 14 cases exclusive of {3} and the artificial case, {16}. (b) Enlarged view of Fig. 4(a) for the original 15 cases of the ABC data.

that reported by Kemerer for the original fifteen data points. Equation (b) is the least-squares line for the original data, excluding case {3} but then adding an even more extreme artificial data point labeled case {16}. Alternatively, one might think of this situation as moving case {3} to an even more extreme and outlying position. Equation (c) is the regression line for the fourteen data points exclusive of cases {3} and {16}.

Visual inspection and intuition tell us that line (b) fits the first fourteen quite poorly in its attempt to accommodate case {16}. Yet, it has the largest R^2 among the three lines at 91.2%. In fact, by making case {16} even more extreme, values of R^2 which are arbitrarily close to 100% may be achieved. To understand this phenomenon, recall that R^2 is the proportion of the total variability about the mean explained by the regression. As case {16} becomes more extreme, the total variability increases, but at the same time the distance of a point from the fitted line is, relatively, a proportionally smaller amount of the

distance of the point from the mean of E. Geometrically, as case {16} becomes more extreme, the first 14 points become, by comparison, clumped together so that they behave as a single point. That is, in a relative sense, they become more and more similar. The regression is essentially fitting only "two" points: the cluster of fourteen and the extreme case {16}.

Eliminating case {3} and case {16} from consideration, we would anticipate the remaining 14 points would be better fit than with one of these extreme cases present. Visual inspection of line (c) supports this view. However, the value of R^2 drops to 46%. Kemerer notes that case {3} is outlying, but upon recognizing the drop in R^2 when case {3} is removed, he concludes that it is better to keep it in. But if we are to follow through with this reasoning, case {16} were it present, would be even more desirable. This reasoning is completely counter intuitive and indeed, faulty.

What factors, in addition to R^2, should be considered when assessing a regression model? For the purpose of estimation, the mse plays a vital role. We observe that though it has the smallest R^2, line (c) also has the smallest associated mse (see Fig. 4). For a fixed level of confidence, the width of the prediction interval is determined primarily by mse. Hence, equation (c) is much more appealing since it will produce narrower prediction intervals over the relevant range of the independent variable. Of course, one should not summarily discard cases simply because they do not fit. The appropriate disposition or accommodation of case {3} requires further investigation. The point is that reliance on R^2 alone for assessing the appropriateness and strength of a regression model is erroneous.

Kemerer also reports that an important finding of his study is that the Albrecht and Gaffney estimation model was validated by his independent study. Specifically, using a single regression on all $24 + 14 = 39$ data points with the units of *Effort* similarly scaled, the null hypothesis that the two models were different could not be rejected at the 95% confidence level. This finding is however, weak on two counts. First, both models are somewhat suspect, as we have demonstrated. Perhaps if case {3} were not present in Kemerer's data, the hypothesis test would have had a different outcome. Secondly, both models are based on relatively small samples with large mse's. As a result, the respective estimated regression coefficients have large confidence intervals which make it unlikely that any differences in the models will be detected unless the differences are dramatic.

We do not mean to be overly critical of either Albrecht and Gaffney or Kemerer; each has contributed significantly to the theory and practice of software development effort measurement. We mean only to point out that the acquisition of a good regression model requires a fair amount of data as well as careful and thoughtful analysis of the underlying model assumptions.

III. LARGE SAMPLE COST ESTIMATION RESULTS

In this section we present the results of our analysis of function point data from 104 projects obtained from a major corporation. There were several reasons for using this

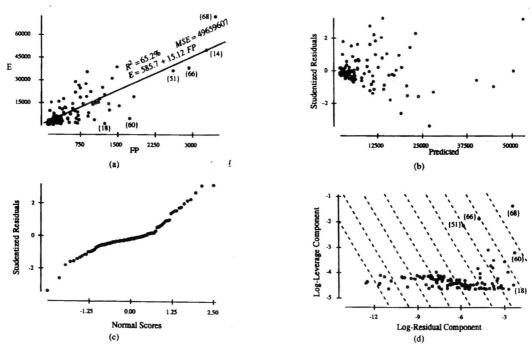

Fig. 5. Regression diagnostics for the original variables in the model (2). (a) Regression of Developmental Effort (E) versus Function Points (FP). Effort is measured in work-hours. (b) Studentized Residuals versus Predicted Values for the model in (a). (c) Normal Probability Plot of residuals for the model in (a). (d) Leverage-Residual plot of Cook's Distance. Cases that lie along the same dashed contour have the same influence. Moving from one contour line to an adjacent line represents an increase or decrease in influence by a factor of 4.

company's data. First, the company has a well-trained and experienced systems development staff and encourages the use of current software development methodologies and tools. Furthermore, the company is interested in the use of function point analysis and has used function points to measure productivity and quality for several years. The accumulated historical project data includes development effort and function points. Managers at this company were willing to provide project data and to participate in the research effort.

The set of project data represents a wide range of software applications. Included are data for systems which run on MVS and UNIX operating systems, which are programmed in COBOL, PL/I, and C, and which use IMS, IDMS, IN-FORMIX, INGRESS, and other data base management systems. Finally, the company has well defined procedures for reporting development hours spent on their software development projects. Since the objective of the study was the estimation of effort using a model based on actual development effort, it was important that the actual effort data be accurate and consistent. The record-keeping procedures at this company ensured that such was the case.

The 104 projects used in developing our cost estimation model represent a large sample compared to most other published studies. According to Moseley [19], "it is not uncommon to find in the literature estimation models that are based on sample sizes of fifteen to thirty projects." The projects in this study represent medium-to-large business applications, ranging in size from 119 function points to 3472

function points. Project data included the following information: software size in function points, development effort in hours, operating system, data base management system, and programming language. We will initially concentrate on using the single independent variable, FP, for prediction and subsequently discuss the inclusion of additional variables.

A scatter-plot of the data (Fig. 5(a)) suggests that a linear relationship is present and we fit our initial model,

$$E = 585.7 + 15.12 \text{ FP} \qquad (2)$$

where the developmental effort is given in work-hours. From the residual plot in Fig. 5(b), the variability of the error terms seems to increase as development effort increases, placing the assumption of homoscedasticity of the residuals in serious doubt. This observation also supports our intuition that the absolute precision with which we may predict the effort for large projects is less than that for small projects. For example, if we consider a large project as merely the sum of several smaller independent projects, the variance of the error terms for the sum is additive. We also note that the normal probability plot of the residuals in Fig. 5(c) departs from the straight line that one would expect were the normality assumption met.

For the data in this study, cases {68}, {14}, {66}, and {51} are high leverage points, as seen in Fig. 5(a). Fig. 5(d) is a graphical display of the leverage component, the residual component, and the resulting influence for each case. For example, case {68} has both the largest leverage component

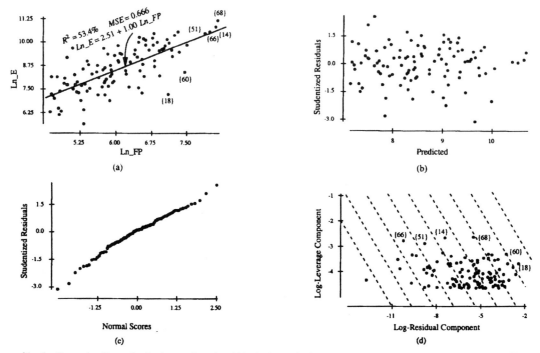

Fig. 6. Regression diagnostics for the transformed variables in the model(3). (a) Regression for the transformed variables, Ln_E versus Ln_FP. Efforts is measured in work-hours. (b) Studentized Residuals versus Predicted Values for the model in (a). (c) Normal Probability Plot of residuals for the model in (a). (d) Leverage-Residual plot of Cook's Distance. Cases that lie along the same dashed contour have the same influence. Moving from one contour line to an adjacent line represents an increase or decrease in influence by a factor of 4.

and the largest residual component, and therefore, the greatest influence. Its influence is approximately five times that of the next most influential point (case {60}) and is certainly large enough to warrant our concern. Case {14} is also a high leverage point, but its influence is negligible since its residual value is close to zero.

In order to overcome the difficulties with the model assumptions and model stability, we applied a logarithmic transformation to both the dependent and independent variables. This transformation is particularly useful in that linearity of the original relationship is preserved while stabilizing the error variance. The resulting data and fitted line,

$$\ln E = 2.51 + 1.00(\ln FP) \qquad (3)$$

are displayed in Fig. 6(a). The plots in Fig. 6(b) and 6(c) indicate that the residuals are more well behaved than those of the original model in (2). Standard tests for linearity and the normality, independence, and homoscedasticity of the residuals confirm the visual analysis.

The stability of the model is also improved. The leverage-residual influence plot in Fig. 6(d) shows that the high leverage cases are now associated with much smaller residuals, so their influence is greatly mitigated. Indeed, the most highly influential point for the transformed data is case {18}, which has an influence value one-tenth that of the most influential case of the original data (case {68}). We conclude that the model using the transformed data (3) is appropriate in all aspects and superior to the model using the original data (2).

Retrospectively, the data sets examined in Section II are now more readily understood. In view of our results here, the log-linear relationship between effort and function points may apply generally to other studies. It is only due to lack of data that the relationship remains hidden in the earlier studies. The apparent lack of linearity in each of those models was primarily a result of very few points with large FP values and an increasing error variance. For example, case {3} from Kemerer's data fits rather well into a log-log transformation. Fig. 7 shows the combined data sets of Section II (with the exception of Albrecht and Gaffney case {5}) with a log-log transformation applied. We caution that this plot is meant to illustrate only a rough, qualitative compliance with the model developed for our own data set. Without further details and reconciliation, it would be presumptuous to combine the data for any confident analysis.

Having established the aptness and stability of the model in (3), we turn our attention to its predictive power. As noted earlier in discussing the models of Albrecht and Gaffney and Kemerer, the width of the prediction interval is a more relevant measure of a model's usefulness than is R^2. For the present model (3) we first construct prediction intervals for R^2 in the usual manner and then apply the exponential function to translate the interval back to the work-hour units of the original dependent variable, E. The prediction interval arrived at in this way is not symmetric about the point estimate. For example, a new observation at FP = 2981 (i.e., ln FP = 8) yields a point estimate of 4964 work hours and a 90% prediction

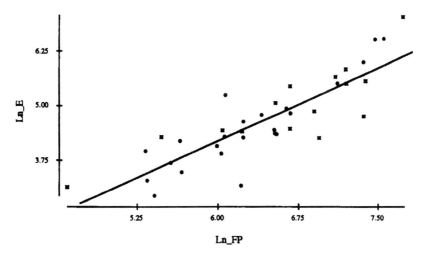

Fig. 7. Combined data sets of Albrecht and Gaffney, excluding case {5} (denoted by •), and Kemerer (denoted by *r*). Regression line is that for log-log transformed data.

interval of from 1287 to 19145 work-hours. In absolute terms, larger function point values produce wider prediction intervals when translated back into the original units; but in relation to the magnitude of the point estimate, the interval widths for a given level of confidence are very nearly constant across the relevant range of function point values. Also, in presenting these results we have considered only the one-sided, upper-tail prediction value since managers are generally more concerned with possible cost overruns than coming in under budget. The one-sided intervals allow for a smaller upper bound. For example, from Table I we see that for FP = 600 the estimated work-hours is 7383 (*i.e.*, the value at $\alpha = 0.50$) with a 90% upper bound of 21275, which is 2.88 times the point estimate. A different value of FP will produce a different interval, but using this model one may say, for example, that a future project will result in work-hours less than approximately twice the estimated value with 80% probability. These prediction intervals apply to the prediction of a *single* new observation. If one is fortunate enough to have several new projects of similar size, the prediction interval for the *average* number of work-hours is significantly tighter.

We next attempted improve the fit by employing a multiple regression model which considered the additional independent variables *operating system*, *data base management system*, and *programming language*. With the FP variable in the model, inclusion of these additional variables resulted in only a modest improvement. Indeed, programming language and operating systems contributed almost no marginal information and only two of the four data base types were significant. The fitted multiple regression equation is given by

$$\ln E = 3.397 + 0.914(\ln FP) - 0.629DB1 - 0.877DB2 \quad (4)$$

where DB1 and DB2 are indicator variables for the presence or absence of the IMS and INGRESS data bases, respectively. The upper confidence bounds and relative interval lengths for this model (at the level FP = 600 and with the IMS data base

TABLE I
PREDICTION INTERVALS FOR EFFORT AT
$FP = 600$, FOR THE DATA SET OF SECTION III

Confidence level $(1 - \alpha)$	Model (3)		Model (4)	
	Upper bound	Relative width	Upper bound	Relative width
0.95	28 822	3.90	18 984	3.44
0.90	21 275	2.88	14 419	2.61
0.85	17 355	2.35	11 989	2.17
0.80	14 770	2.00	10 359	1.87
0.75	12 866	1.74	9141	1.65
0.70	11 368	1.54	8171	1.48
0.65	10 137	1.37	7366	1.33
0.60	9094	1.23	6675	1.21
0.55	8187	1.11	6069	1.10
0.50	7383	1.00	5526	1.00

The point estimate, or value from the fitted line, for a new observation at the level $FP = 600$ using the model (3) is given by the upper bound of the 50% prediction interval. The relative widths are calculated, for example, as 21 275/7383 = 2.88. The value of $FP = 600$ is arbitrary. Other FP values will give different point estimates, but the relative range values are nearly constant.

present) are given in Table I. Comparison with the simple regression model in (3) shows a slight improvement.

When dealing with effort estimation models, there are other approaches to assessing the usefulness of the model for prediction which stem from the basic premise that the seriousness of prediction errors is related to the size of the project. This was, in fact the point of view we adopted in presenting our confidence interval results in Table I. That is, the width of the confidence intervals in absolute terms is larger for larger projects, but the relative widths, given in terms of the predicted effort are nearly constant for a fixed value of α.

Others have suggested similarly motivated summary measures of predictive power. One such approach, suggested by Conte, Dunsmore, and Shen [7], is to measure the (absolute) relative error. That is, the absolute difference in the observed and fitted values for Effort divided by the actual observed Effort. (See the Appendix section for further details.) These authors suggest that the average of these relative errors should be less than 0.25 for a good model. In our study, the model in (3) had an average relative error of 0.87 when transformed back to the original units while the model (4) gave a value of 0.71.

A related measure of Conte, Dunsmore, and Shen [7] is the percentage of observations whose predicted values are within a certain percentage of their actual values. In their judgement, an acceptable effort prediction model will have at least 75% of all predicted values fall within 25% of their actual observations. In our study, only 64% of the predicted values fell within 25% of their observations for the model (3) and only 68% for the model (4). Hence, by both of these relative error goodness-of-fit criteria, the function point models developed here are deemed somewhat less than adequate.

IV. CONCLUSION AND SUGGESTIONS FOR FURTHER STUDY

In the previous sections we have demonstrated some of the pitfalls encountered in developing good regression models and have provided a software cost estimation model based on a relatively large data set. Several questions remain. First, how useful is the model in practice within the environment in which it was developed? Secondly, how portable is the model to other organizations? And finally, can the model be improved by additional data collection?

As for the practical, same site, usefulness of the model, it seems a very broad tool at best. Many experienced managers would likely be able to estimate the final cost of a project (in hours) to within a factor of two nearly 80% of the time without the aid of function points or a cost estimation model. Though perhaps they will not estimate to within 33% of the final cost, on average, 65% of the time (see Table I). In any event, it is still preferable to be able to deliver more precision in an estimate of developmental effort.

In considering this problem, the sources of variability must be identified. Within a single organization, there are sometimes significant differences in the function point counts for the same project as determined by separate individuals. This arises from subjective assessments in both the raw counts and the adjustment factor. Suggestions for reducing or eliminating this source of variability include using a single rater for all projects or using a single *group* of raters for each project to arrive at an average [24]. Kemerer [13] and Matson and Mellichamp [17] have suggested more automated approaches to overcome this inter-rater variability. Another source of variability is the different abilities and productivity levels of various project teams. One possibility for mitigating this variability is to take personnel into account in the adjustment factor.

At a specific site or even within an organization, it may be possible to control variability as described above. However, the use of a model developed from the data of one organization for prediction at another requires more care. For example, the external organization would need to know, specifically, how work-hours were counted. Even so, it is unlikely that the external organization will be able to completely control

for all inter-organizational differences that may impact the model. Therefore, we recommend that organizations using models developed elsewhere begin to collect their own data for model building. Since this may take quite some time, it may be necessary to make use of an "adopted" model from an organization which is qualitatively similar.

As we have demonstrated, function points, even in concert with other predictors, seem only moderately helpful in software development cost estimation. However, we believe that this situation may be markedly improved by making better use of available information. The function point value for a given project is a linear combination of other variables, multiplied by an adjustment factor. The method of FP calculations used for our data set takes a linear combination of 15 variables (see (1)) with predetermined coefficients which are given in Kemerer [13]. For qualitative assessment of productivity, it may be useful to combine the available information into a single measure of utility such as function points. However, for the purpose of estimation, the predetermined coefficients of the individual components unnecessarily constrain the regression to a less than optimal solution. It would be preferable to use all 15 variables (each times the adjustment factor) as predictors in the model since this will allow the estimation method to select the best weights. This will necessitate a somewhat larger minimum sample size than with just the single variable, but the potential improvement in the model may be significant. Certainly, the 104 observations in the data we have presented are sufficient for such an analysis. Unfortunately, we were unable to obtain the individual component values for this data set from which the function point counts were calculated. It may also be useful to first perform a principal components analysis to reduce the number of predictor variables from 15 or more down to a more manageable number. Even if one is intent on a single summary predictor such as FP, the first principal component will provide a set of weights for a linear combination of the components which is likely to be superior to the preassigned weights.

To illustrate the potential improvement, we return to the data of Albrecht and Gaffney, discussed in Section II. The function points calculations for this data set differ from the current definition in several respects. First, interfaces were considered as master files and not counted separately, so that there are only four basic components (inputs, outputs, master files, and inquiries) rather than five. Also, these four components were each held at only one complexity level rather than low, average, and high. Finally, the adjustment factor had a range of $\pm 25\%$ rather than $\pm 35\%$. The resulting function point calculation for the kth observation is,

$$FP_k = (4 \text{ IN} + 5 \text{ OUT} + 4 \text{ INQ} + 10 \text{ FILE })c_k$$

where c_k is the adjustment factor and the coefficients (4, 5, 4, and 10) are those currently used for these components at the *average* level of complexity. The specific values for each of these variables are given in Table II.

In fitting a model using the four components as predictors (rather than FP) we take the position that the adjustment factor, c_k, acts multiplicatively with *each* variable. Denoting the adjusted predictors by, for example, $c_k \text{IN} = \widetilde{\text{IN}}$, we first

TABLE II
CONSTITUENT COMPONENTS FOR FP CALCULATIONS: ALBRECHT AND GAFFNEY DATA

Case No.	IN	OUT	INQ	FILE	ADJ	FP	EFFORT
1	25	150	75	60	1.00	1750	102.4
2	193	98	70	36	1.00	1902	105.2
3	70	27	0	12	0.80	428	11.1
4	40	60	20	12	1.15	759	21.1
5	10	69	1	9	0.90	431	28.8
6	13	19	0	23	0.75	283	10.0
7	34	14	0	5	0.80	205	8.0
8	17	17	15	5	1.10	289	4.9
9	45	64	14	16	0.95	680	12.9
10	40	60	20	15	1.15	794	19.0
11	41	27	29	5	1.10	512	10.8
12	33	17	8	5	0.75	224	2.9
13	28	41	16	11	0.85	417	7.5
14	43	40	20	35	0.85	682	12.0
15	7	12	13	8	0.95	209	4.1
16	28	38	24	9	1.05	512	15.8
17	42	57	12	5	1.10	606	18.3
18	27	20	24	6	1.10	400	8.9
19	48	66	13	50	1.15	1235	38.1
20	69	112	21	39	1.20	1572	61.2
21	25	28	4	22	1.05	500	3.6
22	61	68	0	11	1.00	694	11.8
23	15	15	6	3	1.05	199	0.5
24	12	15	0	15	0.95	260	6.1

The IBM data of Albrecht and Gaffney. The function point values are arrived at by, for example, in case {20}. $FP =$ [4(69) + 5(112) + 4(21) + 10(39)]1.20 = 1572.

considered the model

$$E = \beta_0 + \beta_1 \widetilde{IN} + \beta_2 \widetilde{OUT} + \beta_3 \widetilde{INQ} + \beta_4 \widetilde{FILE} + \varepsilon.$$

However, this model resulted in a fit which exhibited many of the same shortcomings as the original Albrecht and Gaffney model. After some exploration, we selected the model in which each predictor variable is transformed by taking its square. The fitted equation for the transformed data is

$$E = 3.80 + 0.00119 \widetilde{IN}^2 + 0.00210 \widetilde{OUT}^2 + 0.00608 \widetilde{INQ}^2$$
$$+ 0.0045 \widetilde{FILE}^2 \tag{5}$$

This model is superior in several respects. The residuals are very well behaved, although, as before, case {5} appears to be an outlier in need of further investigation. The value of R^2 is 97.5% and the value of mse is 25.7 which is less than one-fourth that of the Albrecht and Gaffney model. This results in prediction intervals less than one-half as wide.

We suspect that the functional form for the model in (5) may turn out differently if more data were available and we cannot recommend any model, based on such a small sample size. The key point is that improved results may be achieved by unbundling the function point variable into its constituent components. This direction seems to offer a strong possibility of more precise prediction in future studies.

APPENDIX
ASSESSING THE PREDICTIVE POWER OF A REGRESSION MODEL

One of the primary uses of any regression model is in the prediction of future values of the dependent variable at some specified levels of the independent variables. For ease of discussion, consider the simple regression model

$$Y_i = \beta_0 + \beta_1 X_i + \varepsilon_i, i = 1, \cdots, n \tag{A1}$$

where the error terms ε_i are assumed to be independent, normally distributed random variables with zero mean and identical variance, σ^2. (Generalizations to more than one independent variable are straightforward.) The least-squares fitted model is denoted by $\hat{Y}_i = b_0 + b_1 X_i$, with residuals $e_i = (Y_i - \hat{Y}_i)$.

Now, the true line in (A1) is unknown and $\hat{Y}_h$ is a point estimate of the true mean at level h. Also, the estimated variance of $\hat{Y}_h$ is given by

$$s_{\hat{Y}_h}^2 = \text{mse} \left(\frac{1}{n} + \frac{(X_h - \overline{X})^2}{\sum_{i=1}^n (X_i - \overline{X})^2} \right) \tag{A2}$$

where mse $= \frac{1}{n-2} \sum_{i=1}^n e_i^2$ is the sample estimate of σ^2. $\overline{\text{MRE}}(1 - \alpha)100\%$ confidence interval on the true mean value at level h is $\hat{Y}_h \pm t_{\alpha/2, n-2} s_{\hat{Y}_h}^2$.

When the goal is the prediction of some single future value at level X_h rather than the mean, one must consider two sources of variability. First is the vaibility associated with the location of the true mean, which is given in (A2) and secondly, the variability for the probability distribution of a single value about its mean, which is σ^2, estimated by mse. Hence, the estimated variance for a future value at level h

is mse $+ S_Y^2$ and the corresponding $(1-\alpha)$ 100% prediction interval is $\hat{Y}_h \pm t_{\alpha/2, n-2}(\text{mse} + s_{\hat{y}}^2)$. From the expression in (A2) we note that values X_h far away from $\overline{X}$ result in larger variances and hence wider prediction intervals.

The width of the prediction intervals gives an indication of the usefulness of the model in assessing future values. For a fixed level of α, a sample size, n, and a given level of future prediction, h, this width is controlled by the value of mse. As illustrated in Section III, mse is sometimes more indicitive of model usefulness than is R^2.

There are other approaches to assessing the acceptability of effort prediction models. Conte, Dunsmore, and Shen [7] introduced a measure, the mean magnitude of relative error, defined by

$$\overline{\text{MRE}} = \frac{1}{n} \sum_{i=1}^{n} \left| \frac{Y_i - \hat{Y}_i}{Y_i} \right| = \frac{1}{n} \sum_{i=1}^{n} \left| \frac{e_i}{Y_i} \right| = \frac{1}{n} \sum_{i=1}^{n} \text{MRE}. \quad (A3)$$

The implicit assumption in this summary measure is that the seriousness of the absolute error is proportional to the size of the observation. For effort estimation models, this seems reasonable. For example, an ablolute error of four days on a small project may be comparable to an absolute error of several weeks on a much larger project. In this setting, the use of relative error may be more appealing. These same authors report that they consider a value of $\overline{\text{MRE}} \leq 0.25$ to be acceptable for estimation effort models.

A companion summary measure related to $\overline{\text{MRE}}$ is the prediction at level ℓ, $\text{PRED}(\ell) = \frac{k}{n}$, where k is the number of observations whose MRE is less than or equal to ℓ and n is the sample size. Conte, Dunsmore, and Shen [7] conclude that a good effort estimation model should have $\text{PRED}(0.25) \geq 0.75$. That is, 75% of the fitted or predicted values should fall within 25% of their actual observations.

These methods are *ad hoc* procedures which make no assumption concerning the distribution of the observations. They are specifically suited to the situation where the errors are increasing with the size of the observation. Indeed, if the model assumptions in (A1) have been met, the relative error measures are inappropriate since the error variance is constant. In dealing with the problem of increasing variance, (i.e., residuals), one approach is to transform the variables in the model in order to meet the assumptions in (A1). This was the approach taken in this article. In this instance, the calculation of the relative error measures $\overline{\text{MRE}}$ and $\text{PRED}(\ell)$ should be done using the original observations and the corresponding fitted values which have been transformed back into the original units.

REFERENCES

[1] A. J. Albrecht, "Measuring application development productivity," in *Programming Productivity: Issues for the Eighties.* C. Jones, ed. Washington, DC: IEEE Computer Society Press, 1981.
[2] A. J. Albrecht and J. E. Gaffney, "Software function. source lines of code, and development effort prediction: A software science validation," *IEEE Trans. Software Eng.,* vol. SE-9, no. 6, pp. 639–648, June 1983.
[3] B. E. Barrett and R. F. Ling, "General classes of influence measures for multivariate regression," *J. American Statistical Assoc.,* vol. 87, pp. 184–191, 1992.
[4] B. W. Boehm, *Software Engineering Economics.* Englewood Cliffs, NJ: Prentice-Hall, 1981.
[5] B. W. Boehm and P. N. Papaccio, "Understanding and controlling software costs," *IEEE Trans. Software Eng.,* vol. 14, pp. 1462–1477, Oct. 1988.
[6] R. D. Cook, "Detection of influential observations in linear regression," *Technometrics,* vol. 19, pp. 15–18, 1977.
[7] S. D. Conte, H. E. Dunsmore, and V. Y. Shen, *Software Engineering Metrics and Models.* Menlo Park, CA: Benjamin Cummings, 1986.
[8] R. D. Emrick, "In search of a better metric for measuring productivity of application development," *Int. Function Point Users Group Conf. Proc.,* 1987.
[9] D. Ince, "Software metrics," *Measurement for Software Control and Assurance,* B. A. Kitchenham and B. Littlewood, eds. New York: Elsevier, 1989.
[10] C. Jones, *Programming Productivity.* New York: McGraw-Hill, 1986.
[11] ——, "A short history of function and feature points," *Int. Function Point Users Group Conf. Proc.,* 1988.
[12] C. F. Kemerer, "An empirical validation of software cost estimation models," *Commun. ACM,* vol. 30, no. 5, pp. 416–429, 1987.
[13] ——, "Reliability of function points measurements," *Commun. ACM,* vol. 36, pp. 85–97, 1993.
[14] L. A. Laranjeira, "Software size estimation of object-oriented systems," *IEEE Trans. Software Eng.,* vol. 16, pp. 64–71, Jan. 1990.
[15] W. E. Lehder, D. P. Smith, and W. D. Yu, "Software estimation technology," *AT&T Tech. J.,* vol. 67, pp. 10–18, July–Aug. 1988.
[16] G. C. Low and D. R. Jeffery, "Function points in the estimation and evaluation of the software process," *IEEE Trans. Software Eng.,* vol. 16, pp. 64–71, 1990.
[17] J. E. Matson and J. M. Mellichamp, "An object-oriented tool for function point analysis," *Expert Syst.,* vol. 10, pp. 3–14, Feb. 1993.
[18] C. E. McCulloch and D. Meeter, "Discussion of Outliers," by R. J. Beckman and R. D. Cook, *Technometrics,* vol. 25, pp. 152–155, 1983.
[19] C. W. Moseley, "A timescale estimating model for rule-based systems," Ph.D. diss., North Tex. State Univ., 1987.
[20] B. Porter, "A critical comparison of function point counting techniques," *Int. Function Point Users Group Conf. Proc.,* 1988.
[21] C. Richards, "Estimating function points," *Int. Function Point Users Group Conf. Proc.,* 1989.
[22] H. A. Rubin, "Macro-estimation of software development parameters: The ESTIMACS system," *SOFTFAIR Conf. Software Dev. Tools, Techniques, and Alternatives,* 1983, pp. 109–118.
[23] J. Sprouls, IFPUG Function Point Counting Practices Manual Release 3.0, Int. Function Point Users Group, Westerfield, OH, 1990.
[24] C. R. Symons, "Function point analysis: Difficulties and improvements," *IEEE Trans. Software Eng.,* vol. 14, pp. 2–11, Jan. 1988.

J. E. Matson received the M.S. in industrial engineering from Mississippi State University and the Ph.D. degree in management science from the University of Alabama.

He is an Assistant Professor in the Department of Industrial Engineering at the University of Alabama. In addition, he has more than 10 years of industrial experience with AT&T and Southern Bell. His research interests include computer systems engineering and simulation.

B. E. Barrett received the B.S. in biology from the College of Charleston and the M.S. and Ph.D. degrees in mathematical science from Clemson University, Clemson, SC.

He is Assistant Professor of statistics at the Manderson School of Business, University of Alabama, Tuscaloosa, AL. His primary areas of research interest are regression diagnostics and statistical computing.

Dr. Barrett has published articles in *Journal of the American Statistical Association, Journal of Computational and Graphical Statistics,* and *Statistics and Computing.*

J. M. Mellichamp received the B.S. degree in industrial engineering from the Georgia Institute of Technology and the Ph.D. degree in engineering management from Clemson University, Clemson, SC.

He is a Professor of management science at the Manderson Graduate School of Business, University of Alabama, Tuscaloosa, AL. His primary areas of research are simulation and knowledge-based systems, with an emphasis in the use of knowledge-based systems and simulation methods to design complex systems.

Dr. Mellichamp has published numerous articles in such journals as *Management Science, Simulation, Expert Systems, Interfaces, Decision Sciences, International Journal of Production Research, Harvard Business Review,* and IEEE NETWORKS. He is a member of the Institute of Management Science and the Society for Computer Simulation.

Function Points in the Estimation and Evaluation of the Software Process

GRAHAM C. LOW AND D. ROSS JEFFERY

Abstract—Measures of project size are a prerequisite to successful quantitative management of software projects. One such measure that is gaining acceptance with commercial organizations is function points. This paper reports the results of an empirical research project into the consistency and limitations of function points as an *a priori* measure of system size compared to the traditional lines of code measure. The paper concludes that function points are a more consistent *a priori* measure of system size. The results also indicate that the function point estimate of size is lower for analysts experienced both in software development and in function point estimation.

Index Terms—Estimation, function points, lines of code, quantitative measurement, software management, software size.

I. INTRODUCTION

A CRITICAL problem facing MIS management in today's competitive environment is project planning [18]. However, planning requires an ability to accurately estimate the effort involved in developing new application systems. A number of effort models have been proposed [19], [12], [3], [6], [11], [8]. Software size is an important parameter in these models with the size measure most often adopted being lines of code.

Expressing software size in terms of lines of code has difficulties [11]. The first is what is meant by a line of code. Jones suggests that there are eleven major variations which may be broadly split into two groups. These are concerned with program level and project level variations. The variations at the program level are:
1) count only executable lines;
2) executable lines plus data definitions;
3) count executable lines, data definitions, and comments;
4) count executable lines, data definitions, comments and Job Control Language;
5) count lines as physical lines on an input screen; and
6) count lines as terminated by logical delimiters.

Jones [10] reports that the program level variations can result in differences of up to five to one in the lines of code count.

Variations at the project level are:
1) count only new lines;
2) count new lines and changed lines;

Manuscript received September 27, 1988; revised May 22, 1989. Recommended by W. Royce.

The authors are with the School of Information Systems, University of New South Wales, P.O. Box 1, Kensington, N. S. W. 2033, Australia

IEEE Log Number 8931762.

3) count new lines, changed lines, and reused lines;
4) count all delivered lines plus temporary scaffold code; and
5) count all delivered lines, temporary code, and support code.

Project level variations are important when the program is not completely new code. Two examples are the addition of extra functionality to an existing program and the use of reused code in a program.

The particular definition of lines of code that is adopted in any particular instance depends on its intended use. For instance, it would be more appropriate to use the project level variation "new lines plus changed lines" rather than "all delivered lines, temporary code, and support code" in estimating *a priori* the effort involved in adding extra functionality to a program. Having decided which project level variation is to be adopted, the analyst must also decide which program level variation to adopt.

The *a posteriori* estimate of system size using lines of code should be totally consistent since there can only be one answer provided the definition of lines of code does not change. However *a priori* estimation of effort required for application systems development requires an estimation of system size early in the system development lifecycle at points such as the requirements and the design specification stages. This *a priori* estimate of system size is usually based on the past experience of the person performing the estimate with similar projects and/or systems. To the best of the authors knowledge the consistency of lines of code as an *a priori* measure of system size has not been tested. Certainly most commercial organizations place little or no faith in its usefulness to the extent that it is almost impossible to locate analysts who can perform a priori estimates of system size using lines of code.

Another difficulty with lines of code as a measure of system size is its language dependence. Consequently it is not possible to directly compare the productivity of projects developed in different languages [14], [4], using lines of code as the measure of system size.

Albrecht [1] introduced the concept of function points in 1979 to measure the functionality delivered by software. Function points can be determined from the requirements specification, design specification, source listing or live system [16]. Since function points measure functionality, they should be independent of the technology and language used for the software implementation. The ability to determine function points *a priori* and their

Reprinted from *IEEE Transactions on Software Engineering*, Vol. 16, No. 1, Jan. 1990, pp. 64-71.

325

technology and language independence overcome two of the main objections pertaining to lines of code as a measure of system size.

The steps taken to arrive at the function point count for a software product are:

1) Classify and count the five user function types delivered by the development project. These are:

   i) external input types. For instance input screens where the user enters data that is added to or modifies data in a logical internal file;

   ii) external output types. For instance output screens or reports;

   iii) logical internal file types. Each major logical group of user data or control information maintained by the application is classified as a logical internal file type;

   iv) external interface file types. These are files passed or shared between applications; and

   v) external inquiry types. These are enquiries where a user request causes and generates an immediate output.

According to Albrecht, these factors are the functional manifestations of any application and they cover all the functions in an application. The counts for each function type are classified according to perceived complexity and are then weighted by numbers designed "to reflect the function value to the customer." For instance a simple external input is weighted at 3 whereas a complex external input has a weight of 6. In comparison a simple logical internal file is weighted at 7. The weights used were determined by Albrecht by debate and trial. The individual weighted counts are then summed up to give what Albrecht called the Raw or Unadjusted Function Points.

The raw function point worksheet proposed by Albrecht and Gaffney [2] is shown below.

Function type	Simple	Complexity Average	Complex	Total
External input	___*3=___	___*4=___	___*6=___	___
External output	___*4=___	___*5=___	___*7=___	___
Logical internal file	___*7=___	___*10=___	___*15=___	___
External interface file	___*5=___	___*7=___	___*10=___	___
External inquiry	___*3=___	___*4=___	___*6=___	___

Total unadjusted function points

2) Adjust for application and environment complexity. The adjustment for complexity can be accomplished in two steps.

   a) The degree of influence of each of 14 general characteristics listed below is estimated.

      i) data communications;
      ii) distributed processing;
      iii) performance objectives;
      iv) operational configuration load;
      v) transaction rate;
      vi) online data entry;
      vii) end user efficiency;
      viii) online update;
      ix) complex processing logic;
      x) reusability;
      xi) installation ease;
      xii) operational ease;
      xiii) multiple sites; and
      xiv) desire to facilitate change.

The degree of influence of each of these factors takes a value from 0 to 5 to signify none to essential.

   b) The 14 degrees of influence are summed giving a total (N) which is used to develop a complexity adjustment factor ranging from 0.65 to 1.35 (this gives an adjustment of $+/-$ 35 percent). The adjustment factor equals to $[0.65 + 0.01 (N)]$ where N is the total degree of influence.

3) Make the function points calculation. The function points delivered by an application program are calculated by:

Function Points Delivered

= (Unadjusted Function Points

× Complexity Adjustment Factor).

Numerous authors [1], [11], [14] quote factors to convert between function points and lines of code for various languages. For instance Jones [11] suggests that it takes 106 lines of code to implement one function point in Cobol while in PL1 it is 80 and in FOCUS it is 40. Using these figures it is possible to estimate software size using function points and then convert the estimate to lines of code.

Function points are currently used by numerous large Australian organizations in the measurement of productivity for project review purposes and effort estimation. Productivity in this instance is defined as function points divided by work effort [5], [13], [14], [11]. Naturally this use of function points is only valid if there is a relationship between function points and hours worked. Numerous authors report such a relationship [1], [2], [9], [15].

This *a posteriori* use of function points appears to be the starting point in many organizations for the use of functions points in project management. Once this relationship between function points (output) and hours worked (input) has been determined for an organization, the next step taken is to estimate a project's size in function points and then use the predetermined relationship to predict anticipated work hours. Unlike *a posteriori* measurement of size which is based on the delivered product, estimation (*a priori* measurement) is based on either the functional specification, logical design specification, or physical design specification.

Little work has been published on the use of function points as a measure of software size prior to project completion with the exception of Rudolph [14]. He reported an experiment where members of the GUIDE Productivity Project Group estimated the number of function points from a requirements specification. In this case the values were within 30 percent of the average judgment. Not-

IEEE TRANSACTIONS ON SOFTWARE ENGINEERING, VOL. 16, NO. 1, JANUARY 1990

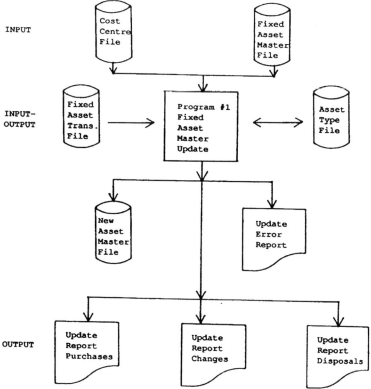

Fig. 1. Fixed asset master file update (program 1) flowchart.

withstanding the lack of published information, organizations are using function points as a project management and estimation tool. They have also been incorporated into commercially available software project management packages such as SPQR [11].

II. RESEARCH OBJECTIVES

This paper reports the results of an empirical research project concerned with function points.

The aim of this research was threefold:

1) To evaluate the consistency of the function point estimate as an *a priori* measure of software size.

It was decided to test consistency in the following ways. Present a set of program specifications to different sets of analysts, and:

a) Determine the consistency between individual counts carried out by different experienced analysts.

b) Determine the consistency between counts on an organizational basis for the different experienced analysts.

c) Determine the consistency between counts carried out by experienced versus inexperienced analysts.

The effect of two different dimensions of experience was studied in the experiment:

i) experience in software development; and

ii) experience in counting function points.

2) To identify any limitations in the use of function points as an *a priori* measure of software size. For ex-

ample prior experience of function points had led us to believe that the complexity assigned to a function point factor (i.e., simple, average, or complex) is heavily dependent on the analyst's previous experience. It was expected that an inexperienced analyst would be more likely to weight a factor as complex than an experienced analyst.

3) To determine if function point estimates are more consistent than lines of code estimates. This was tested by comparing the consistency of function point count and source lines of code estimate.

III. DATA COLLECTION

In this research, function point and source lines of code estimates were carried out on two programs using program specifications prepared according to commercial standards by an experienced professional analyst/programmer. The programs formed part of a complete Fixed Asset Accounting system comprising five programs. The two programs used were:

1) Fixed Asset Master file update (Fig. 1).

2) Fixed Asset depreciation calculation and reporting (Fig. 2).

These program specifications were selected for the research since Jeffery *et al.* [19] reported that the number of function points counted for each of eight student implementations of these programs was close (3 percent Standard Deviation/Mean for program 1 and 6 percent Standard Deviation/Mean for program 2). This indicates

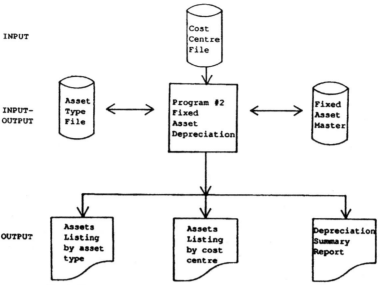

INPUT

INPUT-OUTPUT

OUTPUT

Fig. 2. Fixed asset depreciation calculation and reporting (program 2) flowchart.

that the specifications were quite specific and not subject to differences in interpretation. It was important to ensure that differences in estimated function points and source lines of code could not arise through imprecise specifications.

The data collected and the relationship of this data with the research objectives is shown in Table I.

In summary there are three major data sets.

1) Twenty-two function point experienced analysts counting *a priori* from the program specification.

2) Two groups of function point naive analysts, one group very experienced in analysis; the other group relatively inexperienced in analysis. Both groups counted function points *a priori* from the program specification.

All of the subjects were working as analysts or programmers in commercial Information Systems groups associated with Government or Industry.

3) Twelve analysts estimating source lines of code from the program specification. While all twelve analysts had prior experience in this estimating technique, none currently used this method to estimate system size.

IV. EXPERIMENTAL RESULTS

A. Comparison of Results for Experienced Analysts

The results for the experienced analysts show quite marked variations about the mean, Table II. In contrast, Rudolph [14] reported an experiment where a group of approximately 20 GUIDE Productivity Project Group members estimated functions points using a requirements specification. The variation was found to be within 30 percent of the mean.

Possible explanations for the variation in our estimates include:

1) Complexity of the user function types. Differences in perception of the user function type complexity can

TABLE I
SUMMARY OF DATA COLLECTION

Research objective	Data used
Evaluate the consistency of function points	
1) Between individual counts carried out by different experienced analysts	Twenty two analysts in seven Australian organisations experienced in using function points estimated the number of function points for the two programs using the program specification.
2) Between counts on an organizational basis for different experienced analysts	Data collected for part (1) was analyzed on an organizational basis
3) Between counts for experienced versus inexperienced analysts	
i) Experience in software development	Two groups of analysts trained in the use of function points by one of the authors estimated the number of function points for the first of the two programs (Fixed Asset Master file update program) at the conclusion of their training course. One group (group A) comprised people from a single organisation with experience levels ranging from trainee analyst/programmer to experienced analyst. The other group (group B) was comprised entirely of experienced analysts.
ii) Experience in counting function points	Data obtained for the experienced analysts in part (1) for program #1 was compared with that for the two inexperienced groups.
Limitations in the use of function points	All data previously discussed.
Compare the consistency of function point and source lines of code estimates	The function point data obtained for the experienced analysts in part (1) was compared with lines of code data obtained from twelve analysts in three Australian organisations. In both cases the estimates were for the two programs using the program specification.

IEEE TRANSACTIONS ON SOFTWARE ENGINEERING, VOL. 16, NO. 1, JANUARY 1990

TABLE II
A Priori Mean and Standard Deviation of Function Points for Experienced Analysts

Program	No. of Analysts	Estimated No. of Function Points (Mean)	Std. Dev.	Std. Dev. /Mean (%)	Range
1	22	57.7	26.3	45.5	(26-159)
2	22	39.6	13.4	33.8	(15-76)

have a dramatic effect on the total function point count since the weighting for a complex user function type is on average approximately double that of a simple user function type. For instance if the analysts had rated all user function types as simple for program 1 the mean estimate would have been 45.6 (STD 26.0) whereas if they had been rated as complex the mean estimate would have been 90.5 (STD 55.8).

2) Value judgments made when estimating the number of function points. For example, program 2 produces three reports two of which only differ by the order in which the line items are listed. One analyst suggested that these two reports should only be counted once due to their similarity.

3) Different interpretations of the specification. It is evident that various analysts interpreted the two program specifications in different ways for function point estimation purposes although the program specifications resulted in consistent implementations [9]. The various interpretations of the system *a priori* resulted in differing counts for the number of user function types. For example, many analysts counted four files (whether logical internal or interface files) for program 1 since only four physical files were specified. In a number of instances this count was reduced to three with the Fixed Asset Transaction file counted as an external input. This is in conflict with the information published in the IBM Productivity Measurement Guide [7]. This guide specifically states "do not include input files of records as external input types, because these are counted as external interface file types". In one instance the misunderstanding could be attributed to the analyst's unfamiliarity with batch systems. In another case the analyst concerned commented "not worth a file—it could just as easily have been typed as inputs on a line".

The specifications for program 1 required that the control records be retrieved for each of the four input files (Cost Center, Fixed Asset Master, Fixed Asset Transaction, and Asset Type) to check for file integrity. The Fixed Asset Transaction file is then sorted prior to the creation of a new Asset Master file reflecting the old Asset Master file updated for purchase, adjustment, and disposal orders. In addition, purchase, adjustment, and disposal transaction counts are accumulated during processing and compared with the totals contained in the Fixed Asset Transaction file.

Some analysts counted five files (the four original files plus the New Asset Master file). Another analyst counted

the control records, trailer records, and purchase, adjustment and disposal records for each file as separate logical files. This accounts for the particularly high function point count of 159 for program 1 and 76 for program 2. Other analysts specifically commented that control and trailer records were not counted since they did not directly contribute to user functionality. The different interpretations of what constitutes a logical file for the purposes of counting function points can have a substantial effect on the final count (mean number of logical internal files for program 1 was 4.5 with range 0–20).

4) Perception of the object boundaries. Most organizations surveyed currently perform function point counts on entire systems and not on individual programs. Many analysts indicated that they would normally only count files once for a system. In addition files that may be logical internal files to a system may be considered external interface files to an individual program. In 14 out of the 22 cases the analysts appeared to determine the file type on a system rather than a program basis.

5) Objectives of the function point counter. Since function points are used by a number of organizations to measure staff productivity, there is a tendency to subconsciously adjust the function point count based on the analyst's perception of program difficulty. This was very evident for the analyst who recorded the lowest count for both programs (value of 26 for program 1 and 15 for program 2). This analyst refused to count the update reports as external outputs on the basis they were simple and really "part of input processing."

6) Analyst experience in *a priori* counting. While all analysts were experienced in function point counting, not all were experienced in *a priori* counting. Three of the four analysts participating from one organization (2) had only *a posteriori* experience. This was the only organization surveyed that did not have senior management commitment for the use of function points. These analysts were responsible for the very high counts recorded. In addition this organization had the largest variation in estimates (Section IV-B).

B. Organizational Effect

Tables III and IV show the estimated number of function points by organization for programs 1 and 2 respectively. Organization 2 had by far the largest variation about the organizational mean of all organizations. Senior management has been reluctant to accept the use of function points for estimating purposes in this organization. Consequently three of the four analysts in this organization had only *a posteriori* experience in function point counting.

The variation about the organization's mean for the other 6 organization is 24 percent for program 1 and 16 percent for program 2. Comparing these variations to the variation about the overall mean for the same organizations of 42 percent for program 1 and 30 percent for program 2 suggests that organizational differences may also affect the function point count. Unfortunately it was not possible to statistically verify this conclusion and further

TABLE III
MEAN AND STANDARD DEVIATION OF FUNCTION POINTS FOR PROGRAM 1 BY ORGANIZATION

Organisation	No. of Analysts	Estimated No. of Function Points (Mean)	Std. Dev.	Std. Dev. /Mean (%)	Range
1	7	51.9	8.6	16.5	(40 - 64)
2	4	85.5	53.6	62.7	(34 - 159)
3	4	47.8	2.6	5.5	(44 - 50)
4	2	51.0	0.0	0.0	(51 - 51)
5	3	57.3	13.6	23.7	(49 - 73)
6	1	73.0			
7	1	26.0			

TABLE IV
MEAN AND STANDARD DEVIATION OF FUNCTION POINTS FOR PROGRM 2 BY ORGANIZATION

Organisation	No. of Analysts	Estimated No. of Function Points (Mean)	Std. Dev.	Std. Dev. /Mean (%)	Range
1	7	36.9	2.1	5.7	(33 - 39)
2	4	49.0	23.3	47.5	(23 - 76)
3	4	34.3	3.6	10.5	(31 - 39)
4	2	34.0	0.0	0.0	(34 - 34)
5	3	43.3	6.7	15.4	(36 - 49)
6	1	67.0			
7	1	15.0			

TABLE V
EFFECT OF EXPERIENCE ON FUNCTION POINT COUNTS

Group	No. of Analysts	Estimated No. of Function Points	Std. Dev.	Std. Dev. /Mean (%)	Range
Experienced	22	57.7	26.3	45.5	(26 - 159)
Inexperienced					
Group A	11	83.7	34.5	41.2	(52 - 144)
Group B	9	72.9	30.6	42.0	(43 - 139)

TABLE VI
EFFECT OF EXPERIENCE ON FUNCTION POINT COUNTS EXCLUDING ORGANIZATION 2

Group	No. of Analysts	Estimated No. of Function Points	Std. Dev.	Std. Dev. /Mean (%)	Range
Experienced	18	51.5	11.1	21.6	(26 - 73)
Inexperienced					
Group A	11	83.7	34.5	41.2	(52 - 144)
Group B	9	72.9	30.6	42.0	(43 - 139)

research is planned. The apparent variation may be attributed to differences in training and organizational standards.

C. Comparison of Experienced and Inexperienced Function Point Counters

Two groups of analysts, inexperienced in function point counting, estimated the number of function points for program 1. Their results are shown in Table V together with those for the experienced group discussed previously.

Table VI shows the same results as Table V except the results for organization 2 have been omitted from the group of experienced analysts since three of the four analysts in this organization had no experience in *a priori* function point counting.

Using a t-test, the estimates for groups A and B are significantly higher than for the experienced group excluding organization 2 ($P < 0.05$). This may be attributed to differences in function point estimation experience. However it does not account for the variation between the two inexperienced groups since both groups performed the estimates immediately following the receipt of identical training from one of the authors. Group B consisted of analysts with greater experience in systems development than group A. While the concepts of function point counting were entirely new to both groups, group B had a more practical background on which to build. This concept is consistent with the fact that their counts were closer to those of the experienced function point analysts than group A.

D. Comparison of the Consistency of Function Point Estimates and Source Lines of Code Estimates

Table VII reports the source lines of code estimates for the twelve analysts identified as having previous experience in estimating source lines of code. All source lines of code counts included blank and comment lines. The analysts from organizations A and B estimated directly source lines of code while the analysts from organization C estimated in staff days and used their organizational productivity factor (i.e., source lines of code per staff day) to convert from staff days to source lines of code.

The estimates were for either Cobol or PL/1 implementations. The Cobol source lines of code estimates were performed by two analysts in organization A. The ten analysts who estimated in PL/1 source lines of code were from organizations B and C. The computer type and operating system was similar in all three organizations.

Examination of Table VII reveals significantly differing source lines of code estimates for the two organizations coding in PL/1 (program 1, $p = 0.000$, $t = 9.42$; program 2, $p = 0.000$, $t = 8.88$). The different methods used to arrive at the estimates may be responsible for this difference. Organization B estimated staff days of effort and then used the organizational productivity factor to convert to lines of code. Alternatively the results may reflect different organizational practices and standards which results in dissimilar estimates for the number of lines of code to implement the same functionality.

Table VIII suggests that on an organizational basis source lines of code estimates are no better than function point count estimates when estimating from a program specification. Since function points measure the "functionality delivered to the user" they are suitable for estimating systems size at earlier stages in the systems development. In comparison it is extremely difficult to

330

TABLE VII
A PRIORI MEAN AND STANDARD DEVIATION OF SOURCE LINES OF CODE
ESTIMATES

Program	Language	Organisation	No. of Analysts	Estimated Source Lines of Code (Mean)	Std. Dev.	Std. Dev. /Mean (%)	Range
1	Cobol	A	2	1205	870	72.2	(700–1710)
1	PL/1	B	2	2033	379	18.8	(1600–2300)
1	PL/1	C	8	534	152	28.5	(360–720)
1	PL/1	ALL*	10	984	715	72.7	(360–2300)
2	Cobol	A	2	1265	870	68.8	(650–1880)
2	Pl/1	B	2	1633	321	19.6	(1400–2000)
2	Pl/1	C	8	403	139	34.5	(144–600)
2	Pl/1	ALL*	10	772	624	80.8	(144–2000)

*　　　Data for both organisations B and C.

TABLE VIII
COMPARISON OF FUNCTION POINT AND SOURCE LINES OF CODE VARIATIONS
ABOUT THE MEAN

Program	Estimating Method*	Organisation	Language	No. of Analysts	Std. Dev. /Mean (%)
1	FP	1	N/A**	7	16.5
1	FP	2	N/A**	4	62.7
1	FP	3	N/A**	4	5.5
1	FP	4	N/A**	2	0.0
1	FP	5	N/A**	3	23.7
1	FP	6	N/A**	1	
1	FP	7	N/A**	1	
1	FP	1–7+	N/A**	22	45.5
1	SLOC	A	Cobol	2	72.2
1	SLOC	B	PL/1	10	18.8
1	SLOC	C	PL/1	10	28.5
1	SLOC	B&C++		12	72.2
2	FP	1	N/A**	7	5.7
2	FP	2	N/A**	4	47.5
2	FP	3	N/A**	4	10.5
2	FP	4	N/A**	2	0.0
2	FP	5	N/A**	3	15.4
2	FP	6	N/A**	1	
2	FP	7	N/A**	1	
2	FP	1–7+	N/A**	7	33.8
2	SLOC	A	Cobol	2	68.8
2	SLOC	B	Pl/1	10	19.6
2	SLOC	C	Pl/1	10	34.5
2	SLOC	B&C++		2	80.8

*　　　FP　= function points
　　　SLOC = source lines of code
**　　Function point counts are independent of the implementing language.
+　　　Result for all organisations (1–7) that estimated function points.
++　　Result for both organisations (B and C) that estimated source lines
　　　of code in PL/1.

estimate lines of code prior to the program specification stage. The estimates tend to be based on the past experience of the analysts performing the estimate with similar programs and/or systems and not based on any particular set of procedures or rules. In contrast function point count estimates are obtained using a formalized set of procedures proposed by Albrecht [1] and Albrecht *et al.* [2]. Consequently there is every reason to believe that the function point estimates made early in the systems development lifecycle will be more consistent than lines of code estimates.

As mentioned in the introduction a number of effort models have been proposed to assist management in determining the effort required to develop new applications [19], [12], [3], [6], [11], [8]. A key factor in all these models is software size which has traditionally been measured as source lines of code since the models were developed using data from developed application systems.

Management, however, is interested in obtaining an *a priori* estimate of the effort required to develop new applications. This necessitates the application of these effort models at an early stage in the systems development lifecycle where there is every reason to believe function point counts are a more consistent *a priori* measure of system size than source lines of code. Fortunately many of the commercial estimation packages accept estimates of system size in either lines of code or function points.

V. CONCLUSIONS

1) Function point counts appear to be a more consistent *a priori* measure of software size than source lines of code. As such it is recommended that function point estimates be used in preference to lines of code estimates as the measure of system size, for the type of software investigated here, when estimating *a priori* the effort required for application development.

2) Within organizations the variation in function point counts about the mean appears to be within the 30 percent reported by Rudolph [14]. The variation can be attributed to the analyst's assessment of the complexity of the user function type, interpretation of the specification, value judgments, perception of the object boundaries, objectives of the function point counter and experience in *a priori* counting.

3) There appears to be a variation in function point estimates between companies. This can be attributed to possible differences in training and organizational standards. This variation does not affect the validity of function points as a software estimation metric within an organization provided that the estimates are consistent. However, management should exercise care when comparing productivity figures between companies based on function points, or when using productivity relationships derived from other organizations.

4) Experience in the application of function points is an important factor in their successful application. This is evidenced by comparing the results of the two inexperienced groups to the experienced group. Consequently one should not expect an analyst to undertake a function point training course and immediately be proficient. The analyst should be assisted for a period by an experienced analyst. In this way organizations are more likely to achieve consistent results. This technique has been adopted by some of the participating organizations. However, the technique is not perfect, as evidenced by organization 5 where the analyst showing the greatest variation from the organization's mean was the liaison officer responsible for implementing function point analysis in the organization's development areas.

5) Software development experience influences function point estimates. This can be seen by comparing the results of the two inexperienced groups. The group with the greater software development experience had results closer to those of the experienced group in function point counting.

REFERENCES

[1] A. J. Albrecht, "Measuring application development productivity," in *Proc. Joint SHARE/GUIDE/IBM Application Development Symp.*, Oct. 1979, pp. 34–43.
[2] A. J. Albrecht and J. E. Gaffney, "Software function, source lines of code, and development effort prediction: A software science validation," *IEEE Trans. Software Eng.*, vol. SE-9, pp. 639–648, Nov. 1983.
[3] B. W. Boehm, *Software Engineering Economics*. Englewood Cliffs, NJ: Prentice-Hall, 1981.
[4] R. G. Canning, "A programmer productivity controversy," *EDP Analyser*, vol. 24, no. 1, pp. 1–11, 1986.
[5] D. Case, "Productivity in the university—Scholarly work as information work," *Proc. Ameri. Soc. Inform. Sci.*, vol. 20, pp. 2–3, 1983.
[6] S. D. Conte, H. E. Dunsmore, and V. Y. Shen, *Software Engineering Metrics and Models*. Menlo Park, CA: Benjamin/Cummings, 1983.
[7] IBM Corp., *Development Center Productivity Measurement Guide*, Middlesex, England 1984.
[8] D. R. Jeffery, "A software development productivity model for MIS environments," *J. Syst. Software* vol. 7, pp. 115–125, June 1987.
[9] D. R. Jeffery, C. C. Loo, and G. C. Low, "The validity, reliability, and practically of function points as a measure of software size," Dep. Inform. Syst., Univ. New South Wales, Inform. Syst. Res. Rep. 33, 1988.
[10] T. C. Jones, "Measuring programming quality and productivity," *IBM Syst. J.*, vol. 17, no. 1, pp. 39–63, 1978.
[11] ——, *Programming Productivity*. New York: McGraw-Hill, 1986.
[12] L. H. Putnam, "A general empirical solution to the macro software sizing and estimation problem," *IEEE Trans. Software Eng.*, vol. SE-4, pp. 345–361, July 1978.
[13] R. E. Rice and J. Bair, "Conceptual role of new communication technology in organizational productivity," *Proc. Amer. Soc. Inform. Sci.*, vol. 20, pp. 4–8, 1983.
[14] E. E. Rudolph, "Productivity in computer application development," Dep. Management Studies, Univ. Auckland, Australia, 1983.
[15] "Quoting a software job—by simple arithmetic," *Computerworld*, pp. 33–34, Aug. 1987.
[16] E. E. Rudolph and G. Simpson, "Evaluation of a fourth generation language," in *Proc. ACS & IFIP Joint Sym. Information Systems*, Sydney, Australia, Apr. 1984, pp. 148–165.
[17] Software Productivity Research Inc., *SPQR/20 User's Guide*, 1986.
[18] R. H. Thayer, A. B. Pyster, and R. C. Wood, "Major issues in software engineering project management," *IEEE Trans. Software Eng.*, vol. SE-7, pp. 333–342, July 1981.
[19] C. E. Walston and C. P. Felix, A method of program measurement and estimation," *IBM Syst. J.*, vol. 16, no. 1, pp. 54–73, 1977.

Graham C. Low received the B.E. and Ph.D. degrees from the University of Queensland, Australia.

He is a Senior Lecturer in the School of Information Systems at the University of New South Wales, Australia. He had in excess of 10 years MIS experience in industry prior to joining the School of Information Systems in 1987. His current research interests are in the areas of estimating and the use of CASE tools. His research is based on actual data collected from some of Australia's largest organizations.

D. Ross Jeffery is Professor and Head of the School of Information Systems at the University of New South Wales, Australia. He has been researching the software development process for the last nine years in the areas of cost estimation, productivity, languages, and management. He has also published three books on information systems.

Dr. Jeffery is a member of the Association for Computing Machinery, the IEEE Computer Society, Australian Computer Society, and the Australian Society of Accountants. He was Program Chairman for the 1984 and 1988 IFIP TC8 Conference on Information Systems and is on the Editorial Board of the John Wiley Series in Information Systems.

Capers Jones, Software Productivity Research Inc., 1 New England Executive Park, Burlington, MA 01803-5005; phone (617) 273-0140; fax (617) 273-5176; Internet capers@spr.com; Compuserve 75430,231

Determining software schedules

Capers Jones
Software Productivity Research

mproving software productivity, shortening schedules or time to market, and improving quality are prominent topics in software journals in both contributed articles and advertising copy. Unfortunately, most of these articles and advertisements have dealt with software schedules, productivity, or quality factors in abstract terms such as "Buy our tool and improve productivity by 10 to 1" or "Cut development schedules by 50 percent." But now we can measure these factors with reasonable accuracy and collect empirical data on both "average" and "best-in-class" results. We are particularly interested in the wide performance gaps between laggards, average enterprises, and industry leaders, as well as differences among the various software domains. The function-point metric lets us establish a meaningful database of software performance levels. A simple algorithm raises function points to a total to obtain a useful first-order schedule estimate.

Beginning and end points of software schedules

Considering how important software schedules and time-to-market considerations are, it is surprising that in the past 50 years, this topic has inspired very little solid, printed data. Although many commercial-software cost-estimating tools can predict schedules with fairly good accuracy, as of 1994 only about 15 percent of US software managers—and even less abroad—were using them. So at least 85 percent of the world's software managers jump into projects with hardly a clue as to how long they will take. This explains why about half the major disasters associated with missed schedules and overruns can be traced back to the schedules being incompetently established in the first place.

From collecting schedule information on historical projects, I've observed that establishing a software project's true duration schedule is one of the trickiest measurement tasks in the entire software domain. A software project's shipping date is usually fairly clear, but the date the project actually originated is the hardest and most imprecise data

point in the software industry. For most software projects, there is an amorphous, unmeasured period during which clients and software personnel grope with fundamental issues such as whether to build or buy, and what is really needed. Of several thousand software projects that my colleagues and I have analyzed over the past 10 years, less than 1 percent had a clearly defined starting point. To avoid this ambiguity, our pragmatic approach is to ask the project's senior software manager to pick a date as the starting point and simply use that. If the project has formal, written requirements, we can sometimes ascertain the date they were introduced, or at least the date shown on the first printed version.

Surprisingly, more than 15 percent of software projects are also ambiguous as to when they were truly delivered. One source of ambiguity is whether to count the start of external beta testing as the delivery point or to wait until the formal delivery when this testing is over. (Our general rule is to count the first formal release to paying customers or users that are not participants in beta testing or prerelease field testing.) Another source of ambiguity is whether to count a software product's initial delivery or to wait until deferred functions come out a few months later in what is usually called a point release (such as "Version 1.1").

Not only are both ends of software projects ambiguous and difficult to determine, but the middle can get messy, too. Even with the "waterfall model" of development, there is always overlap and parallelism between adjacent activities, so that a project's end-to-end schedule is never the same as the duration of those activities. Software requirements are usually only about 75 percent defined when design starts. Design is often little more than 50 percent complete when coding starts. Integration and testing can begin when coding is less than 20 percent complete. And user documentation usually starts when coding is about 50 percent finished. Moreover, the newer spiral and iterative models of software development are even more amorphous, since requirements, design, coding, testing, and documentation can be freely interleaved and take place concurrently.

Space does not permit a full discussion of all the factors that affect software schedules or of the schedule durations

Reprinted from *IEEE Computer*, Vol. 28, No. 2, Feb. 1995, pp. 73-75.

Table 1. Nominal power level for schedule duration applied to function-point totals.

Software domain	Best in class	Average	Worst in class
Commercial	0.39	0.42	0.45
MIS	0.41	0.43	0.46
Systems	0.43	0.45	0.48
Military	0.45	0.46	0.50

for all kinds of software projects. But the function-point metric provides a convenient, quick estimator for schedule durations that can be applied early in a software project's development cycle. The schedule interval runs from the project's nominal "start of requirements" to the "first customer ship" date. The activities in this interval include requirements creation, analysis, high-level and detail design, reviews and inspections, coding, integration, all forms of testing, and user-document creation.

Once the application's function-point total has been determined, it is only necessary to raise that total to the power shown in Table 1. For example, an "average" military project of 10,000 function points (equivalent to about 700,000 Ada statements) would use a power of 0.46. Raising 10,000 function points to the 0.46 power, we would estimate the project's nominal schedule at 69.18 calendar months. (Note that for enhancement schedules, we would use the enhancement's—not the original product's—function-point total as the estimate basis. Thus, if we added 100 function points to a 5,000-function-point system, we would use 100 as the starting point.) This simplistic methodology is not a substitute for a true software-estimating tool that can deal with factors such as programming languages, tools, reuse, experience levels, creeping requirements, and other characteristics known to influence a software project's outcome. But it does enable a useful first-order approximation with any pocket calculator that can handle power calculations. In fact, clients who have used this methodology have found that it works reasonably well. However, leading-edge companies whose available volume of reusable material exceeds 50 percent can surpass even the "best in class."

Software schedules in different domains

Software schedules in the four domains—commercial software, management information systems (MIS), systems software, and military software—are strongly impacted by several considerations.

Commercial software. This domain includes products marketed to customers, such as spreadsheets, word-processors, and accounting packages. The average size of modern, windows-based commercial products for typical word-processing and spreadsheet packages is roughly 1,000 function points. However, large mainframe software packages, such as order-entry systems, databases like IBM's DB2 or IMS, and manufacturing-support packages, can exceed 10,000 function points. The primary schedule consideration in the commercial world is quality, and the reason most commercial-software projects run late is that

they encounter too many bugs during testing to be released.

Management information systems. MIS concerns custom software that companies build for their own use or that they commission contractors or outsource vendors to build for them. An MIS project's size ranges from less than 100 function points to more than 20,000 for major systems involving insurance-claims handling, manufacturing control, or full order-entry systems.

The MIS domain's two key schedule drivers, quality and creeping user requirements, tend to interact in unpleasant ways. The rate of unanticipated user-requirement changes in a typical MIS project is about 1 percent per month. So for a three-year project, more than a third of the final functionality may be added midstream. Many MIS shops are not very sophisticated in software quality control and omit important activities such as reviews and inspections. Since quality control on creeping user requirements is even worse than normal, lax development methods coupled with volatile requirements result in many MIS projects running amok around the time testing starts. If the projects are developed carelessly, which unfortunately is the case for many new client/server applications, the resulting poor quality may be passed on to users, because testing is often perfunctory.

Systems software. This domain involves software that controls physical devices such as telecommunication-switching, fuel-injection, flight-control, and operating systems. Software ranges from about 250 function points to more than 50,000 function points for huge systems such as large mainframe operating systems. Because quality levels are high in the systems-software domain, the better systems producers are in a good position to take advantage of reusability and increase the parallelism of their development methods. In fact, some projects are setting new records and improving the "best-in-class" results.

The systems-software community has learned that full quality control, including formal pretest inspections, is necessary to do business. This also implies formal specifications, so the important schedule factors for systems software are creating and reviewing a significant volume of specification material and executing an extended series of defect-removal operations. A typical defect-removal cycle for a large system-software project, such as a telephone-switching system of around 10,000 function points, would include formal inspections of design, code, and documents, and at least seven kinds of testing: unit, new-function, regression, integration, stress, system, and field tests.

Military software. Applications that are required to follow US military standards such as DoD 2167A are included in this domain. Military projects range from those of perhaps 200 function points to the largest software systems in human history, which can exceed 250,000 function points. Military software schedules have four key gating factors: the initial procurement process, enormous volumes of paperwork created in the DoD community, high quality levels for mission-critical applications, and the special activities that only military projects perform. Software (and hardware) is typically procured via external contracts derived from various bids and proposals. This process is both intrinsically time-consuming and rife with challenges and litigation from disgruntled vendors who have not received the contract. Thus, a typical military software project takes about 35 percent longer to get started than a similar civilian project. If the initial procurement leads to major litigation, the schedules can be even longer.

US military standards have been useful in many ways, but they have had some unintended side effects. One of the most significant is the enormous volume of specifications and planning documents. By actual count, military software projects that follow the DoD 2167A standard have averaged about 400 English words for every Ada statement. This is about three times more than civilian norms and twice as much as the second-place paperwork-generating industry (telecommunications).

Quality control for military projects is generally the same as for civilian systems software and includes formal inspections followed by a full suite of testing steps. But military projects also tend to perform many activities that are essentially unique and have no equivalence in the civilian domain. One notable example is an IV&V (independent verification and validation), a structured review of plans and specifications by a contractor different from the primary contractor. The value of this rather time-consuming undertaking has not been formally explored.

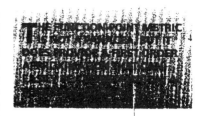

In mid 1994, the Secretary of Defense stated that US military organizations should begin to move toward civilian best practices and away from the somewhat baroque, convoluted defense approaches and military standards that have developed and accreted over the past 20 years. This is a promising concept, but it is too soon to judge whether it will prove effective.

Because military quality levels are fairly high, the military domain is in a position to increase material reusability and perhaps begin to match the civilian sector in schedule results. It remains to be seen whether this will really occur. But at least the military services are exploring civilian best practices, even if they don't fully adopt them.

Schedules and time-to-market intervals are among the most important factors in the software industry. For more than 50 years, there has been a shortage of empirical data and useful rules for estimating software schedules early and accurately. The function-point metric is not a panacea, but it does provide a first-order approximation that can easily be carried out on a pocket calculator. Since function points are derived during requirements and early design, the ability to estimate schedules before committing major resources to a project is a practical way to minimize later problems.

Capers Jones, Software Productivity Research Inc., 1 New England Excutive Park, Burlington, MA 01803-5005; phone (617) 273-0140; fax (617) 273-5176; Internet capers@xanadu.spr.com; CompuServe 7543,231

Activity-based software costing

The study of software economics is not yet mature. For many years, the lines of code (LOC) metrics has tended to conceal major software cost drivers such as the production of requirements, plans, specifications, manuals, and other paper documents. The advent of function point metrics in the late 1970s allowed us to explore the measurement of such noncoding activities, none of which could be properly explored or normalized using LOC metrics. Indeed, we now know that on some projects (such as large defense systems) the cost to produce paper documents is twice as much as the cost to produce the code itself.

The ability to measure all activities associated with software production has led to the concept of *activity-based* studies of software cost. This approach is very promising but still in development.

Activity averages

In activity-based costing, estimators associate an average number of work hours with each activity or task. They can then assemble effort and cost estimates by selecting those activities that will be performed for a given project, aggregating the effort, and applying standard costs. Activity-based costing is used in several other domains, including automobile repair and medical and dental insurance.

For activity-based costing to be accurate enough for use on software projects, estimators must consider several problems. First, software staff compensation levels vary by a ratio of about 3 to 1 in the US, and by more than 10 to 1 throughout the world. However, basic compensation rates for software personnel are readily available from annual surveys that are published by many journals, and most companies know their own rates.

Second, even greater variations affect the *burden rates* or overhead structures that companies apply to recover expenses such as rent, mortgages, taxes, benefits, indirect personnel, and so on. Burden rates in the US can vary from less than 15 percent to more than 300 percent. Unlike basic compensation rates, which are widely published, burden rates are not readily available. Indeed, some companies regard their burden rates as proprietary information.

Wide variations

When the variance in basic staff compensation is compounded by the variance in burden rates, the overall cost differences are notable indeed.

For example, assume that a small software company in a rural area is building an application of 100 function points in size. The company's average annual compensation for programmers is $36,000, and the burden rate is 50 percent. The total cost of producing applications in this shop is $54,000 per year. If the project in question required five staff-months of effort, the project would cost $22,500, or $225 per function point.

Now assume that the same project was developed in a major urban area, where the company's average annual compensation for programmers might be $60,000 and the burden rate 100 percent. Under this cost structure the annual burdened personnel costs are $120,000. A five-staff-month project would cost $50,000, or $500 per function point.

With cost ranges like these it is easy to see why figures cited as "average cost per function point" should not be used without substantial adjustments for local conditions.

Sample metrics

Activity-based costing is a step toward greater precision for dealing with software projects. Rather than considering a project in its entirety, each activity is considered in terms of the normal amount of effort needed to perform it and the burdened cost structures.

My company considers a standard set of 25 activities when we do software cost studies. Our cost structures assume an average monthly compensation for software personnel of $5,000 and an average burden rate of 100 percent.

Although SPR uses 25 activities, we recognize that not every project includes all 25 activities. For example, small end-user applications might perform only one of the 25, coding.

Generally, information-system projects involve between eight and 14 activities; systems and real-time projects between 15 and 20. Only military projects would routinely involve all 25 activities. In fact, two of the activities (independent verification and validation and independent testing) are almost never performed on civilian software projects but are routine in the military world.

To use Table 1, you must know at least the approximate function-point size of the application in question. Select the activities you believe will be performed for the application. Add the work-hours per function point for each activity. You can do the same thing with costs, of course, but you should replace the assumed costs of $5,000 per staff month and a 100-percent burden rate with the appropriate values from your own organization.

Reprinted from *IEEE Computer*, Vol. 29, No. 5, May 1996, pp. 103-104.

Note that the productivity rates and work hours per function point are based on Version 3 of the US function points as defined by the International Function Point Users Group (IFPUG). If you use British Mark II function points, feature points, IFPUG version 4 function points, engineering function points, or some other variant you will need to make adjustments to the basic rates.

Extending activities

The information in Table 1 illustrates the basic concept of activity-based costing. It is not a substitute for a commercial software cost-estimating tool that supports activity-based costs in a more sophisticated way, such as allowing each activity to have its own unique cost structure, and to vary the nominal hours expended on the basis of experience, methods, tools, and so on.

Once you start using activity-based costing, you can extend it to include many other activities. The activities shown in Table 1 are common in development projects. However, if you are concerned with maintaining aging

Activity-based cost analysis can be much more accurate than other estimating methods that lack any internal structure or granularity.

legacy applications, with porting software from one platform to another, or with bringing out a new release of a commercial software package, then you will need to deal with other activities.

You should also be aware that over and above the cost variances already discussed, variances in the real productivity rates might be experienced. These variances are based on many factors, including but not limited to staff experience, tools used, programming languages, and the unpaid overtime that might be part of the project but which not tracked by resource-tracking systems.

Activity-based cost analysis can be much more accurate than other estimating methods that lack any internal structure or granularity. The software industry is developing sets of *activity templates* based on specific companies or industries, on methodologies such as ISO 9000, and on other criteria such as the Software Engineering Institute's five-level Capability Maturity Model.

Activity-based costing will become more widely used and more rigorous as we approach the end of the 20th century.

Table 1. Sample activity-based costs per function point (assumes $5,000 monthly compensation and 100 percent burden rate).

Activities performed	FP/PM mode	Hours/FP mode	Unburdened Cost/FP mode	Burdened Cost/FP mode
01 Requirements	175.00	0.75	$28.57	$57.14
02 Prototyping	150.00	0.88	$33.33	$66.67
03 Architecture	300.00	0.44	$16.67	$33.33
04 Project plans	500.00	0.26	$10.00	$20.00
05 Initial design	175.00	0.75	$28.57	$57.14
06 Detailed design	150.00	0.88	$33.33	$66.67
07 Design reviews	225.00	0.59	$22.39	$44.78
08 Coding	50.00	2.64	$100.00	$200.01
09 Reuse acquisition	600.00	0.22	$8.33	$16.67
10 Package purchase	400.00	0.33	$12.50	$25.00
11 Code inspections	150.00	0.88	$33.33	$66.67
12 Independent V & V	125.00	1.06	$40.00	$80.00
13 Configuration mgt.	1,750.00	0.08	$2.86	$5.71
14 Formal integration	250.00	0.53	$20.00	$40.00
15 User documentation	70.00	1.89	$71.43	$142.86
16 Unit testing	150.00	0.88	$33.33	$66.67
17 Function testing	150.00	0.88	$33.33	$66.67
18 Integration testing	175.00	0.75	$28.57	$57.14
19 System testing	200.00	0.66	$25.00	$50.00
20 Field testing	225.00	0.59	$22.22	$44.45
21 Acceptance testing	350.00	0.38	$14.29	$28.57
22 Independent testing	200.00	0.66	$25.00	$50.00
23 Quality assurance	150.00	0.88	$33.33	$66.67
24 Installation/training	350.00	0.38	$14.29	$28.57
25 Project management	100.00	1.32	$50.00	$28.57
Cumulative results	6.75	19.55	$740.71	$1,409.98
Arithmetic mean	284.80	0.78	$29.63	$56.40